GENGHIS KHAN
AND THE
MONGOL EMPIRE

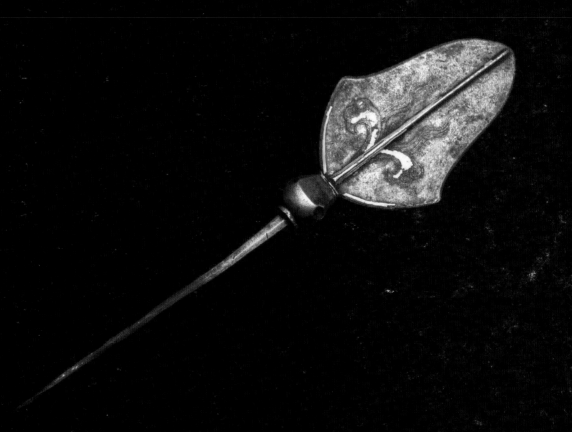

GENGHIS KHAN AND THE

EDITED BY
William W. Fitzhugh
Morris Rossabi
William Honeychurch

PROJECT ADMINISTRATOR
Abigail McDermott

MONGOL EMPIRE

PUBLISHED BY
Arctic Studies Center, Smithsonian Institution
& Mongolian Preservation Foundation
in collaboration with Odyssey Books & Maps

DISTRIBUTED IN USA BY
W.W. Norton & Company, Inc.

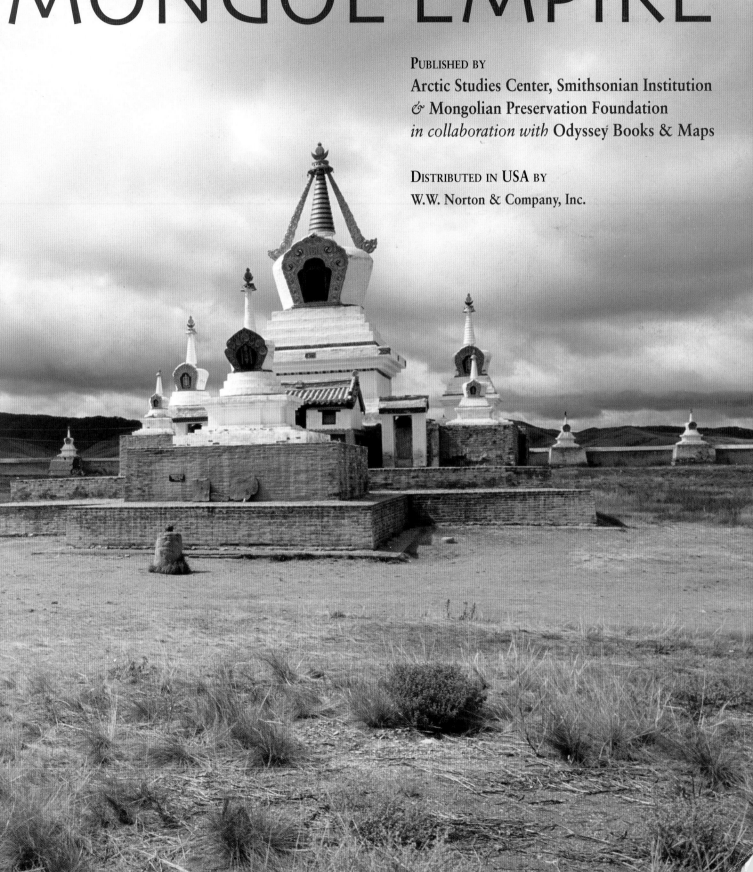

Contents

Part III. The Mongolian Western Empire

Part IV. Kublai Khan and Yuan China

Part V.   Genghis Khan's Legacy

ISBN: 978-962-217-835-9
Library of Congress Cataloging-in-Publication Data
Genghis Khan and the Mongol empire / edited by William W. Fitzhugh,
Morris Rossabi, William Honeychurch

     p. cm.

    Published in conjunction with an exhibition which is first appearing
at the Houston Museum of Natural Science, February-September 2009.
    Includes bibliographical references and index.
1. Genghis Khan, 1162-1227. 2. Mongols--History--To 1500. 3.
Mongolia--Antiquities. 4. Mongols--History. I. Fitzhugh, William W.,
1943- II. Rossabi, Morris. III. Honeychurch, William, 1966- IV. Houston
Museum of Natural Science.
   DS22.G46 2009
   950'.21092--DC22

COVER
Nadaam Riders
Horses have been central to Mongol cultures for thousands of years.
Speed and horsemanship are contested as much today as in the past,
primarily in *nadaam* festivals held annually in early July. Competitive
racing has been an important part of Mongol life for centuries, if not for
thousands of years, and was the basis for training Genghis Khan's 13th-
century cavalry troops.

PAGE 1
Whistling arrow
Mongol battle commanders used whistling arrows as sound signals
to initiate battle orders and for disorienting prey during the hunt. The
sound was created by wind rushing across small cup-shaped hollows in
the arrow stem.

PAGE 2-3
Erdene Zuu Monastery
After its heyday in the 13th century, the Mongol capital city, Khara
Khorum, declined and knowledge of its location was lost. Archaeological
work conducted in the 20th century identified its buried remains under
and north of the Erdene Zuu monastery. Archaeologists believe the
monastery, founded in 1586, is built on the remains of the khan's palace.

BACK COVER:
Paiza
Use of metal *paizas*, or messenger passes, preceded the Mongol period,
but were adopted by Genghis and later Mongol khans to guarantee safe
passage for official representatives and emissaries throughout the Mongol
realm. They were worn about the neck and were inscribed with a silver-
inlaid message proclaiming that anyone harming the bearer could be put
to death. Early *paizas* were shaped as oblong plates, while those of the
Yuan period like this one were round and inscribed with 'Phags-pa script.

Notes on Transliteration

The Editors have adopted a common sense approach toward translit-
eration of foreign words. In general, the following standard systems of
Romanization have been used: pinyin for Chinese, the revised roman-
ization of Korean of 2000, and Hepburn for Japanese. The Royal
Asiatic Society system has been used for the transliteration of Persian.
Antoine Mostaert's scheme for the transliteration of Classical
Mongolian, as modified by Francis Cleaves, has been adopted, except
for these deviations:

ch is used for č
sh is used for š
gh is used for ɣ
kh is used for q
j is used for ĵ

Macrons and other symbols have not been used in order not to impose
on the reader. For contemporary Mongolian terms in the Cyrillic alphabet we use a simplified transliteration system in which some letters and
diacritical marks represent one or more than one Cyrillic letter as follows:

a is used for A
e is used for Э
i is used for И and Й
o is used for O and Ө
u is used for У and Y
y is used for Ы
ye is used for E
yo is used for Ё
ya is used for Я
yu is used for Ю
' is used for Ь

When a Mongolian term has a traditional transliteration in English, such
as the word "gobi," we defer to that form. When authors have requested
specific transliterations, we have done our best to accommodate them.

Lenders to the Exhibition

The Dornod Province Museum, Mongolia

The Dornogobi Province Museum, Mongolia

Natsag Gankhuyag, Arlington, Virginia

Larry and Pat Gotuaco, San Francisco, California

The Institute of Archaeology of the Mongolian Academy of Sciences

Vahid and Cathy Kooros, with the cooperation of the
Museum of Fine Arts, Houston

Arthur Leeper, Belvedere, California

The Military Museum of Mongolia

The National Library of Mongolia

The National Museum of Mongolia

The Qinxuan Collection, San Francisco, California

The State Hermitage Museum, St. Petersburg

Foreword

IT IS REMARKABLE HOW MANY SECRETS OF HISTORY we learn only well after the fact. Mongolians, especially, take the secrets of Chinggis Khaan, the founding father of the country of Mongolia, very close to their hearts. Historians and archaeologists have enriched our lives today with the insights they have gained about Mongolia's past. Despite this, many of us hold deeply to the conviction that no one should ever try to discover the most precious secrets of the great Khans; we prefer their spirits rest in peace.

Perhaps it is the long-lasting enigma of the Great Khaan that stirs the curiosity of every generation of scientists and makes each new piece of evidence of Chinggis Khaan's time a precious legacy. The mystery surrounding Chinggis Khaan and many aspects of the Mongolian empire results from the small quantity of records written from the Mongolian perspective. Many of these records are only now coming to light and being researched. *Genghis Khan and the Mongol Empire* presents new research on the lives, cultures, and adventures of the world's largest land empire and helps us comprehend facets of that past more fully and vividly. Mindful of present sensibilities, the authors show due respect for the feelings of Mongolian people about their past. I appreciate this and applaud the diligent work of researchers, writers, and other team members who participated in this publication.

I extend my special thanks to the Smithsonian Institution for spending its resources and distinguished human capacity to republish this historic volume, which provides more readers a chance to enjoy and learn about Chinggis Khaan, the Mongol empire, and our history from ancient times to the present.

OYUNGEREL TSEDEVDAMBA
Minister of Culture, Sports and Tourism of Mongolia
Member of the State Great Hural (Parliament) of Mongolia

It is an honor to write a preface for this edition of *Genghis Khan and the Mongol Empire*. The touring exhibit bearing the same name introduced Mongolia to a wide audience in many places, including California, Colorado, Illinois, Georgia, North Carolina, Texas and even Singapore. Hopefully, the impact of this book will be at least as far-reaching.

Henti, the reputed birthplace—and possible burial site—of Genghis Khan is one of Mongolia's most beautiful provinces, featuring a scenic mix of mountains, grasslands, forests, lakes and rivers. But other parts of Mongolia are also attractive, not only for the their natural beauty but also for the historical references that they evoke with respect to Genghis Khan and the empire that he established.

Reflecting on my life in the foreign service, I am struck by how often I have encountered traces of that Mongolian past over the last three decades, despite the vast distances involved. Indeed, in virtually every country where I have served—including Pakistan, Afghanistan, Kazakhstan, Jordan and even Cambodia —the Mongol Empire left a lasting mark. For example, in Pakistan I learned that the Moghuls consciously evoked their Mongol roots, even as they expanded their influence across South Asia and built an entirely different civilization. As it happens, Genghis Khan's favorite grandson was reportedly killed at Bamiyan in Afghanistan and that country's Hazara minority continues to claim Mongol ancestry.

Similarly, in Kazakhstan and across Central Asia the impact of the Mongol Empire lingers everywhere. While working in Jordan, I was struck by an inscription on the wall at Ajlun Castle north of

Amman which referred to a thirteenth century battle between the Mamluks and the Mongol cavalry. Even in Cambodia I found traces of a Mongolian connection, this time in a graphic account of historic Angkor Wat, written by a visiting diplomat from the court of Kublai Khan.

My sincere hope is that *Genghis Khan and the Mongol Empire* will spark a broader interest in Mongolia, both past and present. Certainly, those who read it will gain a better understanding of not only Mongolia's historical heritage but also the enduring impact of the Mongol Empire, an impact that continues to the present day.

JONATHAN ADDLETON
United States Ambassador to Mongolia,
2009–2012

Mongolia: The Book and Genghis Khan: The Exhibition

Don Lessem

The debut of the exhibition "Genghis Khan" provides the occasion for the publication of this book. Traveling to science museums across North America, the exhibition is dedicated to both an appreciation of Genghis Khan's long-slighted (at least in the West) contributions to world history and a celebration of traditional Mongolian culture.

The exhibition is centered upon a representation of Mongolian imperial culture and Genghis's own life, and was assembled through the generous loans of the Ministry of Education, Culture, and Science of Mongolia; the State Hermitage Museum, St. Petersburg, Russia; and the collections of Larry and Pat Gotuaco, Vahid and Cathy Kooros, Arthur Leeper, and Terese Bartholomew of the Qinxuan Collection. Many of the more than 200 objects on view in the exhibition are described and pictured here, in addition to other illustrative materials documenting the essays by noted scholars of the Mongolian world.

As the exhibit occasioned this book, this volume's purpose is two-fold: to provide supporting documentation for the exhibition and its objects and to provide an up-to-date and accessible scholarly treatment of Mongolia and its place in the world, focused around Genghis Khan and his legacy. No other such book currently exists.

For many, perhaps all, of the authors of this volume, their contributions are labors of love as well as the fruits of life-long study. The devotion Mongolia inspires in those who work there has multiple and far-from-mysterious origins. The nation is distinctly remote and hence little known— the furthest from the sea of any nation, a geographic feature that the political isolation of the twentieth century has immensely magnified. It is quite empty, with just 2.8 million residents in a stretch of wild and largely open land half the size of the continental United States. The landscapes are awe-inspiring: from the 1,000-mile hard-scrabble swath of the Gobi Desert northward across the oceanic grassland to the pristine deep lakes and evergreen forests beneath snow-capped northern mountains. The culture, arguably the last horse-based society on Earth, is ancient and unfamiliar.

But perhaps most alluring to Mongolia's devotees are its people, with a warmth born of nomads' hospitality, the curiosity and enterprise of constant travelers, the gentle tranquility of adherents to Buddhist principles as well as a lasting shamanistic legacy, and almost unaccountably, an optimistic enthusiasm that belies their struggles in an economically challenged country in the harshest of all continental climates. To Americans in particular there is something in the Mongolian high plateau and its undeveloped nature that evokes the long-vanished American West. For all there is the spectacular irony that what was, for millennia before and hundreds of years after Genghis Khan, a landlocked cipher became the greatest empire the world has ever known (with only the Queen's Navy to contend that assertion). It can also be said with some certainty that this fascination most likely does not stem from the cuisine, unless the visitor harbors an inordinate fondness for boiled mutton.

Frequent visits over twenty years, whether to look for dinosaurs or follow the route of Genghis Khan with friends become lifelong, have engendered that passion for Mongolia in me as well. So it is my privilege and great pleasure to both create and

Dermott of the Arctic Studies Center, who coordinated the efforts of the publication's many literary and photographic contributors. Natsag Gankyuhag was a liaison of great value to all concerned, and the distinguished Mongolian photographer Oktyabri Dash added many spectacular images.

The exhibition, and hence the book, would be impossible without the long cooperation of the Mongolian government, in particular its Ministry of Education, Culture, and Science, efforts coordinated by Assistant Director Z. Oyunbileg. D. Tseveendorj, Director of the Institute of Archaeology of the Mongolian Academy of Sciences, made available a host of newly discovered finds, including

Genghis Khan Mural
This mural, painted for the exhibit by Yu Shan, shows Genghis Khan with his standards, generals, and army. The group is pictured as they set out from the Mongol homeland to attack the Khwarazmian empire in 1219.

On the following pages we have featured some important loans from private collectors to the travelling exhibition "Genghis Khan and the Mongol Empire."

organize the exhibit and support the publication of this book. I trust you will find that same powerful draw in this book that visitors to Mongolia so often discover.

Thanks go to many for making this book possible, in particular editors William W. Fitzhugh, Director of the Arctic Studies Center at the Smithsonian Institution's National Museum of Natural History; William Honeychurch of the Department of Anthropology at Yale University; and Morris Rossabi, who holds faculty positions at both the City University of New York and Columbia University. Letitia Burns O'Connor and Dana Levy of Perpetua Press in Santa Barbara, California, prepared this complex manuscript and designed its eye-catching layout, with the assistance of Abigail Mc-

mummies analyzed by Bruno Frohlich, statistician for the Department of Anthropology in the Smithsonian Institution's National Museum of Natural History, and other objects displayed for the first time in this exhibition. Contributions of precious artifacts and images thereof from the Golden Horde lent by the State Hermitage Museum in St. Petersburg, Russia, are gratefully acknowledged.

Among the many others whose generosity and skill made the exhibition possible are: Sukhbaatar Altantsetseg; Juliana Flower; Yu Shan; Julia Xu; Guan Jian; Lisa Rebori, Rodney Gentry and their colleagues at the Houston Museum of Natural Science; Jodi Schoemer and her colleagues at the Denver Museum of Nature & Science; and the Irving Arts Center.

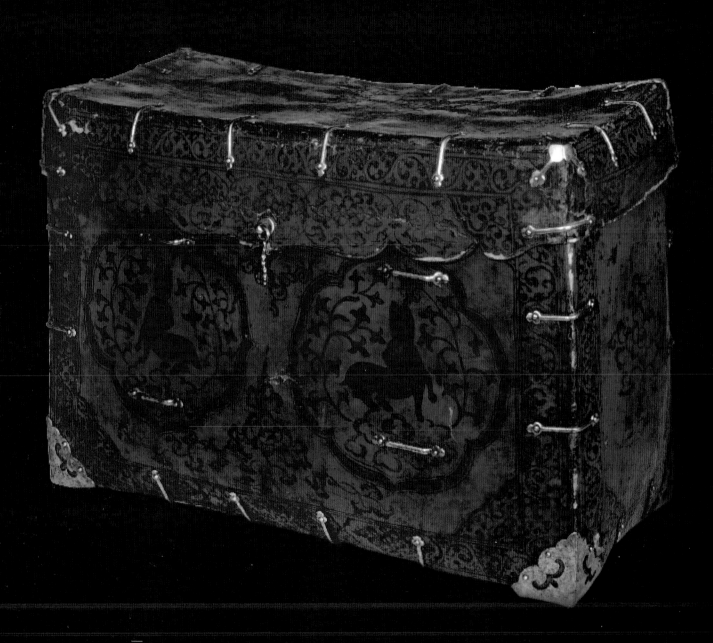

Lacquered Trunk

Lacquer-covered leather trunks like this one from the 15th–16th century with iron fittings were light and kept possessions dry when traveling on horseback. Lacquer was also durable, flexible, and could be elaborately decorated. This design features medallions with rabbits surrounded by floral elements. Its home for centuries was probably a storeroom in a Tibetan monastery.

Seal with Wooden Handle
Personal and official seals were applied widely in Mongolia and China and other Asian countries to authenticate documents and provide proof of authorship. This 14th-century iron seal is a rare example in which the ornamented wooden handle has been preserved.

Saddle Cloth

This textile fragment of a Yuan official's saddle cloth is constructed of silk *kesi* tapestry and *nasij* or "cloth of gold," and was once decorated with gold cording, now lost. The cloth has been radiocarbon-dated to 1263–1395.

< **Coins of the Realm**

This group of coins dating to the 13th and 14th centuries includes silver dirnams and gold dinars minted in Central Asia for Genghis Khan, Mahmud Ghazan, Alghu Khan, Hülegü Khan, and Abu-Said.

Fresco Fragment

This fresco depict warriors in a style of dress typical of northern or western Mongols during the Yuan pe-

Travel Trunk

This trunk made of lacquer-covered leather is decorated with birds centered in medallions. The largest birds are paired and single phoenixes, while the smaller ones are cranes. The decoration resembles textile patterns of the Yuan period. Leather loops were for fastening to a packsaddle. The trunk is of Tibetan origin and has been radiocarbon-dated to the 14th century. Its pristine condition suggests it was kept for centuries in a Tibetan monastery.

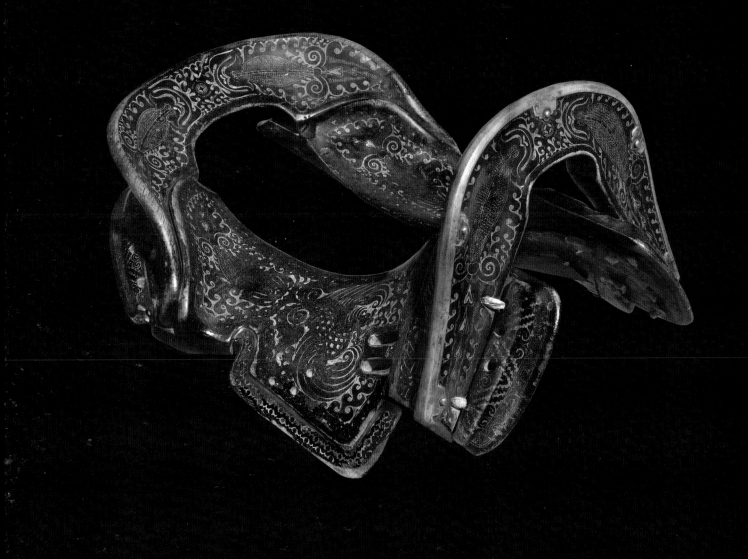

Lacquer Saddle

This saddle weighing less than four pounds has ornate decorations created with the *moxian* or "polish reveal" technique, in which layers of different colors of lacquer are revealed by selectively abrading away the darker surface coat. Its animal motifs include winged dragons with fish tails, nightmarish birds, squidlike figures surrounded by flames or wave patterns, and images of Chinese coins. This is the earliest known example of a lacquer saddle and has been radiocarbon-dated to 1298–1408.

Contributors

Chunag Amartuvshin is a senior research archaeologist at the Institute of Mongolian Archaeology of the Mongolian Academy of Sciences, and Co-Director of the Institute's National Cultural Resource Management Sector. Dr. Amartuvshin is also Co-Director of the Joint Mongolian-American Baga Gazaryn Chuluu Expedition. His research interests include the emergence of social complexity among nomadic groups, the study of mortuary processes, and the preservation of steppe nomadic heritage.

Tsend Amgalantugs is the Director of the Laboratory of Biological Anthropology at the Institute of Mongolian Archaeology at the Mongolian Academy of Sciences in Ulaan Baatar, Mongolia. He is trained as a biological anthropologist and archaeologist, and presently codirects expeditions to survey and excavate Bronze Age burial mounds in Central and Northern Mongolia with Dr. Bruno Frohlich.

Erdene Batshatar is a researcher at the Institute of Mongolian Archaeology at the Mongolian Academy of Sciences. He has worked closely with Bruno Frohlich and Tsend Amgalantugs on several Mongolian projects, including surveying and excavations of Bronze Age burial mounds, forensic investigations, and studies of human mummified remains.

Shagdaryn Bira is a member of the Mongolian Academy of Sciences and serves as General Secretary of the International Association for Mongol Studies. He is a Mongolian historian who has won international acclaim for his multifaceted research that examines the history, culture, religion, and languages of the Mongols. He has made noteworthy contributions to the organization and spread of Mongol research on an international level as a conference organizer and editor of proceedings.

James Bosson is Emeritus Professor of East Asian Languages and Cultures at the University of California, Berkeley, specializing in Tibetan and Altaic languages. Dr. Bosson was a contributor to the Asian Art Museum of San Francisco exhibition catalog, *Mongolia: The Legacy of Chinggis Khan* (Thames and Hudson, 1995).

Manduhai Buyandelger received her BA and MA from the National University of Mongolia, and her PhD from Harvard University. She held a postdoctoral fellowship as a Junior Fellow at the Harvard Society of Fellows, 2004–07. She currently serves as an assistant professor in the Anthropology Department at MIT. Her book, *Tragic Spirits: Shamanism, Socialism, and Neoliberal State in Mongolia*, is under contract with the University of Chicago Press.

Pamela K. Crossley is the Robert and Barbara Black Professor of Asian History at Dartmouth College. She is a specialist on the history of the Qing empire; on this subject she has published *Orphan Warriors* (Princeton Univ. Press, 1990), *The Manchus* (Blackwell Publishers, 1997) and *A Translucent Mirror* (Univ. of California Press, 1999). Her forthcoming book, *The Wobbling Pivot*, is on Chinese history since 1800.

James P. Delgado is the President and Chief Executive Officer of the Institute of Nautical Archaeology (INA). He previously served as Executive Director of the Vancouver Maritime Museum, and before that was with the National Park Service both in San Francisco and Washington, DC. He has authored or edited more than 30 books on maritime history and nautical archaeology and most recently published *Khubilai Khan's Lost Fleet: In Search of a Legendary Armada* (Univ. of California Press, 2008).

Ross E. Dunn is Professor Emeritus of History at San Diego State University and Director of World History Projects for the National Center for History in the Schools, UCLA. His books include *Resistance in the Desert: Moroccan Responses to French Imperialism, 1881–1912* (Croom Helm/Univ. of Wisconsin Press, 1977), and *The Adventures of Ibn Battuta, a Muslim Traveler of the Fourteenth Century* (Univ. of California Press, 1986).

Ruth W. Dunnell is the James P. Storer Professor of Asian History at Kenyon College. A specialist in premodern Chinese history, she helped to launch the interdisciplinary Asian Studies Program at Kenyon in 1991. After publishing a book on the rise of the Buddhist Tangut Xia state between Tibet and China in the eleventh century, she shifted her attention to the Mongol empire in East Asia, and has recently completed a biography of Genghis Khan for Pearson Education's World Biography Series.

Ulambayar Erdenebat is an archaeologist at the Institute of Mongolian Archaeology of the Mongolian Academy of Sciences, and a professor in the Archaeology and Anthropology Department of the National University of Mongolia in Ulaan Baatar. Dr. Erdenebat is also Co-Director of the Mongolian-German Orkhon Project.

William W. Fitzhugh is Director of the Arctic Studies Center and a curator in the Department of Anthropology at the Smithsonian Institution National Museum of Natural History. During his long career as an archaeologist, he has specialized in Arctic and Subarctic prehistory, circumpolar cultures, human-environmental interactions, and the anthropology of culture contact. He has produced many exhibitions and books on northern cultures, including *Inua: Spirit World of the Bering Sea Eskimo* (SI Press, 1982); *Crossroads of Continents* (SI Press, 1988); *Ainu: Spirit of a Northern People* (Univ. of Washington Press, 1999); *Vikings: the North Atlantic Saga* (SI Press, 2000); and *The Deer Stone Project: Anthropological Studies in Mongolia*, SI (Arctic Studies Center, 2005).

Bruno Frohlich, a biological anthropologist, directs the Computed Tomography Laboratory at the Smithsonian Institution National Museum of Natural History. In collaboration with the Mongolian Academy of Sciences, he has directed several excavations of Bronze Age burial mounds, conducted forensic investigations, and examined human mummified remains from the Gobi Desert. His publications include *To The Aleutians and Beyond: The Anthropology of William S. Laughlin* (The National Museum of Denmark, 2002), and *The Early Bronze Age I Tombs and Burials of Bâb edh-Dhrâ, Jordan* (AltaMira Press/SI/NMNH, 2008).

Kenzo Hayashida is the Chairman and Founder of the Asian Research Institute of Underwater Archaeology in Japan. He is internationally known for his discovery of the lost fleet of Kublai Khan, wrecked in 1281. He also played a major role in creating Japan's first graduate program in maritime archaeology at the Tokyo University of Marine Science and Technology.

Janine Hinton is the Manager of Radiographic Services for the Repatriation Office and supports the director of the Computed Tomography Laboratory at the Smithsonian Institution National Museum of Natural History.

William Honeychurch is an assistant professor at Yale University in the Department of Anthropology. His research focuses on interregional interaction and the development of complex political organization, the rise of states and empires among nomadic peoples, and the construction and use of monumental landscapes. Dr. Honeychurch conducts field research in Mongolia with an emphasis on surface survey and bioarchaeology.

Hans-Georg Hüttel is a senior researcher and archaeologist specializing in Asian Archaeology at the German Archaeological Institute in Bonn, Germany, where he is also head of the library. He holds an honorary professorship at the University of Bonn. He has conducted field studies and excavations in Germany, Greece, Indonesia, Nepal, and since 1999, has focused his efforts on the Khara Khorum site in Mongolia.

David R. Hunt serves as the Collection Manager for the Physical Anthropology Division in the Department of Anthropology at the Smithsonian Institution National Museum of Natural History. His areas of research include human skeletal biology and variation, forensic anthropology, and mummies of the world. Dr. Hunt has published on these topics in a variety of professional anthropological journals and edited volumes, and co-authored *Photographic Regional Atlas Of Bone Disease: A Guide To Pathologic And Normal Variation In The Human Skeleton* (C. C. Thomas, 2005).

Gordon C. Jacoby is a leading climate scholar researching tree rings and environmental history. Now retired, he founded the Tree-Ring Laboratory of the Lamont-Doherty Earth Observatory in 1975. He previously held positions at the Institute of Geophysics and Planetary Physics, UCLA, and as a visiting professor at Dartmouth College.

Paul Kahn is an American writer and information architect, working in Paris. He formerly served as Director of the Institute for Research in Information and Scholarship (IRIS) at Brown University, and as an adjunct professor at the Rhode Island School of Design. He is the author of the American English adaptation of *The Secret History of the Mongols: The Origin of Chingis Khan* (2nd edition: Cheng & Tsui, 1998).

George L. Kallander is Assistant Professor of History in the Maxwell School of Syracuse University, specializing in the history of Korea, Japan, and Mongolia. He earned his PhD from Columbia University (2006). Awards include: a Fulbright research fellowship (2001–02); a postdoctoral fellowship at Columbia University's Weatherhead East Asian Institute Expanding East Asian Studies (2005–06); and a research fellowship at the Academy of Korean Studies (2009–10).

Mark G. Kramarovsky is Senior Curator of Central Asian Collections at the State Hermitage Museum in St. Petersburg, Russia. His many publications on the material culture and history of the Golden Horde include *Zoloto Chingisidov: kul'turnoe nasledie Zolotoi Ordy* (Gold of the Chingisids: The cultural heritage of the Golden Horde published by Slaviya, 2001).

Don Lessem published this volume to accompany the "Genghis Khan" exhibition he organized in association with the Mongolian Cultural Ministry and the State Hermitage Museum, St. Petersbug. Mr. Lessem became fascinated with Genghis Khan during his twenty years of expeditions to Mongolia to study dinosaurs. A former Knight Science Journalism Fellow at MIT, he has authored more than fifty books on natural science for adults and children, and has produced international television and radio documentaries. Mr. Lessem has excavated and exhibited the world's largest dinosaurs and created the leading charities for dinosaur research. He has the dubious distinction of having *Lessemsaurus*, a small-brained and large-bellied Argentine dinosaur, named in his honor.

Nomin Lkhagvasuren is a freelance journalist and publisher based in Ulaan Baatar, Mongolia. She writes on issues of culture, poverty, human rights, and gender, and is interested in anthropology, religion, and history. Her articles appear in international publications as well as local print media, and she has served as a Mongolian correspondent for *Transitions Online* magazine and Reporters Without Borders.

François Louis is an associate professor at the Bard Graduate Center in New York, NY. He was previously Editor-in-Chief of *Artibus Asiae* and Assistant Curator at the Museum Rietberg in Zurich, Switzerland. He is currently working on a publication tentatively titled *Dynastic Possessions: The Material Culture of the Khitan Elite*.

Peter K. Marsh is a musicologist and ethnomusicologist on the faculty of California State University, East Bay, specializing in Inner Asian music and culture. He has written extensively on issues of musical tradition and modernity in Mongolia. His latest book is *The Horse-head Fiddle and the Cosmopolitan Reimagination of Tradition in Mongolia* (Routledge, 2009).

Timothy May is an historian of Central Eurasia and the Middle East with a focus on the Mongol empire and nomadic-based empires. He recently published *The Mongol Art of War* (Pen and Sword Publications, 2007) and is on the faculty of North Georgia College and State University.

David Morgan is a professor of History and Religious Studies at the University of Wisconsin-Madison. His works *Medieval Persia 1040-1797* (Longman, 1988) and *The Mongols* (Blackwell Publishers, 1986: 2nd. edition, 2007) have seen numerous reprintings and have been translated into a number of languages including Spanish, Japanese, and Persian.

Ernst Pohl is Curator for the archaeological artifacts collection in the Department of Pre- and Early Historical Archaeology at the University of Bonn in Germany. From 1994 to 1998, he excavated Tibetan settlements in Northern Mustang (Nepal). Recently, he has focused on excavating the Chinese craftsmen quarter of the ancient Mongolian capital, Khara Khorum.

J. Daniel Rogers is Chairman of the Department of Anthropology at the Smithsonian Institution National Museum of Natural History and specializes in the archaeology of complex societies, ethnohistory, and culture contact. He has researched and written on state formation and urban centers in Mongolia and has authored books including *Objects of Change: The Archaeology and History of Arikara Contact with Europeans* (SI Press, 1990), and *Ethnohistory and Archaeology: Approaches to Postcontact Change in the Americas* (Plenum Press, 1993).

Morris Rossabi is a prominent historian of China and Central Asia who teaches Inner Asian and East Asian history to graduate students at Columbia University and the City University of New York. Dr. Rossabi has published extensively, with a special focus on China and the Mongols. His notable publications include *Khubilai Khan: His Life and Times* (Univ. of California Press, 1988); *Voyager from Xanadu* (Kodansha, 1992); and *Modern Mongolia: From Khans to Commissars to Capitalists* (Univ. of California Press, 2005). He has also contributed to exhibitions at The Metropolitan Museum of Art, the Cleveland Museum of Art, and the Los Angeles County Museum of Art. In 2009, he was awarded an honorary doctorate by the National University of Mongolia.

Randall J. Sasaki is a research associate at the Institute of Nautical Archaeology (INA) at Texas A&M University, where he is currently pursuing his PhD in Nautical Archaeology. He has conducted several research projects in Japan, including the analysis of hull remains from Kublai Khan's ill-fated fleet, found off the coast of Takashima, Japan. He has published several articles regarding his research on East Asian shipbuilding traditions.

Myagmar Saruul-Erdene has a PhD in Linguistics and has taught at the Mongolian State University of Education (Ulaan Baatar), the International Center for Language Studies (Washington, DC), and the State Department Foreign Service Institute (Arlington, VA). He has held research positions at Istanbul University and Indiana University.

Theodore G. Schurr is a biological anthropologist on the faculty of the University of Pennsylvania who has investigated the prehistory of Asia and the Americas through studies of mtDNA, Y-chromosome, and autosomal genetic variation in Central and East Asian, Siberian, and Native American populations. Among his publications are papers describing his work with indigenous Siberian peoples, Kazakhs, and Mongolians, as well as archaeological populations from the Lake Baikal region.

Noriyuki Shiraishi is a professor of Archaeology at Niigata University in Japan. He has published a number of reports on his archaeological expeditions to uncover the history of Genghis Khan and the Mongol empire.

Jonathan K. Skaff, an associate professor of history at Shippensburg University, has devoted his career to studying the relationship between Chinese and Inner Asian cultures. His awards include a National Endowment for the Humanities Fellowship (2007–08), and a membership in the Institute for Advanced Study in Princeton, New Jersey (2007).

David Sneath is a social anthropologist and Director of the Mongolia & Inner Asia Studies Unit at Cambridge University. Dr. Sneath has carried out research on pastoralism, land use, and political culture in Inner Mongolia (China) and Mongolia. Among his many books are *The End of Nomadism?: Society, State and the Environment in Inner Asia* (Duke Univ. Press, 1999), and *The Headless State: Aristocratic Orders, Kinship Society, and the Misrepresentation of Inner Asia* (Columbia Univ. Press, 2007).

Isenbike Togan is a member of the Turkish Academy of Sciences, and was formerly a professor of History at Middle East Technical University in Ankara, Turkey. Dr. Togan participated in the UNESCO Silk Road expeditions of 1990 and 1991, and currently resides in Istanbul.

Willem J. Vogelsang is the former Curator for Southwest and Central Asia at the National Museum of Ethnology, in Leiden, The Netherlands. Since 2008, he has served as a cultural and regional advisor to the Dutch ISAF-operation Task Force Uruzgan in South Afghanistan. He has traveled widely in Iran and Afghanistan since 1978, and is also Co-Editor of the journal *Khila*, which focuses on Middle Eastern dress.

Daniel C. Waugh is Professor Emeritus in the Departments of History and Slavic Languages and Literature, and in the Jackson School of International Studies, at the University of Washington. He has published two monographs and numerous articles on his research specialty of pre-modern Russia. He also edits the Silkroad Foundation journal *The Silk Road* and directs the internet project Silk Road Seattle (http://depts.washington.edu/silkroad).

Steven B. Young is Cofounder of the Center for Northern Studies at Sterling College in Vermont. A naturalist and paleoecologist who has devoted his career to the study of polar regions, he has participated in many expeditions to the Arctic, Siberia, and Antarctica and is author of *To the Arctic: An Introduction to the Far North* (Wiley, 1989).

1.1 Lake Khovsgol

Lake Khovsgol is bounded by the Horidal-Saridag Mountains that separate it from the Darkhad Valley to the west. To the north lie the Sayan Mountains, home to Mongolia's Dukha (Tsaatan), an ethnic minority who are the southernmost reindeer herders in the world. The rippling raised shorelines etched into the peninsula record the gradual lowering of the lake from drying climate and increased erosion of its outlet. Khovsgol, at 1,645 meters elevation, holds some of the purest water in the world. Its output flows through Mongolia across the Russian border into Lake Baikal, and from there via the Angara and Yenisei Rivers to the Arctic Ocean.

1. Genghis Khan

EMPIRE AND LEGACY

William W. Fitzhugh

The terms "empire" and "imperial" are rarely heard in modern political discourse. Yet as the world transitions from a post-imperial era into an increasingly global era, knowledge of past empires can be instructive. In their empire, the Mongols controlled the largest contiguous landmass on one continent the world has ever known, challenged only by the scattered colonies of the British empire. But despite its huge size and phenomenal impact, this period of world history, which unfolded only two hundred years before Columbus encountered the New World, is barely known outside of Asia. Many recognize the name "Genghis Khan" as a Mongol warrior and empire-builder, but few know in which century he lived or his military and civic accomplishments. Fewer still know of his grandson Kublai, emperor of China, although some recognize the first line of Samuel Taylor Coleridge's poem of 1798, "Kubla Khan" ("In Xanadu did Kubla Khan / A stately pleasure-dome decree") inspired by Marco Polo's descriptions of his travels in China from 1275 to 1291. Today Asia is no longer the mysterious chimera described by Polo and romanticized by Coleridge; many of its nations are economic powerhouses and world leaders in arts, science, and technology. The Mongol empire that Genghis Khan forged was the most important early link between East and West and began the process of transforming worlds apart into the interconnected, globalized world of today.

Empires have ruled most of the world's territory and population for the past three thousand years. At its zenith during the mid-thirteenth century the Mongol empire created by Genghis Khan and his descendants ruled over the great civilizations of China and Iran and much of the Near East and Russia (fig. 1.2). Even the Roman empire under Trajan (98–117 CE), at 2.3 million square miles, was dwarfed by the Mongol territories, which in 1260 encompassed territories on the order of 10 million square miles, from the Yellow Sea to Budapest. Its grist included other empires, nations, chiefdoms, and tribal peoples; its subjects spoke scores of languages and practiced the world's great religions—Islam, Buddhism, Christianity—as well as many other faiths.

It is generally agreed that the end of a sword does not foster understanding between peoples, and during the Mongol conquest phase millions died and incalculable artistic, cultural, and scientific treasures were lost. Yet, as tragic and disruptive as the initial invasions that took place between 1215 and 1241 were to cultures and societies through-

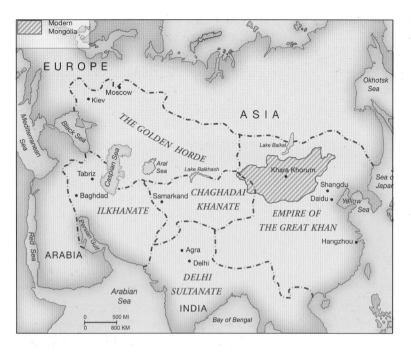

1.2 The Mongol Empire
At its greatest extent in 1276, the Mongol empire included the steppe and nearby forest zones of Russia from Moscow to Lake Baikal and the territories of the Aral, Caspian, and Black Seas, and it briefly reached the Mediterranean. Its northwestern section, where khans ruled over Russians and other ethnicities, was known as the Golden Horde. Its West Asian portion, known as the Ilkhanate, centered on Iran and extended from eastern Turkey and Iraq to the shores of the Persian Gulf and the Arabian Sea. Its central Asian portion, the Chaghadai khanate, included territories south of the Aral Sea and Lake Balkhash as well as much of Afghanistan, Kazakhstan, the Himalayas, and parts of western China. The fourth, the khanate of the Great Khan, encompassed China and Mongolia, stretching from Lake Baikal in southern Siberia to Vladivostok and extending south through Tibet and to the northern border of Viet Nam.

out Eurasia, many benefits also accrued. An era of expanded contacts and exchanges, accompanied by a great expansion of trade, followed the military campaigns for another two hundred years in many of the Mongol-administered territories. More important than cargo was knowledge. Exchanges of medicine, exotic spices, forest products, and industrial products such as ceramics and textiles led the way, but knowledge and information about science and mathematics, arts, and new technologies produced more lasting impacts.[1] Standards of governance and diplomacy, internationalism, long-distance communication systems, promotion of business, and freedom of religion advanced in ways that helped lay the foundation for the modern world. How this was accomplished, who its perpetrators were, and why this story is important is the subject of this book and its accompanying exhibition.

Mongol and Other Empires

Empires are nation-states that "metastasize" beyond their borders. Empires arise when a leader or elite group exerts military power over vast regions and diverse peoples and thereafter maintains control through some combination of military, economic, political, and religious force. Historians and archaeologists have catalogued nearly one hundred empires since the first examples appeared in the Near East three thousand years ago.

One of the most famous is the highly organized and largely secular Roman empire, with leaders chosen, at least initially, by democratic vote from a central governing body, the Senate. Its successor, the Holy Roman empire, ruled Christian kingdoms and waged crusades against Islam by claiming moral authority directly from God, through the Pope, who was elected by vote of the synod, an ecclesiastical council. The British, French, and Spanish empires of the sixteenth to nineteenth centuries used naval power and maritime trade to build vast empires overseas supported by royal courts and a variety of parliaments and legislative bodies. While the Mongol empire's most direct influence was in Asia, where its legacy remains strongest, it also had a powerful effect on Europe and the Western world through direct confrontations in the thirteenth century and by the cultural, demographic, and economic impact of the empire on neighboring regions of Russia, Asia, and the Near East (fig. 1.3).

The Mongol empire, while sharing with other urban-based empires such core characteristics as centralized leadership, imperial symbols and ideology, aggressive militarism, police control, and supra-state governance structures, differed from most of these in a single surprising and fundamental way: it was an empire built and controlled by nomads. Such was not the typical course to empire, which is generally based on a triad of military might, urban bureaucracy, and agrarian production. The Mongol empire followed a different path, one that grew from the grasslands of the Eurasian steppe through the actions of nomads who counted their wealth in horses, sheep, goats, and cattle, along with camels in the south and yaks in the north—the so-called "five muzzles," animals that ensured a herder against catastrophic loss to weather or disease of any one animal group (see Chapters 5 and 9). Mongols preferred living in tents in the open rather than in houses in villages or cities. They were accustomed to mobile life, moving with the seasons across hundreds or even thousands of miles, if necessary. They had few material possessions and little to lose in the constant cycle of steppe warfare—other

1.3 Fra Mauro Mappamundi, 1459
One of the first detailed medieval maps to include geographic information on Asia as well as Europe is the world map commissioned by King Afonso V of Portugal. The original was produced in Venice around 1450 by a local monk, Fra Mauro, and his sailor-cartographer assistant, Andrea Bianco, but has been lost. This copy, 2 meters in diameter, was produced by Bianco and completed on April 24, 1459. The map shows south at the top, in the portolan tradition of Muslim maps, and includes Mongol toponyms gleaned from Marco Polo's travels in Central and Eastern Asia. These place-names emphasize the Mongol legacy in the geography of Eurasia, a landmass conquered and administered by Mongols in the 13th–14th century.

and related arms—is one of nearly incessant competition and war. By Mongol times, men were trained as warriors from the moment they could ride and pull the short but powerful Mongolian bow. With a sleeping robe and a warm *deel*—an all-purpose cloak-like overcoat—a Mongol warrior could ride nearly one hundred miles in a single day. In deserts or on forced marches, soldiers tapped their horses' veins as a substitute for food and water. Trained and marshaled into a disciplined mounted cavalry, self-sufficient Mongol warriors became a Panzer-like army seven hundred years before the Germans reintroduced Mongol tactics with fast battle tanks in World War II. The medieval world had never seen such a blitzkrieg, and the Mongols' battle plans—derived from ancient animal hunting strategies—have been studied by military leaders throughout the world ever since. Armies, cities, and entire civilizations were powerless to check the Mongols as they advanced across Central Asia nearly to the shores of the Mediterranean and the banks of the Danube in Europe.

Warriors and armies need support, and empires need administrators. Mongol women, trained to be independent by virtue of nomadic life, often reared families and maintained hundreds of animals under arduous conditions, often without the help of their husbands, whose campaigns could last for years. Many were hunters, and some became powerful shamans and local leaders. The most influential were wives, mothers, and close relatives of Mongol khans (see Chapter 12). Sorghaghtani Beki, Kublai Khan's mother, ruled for years as regent over a large portion of Inner Mongolia until her eldest son Möngke was old enough to take charge; others played important roles in the power struggles leading up to the elections of khans by the *khuriltai*, the Mongol grand council.

Centralized leadership is a precondition for the growth of empires, and in its early phase, when led by Genghis Khan, the Mongol empire was highly centralized. The Mongol empire embodied the personal vision of its founder throughout the thirteenth century, even more than Julius Caesar, Charlemagne, or Napoleon personified theirs. Long after his death in 1227,

than their families, their honor, or their lives. Their polities were small, except during empire periods, and consisted of clans and small tribes that tended to be fiercely independent and were unlikely to trust their neighbors, who were usually their strongest competitors and fiercest opponents. Inured to hardship and constantly expecting treachery, their alliances were opportunistic and ephemeral. Genghis Khan saw his father poisoned by a rival clan leader and his long-betrothed bride kidnapped on his wedding night. Living on the edge of larger, wealthier societies, Mongols and their neighbors desired exotic gold, jewels, and finery, but found them inaccessible. In short, although lacking material wealth, they were proud, well armed, and in their day unparalleled in open-field battle.

Such was the background of steppe nomadic life and the incipient Mongol polity, which largely through the genius of a single man, became a huge medieval-era empire built entirely on the backs of horses. The pre-Mongol history of steppe peoples since the domestication of the horse 5,500 years ago—and the subsequent refinements of saddles, bridles, reins, stirrups, chariots,

1.4 Khara Khorum Tortoise
Resting outside the north wall of the Erdene Zuu monastery, this large stone tortoise dating to the 13th century is the only outward sign of the great buried Mongol capital city that lies beneath the soil. In Mongol mythology a golden tortoise carries the weight of earth and heaven on its back. Tortoises also symbolize immortality and provide protection against flood and other natural disasters.

Genghis Khan's vision of a world ruled by Mongols continued to inspire subsequent khans, whose two-century rule coincided with the medieval period in Europe.

Beginning life as a member of an honorable but besieged clan, Genghis Khan's youth was one of hardship and privation. Hounded by enemies who drove him and his family into the wilderness, enduring starvation and periods when enemies hunted him like an animal, he miraculously survived to rise in power through a succession of military victories until in 1206 he was elected by an all-Mongol *khuriltai* as "Genghis" (variously interpreted to mean great, oceanic, or universal), Khan of all the Mongols. Thereafter he consolidated Mongols and other steppe tribes into a single Mongol polity by integrating the army across tribal and clan lines, enforcing strict discipline and loyalty, rewarding able leaders without regard to clan or tribal affiliation, and ensuring all a fair share of war spoils (see Chapter 10). He established a quasi-legal code of behavior known as the *Jasagh*, settled disputes, and used his army to improve economic conditions for his people, whose nomadic lives provided little more than food and clothing.

Genghis's earliest campaigns were not initiated to create an empire or new homelands for Mongols but to improve living conditions at home, but soon the subjugation of foreign lands resulted in long-term Mongol presence and extensive foreign influence in Mongolia. These campaigns sought to acquire such necessities as cloth, foodstuffs, iron, and military hardware, as well as precious metals and jewels, fine clothing, and other goods needed by a growing Mongol elite (figs. 1.8, 9, 11). Because Mongolia lay north of the major Silk Road trade routes, Genghis's first target, in 1209, was the Tanghut kingdom of Xi Xia in Gansu and Ningxia, northwestern China (see Chapter 21). Soon after, in 1211, he began attacks on the Jin dynasty of northern China whose capital, Zhongdu (renamed Daidu by the Mongols and now called Beijing) fell in 1215, and then turned west against the Kara-Khitai empire of central Asia in 1218, in part because they were harboring some of his former enemies (see Chapter 22). As the khan's army grew in size, armament, and experience, it marched further west, subduing the Iranian Khwarazmian empire and attacking the Kipchak (Cuman) Türks of the Ukraine. Genghis returned to Mongolia in 1223 and later initiated a devastating attack on the Tanghuts, capturing their Silk Road trade. By this time small nomadic polities, cities, and sedentary states had proved no match for the mobile, well-trained, battle-hardened Mongol juggernaut. All of these subjugations brought increased trade and tribute, raw materials, elite goods, slaves, and supplemental troops needed at home and to support the growing Mongol domain.

Many empires have been transient and remained nameless, lasting only a few decades before collapsing from problems of leadership, succession, or rebellion. When empires disappeared, life often returned to what went before, until another power center formed and a new empire was created. Unlike empires that took decades or even centuries to mature, such as the Roman (27 BCE–395 CE), Holy Roman (962–1806), and British empires (1583–1997), the Mongol empire grew from grass roots to mega-empire status in four decades, from 1206 to 1242, and reached its global limits in 1279. At the end of his life Genghis apportioned different sectors of the Mongol *ulus* (realm) to his sons to govern as khanates under the supervision of an empire-wide Great Khan

1.5 Ulaan Tolgoi Deer Stone Site
Khovsgol province, one of the most productive herding regions in northern Mongolia, has many Bronze Age sites like this one near Lake Erkhel. Deer stones bear carvings of stylized warriors with tool belts and deer imagery on their torsos. Found with the heads of sacrificed horses and often accompanied by stone burial mounds known as *khirigsuurs*, deer stone monuments are among Mongolia's most visible archaeological treasures, dating 1300–700 BCE. The slab-lined square burial in the foreground had been looted in antiquity and probably dates to ca. 800–400 BCE.

elected by the *khuriltai* from among his male descendants. It persisted as a centralized empire for nearly fifty years, until Möngke's reign from 1251 to 1259. By this time, rival western khanates had grown stronger and more independent, and the absence of a clear method for selecting the grand khan resulted in rival claims, civil war, and eventually the empire's decline and dissolution. The Golden Horde khanate centered in southern Russia, Ukraine, and Georgia persisted until 1505, the West Asian Ilkhanate until 1335, and the khanate of the Great Khan (Yuan dynasty, founded by Kublai in China) until 1368. The empire's last gasp was from the Chaghadai khanate, which survived into the sixteenth century, lasting about as long as the Roman and British empires.

The Mongol empire did not have the formal religious core of empires built on Islam or Christianity; but neither could the Mongols' shamanist beliefs be called faithless or heathen. Similar to the Christian belief in a god residing in heaven, the Mongol religion also was based in the firmament. Genghis believed in a supreme, all-powerful deity known as Tenggeri (Eternal Heaven; see Chapter 36), who like the gods of other faiths controlled the world and human affairs, but unlike Christianity and Buddhism, lacked anthropomorphic form. It had no organized priesthood or scripture, no public ceremonies, temples or fixed places of public worship, and was interpreted primarily by shamans trained to decipher visions, interact with the spirits of nature, heal the sick, and generally set things right between the worlds of spirits and humans (see Chapter 6). Shamans performed rituals, animal sacrifice, and divination to cure the sick, change the weather, discern the future, and affect the course of events.

The Secret History of the Mongols (see Chapter 14) makes it clear that Genghis's survival during his childhood and the wars of unification, and his vision of a Mongol-dominated world, came directly from Tenggeri. Genghis seems to have acquired his vision as well as certain shamanistic powers during his periods of enforced isolation hiding from enemies in the wilderness as a young man. After becoming khan, he received spiritual support from the powerful shaman, Teb Tenggeri, who advised Genghis on everything from personnel appointments to when to wage war and engage in battle, although Genghis later perceived him as a threat and had him killed. It was not until the Mongol imperial city at Khara Khorum had become established in the 1240s that Buddhism became influencial among Mongol leaders.

During the early days of the empire religious tolerance was practiced and faith was considered a private matter. Later, as Mongol control expanded into Central Asia, the Near East, and Eastern Europe where more formal religious were dominant, Mongol religious policies changed. When Genghis Khan's grandson Hülegü began the Mongol campaign against the Abbasid caliph of Baghdad in 1256, he turned first to defeat the Assassins, a powerful Ismaili Muslim group whose tactics included murdering enemy leaders by stealth. As his war expanded into Muslim western Asia and the Near East, his campaign began to resemble a crusade against Muslims, but in reality it was always an exercise of power and subjugation. Once an enemy was subdued, Mongol khans rarely interfered with local religious beliefs or cultural affairs. Hülegü then established the West Asian Ilkhanate and proclaimed himself its ilkhan (subordinate khan). Complicating matters and symptomatic of rising internal conflicts within the empire, three years earlier Berke, khan of the Golden Horde, had converted to Islam, in part to facilitate trade with Mediterranean Muslims. Soon Berke and Hülegü were waging war with each other over territory and vassals and as supporters of different factions in the succession battle for Great Khan between Arigh Böke and Kublai between 1260 and 1264. Later, in 1295, Ghazan, khan of the Iranian Ilkanate, also converted to Islam. Mongols who remained in Mongolia continued to practice Buddhism, often together with shamanism, as they still do today. Adoption of local religious beliefs also occurred under Kublai's reign in Yuan China. In short, religion under the khans was as varied as the economics and populations of the empire at large.

Mongols and the West

Genghis died in the midst of the Tanghut campaign in 1227, never living to see construction of the capital city for the new Mongol empire that he envisioned. Still, his armies kept advancing as a succession of khans pursued Genghis's dream. By 1240, when Genghis Khan's son Ögödei was Great Khan, Khara Khorum had been completed with its khan's palace, Buddhist temples, and a Nestorian Christian church, all surrounded by a sea of Mongol felt tents (gers) housing administrators, military guards, traders, and craftsmen brought as volunteers or slaves to serve the Mongol khans (fig. 1.10). By then armies of Genghis's sons and grandsons stood on the banks of the Danube River, poised to march on Europe. While European leaders interpreted the advancing eastern storm variously, the message from the Mongol defeat of King Béla's Hungarian forces at Sajo River (see Chapter 26) was anything but speculative. Genghis's plan for Mongol domination of the world as then known seemed about to be realized. A man, who in death Mongols believed held the status of a deity, had brought Europe face-to-face with Asia. At this point, the fate of Europe seemed to hang in the balance, and diplomacy was initiated as a last resort.

European understanding of the Mongols was plagued by the absence of knowledge based on direct observation. Except when the Mongols were campaigning in Russia, Poland, and Hungary from 1237 to 1242, the menace seemed distant because Europe was not heavily invested in overland trade with China or the Mongol region to the north. The route was long and arduous and beset with many dangers, including deserts, mountain ranges, and huge rivers that impeded passage. Small numbers of merchants had been successfully negotiating the Silk Road since the late first millennium BCE, when its existence was known in Rome and China, although it could only accommodate lightweight prestige cargos such as fabrics, spices, jewels, and other exotic goods.

Religion, compounded by geography and distance, contributed to early European misunderstandings of Mongols. The Mongols, for their part, soon discovered Europeans to be, according to their terms, undisciplined, politically disorganized, and dominated by an impractical Christian ideology. European knowledge of Asia at this time was heavily tinged with exoticism and religious propaganda. To medieval Europeans fixated on

1.6 Mongolian Boots
These elaborate boots, Mongolian *gutal*, have turned-up toes similar to fancy Tibetan footgear. According to Buddhist folk tradition, they permit one to tread softly, doing little damage to the earth and its creatures. Such boots are part of the standard costume worn by Mongolian wrestlers, and it is said that the up-turned toes help wrestlers to throw an opponent by hooking his leg. Others note that they help a rider keep his foot in the stirrup. Such ideas are probably apocryphal. This pair has beautiful lines, colored panels, and handiwork of embossed and appliquéd scrolls.

the Crusades, Genghis Khan became the anti-Christ heralding Armageddon in the form of a wave of murderous Mongols. Mongols felt no compunction about mistreating their enemies, for to them power, bequeathed by Tenggeri, brought its own justice. Because Christian morality meant nothing to them, Mongols were considered demons by Christians, whose medieval mythology included an exotic pagan world populated by one-eyed, one-legged, headless, generally cannibalistic heathens, some of whom did not bleed when wounded, or, alternatively, bled like flowing rivers when killed.

The more historically inclined equated Genghis Khan with Prester John (also known as John the Presbyter), the legendary Christian king of the Orient thought to have descended from one of the three magi who honored Christ's birth. The rumors of such a king's existence may have been stimulated by an early twelfth-century visit to Rome by a prelate named John from a Christian community on the Malabar coast, which was conflated with vague knowledge of a group of Asian Christians known as Nestorians. The Nestorians were a schismatic sect founded by the fifth-century Constantinople

patriarch, Nestorius, whose expelled followers founded the Assyrian Church of the East. Pressured to move again by the expansion of Islam into western Asia, the Nestorians reached Mongolia and China, where they became widely established before the spread of Buddhism. The idea of a long-lost Christian East appealed greatly to Europeans after the beginning of the Crusades, and they came to believe, from rumors of Nestorians, that an imaginary Christian king named Prester John ruled there, waiting for a chance to retake Jerusalem from the Muslims. Such fanciful ideas about an eastern Christian-Muslim front probably originated from garbled reports of Asian traders who had heard about Muslim Khwarazmian battles with the non-Muslim Kara-Khitai empire or with Genghis Khan's western campaigns against both groups. Others saw the Mongol surge as the outcome of a biblical scenario featuring Gog and Magog, giants from the Book of Revelations, who were thought to have been imprisoned somewhere beyond the Caucasus and must have escaped to lead the Mongol attack on Christendom.

The cultural chasm between Christian Europe and the shamanist Mongols on the eve of the Mongol invasion of Europe is dramatically seen in an exchange of letters between Khaghan Güyüg and Pope Innocent IV. Having experienced the Mongol slaughters in Poland and Hungary, in 1245 the pope sent John of Plano Carpini, a 60-year-old Franciscan friar, as an envoy to the court of Khaghan Güyüg (see Chapter 20). Carpini delivered a letter chastising the khan for murdering innocent villagers and asking for clarifications of future Mongol intentions in Europe. In return for peace, the pope offered baptism and forgiveness of the khan's sins. The khan replied in 1246:

> You have…said that supplication and prayer have been offered by you, that I might find a good entry into baptism. This prayer of thine I have not understood. Other words which thou hast sent me: 'I am surprised that thou has seized all the lands of the Magyar [Hungarians] and the Christians. Tell us what their fault is.' These words of thine I have also not understood. The eternal God has slain and annihilated these lands

1.7 Engraved Silver Medallion
During the 13th and 14th centuries, Yuan dynasty officials used silver medallions like this one to certify property ownership rights to individuals. The inscription on this medallion is illegible.

and peoples because they neither adhered to Chingghis [Genghis] Khaan, nor the Khaan [Ögödei], both of whom have been sent to make known God's command, nor to the command of God. Like thy words, they also were imprudent; they were proud, and they slew out messenger emissaries. How could anybody seize or kill by his own power contrary to the command of God?

Though thou likewise sayest that I should become a trembling Nestorian Christian, worship God and be an ascetic. How knowest thou whom God absolves, in truth to whom He shows mercy? How dost thou know that such words as thou speakest are with God's sanction? From the rising of the sun to its setting, all the lands have been made subject to me. Who could do this contrary to the command of God?

Now you should say with a sincere heart: 'I will submit and serve you.' Thou thyself, at the head of all the Princes, come at once to serve and wait upon us! At that time I shall recognize your submission.

If you do not observe God's command, and if you ignore my command, I shall know you as my enemy. Likewise I shall make you understand. If you do otherwise, God knows what I know.[2]

This was not what Western leaders or the pope had hoped for, but it did have unexpected and useful results. The Carpini Franciscan mission, which lasted from 1245 to

1247 was the first important diplomatic exchange between European and Mongol leaders and seems to have been the first official envoy and exchange of relations between European and Asian heads of state. Earlier attempts to reach the Mongols initiated by King Béla of Hungary in 1234–35 and 1237 were thwarted by the turmoil of the Mongol's Russian campaign. A parallel papal mission undertaken by Dominican friars in 1246, following a southern route, reached only as far as the West Asian military camp established by the Mongol general Baiju, who was put off by the envoys' lack of customary diplomatic gifts and their strident demands. Carpini, following a northern route through Russia, was more astute and impressed Genghis Khan's grandson Batu, who gave him safe passage to Khara Khorum. Once there, however, Carpini found his mission in jeopardy. His diplomatic gifts had been expended on Batu, and Güyüg saw little use in receiving him (having already heard of the pope's message from Baiju) or even providing food or shelter. But finally, with the assistance of a Uyghur Nestorian named Chinqai who was secretary to the khan's court, an audience was arranged.

Güyüg's formal response to the papal letter was a stern rebuff, seen above. Both sides believed their god was on their side, and rather than seeking areas of accommodation, they hectored each other. The pope's overture seems particularly condescending because Mongols had yet to be defeated in any major battle and were preparing to storm Europe. To admonish the khan for killing Hungarians and Christians and seizing their lands, offering conversion and baptism, benefits that Güyüg did not understand, shows how little Christian leaders understood Mongols. Güyüg's response was more pragmatic. Recognizing no higher power than Tenggeri, he was in no need of conversion and saw no value in questioning the vision of a Mongol-ruled world received from Tenggeri through Genghis Khan; and anyway, all would be made manifest by battle outcomes.

In spite of its diplomatic failure, the Carpini mission gathered information on Mongol life, technology, religious beliefs,

1.8 Metal Casting Ladle
This cast copper ladle dating to the 14th century was recovered in archaeological excavations at the Mongol empire capital, Khara Khorum. Although it was not capital of the Mongol empire after 1260 and was past its prime in the 14th century, the city remained a center for trade; its many craft shops included metallurgical artisans.

and military organization and capability. His report, *Ystoria Mongolorum*, while notably grim about politics, was optimistic about future missionary work after discovering that many at the Mongol court, both Mongols and Chinese, were Nestorian Christians, worshiped one god, believed in Jesus Christ, and prayed in churches. Carpini dispelled the myth that Genghis Khan was Prester John, describing him as a shamanist and an empire-builder with near deity status, and noted that Mongols worshipped felt effigies of Genghis in their homes. From Chinese informants at the Mongol court he learned that Prester John did not exist in Asia, but held out India as a possibility. For the first time Europeans received a reasonably objective view of their adversary.

Fortunately for Europe the attack west of the Danube never came. Ögödei died in 1241, and his forces massing near Budapest retreated, awaiting the selection of a new khan. Güyüg reigned briefly, from 1246 to 1248, and by the time Möngke was elected in 1251, Mongol forces made the subjugation of China's Song dynasty their priority. Hülegü later began campaigns against Islam in Iran and West Asia. This shift in theater delighted European supporters of the Crusades, and after 1253 relations between the Vatican and Khara Khorum improved for a while. But despite continued exploration of diplomatic contacts, a Mongol-Vatican alliance against Islam failed to materialize; the parties and their philosophical differences were too far apart to be bridged by fleeting accords.

GENGHIS: THE EXHIBITION AND THE BOOK

Recognizing the dearth of knowledge about Genghis Khan, Don Lessem organized an exhibition featuring Genghis Khan, the Mongol empire, and Mongol history, culture, and art. The exhibition, titled *Genghis Khan*, opened at the Houston Museum of Natural Science on February 27, 2009. As part of the project, Lessem asked Morris Rossabi, William Honeychurch, and me to prepare a supporting book presenting Mongolia's geography and history, the resilient nomadic society that produced this remarkable man, and his legacy to the present day. More than thirty international experts from a variety of disciplines contributed environmental, archaeological, anthropological, and art historical perspectives. *Genghis Khan and the Mongol Empire* is organized around the central character in this great historical story. But rather than treating this subject as a biography, or the Mongol empire simply as history, we have chosen to extend the frame, to include artifacts from the exhibition as well as historical documents from libraries, museums, and archives around the world. Unlike other works dealing with Genghis Khan and the Mongol empire that take a primarily historical approach,[3] this volume also includes environmental, archaeological, anthropological, and art historical perspectives.[4]

Written Sources

Reports by traveling scholars and educated religious people provided the first direct written observations on the Mongols. Theirs was a very different process of information transfer than the field education obtained by soldiers on the battlefield. The earliest contacts were primarily European-sponsored. In addition to the report of John of Plano Carpini, his fellow traveler Friar Benedict the Pole prepared a manuscript entitled *The Tartar Relation* that generally parallels the Carpini report. *The Tartar Relation* has become notable mostly because the manuscript was found bound with a manuscript of Vincent of Beauvais's popular world history, *Speculum Historiale*, together with the notorious "Vinland Map," which purports to show eleventh-century trans-Atlantic travel to Newfoundland

1.9 Arrowheads
Each type of iron arrowhead used by Mongols for hunting and war has different qualities. Broad-bladed varieties were for hunting animals and unarmored targets. Narrow, heavy points were used for piercing leather or metal armor.

but that is judged a fake by most scholars.[5]

A few years later, around 1254, William of Rubruck arrived as an independent missionary at the Khara Khorum court of Great Khan Möngke. His *Itinerarium*, while basically a travelogue, was more perceptive than Carpini's and Benedict's reports, especially regarding religious views and culture. Best known is his account of a philosophical debate about the nature of god and faith he had with Möngke and resident Muslims, Nestorians, and Buddhists. By his reckoning, he won and the Nestorians came in last.

Although the information flow from scholar-travelers was largely biased toward the West because of wider distribution of their reports, envoys sent west by the Mongols informed at least the Mongol leadership about Europe. The first of these envoys were Aïbeg and Serkis, who were sent by the Ilkhanid Mongol ruler Baiju to Pope Innocent IV in 1247–48.[6] Forty years later the Nestorian monk Rabban Sauma went to Europe at the request of Arghun, khan of the Ilkhanate, bearing a proposal for joint military action against the Mamluks of Egypt. He reported to the khans on his return (see Chapter 28). During visits to Rome, Genoa, Paris, and other locations, Sauma was much impressed with the magnificence of Europe's churches and the might of its military forces. In a much-noted highlight, he wrote about a naval battle between Neopolitan and Aragonese fleets he witnessed from the roof of his house in Naples

and about the Frankish practice of engaging only combatants rather than civilians in war. His favorable view of Europe was probably influenced by his Eastern Christian faith.[7]

The Secret History of the Mongols is the most valuable and interesting source on the earliest phase of the empire, but it is also the most problematic. This remarkable document, which purports to be the official story of Genghis Khan's life and times, may have been written shortly after Genghis's death in 1227, although a final section seems to have been added between 1240 and 1252 (see Chapter 14). *The Secret History* is also remarkable for being the first piece ever written in Mongolian language, probably using the Uyghur-Mongolian script. Its seamless mix of mythology, epic poetry, history, and gazetteer, with no clear indication of where fact meets fancy, makes it problematic as a primary historical source on Genghis's life and thirteenth-century Mongol culture, geography, and political events. Yet without *The Secret History* almost nothing would be known about Genghis from those who knew him directly, for he died before Iranian sources begin, except what can be gleaned of his values from the *Jasagh* (see Chapter 11), the quasi-legal code he established soon after becoming Genghis Khan. Even his official portrait is fantasy, painted long after his death by a Yuan-era Chinese artist who had never seen him.

Fortunately, parts of *The Secret History* are verified by a few other independent sources. These include *Tarikh-i jahangusha* (*History of the World Conqueror*) an encyclopedic account of Genghis Khan and the Mongol empire by Ata-Malik Juvaini, a high-ranking Iranian administrative official and historian who served under Hülegü and visited the imperial court in Khara Khorum several times between 1249 and 1253. Juvaini's *History*, which was strongly influenced by his official role, provides valuable information on Genghis's life and conquests, on the history of the western empire through the 1260s, as well as on Mongol culture, nomadic life, customs, and law. Rashid al-Din (see Chapter 23), a Jewish-born Iranian who converted to Islam and held powerful government posts under two of Hülegü's

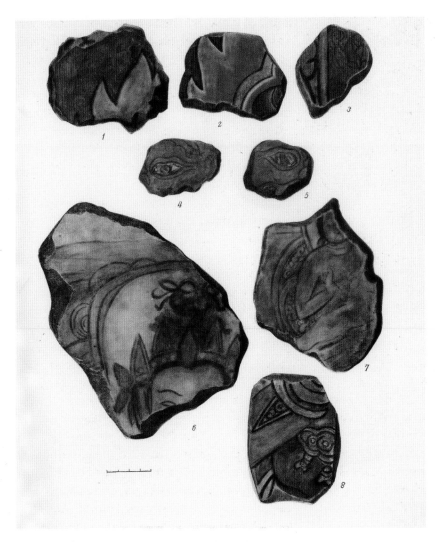

1.10 Soviet Khara Khorum Finds
Soviet archaeologist S. V. Kiselev conducted excavations in 1948–49 at Erdene Zuu and concluded that this indeed was the lost site of Khara Khorum, the ancient capital of the Mongol empire. Among the clues were 13th-century ceramics with painted Chinese designs, reproduced here from Kiselev's monograph of 1965, one of the first major publications to document scientific excavations in Mongolia.

the Euro-Christian bias of Western travelers, are primary sources for what happened within the Islamic and Mongol worlds. Each had access to Mongol informants and now-lost Mongol manuscripts, but neither of them knew Genghis Khan as a living person.

Marco Polo's report, *A Description of the World*, which appeared in 1299, is unlike other traveler reports because Polo's perspective is that of a merchant rather than an ambassador, missionary, or cleric (see Chapter 28). The Polo brothers Niccoló and Maffeo, and Niccoló's son, Marco, traveled with an official permit known as a *paiza*—something like a passport guaranteeing safe passage—granted to the Polos first by Berke and later by Kublai. The three Venetians journeyed extensively between the Mediterranean and the Mongol courts in Russia, Central Asia, China, and West Asia between 1260 and 1294. For sixteen years (1275–91) they were associated with Kublai's court, which was by then a popular meeting-place for world travelers and thinkers. Marco's widely published work was first written as recounted to Rusticello da Pisa when they were imprisoned (with amenities) in Genoa during a Venetian-Genoese war in 1298–99. First published in French, the tale soon became a sensation and was translated widely, providing Europe with its first description of a strange new eastern world. Later versions inspired Geoffrey Chaucer to write about "the king of Tartary" as a noble, merciful leader "blest by Fortune's smile" in his late fourteenth-century *Canterbury Tales*. Expecting to meet Mongol khans when he sailed west from Spain, Christopher Columbus carried a copy of the Polo book on his 1492 voyage. He did not realize that he was still an ocean away and 124 years too late.

The most formidable Asian source by far is the 4,000-page *Yuanshi* (1370), the official encyclopedic account of the Yuan dynasty (1207/71–1368) commissioned by Ming Taizu, founder of the Ming dynasty, immediately after the fall of the Yuan in 1368. Like all Chinese dynastic histories, it emphasizes bureaucratic matters and is thus invaluable for understanding the government's view.

Perhaps the biggest mystery of the Mongol story concerns Genghis Khan's death

Ilkhanate descendants, Ghazan and Öljeitü, also wrote an encyclopedic history of the Mongol empire. Commissioned by Ghazan, who was concerned over the waning knowledge of Mongol life and history in the increasingly Islamicized khanate, Rashid al-Din used Juvaini as a source to describe Möngke's reign (1251–59) the *Jami' al-Tavarikh* (*Compendium of Chronicles*) and translated materials from the *Altan Devter*, known as the Golden Book, an official document of Mongol history that was kept secretly by the Mongol court but has since been lost. A version of the *Altan Devter* compiled in Chinese as *Shengwu qinzhenglu* closely parallels the account known from al-Din and provides some assurance of its validity.[8]

Ibn Battuta, an early fourteenth-century Moroccan traveler, also produced histories that provide documentation on the western khanates (see Chapter 29). The works of these administrator-historians, who lacked and burial. Rashid al-Din ascribes his death to an unspecified illness—possibly resulting from a fall from a horse—shortly before the Xi Xia king surrendered and its capital city and entire population was destroyed in 1227. As Genghis's troops advanced, his decline and death had been kept secret from all but his family. After the victory, Genghis's body seems to have been taken back to Khentii province in northern Mongolia where his life began, to a spot he had chosen many years before. Al-Din adds a macabre detail: "On the way they killed every living being they met until they had reached the *horda* [nomadic palace-tent] with the coffin." The location of the burial is described in relation to Burkhan Khaldun, a mountain where Temüjin, young Genghis, had found refuge as a youth. In this passage al-Din notes the identification of Genghis Khan, the warrior and empire-builder, with his beginning as a hunter. He also notes that it was customary, after Mongol leaders were buried, for herds of horses to be driven back and forth across the site to obliterate all traces of its precise location. The prize of finding Genghis's grave has inspired archaeological searches since the 1870s. Many wild claims have been made, starting with an erroneous report in 1888 that the famous Russian archaeologist P.K. Kozlov had discovered his silver coffin—a notion that may have been inspired by silver finds in the ruins of the destroyed Xi Xia capital.[9] Later, in the 1930s, Owen Lattimore visited a Genghis shrine in Inner Mongolia (see page 37) where an annual festival was held at which his "memorabilia" and "remains" in a silver coffin were on display, although Lattimore doubted their authenticity.[10] Many Mongolians—following Genghis Khan's wishes—hope the location of his grave will remain forever unknown.

New Discoveries
As the survey of historical reports on the Mongol empire reveals, much of the contemporary information about this subject comes from non-Mongol sources. With the gradual decline in the discovery of new written sources, archaeology has begun to offer a promising approach to the still-poorly known history of the Mongols. In the thirteenth and fourteenth centuries Mongolia was a nation whose culture depended largely on oral traditions; it had few institutions comparable to those that existed throughout Europe, India, and South Asia—churches, mosques, palace complexes, libraries, armories—that preserved relics of the past. Almost all tangible materials from this period of empire that existed in places such as Khara Khorum have been destroyed in wars or were carried off, lost, or buried (figs. 1.4, 10). Even knowledge of the location of Khara Khorum was lost. In short, much that remains to be learned about the history of the Mongols and their empire will have to be gleaned from archaeological evidence of material culture.

William Honeychurch, Chunag Amartuvshin, and I present archaeological evidence (see Chapter 8) that shows that by the introduction of metal in the Bronze Age, which dates to around 4,000 to 2,800 years ago, the roots of the horse-based nomadic culture seen today had taken shape. Large burial mounds were erected for the dead and Mongolia's famous "deer stone" monuments, standing stones representing warriors with iconic images of deer carved on their bodies, were being constructed (fig. 1.5). Prehistoric Mongolia experienced occasional bursts of agriculture, urbanism, trade, and craft innovation, and the first state-level developments, represented by the Xiongnu culture (200 BCE–200 CE), whose burial complexes contain chariots and retainer graves also found in South Siberia and China. The Xiongnu were followed by a succession of steppe empires including the sixth- to eighth-century Türk empires and others, separated by periods of decline, until the rise of the Mongol empire in the thirteenth century.

Recent archaeological research has demonstrated promising results, including settlements perhaps relating to Genghis Khan and the Mongol clans. Noriyuki Shiraishi discusses (Chapter 17) the inscription found on a rock surface at Serven Khaalga mountain in Khentii province, a Mongol homeland, that appears to commemorate a battle at the end of the twelfth century

1.11 Blue-and-White Porcelain Dish

Chinese artisans began manufacturing blue-and-white Qinghua porcelain, famous for its deep cobalt underglaze painting, in the 12th century. During the Yuan dynasty established by Genghis Khan's grandson, Kublai, it became a valuable export commodity, sent to Japan, Southeast Asia, and West Asia. It first reached Europe with Portuguese merchants and became a sensation in Holland after being imported by the Dutch East Indian Company in 1603. This 13th-century piece manufactured at the Qinghua kiln in China was recovered at Khara Khorum. Its decoration includes a crane, an ancient Chinese motif symbolizing longevity, surrounded by floral elements.

between the Jurchen-Jin state (1115–1234) and the Tartar enemies of the early Mongol tribes. More relevant to Genghis himself may be the Avraga site located near the Kherlen River not far from Serven Khaalga. Coins minted by the Jurchen-Jin state in 1179 and radiocarbon dates of similar age indicate that Avraga was occupied in the early period of Genghis's life. While there is no direct evidence confirming Genghis's presence at the site, the complex architecture and evidence of craft production and trade goods suggest it was an elite seasonal camp of the sort Genghis would have used.

New information from the very heart of the Mongol Empire is also becoming available. In separate essays, Ulambayar Erdenebat and Ernst Pohl (Chapter 18), and Hans-Georg Hüttel (Chapter 19), present the results of excavations at Khara Khorum documenting the early development of this early imperial city and its architecture, arts, technologies, and external contacts as Mongolia emerged from centuries of isolation to become, from 1235 to 1265, the political center of eastern Eurasia. Excavations in the business district near the city center have uncovered remains of ceramic and metallurgical workshops similar to those described by William of Rubruck, who reached Khara Kho-

rum in the spring of 1254. It was in shops like these that the French goldsmith, Guillaume Boucher—one of many famous foreign artisans brought to Khara Khorum as slaves to build and decorate the new Mongol capital—must have made the tree-shaped silver fountain in the courtyard of the khan's palace that dazzled foreign visitors by dispensing different beverages from its branches. The search for the palace of the Great Khan, an ongoing archaeological effort of the past seventy-five years, has also advanced. A large building once thought to be the palace has recently been properly identified as the Buddhist Temple of the Rising Yuan described in a Khara Khorum stone inscription dating to 1346. The missing palace, described by Marco Polo, seems to have been found exactly where it was supposed to be all along, directly beneath the Erdene Zuu monastery.

Archaeological evidence has also emerged from the relatively unknown Russian portion of the Mongolian empire known as the Golden Horde. Here, as in Mongolia, the paucity of written records has hampered historical research. The Golden Horde, named for the gold-colored *horda* or *ordo*, the nomadic palace tent used by its leaders, was the most distant khanate from Mongolia and became part of the empire with

Batu's and Subödei's invasion of Russia in 1237. An essay by Mark G. Kramarovsky (Chapter 25) reveals the Genghisid heraldic motifs and three- and four-clawed dragons on belt ornaments that identify the graves of Golden Horde leaders and members of the house of Batu. Over time the Golden Horde grew fabulously rich from Russian tribute and from trade that passed through its territory linking southern Russia with the Near East, West Asia, Mongolia, and China. This and Daniel Waugh's essay (Chapter 24) reveal the Mongol role in founding administrative, trade, and craft centers in territories that had previously been tribal lands, and extending Silk Road trade far west of its earlier boundaries, connecting Russia's gold, silver, ivory, and fur resources with the Muslim world and the Orient.

At the other end of the Eurasian continent, Mongols made an even more lasting impact on China, uniting it into a single political entity and modernizing its government, economy, and arts. Morris Rossabi (Chapter 27), François Louis (Chapter 30), and Willem Vogelsang (Chapter 31) discuss the advances in Chinese textiles, painting, ceramics, and sculpture of the Yuan period, which Genghis's grandson, Kublai, encouraged as he also promoted industry and foreign trade. During this period, Chinese goods and art styles penetrated into Iran and other areas of Central and West Asia, finding markets for its blue-and-white porcelain, silk brocade textiles, architecture, and even the art of book-making. Once South China had been subdued, its maritime traditions were harnessed to extend Yuan trade and influence into the coastal areas and island systems of Southeast Asia, and into the Indian Ocean. Archaeologists have recovered cargoes of the famous Yuan porcelain export ware from sunken ships that once sailed these routes.

Despite great progress at the center of the Yuan empire, much of its population continued to suffer great hardship, as seen dramatically in a group of mummies found in a cave in the Gobi Desert near the present China-Mongolia border. Bruno Frohlich and his colleagues (Chapter 34) document the manner of their gruesome deaths, which he relates to struggles between rival herding groups whose lives had not benefited from the growth of imperial elites and luxury trade passing through their territory. The Gobi finds are not unique, for as Ulamba-yar Erdenebat shows (Chapter 35), Mongolia's dry, cold climates have preserved the graves of many Mongolians, mighty and humble, whose bodies and artifacts provide insight into their lives and ancient world.

Archaeologists have also provided information on the ill-fated invasions of Japan that Kublai forced upon his Korean allies in 1274 and 1281. James P. Delgado, Randall J. Sasaki, and Kenzo Hayashida (Chapter 33) describe how underwater archaeologists have recovered traces of the 1281 fleet that was wrecked by a *kamikaze* (typhoon) near Takashima Island just as it was about to disembark its troops on Japanese soil, losing thousands of ships and tens of thousands of men. Researchers excavating ancient shipyards in China and underwater archaeologists working at the invasion site at Takashima Island have recovered remains of vessels, ceramic bombs, Buddha figures, and other materials related to the Mongol-led invasion of 1281.

Genghis Khan's Legacy

Following the decline of the Mongol empire, five hundred years passed during which Mongolia was dominated by the Qing-Manchu dynasty and became increasingly influenced by Tibetan Buddhism (see Chapter 36). During this period the legacy of Genghis Khan remained strong; however, the situation changed dramatically when Mongolia became a Soviet vassal state in 1924. During the 1930s the Soviet-backed Mongolian government destroyed most of the country's Buddhist monasteries and murdered 20,000 to 25,000 monks and lamas as well as many of its teachers and educated class. By the mid-twentieth century, when the Soviet Union and China were engaged in their own cold war, thousands of Soviet troops, advisors, and scientists came to Mongolia. In addition to purges and exploitation, the de facto Soviet occupation brought many benefits—reforms in education and medicine, technical assistance to

"The Shrine of a Conqueror"

"There is a sanctuary in the loop of the Yellow River to which thousands of Mongols make pilgrimage, believing it to be the burial place of the great Chingghis or Genghis Khan. No Westerner had seen the ceremonies of this cult, much less taken part in them..."

So began an article entitled "The Shrine of a Conqueror" written by the famous China and Mongolia scholar, Owen Lattimore, in *The Times*, London on 21 April 1936. In it he describes a visit the prior year to a desolate region of the Ordos in western Inner Mongolia to witness annual spring ceremonies marking the death of Genghis Khan. Local tradition held that it took place at this very location, known as Edjen Khorokha (Enclosure of the Lord), nearly 900 kilometers west of Bejing. Those attending the ceremony told Lattimore that the court traveling with Genghis at the time of his death had been charged with carrying on an annual commemorative ritual. Lattimore describes the ceremonies and notes that they were attended annually by thousands of Mongol pilgrims who come to offer prayers to the conqueror, whom many believe to be a god and whose spirit is thought to be present. Lattimore found relics of the conqueror displayed in decorated *gers*, chief among them being Genghis's State Tent. To its right was the Tent of the Bows and Quivers with its silver-plated bows, armor, and saddles. To the left were the tents of the Greater and Lesser Empresses, the latter dedicated to the Tanghut princess he took from the king of Xi Xia in 1209. There was a stand-in for Genghis's sacred white horse and a cart for dispensing *airag*, the Mon-

gol beverage made from fermented mare's milk. Lattimore, in disguise because foreigners were barred from the rituals, participated in chants and drinking of fermented milk before the relics.

> In the tent, on a silver-plated altar, stand three wooden chests, one upon the other, all plated with silver. One of them by tradition holds the remains of the conqueror. On the hammered silver plating are Mongol inscriptions, in a not archaic lettering. I made out a reference to "the Leagues and Banners of Inner and Outer Mongolia"—a formula which did not exist under the Mongol dynasty, and proves that most of the silver work is not older than the Manchu dynasty.

The Manchu inscription led Lattimore to conclude that Edjen Khorokha was probably not Genghis's final resting place; the alternative tradition, that he was buried somewhere in northern Outer Mongolia, was more likely. At the close of the festival all of the shrine tents were "invited" back to their permanent sanctuaries. Before a

team of two white camels hitched to the cart carrying Genghis's tent was hauled off, Lattimore took the photograph seen here, and later, on the back of a print, wrote "Ger holding the relics of Genghis Khan." Soon after the relics departed, word spread that bandits were about to attack. All ran for their horses, and Lattimore's party made a forced march for several days, finally reaching the Yellow River. Here, safe at last, his guide confided, "We are men of good destiny and can speak the truth; I have ridden this whole journey in fear."

Much has changed since Lattimore's visit. Today the sanctuary of a conqueror, where Genghis's life has been celebrated faithfully by true believers for 800 years, has been turned into a theme park and tourist center.

herders, introduction of irrigation and expansion of agriculture, development of infrastructure and transport, establishment of a stable government bureaucracy, creation of arts and scientific institutions, and imposition of a written form of Mongolian based on the Cyrillic alphabet. By the 1990s most Mongolians could read and had access to radios and televisions, and some received higher education in the Soviet Union.

The Communist Chinese government provided similar benefits to Mongolians living in Inner Mongolia, but unlike the Soviets, the Chinese did not suppress the memory of Genghis Khan or the celebration of festivals in his name such as that witnessed by Owen Lattimore in 1935, noted above. Annexed to China in the early twentieth century, Inner Mongolia became subject to the assimilation policies of its Communist government. Throughout the middle part of the century, hundreds of thousands of Chinese belonging to the ruling Han ethnic group immigrated or were sent to build farms, diluting and sinicizing its Mongol population, which was then two to three times as large as Outer Mongolia's. By 1990 the population of Inner Mongolia was 21 million, of which only 3.8 million were Mongol, the rest being largely Han Chinese. Today there are about 4 million Mongols in Inner Mongolia and 2.8 million in the Republic of Mongolia.[11]

While much social progress was made, the Soviet era brought tragedy and suffering beyond that experienced in the early purges. For the first time in a thousand years, the Mongols found themselves almost completely isolated from the world beyond the Soviet orbit. All information passed through Soviet filters; political life was filled with cronyism and corruption; and freedom of movement and expression was greatly restricted. Mongolians retained memories of Genghis Khan and the empire period, but they were memories.

Among the more unusual aspects of the Mongol legacy is the recent scientific discovery, discussed here by Theodore Schurr (see Chapter 38), that genetic traces of a distinctive Mongol male descent line can be identified today in the genome of more than 16 million Central and East Asian

men—a biological inheritance of the Mongol wars, empire, and the access of its male leaders to large numbers of women.

Despite nearly a century of repression, Genghis's legacy thrives today. In 1990, in the aftermath of the Soviet empire's collapse, the new democratic nation of Mongolia, freed for the first time in hundreds of years to chart its own course, initiated a frenzy for all things Genghis, whose name and/or likeness branded everything from vodka to restaurants, airports to currency (see Chapter 40). Instantly the lives of Genghis and his descendants became as popular to herders as to the urban culture of the rapidly growing regional centers and the capital, Ulaan Baatar. Mongolia again began to look beyond its borders. Nations all around the world reciprocated, sending aid, money, hospital equipment, and mining companies, in particular, began joint ventures in Mongolia.

Some Mongols resettled abroad in Korea, Europe, and the United States, where within the past ten years Mongol communities of 3,000 to 5,000 developed in San Francisco, Los Angeles, Denver, Chicago, and Washington, D.C. Meanwhile, tourism became a major Mongolian industry: thousands of outsiders flock yearly to experience Mongolia's Flaming Cliffs, the snow-capped Altai Mountains, and the pristine waters and forests of Lake Khovsgol. Tourists climb onto the backs of camels, ride horses into the mountains and across the steppe, and visit the haunts of America's 1920s swashbuckler explorer-paleontologist, Roy Chapman Andrews, the first to discover dinosaur eggs. Foreigners enjoy Mongolia's traditional life and cheerful welcoming people, taste *airag*, the famous national drink made from fermented mare's milk, and participate in the annual July Naadam Festival with its "manly sports"—horse-racing, archery, wrestling—all under Tenggeri's great blue sky (fig.1.6).

The wider world's most recent engagement with Mongolia came in 2006 when the nation marked the 800th anniversary of Genghis's investiture, which is now recognized as Mongolia's birthday. A new façade was built to obscure the old Soviet-style parliament building and serves as a

1.12 Reconstructed "Camp of a Conqueror"
The opening of Mongolia to tourism has prompted the development of museums and monuments, along with preservation of historical sites and re-creations such as this 13th-century *ger* camp northeast of Ulaan Baatar. Here, in a dramatic setting amidst craggy granite outcrops, is an encampment of a type that might have been occupied by Genghis Khan, his family, and personal guard, replete with a nearby "shaman's camp." Visitors attend audiences with Genghis, hear throat-singing (*khoomii*) performances with traditional Mongol instruments such as the horsehead fiddle (*morin khuur*), and stay overnight in 13th-century style.

phones, iPods, baggy pants, and cars, cars, and more cars signaled the dawn of a new era.

Although an ancient polity, Mongolia today is in the midst of rapid transformation. The last century was one of turmoil, when Mongolia passed from a semi-theocratic society to a communistic order and, in 1990, to a democratic nation. About half of its 2.8 million people live in the capital city of Ulaan Baatar, while the rest live in the countryside as herders or in regional centers. Not since the days of Genghis Khan have its diplomats, soldiers, and businessmen, traveling to the far corners of the world, been received with respect rather than fear. Little by little Mongolia's resources—cashmere, ore, oil, meat products, and hides—are finding markets beyond its former and proximal trading partners, Russia and China. Its authors and filmmakers are finding readers and viewers in Europe and North America, and outsiders are increasingly traveling to Mongolia to view its spectacular natural landscapes, experience its fascinating traditional cultures, and meet its friendly, resourceful people. In a real way, ancient Mongolia and modern Mongolia have merged. The elemental herding life that continues to sustain most Mongolians today has not changed much since the time when Genghis as a young man struggled to feed and defend his family. Many of Mongolia's ancient ways—its nomadic economy, musical traditions, love of horses, of festivals and sporting events, and openness to the outside world, remain strong, even as Mongolia finds its way into the globalized world. One senses that if Genghis Khan, an early advocate of global integration, returned today, he would approve and would see that little of what was essentially "Mongol" in his day has changed.

backdrop for an immense bronze statue of a regal Genghis seated on his throne flanked by his four sons. A 95-foot high statue of Genghis on horseback was constructed on an open hilltop near the Tuul River, 54 kilometers from Ulaan Baatar near a re-constructed "thirteenth-century village" catering to caravans of tourist buses (fig. 1.12). Tourists from around the world participated in festivities marking the rebirth of a nation, observing special art exhibits and performances of the Buddhist Tsaam dance in which performers wearing oversize papier-mâché heads engage in mock battles and comic antics. In the midst of this festival, which coincided with the annual Naadam in early July, Ulaan Baatar was experiencing an economic boom with the construction of hundreds of new buildings. Ubiquitous cell-

1. Komaraoff and Carboni 2002, 7.
2. Translation drawn from Dawson 1955, 86.
3. Morgan 1986; Marshall 1993; Jackson 2005.
4. Komaroff and Carboni 2002.
5. Skelton et al. 1965.
6. Roux 1993, 316.
7. Morgan 1986, 188-9.
8. Morgan 1986, 11-12.
9. "Secrecy Still Marks Tomb of Genghis Khan," *New York Times*, 20 Nov. 1927.
10. Lattimore 1936.
11. Atwood 2004, 245.

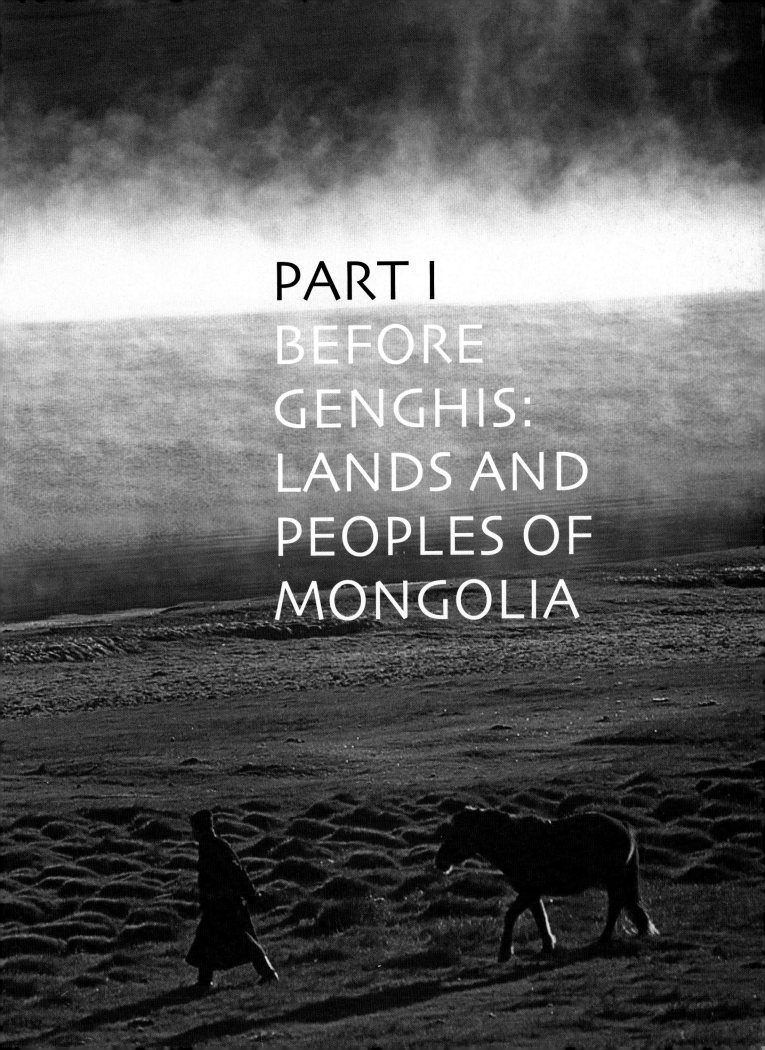

PART I

BEFORE GENGHIS: LANDS AND PEOPLES OF MONGOLIA

2.1 Intertwined History

Recent research has revealed evidence of bit abrasion on horse teeth and horse milk residue in ceramic containers at sites on the Central Eurasian steppe dated to 3500 BCE. Such evidence suggests domestication of horses was well underway by this time, eventually leading to revolutionary changes in transportation, warfare, and social life throughout the world. Mongolia, with its broad expanses of steppe grasslands, is ideal horse habitat, and the rearing and riding of horses remains central to Mongolian life, culture, and economy. Here a herder captures a horse with the traditional *uurga*, a long pole with a noose at its end.

BOSSON

2. Mongolia

HEARTLAND OF ASIA

JAMES BOSSON

FOR THOUSANDS OF YEARS, the rolling Mongolian steppe, like a grassy cradle in the heartland of Inner Asia, has provided sustenance and geographic protection for its animal and human inhabitants. Surrounding this oasis of green, mountains or deserts form distinct but permeable barriers. To the north lie the Sayan Mountains of southern Siberia, the Russian province of Tuva, backed by thick forests and bogs. In the west the Altai Mountains rise to glaciated peaks. To the south lies the Gobi Desert, hundreds of kilometers wide, and to the east the steppe grasslands give way to parched barrens that stretch a thousand kilometers to the Gulf of Korea. Between these natural borders the more hospitable basin-like central Mongolian steppe forms the biological core of the Inner Asian plateau. Watered by winter snows, seasonal mountain rivers, and summer thunderstorms, the Mongolian plain—one thousand kilometers wide, wetter and greener in the northern foothills, and drier toward the Gobi—has nurtured pastoralists for millennia.

Once converted about five thousand years ago from an Ice Age hunters' paradise to a herders' landscape following the domestication of its "five snouts"—sheep, goats, cattle, camels, and horses—the Mongolian culture quickly became established and has changed little over succeeding millennia. Today, half of Mongolia's human population lives outside of the capital city in small towns or settlements of felt tents known as *gers.* They tend the same animals, eat the same food, and converse about the weather, water, their neighbors, and the spirits of the land much as their ancestors did through the ages. And yet, as steady as the Gobi winds, the cross-currents of history have found their way into Mongolian *gers,* just as Mongolian peoples have found their way to other lands, following the steppe grasslands west to the Caspian, Southern Russia, even to the Puszta steppes of Hungary. Mongolia, while particularly susceptible to influences from Siberia and China, has always had natural geographic and ecological continuity via the steppe to the west. The steppe is Mongolia's lifeline—its source of sustenance and its strongest connection to the outside world (fig. 2.8).

The Land

Mongolia's geography is both physically daunting and visually awe-inspiring. Its steppe region averages 1580 meters above sea level,[1] and because it is far from the moderating influence of the ocean, the climate is extreme. The country's landlocked position creates spectacular diurnal and annual ranges in

2.2 Gobi Dunes
High sand dunes like those found in the driest deserts are uncommon but dramatic features of Mongolia's Gobi Desert. Where topography and strong prevailing winds over millennia have concentrated sands, high dune-fields, called *elsen mankhan*, have formed.

temperature and weather systems. Yet, due to the low precipitation and strong winds, there is seldom snow of any depth on the ground, even in sub-zero conditions. In fact, when snow is plentiful, it is a disaster for the herdsmen. This condition is called "white famine" (*tsagaan zud*), a time when the snow is so deep herds cannot kick through to reach the grass. Even more devastating is the "black famine" *(khara zud)*, when an ice crust forms that is equally impenetrable. The storms that produce these conditions are called *zuds* and can last for days and fill the air with a deadly mixture of snow and sand, freezing or suffocating animals over huge expanses of territory. The variety of natural catastrophes—including *zuds*, droughts, fire, and animal disease—is offset by the herdsman's time-tested "five snouts" insurance policy, because each of these animals has different tolerances and abilities to withstand privation.

Throughout most of Mongolia the winds blow almost constantly, with a decreasing intensity only in summertime. In April, the wind velocity in Dalanzadgad, a small town in the southern Gobi region, has been measured at 28 meters per second.[2] Anyone who has visited these steppes comes away with the sound of the constant wind as a souvenir; some believe the wind-song is the source of Mongolia's unique musical traditions, such as the high-pitched operatic "long song" genre (see Chapter 7).[3]

To the newly arrived visitor, Mongolia's landscape can befuddle. Traveling north from Mongolia's capital city, Ulaan Baatar, located in the central steppe region, grassy hills climb one above the other toward the mountains of Siberia (fig. 2.3). But looking in the other direction the vista reverses: all one sees are the northern sides of fully forested hills. This visual paradox has an intricate biological and cultural basis in which grazing and wood-cutting find a balance with precipitation and evaporation that keeps south-facing slopes in grassland and sunshadowed north-facing slopes under forests of Siberian larch (*Larix sibirica*) and birch (*Betula*) trees. Willows (*Salix*) also grow along watercourses. On the steppe, a variety of feather grasses (*Stipa* sp.) and brush are dominant, and rodents, principally marmots and squirrels, are abundant. In northern and mountainous regions arctic vegetation prevails, and permafrost is present sporadically in the ground even in summer. In areas of discontinuous permafrost, large earth-

2.3 Steppe Grasslands
Typical of northern Mongolia are rolling hills covered with grass and brush that form part of the great Eurasian steppe. Cold and snow-covered in winter and temperate with frequent thunderstorms in summer, the Mongolian steppe supported many species of grazing animals during the Ice Ages, and after the domestication of sheep, goats, camels, cattle, and horses, became the economic core of nomadic life. Nearly one-third of Mongolia's population still lives as herders in *gers* and small villages in "the countryside," as the steppe is popularly known.

covered ice mounds called *pingos*, sometimes reaching three meters in height, form under the surface, rising and falling with the seasons. The alpine pastures in the Sayan Mountains around Lake Khovsgol support the southernmost domestic reindeer population in the world. The lower forested mountain slopes are inhabited by bear, antelope, large cats, and the Siberian elk (red deer, *Cervus sibericus*), famed for its huge, graceful antlers.

Mongolia's surrounding mountains create complex drainage patterns, but most of its rivers are small and do not create barriers to flocks, horses, or carts. Snow-melt creates strong spring and early summer run-off from the mountain slopes. In summer many of these rivers and streams are dry, but violent thunderstorms bring torrential rains that periodically flood large swaths of land. But even Mongolia's largest rivers like the Selenge, Orhkon, and Kherlen, can often be crossed in numerous places. Most others draining from the mountain rims surrounding Mongolia eventually disappear into the steppe, either into the ground, into playas and salt marshes, or into saline lakes, which are common in western Mongolia and in the Gobi. However, two rivers, the Khug and the Selenge, rising only a few tens of kilometers

apart in northern Mongolia, flow east and west then northward to form the great Yenisei-Angara drainage of Siberia. Most of Mongolia's lakes are "dead seas." Lake Khovsgol in northern Mongolia is the exception, being the highest large sweet-water lake in Asia. It drains through the Selenge River into Siberia's Lake Baikal, Asia's largest freshwater lake and the world's deepest.

Southern Mongolia is a land of arid sandy deserts with dunes in constant motion, driven by strong winds. The vast Gobi Desert is not as arid as its reputation leads us to believe (fig. 2.2). The term *gobi* refers to a specific type of gravel desert with a flora of low, creeping, drought-resistant grasses, but it also has broad areas of savannah-type landscape with grasslands, brush, and stunted trees. *Gobi* has come to be used as a place-name, which has become synonymous with danger, hardship, and menace. In fact, there are springs and wells in numerous locations that allow the Gobi Desert to be traversed without dramatic difficulties. Water can be found close enough to the surface to quench the thirst of the herdsmen and their animals; although it is often saline and unappetizing, it is nevertheless potable.

The domesticated horse, that most pre-

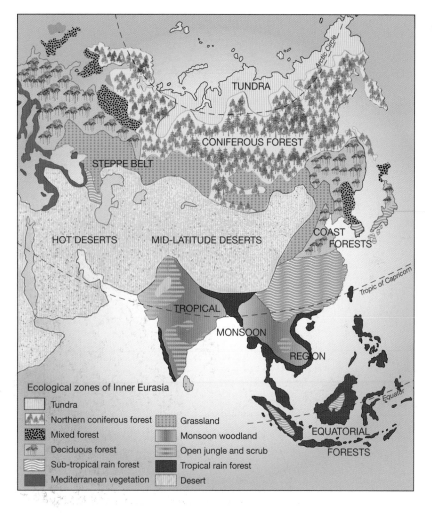

Ecological zones of Inner Eurasia

- Tundra
- Northern coniferous forest
- Mixed forest
- Deciduous forest
- Sub-tropical rain forest
- Mediterranean vegetation
- Grassland
- Monsoon woodland
- Open jungle and scrub
- Tropical rain forest
- Desert

2.4 The Steppe Zone: Highway of Conquest
Running across Eurasia from Manchuria to Hungary between 40–50° N latitude, the grassy rolling steppe is a highway of migration, trade, and cultural influences. Until the development of ocean-going ships, the steppe, like the arid region to the south supporting the Silk Road, was a major artery connecting East and West. Like Scythians and Türks before them, Mongols used the steppe as their highway of conquest in the West.

cious of animals, allowed Mongolian peoples to become nomads par excellence (fig. 2.1). The horse's mobility allowed nomads to seek sustenance where it was most abundant. Game could be found everywhere—from the Gobi through the grasslands to the foothills of the high mountains. The Mongolians' economic survival has always combined animal husbandry and hunting. And what they could not produce locally, over time they learned to acquire by force, making a regular practice of raids into Northern China to obtain such goods as woven cloth, silk, and tea.

Nomads and their Culture

Who then, were the freely moving herdsmen who inhabited this area from ancient times? Nomads leave few physical remains to be found by archaeologists; neither do they commonly leave written records. Although archaeological knowledge is advancing, much that is known of Mongolia's early people comes from Mongolia's literate and sedentary

neighbors, in this case, the Chinese.

Archaeological evidence indicates that the herder had a military alter ego. The warrior-herdsman duality must have been present in steppe societies as early as the Bronze and Iron ages, 3,500 to 2,500 and 2,500 to 1,500 years ago, respectively. During the Late Bronze Age "deer stones"—engraved stone monuments found throughout northern and western Mongolia—were carved, depicting stylized warriors with tools and weapons hanging from their belts and graceful images of the Siberian deer on their torsos. Warfare must have been endemic in these early societies and probably ranged from localized clan rivalries involving disputes over pasture rights, water, women, slaves, and others matters to the scale of regional conflicts and wars between entire ethnic or political confederations.

A tall stone stele known as the Kül Tegin stone, which was carved a little more than 1,200 years ago and still stands in the heartland of Mongolia, offers more direct clues into the early human history of this region. This stone bears inscriptions in letters reminiscent of the Scandinavian runic script, mainly straight-cut lines, vertical and oblique with few horizontal or curved lines. The origins of this script are still obscure, but because this stele bears a parallel Chinese text, the script was deciphered in 1893. The text, which was determined to be an early form of the Türkic language,[4] refers to events in the eighth century is a tangible witness that a nomadic Türkic society inhabited the center of what is now Mongolia. From these inscriptions memorializing famous leaders, and from other documents, scholars have learned much about the political organization of Mongolia's early nomadic peoples.

Confederations were made up of nomadic clans that allied themselves to the local leader, known as khan. If they had other ambitions or were defeated, the khan and his commanders were killed, and a new oath of allegiance was taken by those remaining. The new clan became part of the confederation. In this way, the khan's troops grew by geometric progression, and it was to the advantage of the defeated soldiers

to be on the victorious side with promise of future booty. Because the defeated clan had the same organization and economic structure as the victor, the amalgamation of troops was successful. Although these nomadic clans might have different linguistic backgrounds, the majority spoke Türkic or Mongolian languages. Such confederations were multicultural, although the name of the confederation was that of the ruling khan. These armies of nomads also had other advantages over their more settled adversaries. To begin with, they were not fighting for a nation, in the way a sedentary polity defines this concept (see Chapter 10). The confederation title "Mongol" did not conclusively appear until the time of Temüjin, who later held the title of Genghis Khan.

Because outsiders could not easily breach the Sayan or Altai mountains or the steppe's barrens or deserts, the Mongolian heartland was a natural fortress whose development depended mostly on its own internal affairs.

Yet to Türks, Mongols, and other nomadic tribes who had adapted to these harsh conditions, these barriers were easily passed, and the one-way traffic helped preserve an indigenous life-style. As Owen Lattimore recognized years ago,[5] invaders might destroy a city or lay waste to villages, but the Mongols could slip away into the hills with their *gers* and animals where armies could not find them. Invaders rarely stayed to hunt them down. In time, the Mongols would reassemble and march forward again. In this way Mongolia's geographic isolation was both its greatest boon and its gravest challenge.

Mobility remains at the core of steppe nomadic life, and key to mobility is the felt tent or yurt, known to Mongols as a *ger* (fig. 2.8). The antiquity of the *ger* may reach back more than four thousand years, to the time when nomadic pastoralism began to be practiced. The *ger* had to be light and easily transportable yet strong enough to withstand fierce storms. Today's Mongolian *ger* is prob-

ably similar to its ancient prototype: it has collapsible lattice walls fastened to a conical roof made of slender wooden poles, a rigid wooden door supported by posts, and a hole for smoke and ventilation at the apex of the structure (fig. 2.7). Once the framework is secured by lashings, one or more layers of thick felt matting are tied around the walls and over the roof. The *ger* is heated by burning wood or dung in a small barrel stove, which can keep a *ger* warm in the depths of winter. When storms threaten, heavy rocks are suspended from the walls or roof to hold it down. This exquisitely designed house is ideally suited to the constant winds; they are warm in winter and provide shade and ventilation in summer when the lower felt wall covering can be rolled up a short distance to let the wind blow right through the dwelling. Experienced hands can erect or disassemble a *ger* in thirty minutes. Dismantled, the entire dwelling can be carried on several camels or on carts pulled by yaks. Today's nomads more frequently make their seasonal moves by truck.

The modern Mongol herder's yearly round is also undoubtedly similar to the ancient pattern of seasonal camp moves. In some areas, for example, near forested areas or rivers, herders may move only short distances, or might move only two or three times a year. In less productive regions, such as the Gobi, or in the aftermath of *zuds* or droughts, herders' seasonal moves are more frequent and take place over great distances. In northern Mongolia, nomads frequently locate winter camps in protected valleys near the edge of the forest; in barren hilly regions, people prefer south-facing slopes and hillsides protected from northern winds and where spring snow-melt promotes early grass growth. Water is always an issue, and camps must be accessible to rivers, springs, or wells. If winter snows are too low, summer droughts may force nomads to migrate hundreds of kilometers. Cold climate conditions have been theorized as a major factor in historical social and cultural change on the steppe and have been cited specifically in the rise of Genghis Khan and the expansion of the Mongol empire. More refined studies (see Chapter 4) confirm a cold period before 1206 when Genghis Khan was consolidating the Mongol tribes. Losses of livestock due to such conditions might have enticed people to join a powerful new leader. After Genghis Khan's election in 1206, however, warmer weather returned through much of the early thirteenth century, making climate an unlikely factor in the growth of the Mongol empire.

Mongolian culture and society today retain many characteristics that emerged thousands of years ago in response to its climate, environment, and geography. Its culture type

2.8 Erecting a *Ger*

The *ger*, a felt-covered tent with a lattice-wall frame and roof poles fitted into a central ring, has been the traditional Mongolian dwelling for at least two thousand years. Equipped with a small tin barrel stove and insulated with felt, a *ger* is comfortable in all seasons, even the depth of winter. In summer the felt can be rolled up from the ground to let the breeze blow through. An engineering marvel, a dwelling that is light and easy to move by cart, camel, or truck, the *ger* is strong enough to withstand Mongolia's violent winter and summer storms.

seems to have became established quickly following the adoption of domestic sheep and goats from the western Asian steppe and the addition—perhaps locally derived—of yak and camel domesticates. Wool from these animals stimulated the invention of felt, which provided sturdy material for everything from warm clothing to *ger* coverings and became the focus for an ancient artistic genre of felt appliqué and embroidery that continues to this day. Soon after these core traditions of Mongolian nomadic life were in place, about 5,000 years ago, came the domestication of the horse. Horse-riding was a later development that transformed herding, and it established mounted warfare as another core element of nomadic steppe life, bringing with it new political developments, trade,

and external relations. During the last two thousand years, Mongolia's nomadic economy, traditional adaptations, and military tradition provided the basis for the growth of huge empires and population dispersions, notably that of the Türks in the seventh and eighth centuries and the Mongols in the thirteenth. During intervening periods Mongolia's "fortress" topography, and relative geographic isolation, allowed its grass, its "five muzzles," and its hardy and resilient peoples to preserve an ancient cultural tradition that has become part of the modern world.

1. Murzaev 1954, 133.
2. Murzaev 1954, 246.
3. Levin 2006: Levin and Suzukei 2006.
4. Thomsen 1893.
5. Lattimore 1938.

3. Mongolia: Ancient Hearth of Central Asia

Steven B. Young

In Mongolia, one is as far from the salt seas as it is possible to be on this planet. North lies the broad belt of the Siberian larch forest, extending thousands of kilometers to the Arctic Ocean. To the south, the Gobi Desert rises to the Himalayan mountain complex. To the east physical barriers are less formidable and have long allowed migrations of people, as well as animals and plants, between Mongolia and the Pacific shores in China and Korea. Westward, the old trade routes lead through the steppes and highlands of Kazakhstan into the Caspian Basin and, ultimately, the ancient grasslands of eastern Europe. Long before trade routes were established, these pathways were traversed by camels, wild horses, bison, and a host of other creatures, large and small—as well as human migrants.

New research suggests that Mongolia, once thought of as an isolated marginal region of Inner Asia, may have been a central refuge and source of animal species and a hearth of human peoples and cultures that repeatedly migrated into other parts of the world. Scythians, Türks, and Mongols are only the most recent of these diasporic peoples; others may have included the ancient Americans and Eskimos. The history of early Mongolia and its ancient environments is only beginning to be explored, and the results suggest that a unique combination of high-altitude geography, cold climate, and resourceful peoples have given Mongolia a larger role in history than is generally accorded.

Climate

Mongolia's extreme continental climate reflects its landlocked nature. With none of the ameliorating influence of the sea, the range of seasonal changes is intensified. The range between Ulaan Baatar's mean summer and winter temperatures is three times greater than in Vancouver, also at about 50 degrees North latitude. Conversely, total annual precipitation in Ulaan Baatar is about one-third that of Vancouver (fig. 3.1). Climatic factors, of course, control the type of vegetation. The presence of a temperate rain forest in coastal British Columbia could be predicted accurately from the climatic data, as could the steppe that dominates much of Mongolia north of the Gobi Desert. Scientists have determined that Mongolia's climate has been fairly stable for at least one thousand years (see Chapter 4).

Not only is the Mongolian climate more seasonal than that of coastal regions, it is also colder. This is typical of continental climates at high latitudes; in Mongolia, climate extremes are exacerbated by elevation. Most of the plains and valley floors lie at elevations well above one thousand meters. Northern Mongolia is underlain by permafrost, indicating a mean annual temperature significantly below freezing—even at roughly the same latitude as London. Ulaan Baatar is the coldest national capital of any country on earth. The current climate of many northern Mongolia weather stations, such as Hatgal, is comparable to that of parts of Alaska near the Arctic Circle. According to widely accepted definitions of the Subarctic,[1] much of Mongolia would fall within this region because in most stations no more than four months of the year have mean temperatures above 10 degrees celsius. Stations such as Hatgal display climatic conditions comparable to those of the low Arctic, or to alpine regions in interior Alaska and the Yukon Territory.

A peculiarity of Mongolia's climate is the extreme aridity of the winter season. Many Mongolian

3.1 Comparative Climate Profiles
This graph shows yearly profiles for five climate stations located near 50° N latitude. Of all stations, Mongolia has the lowest average temperatures, the highest amount of variation between summer and winter, and low and highly seasonal precipitation, most of which occurs as rain during summer.

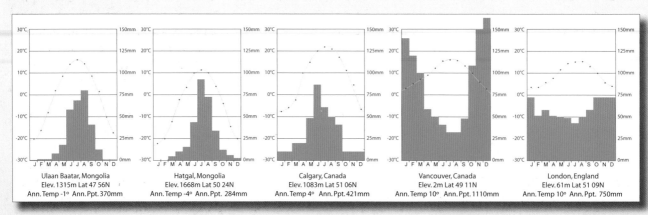

Ulaan Baatar, Mongolia
Elev. 1315m Lat 47 56N
Ann. Temp -1° Ann. Ppt. 370mm

Hatgal, Mongolia
Elev. 1668m Lat 50 24N
Ann. Temp -4° Ann. Ppt. 284mm

Calgary, Canada
Elev. 1083m Lat 51 06N
Ann. Temp 4° Ann. Ppt. 421mm

Vancouver, Canada
Elev. 2m Lat 49 11N
Ann. Temp 10° Ann. Ppt. 1110mm

London, England
Elev. 61m Lat 51 09N
Ann. Temp 10° Ann. Ppt. 750mm

stations report virtually no measurable precipitation during the four to six coldest months of the year. In a normal winter, the steppe may be essentially snow free. Grazing animals that can withstand the intense cold can continue to forage on the dried and frozen grasses and other vegetation without needing any special ability to dig for food sources buried deep under snow.

Pollen and tree ring data show that Mongolia has had a cold, arid, and relatively stable climate extending back through the millennia into the last Ice Age, which reached it greatest extent about twenty thousand years ago, and probably for much longer. We may reasonably hypothesize that the pattern of winter drought and lack of snow cover was also characteristic of the climate back into the distant past.

Beringia and Megaberingia

Early in the twentieth century, scientists realized that the seas to the north and south of the Bering Strait were shallow. The sea floor is actually a shelf of the Asian and North American continents, often lying less than one hundred meters below current sea level. A drop in the level of the ocean's surface of one hundred meters would thus create a broad land connection between the two continents. At the height of an Ice Age, sea level was lowered by at least this much, and Alaska and easternmost Asia became connected. Alaska was also cut off from the rest of North America by immense glacial barriers. Alaska was geographically a part of Asia during the repeated Ice Ages of the past million years or so.

The great Swedish botanist Eric Hultèn in the 1930s called attention

to this area around Bering Strait, which he named "Beringia." He believed that Beringia was an extensive ice-free area lying between the enormous ice sheets of North America and the equally vast glaciers of Siberia.[2] He further postulated that Beringia had served as a refugium, a place where cold-adapted animals and plants could "overwinter" the Ice Age, then repopulate other high-latitude lands to the east and west as the earth warmed and the ice retreated. Hultèn's original idea has been refined and modified over the years as additional evidence has been uncovered.

Most of the major mountain systems of Eurasia as well as North America are connected to Beringia, providing migration routes between the circumpolar Arctic and alpine regions at lower latitudes. This ancient ecosystem, sometimes called the "mammoth steppe," extended from Beringia across Asia westward even to Ukraine, Poland, and Hungary. In this view, Beringia, in its traditional, narrow sense, is an outlier of a great belt of cold steppe that extended nearly half way around the world, from central Europe to the Yukon Territory during the last Ice Age.

Mongolia, situated in the center of this mammoth steppe belt, has

3.2 Southernmost Reindeer
The Dukha, a Tuvan-speaking people closely related to Siberian tribes, occupy mountain regions around Lake Khovsgol in northern Mongolia. Known in Mongolia as Tsaatan (reindeer-herder), they winter in the forest and summer in the mountain tundra. Dukha ancestors may have been the first to domesticate reindeer, probably about 2,000 years ago, perhaps inspired by knowledge of domestication of other animals on the steppe. The Dukha use reindeer for transport and milk, and only rarely for meat. Today they are the southernmost reindeer herders in the world, a traditional lifestyle vulnerable to global warming and shrinking habitat.

been called "Megaberingia" by some paleoecologists. Its current environment is characterized by an extreme continental climate: intensely cold, dry winters and warm summers; vegetation includes many species typical of steppe, cold desert, and semi-desert, and, at least historically, large populations of steppe-adapted animals. These aspects of the present Mongolian environment suggest that it retains many characteristics of the Ice Age mammoth steppe. Studies of Mongolia's past may yield important information about the conditions that influenced its cultural development, including those, such as cycles of drought or harsh conditions that may have contributed to the Mongol empire. And because of its geographic centrality and mountain connections, Mongolia may have been a source for animal and human migrations into other parts of the world.

3.3 **Winter Camp**
With most of Mongolia above 1500m and far from moderating oceans, its winters are long, cold, and dry. In treeless regions, *gers* are heated by dung-fueled fires and by wood in northern or mountainous areas. Animals are often sheltered in low sheds and forage close to home, protected from wolves by dogs and armed herders. Sheep and goats can starve if an icy surface crust forms on pastures. Their survival depends on horses, yaks, or camels whose hooves and feeding breaks up the crust, giving smaller animals a chance to reach the leftovers.

Ancient Hearth of Cultures

One of the perennial controversies regarding the mammoth steppe environment of ancient Beringia involves the carrying capacity of the ecosystem for large herbivores.[3] A productive mammoth steppe ecosystem, supporting herds of large herbivores, carnivores, and scavengers, north central Asia probably supported advanced hunter-gatherer cultures of humans during the last Ice Age. If this were the case, the area that is now Mongolia and its environs could be envisioned as a staging area for human expansion deeper into the north as the climate changed in postglacial times. In this scenario, the thirteenth-century Mongol intrusions into western Asia and Europe would be late manifestations of the kind of human movements that had occurred before, perhaps many times before, and include the earlier advances of the Scythians (700 BCE–500 CE) and the Türks (700–800s). The speed and intensity of these later excursions would, of course, have been augmented by use of the horse and by the increasing sophistication of the skills and technology of horsemanship.

The modern Mongolian steppe is capable of supporting such large populations of herd animals. The modern herds are of domestic animals; presumably, managed herds can utilize the resources more efficiently than wild herds. But even if the wild herds of the mammoth steppe numbered no more than a tenth, in terms of individuals or biomass, of modern herds, they would have indicated a complex and highly productive ecosystem.[4] The high, cold Darkhad Valley today supports well over one hundred thousand individual herd animals.[5] Even if the wild herds were a fraction of that size, they would have provided ample resources for partial support of a semi-nomadic, hunter-gatherer human population.

Given what we know of Mongolia's climate during the last few thousand years and today, a good case can be made that the cold, dry steppe that remains to this day, extends back deep into the last Ice Age, and perhaps earlier. It is clear that there have been major changes in the large animal species, in terms of both species present and population sizes, over the millennia. Many indigenous species, such as Przewalski's horse and the Saiga antelope, have been largely replaced by domestic sheep, goats, cattle, and horses. Although the hunting of wild game was important in the time of Genghis Khan, little information is available on the size and location of game animal populations and how they may have interacted with domestic herds and herders.

When Genghis Khan first began to solidify his main confederacy into outlying regions beyond the main steppe area of Mongolia, he turned his military efforts northward, into the Darkhad and Selenge valleys, the gateway to Siberia and its wealth of animals, fur, fish, and gold. Once again Mongolia found itself reconnected to the northern world. That these areas were given attention suggests that Mongolia's northern regions and nearby Buryatia, where the Central Asian steppe meets the Siberian taiga, were productive and well known. As in earlier periods, these boreal and arctic outliers soon became an important part of another cyclical pulse of Mongolian peoples and cultures facilitated by Mongolia's unique geographic position and environmental connections.

1. Young 1994.
2. Hultèn 1937.
3. Guthrie 1990; Brigham-Grette and Elias 2001.
4. Brigham-Grette and Elias 2001.
5. O. Sukhbaatar, personal communication, 2003.

4. Tree Rings, Climate History, and Genghis Khan

GORDON C. JACOBY

THE RISE AND FALL OF CULTURES and civilizations has been a focus of scholarly debate for hundreds of years. Geographical and climatic factors were among the first explanations to be promoted, followed by Arnold Toynbee's "great man" explanations.[1] The rise of Genghis Khan and rapid spread of the Mongolian empire have often been explained by his charismatic leadership. But were other factors involved? Was Genghis Khan's rise to power due to harsh climate and agrarian privation? Or was it facilitated by optimal conditions and agrarian productivity that promoted demographic and political expansion? Were there other factors?

Most early geographic theories of culture change, such as those promoted by Ellsworth Huntington and Friedrik Ratzel, were seriously flawed and lack scientific merit. Owen Lattimore in the 1930s,

followed by Gareth Jenkins forty years later, developed more objective hypotheses.[2] A gifted pioneer of Asian ethnology and geography, Lattimore understood the delicate balance between precipitation, temperature, storminess, and disease upon which Mongolian herding societies depended. Jenkins, a climatologist with a strong interest in history, and with access to some of the first detailed meteorological records from central Asia, believed there "may have been a steady and deep decline in the mean-annual temperature in Mongolia in the years 1175–1260," the years when Genghis Khan and his sons and grandsons built the Mongol empire. He believed cold conditions may have been an important factor promoting Mongol unification and expansion.

In Jenkins's time the science of paleoclimatology was still rudimentary. Few paleo records

were available, and variations of climatic change were not understood. Today it is possible to reconstruct climate and temperature history in far more detail, from a variety of proxies (comparative records), because it is not possible to obtain direct temperature and weather readings from the past.

One important source of proxy records that relate closely to temperature and precipitation is from annual growth rings of trees. Dendrochronology, or tree-ring analysis, uses the natural record of environmental variations preserved in the growth rings to extend our knowledge of past conditions.[3] The basis of the science is the tendency for trees and some shrubs to form identifiable annual increments. Most sampling of living trees is done by boring a thin core from the outer bark to the center of the tree. There are frequently missing and/or false

4.1 Ancient Larch
The author stands next to a Siberian larch (*Larix sibirica*) tree near the Khoton nuur (Pelican Lake) site in Western Mongolia. Wide and narrow tree rings correspond respectively to wetter and drier years in this region. The core extracted from this tree had 791 rings (1215–2005) but did not reach its inner heart-wood, so the tree may be much older.

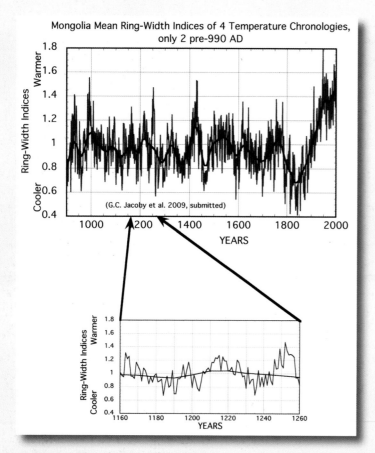

Mongolia Mean Ring-Width Indices of 4 Temperature Chronologies, only 2 pre-990 AD

(G.C. Jacoby et al. 2009, submitted)

4.2 Temperature Record from Tree Rings
The upper graph plots average tree-ring indices based on four tree-ring records. Higher values indicate wider rings and warmer temperatures; lower values indicate narrower rings and colder temperatures. The darker line is constructed from ten-year running averages. The lower graph provides detail on temperature change during Genghis's life time and the expansion phase of the Mongol empire.

rings that must be identified in order to determine the exact calendar year of growth for each ring, however.

A key factor in dendroclimatic tree-ring research is to seek out sampling sites where the variable of interest—usually, either temperature or precipitation—has strong influence on tree growth. Examples are (1) elevational or latitudinal treeline, where temperatures are cold enough to limit the survival of trees at higher levels and (2) the lower forest border, where trees cannot extend into the grassland of the lower elevations due to lack of precipitation and usually higher temperatures. The respective limits to tree growth are temperature and precipitation.[4] The latter correlates with stream-flow, drought, and soil moisture.

Applying this science to paleocli-

matology provides us with a quantitative record of climate for times of history when there are few other records. The question here is what the climate variations may have been in Mongolia at the time when Genghis Khan (1162–1227) was uniting and expanding his empire. Research in Mongolia has resulted in records of temperature and precipitation that extend back through many centuries before the recorded information extant in Mongolia. In addition to temporal variations there are substantial spatial variations of climate throughout the empire and, to a lesser degree, even within present-day Mongolia. Tree-ring studies give us insight to these variations. The following discussion is based on tree-ring records primarily from within Mongolia's present boundaries.

Four independent tree-ring records of year-to-year temperatures, each spanning more than one thousand years, have been developed in Mongolia from trees growing at their high-elevation limits where growth is limited by temperature (fig. 4.2). These records comprise samples from old-aged living trees and relict wood samples, more than 300 individual series. Well-preserved relict trees often fell against rocks after death and had little contact with moist soil. Some samples have been dead and exposed for more than a thousand years but are still sound and useful for tree-ring analyses.

Two living trees from the Khentii Mountains are known to have been alive during the life of Genghis Khan. Due to spatial variations in mountain temperatures, the records from each site do not match exactly year by year, but cooler and warmer times of three to five years are very consistent between the sites.[5] The top graph in fig. 4.2 presents the average ring-width indices of all four sites. One can see the effects of eras termed Medieval Warm Epoch (MWE, from around 1000 to 1400),[6] Little Ice Age (LIA, 1450 to 1850),[7] and recent climatic warming. Several of the lower-frequency temperature declines match similar trends in the weakening of the monsoon as inferred from the isotope data from a cave deposit in the northern margin of the Tibetan Plateau, especially in the late 1300s and around 1600.[8]

The time of Genghis Khan is concurrent with somewhat warmer spells after a brief cooler interval within the MWE. Today, at two of the sites, small, young saplings have migrated above the present elevation of the highest mature trees, indicating unusual recent warmth. These results are similar to high-resolution paleotemperature records from lake sediment studies in Mongolia.[9] In the context of eastern Asia, the Mongolian records also show similarity to the eastern China temperature and China temperature reconstructions.[10]

The tree-ring record of moisture variations is much shorter than the temperature record, producing tree-ring records that go back only 400 to 500 years.[11] Tree-ring studies in other areas of eastern Asia indicate some increase in precipitation and moisture in China in the early 1200s.[12] Unfortunately, we have only found one moisture-sensitive tree in Mongolia that was alive during Genghis Khan's time. Core samples from this tree extend back to 1215 (fig. 4.1). One tree is not enough to use for a firm judgment, but the increasing growth trend in this specimen during the early 1200s is in agreement with results

found by Chinese researchers.[13]

Early discussions on the influence of climate on culture and history suffered from scarcity of accurate paleoclimate records. The relatively recent availability of more accurate sources of information from tree rings and other climate records[14] provides long-term climate contexts for reconsideration of some early hypotheses.[15] Only Jenkins provides quantitative data in the form of temperature and precipitation. His hypothesis that cold conditions promoted Mongol unification may have some merit for the period of 1175 to 1206, that is, during the decades when Temüjin struggled to consolidate his power, prior to being named Genghis Khan.

Jenkins's hypothesis that unusual cold continued during Genghis Khan's actual reign (1206–27) is not supported by modern tree-ring paleoclimate studies for northern Mongolia after the very early 1200s.[16] These tree-ring indices (Figure 4.2) show a decline in temperature from a peak (which may represent the early part of the Medieval Warm Epoch) around 1000 until around the 1120s, followed by some warmer temperatures in the 1150s, and renewed cooling from around 1180 through 1204, with a few intervening periods of increased-growth (warmer). Genghis Kahn's consolidation and expansion of the empire coincided with a period of increased growth (warmer temperatures), although the specter of colder times must have remained with him and his people. After another brief colder interval (1228–45), the warming period climaxed in the 1250s, and then growth rates fell severely, more severely than around 1100.

While new data supports Jen-

kins's data that cooler temperatures were present while Genghis was consolidating his power over the disparate Mongolian tribes, it probably was not a deciding factor in Genghis's rise to power or in the major period of empire expansion. In similar times of colder environs both before and after Genghis Khan, no single leader emerged to unify the empire even though the climatic stresses were as severe, and even worse, in some later intervals, including around 1300, the 1360s, 1460s, and beyond.

1. Toynbee 1934.
2. Lattimore 1938; Jenkins 1974.
3. Fritts 1976.
4. Fritts 1976.
5. Jacoby et al. 2009.
6. Lamb 1995.
7. Grove 1988.
8. Zhang et al. 2008.
9. Robinson et al. 2009.
10. Yang et al. 2002.
11. Pederson et al. 2001; Davi et al. 2006.
12. For example, Zhi-Yong et al. 2007.
13. Zhi-Yong et al. 2007.
14. IPCC 2007.
15. Toynbee 1934; Lattimore 1938; Jenkins 1974.
16. Jacoby et al. 2009.

5.1 Mountain Herding

In most herding families, youngsters do much of the work tending animals. As soon as they can ride a horse, at about age four, children tend flocks in all kinds of weather conditions. Back at camp they milk and help their parents with fleecing, caring for the sick, and butchering and processing foods. This family is camped in one of the upland valleys in the Altai region of western Mongolia. Solar panels store energy to operate a light, a radio, and often a television.

5. Masters of the Steppe

PEOPLES OF MONGOLIA

David Sneath

For thousands of years, the Mongolian steppe has been home to an array of peoples and empires. Since the first millennium BCE, if not before, societies with pastoral nomadic lifestyles populated the belt of steppe lands that stretches across Eurasia from the Black Sea to the Manchurian forests.[1] These peoples lived in dwellings made of felt and wood that could be moved easily. They herded livestock on horseback and traveled from one seasonal pasture to the next. With these strategies, pastoral peoples were able to master the climatic and geographical challenges of the rolling grasslands of Central and Inner Asia. Their mobile lifestyle and talent with horses made these nomads formidable warriors, who did not hesitate to profit from any weakness they detected in their neighbors.

Chinese sources describe the powerful Xiongnu empire that, beginning in the third century BCE, ruled what is now Mongolia (see Chapter 8). To counter the threat of this northern neighbor, the Chinese Qin emperor Shi Huang (r. 221–210 BCE) linked smaller existing fortifications into a huge chain of walls that snaked across much of northern China. For centuries, the Great Wall marked the division between the domains of the Chinese emperors and the lords of the steppe.[2] On either side of this formidable frontier emerged some of the most expansive empires ever known.

Religion and Civil Organization

Far from being a timeless land of ancient, unchanged traditions, Mongolia has had a tumultuous history of sweeping changes. New regimes and religions have transformed political, economic, and ideological life. One of the most important developments was religious conversion. Genghis Khan and his successors had followed the established shamanic polytheistic religion of the Mongols, but since the days of Kublai Khan, Tibetan Buddhism attracted Mongol followers, particularly at court. By the end of the sixteenth century, Buddhism was the dominant religion of the region. Some elements of the pre-Buddhist shamanic religion, including the worship of local deities, may have lived on under Buddhist auspices[3] and some practices may have survived periods of active suppression (see Chapter 6). In some areas, such as remote Khovsgol, some shamanic practices can be found to this day. But from the sixteenth century, Buddhist rulers began to effectively suppress the old faith as a public religion, persecuting shamans and burning their ritual objects. Explicitly non-Buddhist shamanic practices were retained in the northern and eastern fringes of the Mongolian world, among groups such as the Buryats and Daur.[4]

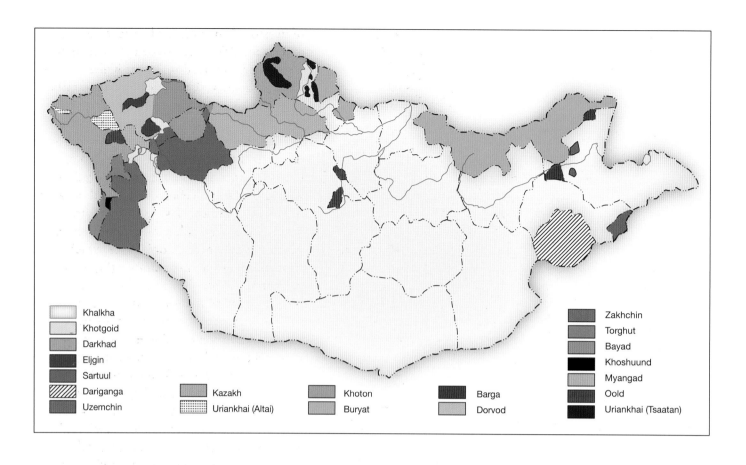

Khalkha				Zakhchin
Khotgoid				Torghut
Darkhad				Bayad
Eljgin				Khoshuund
Sartuul				Myangad
Dariganga				Oold
Uzemchin	Kazakh	Khoton	Barga	Urainkhai (Tsaatan)
	Uriankhai (Altai)	Buryat	Dorvod	

5.2 Mongolian Ethnicity
The largest ethnic group in Mongolia today are Khalkha Mongolians, comprising more than 80 percent of the country's population and occupying most of its core territory. Mountainous northern and western Mongolia holds most of the nation's ethnic diversity, including Buryats, Darkhad, Dukha, and others along its northern frontier with Russia, and Kazakhs in the Altai regions in the west. Khalkhas are mostly Buddhist; Darkhads, Buryats, and Dukha are mostly shamanist; and Kazakhs and some other western groups are predominantly Muslim.

The Buddhist era introduced monasteries throughout Mongolia. These became enormously important ritual, economic, and political centers, and throughout the eighteenth and nineteenth centuries, they became the hubs of small settlements. Great complexes were built in such places as Urga and Erdene Zuu—where Ögödei's imperial capital, Khara Khorum, had once stood (see Chapter 19).

The Buddhist establishment also took over the ritual aspects of relations with the environment. Every year, the local spiritual masters of the land (*gazaryn ezed*) were honored in ceremonies held at ritual cairns (*ovoo*).[5] The district officials might control access to pasture land, but these rites demonstrated that, in some sense, the true owners of the land were spiritual ones, in recognition of which the people, lamas, and officials of districts came together to make offerings to these local deities, who were thought to control environmental conditions.[6] These ceremonies and attendant local games (*naadam*) have been revived throughout much of the country in recent years.

Mobile pastoralism has long required flexible access to grazing land. District authorities (lordly, monastic, or collective) historically have tended to control large tracts of territory within which pastoral families have been allocated complimentary seasonal pastures. This local control of land has allowed for movement and reallocation of pasture in harsh environmental conditions such as drought and the winter freezes known as *zud*. Such flexibility conflicts with rigid and permanent private ownership of land, and until relatively recently, grazing land in Mongolia was never owned in this manner. This tradition reflects the notion of spiritual authority over the land, which makes human claims custodial rather than absolute.

Some areas in Mongolia are suitable for agriculture, but most of this vast land is best used for livestock. Around half of Mongolia's population now relies upon their domestic animals to make a living. Many, but not all, of these pastoralists are still "nomads," moving to different seasonal pastures as part of an annual cycle. Since long before the time of Genghis Khan pastoralists have kept what Mongols today describe as the *tavan khoshuu mal*, the "five types

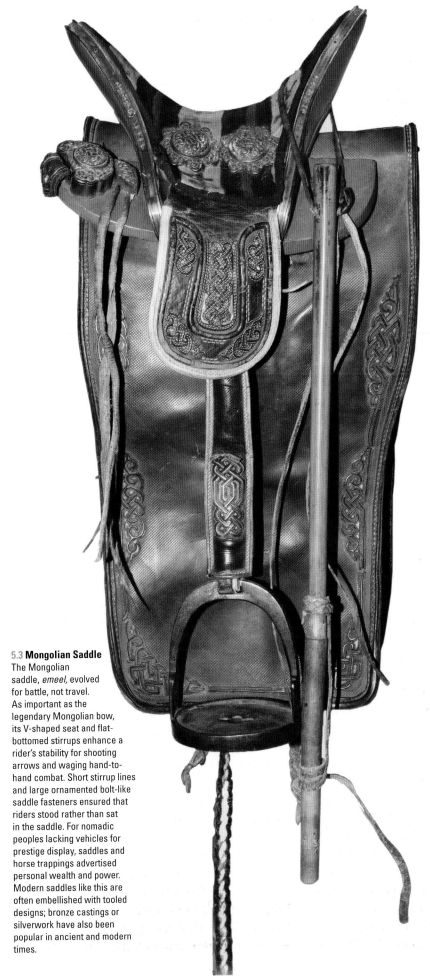

5.3 Mongolian Saddle
The Mongolian saddle, *emeel,* evolved for battle, not travel. As important as the legendary Mongolian bow, its V-shaped seat and flat-bottomed stirrups enhance a rider's stability for shooting arrows and waging hand-to-hand combat. Short stirrup lines and large ornamented bolt-like saddle fasteners ensured that riders stood rather than sat in the saddle. For nomadic peoples lacking vehicles for prestige display, saddles and horse trappings advertised personal wealth and power. Modern saddles like this are often embellished with tooled designs; bronze castings or silverwork have also been popular in ancient and modern times.

of livestock": horses, cattle, sheep, goats, and, in the drier regions, camels, which are used for transportation. In the higher northern regions they also keep yaks, sometimes cross-breeding them with Mongol cattle. But above all, Mongolia remains a land of horses. There are almost as many horses as people living in Mongolia—some two million. No other animal is more honored or valued, and top racehorses sell for thousands of dollars. Until the development of firearms, horses were a key military resource, providing the deadly mobility for which Mongol armies became famous (fig. 5.3).

Steppe "nomadism" should not be thought of as an aimless, wandering subsistence activity. Mongolian mobile pastoralists know very well which seasonal pastures they will use in winter, spring, summer, and autumn. These generally form an established annual cycle, although pastoralists may adapt their pattern in response to changing economic, social, and environmental circumstances. Pastoralism need not be a small-scale activity, limited to one or two households. Large-scale, coordinated, mobile herding systems can involve hundreds of households, thousands of animals, and have ancient roots.

From the seventeenth century until the twentieth, Mongolia was divided into administrative districts called *khoshuu,* or "banners," ruled by a hereditary lord or a Buddhist monastery. Mongol commoners were tied to a district and were required to provide taxes and labor to their noble or ecclesiastical masters. Buddhist monasteries, the nobility, and the imperial administration owned large numbers of livestock, which were herded for them by subjects or servants who received a share of the animal produce. Most commoners also owned their own livestock, and some could be rich, but they were still required to render service to local princely or monastic authorities as part of their political units.[7]

Pastoral systems could also be highly sophisticated. Specialist herders and their families moved large herds of livestock to selected seasonal pastures in an annual cycle. Banner officials regulated pasture allocation. Some movement systems could entail

5.4 Salty Milk Tea
Hospitality is an ancient Mongolian custom that begins with ritual drinking of salty *suutei tsai,* Mongolian tea. Prepared with tea shredded from a compressed block, milk, and a handful of salt, the brew is mixed by repeatedly pouring cascades of steaming tea from a ladle.

5.5 Making *Aaruul*
Mongolians thrive on cheese and other dairy products made from goats, cows, yaks, and even horses, whose milk they ferment into a beverage called *airag.* Various Mongolian cheeses, yogurts, and other dairy products can be stored, depending on fat and moisture content. Here a woman turns cheese blocks drying in the sun. This type of dried cheese provides a nutritious snack for herders on the trail or can be rehydrated to fortify soup or stew.

herd shifts of 150 to 200 km between summer and winter pastures.[8] Because different animals have different grazing habits, species were segregated. Sheep crop vegetation so close that horses and cattle cannot get at what is left, so efficient use of land required coordinated movement of livestock.

This "feudal" system was largely abolished in the early years of the Soviet-style Mongolian People's Republic, and, in the 1950s, pastoralists were organized into large collective and state farms. Although these collectives represented a radical break from the past, in some respects they resembled the large monastic and noble estates. As had their predecessors, they controlled access to grazing land and required herders to provide quotas of produce as part of a district-wide operation. They also supported

seasonal movement and supplied hay using central motor pools. The collectives were disbanded in the early 1990s, using various formulas to divide livestock and other assets among local members. This has allowed some herders to become wealthy, but others now own barely enough animals to make a living, and many pastoral households have struggled to do without collective fodder supplies and motor support in the face of harsh weather conditions.[9]

Mongolian Ethnicity

The modern state of Mongolia has a number of officially recognized ethnic groups. More than 80 percent of Mongolians are registered Khalkha (fig. 5.2). In the western part of the country there are some 100,000 Kazakhs, whose Türkic Muslim ancestors had moved into the region in the nineteenth century, in part to avoid Tsarist Russian rule. The incorporation of subjects of the former Oyirad realms in western Mongolia, after their defeat by the Qing emperor of China in the eighteenth century, left a number of named groups that became officially registered ethnic minorities (*yastan*), mostly in the Mongolian west.

Administrative divisions introduced by the Manchu rulers of China and Mongolia also left their marks on the ethnographic map of Mongolia. At the beginning of the eighteenth century, the Qing emperor Kangxi (r. 1662–1722) established a unit to raise imperial horse and camel herds in the Dariganga region in what is now the eastern part of Mongolia. The people of this region were registered as an ethnic group of 32,000 in the 2000 census. In the north, next to the huge fresh-water Lake Khovsgol, is another ethnic group of around 20,000 who trace descent from the great monastic estate of the Bogdo Gegen "Living Buddha." As part of a religious establishment they were exempt from state taxes and described as the "exempt ones," or Darkhad,[10] as they are known today. Khovsgol province is also home to some Tuvan-speaking people, such as the Dukha (Tsaatan), famous for herding reindeer. In the early twentieth century, many Buryats crossed the border into Mongolia to escape the turmoil of the Russian

5.6 Iron Camp Stove
Ceramic pots appeared in Mongolia during the Neolithic period. The introduction of bronze and later iron vessels provided better cooking service while ceramics persisted as personal eating utensils. This iron pot and brazier from a grave in Inner Mongolia and dating to the Yuan period, ca. 1300 CE, could be fueled by wood or charcoal, but most commonly by dung.

revolution. Today, some 40,000 Buryats live in Mongolia, mostly in the northern provinces of Selenge, Khentii, and Dornod.[11]

Today, many aspects of Mongolian culture remain important in Inner Mongolia, now one of the autonomous regions of the People's Republic of China. Mongolian is an official language, alongside Chinese, and the head of the local government is routinely Mongolian. There are around four million people of Mongolian nationality in the region—many more than in the independent state of Mongolia. The region was subject to Chinese settlement throughout the twentieth century, however, and today about 80 percent of the population of Inner Mongolia consists of Han Chinese.[12]

Farther abroad, people tracing Mongolian descent turn up in some surprising places. On the Russian shores of the Caspian Sea lies the semi-autonomous Republic of Kalmykia, the successor state of the western-most outpost of a seventeenth-century expansion by the Oyirad Mongols. In exchange for guarding Russia's eastern frontier, the tsar granted them a small khanate south of the Volga River. The republic has a rich Oyirad-Mongol heritage—it is the only Buddhist nation in Europe and devoted to the Dalai Lama—although only about half of the republic's population of 300,000 people are Kalmyk, and many of these no longer speak their historic dialect of Mongolian. Having endured the turbulent and brutal tenure of the Soviet Union, diaspora communities of Kalmyks can be found elsewhere in Europe, including Serbia and France, and on the east coast of the United States. The Kalmyk community in New Jersey holds annual festivals to honor their Mongolian heritage.

Mongolia is also a land of settlements—most of them tiny, widely dispersed villages, isolated in the endless grassy sea of the steppe. There are larger urban centers such as Darkhan and Erdenet, but a single city dominates national consciousness: the capital, Ulaan Baatar. The city started life in the seventeenth century as a great encampment around the Bogdo Gegen or "Living Buddha," the head of the Buddhist church. At first, it remained mobile, a city of tents that moved every few years. Only around 1778 did it settle in its present location in east central Mongolia. It was first known as Ikh Khüree (Great Camp) and later called Urga by Europeans (probably from *orgoo*, the Mongol term for a palace yurt). By the end of the nineteenth century, one hundred monasteries and temples of various sizes were located in the vicinity of Urga, with a total population of around 20,000 monks. In the Soviet era, the capital was renamed Ulaan Baatar ("red hero"). The city took on an unmistakably Soviet look, especially in its architecture, and grew at an amazing speed. In 1935, the population of Ulaan Baatar was 10,400. Fifty years later it was fifty times larger, growing to more than a half million people. Since then, the population has almost doubled again to nearly one million.[13]

Mongolia is a relatively unified nation, with a dominant Khalkha culture and language and smaller Kazak, Buryat, and Dukha

5.7 A Fashionable Women's Outfit
The Khalkha seamstress who made this fancy woman's garment in the late 19th or early 20th century created it from silk fabrics. Because Mongolia produced only homespun wool and cashmere made from camel, sheep, and goats, finer fabrics like silk had to be imported. Silk was among the commodities obtained from China in exchange for Mongolian horses, wool, and in recent centuries, cashmere. This outfit consists of a long-sleeved *deel* and a sleeveless outer garmet called *uuj*.

5.8 Woman's Headdress
Head gear has always been a striking component of Mongolian apparel. The Early Iron Age headdress from the Arzhan site in Russia's Gorni-Altai had a gold deer figure on its crest, and the 5th-century BCE Issyk Gold Man from Kazakhstan wore a hat with a towering gold pillar. Chinese portraits of elite Mongol women of the Genghis Khan era also depict hats with high pillar-like tops. The hats of elite 19th- and early 20th-century Mongolian women were more conservative, but were often peaked and highly-styled, such as this hat ornamented with silver, silk tassels, and Chinese silk with embroidered designs.

minorities. Nevertheless, within the Khalkha majority are remnants of many distinctive local traditions, linguistic dialects, beliefs customs, and techniques of managing livestock. Even greater diversity exists if one includes the peoples of Inner Mongolia, most of whom have been heavily influenced by Chinese assimilation policies and the massive influx of native Chinese in the last century. Yet, throughout "greater Mongolia" one finds common threads that are the legacy of a long history of largely nomadic and pastoral steppe life, with roots stretching back for more than two millennia. While keeping step with the increasingly urban,

industrialized world, Mongolia's peoples continue to find countless ways to express their unique history, culture, and way of life.

1. Allard and Erdenebaatar 2005; Levine 1999.
2. Di Cosmo 2002; Jagchid and Symons 1989.
3. Sneath 2007.
4. Humphrey 1996.
5. Heissig 1980.
6. Erdenetuya 2002.
7. Natsagdorj 1978; Boldbaatar and Sneath 2006.
8. Simukov 1936; Sneath 1999.
9. Simukov 1936; Sneath 1999.
10. Atwood 2004, 132.
11. IISNC 2006, 135.
12. Bulag 2002.
13. Gilberg and Svantesson 1996; Campi 2006.

6.1 Shaman Robe

As in modern times, ancient seamstresses often created garments using scraps available from various sources. This shaman's robe is a replica based on a garment from the grave of a Yuan-dynasty shaman in Inner Mongolia and is created from scores of tassels and strips of different materials, each of which flashed and swirled as the shaman danced. The iron headdress is surmounted by antlers or horns, and the many metal discs, probably representing mirrors for seeing into the spirit world, would have enhanced the shaman's powers and ability to foresee the future, cure the sick, or inflict injury upon enemies.

6. Mongolian Shamanism

THE MOSAIC OF PERFORMED MEMORY

Manduhai Buyandelger

IN SHAMANISM, the spirit realm continuously engages with the human world. Because humans unwittingly disturb the province of spirits, inviting misfortune and death, they require shamans to mediate between themselves and the supernatural. To ensure the well-being of individuals and communities, a shaman performs rituals to mediate between humans and the supernatural. Rock art and archaeological finds of human figurines, drums, mirrors, and mouth harps, suggest shamanism has existed in central Eurasia since the Upper Paleolithic period, beginning about 30,000 years ago (fig. 6.2).

Based on twelfth-century documentary information in *The Secret History of the Mongols* (compiled after Genghis Khan's death in 1227) and Rashid al-Din's *Compendium of Chronicles* (*Jami'al-tavarikh*; completed around 1310), anthropologist Caroline Humphrey[1] speculates that shamanistic belief in Eternal Heaven was important for consolidating political power and for the establishment of the Inner Asian states, including the Mongol state in the thirteenth century. Shamanic insight is credited with assisting Genghis Khan's accession to khanship when the legendary shaman Teb Tenggeri announced that it was heaven's will that Temüjin (young Genghis) become the ruler of the nation and receive the title of Genghis Khan. Later, Genghis became adept in discovering heaven's will himself by going into a trance and communicating with the supernatural. He seems, however, to have bent his inspirational abilities to expand and strengthen his power. When Teb Tenggeri became Genghis Khan's rival and declared that Genghis's younger brother Khasar was soon to succeed him as a khan, Genghis had Teb Tenggeri eliminated. In successive Mongol courts, the ruling elite continued to seek shamanic services, while also being influenced by Nestorian Christianity, Buddhism, and Confucianism.[2]

Shamanism not only helped to strengthen the political powers of the elite; among ordinary Mongols of the twelfth to sixteenth centuries it was an everyday religion. Male and female shamans, called *boo* and *udgan* respectively, performed the rituals of offering milk and blood sacrifices to *ongguts*, the shamanic gods and spirits. The *ongguts* of the household, livestock, mountains, and rivers, and especially sky and earth, were evoked and appeased to protect against death, illnesses, and natural catastrophe. They were represented in the forms of figurines and masks made from skin, leather, felt, metal, and multicolored silk, or carved from wood and kept in little boxes or wrapped in cloth or felt.[3]

In those places where *ongguts* are the spirits of ancestors, shamanism constitutes an historical memory. By communicating with those *ongguts* who speak through sha-

6.2 Ancient Spirit Figure
Mongolian rock art provides a window into the past. This spirit figure from the Biluut site at Khoton Lake, Bayan Ulgii province, has large three-fingered hands and an elaborate headdress. It is surrounded by animals and human figures, which are smaller than the spirit figure, perhaps to indicate the powerful nature of the deity.

the shaman to summon spirits and convince the audiences of the authenticity of his or her performance. Throughout Mongolia, shamanic paraphernalia consist of various types of mirrors, drums, headdresses representing an animal or a bird, a gown, and often a cape or an apron (figs. 6.4, 5). Male and female shamans generally use the same paraphernalia and perform similar rituals. Shamans chant elaborate poetry that maps out the hierarchy of the spirit world, the expansiveness of the landscape, and the types and identities of individual gods, demigods, and spirits of particular groups and clans. Shamanic ritual condenses the political, historical, and economic spheres of life into a single cultural event.

mans about their lives in the past, Mongols keep in touch with their history. These *ongguts* are disembodied relics[4] and the verbal archives of the nomadic population. These origin spirits also reside in (or visit) the places of their burial and become the protective deities of their neighboring mountains, rivers, and cliffs. A landscape infused with spirits resembles a mosaic of memory where stories lie dormant and come alive through shamanic rituals of possession. Through communal worship of such landscape spirits, which are either individual ancestors or communal mythical *ongguts*, the Mongol people perpetuate their ancient history.

In places where the origin spirits had become communal *ongguts*, their myths and stories make up regional and clan identities.[5] Among the Buryats there is even a correlation between use of communal pastures and sharing of the same mythical origin ancestor.[6] Almost everywhere in Mongolia, Eternal Heaven and its entourage of gods, demigods, and spirits, constitute a shamanic ruling hierarchy that can be called a celestial court that oversees the rest of the spirit world. The origin spirits and landscape spirits occupy the lower part of this hierarchy and shift freely between the spirit and human worlds.

Shamanic rituals are intended to alter the believer's perception of the world. Ceremonies are layered with meaning. Elaborate shamanic paraphernalia allow

Shamanism and Buddhism

Shamanism had been the dominant spiritual practice in Mongolia until persecution began in the sixteenth century, when Mongol elites began to convert to Tibetan Buddhism under the sponsorship of the Mongol khans. As Buddhism spread from the south to the north, shamanism became less prominent in southern and central Mongolia, and in some places it disappeared altogether. However, in the north, among the Buryat, Dukha, and Darkhad peoples, shamanism remained powerful. That persistence was not only because Buddhism reached these groups later but because their cultural backgrounds were different from mainstream Mongols. Their mobility between Mongolia and Russia and their political prowess also helped the Buryat, Dukha, and Darkhad peoples to retain their practice. For instance, the Darkhat nobility in the seventeenth century successfully negotiated their freedom to practice both shamanism and Buddhism in return for submitting to the lineage of a leading lama.[7]

Shamanism continued to be persecuted under the direction of the third Dalai Lama, who asked the Mongol khans to destroy *ongguts* and punish shamans and believers by taking away their livestock.[8] To attract converts, the lamas took on the roles of shamans by offering rituals of healing, magic, and exorcism adopted from pre-Buddhist Bon shamanism in Tibet, in which lama oracles would go into a trance similar

6.3 Buryat Shaman
This female Buryat shaman, smoking a pipe and wearing a shaman robe and headdress, was possessed by a spirit during her conversation with the elderly client at the left. Mongol shamans, are accustomed to making house calls and perform many of the same services.

to Mongol shamanic spirit possession. The Buddhist missionaries also replaced the functions of shamans by incorporating the local rituals of worshiping mountain cairns (*ovoos*) and by introducing deities that protected livestock and life. Buddhism also substituted the shamanic guardian and ancestor deities with personalized lamaist deities. The lamas taught *tarani* (incantations) for individual protection, destruction of evil, good luck, and healing illness. For each illness and body organ there was a separate *tarani*. Lamas prescribed healing packages consisting of *taranis*, herbal medicine, and rituals of cleansing and deflection that devotees could perform at home. The Buddhism introduced in Mongolia promoted itself as a more advanced spiritual practice because it operated not through the spirits of the deceased or animals and nature, but by communicating with deities (*sahius*). The Buddhist missionaries prohibited shamanic blood sacrifice as barbaric and promulgated ritual offerings of dairy products as humane and superior. Unlike shamanism, which only has a celestial realm, Buddhism's upper (paradise) and lower worlds (hell) were meant to induce consternation among nonbelievers

As Buddhism became prominent by the nineteenth century, shamanism became known as a "black" or evil religion, in contrast to Buddhism, a "yellow" or benign religion.[9] Officially, Buddhism replaced shamanism in most of Mongolia. In places

with communal shamanic *ongguts*, these spirits were replaced by the Buddhist deities in a fairly straightforward way. But in places where, in addition to the communal *ongguts*, individual families also worshipped their own origin or ancestor spirits, Buddhism replaced the communal ones without destroying the origin spirits. Therefore, in many places, Buddhism and shamanism coexisted.

The Buryats were able to maintain their traditional belief in shamanism (fig. 6.3). In addition to their communal shamanic *ongguts*, individual families also have origin spirits who are passed down within the family. Most of the communal *ongguts* acquired their Buddhist versions, but the Buryat origin spirits who are the souls of deceased historical people were not replaced. The shamans who become possessed by these origin spirits impersonate historical personages through dramatic performances by changing their body language, speech, enacting the spirits' gender, age, and narrating historical events. By doing so, these spirits achieve a lasting presence in the Buryat collective memory

Although Buddhism was officially established throughout Mongolia and became the dominant religion by the early twentieth century, shamanism remained covert. Shamanic spirits are considered to be eternal, and while shamans can be removed, the spirits can emerge at any time, request propitiation, and if displeased, they may brutally punish the living. The spirits who possess shamans in the ritual arena recount the clashes between shamans and lamas and the heroic battles shamans fought with lamas. It is particularly in resistance to Buddhism that Mongol shamanism developed creative and undercover strategies that enabled it to endure socialist suppression.

Feminization of Shamanism under Socialism

Shamanism in Mongolia was suppressed during the era of state socialism in the early twentieth century. Under the fledgling Mongol state that had gained its independence after the fall of Qing China in 1911, religion was seen as a hindrance to modernization and nation building. Following the communist lead, the state regarded religion as an "opiate of the masses" and shamanism as the remnant of the most primitive and barbaric past that brought shame upon the nation. To eradicate these scourges, the state launched purges in the 1930s. The official history of Mongolia mostly records the destruction of Buddhism, which was, by then, the most powerful institution and the greatest threat to the young socialist state. But along with Buddhism, shamanism was also suppressed; its practitioners were either killed or forced to renounce their religious affiliations and accept civilian jobs. The state control of the economy also made it difficult to engage in private enterprise, and, with the decrease of economic incentives, shamanism became less attractive. Nevertheless, shamanism was still in demand as a form of healing and a way of explaining misfortune and the vicissitudes of life through ritual. Because shamanism is not a formal religion with an institutional base of support, but rather a fluid practice that is deeply rooted in the domestic sphere of everyday life, it could more easily survive, albeit in condensed and hidden forms.

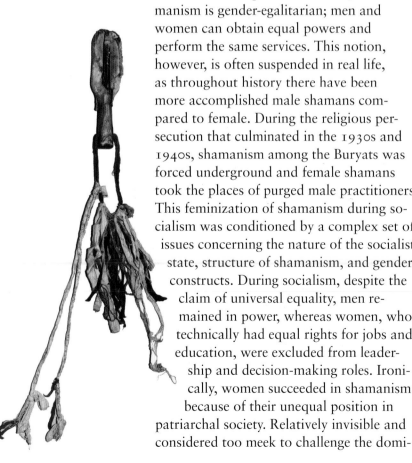

6.4 Drum-Beater
A shaman's drum and drum-beater, like the coat or headdress, had special powers. This beater has a skin covering, a paddle-shaped blade fitted with iron rattles, and suspended amulets.

Unlike the larger society that is constructed around patriarchal rules, shamanism is gender-egalitarian; men and women can obtain equal powers and perform the same services. This notion, however, is often suspended in real life, as throughout history there have been more accomplished male shamans compared to female. During the religious persecution that culminated in the 1930s and 1940s, shamanism among the Buryats was forced underground and female shamans took the places of purged male practitioners. This feminization of shamanism during socialism was conditioned by a complex set of issues concerning the nature of the socialist state, structure of shamanism, and gender constructs. During socialism, despite the claim of universal equality, men remained in power, whereas women, who technically had equal rights for jobs and education, were excluded from leadership and decision-making roles. Ironically, women succeeded in shamanism because of their unequal position in patriarchal society. Relatively invisible and considered too meek to challenge the domi-

nant power, their actions were not scrutinized by the state as closely as that of men.

Engaging in shamanism was a subversive and dangerous activity. The shamans were seen as charlatans and their clients as superstitious and uncivilized. Associated primarily with the domestic sphere, women were afforded less suspicion and scrutiny. Men's greater role in the state limited their opportunities for underground activities. Women's lesser official positions allowed them to engage in secret practices in the mountains and forests at night or, quietly, in the privacy of their own homes. A schoolbag hanging on the wall might hide a shaman's drum; old family trunks might conceal ritual paraphernalia. Some of the herdsmen secretly

SHAMANISM

6.7 Modern Shamans >
During the Soviet period, shamanism was banned in Mongolia, as it was in the Soviet Union, and shamans were persecuted, jailed, or even killed. Nevertheless, many continued to practice in secret and hid their costumes and drums. After 1990 persecution stopped and shamans were able to practice again. In areas where shamanism had ceased, costumes, rituals, and gear had to be reinvented, resulting in new and sometimes non-traditional forms.

< 6.6 Darkhad Shaman
This shaman in the Darkhad valley west of Lake Khovsgol wears a costume with a feathered mask. Chanting to the beat of his drum helps him enter a trance to communicate with the spirits.

attended rituals by night, but supported the propaganda of atheism by day, thus reconciling the uncompromising demands of both the state prohibition and their *ongguts* who demanded commemoration.

Shamanism Today

Following the collapse of socialism in the 1990s, shamanism began reemerging from underground into a public sphere. Shamanism could explain away the ongoing crises as chaos and disorder in revenge for the people's abandonment of the shamanic spirits during socialism. Among the Khalkha Mongols, these spirits are mostly the guardians of landscape, particularly the lords of *ovoos*, while among the Buryats, these are origin spirits. Many of these spirits have been suppressed for five, seven, or more generations, from the time when Buddhism was politically dominant. Today, the Buryats of Mongolia worship both the white and black spirits and shamans draw upon knowledge from Buddhism and shamanism to satisfy the needs of different Mongol groups. Shamanistic rituals are performed publicly for Mongolian travelers and foreign tourists. Shamanism offers modern Mongolians entrepreneurial opportunities, and, more significantly, a source of ethnic pride, historical identification and national identity. Much as it helped Mongolian peoples for centuries to cope with myriad challenges, shamanism has become a popular tool for dealing with the misfortunes and uncertainties of incipient capitalism and democracy. As shamanism became a respected and income-generating practice, more male practitioners emerged and have taken leading roles in an increasingly male-centered society of neoliberal capitalism without the former state rhetoric of gender equality.

1. Humphrey 1994.
2. Atwood 2004.
3. Heissig 1980.
4. Taussig 1997.
5. Buyandelger 2004.
6. Humphrey 1983.
7. Atwood 2004.
8. Heissig 1980.
9. Banzarov 1991–92.

7. Sounds from Nature: MUSIC OF THE MONGOLS

PETER K. MARSH

THE HAUNTING MELODIES of Mongolian "long songs" are said to be the oldest tunes still performed and Mongolian throat-singing the most complex of all musical vocalizations. While these assertions are difficult to verify, evidence of music, song, and dance among the Mongols dates back to the thirteenth century. The *Yuanshi* (the history of the Mongol dynasty in China) describes an enormous staff of singers, dancers, and musicians, at times numbering more than 700, resident in Kublai Khan's palaces in the imperial city of Daidu (modern Beijing). These artists formed enormous ensembles during formal state ceremonies, such as weddings, feasts, and banquets.

Marco Polo, who spent years at Kublai Khan's court, noted the close link between music and the drinking of *airag*, or fermented mare's milk (called *koumis* in Central Asia), a summer drink highly prized by the Mongols (fig. 7.1). When the Great Khan was about to drink from his enormous bowl of *airag*, Polo writes, the musicians would begin to play and all in attendance would kneel in respect. The Franciscan monks John of Plano Carpini and William of Rubruck, who also visited the Mongol court (see Chapter 20), observed similar uses of

music. On his visit to the palace of Batu Khan—one of Genghis Khan's grandsons, then khan of the Golden Horde—Carpini writes that neither the khan nor any of the other princes "ever drinks, especially in public, without there being singing and guitar-playing."[1] Music and song were also tools in warfare of the time. Polo remarks that Mongol soldiers preparing for battle would sing "very sweetly" to the accompaniment of their stringed instruments, a practice that might also have been a means of intimidating their enemies.

Despite the awesome power of their armies and the global reach of their empire, the Mongols were at root a nomadic people of the steppe lands and mountains of their homeland. *The Secret History of the Mongols* (see Chapter 14) speaks of Mongols far removed from war and imperial palaces playing fiddles, singing folk songs, and dancing—in one instance, dancing joyously around verdant trees until their bodies ached. Such is evidence of musical traditions that existed long before and long after the period of empire.

We know little about musical practice during the many years of social and political upheaval that accompanied the end of the empire.

But oral history tells us that by the late nineteenth and early twentieth centuries several distinct, but interrelated, music cultures had formed along ethnic lines, the most significant of which included those of the Khalkha Mongols of central Mongolia and the Oyirad Mongols of the far west. Among the many musical traditions of the Khalkha, the two-stringed fiddle and long song genre have held a special place in traditional society. Among the Oyirad, a confederation of smaller ethnic groups, the plucked lute, *bii* dances, heroic epics, and *khoomii*, or "throat-singing," traditions have held an equally important place.

Whether bowed or plucked, the pear-shaped, two- and four-stringed lute has a truly ancient history in Central Asia. Images of such lutes, as well as lutes themselves, have been found at ancient sites along the Silk Roads, which crisscrossed central Eurasia from ancient times, including the lands of the Türkic nomadic pastoralists. The Mongols, who likely adopted the instrument from their Türkic neighbors, adapted it in truly unique ways. By the end of the nineteenth century, the Khalkha of the south-central Gobi Desert region of Mongolia had highly developed bowed lute

7.1 Marco Polo and Kublai Khan
Marco Polo and his father and uncle, merchants from Venice, noted the importance of music in the Chinese court of Kublai Khan. This image from *Le Livre des Merveilles du Monde* (*Travels of Marco Polo*, 1298/99) shows Kublai giving the Polos a letter for the Pope. It was common for European artists of the day to represent the foreign setting and people in a manner familiar to Europeans.

< 7.2 "Chinggis 800" Festival
7.2 "Chinggis 800" Festival
On the 800th anniversary of Temüjin's investiture as Genghis Khan at the *khuriltai* of 1206, the Smithsonian's National Museum of Natural History staged a festival with traditional Mongolian music and dance. Many of the performers came from the Mongolian community in Washington, D.C.

traditions. Pastoralists constructed their fiddles out of wood covered with animal hide and strung with horsehair. A simple bow was fashioned from a stick also strung with horsehair. These fiddles would often be crowned with the heads of animals and mythical beasts. By the late nineteenth century, the head of the horse was especially popular, lending the instrument the name *morin khuur*, or "horsehead fiddle" (fig. 7.3)." By the turn of the twentieth century, the two-stringed fiddle had become so popular that it is said that every Mongol *ger* in the Gobi had one hanging on its walls.

The central and southern regions are also the home of the Khalkha Mongol long song traditions. This is a genre of folksong characterized by long, ornamented melodic phrases that follow no strict rhythmic patterns. The songs typically have many verses and the lyrics are often about love or horses. Some Mongolian musicologists connect the long, flowing nature of the long song's melodic phrases with the open and undulating surface of the steppe lands of central and southern Mongolia.

The Oyirad Mongols of the far west, a confederation of smaller ethnic groups, also have two-stringed fiddles, but far more common is the two-stringed plucked lute, or *tovshuur*. A narrow and traditionally pear-shaped lute constructed from a single piece of wood, this instrument often accompanies the singing of folksongs and the telling of stories and legends. Also popular, but now disappearing, is the tradition of reciting epic tales, accompanied by the *tovshuur*, which recount the exploits of fabulous, and often mythical, Mongol heroes. Some of these tales are so long that a singer

can require several days to complete the narration.

The *tovshuur* also commonly accompanies dances, the most famous of which in western Mongolia is the *bii*. Traditionally danced in the small space of a pastoralists' *ger*, the *bii* emphasizes the movements of the dancer's upper body, especially the arms, hands, and face. These movements often stylistically mimic the actions of the pastoralists' daily lives. Male dancers might imitate the movement of riding or roping their horses, while female dancers might imitate the movement of brushing their hair or milking the family's animals.

Western Mongolia is also the home of a unique method of singing, which in recent decades has brought the region national and international fame. Throat-singing requires a singer to produce two or more separate tones at the same time. Singers execute a resonant drone above which they "sing" a folksong melody. Musicologists suggest that, like the long song tradition, *khoomii* is intimately connected with the Mongols' close relationship with their natural environment. The pastoralists themselves often say that they learned to sing this way from listening to the world around them, such as to the sounds of water flowing over stones in a brook or wind blowing over rocks on a mountain. Ethnomusicologist Ted Levin suggests that such abilities to hear and imitate the sounds of their ambient environment is a critical survival tool

for pastoralists trying to navigate their ways through a world fraught with physical and spiritual danger.[2]

The twentieth century, which brought revolution, modernization, and urbanization to Mongolia, fundamentally changed the ways in which the Mongolians interacted with their natural and spiritual worlds, and these changes were reflected in musical practice. Western-styled folkloric institutions were established around the country and talented rural folk musicians were sent to the nation's capital for training in music schools and colleges. Students were taught to read music, pay attention to musical style, tuning, and technique, and to perform repertoire written by urban composers. From Ulaan Baatar to rural villages, musical practice slowly migrated from the homes of pastoralists to the stages of newly built theaters and cultural centers, where it was overseen by cultural officials from the local and national governments.[3] This institutionalization and nationalization of folk music has given rise to largely professional and urban-oriented folk music very different from the mostly amateur and locally oriented folk musical traditions still practiced in the countryside.

1. Dawson 1980, 57.
2. Levin and Suzukei 2006.
3. Marsh 2009.

ABOVE

7.3 Morin Khuur
The *morin khuur*, known to English-speakers as the "horsehead fiddle", is still played by many Mongolian musicians. Carrying only two strings, it can be plucked and bowed at the same time to produce a great variety of genres, but most popular are those with a driving, hoof-beat cadence.

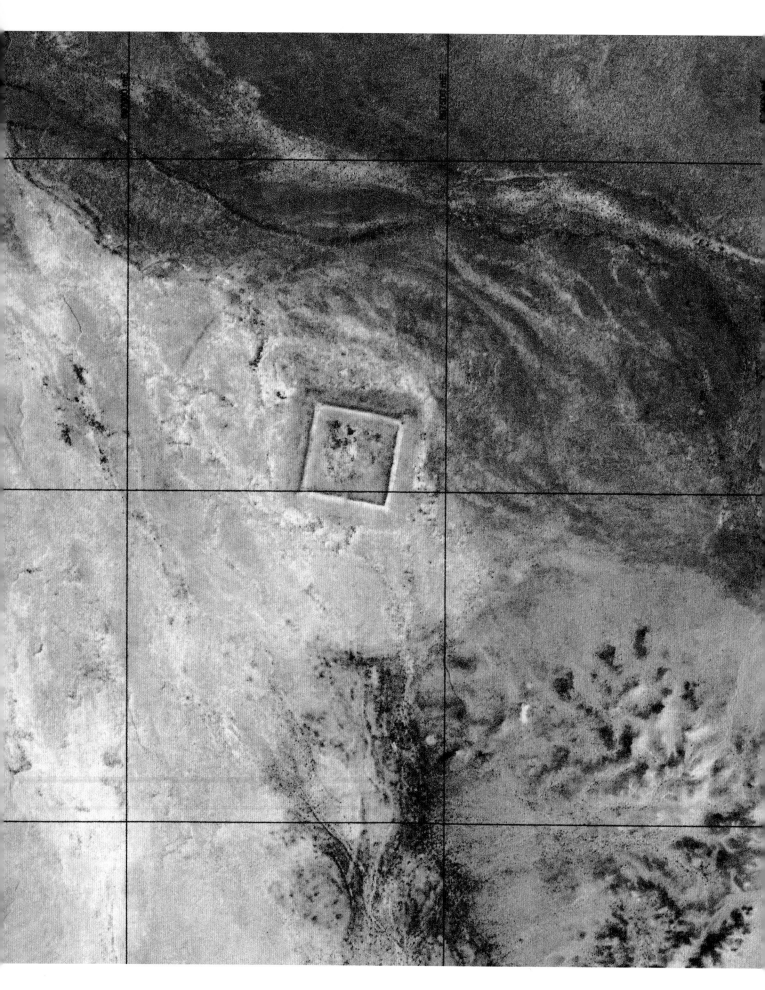

HONEYCHURCH · FITZHUGH · AMARTUVSHIN

8. Precursor to Empire

EARLY CULTURES AND PREHISTORIC PEOPLES

WILLIAM HONEYCHURCH

WILLIAM W. FITZHUGH

CHUNAG AMARTUVSHIN

IN WESTERN POPULAR IMAGINATION, Mongolia has long seemed more a concept than a real place, more a land of myth than of dynamic history. Unlike China, where written records reach 3,500 years into the past, the earliest texts by the people of the eastern steppe begin 2,000 years later, found on isolated standing stones with carved inscriptions, some of which have never been deciphered. Otherwise, the history of Mongolia's steppe nomads has been largely told through the accounts of such foreigners as Marco Polo and John of Plano Carpini. Their sparse words and partial understandings inspired Westerners to romanticize a distant land of imperial khans. Even when scientific knowledge of Mongolia began to accumulate in the late nineteenth and early twentieth centuries, ethnographic and travel accounts of Mongolian horse herders, camel caravans, abandoned cities of crumbling mud-brick, and stately Buddhist temples tended to reaffirm the earlier images of a timeless and unchanging land. While adventuresome accounts of Western expeditions to Mongolia in the 1920s and 1930s popularized this vast steppe region, for the most part, Mongolia's people and history still remained as inscrutable as the Gobi rock that entombed its prehistoric dinosaurs.

8.1 Xiongnu, an Early State
The Xiongnu people, who emerged during the late Iron Age, created a powerful Mongolia-based state that controlled territories from southern Siberia to northern China and the Altai. Their royal cemeteries contain platform mounds with deep shaft graves for burials of leaders, horses, and chariots. Grave goods included artifacts from as far afield as Egypt and China, indicating Xiongnu involvement with the Silk Road trade. This photograph shows the fortified Mangasiin Khuree site, a garrison in the southern Gobi near the Xiongnu-Chinese frontier.

Over the last sixty years, Western understanding of Mongolia has transformed dramatically thanks to innovative studies of the historic and prehistoric past. A few Western archaeologists such as Nels Nelson, who worked with Roy Chapman Andrews on the American Museum of Natural History expeditions in the 1920s, took an interest in the early Paleolithic- and Neolithic-period stone tools found emerging from the shifting sands of the Gobi Desert.[1] Later, Soviet-period researchers, both Russian and Mongolian, advanced the scientific study of the Mongolian past by launching major excavation projects in the mid-twentieth century.[2] These early Soviet projects were devoted to discovering, mapping, and exploring the magnificent royal tombs of the Iron Age Xiongnu peoples and the numerous ancient ruins of cities standing forgotten in the grasslands (fig.8.1). In the 1990s, a virtual explosion of archaeological fieldwork and historical research has followed closely upon the democratic transition in Mongolia.

Spectacular finds have been made across the eastern steppe in the past few years, such as an intact tomb with a frozen mummy dating to 2,500 years ago from the western Altai Mountains,[3] and an imperial medieval palace that some believe was built by Genghis Khan, discovered in the northeast (see Chapter 17). One very important find

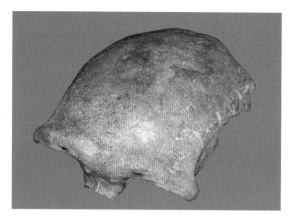

8.2 Salkhit Cranium
In 2006 this fragmentary human skull was found, along with bones of a woolly rhinoceros, in the rubble excavated for a mine at Salkhit in northeastern Mongolia. Subsequent archaeological work failed to recover other evidence. Preliminary results suggest the skull is slightly fossilized, has features of both modern humans and Neanderthals, and probably dates between 40,000 and 100,000 years old, a time when both modern and archaic humans were present in northern Asia. The Salkhit skull is the first early hominid found in Mongolia and one of the northernmost human fossils known from Asia.

8.3 Bayanlig Hunting Art
Rock art is common throughout Mongolia but is most prevalent in the Altai region of western Mongolia. This panel from the Bayanlig rock art site in Bayankhongor province probably dates to the Iron Age and illustrates two people hunting deer with bows, possibly assisted by dogs. Wild goats and sheep are also shown. Such art is believed to have been used to enhance the hunt, which remained an important supplement to the herding economy given the lack or uncertainty of agriculture in many regions.

from northeastern Mongolia may, however, change the very way we understand the origins and spread of our own species. A fragmentary hominin skull uncovered at the mining site of Salkhit in the fall of 2006 along with the remains of a woolly rhinoceros is already causing an international stir among researchers who study human evolution (fig. 8.2).[4] Only the upper portion of the skull remains, and while its species has not yet been identified with certainty, this early individual probably dates to between 40,000 and 100,000 years ago, a period when both modern and archaic forms of human beings inhabited northern Asia.[5] The Salkhit find is the first early hominin

to be discovered in Mongolia and is one of the northernmost human fossils known from Asia. Preliminary reports suggest that because these remains are only lightly fossilized, they may contain analyzable DNA, which could clarify our understanding of the early peopling of Asia and, possibly, of the New World as well. Whatever the ultimate determination of the Salkhit hominin's age and species, such recent discoveries are contributing new chapters to the fascinating and complex archaeological story of Mongolia and to the course of human prehistory. In the following sections we review some of the major contributions made by Mongolian archaeology to an improved understanding of the ancient world.

From Ice Age to Neolithic Domestication of the Steppe

The two million-year era known popularly as the Ice Age—and to scientists as the Pleistocene—was a time of intense cold when glaciers advanced throughout many areas of the northern latitudes (see Chapter 3). The first evidence of the entrance of human ancestors into the region of Mongolia is toward the end of the Ice Age, about 100,000 years ago. Collections from cave sites in Mongolia and Siberia suggest that these first people were probably very similar to the Neanderthals of Europe and western Asia and were adapted, physically and culturally, to survive in frigid environments. The Salkhit fossil, for example, has several cranial characteristics that are distinctive of Neanderthals.[6] Between 45,000 and 35,000 years ago, a technological revolution swept northern Asia, as it had western Eurasia, producing a greatly expanded tool kit that made more sophisticated use of bone and antler and introduced a new stone tool technology on the steppe. These new tools, made from large blades struck from prepared cores of rock, appear in Mongolian sites at the same time as the arrival of modern Homo sapiens. Whether this innovation originated locally or was introduced by migrating Homo sapiens has not been conclusively established,[7] but such technological developments as finely worked clothing, more efficient hunt-

8.4 *Khirigsuurs* and Horse Burials

Stone mounds known as *khirigsuurs* are often associated with deer stones and date to the same period, ca. 1300–800 BCE. Although *khirigsuurs* were used for human burial, grave goods were almost never included. This *khirigsuur* north of Lake Khoton in Bayan Ulgii province is surrounded by a low squared fence of stones. Outside the fence line are twelve small mounds each containing the skull of a sacrificed horse. Encircling the central mound, fence, and horse graves are small hearths where members of the burial party cooked and ate ritual meals.

ing implements, and construction of dwellings suitable for winter occupation propelled a major growth in population. The increased number of late Upper Paleolithic sites from Siberia to the Gobi Desert attests to this surge in human habitation. After 26,000 years ago, hunting on the vast grasslands of Mongolia was bountiful, and well-equipped hunters pursued Ice Age megafauna, including woolly mammoth, woolly rhinoceros, horse, cave bear, reindeer, bison, and musk ox.

The advances in cognitive, symbolic, and expressive skills that identify the Upper Paleolithic revolution include a dramatic new form of cultural representation that emerged at the end of the Ice Age. In the first pictorial records produced by these ancient peoples, petroglyphic carvings and rock paintings show us ancient Mongolia through the eyes of the Upper Paleolithic hunters who once lived there, rather than our having to infer their activities from mute bones and artifacts. Ibex with their elaborate notched horns, mountain sheep, camels,

horses, bears, and several species of cattle leap to life from the surfaces of rocks embellished during the final centuries of the Ice Age. The canyon cathedrals of ancient rock art at Baga Oigor–Tsagaan Salaa[8] and cave paintings deep inside Khoid Tsenkher Cave,[9] both located in far western Mongolia, show an array of animals long extinct from the mountains and steppes of Eurasia. Usually interpreted as a form of hunting magic to increase the abundance of game or hunting effectiveness, petroglyphs became increasingly abundant over the millennia and constitute one of the most informative site types of Mongolian archaeology (figs. 8.3, 6).

The milder climate of the Holocene period, which begins after the Ice Age some 10,000 years ago, stimulated a major change that transformed human societies. Plants and animals were domesticated and various forms of agriculture were adopted. Not surprisingly, however, the Neolithic period seems to have brought less dramatic change to Mongolia than to many other areas of Eurasia, such as China or the Near East. Lack

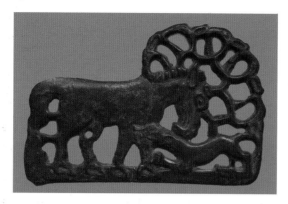

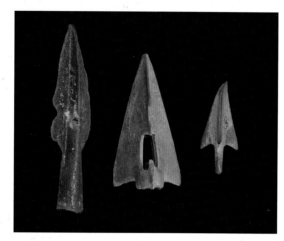

8.5 The Bronze Age
The Mongolian Bronze Age, ca. 1500–700 BCE, brought far-reaching change to society as well as to technology. Bronze arrow tips and battle axes, more durable bits for horse bridles, and more effective knives had both military and practical implications. Producing and acquiring bronze stimulated trade, competition, and warfare, leading to larger political groups, elites, and more rigid social hierarchies. Wealth was displayed on one's person, often in the form of animal-headed knives and ornamental castings affixed to horse gear.

blade industries remained the dominant technology for hunting, processing, and production. Tiny flint blades, hardly larger than slivers, were set into the sides of bone and antler to serve as butchering knives, scrapers, implements for preparing patterned skin garments and embroidery, and many other purposes. Not only these products but the microtools themselves, fashioned from multicolored crystalline stone, were often extremely beautiful.

Pottery began to appear at small open-air sites across the steppe by 8,000 to 6,000 years ago, along with microlithic stone tools and grinding stones.[11] Pottery is sometimes associated with the introduction of agriculture and building of permanent dwellings, but these parallel developments did not occur as readily in Mongolia. Intensification of hunting, gathering, and fishing in many places provided sufficient food resources so that people did not need to maintain a completely nomadic way of life. At least seasonally, longer-term villages could be established. Ceramics, along with more stable living sites, were the key to improved nutrition: more efficient food-processing and cooking techniques could be used for making stews and gruels from cereal grains, whether wild or domesticated. Mongolian Neolithic sites are full of ceramics, most of which were decorated with incisions and the impressions of cordage, textiles, and sometimes painted designs. Although early ceramics were initially poorly fired and fragile, once introduced, pottery remained part of the Mongolian cultural pattern for thousands of years.

During the late Neolithic period, Mongolian culture gradually became invested in the use and management of domesticated herd animals. Cattle may have been domesticated about 5,000 years ago at sites like

of sufficient water, saline soils and lakes, and a short growing season may explain why early to mid-Holocene peoples of Mongolia maintained their earlier subsistence strategies. Hunting and gathering continued among Mongolian steppe dwellers who experimented with the growing of grains and other crops sporadically in the more fertile and well-watered valley locations.

Two important new technologies dominate archaeological assemblages during the Neolithic period: microlithic tools and pottery.[10] By about 6,000 years ago, miniaturization of cores and blades reached a level of efficiency that could only be further improved by the introduction of metal. But with metal smelting still two thousand years in the future, core and

8.6 Biluut Ceremonial Figures
This unusual image, which was pecked into a polished rock at the Biluut site in southern Bayan Ulgii province, displays a central genii-like figure with no legs. It has huge arms, each of which has appendages and holds a crook or hooked implement. Small dancing human figures are seen on either side; the one on the right appears to hold a dagger.

curred, was a critical event that shaped both Mongolian and, eventually, world history.

The Bronze and Early Iron Ages: Warfare and Ritual Landscapes

Highly visible changes in social and religious life—rather than changes in environment, technology, and relationships with animals and plants—marked the final phase prior to the appearance of state-level societies and empires in Mongolia's culture history. These changes, which begin during the early second millennium BCE and develop over the next thousand years, intersect with far-reaching transformations across the Eurasian steppe zone. The first horse-drawn chariots in the southern Russian steppe, the expansion of sophisticated bronze technology across the territory of Kazakhstan and southern Siberia, and the rise of long-distance trade routes and violent warfare were transformations that also occurred over the eastern steppe, but at different rates and at different times. These innovations were facilitated, almost certainly, by increasing mobility made possible by use of horse-drawn carts and, very likely, horse riding.[14]

The ritual use of horses in Mongolia was widespread and intensive by 1500 BCE. Ceremonial stone piles encircling megalithic burial mounds, known as *khirigsuur* (fig. 8.4), punctuate Mongolia's steppe lands from the borders of Manchuria all the way to Tuva and the Russian Altai and into the south Gobi Desert.[15] These stone piles contain horse skulls, vertebrae, and hooves derived from horse sacrifices and feasting that accompanied the building of *khirigsuur* mounds. *Khirigsuurs* have central, stone-mounded burial chambers, surrounded by rectangular or circular stone enclosures, and outlying stone circles, often with horse-head burials.[16] The wide variation of the size and complexity of *khirigsuur* mounds may indicate differences in personal wealth and social status, even though the burials do not contain grave goods. An idea of the labor needed to build a *khirigsuur* can be provided by the larger monuments, which can be 400 meters across and up to five or six meters high.[17]

Khirigsuurs are a specialized form of *kurgan*, a term widely used in northern Eurasia for stone-mounded graves. *Khirigsuurs* are

the late Neolithic village of Tamsagbulag, a small settlement of subterranean pit houses on the far eastern steppe.[12] Microliths and ceramics, as well as artifacts related to cultivation and processing of grain—including grinders, millstones, weights for digging sticks, and stone hoes—were found there. Human burials were also discovered under the floors of some pit houses, along with large quantities of cattle bones.

While the use of cattle was certainly intensive, it is still not yet known whether they were wild or domestic breeds. Sites such as Tamsagbulag may reveal the kind of experimentation and intensive use of wild animal species that eventually results in local domestication. Domestic sheep, goats, and cattle can also be moved over great distances, exchanged, and transferred to groups who primarily survive by hunting. Domestic herd animals may have appeared in Mongolia by way of such exchanges from the northwest, where they are documented 5,000 to 4,500 years ago as part of a mixed hunting-herding strategy of the Siberian Afanas'evo culture.[13] The introduction of herd animals to the Mongolian steppe, however that may have oc-

8.7 Ulan Tolgoi
This site west of Lake Erkhel in Khovsgol province has five deer stones in north-south alignment and many large *khirigsuur* mounds. A joint Smithsonian-Mongolian team excavated here from 2002 to 2006, discovering multiple horse-head burials surrounding Deer Stone 4, all dating ca. 800 BCE. The tall deer stone (DS2), measuring 3.2m high, is one of the largest and one of the most beautifully carved in Mongolia.

ern interpretation of the term, because the word *kereksur/khirgisuuer* does not occur in premodern Mongol written sources.

The large region in which these complexes appear probably indicates greater contacts between local groups, which by the second millennium BCE had adopted horse-riding and more mobile forms of herding, and so were interacting over longer distances. Rock art panels from many parts of Mongolia show riders mounted on camels and horses, often in association with highly stylized deer images that are best known from hundreds of stone steles found throughout northern Mongolia. Deer stone steles are anthropomorphic figures, delineated by earrings, belts, weapon sets, and, sometimes, with human faces, and elegantly carved with stylized deer motifs (figs. 8.7, 9, 11).[18] They have been interpreted as depictions of revered warriors and chieftains whose tattooed bodies may have resembled the individuals found in the frozen Early Iron Age tombs at Pazyryk in the Altai Mountains.[19] These striking monuments were also erected at *khirigsuur* sites and, like them, are often surrounded by horse-head burials, suggesting that in addition to changes in transport and burial customs, new religious and status systems were extending across the steppe.

New technologies were also developed and spread rapidly during the second to first millennium BCE, especially with the advent of bronze and, later, iron metallurgy. Developed independently in several parts of Eurasia, bronze-working was a technology transferred between and among sedentary and nomadic societies. The southern Gobi site of Oyu Tolgoi, dated by the presence of decorated Bronze Age ceramics, is a representative example of early copper mining and bronze production in Mongolia. The site has mine shafts dug into deep copper veins, piles of discarded copper ore, slag-encrusted ceramic and stone crucibles for smelting, and extensive bronze slag.[20] Daggers and knives, bells, arrowheads, saddle decorations, axes, and many ritual items were the types of stunning artifacts eventually produced from such mining and casting activities (fig. 8.5).[21]

similar to *kurgans*, but have a more complicated structure and the term is restricted to Mongolia and adjacent regions. At the present authors request, an etymology has recently been offered by Professor Gyorgy Kara of Indiana University. He notes that Tsewel's Mongol-Mongol dictionary defines *khirigsuur* as an ancient tomb (*ert deer tsagt uexegsdiin xuueriig orshuulsan bulsh*, "a tomb for the corpses of people [who] died in ancient times"). The Uyghur-script, or classical form, of the word is indicated as *Kirgis eguer*, literally, "Kyrgyz (or Kirghiz) nest." The late Mongol scholar Yoengsiyebue Rinchen considered the term a distortion of *Kirgis keguer* (modern *Khirgis khuuer*), the last word meaning "corpse; burial, tomb." Mongol scholarly tradition connected those prehistoric tombs with the medieval Kirghiz people whose empire ruled over what is now Mongolia in the ninth century CE. Its usage today may be based on the mod-

8.8 Square Burial
At the end of the period of deer stone and *khirigsuur* construction, a new culture appeared that can be identified by square burials lined with stone slabs. Their graves are sometimes found at the outer edges of *khirigsuurs* or deer stone sites and occasionally used recycled deer stones as corner posts and retaining walls. In Mongolia square burials appear toward the terminal Bronze Age and Early Iron Age, ca. 1000–600 BCE, but unlike the latter they contain many grave goods. This burial is from the Salkhat site near Ulziit, Khovsgol province.

By the first half of the first millennium BCE, iron objects appear in burial assemblages in both Siberia and Mongolia, as does increased evidence for conflict and violence. The battle axe and war hammer, artifacts once cast from bronze and, later, in iron, were designed specifically for use in armed combat. If the evidence for fractured skulls and other conflict-related trauma from sites such as Chandman in northwestern Mongolia are indicative, violence was increasingly a part of everyday life among many nomadic groups during this period.[22]

Ancient Empires of the Steppes: The Xiongnu

Inter-group conflict may have been one important factor that culminated at the end of the first millennium BCE in the emergence of the first nomadic state, known as the Xiongnu confederation. While violent conflict did not occur in every locale—studies of skeletons from the Egiin Gol Valley in northern Mongolia show mostly healthy individuals[23]—evidence of warfare in some regions demonstrates varying degrees of political stability and instability across the eastern steppe. Conflict could have resulted from many factors, including increased territoriality as small-scale political organizations expanded and controlled specific resources. Another source of political instability may have

been the competition over and disruption of long-distance exchange relationships with Inner Mongolia and China, where highly militarized states were aggressively competing for dominance during the Warring States period (475–221 BCE).

The first references to mounted warriors from the steppe occur in the early Chinese histories around the fourth and third centuries BCE.[24] These fearsome peoples are referred to as "Hu," a generic term for non-Chinese barbarians, and sometimes as "Xiongnu," a specific steppe group. Sima Qian (145–86 BCE), the grand historian of the Han dynasty (206 BCE– 220 CE), provides an account of the rise of the Xiongnu state in 209 BCE under the leader Maodun, a dispossessed younger son of a tribal leader. Maodun escaped from captivity among the enemies of the Xiongnu into which his own father had sent him. Secretly, he trained a small elite force of warriors to loose their arrows toward whatever target Maodun shot at with his own bow. A bone whistle attached to Maodun's arrow screeched menacingly toward its victim, instantly informing the elite warriors of the target's direction. Maodun tested the archers relentlessly, first by letting his arrow loose at his favorite horse, and then at his favorite wife; those who hesitated were summarily killed on the spot. Finally, during a day of hunting along

the forest fringes of the vast Mongolian grasslands, Maodun shot a whistling arrow at his own father and, inevitably, his arrow was answered by twenty-five more, leaving Maodun's father dead in his saddle.[25] Maodun used this moment to seize control of his tribe and neighboring peoples, and quickly consolidated a large and powerful polity, which he used to extract tribute from the neighboring Chinese Han dynasty. The legend of Maodun will probably never be certified as fact or myth, and the story may be colored by Chinese cultural distaste for the northern nomads. However, archaeologists have discovered material culture that can be identified with the historical Xiongnu and have even recovered examples of whistling arrows from tombs of this period.[26]

Archaeological investigation of the Xiongnu has revealed information that is lacking or only hinted in the historical texts. Research in the Selenge River basin of Mongolia and Siberia suggests that the Xiongnu originated from indigenous Early Iron Age groups south of Lake Baikal.[27] Historians describe the huge territory controlled by the Xiongnu as being divided into eastern, western, and central sections, a distribution actually borne out by archaeological site locations. Until recently it was thought that the Xiongnu were specialized herders who moved with their animals; but large, walled Xiongnu settlements are also known from across the steppe, some with agricultural production, as seen at Ivolga in southern Siberia.[28]

The massive cemeteries of the Xiongnu elite, with burials excavated as deep as fifteen or twenty meters below the surface, contain elaborate internal chambers constructed from heavy wooden beams and stone; immediately above the burial chamber complete chariots have been discovered.[29] Inside the tomb chamber archaeologists have not only recovered artifacts of gold, silver, and semi-precious stones but also objects from everyday life such has horse-riding gear, storage pots, domestic grain, and the remains of sacrificed cattle, horses, and camels. Along the walls of the tomb are found long severed hair braids, perhaps symbols of mourning placed by

8.11 Tsagaan Asga Deer Stones
The 3,000-year-old Tsagaan Asga site has the largest number of deer stones in western Mongolia. More than twenty stone slabs with images of antlered deer-bird figures once stood in north-south alignment. Today only a few remain intact, and most are covered with modern grafitti. Little protection is available for such archaeological monuments, but signage and listing as cultural heritage sites would alert local people and officials to their importance and need for preservation.

men or women of the Xiongnu aristocracy. Imported artifacts are also found, many produced in China and others from Central Asia and beyond, including objects from as far away as the Mediterranean (fig. 8.10).[30] These long-distance imports have led scholars to infer that Xiongnu tribute and trade routes extended far into Central Asia and possibly constituted an early form of Silk Road exchange long before the Han dynasty's well-documented Silk Road trade.[31]

The Xiongnu polity, with shifts in structure and in geographical extent, persisted as a regional organization for more than three hundred years. By CE 91 major factional challenges within the Xiongnu eastern flank, supported by the Han dynasty, caused a series of significant defeats and subsequent migrations out of Mongolia into the western steppe. The Xiongnu created a major state on the present-day territory of Mongolia that strongly influenced other regions and peoples of Eurasia. Their political, ideological, and cultural precedents were later assimilated and developed by the imperial Türks, Uyghurs, and Mongols into a unique nomadic civilization.

1. Fairservis 1993.
2. Kiselev 1965; Rudenko 1962.
3. Tseveendorj et al. 2007.
4. Tseveendorj et al. 2006.
5. Etler 1996, 291–93.
6. Coppens et al. 2008.
7. Brantingham et al. 2001, 745–46.
8. Jacobson et al. 2001.
9. Tseveendorj et al. 2003, 56–57.
10. Derevianko 1994.
11. Derevianko 1994.
12. Derevianko and Dorj 1992, 172–75.
13. Honeychurch and Wright 2008, 522.
14. Honeychurch et al. 2009.
15. Frohlich et al. 2009.
16. Allard and Erdenebaatar 2005.
17. Allard and Erdenebaatar 2005.
18. Fitzhugh 2009.
19. Rudenko 1970; Jettmar 1994.
20. Tseveendorj et al. 2001.
21. Erdenebaatar 2004.
22. Tseveendorj 1980; Novgorodova 1982.
23. Nelson 2000.
24. Di Cosmo 2002, 165–66.
25. Sima Qian 1993, vol. 2, 134.
26. Konovalov 1976.
27. Honeychurch and Wright 2008, 529.
28. Davydova 1995.
29. Miniaev and Sakharovskaia 2007.
30. Khatanbaatar et al. 2007.
31. Barfield 2001; Christian 2000.

9. Empire Building Before the Mongols

LEGACIES OF THE TÜRKS AND UYGHURS

Jonathan K. Skaff

William Honeychurch

THE MONGOLS WERE NOT THE FIRST GREAT EMPIRE to rise from the steppes of Central Asia. The Türks and their successors, the Uyghurs, would unify Mongolia from the sixth through ninth centuries and migrate west to build a string of empires, culminating in the Ottoman. Many of their Türkic traditions such as rule from the Orkhon River Valley of Mongolia and worship of a sky god, were adopted by the Mongols. Türkic peoples also were a crucial component of the Mongol empire. Nomadic Türks are thought to have formed the largest contingent of Mongol cavalry. Settled Türks and Uyghurs advised the Mongols on bureaucratic practices essential for administering sedentary societies. The Mongols built on the debt to their Türkic predecessors and contemporaries in honing their skills at empire building, unsurpassed in the history of the steppe.

9.1 Türkic Monument
Authropomorphic figures known as *khun chuluu*—literally, "stone man"—are common markers of the 6–8th century Türkic period of Mongolian history. Like deer stones, which may have provided inspiration, Türkic figures follow a strict formula: the right hand holds a cup of libation; the left rests at the belt; the mustache is thin and curled; robes, belts, and hats are indicated; the face is absent of expression, and the eyes closed, as in death. Such figures are probably stylized portraits of the deceased. They are usually found at burial sites, but some mark ceremonial structures, like this pair wrapped in blue, orange, and gold Buddhist *khadags* (ritual strips of silk signifying respect) at the Dalkha site south of the Selenge River.

Historical records of the ancient Türks date to the early sixth century, when their original tribal groups were living in the Altai Mountains of what is today western Mongolia. They specialized in ironwork, serving as blacksmiths for the nomadic Rouran confederation. By 545, Ashina Bumïn, who would found the first Türk Empire, was establishing himself as an important regional chieftain. He initiated independent diplomatic and trade relations with the Western Wei dynasty (535–557) of northwestern China, marrying a Western Wei princess to forge an alliance that secured his southern borders. Following a victorious attack against the Rouran in 552, he declared himself khaghan, or supreme ruler, the title later adopted by the Mongols. The name "Türk" became the political designation for all tribes under Ashina authority.

Ashina Bumïn reigned for only two years before he died. He was succeeded by his son Muqan Khaghan, who created by conquest the largest imperial confederation in the region since the time of the Xiongnu polity 300 years earlier (see Chapter 8). The first Türk Empire included much of the eastern Eurasian steppe zone along with deserts, oases, and forested regions to the north (fig. 9.2). Türk officials were stationed in the trade-rich oasis states around the Tarim Basin with small garrisons to oversee taxation; often, they became hereditary rulers of these agricultural regions.[1] Like the later Mongols, Türk rulers built their empire through military victories and justified their rule with myths of descent from a legendary wolf ancestor and claims that the supreme sky god, Tenggeri, had appointed them to govern.[2] The khaghans enhanced their prestige by engaging in diplomacy, warfare, and trade with the great sedentary powers on their borders. Muqan, like his father, allied with the Northern Zhou, one

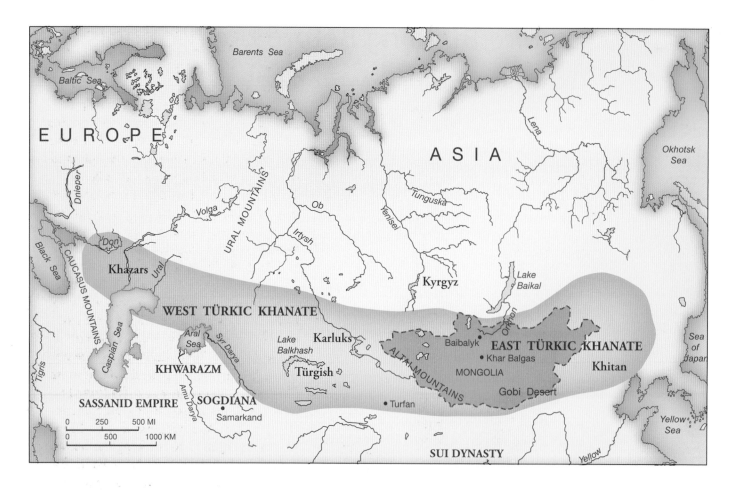

Map of Türkic Empire

9.2 Map of Türkic Empire
Originating in Western Mongolia and the Altai Mountains region, the Türks built a huge empire based on nomadic herding and mounted warriors during the 6th–8th centuries. Expanding throughout the steppe region from the Black Sea nearly to Korea, the Türkic empire and its populations expanded north, where its linguistic, genetic, and cultural legacy is found in today's East Siberian peoples.

9.3 Iron Bits and Stirrups
Major improvements in horse culture, especially the development of stirrups, which enhanced a rider's lateral stability, gave mounted Türkic warriors an advantage in battling infantry soldiers. Since stirrups are rare in Western Asia and Europe before 600 CE, this Asian invention probably was an important factor in the Türkic expansion. These stirrups and bits were recovered from the Bilgä Khaghan treasure dating to ca. 734.

of the important northern Chinese dynasties. He sent one of his daughters to marry the Zhou emperor, a rare honor and a sign of Muqan's power because Chinese rulers usually sent lesser brides to the steppe. The Türks also traded with the Zhou, and the Zhou paid annual tribute of 100,000 bolts of silk to the khaghan during his reign.[3]

Silk Road trade across Eurasia expanded to an extent not seen since the collapse of the Han dynasty of China in 220. Eastern and Western confederations of Türks profited from protecting merchants and facilitating trade. Without them, the Silk Roads might not have been rejuvenated. Although

the goods conveyed over long distances along the Silk Roads were principally luxury products, hence not critical to the survival of the partners, trade did result in considerable cultural exchange. Drugs, aromatics, jewels, precious metals, glassware, and relics reached China from Central Asia and the Middle East and Chinese inventions filtered westward. The Chinese secret of silk production reached Central Asia and the Byzantine empire by the sixth century. Merchants or Buddhist monks probably introduced papermaking to Samarkand, the fabled market of Central Asia, by 700.

Türkic influences on the Tang dynasty (618–907) were dramatic. Türkic soldiers and officers filled the ranks of Tang northern armies. Tang rulers invited Türkic musicians and dancers to perform at court, inspiring fads for foreign music, dance, and dress. Indirect cultural influences from peoples along the farthest reaches of the Silk Road were equally dramatic. For example, the Chinese adapted Middle Eastern musical instruments as part of their own musical repertoire. The Tang fascina-

9.4 Kül Tegin
This carved head of Kül Tegin was found in the Orkhon Valley north of Khara Khorum. Kül Tegin was the younger brother of Bilgä Khaghan and his most important military commander.

the Holy Trinity, attracted many Asian converts, including residents of the Tang capital of Chang'an. The Türk ruler Taspar (r. 572–81) converted to Buddhism, although under the Türk empires many different religions proliferated.[4] Manichaeism, which originated in Iran in the third century and preached of a primordial struggle between light and darkness, spread to the east after being banned at home. This faith found converts in Tang China, but experienced far greater success as the state religion of the Uyghur Empire, which succeeded the Türks in 744.

Much of Türk history, however, was not made of opulence, wealth, and tolerance as much as political discord and violence. Prosperity and stability frequently were interrupted by political factionalism among the Türk elite. Bloody internecine struggles followed the deaths of most khaghans. Succession was a challenge for the entire body politic, as it would be for the Mongols. Another persistent problem was that allegiance to the khaghan was only extended freely by tribes who lived in close proximity; coercion was necessary to ensure the submission of tribes in outer parts of the realm. Rebellion often erupted when there were signs of a khaghan's weakness.

In 630, following several years of harsh winters across the steppe, the Tang emperor Taizong took advantage of divisions among the Türks to launch a lightning cavalry attack that led to the fall of the Eastern Türks.[5] The khaghan and other leaders removed to the Tang capital of Chang'an in the Central Plain of China and were granted positions and titles. Nomadic tribes in Inner Mongolia became Tang subjects and played a prominent role supplying the Tang army with cavalry soldiers. The Western Türks divided into two factions with competing khaghans, making them vulnerable to Tang conquests that took place between 640 and 657. By 648, the Tang had captured all of the oasis city-states of the Turfan and Tarim basins, depriving the Türk tribes of income from taxes and trade, further weakening their authority. Around the same time, fractious tribal groups in the region of Mongolia gave at least nominal allegiance to Uyghur rulers, who in turn supplied cavalry troops to the

tion with foreigners was delightfully realized in the tricolored ceramic figurines of Türks, Arabs, and Silk Road travelers that were made in China and excavated from the tombs of politically prominent individuals.

Through the conduit of the Silk Roads as well as the expansion of the Türk Empire, a profusion of Middle Eastern and South Asian religions found their way to Central Asia and to Tang China. Zoroastrianism, the major Iranian religion, took root in Central Asia and western China before Islam became predominate. The Nestorian sect, a heretical form of Christianity banned in Europe in the fourth century for diminishing the balance of

9.5 Bilgä Khaghan Stele
This stele carved in runic letters and dating to ca. 734 commemorates the life of Bilgä Khaghan, a Türkic leader who created a powerful empire built upon Silk Road trade, military strength, and strategic diplomacy with Tibet and China. He was poisoned in 734, and this huge memorial stele lies fallen in the Okkhon Valley of central Mongolia. The stele covered with runic lettering bears the first account written in an indigenous script in Mongolia, telling history from its own rather than a Chinese perspective. Its text shows that many military and political innovations credited to Genghis Khan were probably borrowed from the earlier Türks or their predecessors.

Tang armies attacking the Western Türks.[6]

Just as it was difficult for Türk khaghans to satisfy all parts of their far-flung domains, Tang emperors likewise faced Türk accusations that "sons of the nobles became slaves of the Chinese, and their lady-like daughters became servants."[7] Adverse weather and drought in 679 caused great hardship on the steppe by killing off massive numbers of livestock. Among the disenfranchised Eastern Türks, the Tang emperor's charisma and legitimacy were waning. Eastern Türks revolted under the leadership of the rebel Ilterish, breaking away from Tang rule and the Türk aristocracy, heading north to Mongolia, where they conquered and reunited the former tribes of the first Türk empire and established a new imperial order. Tonyukuk, the Chinese-educated chief minister of Ilterish, rejected fixed abodes and settlements in favor of traditional steppe ways of life, including hunting and providing for herd animals by "following the water and grass," as Chinese texts commonly described nomadic migrations. The Türks of the second empire also continued the

well-established steppe tradition of raiding China for resources and luxury goods.[8]

Khapaghan Khaghan led the second empire to its pinnacle of power, controlling Inner and Outer Mongolia and Manchuria. In 698 he forced China's Empress Wu to turn over several tens of thousands of her Türk subjects and large quantities of grain seed and agricultural tools. However, Khapaghan severely overextended his military by attacking western Central Asia in attempting to recoup the vast territories of the first Türk empire, which led to major military defeats and his downfall as ruler. His successor, Bilgä Khaghan, relying on the military skill of his younger brother Kül Tegin and the political acumen of the now elderly Tonyukuk, carried out numerous campaigns to force the tribes of Mongolia to subjugate themselves once again to the Türks. Initially, Bilgä allied with Tibet against China, but met with less success in looting the Tang because of their improved frontier defenses. In 725, Bilgä abruptly shifted course in foreign relations and made peace overtures to the Tang. Both sides agreed to trade Türk horses for Chinese silk. Once again, the prosperity and stability was not long lasting. The untimely deaths of Tonyukuk and Kül Tegin strategically weakened Bilgä Khaghan, and he was poisoned in 734.

The deaths of these leaders of the imperial Türks occasioned the construction of three grand funerary monuments on the steppes. The monument to Tonyukuk lies a short distance east of the present-day capital city of Ulaan Baatar. The mortuary monuments to Kül Tegin and Bilgä Khaghan still stand today close together on the open grasslands of the Orkhon Valley in central Mongolia (figs. 9.4, 5). The Orkhon sites contain inscribed stone steles more than three meters tall bearing the most substantial writings in the Orkhon runic script, the indigenous writing system of the ancient Türks.[9] The inscriptions eulogize the lives of these two leaders and in doing so, provide valuable information on history, politics, social life, religion, and military campaigns. The Orkhon steles offer the first glimpses of steppe history from the perspective of the nomadic elite instead of through the eyes of Chinese historians.

Following the demise of Bilgä Khaghan, his successors struggled to maintain political order but by 742 a massive rebellion across the steppe collapsed the second Türk Empire entirely. In place of the Türks and their enormous territories, a politically more stable and geographically smaller organization arose under the Uyghurs, who were one of the disgruntled tribes that had revolted against the second Türk empire. The Uyghurs held sway over their steppe domain between 744 and 840, coexisting with, and at times, propping up, the faltering Tang dynasty to the south.

Uyghur rule instituted great changes on the steppe. They founded such major urban centers as Khar Balgas and Baibalyk, which exist today as magnificent walled ruins in Mongolia[10] (see Chapter 19, fig. 19.3) There is still much to learn from the archaeology of these mostly unstudied urban sites (see Chapter 16). By stabilizing the succession of rulership and by forging close alliances with the Sogdians of Central Asia, a prominent Iranian group known for their trade acumen, the new Uyghur elite fostered economic prosperity and a higher degree of political integration across their empire.[11] Uyghur cities supported markets, craft industries, and intensive agricultural production. However, these important and expansive centers also became vulnerable to attack. Uyghur domination of Mongolia ended in 840, when the capital city of Khar Balgas was conquered by the Kyrgyz tribe of the northern forest regions, and the last Uyghur khaghan of the steppe was summarily executed within his own city walls.

These events had important implications for the later Mongol empire. Some Uyghurs fled westward to take control of the Turfan basin and surrounding oasis states, where they preserved their former administrative traditions and innovated new statecraft to suit their more sedentary way of life. In centuries to come, these Uyghurs of Turfan would communicate the traditions of their empire and those of their Türk predecessors to the Mongols. Not only techniques of governance were shared between these peoples but specific technologies such as writing as well. The Uyghur script, itself improvised from a cursive form of Sogdian writing, was modified by Uyghur scribes to suit the Mongol language.[12] This "Old Mongol" script was not only the imperial writing system of 800 years ago but is still used today in Mongolia and Inner Mongolia.

The Türks and the Uyghurs far outlived their empires. Like the later Mongols, these groups created vast political realms that facilitated long-distance trade and encouraged sharing of political, cultural, and diplomatic traditions between distant parts of Eurasia. The Türk empires also encouraged a cultural identity based upon commonalities of belief, lifestyle, and language among formerly dispersed Türkic peoples. After the fall of the second empire in 742 and the rise of the Uyghurs, the word "Türk" no longer served as the name of a particular tribe, but the name has persisted as an ethnic designation for all speakers of Türkic languages.

The Mongols, fittingly, built their own capital, Khara Khorum, less than a day's ride on horseback from the ruins of the first Uyghur city, Khar Balgas, and the inscribed stones of the Türks standing in the Orkhon Valley (see Chapter 19). The Mongol empire itself took root in the cultural and political legacy left by the Türks and Uyghurs centuries before.[13] Ultimately, the Mongols would surpass these predecessors in empire building because they were more effective at controlling internal factional disputes and more innovative in developing methods to rule sedentary societies.

1. Skaff 2002.
2. Golden 1982.
3. Golden 1992, 127–32; Linghu 1971: 50, 908–12.
4. Sinor 1990, 314–15.
5. Graff 2002.
6. Skaff 2009, 179–89.
7. Sinor 1990, 310.
8. Liu et al. 1975: 194a, 5174.
9. Tekin 1968, 261–90.
10. Honeychurch and Amartuvshin 2007.
11. Mackerras 1990, 323–24.
12. Brose 2007.
13. Honeychurch and Amartuvshin 2006.

بود بخر موجبی یاد کرده شد و پسر داشته طالو قا و نوقا و پسر بوقا او تومن مثل است که شعبه چنکنر خان با او میرود و ذکر او

و د استانش متقاف خواهد آمد و پسر بوقا تی پنجن است که کیفیت شعب و بحقیقت معلوم نیست و صورت نمایش این برین هیات است

د اسپنان و نوم منین بن بوقا ین بود بخر خان و خاتون او و نولون و شعبه فرزندان او و آن برد و قسم است   قسم اول

در دیباچه و شرح حال ایشان د و تومن منین جد معتم چنکنر خان بوده و مغولان جد معتم او د او تان و نه پسر داشته و جون فن

یافت خاتون او مو نو لون نام که مادر پسران بود باز نشر یک به طرفی از قومی دختری پستده و نه براه د لعا می میکرد مده مو لون

نعمتی و ثروتی تمام داشت و او را مقام و یورت د روضعی بود که نوشل ای کوه سپاه خوانده اند و بهر چند روزی فرمودی تا کهارا

کردند و اسب و چهار پا یی از بسیاری شوانستند رفت آن جمند دلکیم جون از سر کوسی که او ی شست تا پایان تا پان برکست چندان چهار پای

با ستادی که زمین از سم ایشان پر شدی شوانستند رفت و نه جمعنی نا تمام جمع والا او نو دی تا طلب کله که در آن تاریخ از مغولانی که نام ایشان جلایریست

و ازد ر اکین بذو شرح شعب و اصناف اقوام ایشان داده شد چند قوم د ر حد و دکلوران می نشسته اند و متفاد کوران بوده اند و معنی کوران

10. Genghis Khan Emerges

POWER AND POLITY ON THE STEPPE

ISENBIKE TOGAN

IN THE ERA DURING WHICH TEMÜJIN, who became known as Genghis Khan, rose to power, alliances between pastoral nomads shifted according to which groups sought power and which preferred to avoid conflict. Most pastoral nomads in twelfth-century Mongolia chose to avoid confrontation rather than to engage in warfare. Conflicts erupted, but warfare was not the norm. In this early nomadic society might made right, and the not-so-mighty simply migrated. There was room to move: nomads were highly mobile and generally lived in sparsely populated areas. In addition to disagreements over hunting, another source of conflict was the control of summer and winter pastures for livestock. Increases in herd size necessitated more land to graze an owner's cattle, but once again, herders who lacked strength preferred to migrate rather than fight.

10.1 Budonchar's Wives and his Sons Buka and Buktal This painting from a *Chinggisnameh* manuscript of 1596 is based on the *Compendium of Chronicles* that Rashid al-Din prepared on commission from the Mughal ruler Akbar. It shows Budonchar's wives with their sons in a courtly gathering. Although the scene is depicted in a Mughal setting, the headgear of the two wives are distinctively Mongolian (*bogtag*), whereas some of the attendants and servants wear Indian outfits. The painting relates to the story of the mythological origin of Genghis Khan's clan, which descended from Alan the Fair, the ancestral mother of the Mongols.

Nine hundred years ago, most steppe families were relatively self-sufficient, living off a wide range of domestic animal products as well as wild game and foraged resources. They caught fish in the rivers and lakes of the northern steppe, and farmed on a small-scale.[1] Steppe families moved their camp possessions seasonally with the aid of horses, camel caravans, and ox-carts (fig. 10.5). The circular tent known as the *ger* could be moved by camel or cart at the slow but steady speed of the entire herd.

Whenever they were not traveling, the family group kept the animals used for milk inside a circular enclosure of carts or *gers* while the other sheep, cattle, and horses were free to move about in herds. During the summer, herd animals spread out widely across the land, but in winter were kept closer to home. Horses were key to winter survival, for their hooves broke up the icy surface of the snow to reach buried grasses, making it possible for cattle, sheep, and goats to graze on what was left below. Horses roamed the steppe in the vicinity of an encampment throughout the year with little supervision, and their independence helped them stay strong enough to withstand winter weather and wolf predation. When the snow and ice was too thick for horses to break up the crust, however, disaster struck animals and people. Known as *zuds*, these times of famine, often weather-related, caused suffering and death to animals and people and initiated massive migrations as people searched for new pastures even as herd animals rapidly weakened and died.

When setting up camp, families erected their *gers* so that the doors faced south, allowing the sunlight from the east, south, and west to shine in. The seat of honor for the master of the house and guests was in the north, opposite the entrance. Male guests and male members of the family sat to the right of the master, and women sat

10.2 Naiman Homeland
The Mongolian valleys on the eastern flanks of the Altai Mountains, once home to Türks, were controlled by the Naiman during Genghis Khan's ascent. This region of Bayan Ulgii province is 500–1,000 meters higher than the steppes of central Mongolia. Its winters are longer and colder than in central Mongolia, promoting the development of large snow mounds with frozen cores of ice known as *pingos*. Melting mountain snow, extended by local irrigation, provides water for animals during early summer when central Mongolia is prone to drought.

to the left. This gendered division was accompanied by an age hierarchy in which elders took their places toward the north—toward the seat of honor—while younger people sat close to the entrance.[2] Directly below the smoke hole at the top of the *ger* was the family hearth, usually in the form of an iron stove. The hearth signified the vitality of the family and also connected to the family's ancestral spirits who were sometimes present in the *ger* in the form of amulets and figurines.

These ancestral spirits were honored with animal sacrifices, and women played an important role in these rituals. Such ceremonies, which were accompanied by the chopping and scorching of meat,[3] could also be used to expel people from the social group. Not inviting someone to the ceremony indicated that they were unwanted and would be forced to move. Decamping was another method of social division; in this case people moved away suddenly, leaving those who were unwanted on their own (fig. 10.4). After she was widowed, Höelün, the mother of the future Genghis Khan, was subjected to such forced isolation. These were traditional methods of conflict resolution on the steppe.

Pastoral nomads of the eleventh and twelfth centuries had been moving between their winter and summer pastures in this manner without centralized leadership since the period of Uyghur leadership in the middle of the ninth century.[4] Interac-

tion with outside states was never totally absent, however, because the Khitan-Liao polity (907–1125) had constructed outposts in these areas. Nevertheless, northern steppe peoples resisted formation of large confederations, preferring to maintain their nomadic life as tribal and clan units.

Steppe Tribes at the Time of Temüjin

At the beginning of the twelfth century, the steppe tribes were scattered and lacked institutionalized political organization (fig. 10.3). Some did not have designated leaders, so anyone from the group could lead based on achievement and dominance, while other groups had several leaders.[5] Strong chieftains began to emerge in areas adjacent to sedentary civilizations,[6] and their chieftains may have acquired the power of hereditary rule. It would have been customary for these leaders to assume the title of khan, a hereditary leadership title that by the twelfth century already had a long imperial tradition in Xiongnu, Türk, and Uyghur polities.

The Kereyid, Naiman, Tanghut, and Uyghur were the most prominent of these local groups (fig. 10.2). Some spoke Mongolian, others Türkic, and many people were bilingual. The bilingual Kereyid had a ruling family supported by retainers and common soldiers led by the commanding elite, which constituted the center of a small-scale polity. The periphery was made up of a larger body of various clans.[7] In for-

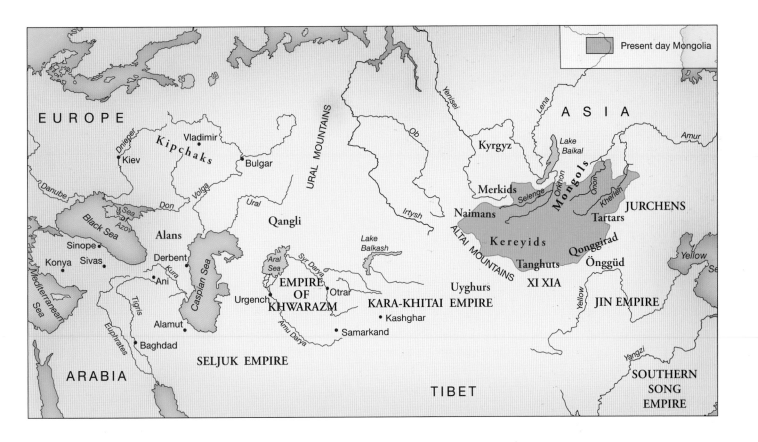

10.3 Tribal Distribution
Mongolia and its surrounding regions were home to many independent tribes at the beginning of the twelfth century, many of which are noted in *The Secret History of the Mongols*.

mer times, discontented tribal people could decamp. However, the creation of a strong multi-group center provided the leader with a military force loyal to the khan that could be employed internally and externally.[8] In this way khans and chiefs acquired methods of enforcement over their subjects such that "voting with their feet" was no longer a means of escape. Competition between polities arose, and as leaders grew more powerful, they sought greater manpower and control of lucrative trade routes.

Some tribes opposed the emergence of strong central authorities, but their options were limited to internal opposition. They resented, in particular, the abandonment of the traditional custom of lateral succession, under which a leader was succeeded by his younger brother after he died, and the former retainers and rank and file continued to wield power as before, partly because there was no generation gap. In contrast, under lineal succession, a son took power but had little connection to his father's followers and often replaced them with individuals from his own generation. This power structure offered greater authority to

the new khan, who controlled the disposition of spoils and kept them under his control without necessarily sharing with others. But internal political dissent was more likely with lineal succession than by following the tradition of lateral succession.

The emergence of a strong central leader almost always provoked strong opposition. When Ong Khan began to assert strong central leadership, many Kereyid opposed him and sought to assert their own authority. As opposition grew stronger, Ong Khan sought help from a young leader named Temüjin.[9] This period was marked by intense military conflict, and many people were killed while others fled to the west or into the Siberian forests. In a matter of decades, all the tribes of Central Asia, whether people of the forest, the desert or the steppe, would be in the thrall of the Mongols and their Khan.

From Temüjin to Genghis Khan

By appealing to the discontented who had left their clans, Temüjin—disenfranchised himself—strategically built up his central command. He recognized and rewarded

10.4 **Camp Scene**
This painting illustrates such Central Asian camp activities as processing entrails and blowing on a brazier fire. A collection of weapons and horses surround a well-dressed man with a saddle; naked figures may represent slaves. It is attributed to Muhammad Siyah Qalam ("Muhammad of the Black Pen"), who is thought to have lived 1469–1525. The attribution is questionable, but this image represents a genre of paintings of outlandish, fantastic, and often humorous figures engaged in various activities, some perhaps inspired by shamanistic séances. Sixty-five such paintings are known, housed in the Topkapi Palace Museum in Istanbul.

loyalty and talent among the more powerful as well as the rank and file, creating an alternative to the traditional model of power. From his personal alliances, political acumen, and structural innovations that fostered an efficient central command, the institution of Mongol leadership evolved, culminating in his appointment as Genghis Khan in 1206.

Genghis recognized the value of horizontal power sharing that constituent tribes desired, as well as the hierarchical structure that drove his rise along with other, newer chieftains. His policies required tribes accepting Mongol rule to integrate with his military administration, a process that was accomplished gradually as the territory of the core Mongol polity grew. Absolute loyalty to the khan, which was reciprocated with redistribution of wealth and power among his followers, was the central pact of the emerging Mongol polity.

The constituent tribes that gave Temüjin his initial rise to power later became major parts of the Mongolian empire in Mongolia, China, Central Asia, Iran, and Russia. Their ideas of self-determination and power sharing did not die out completely, although their ambitions were recast

through an imperial political structure that no one could have foretold in 1206 when Temüjin became Genghis Khan. A century and a half later, the empire fragmented and the same groups re-emerged as steppe tribes once again, mostly under their old names; this time, however, they had the legacy of Genghis Khan and a world empire behind them.

Alan the Fair, Ancestress of the Mongol Tribes

Interactions between families and larger tribal entities in these unsettled times on the steppe are recounted in *The Secret History of the Mongols* (see Chapter 14), as the prologue to Temüjin's emergence. Alan the Fair, whom all the descendants of the successor states of the Mongols recognized as their ancestress, catches the eye of her future husband, Dobun, when she and her family move to the area around Burkhan Khaldun Mountain seeking better hunting grounds. The unusual developments in Alan the Fair's later life are explained to her sons, in a story of miraculous birth that became the basis of the Genghissid legacy (fig. 10.1):

10.5 Silk Road Retirees
Double-humped Bactrian camels were the trucks of the Silk Road trade for almost 2,000 years. Adapted to winter cold and summer drought they reputedly could travel across Asian deserts for thirty days without water, packing loads of people, goods, and, of course, water. In remote regions like the Altai, camels still do heavy lifting when herding camps have to be moved, although they are gradually being replaced by trucks.

In time Dobun passed away
and after he was gone Alan the fair, without a husband,
gave birth to three more sons.
They were named Bughu Khatagi, Bughutu Salji, and Bodonchar the Fool.
The first two sons, Belgunutei and Bugunutei, talked to each other about this:
"Even though our mother has no brothers or kin here
and now has no husband at all
she's given birth to three sons."

[hearing this she said]

"You've said to each other:
'She's given birth to three new sons.
Who is their father and what is their clan?'
You're right to ask questions like this,
so I'll tell you.
Every night a man as yellow as the sun would enter my tent
by the light from the smoke-hole
or by the place light enters at the top of the door.
He'd rub on my belly.

The light from this man would sink into my womb
Then he'd leave me,
crawling out on the sunbeans or the shafts of moonlight,
crawling up like a dog as yellow as the sun.
So now do you believe me?
Now that you know the truth can't you see it's a sign?
These brothers of yours must be the sons of Eternal Heaven.
How can you think these are the sons of a mortal man?
When they become Lords of all people,
Then common men will understand who they are."[10]

1. Honeychurch and Amartuvshin 2006.
2. Kahn 1998, 71–72.
3. Kahn 1998, 17.
4. Golden 1992, 155–73.
5. Rashid al-Din 1998.
6. Scott 1975; Di Cosmo 2006.
7. Togan 1998, 125.
8. Togan 1998, 72.
9. Kahn 1998, 70.
10. Kahn 1998, 5–6.

Naadam Racers

The "three manly games" (*eriin gurvan naadam*) celebrated during midsummer in the national festivals called Naadam include Mongolian wrestling, horse racing, and archery. In older times only men and boys participated; now girls compete in horse racing and archery, but not in wrestling. The horse races are overland events averaging 15–30 miles, depending on the age class of the horse. Riders range from five to thirteen years old. (After thirteen, riders are too heavy for races of this length.) The races test the horses as much as the riders. Horses are fed special diets and young boys sing ritual songs to them throughout the night before the race to protect them and give them strength.

PART II
GENGHIS TIMES

11. Genghis Khan

Morris Rossabi

11.1 Genghis Khan and His Sons
This Iranian miniature painting, taken from a 16th-century manuscript, re-creates the event when Genghis Khan conveyed his precepts of governance to his sons and assigned to them the territories they would rule.

THE LIFE AND CAREER OF GENGHIS KHAN are extraordinary, but his triumphs and his emergence on the historical stage were not inevitable. Temüjin, as he was known before he was granted the title Genghis Khan in 1206, was born in the mid-1160s in a time of considerable turbulence in Mongolia. The Iranian historian Juvaini, writing several decades after Genghis's death, asserts that the people of Mongolia "had neither ruler nor leader."[1] A variety of groups, including the belligerent hunting and fishing Merkid, the Nestorian Christian Kereyid, the pastoral and prosperous Tartars, and the Naiman, probably a Türkic group from Western Mongolia, vied for power. As a result, almost continuous warfare plagued the steppes; the people required a leader who would bring peace.

Temüjin did not, at first glance, appear to be the Mongols' savior. Descended from a family of the minor nobility that had become impoverished, Temüjin had lost his father, been abandoned by his tribal group, and captured several times by rival tribes by his second decade of life. But he overcame his circumstances and used his political skills to rebuild his alliances and popular support.

The Secret History of the Mongols, the only primary source produced by the Mongols, is surprisingly evenhanded in its treatment of Genghis. Written shortly after his death in 1227, it depicts his heroic exploits and his administrative innovations but also describes his murder of his half brother and his execution of former allies. It does not conceal unpleasant decisions, such as his treatment of people who resisted him: "He ordered that the men and women of their cities be killed, their children and grandchildren. . . . As long as I am still alive keep up the slaughter."[2] The principal Chinese source, the thirteenth-century *Shengwu qinzhenglu* (History of the campaigns of Genghis Khan),[3] is based on a Mongol account that has been lost and provides details principally about Genghis's military campaigns. The Iranian historians Rashid al-Din, relying on a Mongol informant and the same lost Mongol account used by the *Shengwu*, and Juvaini, using his own observations and those of other eye-witnesses, describe Genghis with an emphasis on his campaigns in Central Asia. Juvaini offers a decidedly negative account of Genghis and the Mongols' rampage during and after these battles. In general, Iranians, Chinese, and Russians—peoples Genghis and his descendants subjugated—depicted him (and often still do) as a brutal barbarian whose armies plundered states and regions, undermined impressive civilizations,

> *In the time before you were born*
> *the stars in the heavens were spinning around.*
> *Everyone was fighting each other.*
> *Unable to sleep in their own beds,*
> *they constantly stole from each other.*
> *The crust of the earth was pitching back and forth.*
> *All the nations were at war with each other.*
> *Unable to lie beneath their own blankets*
> *they attacked each other every day.*
> *When your mother was stolen by the Merkid*
> *she didn't want it to happen.*
> *It happened because one nation came armed to*
> *   fight with another.*
> — THE SECRET HISTORY OF THE MONGOLS
>   Kahn 1998, 153

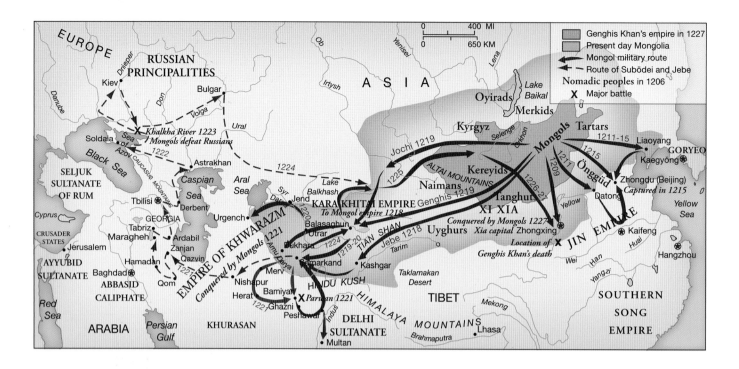

11.2 Genghis Khan's Campaigns, 1209–27
Genghis's first campaign outside the Mongol homeland, which began in 1209, was directed at the Tanghuts, a kingdom also known as the Western Xia (Xi Xia) in Gansu and Ningxia, northwestern China, grown rich by controlling Silk Road travel routes. Genghis attacked the Jin empire in China in 1211 and 1215, the Kara Khitai to the west in 1218, and the powerful Iranian Khwarazmian empire from 1219 to 1221. During 1221–24 his trusted generals Jebe and Subödei campaigned further to the northwest, making a circuit that reached the Dnieper and Black Sea, laying the groundwork for the khanate that became known as the Golden Horde. Genghis returned to complete his conquest of the Tanghuts in 1226-27, and died just as that victory was being realized.

and raped and murdered vast numbers of their citizens. Although these historians offer few, if any, redeeming features of the Mongols' oppressive rule, they are fascinated and horrified by the Mongol leader.

Early Life and Career

Temüjin was betrothed at the age of nine to Börte, the ten year-old daughter of a leader of the Onggirad peoples, who eventually provided consorts for the Mongol khans. As one of its rulers stated, "We don't challenge empires; we don't go to war with our neighbors; we offer our daughters to sit by the khan, and he places them upon the throne. We've survived by the loveliness of our granddaughters, by the beauty of our daughters."[4] Genghis's father Yesügei accompanied him to his future bride's family, where Genghis would reside, and was poisoned on his return journey, when he unwisely accepted an invitation for a meal with a group of Tartars whom he did not recognize as enemies.

News of his death prompted many of his retainers to abandon his widow Höelün, who immediately sent for Temüjin. Without a support network, Höelün's family barely survived, often gathering nuts and roots and hunting marmots to sustain themselves. In these difficult times, Höelün nonetheless taught Temüjin and her other sons basic

military skills required in the demanding environment of Mongolia and drilled into them the need for close bonds with others for survival and strength. She subscribed to the view articulated by one of the Mongols' ancestors in *The Secret History*:

> "You five were born from one womb.
> If, like the five single arrows that you held
> you separate yourselves, each going alone,
> then each of you can be broken by anyone.
> If you are drawn together by a singular
>   purpose
> bound like the five shafts in a bundle
> how can anyone break you?"[5]

However, she could not maintain unity within her own family.[6]

Vying for leadership among the younger generation, Temüjin treacherously surprised and brutally murdered one of his half-brothers.[7]

By age fourteen, about the time he killed his half-brother, Temüjin did not appear to have a great career ahead of him. Lacking any allies or supporters, Temüjin was captured several times by rival tribes. Once he escaped by "hid[ing] in the bed of the River Onon, lying on his back with only his face projecting from the water."[8] The Mongol and Iranian sources recount other of his dashing and colorful adventures. After hiding from his enemies in a forest for three nights, he set forth to escape when "his saddle seemed to fall off by itself."[9] He took this as a sign that Heaven wanted him to stay in the woods. Emerging after three more nights, he found his path blocked when a huge boulder fell a short distance ahead of him. He concluded that "Heaven wants me to stay here." After three more nights, hunger prevailed, and he ground out a path around the boulder only to be captured by enemy soldiers who awaited him. Eventually, he managed to escape.

By the early 1180s, Genghis was basically a minor figure with only a few supporters. However, adherence to his mother's instruction about the need for allies would shape his career. His brilliance at forming the Mongol style of "blood brotherhoods" (*anda*) set the stage for his rise to power. Living in such unsettled and somewhat chaotic times, Mongols recognized that blood brotherhoods were vital for survival, and as early as the age of eleven, Genghis and Jamukha, a noble boy of about the same age, solemnly pledged to assist each other against their enemies. They would become competitors for power and bitter enemies.

When they got back to the tent
Mother Ujin [Höelün] could see on their faces
*   what they'd done.*
She looked at her two sons,
then pointing first at Temüjin said to them:
"Killers, both of you!
When he came out screaming from the heat of my
*   womb*
this one was born holding a clot of black blood in
*   his hand.*
And now you've both destroyed without thinking,
like the Khasar dog who eats his own afterbirth,
like the panther that heedlessly leaps from a cliff,
like the lion who can't control its own fury, . . .
like the tiger who doesn't think before seizing
*   his prey,*
you've killed your own brother!
When we have no one to fight beside us but our
*   shadows*
when there is nothing to whip our horses but
*   their own tails*
when our mouths are filled
with the bitterness of what Tayichiud have done
*   to us,*
and we ask ourselves:
'How can we get our revenge on them?'
you come complaining to me, saying:
'How can we live with these brothers?'
and now you do this!"
This is how she spoke to her sons,
reciting ancient phrases and quoting old sayings to
*   them in her anger.*
——The Secret History of the Mongols
    Kahn 1998, 20.

Becoming Genghis Khan

Temüjin forged "blood brother" relationships with wealthier or stronger Mongol leaders. His first alliance was with the Ong Khan of the Kereyid, a patron and protector rather than a blood brother. The young Mongol appealed to the powerful Ong Khan and to Jamukha, his blood brother, to assist him in recovering his wife Börte, who had been captured during a Merkid raid. Around 1184, their joint forces campaigned against the Merkid and recovered the pregnant bride.

Intermittent failures and successes marked Temüjin's rise to total power. He experienced devastating losses and reversals of fortune: just a few years before the Mongols accepted him as their leader, he had been defeated in battle and left with only a small group of supporters. A Chinese source claims that the Jurchens, who ruled North China as the Jin dynasty, captured and imprisoned Temüjin until the mid-1190s.[10] His virtual disappearance from the historical sources for about seven or eight years after he had assumed the title of khan—sometime between 1187 and 1189—lends credibility to this account, but it cannot confirm it. He reemerged around 1195 and determined to destroy his opponents. *The Secret History of the Mon-*

11.4 Genghis Khan
No actual likeness of Genghis Khan exists. This official portrait was painted during the late 13th century by an anonymous Yuan court painter who had never met Genghis Khan. It is held, along with other portraits of succeeding khans and their wives, painted in similar style, by the National Palace Museum in Taipei.

tell you straight what he's done and here's a man that I'll have in my army."[11] Temüjin recruited him immediately for his army and gave him the new name of Jebe ("Arrow"). His new recruit turned out to be one of his great military commanders.

After some initial successes, his campaign to establish hegemony over steppe peoples suffered setbacks during the decade between 1196 and 1206. The Ong Khan, however, had recognized that Temüjin now had a force to be reckoned with and collaborated with the younger man between 1201 and 1202 to vanquish the Tartars, the people who had poisoned Temüjin's father. In the face of this alliance, the Ong Khan's son and Temüjin competed for power, which eventually led to a break between the Ong Khan and Temüjin. *The Secret History* attributes this split to the duplicity of the Ong Khan and his ambitious son, but since each side sought ultimate authority, all share blame for the severance of relations.[12] *The Secret History* also excuses Temüjin for the feud with his blood brother Jamukha at the same time. The sources record a consistent pattern of ruptures between Temüjin and his allies, accusing them of treachery or disloyalty, which suggests that Temüjin's own ambitions were at least partly responsible.

The Ong Khan, with the support of Temüjin's former blood brother Jamukha, defeated Temüjin in 1203, leaving him with just a few thousand men. Retreating to Baljuna Lake in southeastern Mongolia, Temüjin gathered together the remnants of his forces, and in an emotional speech, he pledged to share the "fruits" when he had "completed this . . . task" of destroying his enemies.[13] News of Temüjin's Baljuna Covenant spread and attracted many Mongol leaders who found his vision of Mongol unity and more equitable division of spoils captivating. His professed asceticism, exhibited by living in a *ger* (yurt), wearing ordinary cloth, and avoiding luxuries, also appealed to his men.

From despair at Baljuna, Temüjin succeeded within three years in becoming the principal Mongol ruler. He launched a surprise attack on the Kereyid, who had become complacent, believing they had

gols subtly criticizes him for his ruthlessness in these bloody encounters. The same text repeatedly praises him for dividing up the spoils of war equally among his forces, a strategy that doubtless prompted many lordless Mongols, including capable military and civilian leaders, to accept him as their leader.

Genghis's ability to attract others, even vaunted enemies, was integral to his success. After his horse was killed in a victorious battle, he rounded up the enemy prisoners and asked the culprit to identify himself, according to *The Secret History*. To his surprise, a lowly soldier accepted responsibility, and Temüjin responded: "Usually a man who's fought against us is the last to admit it. He'll lie about what he's done or simply hide out of fear. But this man doesn't deny that he's fought us; in fact he declares it! Here's a man who'll

totally crushed his forces. Within three days, the Kereyid had been routed and the Ong Khan killed when he tried to escape. This stunning reverse stimulated Temüjin to challenge the Naiman, the last remaining opposition to his supremacy in Mongolia. The Naiman mounted a spirited defense before falling to Temüjin's troops.

Temüjin's last threat was from Jamukha, his blood brother of more than twenty-five years, who had lost favor with many Mongols because he originally had sided with the Naiman, against his Mongol *anda* Temüjin. Jamukha's own subordinates betrayed him and turned him over to Temüjin, who killed these turncoats with the comment, "How can we allow men to lay hands on their own lord to live?"[14] *The Secret History* includes Jamukha's moving speech (inset) in which he absolves Temüjin of any blame for the rupture of their relations and in conclusion, asks for a quick death: "My *anda*, if you want to favor me, then let me die quickly and you'll be at peace with your heart."[15] To honor their previous friendship, Temüjin executed Jamukha without shedding his blood, a "privilege" granted only to rulers, princes, or khans.[16]

To commemorate and legitimize his achievement in defeating the major tribes in Mongolia, Temüjin convened, in the spring of 1206, a *khuriltai*, or assemblage of the Mongol nobility, at the origins of the Onon River in northeastern Mongolia to confirm him as the supreme ruler. The *khuriltai* enthroned him with the title "Genghis Khan," a puzzling term which different scholars have translated variously: from the Mongol term "Ching" as "Cruel Ruler," or "Strong Ruler," and from the Turkish term "Tengiz" as "Ruler of the Ocean (fig. 11.6)."[17] Genghis, in turn, showered rewards on the subordinates who had helped him to emerge victorious.

Temüjin's rise to power as Genghis Khan succeeded not only because of his military prowess, but due to his knack for forging alliances and political deal-making, and his willingness to make an equitable division of spoils. He imposed tight discipline on his forces, a harsh set of rules that mandated severe punishments for those who disobeyed orders. "If we disobey your command during battle/ take away our possessions, our children, and wives./ Leave us behind in the dust,/ cutting off our heads where we stand and letting them fall to the ground."[18] Cowardice resulted in immediate execution, and Genghis ordered similarly draconian punishments for other breaches of discipline. He issued stern warnings to his commanders to avoid conflicts among themselves, and initiated compulsory service for all males from approximately fifteen to seventy years of age, which was meant to signal that everyone should be prepared to give whatever he could, even military service, to the Mongol campaign. Finally, he relied on comprehensive intelligence about the enemy before he initiated a battle or attack. Spying and using psychological warfare, such as undermining popular morale by recounting occasionally apocryphal tales of massacres and destruction by Genghis's forces, were tactics that the Mongols often used to induce voluntary submission.

His military successes were not innovations but based upon centuries-long advances in steppe warfare. Dependence upon an adept and mobile cavalry predated Genghis, as did the effective composite bow, a weapon that had a much greater range than any European bow. The most powerful arrows were adapted from hunting for combat; the so-called whistling arrows induced animals to halt to discover the origins of the noise, a stationary target for a second, deadlier arrow (see Chapter 13). The tactic of feigned retreat by a small detachment, which led the pursuing enemy

> "Long ago when we were chidren in the Khorkhonagh Valley
> I declared myself to be your anda.
> Together we ate the food which is never digested
> and spoke words to each other which are never forgotten,
> and at night we shared one blanket to cover us both.
> Then it was as if people came between us with knives,
> slashing our legs and stabbing our sides,
> and we were separated from each other. . . .
>
> Now, my anda, you've pacified every nation;
> you've united every tribe in the world.
> The Great Khan's throne has given itself to you.
> Now the world is ready for you
> what good would I be as your ally?. . .
>
> I went wrong when I strove to be a better man than my anda."
>
> —THE SECRET HISTORY OF THE MONGOLS
> Kahn 1998, 111

into a deadly trap where they faced a much larger force, was also a traditional ploy that Genghis used but had not originated.[19]

Instead, Genghis's innovations were organizational. Many were designed to subvert the traditional tribal system, which has often been considered the optimal unit in this mostly pastoral society that depended upon considerable flexibility and mobility for survival.[20] These requirements are better suited to relatively small units such as families, clans, and tribes than the much larger organization that Genghis now planned. Members of the same tribe were assigned to entirely different units in order to break down loyalty to their old leaders. Genghis appointed new commanders to these units, who formed a new military elite that owed its advancement to their leader, hence were obliged to him absolutely.[21] Removing the old tribal leaders, he placed his own men in charge and demanded that his forces shift their loyalty to them. Having defeated the major tribes in Mongolia and created a sizable confederation unifying the various peoples in this vast, sprawling territory may have been Temüjin's greatest achievement. His ability to maintain control over such a huge and diverse domain—about three and a half to four times the size of modern France—motivated *The Washington Post* in 1996 to name Genghis Khan the most important man in the past thousand years.

Genghis's Foreign Campaigns

With almost all of Mongolia now under his command, why did Genghis and his forces emerge to attack other lands? The wars leading to his victory devastated the herding economy, with many animals perishing. To recover from these losses, Genghis needed to secure animals and other products from neighboring states. Paul Ratchnevsky characterizes his aim as "the acquisition of slaves, animals, and riches rather than the territory."[22] Another theory for Mongol territorial expansion holds that a drop in the mean annual temperature in parts of Mongolia may have created economic hardships that propelled a small exodus from the country[23] (see Chapter 4). That Genghis had

fashioned such a large group under arms is a condition that would almost ensure inexorable military expansionism. Some assert the existence of a divine plan to bring the world under Mongol hegemony, in which Tenggeri, the Sky God, entrusted Genghis with this Herculean task. Unfortunately, this plan for conquest did not appear to jibe with Genghis's objectives, which often entailed seizure of booty or guarantees of trade concessions.[24]

Genghis's campaigns were generally successful. First, the Uyghurs, a Türkic group that had one of the first written languages and one of the first capital cities of any steppe people, voluntarily submitted.[25] Second, Genghis attacked the Xi Xia dynasty, or the Tanghut peoples, who controlled northwest China. His longest and most demanding campaign in East Asia was his four-year struggle against the Manchurian Jurchens who had conquered North China by 1126, and had established the Chinese-style Jin dynasty, which culminated, in the Mongols' occupation, in 1215, of the Jin capital of Zhongdu, near modern Beijing (fig. 11.2).[26]

After this stunning but debilitating victory, Central Asia, with its network of mercantile centers and potentially lucrative trade became his next target for incursion. Recognizing Genghis's plans, a local governor in Central Asia killed some Mongol merchants whom he accused of spying and psychological warfare. Genghis immediately dispatched official envoys to Muhammad II, the ruler of Central Asia, demanding that he turn over the governor for punishment. Instead Muhammad executed the hapless ambassadors, the most heinous of crimes from the Mongol standpoint.[27]

In 1219 Genghis departed, with a substantial army, to avenge the murders of Mongol merchants and ambassadors and to obtain booty from the rich oases and cities in this region. Muhammad's autocratic rule had alienated many of his top commanders, and Genghis capitalized on this fragmentation by offering favorable terms to those who surrendered without a fight. Urgench and other cities actually defended themselves, killing quite a few Mongol

Having fought hard for his victories in Central Asia, Genghis was now determined to retain control over much of this vast domain. The resistance he encountered may have prompted him to station troops in the oases and towns; Central Asia was the only land where he posted an occupation force. He also devoted two years to devising an administrative system for the newly subjugated territories, which he may have been eager to use as a base for further expansion westward.[30] He may have reconsidered his previous policy about occupations on learning that the Tanghuts, the first foreign group he had conquered, but not occupied, had not lived up to a commitment to support the Mongols' campaigns. He turned eastward from Central Asia to punish them. His troops destroyed the Tanghut state, but Genghis did not witness the final denouement. He died in August 1227, probably of natural causes.

Legacies of Genghis Khan

Despite the stereotypical portrait of Genghis as a great conqueror, he bequeathed a legacy that went beyond the military. Once he had conquered territories beyond Mongolia, he initiated a more sophisticated administrative structure and a regular system of taxation. Recruiting captured Türks, Chinese, and others more experienced with sedentary societies, he began to devise a more stable system that could contribute to a more orderly government, with specialized official positions. He also recognized the need for better communication in the territories he had subjugated and set up postal stations and a courier system that could expeditiously transmit vital messages from one part of his territories to another.

The *Jasagh*, a set of rules and regulations about the military and the systems of governance and justice, may have been his most significant administrative innovation.[31] Although it fell short of a formal written code of laws, it contained his basic precepts and laid down the principles for determination of policy and judicial cases. Genghis added to it over his lifetime as new legal problems arose. Nearly all the provisions concern the lifestyle and regulations relating to the Mongols, the Türkic people, and other nomadic

11.5 Genghis Khan at the Bukhara Mosque
This Persian miniature from the *Shahanshahnama*, a 14th-century collection of epic poems, shows Genghis Khan admonishing the wealthy elite of Bukhara from the pulpit of the Kalon mosque. He told them he was the scourge of God and had come to punish them for their sins. Genghis then razed the mosque, sacked the city, and killed most of its leaders and elite. He was so impressed with the 12th-century Kalon minaret that he ordered it spared, and it stands today.

troops, but Genghis's forces, with the help of Chinese and Muslim experts in the use of catapults and other siege engines, finally overwhelmed them and devastated and plundered these sites. Groups that did not mount such stiff resistance generally escaped the Mongols' wrath. Many merchants and clerics from Samarkand surrendered and were not harmed, but the Türkic troops, who defended the city, were massacred once they were compelled to surrender.[28] By early 1221 cities including Bukhara, Samarkand, and Herat had fallen to Genghis's troops, and Muhammad died of natural causes while fleeing farther west (fig. 11.5).[29]

Jasagh

GENGHIS KHAN promulgated regulations and laws, which came to be known as the Great *Jasagh*, as early as 1202. The *Jasagh* may have originally been in old Mongolian script (although whether it was a written code remains uncertain), but it survives, in fragments, only in Arabic and Iranian sources and is alluded to in *The Secret History* and in Chinese accounts. Genghis and his most trusted advisers added to it as new problems and situations arose. Yet they designed it as final and unchanging laws and regulations, rather than mere judgments relating to individual cases or circumstances. Its final version mandated behavior and specified rules for organization of the military and the system of justice. However, it "gradually lost its importance, the main causes of its decline being the political fragmentation of the Mongol empire, and alien (local) cultural influences."[1] Thus the *Jasagh* applied principally to pastoral nomadic life but did not suit the requirements of more complex sedentary civilizations. Later khans recognized the need for more comprehensive legal codes for the counties they had subjugated. For example, Kublai Khan commissioned Chinese officials to devise a code of laws for China, which appeared in 1291.

MILITARY AND ORGANIZATION

The military must be organized into units of ten, hundred, and thousand.

Soldiers will be punished for negligence or cowardice.

Commanders need to establish postal stations in their domains.

Commanders must personally examine troops and their weapons before departing for battle.

SOCIAL

All religions must be treated with deference and not discriminated against.

Women must assume all the chores when men go to battle.

Children of a concubine have the same inheritance rights as children of a wife.

Clerics, scholars, physicians, and muezzins and those who wash the bodies of the dead should not be taxed.

A son may marry the widows of his father except for his own mother.

Slitting an animal's throat in the Muslim way is forbidden and punishable by death.

Murderers may ransom themselves by paying forty gold coins in the case of a Muslim and a donkey for a Chinese.

A horse thief must compensate the owner with ten horses. If he cannot provide the horses, he must turn over his children to the owner. If he has no children, he is to be executed.

Travelers must always be welcomed as guests and given food.

INDIVIDUAL BEHAVIOR

Adultery and sodomy are punishable by death.

Urinating in water or ashes is punishable by death.

One who finds a captive must return the captive to the captor or face execution.

Clothes must not be washed until they are worn out.

1. De Rachewiltz 1993, 103.

peoples who originally joined them. There are few decrees that deal with land ownership, contractual obligations, agriculture, and the principal issues facing sedentary societies that Genghis and the Mongols would eventually subjugate, but the *Jasagh* began the codification of customary laws that would regulate and bind the Mongols.[32]

This set of regulations was originally written in a Mongolian script, although the remaining fragments are found in Islamic sources.[33] The Mongolian script was devised to fill the need for a written language for administrative and governmental purposes, which Genghis recognized when he was on the verge of unifying the Mongols. In 1204, he instructed one of his Türkic counselors to devise such a written language. Within a short time, his Türkic adviser had adapted the Uyghur script for the Mongolian language, and Türkic secretaries began to record Genghis' pronouncements, edicts, and laws.

Herders needed a steady supply of goods from sedentary civilizations for their very survival, which impressed upon Genghis the value of commerce for his nomadic pastoral peoples. This favorable attitude toward trade translated into advocacy for merchants and efforts to foster commerce, another of his important legacies, perpetuated by all of his successors. Kublai increased the amount of paper money in circulation in China and reduced the punitive taxes previously imposed on merchants. The Mongol rulers of Iran were hospitable to foreign traders and

11.6 Installation of a Mongol Khan
A Mongol khan, his wife, and court are shown during enthronement ceremonies in this illustration from *Jami 'al-Tavarikh* (Compendium of Chronicles) by Rashid al-Din. Ghazan Khan (r. 1295–1304) commissioned al-Din to write a history of the Mongols and gave him access to confidential court records to do so. This work was completed during the reign of Öljeitü (1304–17), and when he finished, Öljeitü asked al-Din to expand it to include all the known world.

constructed caravanserais partly to serve as hostelries for trading caravans. Mongol support of commerce eventually resulted into the greatest flow of goods and people in history until that time, leading to the first direct interactions between Europe and China.

Genghis's interest in new technologies contributed to their diffusion throughout the Mongol domains. Chinese and Muslim advisers introduced catapults, battering rams, and scaling ladders, which proved invaluable to his forces in besieging the larger cities in the sedentary civilizations. His interests were not limited to military technology. Good medical care was essential to maintaining the demanding lifestyle he mandated and to treating the wounds his soldiers suffered. He recruited physicians to remedy the ailments such as gout and liver disease that resulted from obesity and alcoholic binges, in which he and his people indulged.[34] Knowledge of astronomy, another practical field that Genghis prized and patronized, enabled his subjects to gather information about climate and weather conditions that might, on the one hand, bolster their economy and, on the other hand, allow them to make adequate preparations to counter calamities.

Genghis supported the creation of craft articles and repeatedly instructed his soldiers not to harm captured craftsmen. In Samarkand, the Mongol troops, following his orders, reputedly spared 30,000 artisans.[35] Some of the craftsmen who survived were moved to northern China and contributed to an artistic renaissance during the Mongol era. Like Genghis, his descendants treated craftsmen generously, fostering an efflorescence in Chinese porcelain and textiles and in Iranian tile work and illustrated manuscripts in the fourteenth century[36] (see Chapters 30, 31).

Genghis adopted a policy of toleration toward foreign religions, perhaps to ingratiate himself with foreign clerics who could facilitate his rule over the territories he had subjugated. However, his genuine interest in foreign ideas, particularly if they had practical implications, should not be ruled out. In general, Genghis did not seek to impose a particular religion or philosophy on his new subjects. As long as they did not create disturbances or instability, he did not intrude on the beliefs, values, and customs of the subjugated peoples.[37] He also had a personal interest in religion, particularly as he aged and began to fear death. Hearing that Daoists had developed elixirs of immortality, he invited the renowned Daoist monk Changchun to his encampment. Although Changchun traveled with Genghis's entourage in Central Asia, he disclaimed knowledge of formulas for prolonging life. The account of his journeys is an important primary source on both Genghis and Central Asia.[38]

Many, though not all, of Genghis's successors adopted a policy of religious toleration. Kublai proclaimed that he believed in a variety of the Chinese religions.[39] The first Mongol khans in Iran employed Jewish, Nestorian Christian, and Buddhist officials in ruling their principally Muslim populations. Khans throughout the Mongol domains subsidized the construction of monasteries, churches, and mosques and ordered translations of important texts from a wide variety of religions.

Perhaps Genghis's most audacious, yet positive, legacy was recruitment of foreigners. Early in his career, he recognized that the Mongols lacked expertise in various fields. For example, they initially had no experience in besieging cities and did not have the proper equipment to do so. Thus Genghis secured the services of Chinese and Muslim "engineers" who could construct and deploy catapults and other siege engines. He also recognized that the Mongols did not have the requisite skills to devise administrative systems for sedentary empires. If they were to conduct censuses, develop a steady stream of revenue through regular taxation, and organize a system of justice that met the approval of the local population, they would have to recruit knowledgeable foreigners.[40] Similarly, he employed foreign merchants and craftsmen to provide the goods and artifacts the Mongols needed and cherished.[41]

How is one to take the measure of this seemingly larger-than-life figure? Genghis was responsible for remarkable accomplishments. He united, either by force or by negotiations, the diverse Turco-Mongol peoples who inhabited a vast terrain in Mongolia. Capitalizing on the advice of a multiethnic group of counselors, he set up a hierarchical governing structure, established a regular military administration, ordered the development of a written language for Mongolian, and devised regulations that eventually formed a legal code. His occupation of Central Asia paved the way for the creation of the largest contiguous land empire in world history and, perhaps as important, the most extensive East-West commercial and cultural exchanges until that time. He himself lived a relatively simple life for a ruler of such a vast domain, though he married or took many women from his defeated enemies as concubines. He did not take a disproportionate share of the booty that accrued to the Mongols and ensured an equitable division of such riches.

On the other hand, the loss of life and destruction of oases, settlements, and towns wrought by his conquests and occupation cannot be ignored. Though contemporaneous sources sometimes inflated the numbers killed and the damage inflicted, his military campaigns in East and Central Asia were devastating to many areas. Moreover, his words, as quoted in *The Secret History of the Mongols*, occasionally reveal a disdain for human life.

In short, neither hagiography nor condemnation is sufficient to characterize Genghis Khan.

Succession

One of Genghis's glaring failures was his inability to bequeath a regular and orderly system of succession to leadership. Because the Great Khanate was a new institution, no specific structure had been devised to ensure continuity. Clans and tribes had often based succession to the father's status and some of his wealth on the principle of ultimogeniture, that the last born will inherit first. The underlying logic was that the youngest son would not have had the time to establish himself and needed the father's inheritance more than his siblings did. But Genghis did not adhere to such a formula, instead calling together his principal wife Börte's four sons to select his successor on the basis of merit (fig. 11.1). Thus, he chose Ögödei, rather than choosing his youngest son Tolui, the father of Kublai Khan. Although Ögödei did succeed his father, all future successions were contested because it proved impossible to achieve unanimity in determining who was the most talented among Genghis's descendants in each successive generation. Adhering to a less contentious system, such as ultimogeniture, might have averted such disputes. At the death of each leader, assemblages of the Mongol nobility would be convened to choose one of Genghis's descendants as the new Great Khan. At these convocations, Mongol noblemen would express different views about the most meritorious of these descendants, leading to disputes and, eventually, wars. Such conflicts and the ensuing disunity would be prime factors in the collapse of the Mongol empire.

His Tatar wife, Yesui Khatun, spoke:

"The Khan will cross the high mountain passes,
cross over wide rivers,
waging a long war far from home.
Before he leaves has he thought about setting his
*   people in order?*
There is no eternity for all things born in this world.
When your body falls like an old tree,
who will rule your people,
these fields of tangled grasses?
When your body crumbles like an old pillar
who will rule your people,
these great flocks of birds?
Which of your four heroic sons will you name?"

——THE SECRET HISTORY OF THE MONGOLS
    Kahn 1998, 152

1. Juvaini 1958, 21.
2. Kahn 1998, 165.
3. Shengwu 1951.
4. Kahn 1998. 15
5. Kahn 1998, 6.
6. Rossabi 1979, 156.
7. Kahn 1998, 18–20.
8. Ratchnevsky 1991, 21.
9. Kahn 1998, 23.
10. Ratchnevsky 1991, 50; Zhao Gong et al. 1980.
11. Kahn 1998, 59–60.
12. Kahn 1998, 72.
13. Cleaves 1955.
14. Kahn 1998, 110.
15. Kahn 1998, 112.
16. Kahn 1998, 113.
17. Pelliot 1959–73, 301.
18. Kahn 1998, 44.
19. Chambers 1979.
20. Fletcher 1986.
21. Ratchnevsky 1991, 93.
22. Ratchnevsky 1991, 103, 115.
23. Jenkins 1974.
24. Humphrey and Hürelbaatar 2005, 9.
25. De Rachewiltz 1983, 285; Brose 2005.
26. Allsen 1994, 350–52.
27. Juvaini 1958, 79.
28. Ratchnevsky 1991, 132.
29. Juvaini 1958.
30. Buell 1979.
31. De Rachewiltz 1993, 102.
32. Riasanovsky 1965, 33.
33. Ayalon 1971–73; Morgan 1986a.
34. Smith 2000; Hymes 1987.
35. Juvaini 1958, 122.
36. National Palace Museum 2001; Komaroff and Carboni 2002.
37. Ratchnevsky 1991, 185.
38. Li Zhichang 1931.
39. Polo 1938, 201.
40. De Rachewiltz 1983.
41. Rossabi 2002.

12. Mongol Women

Morris Rossabi

On the Mongol division of labor Marco Polo judged that the women "do all the work that is needed for their lords and family and for themselves" and that the "men trouble themselves with nothing at all but with hunting and with feats of battle & of war and with hawking . . . ."[1] The Mongols' demanding and fragile pastoral economy required each household member, even young children, to assume heavy workloads. Women had dual full-time occupations, for they not only performed domestic duties but also milked the animals and produced the household's butter, cheese, and yoghurt. The women could manage the animals, permitting the men complete availability for hunts and warfare, thus contributing to the Mongols' military successes. A few women were even trained in combat and accompanied the men to battle. One of Genghis Khan's daughters commanded a force in April 1221 that razed the city of Nishapur.[2]

Such vital contributions translated into relatively more rights and greater freedom, at least for women of the elite and perhaps even for ordinary women. Unlike Chinese women, Mongol women were not hobbled by bound feet. They differed from almost all women of their era because they could own property, although men generally controlled a household's assets. Although widows faced pressure to remarry the deceased husband's brother or another member of his family to preserve the family's property, such prominent widows as the mothers of Genghis and Kublai ignored the practice of levirate and never remarried.[3] When the Mongols occupied China, they enacted a law code designed to extend the rights of Mongol women to the Chinese and to prohibit the most flagrant abuses against women. They forbad female infanticide, the forcing of women into prostitution, and the sale of daughters into prostitution or servitude.[4] The effectiveness of these provisions for the protection of Chinese women is unknown.

The available historical evidence precludes a comprehensive and definitive assessment of the status of women of the lower strata. The elite women addressed in this essay scarcely confronted restrictions on their mobility and their decision-making. One of Ögödei Khaghan's widows was the de facto ruler of the Mongol empire from 1241 to 1246, when her son was prepared to assume the title of khan. However, she and all the influential women known were directly related to Genghis or his male descendants. It is impossible to determine whether ordinary women enjoyed similar rights and power within their own households. The Mongol women who figure in the Chinese and Iranian histories and in the travel accounts of the Franciscan John of Plano Carpini and of Marco Polo may have been exceptions in their prominence and influence.

Sorghaghtani Beki, the mother of Kublai Khan, is the best known of these extraordinary women. All four of her sons became khans and owed much of their success to her. A Nestorian Christian captured by Genghis's troops and then turned over in marriage to his son Tolui, she took charge of her sons' educations, ensuring that they not only applied themselves to military training but learned to read and write. Attempting to prepare them for rule of a multiethnic and multireligious empire, she also encouraged them to adopt a policy of religious toleration, an attitude that would be invaluable when they became khans.[5] After her husband's death, Sorghaghtani Beki requested and received control over eighty thousand households in North China. Recognizing that exploitation and plunder of the fields of the Chinese peasants in her control would eventually decrease production, she fostered local agriculture and employed Chinese as local officials.[6] In sum, she sought to govern, and it is no accident that two of her sons founded dynasties and devised governments in the domains they subjugated: Hülegü established the Ilkhanate in Iran and the Middle East, his brother Kublai created the Yuan dynasty in China. Their mother also attempted to find her sons suitable mates who would prove to be wise counselors.

Hülegü's wife Dokhuz Khatun was a widow of his father and was passed on to him in leviratic custom. An ardent Nestorian Christian, she championed the recruitment of Nestorians for the Ilkhanate government. Partly due to her convictions, Hülegü employed an international coterie of officials, including Nestorians, Jews, and Buddhists, though most, befitting his location in Iran, were Muslims. She and Hülegü negotiated a marriage alliance between her son and Maria, the natural daughter of the Byzantine emperor.[7] Although the two ruling families were related and Christian (but of different orders), territorial disputes caused a rift between the two empires. Nonetheless, Nestorian Christianity, due to the patronage of Dokhuz Khatun and her descendants, remained a vital religion in the Ilkhanate, with Baghdad becoming the seat of a patriarchate of the Nestorian church.

Kublai's wife Chabi, whose portrait can be found in the National Palace Museum in Taipei, was even more influential, judging from her biography in the Yuan dynastic history, the *Yuanshi* (fig. 12.1).[8] According to that text, her timely warning to her husband led to his accession as the Great Khan. His older brother, the Great Khan Möngke, died during an assault on Southern Song China in 1259. Arigh Böke, their other sibling, quickly capitalized to convene a *khuriltai*, congress of Mongol nobles, to ratify his claim to the throne. Meanwhile, Kublai persisted in his campaign against the Song until Chabi dispatched a messenger to inform him of Arigh Böke's plans.[9] Abandoning his attack on the Southern Song, Kublai traveled north to organize his troops for war against his brother, a war in which he vanquished Arigh Böke's forces in 1264. Chabi's sound political skills may also be observed in her intercession after Kublai defeated the Southern Song and captured the dynasty's dowager empress and empress. When Kublai offered Chabi the Song's jewelry and other imperial treasures, she responded, "The men of the Song saved these objects to bequeath them to their sons and grandsons . . . How could I bear to take one thing?"[10] She insisted that the Song imperial family be treated with proper respect. This account could be considered hagiography, but it certainly conveys the image and the values the Mongols wished to transmit.

Chabi's reported advocacy of Tibetan Buddhism is not mythmaking. She provided funds for the construction of monasteries and the translation of Buddhist texts and received instruction from Tibetan monks. Her most renowned contribution is the resolution of a dispute concerning status between her husband and the 'Phags-pa lama, the eminent Tibetan Buddhist of that time. She helped to devise a compromise by which Kublai would sit below 'Phags-pa in private religious ceremonies but would be seated higher in public court appearances.[11]

Khutulun, the daughter of one of Kublai's cousins, exemplifies the strength, pride, and assertiveness seen in one type of Mongol women. Described by Marco Polo as "very beautiful, but also so strong and brave that in all her father's realm there was no man who could outdo her in feats of strength," she took an active role in combat.[12] Relishing a hardy and active life, she required that a suitable mate defeat her in an athletic contest. She demanded a wager of one hundred horses for the challenge, and, in time, accumulated ten thousand steeds. Finally, a handsome and powerful prince bet one thousand horses on a wrestling match with her. Her parents begged her to lose, but she refused. After a long, grueling competition, she managed to wrestle her opponent to the ground. The prince quickly left. Khutulun assessed her new thousand horses.

Mongol women today, many of whom face poverty, unemployment, domestic abuse, and a shredded social safety net, may yet look to Khutulun as a model. However, they have turned to education— currently comprising more than seventy percent of university students—to improve their prospects in the tradition of women who contributed to an empire.

1. Polo 1938, 169.
2. Juvaini 1958, 177.
3. Ratchnevsky 1968.
4. Ratchnevsky 1937–72, 80, 108–109.
5. Rossabi 1979, 164–66.
6. Song 1976, 35, 912.
7. Spuler 1985, 59, 151.
8. National Palace Museum 1971.
9. Song 1976, 62–63.
10. Song 1976, 2871.
11. Song 1976, 68.
12. Polo 1903, vol. 2, 463.

13.1 Faramurz Pursuing the Kabulis
This Great Mongol *Shahnama* (Book of Kings), an epic work presenting a legendary account of the dynasties of Iran, was first written ca. 1010 by Firdausi (935–1020), but has been lost. A revision with illustrations was produced by Hamdullah Mustaufi Qazvini in ca. 1328–36, during the reign of Ilkhan Abu Sa'id (r. 1316–35). The Demotte *Shahnama*, so called because this illustrated copy of the *Shahnama* was cannibalized by Demotte for the art market, exists today only as fragments—but these exemplify some of the finest book illustrations ever produced.

13.2 Desert Horsemen >
From the moment a youth, whether male or female, is able to sit upon a horse, he or she is taught to ride and manage horses. Here, a young boy on a horse is led by his father along a river in wind-swept dune-field. Mongols name their horses by their colors, not behaviors or terms of endearment.

13. "All the Khan's Horses"

MORRIS ROSSABI

GENGHIS KHAN AND HIS DESCENDENTS could not have conquered and ruled the largest land empire in world history without their diminutive but extremely hardy steeds. In some respects, these Mongolian ponies resembled what is now known as Prezwalski's horse. Mongols held these horses in highest regard and accorded them great spiritual significance. Before setting forth on military expeditions, for example, commanders would scatter mare's milk on the earth to ensure victory. In shamanic rituals, horses were sacrificed to provide "transport" to heaven.

The Mongols prized their horses primarily for the advantages they offered in warfare. In combat, the horses were fast and flexible, and Genghis Khan was the first leader to capitalize fully on these strengths. After hit-and-run raids, for example, his horsemen could race back and quickly disappear into their native steppe. Enemy armies from the sedentary agricultural societies to the south frequently had to abandon their pursuit because they were not accustomed to long rides on horseback and thus could not move as quickly. Nor could these farmer-soldiers leave their fields for extended periods to chase after the Mongols.

The Mongols had developed a composite bow made out of sinew and horn and were skilled at shooting it while riding, which gave them the upper hand against ordinary foot soldiers. With a range of more than 350 yards, the bow was superior to the contemporaneous English long bow, with a range of only 250 yards.[1] A wood-and-leather saddle, which was rubbed with sheep's fat to prevent cracking and shrinkage, allowed the horses to bear the weight of their riders for long periods and also permitted the riders to retain a firm seat. Their saddlebags contained cooking pots, dried meat, yogurt, water bottles, and other essentials for lengthy expeditions. Finally, a sturdy stirrup enabled horsemen to be steadier and thus more accurate in shooting when mounted (fig. 13.3).

Genghis Khan understood the importance of horses and insisted

13.3, 4, 5 Bridle Bit, Stirrups, and Saddle
This bit and set of stirrups were recovered from a 13th–14th-century grave at the Artsat del cave burial site in Bayankhongor province (see Chapter 35). Stirrups originated in Asia in the early centuries CE, and by the 12th century their bases had become flattened to provide better foot support. The saddle from a 14th-century grave in Khuiten Khoshuu in Khentii province is made of wood, tooled leather, and bone. Its sturdy front and back arches helped support the rider and eased the burden on the horse.

that his troops be solicitous of their steeds. A cavalryman normally had three or four mounts, so that each was, at one time or another, given a respite from bearing the weight of the rider during a lengthy journey. Before combat, leather coverings were placed on the head of each horse and its body was covered with armor. After combat, Mongol horses could traverse the most rugged terrain and survive on little fodder.

According to Marco Polo, the horse also provided sustenance to its rider on long trips during which all the food had been consumed. On such rare occasions, the rider would cut the horse's veins and drink the blood that spurted forth. Marco Polo reported, perhaps with some exaggeration, that a horseman could, by nourishing himself on his horse's blood, "ride quite ten days' marches without eating any cooked food and without lighting a fire."[2] And because its milk

offered additional sustenance during extended military campaigns, a cavalryman usually preferred a mare as a mount. The milk was often fermented to produce kumiss, or *airag*, a potent alcoholic drink liberally consumed by the Mongols.

Mobility and surprise characterized the military expeditions led by Genghis Khan and his commanders, and the horse was crucial for such tactics and strategy. Horses could, without exaggeration, be referred to as the intercontinental ballistic missiles of the thirteenth century. The battle of the Khalkha River (now renamed the Kalmyus River) in southern Russia is a good example of the kind of campaign Genghis Khan waged to gain territory, and of the key role of horses.

After his conquest of Central Asia from 1219 to 1220, Genghis Khan dispatched about 30,000 troops led by Jebe and Subödei, two of his ablest commanders, to conduct an exploratory foray to the west (See Chapter 11, fig. 11.2). After several skirmishes, the advance force reached southern Russia. In an initial engagement, the Mongols, appearing to retreat, lured a much larger detachment of Georgian cavalry on a chase. When the Mongols sensed that the Georgian horses were exhausted, they headed to where they kept reserve horses, quickly switched to them, and charged at the bedraggled, spread-out Georgians. Archers, who had been hiding with the reserve horses, backed up the cavalry—with a barrage of arrows as the cavalry routed the Georgians.

Continuing their exploration, the Mongol detachment crossed the Caucasus Mountains, a daunting expedition during which many men and horses perished. They wound up just north of the Black Sea on the southern Russian steppe, which offered rich pasturelands for their horses. After a brief respite, they first attacked Astrakhan to the east and then raided sites along the Dniester and Dnieper Rivers, inciting Russian retaliation in May 1223 under Mstislav the Daring, who had a force of 80,000 men. Jebe and Subödei commanded no more than 20,000 troops and were outnumbered by a ratio of four to one.

Knowing that an immediate, direct clash could

be disastrous, the Mongols again used their tactic of feigned withdrawal. They retreated for more than a week, because they wanted to be certain that the opposing army continued to pursue them but was spaced out over a considerable distance.

At the Khalkha River, the Mongols finally took a stand, swerving around and positioning themselves in battle formation, with archers mounted on horses in the front. The Mongols' retreat seems to have lulled the Russians into believing that the invaders from the East were in disarray. Without waiting for the remainder of his army to catch up and without devising a unified attack, Mstislav the Daring ordered the advance troops to charge immediately. This decision proved to be calamitous. Mongol archers on their well-trained steeds crisscrossed the Russian route of attack, shooting their arrows with great precision. The Russian line of troops was disrupted, and the soldiers scattered.

After their attack, the archers turned the battlefield over to the Mongol heavy cavalry, which pummeled the already battered, disunited, and scattered Russians. Wearing an iron helmet, a shirt of raw silk, a coat of mail, and a cuirass, each Mongol in the heavy cavalry carried with him two bows, a dagger, a battle-ax, a twelve-foot lance, and a lasso as his principal weapons. Using lances, the detach-

ment of heavy cavalry rapidly attacked and overwhelmed the Russian vanguard, which had been cut off from the rest of their forces in the very beginning of the battle.

Rejoined by the mounted archers, the combined Mongol force mowed down the straggling remnants of the Russian forces. Without an escape route, most were killed, and the rest, including Mstislav the Daring, were captured. Rather than shed the blood of rival princes—one of Genghis Khan's commands—Jebe and Subödei ordered the unfortunate commander and two other princes stretched out under boards and slowly suffocated as Mongols stood or sat upon the boards during the victory banquet.[3]

The battle at the Khalkha River resembled, with some slight deviations, the general plan of most of Genghis Khan's campaigns. In fewer than two decades Genghis Khan had, with the support of powerful cavalry, laid the foundations for

an empire that was to control and govern much of Asia in the thirteenth and fourteenth centuries. He died on a campaign in Central Asia, and his underlings reputedly decided to return his corpse to his native land. Any unfortunate individual who happened to encounter the funeral cortege was supposedly killed because the Mongols wished to conceal the precise location of the burial site. At least forty horses were reputedly sacrificed at Genghis Khan's tomb (although his body may have been left behind in Central Asia);[4] his trusted steeds would be as important to him in the afterlife as they had been during his lifetime.

This article, which first appeared in *Natural History*, October 1994, was reprinted with permission.

1. Chambers 1979, 71.
2. Polo 1938, 173.
3. Chambers 1979, 32–34.
4. Ratchnevsky 1991, 142–44.

14.1 Defeat of the Naiman
According to *The Secret History,* the final battle in Temüjin's ascent to leadership was against the Naiman tribe and took place at Baidragiin bulcheer, Zag sum, in Bayankhongor province. Today the battleground is marked by a large *ovoo* (cairn) with a staff bearing prayer flags and a replica of the Mongol imperial white standard.

KAHN

14. Introduction to "The Secret History of the Mongols"

PAUL KAHN

SOMETIME DURING THE FIRST HALF of the thirteenth century an extraordinary literary event took place. The life story of the man who came to be known as Genghis Khan was written down in the language he would have spoken. Six hundred years later, this story, by then entitled by Chinese scribes as *The Secret History of the Mongols*, was discovered on the shelves of a library in Beijing.

Born with the name Temüjin, Genghis had come from a culture that thrived on the steppe to the north of China, to the east of the Christian and Islamic worlds. During the seven decades of Temüjin's life, he and his descendents organized the steppe peoples of this region into a single military force whose leaders were to become the khans of Central Asia, the Ilkhanid rulers of what we know today as the Middle East, the Golden Horde of Russia and the Ukraine, and the emperors of the Yuan dynasty in China.

This was a literary event because *The Secret History* was the first text to be composed in the Mongolian language. Its composition marked the transition from oral to written tradition in a bio-geographical region where human culture had thrived without written literature for thousands of years. The peoples of north and central Asia had been in continuous contact with literate cultures, and several preceding cultures in the same bioregion, notably the Türks and Uyghurs (see Chapter 9), had developed their own forms of writing. But the impetus for this manuscript was not merely contact with other writing systems; the new element was the motivation, perhaps even the necessity, to record recent events in their own language for posterity.

The narrative of the book is extraordinary because of its immediacy. In Homer's *Iliad,* the legends of Alexander the Great, or the sagas of Icelanders, the adventures of cultural heroes are recorded centuries after the events themselves occurred. But in this case, the stories seem to have been written down within a few decades, and by an author familiar with the events. Details of steppe life are rendered with intimate detail, and men and women directly express their feelings and thoughts. The way of telling the story is shaped by frequent use of parallelism and repetition, both well-known techniques of oral storytelling. Events occur in groups of three. Characters justify their actions by repeating entire passages found earlier in the text. Attributes of characters are described in pairs: Börte is introduced as "a girl whose face filled with light, / whose eyes filled with fire,"[1] a phrase that is an inversion of an earlier description of Temüjin himself. Formulas used to describe a character are frequently repeated with slight variation each time the character appears. By capturing the form of oral literature in writing, the story from 800 years ago speaks to us directly.

Evidence suggests that *The Secret History of*

the Mongols was the property of the Mongol ruling family and was never intended to be viewed outside the inner court. Two Iranian histories, written during the Mongol empire period, hint at the book's existence by making reference to its stories. *The History of the World Conqueror* by Ata-Malik Juvaini and the *Compendium of Chronicles* by Rashid al-Din were available in Mongol Iran and later copied in Islamic courts from Turkey to India, transmitting detailed accounts of the origins and lives of the first generations of Mongol rulers. But no copy of the Mongol source from which these Iranian books quote survived in the Islamic world.

In the late fourteenth century the Han Chinese regained political and military control over their own land and forced the Mongol ruling class back to their homeland in the north. A copy of the Mongolian book about Genghis Khan, presumably written in the old Mongolian script adapted from the Uyghur alphabet, remained in Chinese libraries after the transition of power. Following Chinese tradition, scholars of the newly established Ming dynasty compiled the *Yuanshi*, to record the history of the previous Yuan dynasty founded by Kublai Khan. Because Mongolian and Chinese are unrelated languages, with completely different writing systems and grammar, as well as little common vocabulary, scholars from the College of Literature created training materials in the Mongolian language for Chinese diplomats. One of the texts they chose was what we know today as *The Secret History*.[2] The copy they created was written in Chinese characters and incorporated three parallel texts: Chinese characters transcribing the sounds of Mongolian words, a Chinese translation of each word or phrase, and a Chinese summary of each passage (fig. 14.2). The result was quite similar to the way anthropologists from the Bureau of American Ethnography produced transcripts of Native American tales in the early twentieth century—transcribing the sounds of the language, literally translating individual words, and then writing a summary of the meaning.

The Chinese version of the Mongol book was given the title *Yuan bishi* meaning "The Secret History of the Yuan [Mongols]." The text was divided into 282 sections, arranged in twelve chapters. This organization seems to have more to do with the way the book was copied in Chinese than any divisions in the original text. The scribes and printers divided the new version of the book into numbered paragraphs and chapters. The same scholars from the College of Literature incorporated this into a Mongolian-Chinese language-training manual. In the first decade of the fifteenth century, both the Chinese version and the training manual were copied once again into a larger encyclopedia. This encyclopedia survived in both manuscript and printed editions held privately by Chinese scholars and in the Imperial Library. The title of the book was changed to *Yuancho bishi*, meaning "The secret history of the Yuan dynasty." The title was later reinterpreted by Western translators as "The Secret History of the Mongols."

From the fifteenth until the late nineteenth century, knowledge of the book was limited to Chinese intellectual circles, perhaps akin to the way rare Aztec codices are known only in the libraries of Spain. Its existence was a curiosity that attracted a few devoted readers. Chinese scholars who owned the book note repeatedly that it contained information that should be of interest to historians and is not to be found in the official history, the *Yuanshi*. Francis Woodman Cleaves translated a typical remark by the eighteenth century scholar, Qian Daxin:

> Yüan T'ai-tsu [Genghis Khan] was the creator of an empire, yet the account of his deeds in the Yuan History is very careless and contradictory. Only the narrative in the Secret History seems to come closer to the truth, yet its language is vulgar and uncouth, not having had the benefit of polishing by a literary person. Hence, those who know [of] it[s existence are] few. It is very regrettable![3]

As Qian remarks, a factor that contributed to the book's obscurity was that many of the events and actions it described were outside the boundaries of Chinese taste. The following passage illustrates aspects of the text that the Chinese characterized as "vulgar and uncouth." Höelün, mother of Genghis Khan and a woman in her sixties, rides into the camp in a cart drawn by a white camel to confront her eldest son, who has arrested his younger brother, Khasar, on suspicion of plotting to seize power.

> Unable to control the anger she felt,
> Höelün sat down before Genghis,
> crossing her legs beneath her,
> brought out her two breasts from under her
>   coat,
> lay them on her two knees, and cried:
> "Do you know these breasts?
> These are the breasts you sucked from!
> These are the source of your life,
> and like the mother of the wolf
> I ate the afterbirth,
> I cut the navel cord for you both.
> What could Khasar have done to deserve
>   this?
> Temüjin could empty one of my breasts with
>   his drinking,
> and Alchidai and Odchigin together couldn't
>   even empty one.
> But Khasar could drink all the milk from
>   both breasts.
> He eased my pains and brought me rest.[4]

This kind of physical detail was as natural to Mongolian sensibilities as it was alien to Chinese taste. The intimacy of the scene (we are there) and the directness of the speech (the mother is speaking directly to her sons) are fundamental to the style of the book. The implied inner strength of a child who could empty one or both of a mother's breasts is a particularly Mongolian turn of phrase.

The entire language of the story is an expression of Mongolian experience and thought. Images of predatory animals (wolves, panthers) and birds (eagles, falcons) are used to describe human actions, mothers are shown caring for their children as they care for sheep and horses, husbands and wives share each other's resources, and blood or spiritual brothers defend each other's lives. Each man and woman has the obligation to protect the ruler of his/her tribe or clan. Betraying that ruler is an anti-social act punishable by death, and many examples are given to prove this point. But this loyalty is both absolute and transitory. Once a

battle is over, each person is free to change allegiance. The defeat of one group by another certainly resulted in the death of some of the enemy, but victory is also portrayed as a form of redistribution, the absorption of one group by another. Former enemies who pledge allegiance to the victor after a proper fight are rewarded. Enemies who do not recognize redistribution, who flee and continue to resist, are dealt with ruthlessly. A woman's loyalty, whether given in marriage by her parents or taken through abduction or warfare, is also to the victor. The quality of the people rather than the way in which a marriage begins determines the bond of loyalty between husband and wife.

The Portrait of Genghis Khan

The young Temüjin, who becomes the mature military leader Genghis Khan, is the main protagonist of the book. He is portrayed as a human character with strengths and weaknesses. While many incidents in his early life suggest that he is protected or favored by spiritual forces, it is never suggested that he has been given supernatural powers. His strengths are stamina, determination, and shrewdness. He repeatedly demonstrates that he knows when to run, when to attack, when to make peace, and how to manipulate alliances to his own advantage.

His appearance and his actions clearly inspire devotion. The text includes many stories about the men who chose to join him. These men come from all the strata of steppe culture, wealthy and poor, princes and foundlings, close kin and unrelated tribes. A common factor is that all the major characters are people of the steppe, horse nomads who live off their herds and the hunt. The assumption that any band of people benefits from having a strong leader is presented as a self-evident truth, introduced as a prologue in the tales of Mongol ancestors.

The story demonstrates how Genghis Khan, his first wife Börte, and his loyal retainers embody and extend these principles of Mongol culture. Their actions bring peace and stability to a culture that seemed to thrive on and suffer from constant conflict driven by cycles of revenge. We see how Genghis Khan ends discord by absorbing

14.2 *Yuanchao bishi*

The Secret History of the Mongols (subtitled "The Origin of Genghis Khan") was part of a Chinese manuscript known as *Yuanchao bishi* (the Secret History of the Yuan [Mongol] Dynasty). The work was described by early Chinese compilers as "secret" because it was intended for court use only. Until the manuscript was published fully in Chinese in 1933, it was known to only a few scholars. The original Chinese work was presented in three parallel sections on each page: one, a phonetic transcription of Mongol using Chinese characters, another in Chinese, and a third consisting of Chinese summaries of the Mongol text.

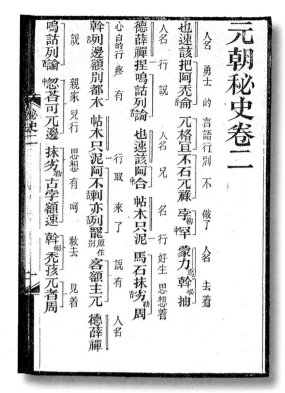

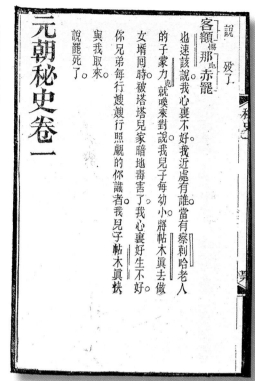

and redistributing the tribes into a Mongol nation, organized through complementary practices of hunting and military discipline, to be fed by constant expansion of territory, trade, and the rewards of conquest. In this world, all the spoils of hunting and warfare belong to the leader, who justly redistributes the wealth among his people.

The story teaches us that Genghis Khan is a great ruler because he inspires his followers, he listens to good counsel, and he keeps his promises. He is always ready to face the next challenge to his leadership role, he acts decisively, and finally he succeeds. The fact that he is favored by heaven is self-evident. It is both the cause and the result of his success as a leader and definer of a nation described as "these fields of tangled grasses."

Rediscovery

Today we know that some of the old Mongolian sources found in *The Secret History of the Mongols* were incorporated in later Mongolian texts, but these works were not read in Chinese intellectual circles and were unknown in Europe. International political and social dynamics at the start of the twentieth century finally brought the book to the attention of Chinese and non-Chinese audiences.

As the twentieth century began, explorers, archaeologists, linguists, and religious missionaries from Russia, British India, France, Germany, and Japan were active in China and the border regions then known as Russian Turkistan, Chinese Turkistan, and Outer Mongolia. All were motivated by a mixture of nationalistic competition, scientific discovery, military intelligence, and religious mission. Both secular scholars and Christian missionaries were studying the native languages of the non-Chinese groups living on the borders of the British, Russian, and Chinese empires. The region, newly accessible along its margins by railroad, was being explored and mapped to prepare for possible military incursions. British, French, German, American and Russian archaeologists and explorers were excavating sites that had been ignored for centuries. Inscriptions and fragments of writing in known and previously unknown languages were found among the paintings, sculptures, cloth fragments, and objects of daily life. Hundreds of crates were being packed and shipped to London, Paris, Berlin, and St. Petersburg for further examination in national libraries and museums.

Most of these archaeological sites predated the Mongol empire, and the book

14.3 Darkhad Winter Rider
This image captures the winter twilight ride of a herder in the Darkhad Valley. Soon after his rise to power, Genghis sent his eldest son Jochi to subjugate the people of this region and those living in what is today Tuva, to the north, who became some of the Mongol's early subjects.

sand. The book was in libraries and private collections of the Chinese capital, Beijing. In 1866 Archimandrite Palladiĭ (Palladius), a member of the Russian religious mission, became the first non-Chinese to find a copy.[5] Palladiĭ could read Chinese but not Mongolian, so he translated the book's Chinese summary into Russian. As a result of his work, the first European edition of the book was a Russian translation based on the Chinese summary of Chapter 1, published in St. Petersburg by A. M. Pozdneyev in 1880.[6] From that moment on, *The Secret History of the Mongols* was "injected into the bloodstream of Western scholarship."[7] However, it remained obscure until a full Chinese version was published in 1933 followed by the first translations into European languages in the 1940s.

Once the Chinese text was available, several obstacles kept the book from being read by all but a few specialists. To translate the book into a modern language, the translator must be fluent in both classical Chinese and Mongolian. The Old Mongolian to be translated is a vernacular language of the thirteenth century, related but not identical to contemporary Mongolian. *The Secret History* itself is the key to that language, being the single large work from that period

that survives. The task is further complicated because the scholars at the College of Literature left in place but did not translate words and place-names they did not understand. To interpret these words, a translator must also possess knowledge of the Altaic family of languages related to Mongolian. Many of the fourteenth-century sources that could be used to explain or verify obscure passages are in Iranian, a language that is unrelated to Chinese or Mongolian. Most of these sources were not translated into European languages until recently.

In addition to the language challenges, the book was difficult to place in the context of any literary or historical tradition. Being in a language spoken by a few million people, with no literary precedent or successor, *The Secret History* does not fit clearly into any larger body of literature. It is not an epic poem, a work of fiction, or a cycle of tales. Some passages are alliterative poetry, intended to be recited, but much of the text seems to be narrative prose. While its subject is the life of a nation-builder, it does not resemble medieval romances such as *La Chanson de Roland* or *Cantar del Mio Cid*, both considered precursors to later European literature.

If the place of *The Secret History* as literature has been unclear, its place as history

If the place of *The Secret History* as literature has been unclear, its place as history has also been suspect. The text does not fit the definition of history as that term is used by our own Greek-Roman-European tradition, nor by the standards of the Chinese or Islamic worlds. The descriptions of people and events inside and outside of Mongolia contain many chronological details that are contradicted by Iranian or Chinese sources, leading many historians to question its value. Sections such as those describing the reign of Ögödei, Genghis Khan's son and first successor, were probably not part of the original. The text we have appears to have been altered or added to during the Yuan period, but there is no clear evidence as to why or when these alterations were made.

A printed edition of the Chinese version of *The Secret History* was produced by The Commercial Press in Shanghai in 1933. Within a decade, scholars were translating the work into German, French, and English. The first European scholars who dedicated themselves to the task were Erich Haenisch, whose work was published in German in 1948, and the French Sinologist Paul Pelliot, whose incomplete translation was published in French after his death in the same year. Father Antoine Mostaert, a Belgian Catholic missionary in Inner Mongolia, and Francis Woodman Cleaves, an American who later became a professor of Chinese and Mongolian language at Harvard University, began similar work. The Cleaves English translation (1982), copies of which had been circulating since the 1950s, is the primary source for my adaptation, *The Secret History of the Mongols: The Origin of Chingis Khan* (1984; 1998), quoted in this chapter and throughout this volume.

The 2004 English translation by Igor de Rachewiltz deserves special mention. His fine translation is accompanied by a historical and philological commentary on each passage to which he devoted four decades. The result is arguably the most complete scholarly work on the subject in any language, a veritable encyclopedia of the field. His introduction summarizes the various arguments put forward regarding when *The Secret History* was written

and by whom. De Rachewiltz agrees with Cleaves and several other scholars that the cyclical date, Year of the Rat, given in the book's final paragraph, corresponds to 1228, which suggests that composition was completed within one year after Genghis Khan's death. By choosing 1228, de Rachewiltz agrees with other scholars that the last few sections, which describe events during the reign of Ögödei, were added to the text at a later date. To consider these passages about Ögödei later additions does not make them less interesting, but does give us a better sense of the shape of the original text, which ends at Genghis Khan's death and contains no account of his funeral or the events that followed.

The location and date of composition are stated in the final paragraph of the text as it was found, but there is no statement in the book that directly identifies the author. Therefore, any identification of the author is speculative and deductive. De Rachewiltz deduces that Shigi Khutukhu, a foundling adopted from the Tatar tribe into Genghis Khan's immediate family and described in the book as chief judge and record keeper, is the author. De Rachewiltz's attribution is the generally accepted one, based on a summary of arguments by a broad range of previous scholars, including Cleaves.

The more significant question may be why the book was written at all. To understand what the book meant to the author and his intended audience, we need some concept of motivation. Is *The Secret History of the Mongols* to be considered literary composition, a work of history, or a group of tales compiled by a committee? Why does some of the chronology not agree with Iranian and Chinese sources? In his biography of Genghis Khan, Paul Ratchnevsky concludes, "The chronology of the *Secret History* is unreliable because the author considers the individual episodes of his epic to be more important than either their interrelation or correct chronological order."[8] To understand what the author did consider important, we must recognize that the book was written for posterity not as a chronology but as a cultural instruction to generations who would inherit a new political state. Its

14.4 Bronze Mirror
This mirror was recovered during excavations at the Mongol capital, Khara Khorum, and dates to the late 12th or early 13th century. Its decoration presents a stylized scene of two standing people, a horse or donkey and rider, and other animals under the overarching branches of a tree.

essential purpose was didactic, to transmit in a dramatic form the information it contains.

The characters of the book explain their motivations very carefully each time they act. An attack today is always justified by a previous transgression or just cause for revenge. The repeated parables of how to treat members of one's family, clan, and tribe; the details of just punishments and rewards; and the many acknowledgments of and invocations for the protection the Eternal Blue Sky —the Mongol deity—all are meant to teach future generations crucial cultural values. It is significant that people of the steppe, having accomplished an unprecedented cultural, military, and material transformation, chose to record these lessons in a literary form.

De Rachewiltz draws a similar conclusion, calling *The Secret History*:

> … an heroic epic, aimed at recording not only the deeds and pronouncements of Chinggis Qan [Genghis Khan], but also those of his faithful companions in a language and style that reflect the attitudes and values of contemporary Mongols. It is at the same time a glorification of the conqueror's clan for the sake of posterity, especially of his immediate successors, and the mere fact that

it was put down in writing so soon after his death (in the form which it still largely retains) indicates, in my view, that it was also meant to serve as a guide and instruction, not just as a plain record or entertainment. [9]

In Mongolia today, the life and accomplishments of Genghis Khan are well known and freely celebrated in books, music, drama, and the plastic arts. Increasingly this is also true throughout the world. In each case, *The Secret History of the Mongols* is the primary source. In her 2006 catalog of translations of the *The Secret History of the Mongols,* Ts. Sarantsatsral lists nearly every major, and many minor, European and Asian languages including English, French, Spanish, German, Russian, Hungarian, Polish, Japanese, Modern Mongolian, and Modern Chinese. [10] More than forty translations have appeared since 1990.

The version we read today is a record, albeit a selective one, of actual people and events. It is epic in scope, joining the story of a man who was a conqueror, his allies and enemies, and the diverse nomadic nations they united. It is weak in its depiction of the sedentary Chinese, Tanghut, and Islamic cultures the Mongols fought because it is not about them. The book's intended audience was the members of those families who carried on the cultural transformation that Genghis Khan began. With this in mind, we can better understand why it is a book worth reading in any language. It enables us to hear the voice of a culture barely understood by the people that it conquered, and to read that culture's view of a man of extraordinary complexity and unique global influence. As the twenty-first century begins, nearly everyone on the planet can read the book that was once the private property of the descendants of Genghis Khan.

1. Kahn 1998, 15.
2. De Rachewiltz 2004, xliv-xlv.
3. Cleaves 1982, xxxiv.
4. Kahn 1998, 140.
5. De Rachewiltz 2004, vol.1, lxx ff.
6. De Rachewiltz 2004, vol.1, ci, note 246.
7. Cleaves 1982, xix.
8. Ratchnevsky 1991, 61.
9. De Rachewiltz 2004, lxix.
10. Sarantsatsral 2006.

15. Rule by Divine Right

SHAGDARYN BIRA

GENGHIS KHAN AND HIS IMPERIAL heirs linked the eternal power of the Sky God Tenggeri with the temporal rule of his designate, the Mongol khan. Whether from political convenience or exalted self-regard, the khans drew from traditional Mongolian shamanism and appropriated some of the rituals of the dominant religion in the East, Buddhism, in spiritual justification for their rule. The idea that the Mongols harbored a cohesive religious concept has emerged in recent years from study of documents relating to the Mongol empire in the thirteenth and fourteenth centuries. Although contro-

versial as a formal religious philosophy, Tenggerism motivated at least the early phase of Mongol expansion and political domination.

The worship of the Eternal Blue Sky is a fundamental concept of ancient Türkic and Mongolian shamanism. Tenggeri represents supreme masculine power in the universe, ruling all natural phenomena (fig. 15.1). Earth is a subordinate feminine force called Etugen, giving rise to the couplet: *etsege Tenggeri* (Father Heaven) *eke Gajar* (Mother Earth). The thirteenth-century traveler Friar William of Rubruck, observed that the Mongols believed in

a god who created all visible and invisible beings as well as all happiness and suffering in the world.

While the theory of divine origin of khanship was perpetrated among the nomadic people, the Mongols refined the oldest version of the credo on the basis of their own perceptions and the achievements of civilizations they encoun-

15.1 Spiritual Elements
Water, earth, and sky were essential elements in Mongol religious beliefs and became fundamental to Genghis's philosophy of life and power. Central also to shamanism and Buddhism, they are ever present and strongly expressed in the Mongolian landscape, framed by the arc of Tenggeri's Eternal Blue Sky.

tered. The totemistic belief in the origin of a leading clan changed into an affirmation of the khan's divine origin from Tenggeri under Genghis Khan. In *The Secret History of the Mongols*, written shortly after Genghis's death in 1227, his descent is attributed to a bluish wolf from the heavens. By this account, Alan the Fair, the mythical ancestress of the Mongols, gave birth to three sons, the youngest of whom was the direct progenitor of Genghis Khan's Golden Family.

Buddhism was to entwine with, rather than replace, shamanism in this theology, as both beliefs have done to this day. With the expansion of the Mongols and their empire, the worship of Tenggeri adopted more sophisticated ideology as Mongol military and political successes brought them into contact with the religions of sedentary peoples such as Christianity, Islam, Buddhism, and Daoism.

Genghis Khan and his successors believed in the omnipotence of Tenggeri, who had invested them with the divine mission and fortune to rule over all countries and peoples. Mongolian khans felt justified in expanding their conquests wherever Blue Sky (Koke Tenggeri) extended and believed their domination was as permanent as the Eternal Blue Sky (Möngke Tenggeri) itself.

Official documents of the Mongol khans in the thirteenth and fourteenth centuries begin with a stereotypical proclamation, such as the opening of Güyüg Khaghan's letter to Pope Innocent IV of around 1247: "This is the order of the everlasting God (Möngke Tenggeri). In heaven, there is only one eternal God: on earth there is only one lord, Chinggis Khan. This is the word of the son of God, which is addressed to you."[1]

This formula distills the dualistic concept that Tenggeri and Khan constitute the two elements of supreme power in the world. Tenggeri is the divinity with absolute power in the universe who protects and sanctifies the khan to act on his behalf. The khan is the absolute embodiment of Tenggeri.

To the Mongols, those who did not accommodate to the divine order of Tenggeri were rebels, not only against the khan but against god. Therefore, Mongols had a divine right to punish their enemies and the obligation to subjugate them to their khans, much as Western Christians in their crusades and the Muslims in *jihads* justified imperial conquests.

As the empire expanded under Kublai Khan, this duality underwent a transformation. After conquering China, Kublai turned to the problems of pacifying and consolidating an immense empire. During the Yuan dynasty he established, Mongols came into direct contact with Chinese, Indo-Tibetan, Arab-Islamic, and Central Asian cultures. Travelers from many areas of the world—most famously, Marco Polo—came to visit his court, acquainting Kublai with new ideas and philosophies. Kublai embraced not only the shamanistic beliefs of his nomadic roots but also personified a religious pragmatism that tolerated Buddhist, Daoist, Arab-Islamic, and European-Christian religions among his subjects. Mahakala, the protector deity of Tantric Buddhism—who is commonly depicted as a frightening black figure with fangs, wearing a crown of skulls, a garland of severed heads, and bracelets of snakes—is still widely regarded as the defender of the Mongolian nation, and paintings and statuettes of Mahakala are kept in the homes of most Mongolian families today.

This essay is condensed from the author's *Mongolian Tenggerism and Modern Globalism: A Retrospective Outlook on Globalisation* delivered to the Royal Asiatic Society, London, 10 October 2002 on the occasion of his receiving the Denis Sinor Medal, and published in *Journal of the Royal Asiatic Society* series 3, 14, no. 1: 3–12.

1. Rubruck 1990, 236.

16.1 Water, Cities, and History
Water, central to the herding economy, also
controls the potential for complex social
life. Small-scale irrigation has long been
practiced in some areas of Mongolia to
prolong winter run-off or conserve summer
rains. Changes in rainfall, shifts in river
courses, and floods have often caused cities
to be abandoned or relocated periodically
throughout history.

16. Ancient Cities of the Steppe

J. Daniel Rogers

EVEN BY TODAY'S MEASURE OF NATION STATES and globalized interaction, the geographic extent of the Mongolian empire is breathtaking. Though it was to last no more than 150 years, the Mongols controlled the largest contiguous landmass of any empire. At different times throughout their imperial history, and at opposite ends of the earth, Mongol regiments took on Egyptian armies of Mamluk slave-soldiers, Polish armored knights, and Japanese samurai. Until today, the Mongol empire has been known largely through the biased historical records compiled by the peoples they defeated. Combining environmental and archaeological research with the study of early documents is producing a more complete and objective understanding of how societies change within empires, of the imperial state established by Genghis Khan, and of the legacy of the Mongols in the modern world.

Archaeological research, in particular, has begun to modify the image etched into the Western collective imagination of hordes of Mongol warriors descending with bows drawn upon peaceful farm villages, or laying waste to the walled cities of China and Persia with catapults and siege machines. Indeed, such events occurred during the initial and most destructive phase of conquest, which wrought havoc on vibrant cultures and civilizations. But these events are only short chapters in the long story of the Mongol empire. Many essential questions remain. What was the empire like internally and across its different regions? How was it organized and who made decisions? How did it evolve and change through time? How was it different from other great empires? Answers to some of these queries are only hinted in documents as revealing as *The Secret History of the Mongols* (see Chapter 14).

Recent studies of settlements and urban sites on the Mongolian steppe have begun to raise—and sometimes answer—questions about the economy, agriculture, manufacturing, and trade with far-flung peoples. The Mongol empire and the early Inner Asian empires that preceded it established a new model for large-scale political organization. The steppe statecraft arose from nomadic and pastoral production; seasonal movement of camps and settlements; and horse-based transport and communication systems all adapted to the ecology of the vast steppe regions of Inner Asia. These characteristics produced both a range of novel options and unique problems for political integration and centralization across large regions and diverse populations.[1]

The Mongols did not emerge as lords of the steppe without substantial political experimentation and precedent on the part

16.2 Gol Mod II
The Xiongnu royal cemetery at the unexcavated Gol Mod II site in the Khanui Valley has scores of burial features ranging from small mounds to huge ramped platforms. Excavations at the nearby Gol Mod I royal cemetery revealed deeply buried internments flanked by subsidiary royal graves. Xiongnu tombs contain lavish grave offerings, including chariots, horses, and spectacular personal artifacts.

of former steppe peoples, many of whom, like the Mongols, constructed empires.[2] Without the long legacy of unique mobile statecraft that had developed over a thousand years on the eastern steppe, the Mongols probably would have been hard pressed to conquer, much less manage, the massive swath of Eurasia that became their political domain. The first example of large-scale and centralized polity building on the territory of Mongolia arose through the efforts, fortunes, and strategies of the ancient Xiongnu (ca. 200 BCE–155 CE)[3] (see Chapter 8). The historical record of these peoples is neither indigenous nor copious; archaeology is the major source of information about Xiongnu ways of life and techniques of organization—and there is still much to learn (fig. 16.2). Some of the principle themes of Xiongnu organization become part of a long-term political repertoire in later steppe empires. Two examples that are repeated time and again are the creation of military-administrative units based on decimal organization (units of 10, 100, 1,000, etc.) and geographical divisions of large-scale polities into "right hand" (western), "left hand" (eastern), and central administrative units.[4]

Cities, Palaces, and Seasonal Camps

The Xiongnu began the tradition of building large walled sites on the open steppe. Several of these structures have been recorded and a few examined by excavation.[5] Several other walled sites were later built by the Khitans, among others (fig. 16.3). Although little is known about the function of these sites, preliminary studies based on archaeological surveys argue that the relationships between walled centers and pastoral nomadic hinterlands change dramatically and strategically over time.[6] Such changes were part of long-term innovations to older techniques that the Mongols carried on in every sphere of life, from trade, to manufacture, to statecraft. Like prior empires, the Mongolian khanate arose from the pastoralist tradition, but evolved different types of settlements and spatial geography as appropriate for its time, setting, and needs. These sites were often planned and built to serve central administrative, military, manufacturing, and trade purposes. Steppe settlements had much smaller populations than the great cities of China or other sedentary states, and the layout of these settlements reflected the pastoralist preference for open spaces and distaste for the narrow confines of the city.

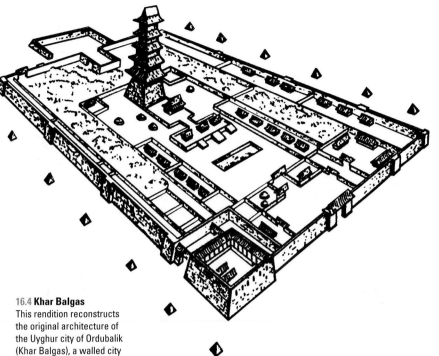

16.4 Khar Balgas
This rendition reconstructs the original architecture of the Uyghur city of Ordubalik (Khar Balgas), a walled city that was the residence of the Uyghur khan, Bögü (r. 759–79 CE). The site is located in the Orkhon Valley, 24 km north of Khara Khorum. According to Ata-Malik Juvaini, the Persian scholar and administrator, the Mongols confirmed its identity from an inscription, then built Khara Khorum nearby as proximity to the once-powerful Uyghur capital would add prestige to their city. Recent research suggests the high tower may not be an accurate projection; instead, a much smaller stupa or an elevated part of the citadel may have existed.

16.3 Kherlen Bars Stupa
The walled city of Kherlen Bars in Dornod province, far eastern Mongolia, was a leading Khitan urban center dating to ca. 10th–12th century. The Khitans, who created the Liao empire in northeastern China, had a language that was expressed in two independent writing systems but is now extinct and only partially deciphered. Many Khitan documents have been recovered from the Kherlen Bars ruins; further progress in deciphering the language depends on the acquisition of more texts. To protect these rare archaeological resources, the site has been listed for protection as a world heritage site by UNESCO. Its Buddhist stupa is the largest standing in Mongolia today.

Genghis Khan continually moved his court from one outlying palace site to another, a practice reminiscent of the seasonal movements of individual herder households. Japanese archaeologists have posited the identification of seasonal sites associated with Genghis Khan's itinerary from evidence recovered in these places. These include a settlement site on the Avraga River as a possible winter and spring camp (see Chapter 17); the site of Sa'ari Ke'er, a possible summer palace, located about 110 km southeast of Ulaan Baatar; and Khara Tün, a possible autumn palace, located 30 km southwest of Ulaan Baatar.[7] While it is sometimes difficult to match archaeological sites with places mentioned in early sources, the work on these potential seasonal encampments continues, and their association with Genghis Khan's seasonal travel is an intriguing theory.

When the need for a more permanent central place was determined—after the death of Genghis Khan—construction of a capital for the Mongol empire began at a site along the Orhkon River in central Mongolia. It was completed during the rule of Ögödei Khaghan, Genghis's third son and successor, in 1234. The construction of the Mongol

walled capital of Khara Khorum did not put this region on the map: the Orhkon Valley is a natural crossroads, where mountain fringes, major rivers, and the steppe edge intersect at the center of the eastern grasslands, and had long been a place of ceremonial significance for the Türks and Uyghurs prior to the Mongols (see Chapter 9). The broad well-watered valleys and grasslands of the Orhkon River area accommodated horse breeding, a practice of the Uyghur and Türk elites.[8] The Uyghurs established the largest of their steppe urban centers at Ordubalik (Khar Balgas), 24 km north of the future location of the Mongol capital (fig. 16.4). Another objective of Genghis Khan's heirs in selecting the Orhkon may have been to accrue political legitimacy through geographic association with the former Uyghur walled capital. Prior to the building of Khara Khorum, the Mongols conducted what was undoubtedly the first archaeological excavation ever to take place in Mongolia to confirm that the ruined and toppled walls were indeed those of Ordubalik. Through their work an inscribed stele was unearthed that identified the site as Ordubalik, the residence of the Uyghur khan Bögü, who reigned from 759 to 779.[9]

Khara Khorum is the best-known settle-

16.6 Pharaonic Maskettes
Two small Egyptian masks with classic pharaonic features were found in the 1970s in the vicinity of Khara Khorum by construction workers. They probably arrived at Khara Khorum during the Mongol era when the city received foreign visitors and gifts from Western envoys.

16.5 Mongolian Central Air
Excavations below the floor at Uglugchiin Kherem, a site in Khentii province of probable Khitan affiliation, revealed stone-lined ducts for delivering heated air to the floors or rooms above. Similar heating systems were employed in Korea and China and have come to light in excavations at the crossroads in Khara Khorum.

ment of the Mongol empire, but there are other large and small sites that have attracted much less attention from researchers (fig. 16.6). Khar Khul Khaany Balgas, covers about three square kilometers on the Khanui River, slightly northwest of the Orhkon Valley.[10] There are ten square enclosures—the largest has earthen walls, built for defensive purposes, standing four to five meters high. Remains of the walls and of glazed roof tiles indicate that buildings once stood on low earthen platforms within most, if not all, of the enclosures.[11] The function of this site is not mentioned in any written sources, but the investment in sizable buildings suggests it was a royal administrative center.

The chronology of Shazaan Khot, a possible Mongol-period palace site, is established by the presence of Chinese coins dated to 1064–66, 1078–85, and later. The ceramics, especially various types of Chinese porcelain, date to the Yuan dynasty (1279–1368).[12] Like other outlying palace sites, Shazaan Khot is not fortified by a major exterior wall but organized as an irregular assortment of building platforms arranged along a central street, similar to that found by archaeologists at Khara Khorum (see Chapter 18). At the end of the street, enclosed by a wall, is a large platform mound with column bases and other evidence of a major building.

Mongol steppe settlements incorporated design principles from China and other regions, but their layout and architecture had unique attributes (fig. 16.5). The royal courts constructed by Genghis Khan's grandson, Kublai Khan, were designed to invoke the steppe origins that lay behind the founding of the Mongol Yuan dynasty of China in 1271. Both Shangdu, where Kublai had already moved his seat of government in North China by 1256, and Daidu, which we now know as Beijing,[13] were built with Chinese principles in mind, but employed uniquely Mongol elements.[14] With the relocation of the capital to Daidu, principles of Chinese construction were emphasized, as Kublai realized that to rule China he must at least have the appearance of being a Chinese emperor (fig. 16.7). Inside the Chinese façade of the imperial compound, the young Mongol princes lived in traditional steppe tents.

Archaeological work on the urban centers of Mongolia continues to yield important discoveries. Based on preliminary research using survey and excavation techniques, a few common characteristics in the design of Mongolian settlements can be identified. Defensive walls with gates at midpoints are typical of large Mongol cities. Inside the walled enclosure, a Mongol settlement generally has a square or rectilinear layout organized around a central street that connects the gates and bisects cross streets. In general, public buildings,

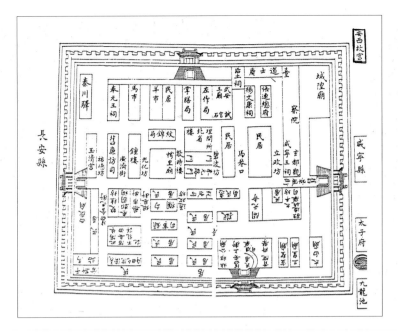

16.7 Plan of a Chinese City
Illustration of the Yuan Dynasty City at Qin showing principles of Chinese city plannings, such as a squared layout with gates in the middle of the four walls and a gridded interior plan of streets and enclosures. Some Mongol urban sites follow this general plan, but little detailed research has been conducted to understand the great variation found in them.

including palaces, are not centrally located but at one edge of the urban matrix. Low earthen platforms formed the typical foundations for tents or royal buildings and other administrative structures. At some sites there is no evidence of buildings or habitations within large sectors of the city that were probably occupied as tent neighborhoods, which leave little or no archaeological trace, but are well known from written sources.[15]

The Mongol empire drew on ancient steppe customs both in the construction of urban centers and in the creation of political and economic systems. The bustling center of Khara Khorum became a destination for the many foreign embassies bringing tribute to the burgeoning empire, and for the bureaucracy of government, notably, services to support the royal court. Like the empire, Khara Khorum was a multiethnic town that drew on many traditions and cultures across half the globe—the vast Eurasian steppe, the forests of Siberia, the Middle East, the Manchurian plain, and China. Archaeology continues to add to our understanding of how and when these traditions developed and how they contributed to the sweep and power of the Mongol empire.

1. Honeychurch and Amartuvshin 2006; Rogers et al. 2005.
2. Di Cosmo 1994.
3. Barfield 1981.
4. Honeychurch and Amartuvshin 2006.
5. Rogers et al. 2005; Perlee 1961.
6. Honeychurch and Amartuvshin 2006.
7. Shiraishi 2002.
8. Rogers et al. 2005.
9. Juvaini 1912–37, vol. 1, 39–46; 191–92; Juvani 1958.
10. Tseveendorj et al. 1999.
11. Rogers et al. 2005.
12. Moriyasu and Ochir 1999; Tseveendorj et al. 1999.
13. Rossabi 1988.
14. Steinhardt 1988.
15. Rogers et al. 2005.

17. Searching for Genghis: EXCAVATION OF THE RUINS AT AVRAGA

Noriyuki Shiraishi

As Genghis Khan and his Mongols rode forth from the arid steppe of far northeast Asia, they changed world history. They left little information about their origins, their forbearers, or even of their intentions. How and why an obscure group of shepherds conquered much of Eurasia is a genuine and fascinating historical mystery, about which the medieval Mongols themselves were almost silent. *The Secret History of the Mongols,* a handful of text fragments and a few inscribed stones on the windy steppe are the only indigenous testament to world conquerors—words drowned in an ocean of disparaging histories about the Mongols penned by those they had conquered and dominated. Archaeology is one of the sources that helps fill gaps where histories are lacking.

Northeastern Mongolia, and the modern province of Khentii, has long been identified as the homeland of Genghis Khan, as well as a possible place for the location of his tomb (fig. 17.1). While large-scale excavations are continuing at the ancient Mongolian capital of Khara Khorum (see Chapters 18, 19) 600 km to the northeast in Khentii province, systematic archaeological research is just beginning to reveal how and

why Mongolia became the political and cultural center of Eurasia during the thirteenth century.[1] On the rocky slopes of Serven Khaalga Mountain, halfway up the mountainside, carved into the rock, is a text in the Jurchen script; 20 meters to the east is another inscription in Chinese characters (figs. 17.2, 3). The texts are difficult to read because of heavy weathering of the stone. Preliminary studies suggest they may commemorate a famous battle at the end of the twelfth century between the Jurchen-Jin state (1115–1234) and the Tartar enemies of the early Mongol

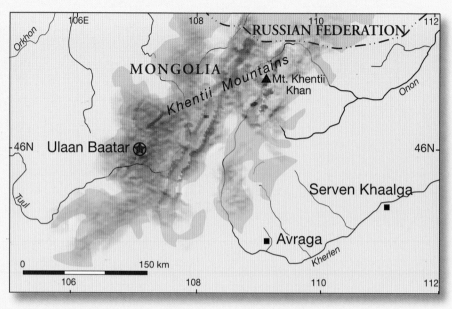

17.1 Khentii Homeland
The Secret History and other sources identify the Khentii Mountains and the Tuul, Kherlen, and Onon River valleys as important places in Genghis Khan's early life and during the initial development of the Mongol empire. Although no archaeological sites have been linked directly to Genghis, a rock inscription on Serven Khaalga Mountain and an archaeological site at Avraga date to this time period.

17.2 Serven Khaalga Inscription
The discovery of an unknown inscription is an important find because it can add immeasurably to the interpretation of mute physical remains. The faint traces of two inscriptions found in 1991 on a rock surface at Serven Khaalga Mountain are eroded and difficult to read.

17.3 Serven Khaalga Rubbings
Parallel texts in Chinese (right) and Jurchen (left) commemorate a battle between the Jurchen-Jin state (1115–1234) and the Tartars. Genghis was living in the area during the period when this battle occurred.

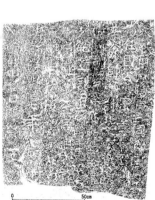

tribes.[2] These texts suggest that the region of Khentii is the place where the earliest history of the Mongols began to unfold upon a world stage.

During the socialist period in Mongolia (1921–90), this region was politically dangerous for archaeologists and historians because of its association with the Mongolian empire. Because attention to the history of Genghis Khan could easily have evoked strong nationalist sentiment in Mongolia, research in Khentii was discouraged by authorities in Moscow, and the archaeology of this fascinating homeland is today still very much in the making.[3] One fascinating site in the homeland of Genghis Khan that was only superficially investigated during the socialist period is the mysterious ruins beside the river Avraga, about 140 km to the west of the Serven Khaalga inscriptions (fig. 17.4). Genghis Khan led a typical nomadic lifestyle, shifting the location of his residence in accordance with the change of seasons. These movements were not haphazard, but involved traveling, with all his wives, retainers, and livestock,

between fixed seasonal camps within a specific area. *The Secret History of the Mongols* identifies one campsite, called Yeke a'uruq, as an important camp in the basin of the Kherlen River. Linguistically, the ancient Mongol *a'uruq* is very similar to the modern name of the river, Avraga.

Since 1992 Mongol-Japanese excavations at the Avraga ruins revealed chronological evidence that the site had been in use during the pre-imperial period of the twelfth century. However tempting it may be to hypothesize that Avraga might have been an important site on the early migration route of Genghis, archaeologists can now only confirm that it was a major center in the early Mongol heartland, even if they have yet to find a direct connection to the Great Khan. Many square earthen mounds can be seen on the site, which covers an area of 60 hectares. These mounds have been identified as the remnants of foundations of substantial buildings (figs. 17.5, 6). Since architecture is rare in this region, these ruins suggest that this place was connected

17.4 Avraga, a Possible Genghis Camp
Historical sources of the Mongols are fragmentary, making it difficult to match established events and people to archaeological sites. Excavations on the Avraga River 140 kilometers west of Serven Khaalga suggest this may have been the camp Genghis used that is named in *The Secret History* as Yeke a'uruq. It also matches a description in *Heida shilu* by Peng Daya, a Southern Song Chinese emissary who traveled in this region in 1232–33 and visited Ögödei Khaghan at a settlement used earlier by Genghis.

with activities of the Mongol elite.

Areas surrounding the main buildings of the Avraga site held evidence for other activities carried out by the people who once lived there. Extensive remains of iron working and ceramic production have been found, showing that Avraga was used for craft manufacture as well as for residences. Clay bricks, made at the site and baked in a kiln or dried in the sun, were used to construct the walls of the buildings. Fine gray earthenware water vessels and storage jars were also made locally. A fragmented inscribed bone object unearthed at the site is similar in shape and design to rulers used for standardized measurement and may have been

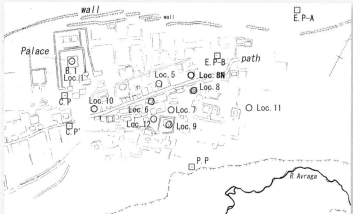

17.5 Avraga "Palace" Complex
 Excavations at the large central mound uncovered foundations of three buildings. The Upper Building (A) has stone walls; stone column bases seen to the right are part of a Lower Building (B); and beneath these buildings are remains of an earlier structure (C). The site's complexity, use of stone walls and columns, and changing construction styles indicates a lengthy period of occupation by high-ranking people. Artifacts and radiocarbon samples from the lowest levels date to the late 12th or early 13th century, the period when Genghis was living in this region

17.6 Avraga Site Plan
Archaeological work in Khentii province, Genghis's homeland and the likely location of his grave, was discouraged during the Soviet era because of concern it might boost nationalistic fervor. In 1992 when these restrictions were lifted, work began at Avraga. The site is large and complex, with numerous raised platform mounds in a 60-hectare area. The largest mound is probably a palace structure. Most of the artifact finds have come from smaller dwellings or workshops.

example of the kinds of tools needed to construct the buildings. The markers on this artifact show that one unit of measure was a little less than 3 centimeters (fig. 17.7). Numerous iron bars, in standard size and weight, may have been ingots used to manufacture iron weapons, tools, and domestic implements.

Numerous other artifacts found at Avraga probably arrived there in the saddlebags or carts of long-distance traders. These include several kinds of high-quality glazed ceramics from the famed Junyao and Cizhouyao kilns in China, all manufactured between the latter half of the twelfth and the first half of the thirteenth century. Coins first minted by the Jurchen-Jin state in 1179 also provide a temporal context for the ruins.[4] Radiocarbon analysis corroborates this dating for the ruins. The presence of such trade goods implies that the upper stratum of Avraga encouraged and was involved in intercultural exchange at a very early time.

The arrangement of the Avraga settlement is dominated by a large central structure made up of a platformlike foundation surrounded by a rectangular earthen enclosure. The central platform was made from hard-packed earth and clay; holes with stone supports for columns were found around the periphery of the platform. Excavating small but deep pits in the surface of the platform revealed that the stonework foundation visible in the uppermost level was only the final and latest phase of construction in the history of this building. Below this surface, another two phases of earlier platform construction were discovered, showing that this structure had been remodeled periodically throughout the empire period. Given its large size and centrality, its special architectural features such as the standing columns, and the great attention given to its maintenance over time, this building probably represents the residence of a nobleman and perhaps even an early Mongol palace.

A huge quantity of bone fragments excavated at Avraga indicates the presence of horses, cattle, sheep,

17.7 Measuring Device
Among the finds was this small, inscribed bone that appears to have been a measuring device. The author contends that Mongolian urban centers from the 8th century to Genghis Khan's reign were constructed with a standardized system of measurement, perhaps the Chinese *chi* (29.6 cm). More work is needed to determine whether this unit or a local Mongolian system was used.

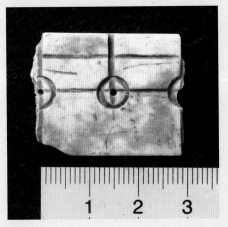

goats, dogs, as well as rodents and fish. Bird bones and eggshells were also unearthed. Some of these animals were being consumed as food, but many others may have been used for ritual purposes. Remains of sheep and goats are found in much greater quantities than those of cattle and horses, and most of the horse remains were recovered in the vicinity of the central platform "palace" structure. While all of these herd animals were used for food and feasting, historical texts, like the *Yuanshi*, state that sheep and especially horses were also used for ceremonies involving the Mongol elite. Most of the horse bones excavated were fragments of skulls, necks, and ribs, which in the Mongolian tradition were honored parts of an animal and offered to noble personages.[5]

From the bottom ash layer of a pit filled with burnt animal bones, we also found charred cereal grains, including barley (*Hordeum vulgare*), wheat (*T. aestivum*), and millet (*P. miliaceum*) (fig. 17.8). Radiocarbon analysis dates these grains to the first half of the thirteenth century, in keeping with all other chronological evidence.[6] The presence of multiple sections of the cereal plants—ears, stems, leaves, even roots—argue that these remains derive from local agriculture and were not obtained through exchange. Since there was, and still is, fertile land and plentiful water nearby, Avraga may have been an agricultural center, not only a destination for rich craft goods and far-off trade.

We know from *The Secret History* that the early life and initial political career of Genghis Khan played out in northeastern forest steppe in what is today called Khentii province. Mongolian people still

17.8 Charred Grain and Crops
The Avraga excavations recovered large amounts of carbonized wheat, barley, and millet, probably of local origin. William of Rubruck reported merchants at the gates of Khara Khorum selling millet and other kinds of local grain. Archaeologists have tended to underestimate the importance of agriculture in Mongolian history, particularly during its periods of centralization and empire.

make pilgrimages to this region to ask for the blessing of Genghis in their daily pursuits, believing that in one of Khentii's forgotten valleys lie the tombs of all the great khans of the empire. These stories, however, can only hint at the evidence that archaeologists must unravel from the damp earth. At the Avraga ruins we find one of the first and earliest indications of the organizational investment made by the Mongols in subjugating the peoples of the vast eastern steppe. By 1206 those people, with the newly anointed Genghis Khan before them, rode forth to conquer Eurasia, though they never forgot their distant steppe homeland.

1. Shiraishi 2004; 2006.
2. Matsuda 2006; Aisin-Gioro 2006.
3. Bawden 1989, 417–49.
4. Miyake 2005.
5. Kato 2005.
6. Obata 2007.

18.1 Unearthing Khara Khorum
The Franciscan monk William of Rubruck arrived at Khara Khorum in the spring of 1254, finding the city a cosmopolitan place full of people from all over the world. Excavations at the city center are revealing much about its early history and the activities of artisans who worked there. Founded in 1235 and razed by the Ming Chinese in 1388, the Mongol capital city is now deeply buried beneath flood deposits and wind-blown sand and silt.

18. The Crossroads in Khara Khorum

EXCAVATIONS AT THE CENTER OF THE MONGOL EMPIRE

ULAMBAYAR ERDENEBAT

ERNST POHL

Regarding the city of Caracorum, you should know that, discounting the Chan's palace, it is not as fine as the town of St. Denis, and the monastery of St. Denis is worth ten of the palace. It contains two quarters: one for the Saracens [Muslims], where there are bazaars and where many traders gather due to the constant proximity of the camp and to the great numbers of envoys; the other is the quarter of the Cataians [Chinese], who are all craftsmen. Set apart from these quarters lie large palaces belonging to the court secretaries. There are twelve idol temples belonging to different peoples, two mosques where the religion of Mahomet [Muhammad] is proclaimed, and one Christian church at the far end of the town. The town is enclosed by a mud wall and has four gates. At the east gate are sold millet and other kinds of grain, though they are seldom imported; at the western, sheep and goats are on sale; at the southern, cattle and wagons; and at the northern, horses.

—WILLIAM OF RUBRUCK (1990: 221)

WHEN THE FRANCISCAN MONK WILLIAM OF RUBRUCK reached the Mongol capital of Khara Khorum in the spring of 1254 after crossing large areas of the Eurasian steppe, he perceived the city as a cosmopolitan community (fig. 18.1). Within its walls members of the Mongol empire's many ethnic groups were living and working side by side. Rubruck's account testifies to religious freedom and tolerance and describes numerous houses of worship, including two mosques, several Daoist and Buddhist temples, and a Nestorian Christian church that Rubruck frequented during his stay.

Although he mentions Europeans of different nationalities, Muslims, and Chinese, Rubruck omits the fact that most of these foreigners lived in the Mongol capital involuntarily, conscripted into service to the court of the Great Khan. People from settled cultures were always in demand to fill jobs that nomadic people were not able or willing to do. Foreign craftsman were vigorously, sometimes forcibly, sought (fig. 18.4). Perhaps the most famous of these was the French goldsmith Guillaume Boucher, who created for the khan's palace the silver and gilt fountain in the form of a tree that dispensed fermented mare's milk *(airag)* and four other liquors from its branches. Boucher had arrived in Khara Khorum as a prisoner of war, captured in Belgrade during the European campaign.

According to both the *Yuanshi*, the official history of the Yuan dynasty, and an inscribed stone of 1346, the earliest building activities at Khara Khorum can be dated to 1235, when the son and successor of

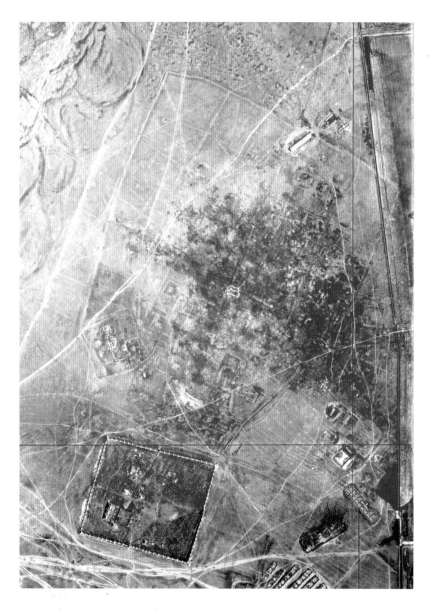

18.2 Khara Khorum from the Air
Patterns in the surface vegetation indicate the buried remains of Khara Khorum, which lie north of the walled enclosure of Erdene Zuu Monastery in this Soviet-era aerial photograph. The remains of the temple enclosures excavated in earlier days are to the left. The khan's palace probably lies directly beneath the monastery.

the Buddhist monastery of Erdene Zuu, which was founded in 1586 in the southern part of the city (see Chapter 19).

According to the written sources, building the Mongolian capital was a protracted process that took many years to complete. One of the first orders Möngke Khaghan issued after his enthronement in 1251 was to discharge some 1,500 workers who were still engaged in constructing the city walls more than a decade after the project had begun. One year later, 500 families of craftsmen were resettled at Khara Khorum to begin another phase of construction on the palace.[2]

As Rubruck makes clear, travelers who journeyed to Khara Khorum two decades or more after the death of Genghis Khan encountered a city of flourishing and diverse communities. Yet, only a few years later, after the death of Möngke during a military campaign in China, Khara Khorum's prospects darkened. Rival claims to the title of khan were staked by two of his younger brothers: Arigh Böke, who had remained at Khara Khorum with the charge to protect the city and maintain order, and Kublai, who had been sent to China to consolidate the empire's southern domains. Each convened a congress, or *khuriltai*, to elect himself Great Khan (*khaghan*).

Discord roiled the royal clan. Khara Khorum was the scene of many military clashes during the nearly four-decade civil war that ensued between the nomadic faction, led at first by Arigh Böke, and later by his nephew, Khaidu, and the "China faction" of Kublai Khan and his successors.[3] The rivals inflicted serious damage on the residents and structures of the city as they took turns overtaking it.

The first military clash took place directly after the investiture of Kublai in 1260. Arigh Böke tried to defeat his brother's forces, but Kublai's army won, then moved north to besiege Khara Khorum. During this first campaign, the surrender of the city appears to have taken place without any destruction because members of the resident religious communities

Genghis Khan, Ögödei Khaghan, began to build walls to enclose the area of the future city.[1] In the same year, construction began on a royal palace, later called Wan-an, and on the foundation of a Buddhist temple. While the first iteration of the palace was completed promptly and inaugurated in the spring of the following year, construction of the temple was not finished until 1256, during the reign of Möngke Khaghan. During the past several years, archaeologists from the Mongolian Academy of Science and the German Archaeological Institute have been excavating this temple area, where the royal palace was also thought to be. However, recent research has shown that the palace is more likely located within the area of

convinced Kublai to take the city peacefully. Arigh Böke reconquered the city the following year, but failed in a second attempt to defeat Kublai, losing a battle to Kublai's forces in the Gobi Desert. When Arigh Böke returned to Khara Khorum, Kublai cut off the supply of food to the city from his Chinese territories and, within a short time, famine and a horse plague broke out, forcing Arigh Böke to submit to Kublai's rule in the spring of 1264.

A second stage of the civil war began in 1277, when Kublai's nephew Khaidu, who belonged to Ögödei's side of the family, took Khara Khorum. Bayan, the commander in chief of the Yuan, recaptured the city in the following year. These campaigns devastated the city, as did another conquest by Khaidu ten years later. Only after Khaidu's death did the relationship stabilize between the nomadic population of the steppe lands around Khara Khorum and the central government in Daidu (modern Beijing). The *Yuanshi* dynastic history reports the start of new construction at Khara Khorum by 1299.

During the fourteenth century, written sources repeatedly mention different administrative divisions in Khara Khorum such as a General Regional Military Command or a Branch Central Secretariat.[4] Traditionally, the heir to the throne had to live in the city for some time before ascending to the throne of the Great Khan. In addition to being the center of the northern province of the Yuan empire, Khara Khorum was the homeland of Kublai's ancestors. According to the stele inscription of 1346, Khara Khorum received regular donations for the restoration of the Buddhist temple after 1311 (fig. 18.10). However, statistics about the size of the city and about construction activities in the intervening decades have not been discovered.

In 1368 the last emperor of the Yuan dynasty, Toghon Temür fled the advancing Chinese army from Daidu to Inner Mongolia, where he died in 1370. His son and successor, Ayushiridara, moved the seat of the Mongol government back to Khara Khorum, where he was anointed Biligtü Khan. Even after this return of the Great Khans to Khara Khorum, the sources provide only a fragmentary picture of the city's history. Biligtü Khan's multiple defeats of the Chinese forces are recorded, but these victories failed to lead to reconquest of China. When the army of the Ming dynasty defeated the Mongolian troops in 1388, the Chinese obliterated the old capital of Khara Khorum.

It is unclear if any permanent reconstruction of Khara Khorum was made during the fifteenth and sixteenth centuries. Written sources of the era mention the former capital several times, but no archaeological evidence of occupation has been uncovered.[5] However, the site of the old capital was still important to various Mongol clans. In 1415 several clans

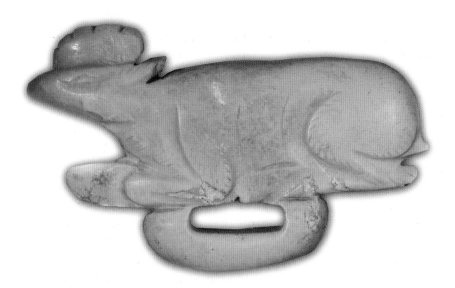

18.4 Strap or Belt Ornament
This 14th-century jade ornament is decorated with the carving of a reclining deer. During the 13th century Mongol khans brought artists and craftspeople from conquered lands to Khara Khorum to manufacture goods for the growing Mongol elite. Whether this piece was imported or produced locally from Chinese or Mongolian jade is not yet known.

reportedly decided to "rebuild" the city, whatever this claim means. By the end of the fifteenth century, during the reign of Dayan Khan, Khara Khorum was established again as the capital and seat of the Mongol khans, but permanent buildings were erected in the vicinity of the old capital only after Abtaj Khan founded the monastery of Erdene Zuu in 1586.

Discovering Khara Khorum
Today, the remains of palaces, temples, shops, and storehouses of ancient Khara Khorum described by William of Rubruck lie nearly invisible beneath several meters of windblown sands and scrublands. Nevertheless, aerial photographs, digital surface modeling, and geophysical surveys provide considerable detail about parts of the Mongols' former capital. Looking at an aerial picture, the long walls and one hundred stupas of the Buddhist monastery Erdene Zuu are visible in the southern part of the site. A wall runs north from the northeastern corner of the monastery before turning west after 1.5 km, and, after another 1.2 km, angles to the south.

The area of the Buddhist temple lies in the southwestern part of the city and is oriented differently from the main axis of the site, formed by the intersection of two main roads that divides the city into four quarters (fig. 18.2).

Archaeologists from the Institute of Archaeology of the Mongolian Academy of Science and from the University of Bonn carried out excavations of Khara Khorum beginning in 1999. Our team began in the center of the walled city to uncover the chronology of the city's development and occupation. We selected an area for excavation immediately south of the central crossroads. The surface topography here is marked by elevated terrain with numerous platforms, piles of rubble, and trackways, suggesting that remains of buildings and courtyards that once stood along the main north–south road would be found underneath the rubble. These mounds stand higher than the surrounding lands of the river valley and probably represent several periods of construction at the site. By excavating here, archaeologists hope to augment the limited historical accounts of Khara Khorum and expose the details of daily life in the city over its many generations.

The Russian archaeologist S.V. Kiselev and his Mongolian colleague Kh. Perlee were also drawn to these large piles of rubble in the southeastern corner of the center during their 1948–49 expedition, excavating a trench of around 20 by 30 meters at the so-called "House of the Crossroads."[6] While their excavation methods would not stand up to scientific scrutiny today, their work did reveal a stratigraphic sequence several meters deep, with different layers of occupation. Needless to say that exca-

18.5 Dragon Ornament
This 5cm carving of a scale-covered dragon dating to the 13th–14th century was recovered during excavations at the Khara Khorum site. It appears to have been used as an ornamental plug or handle

18.6 Handled Mirror
Decorated mirrors appear in the Bronze Age and were probably preceded by Neolithic jade prototypes. Mirrors cast with a polished side and a decorated back were used for both personal and ritual functions. Shamans used mirrors in séances and they are often found as grave goods. This copper alloy mirror dating to the Song or Yuan Dynasty is from a site at Khanan Uul, Khentii province. Its decoration includes two antlered stags, a goose or swan, and two people beneath a tree with a sun symbol to the left. Similar mirrors were made in Korea during the 12th–13th centuries.

18.7 Porcelain Lion
This porcelain lion with a light blue glaze was made at the Qingbai Kiln in China in the 14th century. Its ferocity is compromised by features both humorous and fantastic and its human-like pose. The presence of such exotic artifacts in the upper level of the crossroads excavations may mark the return of elite Mongols to the old capital in 1368 when they were expelled from China at the end of the Yuan dynasty.

vation at the same area would produce a comparable stratigraphy, which—based on modern excavation techniques—could lead to more refined understanding of the city's development.

One of the most exciting discoveries of the excavations by our team was proof of the north–south boulevard of Khara Khorum. Three different road levels were uncovered along a portion of that street. It was clear that the road had been reconstructed several times, providing an important key to the chronological progression of the city center. The oldest surface is paved with irregular limestone blocks separated by wood dividers that may have helped protect the road from Khara Khorum's drastic variations of seasonal temperature. The limestone pavement rests on several gravel layers similar to a Roman-style embankment that slopes on each side toward the habitations lining the avenue. Artifact finds suggest that this kind of road construction was laid down in the first half of the thirteenth century and continued to be traveled into the second half of that century, when Khara Khorum flourished from international trade, requiring arteries worthy of an imperial capital.

In the Mongolian climate, with its periodic sandstorms and rainy summers, these roadways required regular maintenance. The stratigraphic levels above the limestone pavement indicate that road maintenance grew worse over time. Layers of grayish sand interspersed with thin layers of gravel, bones, and potsherds show that the roadway slowly silted up, forcing residents to continually compact its muddy surface lest it become impassable. The main architectural feature of this period, drainage ditches running along each side of the road embankment, testify to the city's con-

cern for water management. These ditches were covered by wooden boards that had been repaired repeatedly. Multiple layers covering both the embankment and drainage ditches show that, over time, the road level continued to rise gradually as more material accumulated. The second phase of road construction occurred in the latter half of the thirteenth century, when Khara Khorum was enduring decades of military confrontations. Eventually, the drainage channels filled up with sandy materials that precipitated the third phase of road construction phase in the fourteenth century, when it became simple, rough pavement.

Chinese roof tiles and roof ridge ornaments excavated on both sides of the road suggest that this was the vibrant quarter of Chinese craftsmen described by William of Rubruck, even though excavations have not yet produced a complete "footprint" for a single building (fig. 18.3). The regular size and arrangement of various plots or enclosures indicate that the

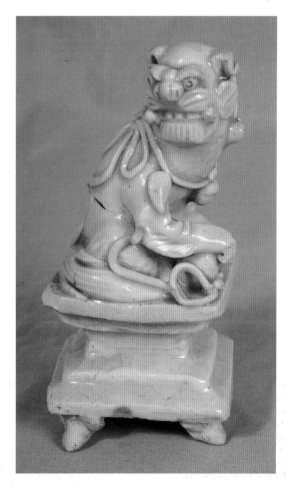

18.8 Storage Vessel
Found set into the floor of a metal workshop at Khara Khorum, this storage vessel dates to the latest period of the city's occupation. It contained a small bronze Buddha (fig.18.9) and a necklace, valuable objects that may have been abandoned as a result of the city's turbulent ending.

18.9 Buddha Sakyamuni
This corroded 13th-century bronze Buddha was found with the storage vessel (fig. 18.8) in a workshop dated to the latest occupation of the Khara Khorum site. The 3.5cm figure is seated in the meditation pose.

settlement was organized by a central plan. Rectangular areas with short sides of three to four meters were placed next to each other on both sides of the road. These plots were first occupied by craftsmen who do not seem to have constructed workshops, as remains of wooden fencing enclose installations for various manufacture. Similar land use is typical in modern Mongolia, where residential or work areas are first surrounded by wood fencing to delineate land ownership.

The borders between the enclosed plots do not appear to have changed during the time of occupation. Four to five periods of settlement have been identified in the area east of the road, and as many as six periods to the west. The outer walls of the houses were built mostly of sun-dried mud bricks. The early buildings are characterized by smaller brick walls stabilized by wooden beams in what may be described as frame construction. The most recent constructions, of the fourteenth century, are marked by brick walls laid out in a square. Smaller brick walls form the internal structure of the buildings. Roofs were supported by wooden beams placed on flat stone slabs. Behind the houses are open courtyards.

Extensive evidence of handicraft production was uncovered during the course of the excavation. Technical installations, such as fireplaces and various types of ovens, as well as a spectrum of artifacts were found from all periods of occupation. Metalworking seems to have been a popular trade. We also found evidence of ateliers specializing in glass working, gems and precious stones, bone carving, and processing of birch bark, attested by the recovery of raw materials, semi-finished objects, and workshop debris (fig. 18.4). One of the most interesting of these ateliers is a metalworking site on the east side of the road. During the 2004 excavation season, several blocks of wood were discovered in the front of two structures. Each measured 30 to 40 cm wide and 80 cm high and had been erected side by side,

parallel to the road. The blocks and the surrounding sediment were covered with bronze powder. The tops of the blocks have rectangular slots for anchoring an anvil.

Several types of kilns and fireplaces were found within both of these enclosures. Two single-shaft furnaces for smelting metal were excavated at the rear of the southern workshop. Smaller furnaces of a different shape found at the front of the workshop near the blocks were used for later stages of metal processing. The dome-shaped furnaces may have been employed to melt raw materials; the round furnaces without domes were likely used to reheat metal for forging. These sites demonstrate that different stages of bronze working were done in close proximity, from smelting copper or bronze through final production of finished, hammered bronze objects. The latter finishing work is indicated by fragments of sheet bronze found together with leather and textile fragments used as padding.

Perhaps the most intriguing discovery was a silver coin with Muslim inscriptions that mentions the name Khara Khorum, which was found on the floor of this metalworking shop (fig. 18.14). This coin is the first to be found carrying the name of the Mongolian capital and dates to 635 in the Muslim calendar, or 1237–38 in the calendar of the Common Era.[7]

Trade and Commerce

William of Rubruck's account of Khara Khorum makes clear that trade and commerce were some of the engines of Genghis Khan's capital city; archaeological evidence confirms his assertion. A gold bracelet made of two rectangular plates decorated with a central phoenix flanked by demon masks is one of the most exquisite objects recovered by our Mongolian-German excavations. The bronze sheet mold used to shape the bracelet was also found (fig. 18.12). Molds with various decorative motifs, a cast bronze spoon, and a small ceramic pot filled with mercury found nearby help elucidate the fabrication techniques of the gold and silversmiths. Elsewhere at the site, evidence of iron production has also been found in the form of a large number of complete or fragmented iron wheel hubs, along with farm tools like spades, and parts of a single-share plough.

In 2005 a well-preserved storage vessel set into the floor of the metal workshop was found to contain the bronze figure of the Buddha, Chinese coins, and an entire

18.12 Gold Bracelet and Mold
High-quality finished products, like this embossed and tooled gold bracelet, continued to be produced at Khara Khorum into the 14th century. The decoration features a phoenix flanked by demon masks. The bronze mold used to make this piece was also recovered, indicating local manufacture.

18.13 Treasury Seal
This treasury stamp made of copper alloy was found in the upper level of the Khara Khorum crossroads excavation. Writing in the 'Phags-pa script dates it to 1371–72, only three years after the return of Mongol leadership from China.

necklace (figs. 18.8, 9). Given the high value of these objects in the fourteenth century, it is unlikely that the owner parted with them willingly. Perhaps work came to an abrupt halt during a sudden raid on Khara Khorum that the owners did not survive or that prevented them from returning to collect their possessions.

After 1368 the city regained its former status as a capital after the return of the Mongol khans who had been driven out of China. The excavation recovered a critical historical document that dates to this time: a treasury seal produced in Khara Khorum in 1371-72 (fig. 18.13).[8] The remarkably high quality of other artifacts of that period, including several bronze mirrors, a porcelain lion, and the finds associated with the above-mentioned workshop, found in the uppermost layers of the excavation areas, suggest that members of the former royal court may have returned to Khara Khorum with the family of the Mongolian khan (fig. 18.7). After hard-fought battles, the Ming Chinese laid waste to Khara Khorum in 1388; no other city was established as the Mongolian capital until construction of Ulaan Baatar began at the end of the nineteenth century.

1. Cleaves 1952; Abramowski 1976.
2. Abramowski 1979
3. Pelliot 1959–73, 126–28; Rossabi 1988: 53–62, 103–14.
4. Cleaves 1952, 25–26; Pelliot 1959–73, 168; Farquhar 1990, 396–98.
5. Pelliot 1959–73, 169.
6. Kiselev et al. 1965, 173–82.
7. Heidemann et al. 2006.
8. Nagel 2002.

18.14 Silver Coin
This Muslim silver coin (both sides shown) was found in a metalworking shop at the Khara Khorum crossroads. It carries the name Khara Khorum and is dated 635 in the Muslim calendar (1237–38 in the Common Era), only a few years after the founding of the city.

19. The Search for Khara Khorum and the Palace of the Great Khan

Hans-Georg Hüttel

UNTIL RECENTLY the precise location of Khara Khorum, the capital of the medieval Mongol empire, was controversial. Although ruins are found throughout the Orkhon Valley in central Mongolia, the exact locations of the city and the palace of the Great Khan have remained a mystery. In the early eighteenth century, the French scholar A. Gaubil, citing Chinese historical sources, correctly identified the Buddhist monastery of Erdene Zuu as the site of the ancient capital.[1] Most scholars of the nineteenth and early twentieth centuries, however, mistook the conspicuous ruins of Khar Balgas (fig. 19.3), the capital city of the Uyghur empire (CE 745–840; see Chapter 9), for those of Khara Khorum. This argument is supported by the account of Ata-Malik Juvaini, a high-ranking Persian official and historian who visited the imperial court in Khara Khorum several times between 1249 and 1253 and wrote *History of the World Conqueror,* one of the most important sources of Mongolian history.[2] Therein he reports that the Great Khan Ögödei chose "for his [new] residence and the capital of the kingdom a place in the region of the river Orkhon and the Khara Khorum mountains. There had previously been no town or village in that place except for the remains of a great wall called Ordubalik."[3]

Ordubalik (Ordu-Baligh) was the ancient name of the Uyghur capital city before it was renamed Khar Balgas. Ordubalik was constructed 450 years before the Mongol empire emerged in the early thirteenth century, and the site is even today much more than a single wall, comprising ruins of a massive town with central walled palace or citadel. Juvaini's description leaves no doubt about which ruins were meant: "Outside the ruins of the palace opposite the gate there lie stones engraved with inscriptions which we have seen ourselves." J.A. Boyle is probably right in asserting that these stones are the fragments of the famous inscribed stele of Khar Balgas, which still stands near the walled citadel.[4] This inscription, in Chinese, Uyghur, and Sogdian, relates the conversion of the Uyghur people to the Persian Gnostic religion of Manichaeism.

The first field scholar to search for Khara Khorum was I.O. Paderin, the Russian consul in Urga (the modern Mongolian city of Ulaan Baatar). Paderin visited Khar Balgas in 1871. Viewing its monumental earthen walls and 12-meter high "tower" (a stupa) looming high on the Orkhon steppe, he became convinced that he stood before ancient Khara Khorum.[5] Not too long after Paderin's visit to the Orkhon, however, discovery of the inscriptions linked to the Mongol city within Erdene Zuu monastery raised new questions about whether Mongol Khara Khorum had ever been established atop the old Uyghur city. Visiting Erdene Zuu in 1877, the Russian scholar Alexei M. Pozdneyev observed several stone inscriptions related to ancient Khara Khorum in several temples of the impressive sixteenth-century monastery. This material evidence, in addition to information from Mongolian chronicles, led Pozdneyev to conclude that Erdene Zuu monastery had been established above the ancient Mongolian capital city and consequently that the ruins of Khara Khorum should lay beneath Erdene Zuu.[6] Pozdneyev had obviously not taken careful notice of

19.1 Khara Khorum and Erdene Zuu
This oblique photograph showing Khara Khorum in the foreground and the walled Erdene Zuu monastery toward the hill reveals little of the buried city. A similar view, shot with digital terrain imaging (fig.19.2), exposes more of the site's archaeological features.

19.2 Terrain Model
Digital terrain analysis enhances minute changes in vertical topography, using color to simulate stereo and shadow effects. The rectangular outline of the Erdene Zuu monastery enclosure is seen in white. The crossroads at the center of the city, its rectilinear temple compound, and other urban features stand out more clearly in this image than in standard aerial photographs. Like other cites of this period, Khara Khorum was laid out on a rough square or rectangular plan, a central crossroads, and a grid plan of temple and dwelling enclosures.

19.3 Khar Balgas
The confusion surrounding Khara Khorum's location begins with Khar Balgas, a well-preserved urban site in the Orkhon Valley. Its walled citadel was the most impressive ancient site in the valley, and its inscribed monuments gave it an aura of greatness. When its inscriptions were translated, however, its true identity was found to be Ordubalik, capital of the 8th–9th–century Uyghur empire.

artifacts of a ruined town extending north of the monastery (fig. 19.1).

If credit must be assigned for discovery of Khara Khorum then the Russian geographer Nikolai M. Jadrincev must be regarded as the discoverer. In July of 1889, he became the first scholar to identify the physical ruins of the Mongolian capital based on topographical features and stones with inscriptions related to events in the history of the famous city. The first plan of the ruins of Khara Khorum was prepared by the German-Russian Turkologist, Wilhelm Radloff, head of the Russian Orkhon expedition. Radloff's *Atlas der Alterthümer der Mongolei*, published in 1892, marks the true beginning of Mongolian archaeology. Like Jadrincev, Radloff recognized the ruins north of Erdene Zuu as the remains of Mongolian Khara Khorum, and he proposed that the palace of the Great Khan might lie somewhere under Erdene Zuu.

The first excavations at Khara Khorum were carried out in 1933 as part of a Russian-Mongolian collaborative expedition. The area was investigated systematically with small test pits, but the results were disappointing because finds were almost entirely from Buddhist-related contexts. Consequently, the leader of the expedition, D. Bukinič,

began to question the Khara Khorum identification. His report was never published but was obviously known to the Russian archaeologist, Sergej Kiselev, who directed Soviet-Mongolian excavations at Khara Khorum in 1948 and 1949. Kiselev was the first to carry out larger-scale excavations intended to confirm that the site was indeed Khara Khorum and to discover the location of the khan's palace within the ruins. He chose to investigate a walled area in the southwestern part of the site, which he supposed to be the ancient "palace area" (fig. 19.2). In this area as large as two soccer fields, he excavated several large trenches in the summer of 1949. Based on archaeological observations and drawing on statements in the Persian, Chinese, and European historical texts, Kiselev advanced his "palace hypothesis" concluding that the larger and more elevated central building in this area must have been the palace of the Great Khan.[7]

After Kiselev's breakthrough, imperial Khara Khorum lay untouched for more than fifty years. In 2001, at the invitation of the Mongolian government, a team from the German Archaeological Institute in collaboration with Mongolian archaeologists began to reexamine the "palace hypothesis." Our results have pro-

19.4 Kiselev's "Palace" Redefined
In 2004 archaeologists reopened the area where Sergei Kiselev in 1949 thought the Khan's palace would be found. Instead of palace materials and remains of the famous Guillaume Boucher "silver tree" beverage fountain described by William of Rubruck in 1254, the finds proved to be the foundation and central hall of an early 13th-century Buddhist temple.

19.5 Votive *Tsha-Tsha*
Among the finds recovered from the so-called khan's palace were masses of *tsha-tsha*, tiny molded clay stupas and figures of the Buddha. These objects connected with Tibetan Buddhist ritual served to ward off evil and provide good fortune and add evidence that the site was a Buddhist temple, not a palace.

19.6 Temple Frescos
Many fragments of painted wall frescos were found in the temple courtyard. Visitors in the 13th century reported that artisans from all corners of the Mongol empire were brought to the city to build and decorate its temples and palace and develop industries and fine arts.

vided a very different perspective on this sector of the imperial city. Nearly all of our stratigraphic observations, as well as most of the artifacts found in the "palace" area, contradict Kiselev's contentions. The stratigraphy of the palace area is much more complex than originally interpreted (fig. 19.4). About 90 percent of our discoveries, as well as most of the interior architectural features of the "palace-level" strata, belongs to a Buddhist inventory that is very different from that used in the construction of Erdene Zuu monastery. The stratigraphical evidence as well as the dating of the Buddhist antiquities places this area of the site between the twelfth and fourteenth centuries and proves that Kiselev's so-called palace sector in fact holds the ruins of a Buddhist temple contemporary with the imperial city of Khara Khorum (fig. 19.5).

All of the ceramics and wall painting fragments (fig. 19.6) found by Kiselev and by the Mongolian–German expedition display features of the "International style" of the twelfth to fourteenth centuries that incorporates Indo-Nepalese, Tibetan, Tanghut, and Chinese elements. Our stylistic chronology is confirmed by dates of Chinese and local ceramics associated with the Buddhist antiquities (fig. 19.9). We found no Chinese pottery in the structure dating later than the second third of the fourteenth century. The stylistic and typological data are also consistent, with two different kinds of laboratory dating (radiocarbon and thermo-luminescence analyses) pointing to a date at the beginning of the thirteenth century. All of these data confirm that the great hall unearthed in the palace area was in fact the central hall of a Buddhist temple of the early thirteenth century.

These results suggest we have found the "Temple of the Rising Yuan" commemorated in the inscribed stone of 1346 or at least a very large temple of the same type. One fragment of this important Khara Khorum inscription was discovered a few meters from the large granite sculpture of a tortoise standing in front of the excavated temple, while other fragments of this inscription had been reused as building material in Erdene Zuu monastery. According to this inscription, the temple hall, its roof, and the great stupa inside were completed in 1256. The temple hall is described as having seven open chambers on each side, which suggests that the temple must have been a quadrangular construction of eight by eight

19.7 Erdene Zuu Stratigraphy
A trench cut in 2005 into the outer side of Erdene Zuu's north wall revealed a buried wall made of bricks identical to those found in the early 13th-century temple. More importantly, stamped marks on bricks indicated their use in palace construction.

19.8 Beneath Erdene Zuu, Palace of the Khan
Identification of the temple renewed interest in earlier suggestions by Wilhelm Radloff that the khan's palace was beneath Erdene Zuu.

gular construction of eight by eight columns, corresponding exactly to the ground-plan of our excavated hall. The inscription explains that the temple was restored between 1342 and 1346, which occasioned the commission of the inscribed stone.[8] These dates match the archaeological evidence for a reconstruction of the hall around 1340.

19.9 Porcelain Dragon Bowl
This early 13th-century blue-and-white bowl with an elaborate dragon motif, which was found in the temple, is a glazed ceramic known as Qingbai ware. This highly prestigious class of porcelain with pale blue underglaze decoration, produced in Song and Yuan periods in China, was a popular commodity in Khara Khorum, as it was elsewhere in Asia.

Unfortunately, by identifying Kiselev's palace as a Buddhist temple we are left once again with the original problem of locating the palace of the Great Khan. The Persian sources describe the palace sub-sector as a walled area with four main gates oriented in cardinal directions. All written sources indicate that the palace was situated outside the city proper, but near or beside the city wall, and was known to have had an artificial river flowing through it. The only construction in the vicinity matching these features is Erdene Zuu monastery itself.

Reconsidering Wilhelm Radloff's original and mostly forgotten hypothesis that Erdene Zuu was constructed above the Khan's palace of Khara Khorum, we excavated six trenches into the monastery's foundation walls (fig. 19.8). Here, we discovered the bases of much earlier 8-meter-thick walls of mud brick with masonry facing (fig. 19.7). Recognizable stamps on the bricks indicate they were made as part of a palace construction. The bricks facing the clay walls are similar to the

bricks of the great Buddhist temple hall, and both brick types have been dated by thermo-luminescence analysis to the early thirteenth century. This result is also confirmed by radiocarbon dates and by the pottery found in the wall excavations. Based on the evidence available so far, the walls discovered below Erdene Zuu were constructed in the early thirteenth century and most probably surrounded what Marco Polo described as the mighty castle or palace city near Khara Khorum, which was indeed the palace of Ögödei and Möngke Khaghan.

1. Cordier 1893.
2. Juvaini 1958.
3. Juvaini 1958.
4. Juvaini 1958.
5. Paderin 1874
6. Pozdneyev 1997.
7. Kiselev 1965
8. Cleaves 1952; Sagaster 2005, 150–52.

20. John of Plano Carpini and William of Rubruck

DAVID MORGAN

POPE INNOCENT IV was elected in 1243, in the immediate aftermath of the Mongol invasion of eastern Europe. He convened a church council at Lyons, which met in 1245. The menace of the Mongols was inevitably on the council's agenda; no one then knew that the Mongols would not return to invade the rest of Europe. Pope Innocent was so concerned that, even before the council met, he had dispatched three separate embassies to Mongol-held territory. Of these, the best known and most momentous was that headed by the Franciscan friar John of Plano Carpini (1180–1252).

Carpini traveled through the devastated lands of eastern Europe, eventually arriving at the camp of Batu, khan of the newly established Golden Horde. He had expected to hand over the Pope's letter and then return home, but Batu decreed that Carpini should go on to Mongolia, to the court of the Great Khan. After a long and arduous journey, he arrived in time to witness the enthronement in 1245 of Güyüg.

The letter that Carpini brought back to the Pope (see Chapter 1) was characteristically uncompromising. The Great Khan professed not to understand Innocent's complaints about Mongol destruction and massacre, and ordered him, together with the kings of Europe, to proceed to Mongolia forthwith, to offer their submission (fig. 20.2).

20.1 William of Rubruck
This illumination appears in a manuscript copy of William of Rubruck's *Itinerarium*, an account of his trip to Mongolia in 1253–55, which included a six-month visit at the court of Möngke Khaghan in Khara Khorum in 1254. The top panel shows Friar William and his companion meeting with King Louis IX of France, who was residing in Acre leading a crusade against Egypt. The lower panel depicts the two friars on their journey.

This letter[1] is among the first unequivocal pieces of evidence for the Mongol view of the world: that, by divine commission, the world and the Mongol empire were identical. Carpini followed much the same route back, and was received on his return to Europe with extraordinary interest. His journey to report to the Council at Lyons was something like a lecture tour.

Several accounts of the embassy have survived. The most important is Carpini's own report, called *Ystoria Mongolorum*,[2] which provided a systematic account of what he had learned about the Mongols, their history, their military organization, and—potentially, most important of all—a series of recommendations about how the Mongols might best be resisted.

William of Rubruck was, like Carpini, a Franciscan friar. But unlike him, he was not an officially accredited ambassador. Rubruck went to Mongolia at his own initiative, though he reported to King Louis IX of France (fig. 20.1). Louis's earlier contacts with the Mongols had not encouraged him to believe that they were truthful or reliable, so he withheld the title of ambassador from Rubruck, who was always careful to emphasize this lack of status (whether the Mongols believed him is another matter). Instead, he traveled as a missionary, in the first instance to minister to some German Christians who had been captured during the invasion of 1241 and deported to Central Asia.

The early stages of Rubruck's journey were different from Carpini's. He left in 1253 from Acre, capital of what was left of the crusader kingdom of Jerusalem, where King Louis was residing at the time. He then went to the Crimea by way of Constantinople, on to the court of Batu's son, Sartaq, who sent him to Batu, who sent him on to Mongolia as he had Carpini some years previously. By now, the political situation in the Mongol empire was very different from when Carpini had visited: in 1251, Batu's cousin and ally

Möngke had seized the throne. Rubruck met him at the Mongol capital, Khara Khorum, which by this time had been transformed from a camp to a small city. He remained at court for around six months. He was not much impressed with the capital of the world's largest empire, which he compared unfavorably with St. Denis, north of Paris (see Chapter 18). But he found many people of interest there, notably, a Parisian goldsmith, Guillaume Boucher, who had constructed a drink fountain of gold and silver for the Great Khan. He also encountered many local Christians. But these were Nestorians, heretics from Rubruck's Roman standpoint, and he formed a very dim view of their characters and attainments. Some of them participated, at Möngke's instigation, in a religious debate in his presence, between Christians, Muslims, and Buddhists. The various monotheists ganged up against the Buddhists, with Rubruck as their spokesman. Rubruck was the debate's runaway winner. Or so he says.

Rubruck returned, bringing with him a letter from the Great Khan to King Louis. This has not survived, but to judge from Rubruck's own account of its contents, it was rather less harsh in tone than Güyüg's letter to Innocent IV had been. He did not receive anything approaching the reception with which Carpini had been greeted; the Mongol menace had receded a little, Rubruck was not an ambassador, and, in any case, he reported to King Louis in Acre, out of Europe's mainstream. He did write an account of his journey, the *Itinerarium*,[3] which never achieved the celebrity of Carpini's *Ystoria*. Four independent manuscripts of it have survived, and they are all in England, perhaps because Roger Bacon, the English Franciscan polymath, knew Rubruck and incorporated some of his information in his *Opus Maius* of around 1258.

It is very fortunate that the *Itinerarium* did survive; it is almost twice as long as Carpini's *Ystoria*, and in the judgment of many, a good deal more than twice as interesting and valuable as a contemporary source on the Mongol empire at its height. Carpini's account is a period piece which reflects faithfully the concerns, even the panic, which Europe's initial uncomprehending contacts with the Mongols had inspired. Rubruck's book is much more a straightforward travel narrative. It is full of fascinating detail, and is the work of the most perceptive and penetrating of all the European travelers who have left us their impressions of Asia under Mongol domination.

20.2 Güyüg's Letter to Innocent IV
One of the most interesting Mongolian documents to survive is this letter of 1246 from Güyüg Khaghan to Pope Innocent IV (see Chapter 1). Bearing Güyüg's personal seal, it is written in Persian and responds to a letter from the Pope that had been delivered by John of Plano Carpini. The khan, who had just been enthroned and was relatively tolerant of Christians, chastizes the Pope for complaining about Mongol attacks in Europe and demanding that the khan convert to Christianity. Güyüg closes with: "Thou thyself, at the head of all the Princes, come at once to serve and wait upon us! At that time I shall recognize your submission. If you do not observe God's command, and if you ignore my command, I shall know you as my enemy. Likewise I shall make you understand. If you do otherwise, God knows what I know."[4]

1. Tr. in De Rachewiltz 1971, 213–14.
2. Tr. in Dawson 1955.
3. Tr. in Dawson 1955; Rubrick 1990.
4. Dawson, 1955, 86.

21.1 Twin Stupas of Baisikou
These twin towers are all
that remain of the large royal
cloister nestled in the Alashan
foothills at Baisikou, about 50
km northwest of the former
Tanghut capital.

21. Xi Xia

THE FIRST MONGOL CONQUEST

Ruth W. Dunnell

In August 1227, after a long campaign led by Genghis Khan, the Mongols celebrated their first victory over a non-Mongol state in East Asia. The victory, however, had a bitter coda for both sides. While the Tanghuts, or Xi (western) Xia, as they are called in later Chinese records, suffered devastation of their long-resisting capital and its environs, the Mongols lost their revered leader, who died around the time of the surrender (fig. 21.2). Much of the material record of Xia civilization disappeared in the carnage of the prolonged Mongol campaign. Yet, from bits and pieces of the rubble recovered over the past one hundred years, scholars have begun to reconstruct the contours of a creative and devoutly Buddhist culture.

Xia on the Eve of Mongol Expansion

Xi Xia refers to a state in the northwest of present-day China that was founded in the early eleventh century by people who had migrated during the Tang dynasty (618–907) from the eastern Tibetan plateau into the modern province of Gansu. Western writers call the people Tanghuts (the Türk version of their ethnonym). The Tanghuts, in turn, named their state the Great White High State of Xia (1038–1227). Its meaning eludes us, but perhaps it invoked the snow-clad mountains, extolled in Tanghut literature, of Gansu and northeastern Qinghai, their ancestral homeland.[1] Mostly consisting of elevated plateau, deserts, mountains, and a few arable river valleys, the land was dry and windy, the temperatures extreme, and rainfall and vegetation were scarce, though not as scarce as today. Snowmelt from the mountains that fed rivers and springs was the crucial resource that made life and civilization possible.

A multiethnic, multilingual state with a mixed economy based on herding, agriculture, and trade, Xia was home to hardy people of Chinese, Türk, and Tibetan, as well as Tanghut, origin, all of whom later writers subsume under the label "Tanghut." Though small in size compared to its East Asian neighbors, Xia marshaled sufficient military prowess to command respect and guard its independence. At home the Tanghuts displayed their own Chinese-style sovereignty, while abroad they acknowledged tributary status to the Song (960–1127) and the Liao (907–1125), a north Asian steppe empire founded by Khitans, a proto-Mongolian federation, in the eleventh century. In the twelfth century, the Tanghuts accepted a subsidiary relationship to the Jurchen Jin state (1115–1235), which served them well when the Jurchens overthrew the Liao and took over all of North China from the Song dynasty, with which the Tanghut had warred for over a century. Cut off from the Song, which had regrouped

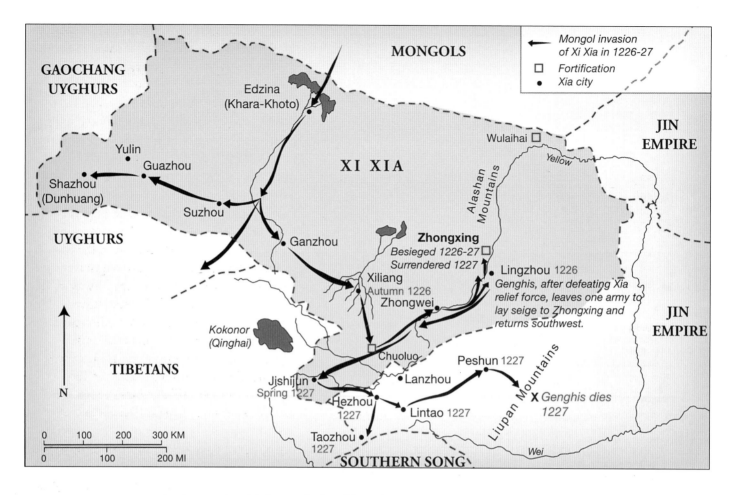

MONGOLS

GAOCHANG UYGHURS

Edzina (Khara-Khoto)

Yulin
Guazhou
Shazhou (Dunhuang)
Suzhou

UYGHURS

XI XIA

Wulaihai

Yellow

JIN EMPIRE

Alashan Mountains

Zhongxing
Besieged 1226-27
Surrendered 1227

Xiliang
Autumn 1226
Zhongwei

Ganzhou

Lingzhou 1226
Genghis, after defeating Xia relief force, leaves one army to lay seige to Zhongxing and returns southwest.

JIN EMPIRE

Kokonor (Qinghai)

TIBETANS

Chuoluo

Peshun 1227

Liupan Mountains

N

Jishijun
Spring 1227
Hezhou
1227

Lanzhou

Lintao 1227

X Genghis dies 1227

Taozhou
1227

Wei

SOUTHERN SONG

0   100   200   300 KM
0   100   200 MI

Mongol invasion of Xi Xia in 1226-27
□ Fortification
• Xia city

21.2 Map of Xi Xia, 1226–27
This map illustrates Genghis Khan's second campaign against the Tanghuts of Western Xia, which coincided with his death in 1227.

in the south with its capital at Hangzhou (1127–1279), the Tanghuts entered an age of peace and cultural efflorescence.

Although heavily indebted to Chinese models, the Tanghuts carved out a unique identity, symbolized in the complex script they invented to write their Tibeto-Burman language. Numerous books and manuscripts in Tanghut and Chinese have survived, but unfortunately none of them is an historical chronicle. In the early twentieth century, Russian explorers unearthed a vast library in a Buddhist stupa buried in the sands of Khara-Khoto, along the Sino-Mongolian border (fig. 21.3). The books, manuscripts, drawings, religious objects, and paintings found there are today housed in St. Petersburg.[2] Khara-Khoto also yielded items of Yuan origin, indicating continuous occupation of this border fortress. Smaller-scale finds in Ningxia, Gansu, and Inner Mongolia continue to augment the archive of Xia culture, an archive predominantly Buddhist in content.[3] These finds include the world's earliest extant texts printed with moveable type, which was invented in

China in the eleventh century (fig. 21.7).[4]

Glimpses of the Xia royal court—in woodblock-printed illustrations to Buddhist texts and in donor portraits set in the lower corners of Buddhist paintings illuminate the throne's and its courtiers' involvement in devotional projects (fig. 21.5). From its beginnings, the Tanghut dynastic clan made Buddhism a foundation of the state,[5] devoting scarce resources to temple construction, repair, and staffing, and to translating texts from Chinese and Tibetan into Tanghut and Chinese (fig. 21.6).[6] Such largesse spread the reputation of the Xia monarch as a saintly Buddhist king, a "dharma lord" in Tibetan sources, and a "burhkan-khan" (Buddha-king) to the Uyghurs and Mongols.[7]

Beyond the capital region, the stark rocky landscape was studded with Buddhist monasteries and shrines (fig. 21.1). Among them, the famous cave temples at Dunhuang and Yulin, which date from the fourth century, preserve in murals the artistic genius of Tanghut culture and its contributions to Chinese temple art.[8] Devotion to religion permeated all levels of

21.3 Khara-Khoto Fortress
This photograph, taken during a 1908 Russian expedition led by P.K. Kozlov, shows the ruins of the walls and stupas of Khara-Khoto, the "Black City." This complex was a Tanghut city located near today's Eljin Banner, Alxa League, Inner Mongolia. After its conquest by the Mongols it took on the name, Edzina. Khara-Khoto was one of the first cities attacked by Genghis in the 1226-27 campaign. Once an irrigated land, the region was ravaged by Mongols and was later subsumed by dunes.

21.4 Tanghut Royal Cemetery Complex
The ruins of the 12th-13th century Tanghut royal cemetery stand out clearly in the desert lands near modern Yinchuan City, in China's Ningxia Hui Autonomous Region. The cemetery includes nine royal tomb complexes and two hundred other burial features. Each tomb, like the two shown in this aerial view, had rectangular walled enclosures that once contained decorated buildings, gates, engraved steles, and watchtowers. An ornate pyramidal mound at the center of each enclosure marked the site of the burial chamber. Although plundered by Genghis Khan's troops, and many others over the centuries, the ruins are a vivid reminder of the advanced architecture and artistic achievements of this strongly religious Buddhist kingdom.

this highly stratified society. In a natural environment so seemingly ill-endowed to the manufacture of fine books, the karmic merit accrued through reproducing religious texts ensured a steady supply of customers, copiers, engravers, and the refinement of production technologies from the materials at hand.[9] Ownership of books and manuscripts conferred social and religious power, which was channeled through monasteries and temples, the repositories of most books. Close ties with local monasteries enabled even those of modest means to advance their religious practice, be it through group sponsorship of a text or a ritual service.

All these streams met in the royal cemetery, where today ruins with nine imperial tombs and some 200 smaller satellite tombs occupy 10 square kilometers in the Alashan foothills west of the capital.[10] Each rectangular walled park encloses an elaborate layout of lavishly adorned buildings, halls, formal gates, and watchtowers. Ten meters north of the underground burial chamber, one majestic pyramid-shaped mound, evocative of Buddhist stupas (shrines for the relics of the Buddha), marks each imperial tomb. Remains of kilns and a compound for tomb priests and guardians lie to the east and north of the cemetery. Mongol armies and later grave robbers stripped away most of the structures and their decorations, smashed the steles inscribed in Chinese and Tanghut eulogizing the deceased emperors, and plundered many burial chambers. Yet the dignity and domesticity of Tanghut sovereignty still suffuses the vestiges of this once-sacred space (figs. 21.9, 10).

Tanghuts: The First Mongol Conquest in East Asia

In the 1170s, the political landscape of East Asia showed few signs of the profound transformations soon to overwhelm it. The currents that brought Genghis Khan to power in north Asia rippled throughout the subcontinent, washing refugees up on the shores of civilizations south of Mongolia.[11] Early portents

21.5 Portrait of a Monk
This fragment of a 12th–13th century tanka, a Tibetan-style painting on cotton, was found at Khara-Khoto. Depicted in the lower corners are a monk, honored by the donors, who are also seen, dressed in the opulent garb and hairstyle of the Tanghut aristocracy.

reached Xia and Central Asia in the form of nomad aristocrats driven out of the Mongolian plateau by rival contenders to power. The winds of change reached Jin and Song as rumors of plots against those courts by schemers colluding with the Kara-Khitai, a Khitan state in Central Asia established by royal remnants of the fallen Liao dynasty. Suspicion that the Tanghuts were spying at the border figured in the Jin closure of several frontier markets with the Xia, which severely restricted Tanghut access to prized Chinese goods.[12]

These tremors echoed clan struggles over the Kereyid throne in central Mongolia that impinged so closely on the fortunes of the future Genghis Khan. Disinherited

Kereyid princes sought shelter among the Kara-Khitai and Xia. One of these refugees, Toghril (or Ong Khan, a title he earned from the Jin), had been restored to his throne with help from Temüjin's father and later became Temüjin's senior ally. His rivals, taking their turns in exile, cultivated ties in Xia governing circles. One, Toghril's younger brother, gave a daughter in marriage to the Tanghut emperor.[13]

After Temüjin defeated and absorbed his Kereyid allies in 1203, the flight of the Kereyid crown prince into northeastern Tibet, abutting Tanghut territory, opened Xia to direct probing by an expansive Mongol power. In early spring of 1205, a Mongol raiding party plundered some western Xia forts and drove off cattle and camels. Its aftershocks may have figured in the 1206 coup that put a new ruler on the Xia throne, the first but not last usurpation of Xia history. The formalization of Mongol unity under Genghis Khan in 1205–1206 heightened tensions both within and among the East Asian states of Xia, Jin, and Song, exposing the fault lines of their triangular division of power to Mongol plucking.

In winter of 1207, Mongol cavalry targeted the northern Xia outpost of Wulahai, on the edge of the Gobi near the Jin frontier, withdrawing early in 1208 with more camels. The Xia turned to the Jin court, seeking support against a common adversary. Harried by a brief but disastrous war with the Song, by defections to the Mongols in 1207 of tribal groups serving as border wardens, and by food shortages owing to flood and drought, the Jin snubbed the proffered alliance against their underrated outer vassal.[14] A new Jin emperor of disputed legitimacy supposedly opined, at the end of 1208, "It is to our advantage when our enemies attack each other. Wherein lies the danger to us?"[15] Long-standing relations between the courts of Xia and Jin rapidly crumbled. Taking advantage of this disarray, Genghis launched the first real test of Xia intentions.

In winter of 1209, Genghis's armies seized the border fort at Wulahai; then the invaders pressed south to lay siege to the capital, defeating several armies along the way. Having, as yet, little experience with

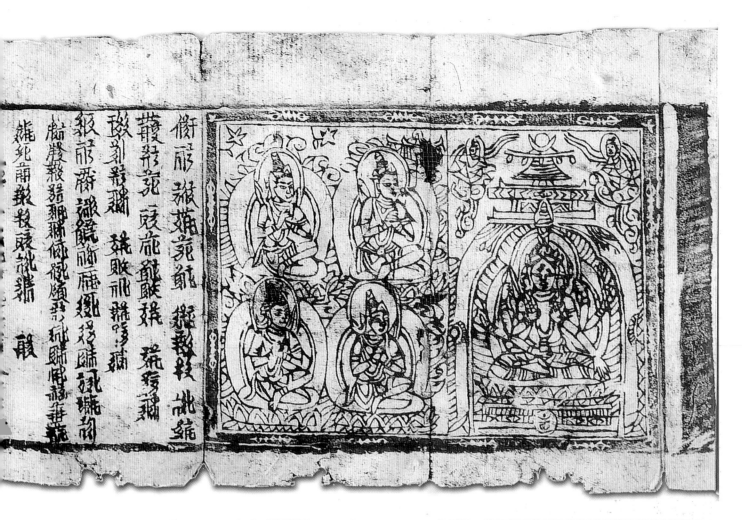

21.6 Buddhist Ritual Text

This sheet is one of nine surviving pages from a late 12th-century Buddhist ritual text from Khara-Khoto, printed in Tanghut script and accompanied by engraved illustrations. The engraving depicts an eight-armed Ushnishavijaya (the embodiment of a powerful *dharani,* or incantation), a popular cult figure in Xia, with a stupa over her head, and four figures in two rows to her right side. Depictions of Ushnishavijaya are rare in East Asian Buddhist art; her image also appears in cave murals at Yulin (Anxi, Gansu), suggesting court sponsorship of her cult.

21.7 Moveable Type Printing

The Tanghuts were a learned society who used moveable clay type to produce publications like this late 12th-century translation of a Tibetan version of the *Samputa tantra*. This document in the Tanghut language was found in the ruins of the square stupa at Baisigou, in the Alashan, about 50 kilometers northwest of the Xia capital at present-day Yinchuan.

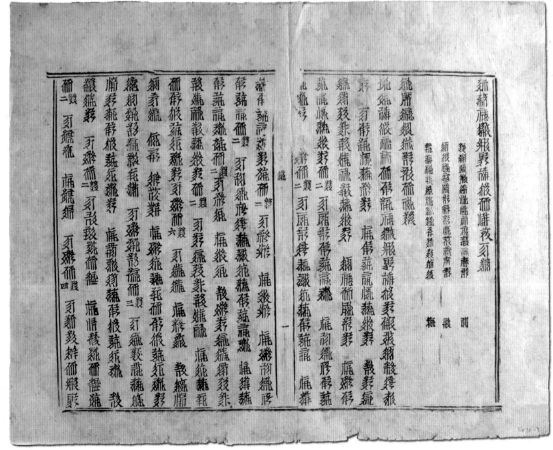

21.8 Gold Bowl
This lovely bowl with its rolled rim and engraved flower-and-scroll decorations closely resembles designs on Yuan silver and gold cups and bowls, but it is attributed to the Xi Xia period.

walled fortifications, the Mongols could not breach the city's defenses. Instead, they diverted the Yellow River canals nearby to flood it, but when the dikes broke, inundating their own camps, they had to withdraw. First, however, Genghis sent a Wulahai captive into the city to negotiate. The panicked ruler tendered his allegiance and a daughter to Genghis Khan, along with much livestock and goods.

The Secret History of the Mongols recounts the Tanghut emperor's offer, although not the campaign, perhaps because of its inglorious conclusion. Styled "Burkhan-khan" (the Uyghur word for "Buddha" [*Burkhan*] elided with the steppe royal title), the Xia ruler mentioned above promises Genghis, "[w]e shall become your right wing and we shall serve you." But he warns that because the Tanghuts live in permanent camps and walled towns, when the Mongols go to combat, "We won't be able to rush off and fight beside you. But if Chinggis Khan will spare us, we Tanghut will give him the camels we raise… We'll give him the woolen clothing and satins we weave. We'll give him the best of the birds we've trained for the hunt."[16] Evidently, the Tanghuts hoped to minimize their commitment, promising provisions rather than manpower. With Wulahai now neutralized, the Mongols secured their rear flank and an open route to North China.

A three-sided war ensued between the Xia, Jin, and Mongols. In 1211, the Mongols launched a reconnaissance campaign against the Jin; another coup in the Tanghut capital brought a learned prince to the throne at a time when no good choices remained. The Tanghuts' promised role as "right wing" to the Mongols materialized only opportunistically, after Mongol operations against the Jin opened in earnest from 1212. Tensions arose again when the Xia rebuffed a Mongol demand for troops to support their Central Asian campaign (1219–23). *The Secret History* puts "haughty words" in the mouth of a certain Asha Gambu, a powerful court minister, who during the interview with Genghis's envoy (late in 1217) rudely asks why the khan comes begging help if he thinks he's so mighty?[17] Genghis departed westward in 1219, vowing to deal with the Tanghuts later. Compounding their earlier defiance, the Tanghuts refused to send a hostage son to serve in Genghis's guard, as Mongol custom required.[18]

21.9 Copper Cow
This large bronze cow was found in the ruins of the royal Tanghut cemetery at Khara Khoto, apparently too sturdy to be carted off by thieves or destroyed by marauding armies. Animals important to the pastoral economy of the Tanghuts often accompanied their royal masters to the afterlife.

21.10 Stone Horse
Like the cow, this sculpture of a resting horse was recovered from the ruins of the royal Tanghut cemetery of Khara-Khoto.

his death was carefully concealed. Following his final instructions, the Mongols sacked Zhongxing, slaughtered the remaining population, and ravaged the royal Buddhist tomb complex west of the capital (fig. 21.4). With the execution of the surrendered monarch, both the Xia dynasty and state ended. The extreme carnage of this last battle may have been intended to tame and tap the religious potency of the Xia royal house, thereby to provide the khan "a suitable escort in the afterlife,"[20] suitable in the sense of noble and (once) powerful.

Despite the devastation of their civilization, the surviving Tanghut people were to influence Asian culture for centuries. When it came time to govern the vast domain that Mongol-led armies had wrested from the Chinese, many Tanghuts who had entered imperial Mongol service, before and after 1227, made distinguished careers as privileged members of the new ruling elite, well prepared by their cultural and linguistic versatility, and background as synthesizers of diverse traditions, Chinese, Tibetan, and steppe. Moreover, emerging forms of tantric Buddhism being developed by Tanghut and Tibetan lamas in the twelfth and thirteenth centuries passed into the purvey of their new patrons, the Mongol rulers of China, and became a prominent feature of the Yuan dynasty's imperial landscape.

Mongol armies invaded in the spring of 1226 and reduced the northern and western garrisons of the Xia one by one (fig. 21.2). Summering in a mountain retreat, the khan directed military operations. After early resistance and the slaughter that inevitably followed, cities and towns began surrendering as the invaders worked their way south and east to conquer districts along the Xia–Jin border.[19] Genghis, by this time very ill, was camped in the Liupan Mountains of southeastern Ningxia, from which his generals oversaw the six-month siege of Zhongxing, the Xia capital. By the time the Tanghut king capitulated in summer of 1227, Genghis had perhaps already succumbed, although

1. Kychanov 1997, 30–37.
2. Piotrovsky 1993; Kychanov 1999; Samosiuk 2006.
3. Lei et al. 1995.
4. Shi and Yasen 2000.
5. Shi 1993; Dunnell 1996.
6. Lei et al. 1995, 76–101, 250.
7. Dunnell 1992, 94–95; Kahn 1998, 162.
8. Liu Yuquan 2002.
9. Kychanov 1998.
10. Xu and Du 1995.
11. Dunnell 1991; 1994.
12. Tuotuo et al. 1975, vol. 50, 1114.
13. Dunnell 1994, 206.
14. Buell 1979b.
15. Yuwen Maochao 1986, vol. 21, 23–24.
16. Kahn 1998, 149.
17. Kahn 1998, 157.
18. Song et al. 1976, vol. 1, 23.
19. Dunnell 1994, 211–13.
20. De Rachewiltz 2004, 975–77.

ساعة فاظهر بها آثار العدل والانصاف بين ... في رعاية الرعية وايالة البلاد و
... الخلاف ... اعمادها وتقرضوا جدار البلاد، وعرضوا العضهم للعطا، ف
... ان ... احكام نوابه نع ملك الاعمال نو... الى الاسقاص ... الحيث ...
... تحت ظل رايته ... من ... ناصر الدين وابت...ناش الحاجب، وابو عبد ...
... قتالهم نوم الجمعة منتصف ذي الحجة سنة ثلث وتسعين وثلثمائة وبعد ساعة من الجاربة

الى غزنة وترك فتحا الحلب الذي كان من ثقات دوك هناك
جماعة من رجوم الفساد ونجوم العناد نقصيان السلطان وسلق
السفا، لما حصل لهم من بطن الرفاهية وشيطنه العصبية فلما عرف
اولئك المدا بمشى إلى بجستان سبع عشرة الاف فارس وكان
الطائى زعيم العرب نحاصرهم واولئك المردة فى قلعه ارك وشرء

PART III

THE
MONGOLIAN
WESTERN
EMPIRE

< Previous Pages Mongols Besiege a Walled City

This detail from Rashid al-Din's *Jami'al-Tavarikh* (Compendium of Chronicles, 1309) was used to illustrate an historic battle that took place in Sijistan in 1003. The illustration is anachronistic in that it uses a familiar scene from al-Din's time showing Mongol troops, catapults, and engineers to illustrate this earlier event. Mongols, at first unfamiliar with siege tactics against fortified targets, recruited Chinese and Iranian experts and utilized their technology, including ceramic bombs and catapults. The painting also shows the black standard, the Mongol signal for a declaration of war.

22.1 Mausoleum of Ilkhan Öljeitü, Sultaniyeh

In addition to supporting the arts, the Ilkhanids were great builders. The lavishly decorated Ilkhanid summer palace at Takht-i Sulaiman (ca. 1275) is a masterful example of secular architecture. The mausoleum built for Öljeitü at Sultaniyeh in 1307–13, seen here, is the architectural masterpiece of the period. This view of an interior bay shows stucco painted with intricate patterns suggesting mosaics.

MORGAN

22. The Mongolian Western Empire

DAVID MORGAN

BY THE TIME OF THE *KHURILTAI* (CONGRESS) of 1206, at which Genghis Khan was proclaimed supreme ruler of the Mongols, what may well have been the most difficult part of his career had been successfully concluded. There were still some loose ends to tie up, but Genghis's dominance in Mongolia was now unchallenged.

Historians have long and inconclusively debated whether or not Genghis and his followers were, from the very beginning, convinced that they had a divine commission to conquer the world. If they did not originally suppose themselves to be the rightful universal rulers, they soon came round to that opinion when they found that they were on their way. What was certain was that expansion beyond Mongolia was inevitable. Genghis had unified a collection of Mongol and Türkic tribes that previously had been constantly at odds with each other. If their military energies were not directed outward, they would soon be directed inward again, and the new confederation would prove as short-lived as many of its steppe predecessors.

The first targets for raids and, in due course, permanent conquest were the realms of the Xi Xia (Tanghut peoples) and Jin (Jurchen peoples) in North China; Central Asia and the lands to the west had to wait their turn. There were two major empires that would eventually succumb to Genghis's armies: Kara-Khitai and the empire of the Khwarazm-shah.

Kara-Khitai was a large and amorphous state, occupying a vast territory in Central Asia. It had been founded by an exiled prince of the Khitan Liao dynasty, which had been evicted from North China by the Jin from Manchuria in the early twelfth century.[1] The Khitans, ethnically and, so far as their tongue is understood, linguistically, seem to have been related to the Mongols. They were Buddhist, but did not insist on any religious uniformity in their empire: many of their subjects were Muslims, and some were Christians. On their western frontier they had had as a vassal the Khwarazm-shah.[2] Khwarazm is the fertile province in the area where the Amu-Darya River flows into the Aral Sea. Its ruler had originally been the governor appointed by the Seljuk rulers of much of the eastern Islamic world. Seljuk rule had collapsed after the death of Sultan Sanjar in 1157, and the governor of Khwarazm, taking the ancient local title of Khwarazm-shah, was able to assert his independence and establish himself along with his heirs as the principal successors to the Seljuks in the east. Under Ala' al-Din Muhammad, who came to the throne in 1200, the Khwarazmians put together, in a matter of a few years, an enormous if unstable empire that included much of the territory of modern Iran and Afghanistan, as well as throwing off their vassalage to the Kara-Khitai. Ala' al-Din Muhammad was thus

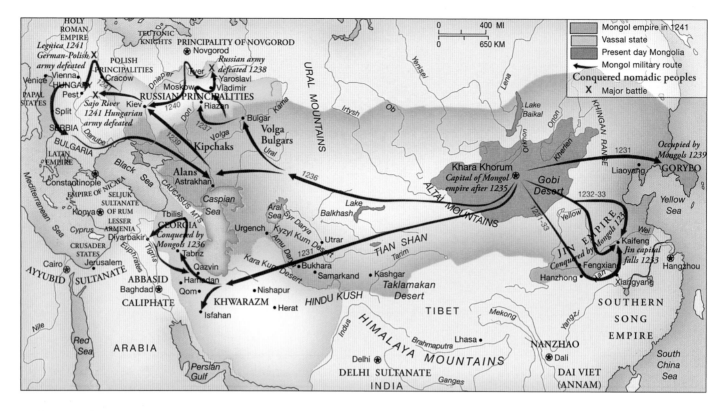

22.2 The Mongol Empire in 1241

Ögödei, Genghis's chosen successor, pursued his father's quest of world dominion by expanding the empire into western Asia, Russia, and Eastern Europe, as well as northern China. After 1235 he abandoned field campaigns and guided the empire from the newly founded Mongol capital in Khara Khorum. His death in 1241 stayed the planned Mongol campaign on western Europe; subsequent khans turned their attention to attacking the Muslim world and Song China.

able to establish his capital at Samarkand.

One of the loose ends of 1206 was the Naiman prince Güchlüg who, after his people had been conclusively defeated by Genghis Khan, had fled westward and had taken refuge with the Kara-Khitai. Here he was hospitably received, an act of generosity that he rewarded by overthrowing the ruler and seizing power. He proved to be an oppressive monarch, not at all in line with Kara-Khitai tradition. He had been converted to Buddhism, apparently in an unusually aggressive form, and proceeded to require his subjects to adopt either that faith or Nestorian Christianity. He attempted to close his kingdom's mosques.

All this did not escape the notice of the Mongols, many of whose victories owed as much to accurate intelligence as to military competence. In 1218, a fairly small Mongol force crossed into Kara-Khitai, reopening the mosques as it went. The population rose against Güchlüg, and the Mongols achieved an easy conquest (see Chapter 11, fig. 11.2); it would appear that a substantial part of Asia joined the Mongol empire by the will of its people.

Genghis Khan may have had no wish to confront the Khwarazm-shah at this stage because he had enough to deal with in China at the time. But his hand was forced when a caravan of merchants from Mongolia was intercepted at the Khwarazmian frontier city of Utrar; its governor killed the merchants and seized their goods. Genghis sent three ambassadors to the shah to demand recompense and retribution for the governor. Muhammad executed the chief envoy and sent his colleagues back to Mongolia with their beards shaved off—a serious insult. The Mongols, throughout their expansion and after, took a particularly strong view regarding the inviolability of ambassadors, especially their own. After such treatment, war was inevitable.

The campaign that followed, between 1219 and 1223, visited colossal death and destruction on much of the eastern Islamic world.[3] In recent years, historical study of the Mongol empire has tended, much more than ever before, to stress the positive features of Mongol rule—and rightly so. But that is no reason for attempting to play down the horrors of such campaigns of initial conquest as this one. Contemporary chroniclers quote enormous figures, both for the massacres inflicted by the Mongols, and for the size of their armies. Such figures should not be taken literally: it would not have been possible to accom-

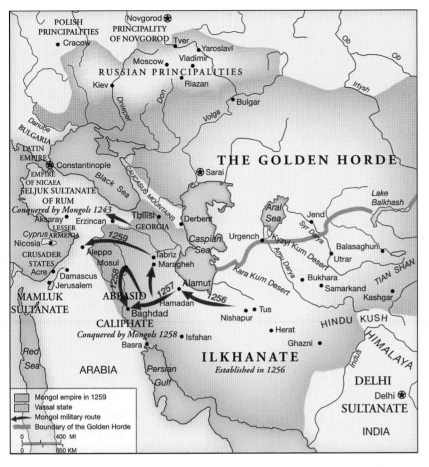

The Golden Horde map showing Mongol empire in 1259

22.3 Western Asia Campaigns
During the early campaigns in western Asia Mongols pushed across the steppes into southern Russia, pursuing rival nomadic groups, especially the Türkic Kipchaks, known in the western steppe as Cumans and in Russia as Polovtsi. After the ascension of Güyüg in 1246, the western Mongol armies turned away from Europe and toward Iran, Turkey, and the Near East, waging a series of campaigns that devastated the Muslim population and the region's cities, institutions, and cultural treasures. These campaigns ended soon after the establishment of the Mongol-led Ilkhanate in 1256, which remained in power until 1335.

modate 2,400,000 people in the city of Herat (in modern Afghanistan), which is what one observer, Juzjani, tells us was the body count when the Mongols took the city. Nor should his figure for Genghis's army—800,000—be received credulously. But that intelligent contemporaries made these estimates indicates the pervasive sense of shock. Nothing comparable to the Mongol invasion had ever happened in the experience or the historical memory of those who bore the brunt of its impact.[4] This was, after all, both a punitive expedition and an attempt—a highly successful one—to destroy a major power, which might otherwise have proved a dangerous rival to the rising Mongol imperium. Over several years, mostly under the direction of Genghis's youngest son Tolui, much of eastern Iran was comprehensively wrecked. The great and historic Persian cities, the capitals of the four quarters of the province of Khurasan—Marv, Balkh, Nishapur, and Herat—were destroyed and their inhabitants put to the sword.

Genghis himself withdrew eastward in 1223 to deal ferociously with disaffection in

Xi Xia; he died in 1227. His son and successor Ögödei (r. 1229–41) expanded Mongol power in the western regions, and not long after his death in 1243, the Mongol general Baiju inflicted a serious defeat, at the battle of Köse-Dagh, on the Seljuk sultanate of Rum. This extended Mongol influence into Anatolia, the modern nation of Turkey. Mongol viceroys presided over the northern tier of Iran, but the country as a whole was not yet brought fully under Mongol government. The main priority of Ögödei's reign, in terms of new conquests, was the great invasion of the Pontic steppe, the Rus principalities (modern Russia) and eastern Europe (1237–42), led by his elder brother's son, Batu (fig. 22.2). So alarmed were the European powers—who could not know that after 1242 the Mongols would never return to conquer the rest of Europe—that they dispatched a series of embassies to the Mongols, notably the envoys of Pope Innocent IV. The best known of these is the Franciscan friar John of Plano Carpini (see Chapters 1, 20). The Mongol response was ominous and uncompromising: submit or perish.

By the mid-1240s Mongol unity was already fraying at the edges. Batu, Genghis Khan's senior grandson, was established in his conquests in southern Russia, later to be known in the West as the Golden Horde. And he was at daggers drawn with Güyüg, Ögödei's son and eventual successor as Great Khan. Only Güyüg's early death (he reigned just two years, 1246–48) averted open conflict with Batu. In 1251 a coup d'état in Mongolia (dressed up as a legitimate *khuriltai*) overthrew the Ögödeid branch of the imperial family. With the support of Batu, Möngke, son of Genghis's youngest son Tolui, became Great Khan; and the title remained permanently in that branch of the family.

Möngke initiated what seems to have been a series of administrative and financial reforms, with the result that the resources available to the empire could be much more effectively mobilized.[5] Thus, he was able to embark on two colossal campaigns of military expansion. One of his brothers, Kublai, was entrusted with the conquest of the Song empire in South China;

22.4 The Siege of Alamut
Alamut, the last major stronghold of the Islamic Shi'a sect known as the Ismailis, or Assassins, was besieged and fell to the Mongols in 1256. The destruction of this group, whose members made a specialty of political murder, had become a major focus of Mongol military action in Western Asia. The siege is said to have involved 1,000 catapult and explosive experts from northern China. Projectiles from this siege still litter the surrounding hillsides.

another, Hülegü, with forces of equivalent size, was to bring large parts of the Muslim Middle East to submission (fig. 22.3).[6]

Our sources suggest that Möngke had two enemies particularly in mind in the Middle East: the Nizari Ismailis of northern Iran, a Shi'ite Muslim order known, from their supposed addiction to hashish, as the Hashshashins or Assassins (the word entered European languages from this source), and the Abbasid caliph, titular head of Sunni Islam, in Baghdad. The story went that the Ismaili Grand Master had sent a number of Assassins to Khara Khorum to murder the Great Khan: a very dim view was taken of this, and the order was marked down for extermination. The caliph was to be summoned, like so many other potentates before him, to submit: he would be attacked if he refused.

Hülegü set off from Mongolia in 1253, crossed the Amu-Darya and headed toward northern Iran with, by Mongol standards, uncharacteristic slowness. In 1256 most of the Assassin castles were captured or surrendered, their Grand Master executed and many of his followers also killed, though they were by no means totally extirpated; the sect still exists today, now a highly respectable branch of Shi'i Islam headed by the Aga Khan. Some of the massive stone missiles hurled at the main Assassin castle, Alamut, may still be seen on the slopes below the castle (fig. 22.4).[7]

Hülegü marched on toward Baghdad, arriving outside the city in 1258. The faction-ridden caliphal court had proved hopelessly indecisive, with the end result that the city was taken and sacked. Hülegü, in a letter a few years later to Louis IX of France, claimed, if implausibly, that two million people had been killed. They included the last Abbasid caliph, who was wrapped in a carpet and kicked or trampled to death: a mode of execution which, as it did not outwardly shed the victim's blood, was regarded by the Mongols as especially honorable (though there is no surviving evidence that this was pointed out to the caliph). Hülegü soon had Baghdad rebuilt. For a quarter of a century its governor was the Persian historian Ata-Malik Juvaini, whose *History of the World Conqueror*, completed around 1260, is one of our most important primary sources.[8] Juvaini's brother became a leading minister of the conquered territories of the Middle East known as the Ilkhanid, "subject khanate," in deference to the Great Khan.

From Baghdad the army moved on to Syria. The primary targets had been eliminated, but there were still powers further west that had not submitted to Mongol rule: most notably, the Mamluk sultanate in Egypt and Syria. Aleppo and Damascus were taken speedily, and by 1260 it must have seemed that nothing could stop the Mongol steamroller. But at that point Hülegü received news that, in 1259, his brother the Great Khan had died in China. An internal Mongol political crisis over the succession loomed, and for safety's sake Hülegü withdrew with most of his forces

22.5 Paper Money
Paper currency originated early in the Song dynasty, about 1000, but its use became complicated as different types of currency with different units of measure were introduced. Yuan reforms produced a single, unified, state-controlled monetary system, the *Zhi-yuan baochao,* which was the earliest and most extensive system of paper money in circulation in the world. Although successful at first, paper currency was periodically compromised by inflation, and metal coins had to remain in use as standards of value.

haps deliberately, a little murky on the issue, but it is probable that Möngke's original commission to his younger brother was that he should conquer the Middle East and reduce it to submission—then return to Mongolia, not remain as ruler of his own kingdom.[10] It was the Mongol political crisis of 1259–64 that gave Hülegü his opportunity to establish his own authority.

The second consequence of the turbulence in the east was what has been termed the "dissolution" of the Mongol empire.[11] The new Mongol ruler of the Golden Horde, Batu's brother Berke, was disinclined to accept Kublai's triumph, disputed Hülegü's occupation of territories in the Caucasus, and, being a convert to Islam—the first member of the Mongol ruling family known to have become a Muslim—he was not entranced by his cousin's treatment of the caliph. Nor were the rulers of the fourth Mongol khanate, that of Chaghadai in Central Asia, any more enamored of Kublai and Hülegü; until after the end of the century, the dominant figure in Central Asia was Khaidu, a member of the deposed Ögödeid branch of Genghis Khan's Golden Family.[12] The Golden Horde made a long-standing anti-Ilkhanid alliance with a non-Mongol power, the Mamluk sultanate in Egypt; this alliance was attractive to both sides because the territory of the Golden Horde was the main recruiting ground for mamluks, or Turkish military slaves, on which the Egyptian regime depended.

Mongol expansion in the west ground to a halt from the 1260s, as members of the Golden Family spent their energies on fighting each other rather than the remaining unconquered powers of the area. When Hülegü withdrew from Syria in 1260, he had left behind a fairly small detachment that was defeated by the Mamluk sultan Qutuz at Ayn Jalut (the Spring of Goliath) in what is now northern Israel.[13] The battle was hardly decisive strategically—after all, Qutuz had by no means defeated the main Mongol army—but it attained great symbolic significance as one of the Mongols' rare defeats. Although the Mongols of the Ilkhanate continued to invade Syria regularly for many decades, some-

to Azerbaijan in northwest Iran to monitor events as they unfolded further east. Kublai and a fourth son of Tolui, Arigh Böke, contested for the position of Great Khan. A civil war ensued, in which Kublai was victorious, but which did not end until 1264.[9] Fortunately, for his and his family's future prospects, Hülegü backed the winner.

Those momentous events in the east had two consequences for the western Mongol empire. One was that Hülegü was able to establish himself as, in effect, an independent ruler and dynastic founder in Iran and Iraq. His kingdom is generally known as the Ilkhanate, and for the whole of its existence it remained on close and, at least in theory and at first, subservient terms with its senior partner in China, the center of the Great Khan's power. The sources are, per-

22.6 Currency Decree of Ilkhan Geikhatu

This edict prohibiting the use of coins was issued at the end of the 13th century, when a paper currency system modeled on the Chinese one was introduced by Mongols. The new Mongol currency was called by its Chinese name, *chao*, and had Chinese words printed on it. In theory, the use of paper currency was supposed to drive gold and silver coinage into the hands of the government, enriching its treasury. However, merchants resisted, and the experiment failed. Commerce came to a standstill; paper *chao* was recalled; and Geikhatu's edict was repealed.

times with success, they never permanently annexed those lands; one relevant consideration may well have been the absence in Syria of sufficient pasture on which to maintain permanently the horses of a large Mongol army.[14] At any rate, in retrospect, Ayn Jalut marked the high water mark of Mongol advance in the Middle East.

Nevertheless, the rule of the house of Hülegü was firmly established over Iran, Iraq, and eastern Anatolia for the next seven decades. Until the accession of Ghazan as ilkhan in 1295, the Mongol rulers were, with one brief exception, non-Muslim and Buddhist (in a Tibetan lamaistic form, as in Mongol China) as much as anything else. Hülegü is said to have favored Buddhism, although this may not have run very deep because his funeral involved human sacrifices. On the other hand, Ilkhan Arghun (r. 1284–91) seems to have taken his Buddhist beliefs seriously. This was a problem for a Muslim people because Islamic theory did not provide for the inexorable process of expansion of the Dar al-Islam to go sharply into reverse. And the experience of the first Muslim ilkhan, Tegüder Ahmad (r. 1282–84), was not encouraging: he was speedily deposed and killed, though perhaps more as a result of incompetence than of his religious preferences.

The forty years of pagan or Buddhist rule traditionally have been portrayed as a period of ruthless and shortsighted exploitation of their subjects by the Mongols. It has long been apparent that this view owes a worrying amount to the testimony of one primary source, the *Jami' al-tavarikh* (Compendium of Chronicles) of Rashid al-Din, who was not only the most important historian of the Mongols (in the Ilkhanate and elsewhere), but also Ghazan's chief minister and, very probably, the chief architect of that ilkhan's program of administrative reforms. That is, he had an all too obvious interest in painting the reigns of the preceding ilkhans in colors as unflattering as possible.[15] The trend in Mongol empire studies in recent years has tended, while not in most cases being in denial about the all-too-evident death and destruction of the initial invasions, to emphasize the more

MORGAN

positive aspects of Mongol rule, especially in the cultural and cross-cultural sphere.[16] Hence, even Hülegü and his son and successor Abaqa have now found an eloquent defender.[17] One notable piece of evidence of Hülegü's interest in construction rather than mere demolition is the observatory that was erected outside his capital, Maragheh, for the Shi'ite polymath Nasir al-Din Tusi.

However, it would be wise not to dismiss Rashid al-Din's historical narrative. Sources show that Ilkhanid rule was far from positive. The evident financial chaos that characterized the reign of Geikhatu (1291–95) included the disastrous experiment of attempting to introduce paper money on the Chinese model,[18] a significant indicator of the close relations between distant sections of the Mongol empire (fig. 22.6). Still, in general, the Mongol regime is now considered a good deal more benevolent and even competent than was once thought. It was long supposed that the Mongols took little or no interest in the actual administration of their realm, leaving it to their experienced Persian officials to ensure that taxation revenues continued to roll in; this too, it has been argued, has been much exaggerated.[19]

How, then, are we to evaluate the achievement of Ghazan, whose reign has traditionally been portrayed as the high point of the Ilkhanate? First, there can be no doubt that his conversion to Islam, and, ultimately, that of the Mongols of the Ilkhanate generally, went far toward making the Mongols' rule acceptable to their subjects. Even so, it now seems that Ghazan was following, not leading, the trend toward Islamization.[20] Perhaps it was partly conversion that made him worry about the Mongols losing their sense of a separate identity, because of which he is said to have commissioned Rashid al-Din's history of the Mongols. Muslim as Ghazan may have become, according to Rashid al-Din he had a formidable knowledge of Mongol history and traditions.

The reforms of the reign are more difficult to assess.[21] To have the texts of reforming edicts is one thing; certainty that they were effectively implemented is quite another. A well-informed bureaucrat, Hamd Allah Mustawfi Qazwini, writing in 1340, a few years after the collapse of the Ilkhanate, reckoned that the reforms achieved a modest but real improvement; this may well be right. In foreign affairs Ghazan did, momentarily, achieve something that had eluded all his predecessors: in 1300, his invading armies cleared the Mamluk forces completely out of Syria causing a flutter of optimism in the West: could Jerusalem perhaps be recovered after all, courtesy of the Mongols? But Ghazan withdrew, and nothing came of it.

In 1304 Ghazan died young, as Mongol rulers (with the conspicuous exception of Kublai) tended to do, even when they died of natural causes. He left no surviving sons (another perennial Mongol problem), and was succeeded by his brother Öljeitü, whose reign was in many ways a continuation of his brother's (with Rashid al-Din remaining in office throughout). Öljeitü left one striking memorial: he moved the capital from Tabriz to Sultaniyeh. Little of the new capital remains, but Öljeitü's mausoleum, one of the most magnificent medieval buildings in Iran, is substantially intact (fig. 22.1). It has even been argued that its innovative double-skinned dome may have provided the model for Brunelleschi's dome of Florence's cathedral, erected a century later.

In 1316 Öljeitü's son Abu-Said, still a child, succeeded him. It was a long reign by Ilkhanid standards—twenty years—but Abu-Said was to be the last ruler of the direct line of Hülegü. Views of the reign have differed substantially. One significant achievement was bringing to an end the long series of wars between the Ilkhanate and the Mamluks.[22] Many contemporaries saw the reign as a kind of Golden Age, perhaps retrospectively and by contrast with the chaos that followed. Some recent historians have discerned signs of "decline and fall" in the factional struggles that began during Abu-Said's minority.[23] What is certain is the disastrous result of Abu-Said's failure, like his uncle, to leave a male heir. The Ilkhanate collapsed as different Mongol warlords, sometimes members of one branch or other of the Mongol royal family, struggled for the Ilkhanid inheritance. None succeeded.

What was the Ilkhanid legacy? Many Iranians, to this day, would blame the Mongols for the long-term devastation and impoverishment of their country. The first Mongol invasions were undeniably grim, but this kind of scape-goating of foreigners is too easy and convenient. It has been suggested that, in many respects, the Ilkhanid legacy was modern Iran, in terms of nomenclature, political geography, language, and ethnic composition.[24] And the incorporation of Iran, Iraq, and much of Anatolia into an Asia-wide empire certainly had significant benefits in terms of cross-cultural contacts. It has even been argued that the last of the great Muslim empires, that of the Ottomans, owed its still-mysterious origins in around 1300 to the vagaries of intra-Mongol political struggles[25] —a major legacy indeed, if an inadvertent one.

1. Biran 2005.
2. Bosworth 1968.
3. Morgan 2007, 60–64.
4. Morgan 2007, 64–73.
5. Allsen 1987.
6. Morgan 2007, 130–139.
7. Marshall 1993, 175.
8. Boyle 1997.
9. Rossabi 1988.
10. Morgan 2007, 130–131.
11. Jackson 1978.
12. Biran 1997.
13. Smith 1984.
14. Morgan 1985.
15. Morgan 2007, 142–43.
16. Allsen 2001.
17. Lane 2003.
18. Jahn 1969.
19. Morgan 1996.
20. Melville 1990.
21. Morgan 2007, 146–48.
22. Amitai 2005.
23. Melville 1999.
24. Fragner 1997.
25. Heywood 2000.

23. Rashi al-Din

Dᴀᴠɪᴅ Mᴏʀɢᴀɴ

Tʜᴇ Mᴏɴɢᴏʟ ᴘᴇʀɪᴏᴅ in the history of Iran, the thirteenth to fourteenth centuries, is generally regarded as the Golden Age of historical writing in Persian. This reputation is owed, more than to any other single figure, to the remarkable Rashid al-Din (c. 1247–1318). He was far more than the greatest historian of Mongol Iran. His major work, the *Jami' al-Tavarikh* (Compendium of Chronicles), is the most significant primary source for the history of the Mongol empire as a whole, not just its Iranian component. He went on to write the history of everywhere else he could think of, and all this was his spare-time occupation (fig. 23.1). While he was writing, his principal office was that of one of the two chief ministers of the Ilkhanate, the Mongol domain in Iran.

Born a Jew, Rashid al-Din converted to Islam at the age of thirty. His enemies often tried to make something of his Jewish background, which may explain his authorship of a number of short and tedious, but impeccably orthodox, Muslim theological treatises. He was trained as a physician, and it seems to have been in that capacity that he first came to work at the Ilkhanid court in Tabriz. In 1295 Ghazan became ilkhan and declared his conversion to Islam. In 1298 he made Rashid al-Din one of his two viziers. Rashid al-Din retained that position throughout the reigns of Ghazan (to 1304) and his brother and successor Öljeitü (to 1316), only to fall from power and be executed in 1318, early in the reign of Öljeitü's son and successor Abu-Said, the last fully fledged Ilkhan of the house of Hülegü. This was a fate that, as was noted at the time, befell every Ilkhanid vizier except one (and there is some doubt about his end too).

At the suggestion of his master Ghazan, Rashid al-Din embarked on his parallel career as a historian. Ghazan seemed to fear that the Mongols, who were now settled permanently in Iran, were in danger of forgetting who they were and where they had come from. Rashid al-Din was therefore commissioned to write the history of the Mongols as a kind of aide-memoire—and in Persian, the language of the land that had become these Mongols' home.[1]

The history[2] begins with an account of the Mongol and Turkish tribes whom Genghis Khan had come to dominate. It then recounts the life of Genghis, the story of the Mongol conquests, and the reigns of Genghis's successors. The long concluding section is a detailed history of the rule of the Mongols in Persia, from Hülegü's invasion and establishment of the Ilkhanate to the death of Ghazan (there was supposed also to be a history of the reign of Öljeitü, but if this ever existed, it has yet to come to light). For historians of Iran in the period, perhaps the most important part is the texts of the reforming edicts by means of which Ghazan attempted (with the aid of his chief minister) to reform the administrative abuses of the previous decades.

When Öljeitü succeeded his brother in 1304, he asked Rashid al-Din, as a tribute and memorial to Ghazan, to add histories of all the peoples with whom the Mongols had come into contact. The complete *Jami' al-Tavarikh* includes histories not only of the Mongols, but also of Adam and the Biblical patriarchs, pre-Islamic Persia, Muhammad and the caliphs, the Persian

23.1 *Mountains Between Tibet and India*
This image accompanies the text on India in Rashid al-Din's *Jami' al-Tavarikh* (Compendium of Chronicles). The artistic conventions show the influence of foreign lands on Iranian artists: the landscape includes a Chinese-style mountain; the buildings display architectural styles of Nepal (left) and China (right), and the two figures are shown with costumes, jewelry, and poses characteristic of Chinese, Tibetan, and Indian cultures.

dynasties of the Islamic period, the Oghuz and the Turks, China, the Jews, the Franks (of western Europe), and India. There was no real precedent for such a work in the Muslim historical tradition—nor was there a precedent for an empire the size of the Mongols'. It was an achievement that prompted one of Rashid al-Din's leading modern students, J.A. Boyle, to term him "the first world-historian."

Rashid al-Din himself was well aware that he had achieved something very much out of the ordinary. He had all his Persian works translated into Arabic, and vice versa, and had copies made that were sent all over the Islamic world. Some of the surviving copies made in the author's lifetime contain miniature paintings that are of great importance for the study of the development of Persian art: for example, they include motifs characteristic of Chinese art, which would hardly have found their way into a Persian painter's repertoire were it not for the cross-cultural contacts of the Mongol empire (see Chapter 31).

The independent historical value of the different sections varies a good deal, however. The interest of many of the "world-history" parts is more historiographical than historical: one would hardly go to Rashid al-Din to find out what happened in China. But his account of the life of Genghis Khan, although it was written a century after the events, is second in significance only to the indigenous and near-contemporary *The Secret History of the Mongols*, because it was based on an early Mongolian chronicle, the *Altan Devter* (Golden Book), which is now lost; the contents of it were conveyed to Rashid al-Din by Bolad Chingsang, the Great Khan's representative at the Ilkhanid court. Rashid al-Din's account of the Ilkhans, especially that of Ghazan, is fundamental to all study of the period—though those who use him need to bear constantly in mind that Rashid al-Din was Ghazan's minister, not an "impartial" historian.

Rashid al-Din is said to have written his history between morning prayer and sunrise. Many have wondered how so busy a bureaucrat found the time for the necessary research and writing. A possible answer is that he employed a team of research assistants. One may have been Abu'l Qasim Qashani, author of a history of Öljeitü, who in it claimed that he was the real author of the *Jami' al-Tavarikh*. This claim is stylistically implausible and does little to damage the reputation of one of the most outstanding intellectual and practical figures to arise from the Mongol cataclysm.

1. Morgan 1997.
2. Rashid al-Din 1998.

WAUGH

24. The Golden Horde and Russia

Daniel C. Waugh

Genghis Khan had assigned the western portion of the Mongol empire to his oldest son, Jochi, but when Jochi predeceased his father, his share fell to his son Batu. The extent of his domains was yet to be defined, as major portions of the territory given to Jochi (*ulus Jochi*) in Russia and Ukraine had not yet been conquered by the Mongols. Batu's armies eventually reached the Adriatic and the valleys of Austria before they retreated in 1241. He began to rule his state—better known as the "Golden Horde," a name given it much later by non-Mongols—from Sarai, a city he founded not far from the mouth of the Volga River. The power and prosperity of the Golden Horde peaked during the second quarter of the fourteenth century, but were shattered by Tamerlane's invasion in 1395. Successor states in its territory—the Crimea and Khiva—were ruled by Ghengissid dynasties far longer than were any other parts of the empire, the first remaining independent until the late eighteenth century, and the second lasting until the twentieth century.

The example of the Golden Horde highlights important aspects of society, the economy, and imperial politics in a large region of the empire. Since the relationship between the Mongols and urban centers is often misunderstood, it is of particular interest to learn about the cities of the Golden Horde. The relations between the Mongol rulers of Ulus Jochi and their Russian subjects evolved from policies of direct political control to those of indirect rule. There is considerable controversy over the impact of Mongol rule in Russia and Ukraine, since the national myths of the conquered paint a picture of unrelieved oppression, the effects of which were still being felt into modern times. Such one-sided assessments of the Golden Horde need to be reconsidered.

When Mongol armies first appeared in eastern Europe in 1223, the steppe nomads who lived there, the Polovtsy (Cumans), turned to the east Slavic princes for aid. The Mongols' shattering victory over this combined force on the River Kalka near the Sea of Azov foreshadowed their conquest in the 1230s (fig. 24.2).

Genghis's son Ögödei sought to follow up on his father's conquests, and, in particular, to extend his empire westward. After defeating the Jin dynasty and seizing North China, Ögödei launched an invasion west, with his nephew Batu and other grandsons of Genghis joining in the campaign. Although the cousins were often at odds, the campaign proved remarkably successful, in part because they did not face a united Russian

24.1 Silver-Gilt Plate
Few objects of Italian manufacture have been found at Golden Horde sites, although Italian merchants were prominent in the Golden Horde trade network. This platter, which bears the arms of the Vento family in Genoa, was found at Belorechenskaia, in the Kuban region near the Sea of Azov, and based on its style probably was made in northern Italy or Dubrovnik between 1390 and 1450.

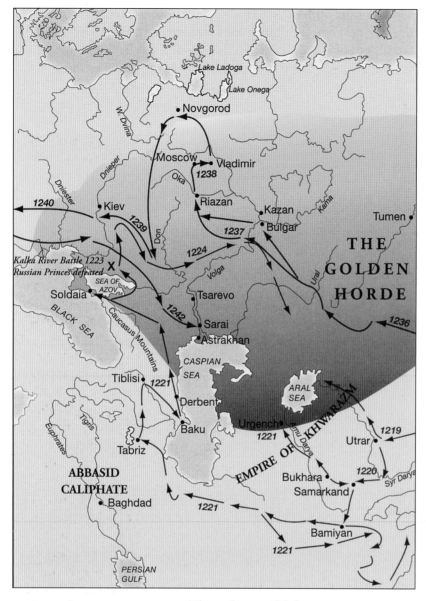

24.2 The Golden Horde
The vast northern lands bequeathed to Genghis's oldest son, Jochi, became known as the Golden Horde. The first Mongol invasion of these territories was essentially a probe, conducted in 1221–24 by Subödei and Jebe, whereas the campaign of 1237–41 led by Jochi's sons Batu and Berke was an invasion with intent to settle and rule. This campaign crossed the northern steppe and reached Moscow and Novgorod, and in 1239–41, Budapest and Austria. Batu and his successors established Sarai, north of the Caspian, to administer the Golden Horde until the Black Death ravaged the region in 1346. The eastern territories, known as the Blue Horde, remained under Mongol control until 1503. In unifying these lands, Mongol administration brought order, prosperity, and political stability to the region's diverse lands and peoples for the first time.

state. Thus, they could focus on one group or territory at a time. In short order in the late 1230s, they defeated the Bulgars, who occupied the middle Volga region, and the Polovtsy, who controlled the steppes north of the Sea of Azov and the Caucasus. Batu then moved on the Russian principalities, destroying Riazan in late 1237, and in the following year conquering the important center of Vladimir-Suzdal and the as-yet insignificant Moscow. The Mongols then swept through Kiev, the once great economic and cultural center of the Russian lands. By 1241 their forces had reached Budapest in the south and Liegnitz in Poland in the north. Mongol detachments were already scouting the routes further west when Batu learned of Ögödei's death and abruptly withdrew to the east, hoping to influence the

choice of the next Great Khan. Rather than resume the campaign to western Europe, he chose to consolidate his rule over the Ulus Jochi from the lower Volga (fig. 24.2).

Once the Mongols had pacified Russia and Ukraine, they took over the traditional nomad routes used by the Polovtsy up and down the main rivers. Batu would spend summers near Bulgar on the middle Volga and winters at his new capital, Sarai. The Franciscan John of Plano Carpini, who traveled as a papal emissary, visited Batu in 1245 en route to Mongolia and recorded how other members of the Mongol elite set up nomad camps along the Dnieper, Don, and Ural (Yaik) Rivers.[1]

The chaos and destruction of invasion had disrupted flourishing commercial and craft emporia that were central to the Mongol empire's sustainability. In the consolidation and reconstruction of the following era, the Mongols, unlike earlier nomadic polities, incorporated into their domain long-established cities on the edge of the steppe world. Thus, Bulgar, at the border between the forest and steppe; Kaffa, a port in the Crimea; and Urgench, in the lower reaches of the Amu-Darya River in Khwarazm south of the Aral Sea, were important cities of the Golden Horde. The khans also founded new cities where previously there had been none. Prime examples are Batu's Sarai (associated with the Selitrennoe Fort site) and the city founded under Khan Özbeg in the 1330s some 200 km further north on the Volga at the Tsarevo Fort site, a strategic location where that river comes closest to the river Don. The fate of these cities is a barometer of the political and economic strength of the Horde. Their decline coincided with the onset of civil war in the second half of the fourteenth century, and their destruction in 1395 marked the end of the Golden Horde's real political power.

Our knowledge of Golden Horde cities derives in part from records such as the eyewitness account by the Moroccan traveler extraordinaire, Ibn Battuta (see Chapter 29). When he arrived in the Golden Horde in the early 1330s, he reported that Kaffa, a city controlled by the Genoese under Mongol suzerainty, was "a wonderful harbor

24.3 Paiza of Khan Özbeg
This medallion commanding safe passage to the bearer was issued by Özbeg, Khan of the Golden Horde (r. 1313–41), and reads: "By the order of Eternal Heaven, the decree of Khan Özbeg [is that] a person who does not submit to the Mongols is guilty and shall die."

with about two hundred vessels in it, both ships of war and trading vessels, small and large, for it is one of the world's celebrated ports."[2] Indeed, an Italian presence—earlier, it was the Venetians—in the ports of the Crimea well antedated the arrival of the Mongols, and the Genoese had been granted trading privileges by the rulers of the Golden Horde through an important international treaty concluded in 1267 (fig. 24.1). Later in his travels Ibn Battuta would describe Khwarazm/Urgench as "the largest, greatest, most beautiful and most important city" of the Mongols.[3] Of course, he was describing the Golden Horde at its peak during the reign of Özbeg Khan; approximately a century had passed since Mongol invasions had devastated the lands of the Khwarazm-shah and destroyed Bulgar on the Volga:

The Khan's court and Sarai impressed the Moroccan visitor as:

one of the finest of cities, of boundless size . . . choked with the throng of its inhabitants, and possessing good bazaars and broad streets. We rode out one day . . . intending to make a circuit of the city and find out its extent. Our lodging place was at one end of it and we set out from it in the early morning, and it was after midday when we reached the other end. We then prayed the noon prayer and ate some food, and we did not get back to our lodging until the hour of the sunset prayer. One day we went on foot across the breadth of the town, going and returning, in half a day, this too through a continuous line of houses, among which there were no ruins and no gardens. The city has thirteen mosques for the holding of Friday prayers, one of them being for the Shafi'ites; as for the other mosques, they are exceedingly numerous. . . . [I]ts inhabitants . . . include the Mughals, who are the dwellers in this country and its sultans, and some of whom are Muslims, then the As, who are Muslims, the Qifjaq, the Jarkas, the Rus, and the Rum [Greeks]—[all of] these are Christians. Each group lives in a separate quarter with its own bazaars. Merchants and strangers from the two Iraqs, Egypt, Syria and elsewhere, live in a quarter which is surrounded by a wall for the protection of the properties of the merchants.[4]

Sarai's population at the time when Ibn Battuta visited is uncertain. One Arab source estimates 75,000[5]; archaeology confirms that the city was a flourishing multiethnic center of commerce and craft production (fig. 24.4). The outward appearance of urban development and prosperity did not reflect an ideal social and political order. Building and populating the new cities involved forced labor and conscription. Much of the initial labor was performed by the previous steppe inhabitants, the Polovtsy, who had been enslaved when they were driven off their grazing lands.

In many areas of the empire the khans conscripted artisans at will, a practice that has been well documented. A Russian goldsmith had made the khan's seal at his court in Mongolia; the famous fountain in the courtyard of the palace in Khara Khorum was the work of a captured Parisian master; weavers from the Middle East were resettled in northern China. In Sarai, ceramic crafts reflected the techniques and designs of such centers as Bulgar and Khwarazm and, at least initially, were probably the work of craftsmen conscripted from those cities (fig. 24.7). While such conscription must have inflicted serious damage on the older craft centers, many of them revived and flourished. The initial minting of coins by the rulers of the Golden Horde seems to have been in Bulgar, only a generation after the invasion. Minting at Sarai, the capital, began later. By the time Özbeg became khan (r. 1313–41), the Muslim architecture of Volga Bulgaria already surpassed what it had been in the century of the Mongol invasion (fig. 24.3).

The specialization of the numerous workshops in Golden Horde cities is impressive and probably reflects a substantial market for metalwork, jewelry, and glass. Ceramics production met demands for building materials such as bricks, decorative tiles, and drain pipes, as well as a broad range of dishes. While imported ceramics formed only a small percentage of what was in common use, local designs responded in creative ways to examples such as Chinese porcelain with its cobalt blue patterns (fig. 24.5). In some parts of the Mongol dominions (for example, northwest Iran) an effort

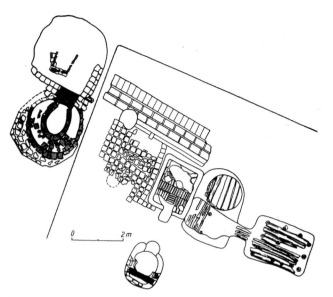

24.4 Ceramic Production
Batu's and Berke's settlements at Sarai, located on the lower Volga River north of the Caspian Sea, served as capital of the Golden Horde. These camps were gradually transformed into huge cities and important commercial centers for Silk Road traffic. This archaeological plan illustrates kilns, storage cellars, wooden kegs, and remnants of a floor excavated at the Selitrennoe Fortress (possibly Sarai).

24.5 Ceramics From Sarai
This glazed vessel with hanging loops represents one of the many ceramic types produced by craftsmen at the Selitrennoe Fortress ceramics workshop.

was made to replicate the Chinese blue-and-white ware. The Golden Horde workshops tended to incorporate some of the motifs, but often with different color combinations.

The steppe cities of the Horde included elite "estates," often on the outskirts of town, with multiroom mansions built of substantial masonry and their own craft shops and servants' quarters. Some of these compounds have the remains of *ger* platforms, a reminder that the Mongol elite did not completely adopt sedentary life. Although Ibn Battuta was impressed by the urban culture in Sarai, he was taken aback by the open observance of nomadic social customs that violated Islamic norms. The elite residences seem to have flourished into the second half of the fourteenth century, at which time growing political instability led their owners to build defensive walls in the same way that previously unfortified cities were then being walled. The bubonic

plague undoubtedly played a major role in the cities' decline. As early as the 1370s, many of the mansions fell into disrepair and their compounds were being converted into cemeteries, well before the wars of the next decades destroyed the cities of the lower Volga and Crimea. The study of the elite residential complexes sheds light on other aspects of social and economic change. Modest structures that probably were living or working space for servants and craftsmen evolved over time from semi-dugout huts with no heating system into more sophisticated houses with stoves. Whether this means slave families were now gaining their freedom and moving up in social and economic terms is difficult to prove.

Ibn Battuta had noted only in passing that the residents of Sarai included Russians. He had no interest in the fact that there was a Russian Orthodox bishop there whose main function was probably to facilitate relations between the khans, on the one hand, and the Russian principalities and the Byzantine empire, on the other. Of greater interest to the Moroccan was the fact that one of the khan's wives was the daughter of the Byzantine emperor. Indeed, Byzantium, by virtue of its strategic control over communications with the Mediterranean, must have been more important to the Horde economically and politically than were the Russian principalities. But even Byzantium was incidental to the main political concern of Sarai: its hostility with Ilkhanid Iran, where the prize, never achieved, was domination of western Asia.

The Russian example illustrates well Mongol relations with subject peoples. However, establishing the exact nature of those relations and their long-term consequences is difficult: the medieval sources often are silent about important topics, and when they do speak, they have a pronounced anti-Mongol bias. Trying to discern the truth is further hindered by the anti-Mongol bias of too many modern assessments.[6] Long after the Mongol invasion of the Russian principalities in the years 1237–40, a monk described how "there is nothing to be seen in [Riazan] excepting smoke, ashes, and barren earth . . . instead of joy,

24.6 Gold Filigree Emblem
Ornaments and personal items of gold, silver, and precious stone were a large part of the huge treasure found accidentally in Simferopol, Crimea, in 1967. The hoard, thought to have belonged to a Jochid khan who ruled the Crimea in the early 14th century, included objects of manufacture and design that show influences from many distant regions.

there are only uninterrupted lamentations."[7] Other cities that resisted met the same fate, although the impact was uneven. The important city of Novgorod in the north escaped destruction, ostensibly because the spring thaw melted the ice on the rivers, which the Mongol horsemen had been using to travel through this unpromising land of swampy, roadless forests. In a territory where the population still lived largely in isolated villages, the destruction of what was only a handful of towns could not be expected to have a permanent impact on social and economic development. Neither could this inhospitable region of modest resources have contributed much to the prosperity of the Horde.

Initially, the Mongols ruled their territories in Russia directly from the center of the empire that was being built at Khara Khorum, with only a limited local presence of Mongol administrators, census takers, and military contingents. Russian princes had to travel to Mongolia to receive their patents of office (*jarlyks*) from the Great Khan. John of Plano Carpini reported on the poisoning there in 1246 of Prince Iaroslav of Vladimir, the senior principality of northeastern Russia. His son, Alexander Nevsky (1220–63), a Russian hero for

his defeat of the Swedish knights on the River Neva in 1240, managed to survive his own visit to Mongolia and went on to become a dutiful servant of the khans in helping to put down Russian resistance to their rule. His descendants ruled Moscow.

By the fourteenth century, the locus of political and fiscal control over Russia had shifted to Sarai, although some tax revenues continued to be sent to the Great Khan. Russian princes still were expected to appear when summoned to the khan's court, either in Sarai or at his summer camp in the Caucasus foothills. The khans bestowed the patents for rule and approved the princes' wills, but largely did not interfere in the established patterns of princely succession. Intermarriage often strengthened the ties between Russian princes and their overlords. The relationship was one that could be manipulated successfully on both sides for political advantage especially as the Horde itself weakened. The emergence of Moscow as the preeminent Russian principality may be explained by its princes' success in cultivating their relations with Sarai.

There is little evidence to show, as some scholars would have us believe, that the khans were continually plotting ways to keep the Russian princes weak. Nor is it the case that the Russians seized every opportunity to rebel in order to throw off the "Mongol yoke."[8] In the national mythology, the high point of this struggle was the battle of Kulikovo in 1380, where Moscow prince Dmitrii Ivanovich "Donskoi" ("of the Don River") is portrayed in hagiographic terms. Yet the battle was not simply a victory of good, Christian Russians over "pagan" Mongols, but a complex affair involving conflicting allegiances on both sides in a period when the Golden Horde had already been substantially weakened by internal strife.[9]

Beginning around 1330, the Moscow princes became tax collectors for the khans and took advantage of administrative mechanisms that would later help them consolidate increasingly independent political power. Evidence that they adopted Mongol bureaucratic procedures does not necessarily mean, as some have claimed, that they also borrowed larger political structures or

24.7 Bronze Mirror
This mirror, found at Bulgar, a city on the Volga, carries an image of two sphinxes and was probably made in northern Iraq or eastern Anatolia in the 11th–13th century. The sphinx was a popular motif in western Asia before the rise of Islam.

political theory.[10] By the time the Russian princes emerged as autocrats in the seventeenth century, the Golden Horde had long ceased to be a viable political model.

Many myths about the Mongol impact in Russia have been invoked to explain uncomfortable facts about the country's subsequent history. Although the impact of the Mongol invasion and ongoing payment of tribute (fig. 24.8) unquestionably was severe, the Mongols have been blamed for Russian "economic backwardness" right down to the twentieth century. The one quantifiable, if imperfect, measure of economic prosperity in Russia—the building of masonry churches in a country where most construction was of wood—bottoms out in the 1230s but shows a dramatic recovery within two or three generations of the invasion.[11] Russian trade through Novgorod to the Baltic and through the Crimea to Byzantium continued and, at least in the south, was in the interests of the khans to promote. The Russian church was among the beneficiaries of this trade; the Italian merchant network, based in the Crimea, reached all the way to Moscow. There is ample evidence of Russian eco-

nomic recovery even before the demise of the Golden Horde in the late fourteenth century. Russian economic woes of later centuries have little to do with the Mongols.

Nor is there justification to support the myth that the Mongols "cut Russia off from the West," thus condemning the Russians to miss out on the Renaissance and the scientific revolution. This idea is encapsulated in an oft-quoted observation by Russia's national poet Alexander Pushkin that, unlike the cultured Muslim rulers in Spain, who were intellectually ahead of the medieval Christian West, "the Mongols gave Russia neither Aristotle nor algebra."[12] Yet, Islam, by the fourteenth century, had become the official religion of the Horde, mosques were being built, and Islamic learning promoted: Ibn Battuta records at length his interactions with learned Muslim clerics. There was no policy of cutting off non-Muslims either from their religious or, if they had any, their intellectual traditions. Indeed, Greek and southern Slavic clerics and artists continued to contribute to Russian culture, and there was active involvement with the Hansa in Novgorod and Italian merchants in the south. The khans even granted the Russian Church immunities from taxation and judicial interference by the secular authorities. Whatever were the intellectual accomplishments of the learned Muslims of Sarai, for perfectly good religious reasons that learning was off limits to the Russian Orthodox. The real barrier to the emerging culture of the Renaissance was that Russian Orthodoxy likewise blocked any intellectual borrowing from the Catholic West.

The fall of the Byzantine empire to the Muslim Turks in 1453 reinforced the Russians' belief in the purity of their faith. Now, more than ever, Moscow felt compelled to defend its traditional religion and culture. The Muscovite state had barely survived a civil war in the first half of the fifteenth century, thanks to some timely help from remnants of the Golden Horde. Grand Prince Ivan III (r. 1462–1505) consolidated his power, absorbed most of the remaining independent Russian principalities, established a degree of political control over the Genghissid successor

24.8 Stemmed Cup

A surprising amount of silver has been found in burials and sacred sites in the Russian forest and arctic regions. This silver cup with gilded decoration was found in 1869 at Ust-Erbinskoe, in the Yenisei drainage of northern Siberia, and dates to the late 13th or first half of the 14th century. Although not directly administered by the Golden Horde, such distant regions became economically engaged with it through the tribute system: fine objects acquired by exchange in the Golden Horde were used as gifts or payment to tribal leaders in return for northern fur, ivory, amber, and gold.

state of Kazan, and waged a successful war against Lithuania. Given his successes, Ivan had every reason to think that his endeavors enjoyed divine sanction and that he was the real heir to the khans in Sarai.

Whether Ivan or his Muscovite heirs consciously articulated claims to that succession is uncertain.[13] The term, "White Tsar," with which rulers in the steppe, the Ottomans, and even princes as far away as Italy at times addressed the Russian ruler, might be taken in the Mongol color- and directional-coded terminology to mean the "Khan of the West." The Muscovite princes had an interest in regalia associated with the khans of the Golden Horde. Of

the many royal crowns in the treasury of the Kremlin, the most important is the so-called "Cap of Monomakh," which some have argued is a prime example of the filigree gold work that was popular among the Mongol elite. Whether it was once part of the khan's regalia before being acquired by Ivan's Muscovite ancestors in the fourteenth or fifteenth centuries is still debated.[14] Although the crown probably dates from the thirteenth century, Russian legends associate it with the eleventh-century Byzantine Emperor Constantine IX Monomachos rather than admit to any Mongol connection.

When Grand Prince Ivan IV (r. 1533–84) became the first Russian ruler to be crowned tsar in 1547, the title, which derives from "Caesar," asserted the prestige associated with imperial Rome, not the tradition by which Russians had termed the khan "tsar." Having incorporated the successor states of the Golden Horde—Kazan (1552), Astrakhan (1556), and Siberia (ca. 1581)—Ivan IV then added the titles Tsar of Kazan, and so on, as explicit recognition that he had replaced the Genghissid khans. Where it served their purposes, the Muscovite rulers respected the imperial charisma of the Genghissid line, even if they did not shape their policies after those of khans whose rule in Russia had long ago ended. The characteristic institutions Muscovy bequeathed to the Russian empire—notably, autocracy and serfdom—developed later and gradually as responses to internal needs of the evolving state, not as a result of Mongol rule.

1. Dawson 1955, 55.
2. Ibn Battuta 1958–2000, vol. 2, 471.
3. Ibn Battuta 1958–2000, vol. 3, 541.
4. Ibn Battuta 1958–2000, vol. 2, 515–16.
5. Fedorov-Davydov 1984, 22.
6. Grekov in Grekov and Iakubovskii 1950; Vernadsky 1953; Halperin 1985.
7. Zenkovsky 1974, 205.
8. Nasonov 1940; Cherepnin in Tikhvinskii 1970, 191–200.
9. Petrov 2005.
10. Ostrowski 1990; Rakhimzianov 2005.
11. Miller 1989.
12. Grekov and Iakobovskii 1950, 177.
13. Halperin 2003.
14. Zhilina 2001.

25. Conquerors and Craftsmen

ARCHAEOLOGY OF THE GOLDEN HORDE

MARK G. KRAMAROVSKY

THE TERRITORIES COMPRISING MUCH OF MODERN-DAY RUSSIA, Ukraine, and Central Asia that Genghis Khan presented to his son Jochi and his heirs became known under Mongol domination as the Golden Horde. Legend holds that Jochi's son Batu lived in an imperial golden tent while he fought for dominion in this region and *orda*, the medieval Mongol term for a political sub-domain and well as the place where a Mongol khan established his base camp, entered into English as "horde." The three hundred-year tenure, until 1502, of the Mongolian Jochid dynasty over the Golden Horde is one of the least-known fields of medieval Eurasian history, largely due to the scarcity of pictorial and written records.

In recent decades, archaeological evidence has provided a new source of information, allowing us to piece together an outline of the political and cultural development of this northern tier of the Mongol empire. The Golden Horde, which extended from west Siberia and Kazakhstan to the Carpathians, was the first, the largest, and the most ethnically diverse of the Mongol khanates. It included the Siberian taiga forests; high mountain ranges; steppe and forest steppe lands; the Volga, Dneiper, upper Ob, and Irtysh river systems; and several inland seas. Among its peoples were scores of cultures and language groups that until the Mongols arrived had experienced little higher-level political organization. Mongol subjugation brought central authority to many in this region for the first time (see Chapter 24).

Developing a distinctive set of imperial dynastic symbols was crucial to establishing Mongol authority over this diverse region. New archaeological investigations have revealed early Jochid heraldic symbols that shed light on the political identity of this Mongol elite and the cultural and economic development of the Golden Horde. Powerful and widely recognized symbols of unity and legitimacy used across the Mongolian empire played a particularly important role in the heterogeneous khanate. It was not until 1257, when the campaigns of Batu were concluded on the shores of the Adriatic, that Jochids grasped the true extent of their domain. Their new state consisted of two primary military-political entities—the eastern Kok ("Blue") Orda and the western Ak ("White") Orda—and contained no fewer than sixteen administrative districts across the heartland of Eurasia.

The steppe territories that formed the core of the *ulus Jochi,* as the domain left to Genghis's son Jochi was called by the Mongols, lay on the outskirts of the Eurasian cultural world. The transformation from village to urban life in the economi-

25.1 Saddle Arch Front
Several elite Mongol women's graves have been found with saddles with front and back arches decorated with embossed gold plates. The front panel of the saddle found at Khailin Gele features two Mongol horses—distinguished by their short legs and large heads—surrounded by plants and flowers.

25.2 Saddle Arch Back
This embossed-gold back panel of the Khailin Gele saddle, is illustrated with two hares surrounded by floral designs and decorative border friezes. In Asian mythology, rabbits or hares symbolized fertility, the moon, and long life. Such wealth found in elite Mongol women's graves from northern China to the Golden Horde indicates the high status held by women in Genghissid society.

cally more developed western steppe was the first stage in overcoming the Golden Horde's physical marginality to its Central Asian core. Although nomadic groups continued to predominate, dozens of cities appeared in the traditional winter-settlement areas of the steppe by the first half of the fourteenth century. The cultural and economic forces that created these cities soon stimulated urban craft centers and trade markets. The interaction within a single political structure of nomadic groups, settled villagers, and urban peoples established the economic and social basis for Jochid culture. Three historical periods representing cultural stages in the evolution of the Golden Horde can now be identified.

Epochs of the Jochid Dynasty

The early Jochid period (1230s–50) is characterized by the administrative separation of Jochi's legacy (*ulus Jochi*, later, the Golden Horde) from other territories that belonged to Genghis Khan (*Ikh Mongol ulus*, or Great Mongol Territories) between 1211 and 1264. During these decades, many of the political, economic, and cultural foundations of the Golden Horde were initiated with little disruption to the overall unity of the larger empire. Traditions originating in Central Asia and northern China transformed the region's material culture during this period. Most of the formerly nomadic Mongol elite settled in permanent steppe communities when the Golden Horde was ruled by Berke

(r. 1257–67). Many innovations during the middle Jochid period, from the second half of the thirteenth through the first two-thirds of the fourteenth century, created a new social environment. Between the late 1250s and early 1260s the Jochids introduced their own monetary system, consolidated the formation of their state, and began achieving a distinct cultural signature. The resumption of trade along the northern branch of the Silk Road, which joined China and Central Asia with the markets of the Mediterranean, was central to these developments. Between the second half of the thirteenth century and the early fourteenth century, the first coins were minted in the Golden Horde.[1] Regional currencies circulated within the provinces of the former Volga Bulgaria, Middle Volga region, Lower Volga region, the Crimea and northwestern Black Sea, and the Danube and Dniester regions.

Sarai, the thirteenth-century capital of the Golden Horde, is mentioned for the first time in 1253 by William of Rubruck (see Chapter 20). Purportedly, Sarai was located at the ancient site of Selitrennoe Fort on the left bank of the Akhtuba River, about 115 km north of modern Astrakhan, although the latest archaeological and numismatic data cast doubt on this identification.[2] Toward the end of the administration of Khan Özbeg (r. 1312–42), the city of Gyulistan-Sarai, located near the site of Tsarev in the Volgograd district, came to life amidst great strife, only to die out at the beginning of the 1360s.[3] During this period, the steppe and urban sectors became more closely integrated, and the Islamized urban communities of the khan's domain and the regional centers of the Azov region, northern Caucasus, and Crimea produced a new model for trade and cultural interaction. These novel regimes of interaction and stability encouraged settlement and a higher degree of permanence. More than 140 communities appear in the register of the Golden Horde cities.[4] Trading centers and the material culture of the steppe begin to reflect these changes as well.

Islamic communities ushered in a flowering of urban life from the 1360s to 1395, the initial stage of the late Jochid period. Traditional cultural elements of Central Asia gradually died out through the end of the fifteenth century, replaced in the steppe lands by Islamic innovations flowing in from the south and southwestern regions, including Khwarazm, in the Caspian area; Mamluk Egypt; and Asia Minor (via the Crimea). The Jochid elite impetuously shed their connections to the homeland of Genghis Khan and lost many ties to their distant Mongol identity, including the Mongolian language. By the eighth to ninth generations of Jochid rule, during the time of Tokhtamysh (r. 1376–95), Türkic had become the official language. Urban trade was the dominant force of change, spurred not by outside production but by commercial centers within the Golden Horde. Under the khans Tokta, Uzbek, and Janibek, the mints of Sarai, Sarai al-Jedid, and Gyulistan-Sarai became important centers of economic development, and Golden Horde coinage, known as the dirkhem, began to circulate in the markets of Eurasia.[5]

The 1395 military victories of Temür (Tamerlane) (r. 1369–1405) precipitated the second stage of the late Jochid period and the slow decline in international trade and urban civilization in the central regions of the Khante. The monetary system began to crumble, initiating a century of collapse and cultural stagnation. Only in the eastern Crimea did local trade centers continue to function and expand. By 1440 political fragmentation had divided the original territory of the Golden Horde into a number of smaller princely khanates that continually competed for prominence. Within this splintered political landscape of Central Eurasia, Russian power and influence, centered in Moscow, was rapidly emerging as a dominant force in the region. The final remnant of the Golden Horde (which by the late fifteenth century was known as the *Bol'shaya Orda,* or Great Horde), comprised those lands surrounding the old capital of Sarai, though this successor state of the Great Khanate was significantly weaker in military, economic, and political capability. In 1502 another successor state, the Crimean khanate, launched a devastating attack against the neighboring Great Horde and successfully destroyed the final political vestiges of the westernmost descendants of Genghis Khan.

25.3 Military Belt of the House of Batu

The three- or four-clawed dragon emerged from 1204–17 as an emblem of the early Genghissids and their elite guard. This and other imperial symbols spread throughout the western steppe during the conquests of the 1220s–40s. This richly ornamented gold belt from a grave at Gashun-Ust near Stavropol features elements from various cultural traditions: the stag probably originated from an east Asian–Jurchen prototype; the flower designs reflect Muslim tradition. The stag became the heraldic sign of the House of Batu, Jochi's son and founder of the Golden Horde.

While the dynastic and military-political life of the Golden Horde had effectively ended, the cultural traditions of the Mongol state continued to have long-lasting influence. Trends and precedents established during the fourteenth century in the spheres of politics, economy, trade, and ideology maintained their importance and, in many ways, still defined the post-Horde period. These traditions are manifested chiefly in centers where the authority of the Genghissid identity lived on: in the steppes of Kazakhstan, the forest steppe of western Siberia, the central Volga region, Riazan, and, even more strongly, in Crimea. During the fifteenth and sixteenth centuries, the dynastic identity also continued to influence the culture of Moscow. In diplomatic cor-

respondence with eastern neighbors Moscow sovereigns referred to themselves as the "White Tsars," associating their legitimacy with the Mongol geographical/color symbolism of the Golden Horde, under which "west" was the seat of the "White" Orda.[6]

Symbols of the Golden Horde

While historical sources are of immense importance, they can be supplemented by other sources of information on the past. Archaeology is particularly well suited to understanding trends in material culture and demonstrating how new styles and motifs supported the authority and legitimacy of the Mongol overlords. Costume, coiffure, headdress, and ornaments worn by the elite constitute symbols of association with the imperial Mongol lineage. Gold and silver treasures found in Central Asia provide important information about the first generations of Genghis Khan's heirs in this region. The discovery in 2005 of a grave from the early Mongol period, probably dating to the first decades of the thirteenth century, of a female buried with a horse and saddle inlaid with gilded four-clawed dragons (Grave No. 5, near Tavan Tolgoi in Sukhbaatar province, southeastern Mongolia) is of great importance).[7] The high status of this young woman, who was about twenty years old, was conveyed by golden earrings, a filigree decoration for her hair, a pectoral ornament, and a Buddhist implement called a *vajra*. The absence of a *bogtag* hat suggests the lady was unmarried. The lavishly decorated woman's saddle—of a type from this period also found at Khailin Gele and near Melitopol' (figs. 25.1, 2)—offers clear evidence of the high status of some women in the early Mongol period. The dragon motif of the inlays on the saddle is imperial regalia, also found on military belts and drinking cups.

Use of the three- or four-clawed dragon as an emblem of the Great Khan and his guard originated between 1204–06 and 1217 (fig. 25.12). Military guard belts with dragons have been found in archaeological materials from the European zone of the steppes (fig. 25.11); documentary evidence dates them to the first generation of Mongol conquerors in the Mongol heartland

25.4 Cup with Dragon Head
This gold cup could have been carried in a leather bag attached to a warrior's belt. It dates to the second half of the 13th century and was found in 1890 in a *kurgan*, or rock mound burial, that was probably the grave of a Golden Horde leader, in Gashun-Ust near Stavropol. Its handle is a dragonhead; fish-scale and plant patterns ornament the cup rim and bottom. Similar cups have been found in Genghissid contexts from across Central Eurasia.

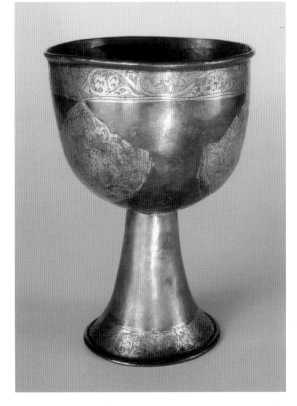

25.5 Stemmed Goblet
This footed silver cup with gilded decoration was found at Tsarevskoe Gorodishche and dates to the turn of the 14th century. It has Byzantine form and Islamic decoration—a gold band and three gold panels with interlaced tendrils and leaves. This style of cup and related silver wares were produced by craftsmen working at Jochi's base camp on the Irtysh River near Tobolsk before his death in 1227. Production of Irtysh silver may have continued into the late 13th century.

from the 1220s to 1240s. The geography of the archaeological finds is circumscribed by the Dnieper, the middle Don, the steppe north of the Caucasus, and the middle Volga.[8] Related finds from Gashun Usta at Stavropol include a golden belt with a heraldic sign of the house of Batu (fig. 25.3) and a ladle or cup with a dragon-headed handle (fig. 25.4); a double-handled wine cup of similar type was found during excavations at Tsarevskoe Gorodishche.[9]

Saddles and belts with dragonlike heraldry appear very suddenly in the Mongol sphere. The reforms of 1206, which established new branches of tribal aristocracy, made it necessary to identify Genghis Khan's regime with special unifying symbols. These belts were inherited by a generation whose fathers and grandfathers had been companions of Genghis Khan, prior to the conquest of the Golden Horde, and who made up the command corps of the Jochids in the 1230s. The belts are emblematic of the equestrian culture of subsequent generations, who, having returned from the western campaign about 1240, established the Golden Horde as an independent state.

The Ilkhanid minister Rashid al-Din reports in his *Compendium of Chronicles* that just prior to Jochi's death in 1227 "the capital of his state" was on the Irtysh River.[10] A group of particularly fine silver articles found in the Tobolsk Irtysh area apparently were made in craft shops located within the personal estate of Jochi and his wives on the Irtysh sometime before 1227.[11] The originality that makes this group impressive derives from the fusion of artistic traditions from northern China and regions west. The forms of the cups evoke those of Byzantium, and the decoration of some of the vessels shows influences from Islamic Asia Minor. It is possible that the Irtysh craftsmen continued to work even after the death of their patron, into the

25.6-7 Glazed Polychrome Bowls
Among the finds from the site of Selitrennoe (possily the ancient city of Sarai) are glazed ceramics with styles that reflect Iranian craft traditions. Ikhanid craftsmen produced these geometric and flower-patterned bowls in the late 14th to early 15th century.

last decades of the thirteenth century.[12]

The archaeological finds from burial complexes of the early Jochids and from contemporaneous layers at some settlements and old villages reveal rare materials identified directly with the Jochids proper and characteristic of the greater Mongolian empire, not unique to the Golden Horde. Belt assemblies and saddle inlays with Central Asian motifs belong to the equestrian culture of the first generation of Mongols, which spread Jochid authority to the steppes of eastern Europe. These artifacts functioned as badges of the empire's military elite during the formative stage of their regime.

A marked change in material culture results from active Islamization in the Golden Horde under Khan Özbeg (r. 1312–42) in the first half of the fourteenth century. Only one of three belt assemblies in the Simferopol find, which belonged to the Golden Horde ruler of the Crimea region, comes from the Golden Horde.[13] This elaborate archer's belt, dated to the first half of the fourteenth century, displays no features of the early Jochid type that were made during unification of the greater Mongol empire.[14] Rather, it belongs to one of the largest groups of finds dating to the middle

Jochid period and was probably made in Crimea; the style is also consistent with urban workshops of Volga Bulgaria.[15] Solkhat and other craft centers of the Golden Horde transmitted the Seljuk–Anatolian Turk style of belt decoration, which was used widely in the northwestern Caucasus.

The gold and silver items manufactured in the Mongol style, representing khanate authority and the Mongol equestrian elite, were gradually replaced over the course of the middle Jochid period with regalia that did not conflict with the dictates of Islam. The author Ibn Tagriberdi, writing in Cairo during the second half of the fifteenth century, offered the wry remark that Khan Özbeg, once he had converted to Islam, preferred decorative belt plates of iron and condemned others for their devotion to gold. The khan's modesty is refuted by Ibn Battuta, who observed that Özbeg's summer quarters were bursting with gold and silver, and that the khan himself arrived late and half-drunk at the mosque for daily prayer[16] (see Chapter 29). Despite the khan's predilections, the material culture of the realm already reflected the political need to convey legitimacy and propriety in the Islamic cultural idiom.

25.8-9 Blue Glazed Bowls
Deep blue-glazed bowls with dark underpainting were also recovered archaeologically at the site of Selitrennoe. The great variety of ceramic styles is an indication of the diverse markets these products served. Crafts made in Sarai, situated on the Silk Road, were positioned to reach markets in Russia, Asia Minor, the Near East, Central and western Asia.

Towns, Cities, and Crafts

Due to its vast territory and multiculturalism, the Golden Horde had no standardized urban planning. Several variations of town construction across the region have been identified by archaeologists. In the Volga steppe, what is thought to be the Golden Horde capital of Sarai—as well as the cities of Gyulistan-Sarai, Ukek, and Beljamen—typify large-scale urban layouts in the central region of the Golden Horde.[17] Cities and villages around the Dniester, Crimea, and Azov regions, and in the northern Caucasus, are in many respects distinct from the cities and communities of the rest of the khan's domains. More than thirty medium and small cities from the fourteenth century have been discovered in the Volga area, including Mokhshi, Ukek, Beljamen, and Khadzhitarkhan.[18] Large and small urban sites have been identified by their official buildings, evidence of trade, and high-quality craftsmanship. The panorama of ancient cities displays a sharp rise in urban life during the fourteenth century.

The cities and villages of the Golden Horde, although diverse, were all activated by the vibrant trade coursing throughout the territory. Archaeologically recovered artifacts, especially ceramics, attest to the links between urban centers in different parts of the state during the fourteenth century (figs. 25.8, 9). Vessels (*khumy*) bearing the stamp of one master craftsman have been found in five different ancient cities: Tsarevskoe (Gyulistan-Sarai city), Sarepty (part of medieval Ukek), Vodyanskoe city, Khadzhitarkhan, and medieval Saraichik. An Arabic inscription on the stamp identifies this artisan or shop owner by his name: Anand, son of Sarkis, a widely known Armenian master in the Volga area whose works reached the banks of the Ural River.[19]

Ceramics provide further evidence of relationships between the Golden Horde and distant regions in the Middle and Near East (figs. 25.6, 7). An exquisite wine goblet found at the Golden Horde site of Azak was probably intended for a palace or noble manor. It has a body employing *kashin*, a silicate material which approximates the fine surface and white color of Chinese porcelain, and is painted in polychrome glazes with images of Islamic paradise. Judging from its fine workmanship, it was very likely made in a workshop of the capital city, Sarai.[20] The marked advances in ceramic technology in various regions of the Golden Horde

25.10 Sgraffito Vessel
Among the local ceramics produced in the Golden Horde were sgraffito wares inlaid with red paste that are reminiscent of Egyptian Mamluk ceramics of Seljuk and Byzantine style. This vessel, which illustrates elaborately dressed people, fish, and plant tendrils, was reassembled from fragments and missing portions were reconstructed.

25.11 Warrior Belt with Dragon Emblem
The dragon motif on this military belt, a symbol of the early Genghissid leadership, identifies it as belonging to one of the 13th-century rulers of the Golden Horde.

were stimulated by trade and the resulting influx of Middle and Near Eastern master craftsmen. Technological progress was rapid, fueled by the increased profitability of ceramic production of both glazed wares for the table and unglazed pots for utilitarian use. High-temperature ceramic kilns, which used the most advanced systems for distributing heat via vertical ducts within the firing chamber, have been found in the ancient city of Selitrennoe.[21] The two kilns excavated there are reported to be of the *karkhana* type usually found in ceramic workshops of the Ilkhanate in Mongol Iran, thousands of kilometers to the south (see Chapters 22, 23). The archaeological contexts of these furnaces suggest that the workshops belonged to high officials, merchants, or even to estates of the khans.[22]

Distinctive ceramics were produced in the eastern and western regions of the Golden Horde. *Kashin* vessels have been found only in Khoresm, Saraichik, and the cities of the lower and middle Volga area. The *kashin* of the Golden Horde in the end of the thirteenth and fourteenth centuries are of equal quality to the ceramics made by master craftsmen of the Near and

25.12 Tsar's Dragon Emblem
Among the emblems found on the throne of the Russian tsars in the St. George Room of the Winter Palace in St. Petersburg is the image of a dragon-like creature with a yellow tail and golden wings. This creature is believed to be a heraldic symbol of the Kazan khanate, a successor state to the Golden Horde that Tsar Ivan IV absorbed into his domains in 1552. While the origin of this dragon-like creature in Kazan iconography is not entirely clear, there is no doubt that its symbolism can be traced back to the Mongol rulers of the Golden Horde.

novel and widespread identity shift within the maturing imperial state. The affinity for the Islamic world and the loosening of ties with the original homeland of Genghis Khan created religious, economic, and political precedents that were inherited by the successor states of the Golden Horde. After the 1360s, a series of calamities befell the Golden Horde that effectively halted the innovative pace of cultural interaction. The ravages of the black plague, destruction in the east by the onslaught of Temür (Tamerlane), and the cessation of Silk Road trade after the fall of the Mongol Yuan dynasty in China forever altered the vibrant character of urban and village life. The hardships of the second half of the fourteenth century cut short a burgeoning era of progress that had transformed small and isolated farming, herding, and hunting societies into the Golden Horde.

The author's text was translated by Richard Bland.

1. Fedorov-Davydov 2003, 45–46.
2. Pachkalov 2001; Goncharov 2000, 345–49.
3. Evstratov 1997, 88–118; Varvarovskii 2000.
4. Egorov 1985, 139.
5. Fedorov-Davydov 2003, 46–47.
6. Trepavlov 1993.
7. Navaan 2005, 18–27; Silk Road 2006, 55–60.
8. Kramarovsky 2001, 35–45, fig. 14:1–19.
9. Piotrovskii et al. 2000, 59, cat. no. 15.
10. Rashid al-Din 2003, 418.
11. Kramarovsky 2001, 93–108.
12. Kramarovsky 2008a, 101–3, fig. 1.
13. Kramarovsky 2001, 114–20.
14. Piotrovskii et al. 2000, 83, cat. nos. 527–64.
15. Kramarovsky 2001, 130, 140.
16. Ibn Battuta 2003, 138–39.
17. Fedorov-Davydov 1984; Blokhin and Yavorskaya 2006.
18. Egorov 1985, 106–20.
19. Kramarovsky 2005, 119; nos. 164, 575, 576; Tasmagambetov et al. 2001, 240; Trepavlov 2002, 225–44.
20. Kramarovsky 2007, 182–89.
21. Fedorov-Davydov and Bulatov 1989, 155–60.
22. Fedorov-Davydov and Bulatov 1989, 239.
23. Zilivinskaya 2003, 41–56; Kramarovsky 2005 112–16.

Middle East. These same workshops in the Golden Horde produced high quality ceramics for daily life, including tableware, cups for rose water, druggists' vessels (*al'barello*, adopted by the Italians as *albarello*), and inkwells. The production of ceramics and glazed tiles for architecture was also highly developed in the region. In other areas, however, ceramic technologies and styles assumed quite different trajectories. Pottery workshops in the region that includes the Crimea and the Azov specialized in glazed sgraffito vessels engraved and inlaid with red clay reminiscent of Mamluk ceramics of the Seljuk and Byzantine styles (fig. 25.10).

Most *madrassas*, mosques, and other public structures in the cities of the Golden Horde date from the first half of the fourteenth century.[23] The Islamization of Jochid urban areas and material culture signifies a

26. The Mongols at War

Timothy May

IN THE POPULAR IMAGINATION, the Mongols are remembered primarily for their militarism—often as a horde of fur-clad, weapon-wielding warriors on horseback, howling as they descend upon civilization with little else on their minds but raping, routing, and plundering. Although the Mongol military did fit that description, at least on occasion, it was also one of the most impressive armies in history—because of its success in conquering other lands and extending its domain, as well as its precise organization and skillful execution of military actions. The military was the primary institution of the Mongol empire. Without it, the empire could not have existed: the extent of conquest would not have been possible, and it was the training ground for many key leaders in the upper levels of the administration.

Training

The Mongols, and the Türkic nomads who were conscripted into the Mongol army, had many natural talents for war. Their nomadic lifestyle had already made them excellent horsemen and inured to a life of hardship in the challenging climate of the steppe. Hunting had developed their skills in using the composite bow, which was to become their primary weapon in war (see Chapter 13). Relying on its range of 300 or more meters and a pull capacity from 45 kg to 68 kg, the Mongols proved to be formidable foes (fig. 26.9). Still, it takes more than a harsh life and natural ability to turn individuals into an army.

The hunting culture of the Mongols ensured a shared familiarity with the techniques of the hunting circle, *nerge* or *jerge*, which the military adapted to ensure cooperation among their units.[1] The *nerge* was a flexible technique that could involve hundreds to thousands of riders who formed a massive circle stretching over several kilometers. The line gradually contracted, herding all animals toward the center of the circle. Riders established their prowess by preventing any animal from escaping, be it a tiger or the smallest rabbit. Anyone who lost control of his section was punished. Once the circle had contracted, a man demonstrated his personal bravery and warrior skills by slaying the animals. The *nerge* required excellent communication skills among mounted riders. If they did not act as a single unit, gaps formed in their lines, allowing animals to escape.[2] This effective hunting strategy, learned by all Mongol males, became a definitive tactic of the Mongol army.

Games that every Mongol played throughout his life also honed his warrior skills. Archers learned to shoot at targets—usually leather bags set atop poles or skins stretched on frames—while riding. They practiced their skills while approaching,

26.1 Mongol Siege Tactics
This illustration from Rashid al-Din's *Jami'al-Tavarikh* (Compendium of Chronicles) shows Mongols attacking Baghdad using siege catapults and bows and arrows. Mongols are dressed in cloth-covered armor plate and wear domed helmets with yellow plumes. Depictions of swords and recurved bows are standardized . Defenders use similar armor and bows, but lack Mongolian features and can be identified by black-plumed helmets and colored shields.

26.2 The Chisel Attack
Similar to the European cavalry tactic known as the caracole, the Mongol chisel attack also involved wheeling horsemen: parallel files of cavalry charge the enemy position, discharging their arrows, and then turn to the rear to reload while those behind them continue a rolling charge. The tactic concentrated heavy fire power on a small area, facilitating penetration and fragmentation of the enemy line.

Caracole Tactic

Enemy Formation

40 -50 meters

Mongol line

Fires in Parthian fasion while turning

26.3 The Feigned Retreat
A classic cavalry tactic used by Mongols in many different situations, the feigned retreat lured enemy forces out from fortified or advantageous positions during a siege or on the field of battle. In the Battle of Sajo River, this tactic led a pursuing army into an ambush and entrapment by hidden troops.

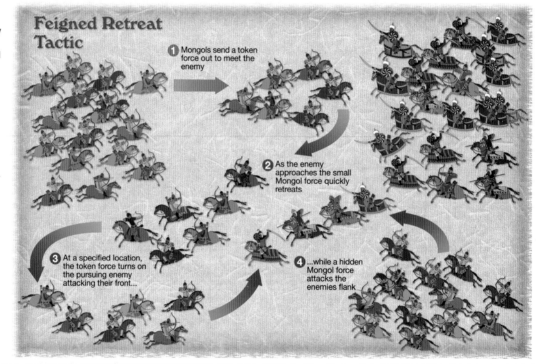

Feigned Retreat Tactic

1 Mongols send a token force out to meet the enemy

2 As the enemy approaches the small Mongol force quickly retreats

3 At a specified location, the token force turns on the pursuing enemy attacking their front...

4 ...while a hidden Mongol force attacks the enemies flank

passing by, and then, by turning around and taking a "Parthian shot" after passing the target. The constant practice developed the upper body strength that allowed the Mongols to pull their powerful bows.

Discipline is what truly set the Mongols apart from most medieval armies. Draconian punishments, including death, awaited those who failed to obey orders or stay with their units during battles. Discipline made the *nerge* successful and allowed the Mongols to develop archery tactics that maximized their effectiveness and mobility. New recruits were trained to execute these properly and to function as units rather than as individuals (fig. 26.4). Early in his career, Genghis Khan recognized the importance of maintaining discipline to ensure that the enemy had been destroyed before the Mongols began plundering their camp.[3]

Command and Leadership

The Mongol army was organized into decimal units of tens (*arban*), hundreds (*jaghun*), and thousands (*minggan*). The *minggan* was the primary unit of operation, but as the empire increased, commanders of *tumen*, or units of ten thousand, were more common.[4] The decimal structure made Mongol commanders immensely flexible. The commander only had to give orders to his ten subordinates, who then did the same to the ranks under his control. Ultimately, the *arban* commanders disseminated orders to the rank and file. Any individual could rise through the ranks, and if a commander did not obey his superiors or failed to execute his duties, he would be replaced.

Mongols gathered together before campaigns to establish strategic goals and a schedule, but commanders in the field were given independence to respond to the climatic, geographic, and political circumstances at hand.[5] Commanders needed to adhere to the agreed schedule to coordinate some aspects of the campaign, but Mongol generals had the flexibility to split off their forces because they all knew when and where to rendezvous. Mongol generals rarely fought in the front lines in battle, unlike many of their contemporaries. In-

26.4 Mongolian Cavalry
Genghis Khan established a rigorous training regime for his cavalry and required his horsemen to maintain horse gear and arms in top condition. From the time a boy could ride, he practiced the art of shooting from a galloping horse, in the process learning to use the principal cavalry weapon, the composite Mongolian bow. Sabers and spears were also used for close combat. Cavalry operations were coordinated across the battlefield by use of whistling signal arrows.

26.5 Mongol Horses
Mongol horses today are little changed from the time of Genghis Khan. They have had less genetic manipulation by humans than Arabian horses, but although similar in size, build, and behavior to such wild Asiatic horses as the Przewalski horse, their DNA is different. For much of the year they roam in herds, feeding off the land, even in the depth of winter. Consequently they have great endurance, are accustomed to rocky terrain, and being small and stocky, are agile in battle.

26.6 The Citadel of Aleppo
Aleppo, west of the upper Euphrates River, was the key stronghold the Mongols needed to gain access to Damascus, the Levant, and Turkey. Mongols attacked it twice, once in 1260 and again in 1299. The successful 1260 attack, under Hülegü, employed twenty siege machines and lasted only five days, after which the Mongols advanced south, taking Damascus. Their later defeat by Egyptian Mamluks at the Battle of Ayn Jalut ended their conquest of the Near East. The second attack of Aleppo, in 1299 during the ilkhanship of Ghazan, secured the fortress again and captured Damascus. Military concerns in the east caused the Mongol forces to withdraw from the city shortly after.

stead, Mongol commanders remained at a vantage point where they could direct the battle through the use of whistling arrows, messengers, drums, and signal flags.

Most of the generals originated from the khan's bodyguard, or *keshik*, which eventually became ten thousand strong. More than a protection detail, the *keshik* served as a military training center, where the future commanders developed loyalty to the khan and earned his trust. From this experience, they also learned standard strategies and tactics, which provided a uniformity of training, and, ultimately, command practices that are unique in the premodern era. Junior officers learned the tactics of warfare from being included in discussions of battles. Mongol princes and promising generals served under the tutelage of more senior commanders. Even Genghis Khan underwent an apprenticeship under Jamukha before the two blood brothers became rivals.[6] Between their experiences in the *keshik* and through apprenticeship, the generals not only proved themselves on the battlefield but also gained the confidence of the khan and the rest of the military staff to lead an army of thousands in hostile territory.

Invasion and Siege Warfare
Invasions followed a set pattern. A screen of scouts who constantly relayed information back to their main column preceded the in-

vading forces. Such gathering of intelligence enabled the Mongols to locate enemy armies rapidly. Because of their preplanned schedule and the information provided by the scouts, the Mongols were able to march divided but fight united. Their forces marched in smaller concentrations, which enhanced Mongol mobility. The use of columns concealed their troop strength, but the Mongols could usually reunite their forces before the enemy was cognizant of all the different invasion forces. Rarely were their opponents' forces prepared to engage the enemy on many fronts at the same time. Essentially the Mongols used the *nerge* hunting technique on a wider scale and with human targets.[7]

The multipronged invasion, which permitted the Mongols to deal with all field armies before moving deep into enemy territory, was a favored method of engagement. Using this technique was contingent upon luring the enemy out to meet the Mongols before they destroyed an entire province. When the Mongols did encounter their enemies in the field, they would try to time the encounter to benefit themselves, by delaying the attack until sufficient troops arrived, or by luring the enemy to another location more suitable for the Mongol horsemen. The deployment of smaller mobile units also facilitated sending reinforcements to an embattled force, or, in the

26.7-8 Helmet and Firearm
Persian illustrations from the late 13th century show Mongol helmets as brimmed, low-domed, and with a spiked or turreted top. Mongols adopted the stockless firearm from the Chinese, but they were difficult to aim and inefficient to reload. Their primary effect may have been for shock and awe.

event of defeat, avenging fallen comrades.

By concentrating on the dispersion and movement of enemy field armies, the assault on strongholds was delayed. Smaller fortresses or locations vulnerable to surprise were taken as the troops progressed, which provided the Mongols with extensive siege experience, valuable for perfecting their tactics. During the Khwarazmian campaign between 1219 and 1222, many smaller cities and fortresses were taken before the Mongols eventually captured Samarkand. The use of multiple columns and raiding forces prevented the main cities from assisting their smaller neighbors, as to do so in any strength would leave them open to attack. This strategy also cut off communication between the principal city and other cities that might have been a source of aid. Like the *nerge*, which forced the surrounded animals inward, this process encouraged refugees from these smaller cities to flee toward the last stronghold. The reports from these defeated cities and the streaming crowds of refugees not only dampened the morale of the garrison forces and inhabitants of the principal city but also strained its resources. Food and water reserves were taxed by the sudden influx of refugees.

Without the interference of a field army, which had been destroyed in advance of the attack, the Mongols were free to lay siege (fig. 26.6). Forces from smaller forts and cit-ies could not harry the Mongols. The capture of the outer strongholds and towns provided captives to either man the siege machines or to act as human shields for the Mongols. Prisoners were also forced to build a palisade around the town under siege, thus preventing the besieged from escaping. Meanwhile, Chinese and Persian engineers assembled trebuchets and catapults to bombard the city. Concentrated firepower, focused on one or two points in the city's defenses, was characteristic of Mongol siege warfare. With repeated bombardment, breaches in the defenses opened quickly and the Mongol troops stormed the city (fig. 26.1).

Tactics

Psychological warfare, particularly in the form of terror, underlay the Mongol form of "diplomacy": enemies were offered the choice to submit or die. If the enemies submitted, they were then required to pay tribute and provide troops and supplies when requested. Those who resisted or rebelled could expect the Mongols to attack without restraint. Massacres and the razing of cities became a tool calculated to encourage submission and as a warning to other cities not to resist. Typically, Mongol acts of cruelty were not performed in a blind rage, but for pragmatic reasons that accelerated the act of conquest: a single massacre could procure the submission of a dozen cities.

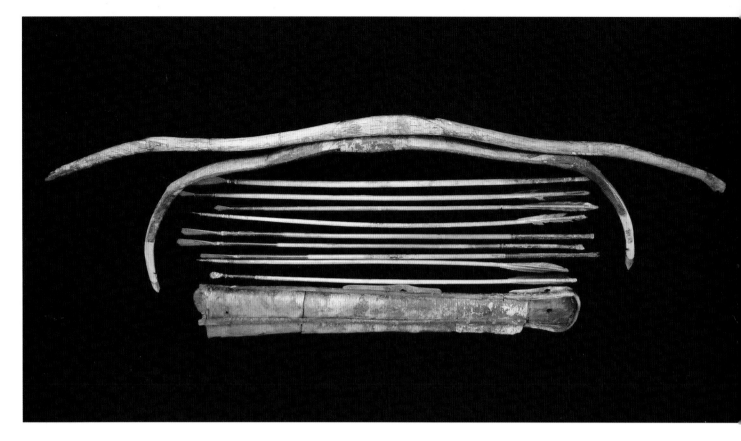

26.9 The Mongol Bow
The distinctive composite bow, with curved tips and double bend, appears in Mongolian rock art more than 2,000 years ago. By Mongol times it had been refined into an extremely powerful weapon whose strength came from laminating together three different materials—horn on the inside facing the archer, wood in the middle, and sinew on the outside—all bound with animal glue. The Mongol bow was shorter than modern Mongolian bows to facilitate shooting from horseback. Arrows were usually made of birch with eagle or crane fletching, and had different types of points for different uses. These bows, arrows, and birch-bark quiver date to the 13th–14th century and were recovered from a grave or cache in Shiluustei sum in Zavkhan province.

In addition, the Mongols relied on three basic tactics, used in a variety of permutations. The first was the feigned retreat, a classic steppe tactic (fig. 26.3). A force of Mongols would attack and harass the enemy, occasionally even charging the enemy. After a brief attack, the Mongols retreated in full flight to a designated location where the rest of the Mongol army waited. When reunited, the forces would wheel around and resume the attack while other units attacked the rear and flanks of their enemies. This process could last for days, as it did in the Battle of the Khalkha River against the Russians in 1223. The goal was to exhaust the enemy and also to break the enemy's formations, thus making them less effective.

Enveloping or surrounding the enemy was another important tactic, often affected by a feigned retreat or by using the *nerge*. During a battle the Mongols executed a flanking maneuver on both sides or a strike to the rear. Their mobility and system of communication on the battlefield allowed a general to order such an attack at any given moment. That mobility also ensured that troops who were operating several kilometers away could be called upon to make the flanking maneuver and appear promptly behind the enemy.

The "chisel," or *shi'uchi*, maneuver was the Mongols' primary form of attack (fig. 26.2).[8] Troops would advance unit by unit in ranks with space between their files. Each man would charge in sequence, shooting arrows until they were roughly thirty to forty meters away, then turning and riding to the end of his file. Each Mongol warrior could shoot three to five arrows during the course of that maneuver, and the next began his charge as the preceding turned back, creating a constant barrage on the enemy. This constant attack pinned the enemy to one location, thus allowing the Mongols to follow up with an enveloping maneuver.[9] As each Mongol warrior also possessed three to five extra mounts on average, the army could maintain the attack for long periods. Eventually, the enemy either broke and fled, or charged the Mongols, who then switched to a feign retreat. The *shi'uchi* chisel attack required an intense discipline and training to execute without men straying from their attack and retreat lanes, thus disrupting the attack of fellow warriors.

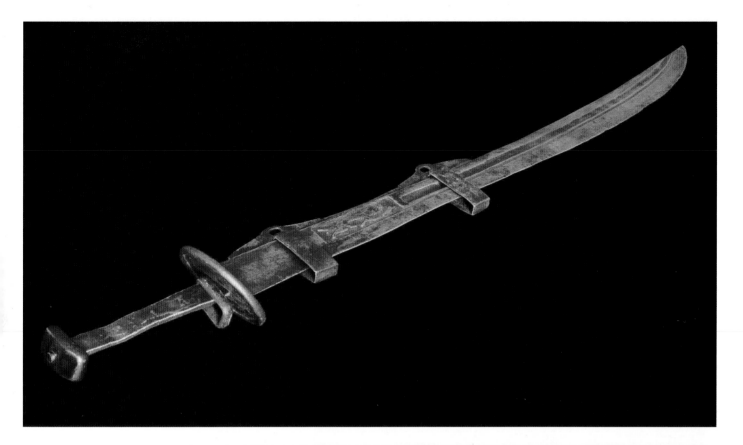

26.10–13 Swords, Spears, and Bombs

Swords were most effective for fighting at close quarters, either on horseback or on foot, and were equally good for offense and defense. Spears, requiring two hands, were useful for cavalry and infantry advances but were dangerous to use in hand-to-hand combat. Ceramic bombs or grenades were pioneered by the Chinese and adopted by the Mongols for use with catapults. It is said that Yuan warriors stiffened their resolve with liquor carried in small ceramic bottles.

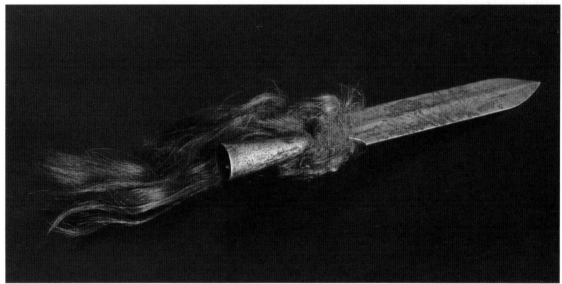

26.14 Plate Armor Vest
Metal plate armor has a long history in Asia, beginning in the Bronze Age. Unlike medieval European armor, which was generally made of chain mail covered with large molded plates articulated at the joints, Asian plate armor was made of small flat or convex plates sewn overlapping to an undergarment, as in the armored vest pictured here. Asian-style plate armor was lighter than European armor, more akin to chain mail, and because it permitted more body movement, was more effective in hand-to-hand combat.

Strategy of Conquest

Over time, the Mongols came to believe that they were destined to rule the world. Their invasions became conquests, notably under the rule of Ögödei Khaghan (r. 1237–41). By fighting on multiple fronts, the Mongols risked overextending their forces. Although they could mobilize large armies—for instance, 150,000 men to invade Russia and eastern Europe from 1236 to 1240, conducting war over such a broad front was a risk, even with the assistance of allies and vassals.

It was in the interest of the Mongols not to overextend themselves. The key to their strategy of conquest was a unit known as the *tanma*. This was a unit, often of non-Mongol nomads, but commanded by a Mongol, known as a *tanmachi*, that was situated on the border of the Mongol empire, often between steppe and sown or agricultural lands.[10] Its goal was not to defend the empire from attack, but to extend Mongol power and influence. At times, this was conducted through additional conquests, but it could also be accomplished through diplomatic means. Large swaths of territory, how-ever, were conquered by the main army.

With the enemy disorganized and much of its military capacity destroyed, what remained was not a major threat. Continued raids by the *tanma* further eroded it. Resistance was often minimal when the Mongols invaded again. A civil administration eventually supplanted the *tanma* and helped to incorporate conquered territory into the empire. The *tanma* would then move forward to the new border, always occupying territory that had not yet been formally integrated into the empire.

In popular literature, the Mongols are often compared to a force of nature because of the speed and ferocity of their conquests.[11] Usually, the descriptor is a whirlwind or storm, but this process of conquest also recalls a tidal wave or tsunami.[12] Like the ocean, Mongol forces were always present. When conditions were appropriate, the full might of the Mongol army struck, and then retreated. Like the wake, a portion of the conquered land remained "flooded" with some of the Mongol troops in the form of the *tanma*, but the rest went back to the empire. The territory remained devastated and weak, like the aftereffect of a tsunami.

Because of the training and quality of leadership within the Mongol army, it was well positioned for conquest. The discipline of the forces allowed the Mongols to use more advance tactics than their opponents and overcome them, even if the individual military skills of their opponents were greater. The more cerebral aspects of warfare, such as order, leadership, and organization, separated the Mongols from their contemporaries and allowed them to become the most formidable military of the premodern world

1. May 2006a; May 2007.
2. Allsen 2006.
3. De Rachewiltz 2004.
4. Buell 1980.
5. Sinor 1971.
6. May 2006b.
7. May 2006a.
8. De Rachewiltz 2004.
9. Smith 1984; May 2006a; 2007; Da 2001.
10. Buell 1980.
11. Marshall 1993; Dupuy 1980.
12. May 2004.

The Battle of Sajo River

William W. Fitzhugh

In the spring of 1241, twenty-two years after Genghis Khan began the invasion of Western Asia, Mongol armies stood on the banks of Danube (see Chapter 22, fig. 22.2). Subödei, Batu, and other Mongol generals paused to contemplate the invasion of Europe. The Mongols had been pursuing the last of the opposing steppe forces, the Kipchaks (known as the Cumans in Latin sources and Polovtsy to Russians), who had been given refuge by King Béla, the easternmost king of Christendom. Batu's envoys demanded that Béla turn the Kipchaks out, but instead Béla rashly took the Mongol envoys prisoner and had them executed. To Mongols this was an act of war, and Batu and Subödei, the greatest of all the Mongol field generals, prepared an elaborate attack.

Arraying their armies along a 300-mile front, the Mongols initiated diversionary attacks on the Hungarian flanks before converging on Budapest, where they camped in full view of Béla's puzzled scouts. After some days the Mongols broke camp and slowly withdrew to the east, drawing Béla's inexperienced army out of their stronghold and into a trap set near the Sajo River where catapults and other devices unfamiliar to Europeans were set. Their forces engaged on 10 April 1241. After initial Mongol advances, the Hungarian army counterattacked, and just as they were about to overwhelm Batu, Subödei's cavalry appeared at the Hungarian rear, cutting off retreat. The two Mongolian armies then encircled the entire Hungarian force and began to tighten the noose in the manner of the *nerge,* a classic Mongol hunting technique of surrounding prey. By the end of the day the Hungarian force had been annihilated,

26.15 Chain Mail Shirt
Most body armor used by Mongolian rank-and-file soldiers was made of heavy hide or padded cloth. Chain mail armor provided much more protection against swords and broad-bladed arrows, but it could be penetrated by heavy, small-bore iron arrowheads.

losing as many as 60,000 men and much equipment. Miraculously, Béla escaped through the cordon, swam the Sajo, and found his way to safety. With the destruction of the Hungarian army and sack of Budapest, the Mongols were poised to invade Europe. It seemed possible, and to some, inevitable, that all of Europe would fall to Mongol domination.

The Battle of Sajo River was indeed a turning point, but not the one Europeans feared. One year later, just as they were mobilizing to march into Europe, the Mongol forces suddenly broke camp and turned back east, abandoning their newly conquered territories. Word had reached them that Grand Khan Ögödei, Genghis Khan's designated successor, had died, and a new khan had to be selected. Batu settled permanently with his army at Sarai, on the Akhtuba River north

of the Caspian Sea, from which he administered the Golden Horde, while Subödei led the remaining imperial troops 6,000 miles back to Khara Khorum to participate in the selection of a new Khan. When military action began again after Güyug became Grand Khan in 1246, Mongol attentions turned away from Europe and toward Persia and the Near East, while in Asia they targeted China, Korea, and Japan. The Golden Horde continued to control Russia and eastern Europe, but Europe had been saved and its Crusaders subsequently became occasional allies of the Mongols in their struggles against Islam and the Muslims.

PART IV
KUBLAI KHAN AND YUAN CHINA

Kublai Khan
In this portrait Kublai is shown
as he was in the 1260s, robust
and in his prime. His simple
white costume, without elegant
furs and trappings, may have
been intended to convey that
the new Mongol khan was a
leader who exuded practicality
rather than pomp and ceremony.

202

27. The Vision in the Dream

KUBLAI KHAN AND THE CONQUEST OF CHINA

MORRIS ROSSABI

GENGHIS KHAN'S GRANDSON KUBLAI KHAN (1215–1294) is one of history's most intriguing heroes. He is a central character in his contemporary Marco Polo's account of his travels through Asia, along with his magnificent marble palace where the "halls and rooms and passages are all gilded and wonderfully painted within with pictures and images of beasts and birds and trees and flowers and many kinds of things, so well and so cunningly that it is a delight and a wonder to see."[1] Kublai and his domain were further romanticized in Samuel Taylor Coleridge's 1798 poem, which generations of English-speaking schoolchildren have memorized:

In Xanadu did Kubla Khan
A stately pleasure-dome decree:
Where Alph, the sacred river, ran
Through caverns measureless to man
Down to a sunless sea.
—Kubla Khan. Or, A Vision in a Dream: A Fragment

27.1 *Kublai Khan Hunting*, 1282
This famous painting by the celebrated Yuan court artist Liu Guandao shows Kublai and his empress during a casual moment on a hunting excursion. They pause to watch one of the royal party shoot a bird from the sky, while a camel caravan passes in the distance. The artist has paid great attention to clothing: Kublai wears a fur robe and fine silk garments. The hunting party is of mixed ethnic origin, befitting China's diverse nationalities, and its animals include horses, a hound, a trained leopard, and a hunting eagle or falcon.

Most in the Western world are familiar with his name and, to some extent, with his exploits. Yet, little is known of Kublai the man. The Chinese sources, including the most important account of his reign (1260–94) in the *Yuanshi*, the record of the dynasty he founded, portray his bureaucratic role, offering abundant details about his meetings with foreign envoys, his intention to waive taxes on regions afflicted by natural disasters, or his decisions in cases involving capital punishment. On occasion, his own personality—that of a visionary with a pragmatic bent—emerges from these passages. Piecing together Chinese, Iranian, Korean, and Western-language accounts, it is possible to offer a glimpse of his life and his family, but even this view focuses on his career.

Early Life and Career

Kublai's mother Sorghaghtani Beki profoundly influenced him. She was the wife of Genghis's son Tolui, a great commander but also a lover of alcohol, who died around 1232. Mother of four sons who played important roles in the thirteenth century, Sorghaghtani Beki received compliments from numerous contemporary observers. The Persian chronicler Rashid al-Din lauds her as "extremely intelligent and able" and claims

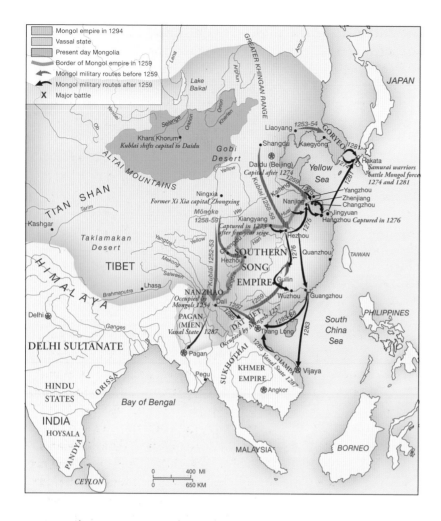

Mongol empire in 1294
Vassal state
Present day Mongolia
Border of Mongol empire in 1259
Mongol military routes before 1259
Mongol military routes after 1259
X Major battle

GREATER KHINGAN RANGE
Lena
Argun
Amur
JAPAN
Lake Baikal
Yenisei
Selenge
Onon
Kerulen
Orkhon
Khara Khorum
Kublai shifts capital to Daidu
Gobi Desert
Liaoyang 1253–54
GORYEO 1281
Shangdu
Kaegyŏng
Hakata
Samurai warriors battle Mongol force 1274 and 1281
ALTAI MOUNTAINS
Daidu (Beijing)
Capital after 1274
Yellow
Yellow Sea
TIAN SHAN
Ningxia
Former Xi Xia capital Zhongxing
Möngke 1258–59
Kaifeng 1259
Yangzhou
Zhenjiang
Changzhou
Nanjing
Kashgar
Tarim
Wei
Xiangyang
Captured in 1273 after five-year siege
Jingyuan
Hangzhou *Captured in 1276*
Taklamakan Desert
Yangtze
Yellow
Chengdu
Han
Hezhou
1276
Quanzhou
TAIWAN
TIBET
Mekong
Salween
SOUTHERN SONG EMPIRE
Lhasa
HIMALAYA
Brahmaputra
NANZHAO
Occupied by Mongols 1254
Dali 1257
Hezhou
Guilin
Wuzhou
Guangzhou
Delhi
Ganges
PAGAN (MIEN)
Vassal State 1287
DAI VIET
Occupied by Mongols 1257
Thang Long
1283
South China Sea
PHILIPPINES
DELHI SULTANATE
Pagan
Pegu
SUKHOTHAI
1285–88
1295 *Vassal State 1287*
CHAMPA
Vijaya
HINDU STATES
ORISSA
Bay of Bengal
KHMER EMPIRE
Angkor
INDIA
HOYSALA
PANDYA
MALAYSIA
BORNEO
CEYLON
0 400 MI
0 650 KM

in fostering the native, mostly agricultural, economies instead of forcing peasants to convert the land to pasturage. Understanding that confiscatory taxation and ravaging of the land would ultimately translate into less income for the Mongol rulers, Sorghaghtani Beki advocated support for agriculture.

She abided by Genghis Khan's policy of religious toleration and ensured that her sons, Kublai, in particular, adopted the same view. Although she herself was a Nestorian Christian, she provided funds alike to Buddhist monasteries, Nestorian churches, and *madrassas* (Islamic theological schools). By supporting a variety of religions, Kublai imitated his mother's ecumenism toward religion.

Sorghaghtani Beki's involvement in politics paved the way for her sons' careers. Disunity within the Mongol elite had flared up almost as soon as Genghis Khan had died, and Sorghaghtani Beki skillfully used alliances and adroit political maneuvering to position her sons to succeed their grandfather as Great Khan.[5] A few months after her son Möngke was enthroned as the Great Khan, the fulfillment of her lifelong dream, she died.

Kublai had scarcely made an appearance on the historical stage when his brother Möngke became Great Khan in 1251. In 1253 Möngke entrusted his younger brother with his first major assignment, the pacification of the Dali state in the modern Chinese province of Yunnan. Diplomacy, threats, and a modicum of violence prompted Dali's king to submit, offering the Mongols a base in southwest China from which to initiate an assault on the still-independent Southern Song dynasty of China.[6] Impressed with Kublai's success in this campaign, Möngke next commissioned him to resolve disputes between the Buddhist and Daoist monasteries, controversies that had frequently erupted into violence. In 1258 Kublai presided over debates between the leading Buddhist and Daoist monks in China and Tibet; eventually, he sided with the Buddhists and imposed restrictions on the Daoists.[7] Even more impressed with his brother's skills, Möngke now recruited Kublai for a major three-pronged assault on the extraordinarily

27.2 The Mongol Conquest of China
This map shows the eastern portion of the Mongol empire at the time of Kublai's death in 1294: the present-day nation of Mongolia; the vassal states; and the two military campaigns conducted by Möngke and Kublai in the 1250s and by Kublai against the Southern Song empire in the 1270s–80s. Following almost 400 years of fragmentation, the Mongol conquest brought China together under a single administration. Although not of Chinese origin, the Yuan dynasty produced lasting benefits to the Chinese: foreign trade, open markets; freedom of religion; support for arts, culture, and science; currency reform; and stable, effective government and statecraft.

that she "towered above all the women in the world."[2] The Hebrew physician Bar Hebraeus describes her as "a queen [who] trained her sons so well that all the princes marveled at her power of administration."[3] She certainly devoted herself to proper training for her sons. Eventually, three of her sons moved to the territories subjugated by the Mongols, while one, Arigh Böke, remained in Mongolia to be the upholder of Mongol traditions. Although she herself was illiterate, she recruited a tutor to teach Kublai and his brothers how to read and write Mongolian. Kublai also learned to speak, though not read, Chinese but whether her mother influenced his decision to learn spoken Chinese is unknown.[4]

Starting in the 1230s, Sorghaghtani Beki governed the North China domains that the Great Khan Ögödei gave to her after her husband's death. She recognized, earlier than many in the Mongol elite, the need to govern rather than merely to plunder the regions they had subjugated. She believed wealthy Southern Song dynasty. Kublai's assignment was to lead a battalion across the Yangzi River, the dividing line between Mongol-controlled North China and the Song Chinese, and attack the Southern Song forces. Möngke himself opened a front in Sichuan, and another force moved from Yunnan. The campaign started in late 1258, and progress was made on all fronts until Möngke's death on 11 August 1259 (fig. 27.2).[8]

Military operations against the Song were suspended because Möngke's brothers now jockeyed to succeed him as the Great Khan. Kublai was one of the contenders; his younger brother Arigh Böke, who had remained in Mongolia and represented the traditional interests and values of the herders, was the other. In 1260, rival *khuriltai* assemblages of the Mongol nobility were convened—Kublai's in his summer capital at Kaiping (later known as Shangdu) and his younger brother's in the Mongol capital at Khara Khorum—to choose the ruler from among Genghis's direct descendants. But as an orderly system of succession had not been devised, diplomacy and raw military power were essential for victory.

The civil war between the backers of Kublai and Arigh Böke lasted for four bloody years and ensured that the winner would be tarred with an aura of illegitimacy. The various khanates of the Mongol empire divided their support between Kublai and Arigh Böke, contributing to the disarray. The Ilkhan rulers of Iran and the Middle East opted for Kublai, while the Central Asian khanate and the Golden Horde of Russia chose Arigh Böke. However, the Iranian, Central Asian, and Russian khanates' troops were too far away to influence the conflict, and Kublai, using the abundant supplies and resources of North China, together with his Mongol archers and cavalry, finally crushed Arigh Böke's forces in Khara Khorum and the rest of Mongolia. Arigh Böke's life was spared, but he died two years later, in 1266, under what some scholars believe to have been mysterious circumstances.[9] Kublai, recognizing that Khara Khorum was too small and did not have the required food supply for a great capital, moved the seat of the empire to Daidu.

Kublai, who had devoted much of his career to governing in North China, appreci-

ated that Chinese practices and institutions fostered stability and effective rule. Indeed, he had developed an appreciation of many refinements and luxuries of Chinese civilization, as evidenced by his construction of a summer capital, with elaborate palaces, Buddhist and Daoist temples, and a hunting preserve. The complex in Shangdu, which Marco Polo called "Ciandu" and described as "a wonder and delight to see," entered the English language as Xanadu, a synonym for a place of idyllic beauty.[10] Kublai was very willing to accommodate to features of Chinese civilization to ingratiate himself to the Chinese—too much so, according to leaders who wished to preserve the traditional Mongol ways and style of life. His struggle with Arigh Böke presaged conflicts between these forces and others who acknowledged the need for acceptance of the practices and beliefs of the subjugated Chinese population.

Kublai now faced the daunting task of buttressing his legitimacy among the traditionalists who had questioned his allegiance to Mongol values while signaling his support for stability and effective governance for the much more populous and recently conquered Chinese population. In the first two decades of his reign, from 1260 to 1280, Kublai performed the delicate balance between his roles as Great Khan of the Mongols and emperor of the Chinese admirably. Hostilities between these two groups would eventually contribute to the collapse of the Mongol empire.

Kublai as Khan

Kublai practiced religious toleration in governing a multiethnic empire. By supporting a variety of religions, he gained the confidence of clerics, facilitating rule over the non-Mongol populations. Kublai explained his ecumenical views to Marco Polo:

> There are four prophets who are worshipped and to whom everybody does reverence. The Christians say their God was Jesus Christ; the Saracens Mahomet; the Jews Moses; and the idolators Sagamoni Burcan [the Shakyamuni Buddha], who was the first god to the idols; and I do honor and reverence to all four, that is to him who is the greatest in heaven and more true, and him I pray to help me.[11]

To gain the support of Mongol tradition-

余嘗畫馬未嘗畫羊因
仲信求畫余故戲為寫生雖不
能逼近古人頗於氣韻有遊

27.3 *Sheep and Goat*
Kublai's support for the arts included a court appointment for the famous Yuan artist, Zhao Mengfu (1254–1322), a descendant of the first Song emperor, Taizu. Zhao came to Daidu, the Yuan dynasty capital, at the request of Kublai, who wanted to recruit talented young people from the Southern Song he had conquered. Zhao had an illustrious career in the Yuan administration, but he is best known today for his poetry and art. He was a versatile artist and worked in many media. His subjects ranged across landscapes, calligraphies, and handscrolls like this painting of a sheep and goat, painted ca. 1300.

alists, some of whom had sympathized with Arigh Böke, Kublai recruited shamans for his court and had them perform the proper rituals for various important occasions. To ensure a good year, Kublai himself scattered auspicious mare's milk on the ground at the beginning of the Mongols' late summer migrations to their winter abodes.[12] When his troops set forth on a military campaign, he conducted similar rituals and, again, poured out mare's milk to secure the Sky God's blessings. He organized elaborate banquets for Mongol festivals, with the guests consuming vast quantities of food and alcohol in what foreign visitors portrayed as drunken orgies (fig. 27.10). His fondness for the traditional hunt was still another endorsement of Mongol practices. As these well-organized hunting expeditions, which had originally served as training exercises for the Mongol military, became increasingly ritualized, they were more an affirmation of Mongol identity than preparation for combat (fig. 27.1).[13]

Kublai either restrained or discouraged Mongols from adopting Chinese customs. For example, Mongol women did not imitate the Chinese practice of binding women's feet, nor did many Mongols intermarry with the Chinese. Kublai himself continued the traditional practice of choosing consorts and concubines. According to Marco Polo,

"The great Khan sends his messengers to . . . find him the most beautiful girls according to the standard of beauty . . . And he has them kept by the elder ladies of the palace . . . and makes them lie with them in one bed to know if she has good breath and sweet, and is clean, and sleeps quietly without snoring, and has no unpleasant scent anywhere, & to know if she is a virgin."[14]

Kublai recognized that success in military campaigns was the most credible means to achieve legitimacy. His grandfather Genghis Khan had, in part, secured renown and earned his people's respect because of his military exploits in China and Central Asia. His brother Möngke had played an important role in the annexation of the Golden Horde territories in Russia. His brother Hülegü had been granted the title of Ilkhan, or subject khan, because he defeated the Ismaili (commonly, perhaps misleadingly, known as the Order of the Assassins) and conquered the Abbasid caliphate, which had previously ruled a vast Middle Eastern and North African empire (and, for a time, governed Spain). By 1264 Kublai had engaged in only one significant military campaign, which resulted in the annexation of the Dali kingdom, but it had been secured by a

27.4 *A Modest Hunting Party*
In contrast to the refined taste of Liu Guandao's bird hunt, this illustration of a later hunting excursion from *The Travels of Marco Polo* was visualized by European artists working only from Polo's inventive prose. Kublai is seen traveling in splendor (though precariously balanced) in a howdah carriage mounted on the backs of four elephants in the midst of a huge entourage. European artists were as unfamiliar with painting Asians as they were with elephant anatomy. Polo described 10,000 "watchers," 10,000 gyrfalcons and falconers, 500 gyrfalcons, plus peregrines and other hawks in great numbers. But it was the size, weight, and intelligence of the elephants, "surpassing all other animals on earth," that most impressed Polo.

voluntary submission rather than a major conquest. However, the Southern Song, the Chinese dynasty directly across the Yangzi River from his domains in North China, offered an opportunity to burnish his legitimacy among the Mongol elite. The Mongols clearly valued extraordinary military achievements, and a forward-looking leader could bolster his credentials through conquests.

The Southern Song ruled the most populous country on Earth, and its prosperous capital in Hangzhou had the largest population of the world's cities. The South was the agricultural heartland of China and had excellent ports, which welcomed Iranian, Arab, Indian, and Southeast Asian merchants. The printing, porcelain, and silk industries were lucrative, and the Southern Song had made striking technological progress in navigation, engineering, and astronomy. In short, the Southern Song dynasty was extremely wealthy and accomplished. Even Marco Polo was overwhelmed by the theaters, the restaurants, the inhabitants' elegant clothing, and the sanitation system in Hangzhou—not to mention its beautiful setting adjacent to the West Lake (fig. 27.4).[15] The capital's intellectual life sparkled and attracted some of the greatest painters, philosophers, poets, and craftsmen in Chinese history. Conquest of this civilization could not only yield considerable booty for the Mongols but also serve to demonstrate Kublai's military prowess.

Although Kublai was determined to occupy the South—in part because he feared a Southern Chinese revanchist movement to oust the Mongols and to recapture North China—fifteen years elapsed after the defeat of Arigh Böke before his troops overwhelmed the Song. The Song mounted a formidable defense, utilizing the armada that protected the seaborne trade, and its powerful navy to advantage in combat on lakes, rivers, and seas. The Mongols, who came from a landlocked domain, had never needed a navy. Kublai commissioned Chinese shipbuilders to build vessels, but that construction, as well as training the Mongols for combat on water, required considerable time. Conditions in the Song territories presented other problems. The Mongols and their horses were not accustomed to the semi-tropical heat of South China, nor had they developed resistance to the region's infectious and parasitic diseases. Horses, central to the Mongols' battle strategies, were not as effective in the hilly and forested southern Chinese landscape as on the Mongol steppes.[16] The steeds could find scant forage to graze because Chinese peasants had used almost all the available land to plant their crops. Despite the political infighting, revenue shortfalls, and rampant corruption at the Song court, Kublai's forces could not immediately gain control over China.

Crucial military encounters took place along the Yangzi River where Kublai's forces had to control the two cities of Xiangyang and Fancheng to enter the Yangzi River basin, and, from there, assault the rest of South China. These campaigns lasted from 1268 to 1273, an excruciatingly long time, because Song naval forces were initially able to evade the Mongol blockade of the two cities and supply the inhabitants and troops (fig. 27.2). As the Mongol–Chinese navy was developed, however, the blockade became increasingly effective and supplies in Xiangyang began to run out. The Song base in a castle and fort made Xiangyang seem impregnable until the Mongols recruited Muslim engineers, who designed siege engines for an assault on the city.[17] These weapons—a mangonel and a catapult that could hurl enormous boulders and projectiles—were devastating, which forced the two cities to surrender.

After the occupation of Xiangyang, the Mongols moved forward but at a less rapid pace than in other military campaigns. With cavalry playing a lesser role than in their other invasions, the Mongol forces relied on the more cumbersome and time-consuming tactic of besieging the many densely populated cities in South China, which were rather numerous. The inhabitants' growing disillusionment with Southern Song corruption and mismanagement, as well as the demoralization of the Chinese armies, were a great boon to the Mongols—a number of towns submitted without putting up stiff resistance. Even the capital city of Hangzhou fell without much of a fight: in January 1276, the empress dowager, who acted in the name of the six-year-old emperor, surrendered the dynasty's seal to a Mongol commander.[18] Kublai treated the imperial family with deference and generosity, which encouraged more Chinese soldiers to defect and other towns and regions to submit.

Kublai's forces still had to subdue a small group of loyalists, who claimed the throne on behalf of royal children. A few Song loyalists in June 1276 enthroned the captured emperor's seven-year-old half-brother as the new emperor.[19] Mongol navies and armies pursued these remnants of the Song court as they fled from one port to another along the southeast Chinese coast. The constant movement and anxiety wore down the fragile young emperor, who suddenly died in May 1278. The undeterred loyalists named another child, the deceased emperor's half-brother, as the new emperor and persisted in their peregrinations along the southeastern Chinese coast. In 1279 the Mongol forces finally caught up with the imperial party on an island near Guangzhou. With the young emperor in tow, the leading Song official attempted unsuccessfully to break through the Mongol blockade around the island, but he and the last ruler drowned.[20] Three centuries of Song governance over China came to an end.

Kublai had proven himself to his fellow Mongols, who prized martial virtues and the annexation of territory. He had earned their plaudits by conquering Song China, the world's most populous country and one of its most prosperous and powerful lands. In 1273 he had also crushed a rebellion in Korea and cemented relations by sending a Mongol princess in marriage to the Korean king[21] (see Chapter 32). He had tightened control over Tibet, which allowed his administration to collect taxes and demand forced labor from Tibetans.[22] In short, Kublai conclusively established the legitimacy of his once-controversial succession as Great Khan.

Kublai and the Yuan Dynasty

Simultaneously, Kublai was largely successful in ingratiating himself to the Chinese by portraying himself as a typical Chinese emperor. He was determined to be not only a universal leader but the founder of a new Chinese dynasty. Kublai was largely successful in persuading many Chinese that he found their civilization attractive and that he was becoming increasingly sinicized. Kublai recognized that the Chinese expected performances of Confucian music and dance at court and used such patronage to signal that he would not trample over their culture's most valued customs and practices.[23]

Even before he had defeated his younger brother in 1264, Kublai had begun to organize a Chinese-style court. He first recruited

27.5 Messenger Passport
This passport takes a different form than most 13th-century Mongol safe-passage *paiza*. To cover contingencies, it is written in several languages, including the official 'Phags-pa script. A bird of prey, perhaps a gyrfalcon, serves as a crest figure.

knowledgeable advisers who could assist him to develop institutions and re-create practices reminiscent of the ones championed in the Chinese dynasties. Kublai hardly needed these counselors' prodding to restore Confucian rituals of earlier dynasties such as the imperial services at the Altars of the Soil and Grain and to assume the role of emperor in these rites. He understood that rituals needed to be properly conducted to avert an imbalance in nature, which resulted in floods, earthquakes, and other disasters according to Chinese beliefs. The emperor was the most important figure for these observances.

Kublai adopted other policies to fashion himself as a typical Chinese emperor. Abiding by the Chinese reverence for ancestors, he built a Great Temple in Daidu (which has not survived) to honor his forebears, including his grandfather Genghis Khan.[24] He curried favor with the Chinese elite by constructing a shrine for Confucius and commissioning a group of academicians to write histories of three earlier dynasties, a vital obligation for Chinese Confucians.[25]

In 1271, on the advice of his Chinese counselors, Kublai selected a Chinese name for his dynasty: Yuan. The name "Yuan" derives from the *Yijing*, better known in the West as *I Ching* (Book of Changes), one of the earliest Chinese classical texts, and is defined in that work as "origins of the universe" or "primal force."[26] The Yuan government that Kublai organized closely resembled those of the Chinese dynasties: the ministries of Rites, War, Revenue, Public Works, Personnel, and Justice were identical to those bureaucracies that had regulated the Chinese population for centuries.

Moving his capital from Mongolia to Daidu, the area around modern Beijing, indicated that Kublai recognized China as the true center of his domains. Although foreign Muslims and other non-Chinese helped design and build the city, Daidu was modeled on earlier Chinese capitals. Built on a grander scale, the gates and the walls surrounding the city resembled earlier Chinese capital cities in design. Numerous Confucian shrines and Buddhist temples were constructed in Daidu, which also had the requisite pavilions, bridges, and parks of a Chinese city. Dragons, phoenixes, and other Chinese motifs adorned Kublai's palaces in the Forbidden City. Daidu's principal drawback was the lack of fertile land in the region, which necessitated the import of food and other provisions.[27] By 1289 Kublai had solved this problem by extending the Grand Canal about 135 miles from Shandong province to the Wei River, which created a continuous waterway to a site near Daidu. This major public works project facilitated the transport of grain and rice from the more fertile South.[28]

Kublai was well aware that he ruled subjugated peoples, some of whom opposed acquiescence to Mongol rule, and he recognized that a few might attempt to subvert the Yuan dynasty. To control and avert disloyalty among his Chinese subjects, he altered some traditional practices and imposed restrictions, eliminating, for example, the civil service examinations, a key institution in traditional China, which had provided most government officials.[29] Realizing that the examinations would have produced a bureaucracy that consisted exclusively of Chinese, a few of whom could have been disloyal, Kublai recruited Central Asian and

Iranian Muslims and Tibetan Buddhists, among others, for government positions.[30] To ferret out corrupt, ineffective, or subversive officials in his government, which included a sizable number of non-Mongols, both Chinese and other foreigners, Kublai established a Censorate, which was far more pervasive than any preceding one, with agents who traveled incognito throughout the country, especially to spy on the bureaucracy.[31] Finally, Kublai divided the population into four classes and allocated positions and privileges commensurately. Mongols comprised the first class; non-Chinese Muslims and a few other foreigners constituted the second class; northern Chinese were the third tier; and southern Chinese the fourth. The lower two classes could not reach the highest levels in the military or some of the leading posts in government.[32]

Kublai attempted, through his economic and social policies, to overcome the hostility engendered by such discrimination against the Chinese. Disdaining advice from traditional Mongols, Kublai did not attempt to convert the Chinese peasants' land to pasturage. One of his first edicts prohibited Mongol herders from permitting their animals to encroach upon China's arable lands.[33] He designed his agrarian policies to benefit peasants, starting with tax-relief measures for those whose lands had been devastated. Once these relief measures had stabilized the countryside, Kublai focused on the *she*, a village organization consisting of approximately fifty households, to promote innovations in agriculture, to plant trees, to reclaim land, to initiate flood-control projects, and to increase silk production.[34] In addition, he charged the *she* leader with the conduct of censuses; the provision of welfare for orphans, widows, and the destitute; the collection of taxes; and an abortive utopian scheme for the establishment of schools for peasant boys. Until the court began to face revenue shortfalls and Kublai had to increase taxes and limit his support for the *she*, agricultural production burgeoned and the countryside remained stable.

Similarly, Kublai's policies bolstered trade. The Confucian Chinese elite, which derived most of its wealth from land ownership, had traditionally disdained commerce, imposed restrictions on trade, and relegated merchants to a relatively low social status. The herding society of the Mongols produced a limited variety of goods, and so required trade with other cultures to improve its standard of living. Kublai built roads and bridges to facilitate transport, and permitted merchants who traveled from one market to another to reside and obtain supplies at one of the more than 1,400 postal stations that were constructed to expedite the delivery of official mail.[35] He set about to foster trade by reducing taxes on merchants, providing low-interest loans to merchant associations involved in risky long-distance trade, and increasing the use of paper money (a system of currency that the Chinese had developed). Marco Polo was the first Westerner to be impressed by and to report that "in almost all the kingdoms subject to his rule none is allowed to make or spend any other money" and that merchants could use these "sheets" to "make payments . . . for gold and . . . silver and for all other things which they carry and sell or buy, of however great value (fig. 27.7)."[36]

These policies led to the first extended regional and international trade and increased contacts between Europe and East

27.6 Standard Weights
Among the reforms instituted by Kublai to assist business and trade was a standard system of weights.

27.7 Yuan Coinage
Kublai's reforms of the earlier paper monetary system improved but did not solve all currency problems, particularly inflation, and coins remained in circulation. This Yuan dynasty coin reads *da yuan tong bao* (currency of great Yuan) in 'Phags-pa script.

Asia. China received or dispatched embassies to and from numerous lands in Asia and Europe. A Chinese envoy wrote the first account of Angkor Wat and the rich Khmer culture;[37] Chinese embassies reached India's Malabar coast;[38] and a Nestorian Christian monk named Rabban Sauma was the first attested voyager from China to travel to Europe and to write a report about his sojourn in Italy and France, earning him the sobriquet "reverse Marco Polo."[39] At the same time, numerous foreigners traveled to China. Marco Polo is the most renowned of these travelers, but other European merchants and missionaries also reached China. Kublai himself invited Central Asian and Iranian astronomers and physicians to introduce advances in those fields to the Chinese, and he recruited talented Turkic peoples and Iranians to serve as officials in the empire's financial administration.[40] Kublai and his wife Chabi pressed a Tibetan Buddhist monk named 'Phags-pa to come to China, and he, in turn, introduced them to the Nepalese architect/artist Anige, who designed a number of buildings in Daidu with a foreign aesthetic reflecting his Nepalese heritage; Anige may also have painted portraits of each of them (illus. p 200).[41] Yuan China became extraordinarily cosmopolitan, and Kublai's policy of toleration for all religions except for Daoism contributed further to its sophistication.

The economic and cultural significance of such cosmopolitanism has been over-emphasized in recent works. China's long-distance trade consisted principally of exchanges of luxury goods, and both domestic and international commerce was only a small fraction of the country's economy. Agriculture remained the major occupation of 85 to 90 percent of the population and generated most of the country's wealth. Mongol rule over much of Asia contributed to unparalleled flows of travelers, ideas, religions, technologies, and artistic motifs, which fostered artistic, technological, and cultural diffusion. But the impact of such interchanges on China and other Eurasian civilizations was limited.[42] Chinese culture remained distinct and did not change radically as a result of contact with other civilizations during the Mongol era.

The Mongol empire and its subjects in Central Asia, Tibet, and Iran influenced China's economy and culture during Kublai's reign, but it would be misleading to assert that such foreign impact on the Yuan dynasty transformed Chinese civilization. To be sure, China benefited from commercial and cultural exchanges facilitated by the so-called *Pax Mongolica*. New products from various regions in Asia reached China: Iranian astronomers and physicians did introduce useful technological innovations, while, simultaneously, Chinese agricultural and medical texts were translated in Iran. A few Chinese merchants were enriched, but the impact of such international trade on the large majority of the Chinese population was minimal; most were not even aware of these exchanges. Chinese artisans prospered by producing goods for Mongols and for foreign trade, but their most important market remained their own people. Such Chinese motifs as the dragon and the phoenix, which were transmitted by the Mongols, began to appear in Iranian art.[43] Yet, neither Chinese nor Iranian culture was fundamentally altered by interchanges with the other.

In their roles as patrons and consumers the Mongols did contribute to Chinese culture, rather than simply transmit new ideas and technologies. To influence Chinese law and written language, Kublai commissioned Chinese and Mongols to fashion a legal code for China that, at least on paper,

27.8 Stemmed Cup
Throughout the empire Mongols preferred using drinking cups with broad conical stems like this one. Although made of gold rather than silver, and lacking engraved decoration, this stemmed cup found in Inner Mongolia has a style similar to those produced and used by Mongols in the Golden Horde territory at the opposite end of the Mongol empire.

appeared more flexible and lenient than traditional Chinese codes and incorporated such Mongol practices as allowing criminals to pay a fine to avoid prison.[44] Kublai, who conceived of himself as a universal ruler, commissioned the 'Phags-pa lama to devise a written script that could be used with the languages found throughout the Mongol domains. In 1269, the 'Phags-pa lama presented Kublai with an alphabet composed of forty-one letters, which provided a better system of transcription for

Mongolian than the prevailing Uyghur script (which had been devised during Genghis Khan's era) and could also be used for Chinese. Despite repeated proclamations urging officials and the educated to employ the script, few Chinese or Mongols actually adopted it. A state-imposed written language could not overcome the desire to maintain a literary tradition; essayists, for instance, never used the 'Phags-pa script. The government turned out to be the major user, employing it on official seals,

ROSSABI

steles, and paper money (fig. 27.5). 'Phags-pa inscriptions were also found on passports that guaranteed safe passage through the Mongol territories.[45] The 'Phags-pa script experiment failed, but it revealed Kublai's aspiration to be a Great Khan who ruled the vast Mongol domains, not simply China.

The Mongols supported specific Chinese literary and artistic forms. Poetry and essays, traditional Chinese literary genres, were too recondite to appeal the Mongols, who more readily appreciated theater, which often included acrobatics, swordplay, music, dancing, and elaborate and colorful costumes. Mongol court patronage resulted in a golden age of Chinese drama, and many of these plays continued to be performed for centuries.[46] Kublai's support for visual arts and crafts prompted a glorious artistic era. He provided an official position to Zhao Meng-fu, the greatest Yuan painter. Kublai recruited other prominent painters, but some refused to serve the Mongols (fig. 27.3). They abstained from public life, and produced paintings infused with symbolism reflecting covert criticism of their Mongol overlords.[47]

Kublai and the Mongol nobles played a more direct role in fostering Chinese crafts. The Mongol conquest of Central Asia and Iran offered Chinese potters access to the cobalt blue used in the production of the first blue-and-white porcelains. The motifs of plants, fruits, and landscapes used as surface decoration on these porcelains were predominantly Chinese, partly because local people purchased or commissioned most of these plates, jars, and other vessels.[48] Even on porcelains exported to Korea, Southeast Asia, and the Middle East, the motifs remained, in large part, Chinese. Textiles designs did evolve in response to the tastes of the Mongols, who persisted in their nomadic lifestyle, so appreciated the portability of textiles. Mongol nobles were important consumers, specifically of "cloth of gold" or articles using gold thread; patrons who favored motifs found on Central Asian and Iranian textiles moved several communities of weavers from those regions to China to collaborate with Chinese counterparts. The textiles they produced blended Chinese, Central Asian, Tibetan, Indian,

and Iranian motifs[49] (see Chapters 30, 31).

By 1279 Kublai had achieved his principal objectives as Great Khan and Emperor of China. His conquest of the Southern Song was the Mongols' greatest military success and offered him credibility with the traditional Mongol elite. His restoration of a Chinese-style government and of Confucian rituals, his construction of a capital in China, his support for Chinese peasants, merchants, and artisans, and his embrace of a variety of religions were enduring achievements. His apparent fondness for Chinese culture and patronage of the theater, painting, and the decorative arts persuaded many Chinese that he was becoming increasingly sinicized.

Kublai's Failures

The high point of Kublai Khan's reign came in 1280; in the successive fourteen years of his dynasty fortunes drastically deteriorated. His domestic and foreign policy ventures went awry, and his decisions appear to have been self-destructive. What precipitated this dramatic turn? Was he plagued by medical problems such as gout, which is associated with obesity? A Chinese painting dated 1260 portrays him as robust and of normal size, but another painting dated 1282 depicts him as grossly overweight and deeply lined.[50] Was the death of his favorite wife Chabi in 1281 a factor in his decline? Chinese and Iranian sources attest that Kublai often consulted her regarding major policy decisions, and that he valued and implemented her advice. The death of his son Jingim in 1285 was similarly disturbing and doubtless contributed to his excessive drinking and weariness. In addition, his most trusted advisers either died or retired in the late 1270s and early 1280s.

Would his wife, son, and counselors have dissuaded him from undertaking the disastrous military campaigns that marred Kublai's last years? Emphasis on expansion and subjugation of additional states and territories had become so important in the Mongol empire that his closest relatives and advisers could probably not have deterred him. That Kublai embarked on these foolhardy campaigns starting in the early 1280s was no accident; he was driven to expand the empire, the key in Mongol eyes to his attempts

27.9 Sartorial Splendor
This detail of Kublai and his empress in Liu Guandao's painting *Kublai Khan Hunting* shows attention to Yuan-era royal attire and horse trappings. Kublai wears a Chinese rather than a Mongol style hat, and an elegant fur robe edged with sable; his boots and silk *deel* are embroidered in matching patterns; his felt saddle pad is also decorated; and his horse sports orange fur ornaments. His empress is more simply attired, wearing a *deel* embroidered with gold; her horse wears balls of red fur. The blend of Mongolian and Chinese elements suggests the political fusion of Mongol and Chinese cultures Kublai sought for his dynasty.

to bolster his legitimacy. Over the past twenty years, scholars and popular writers have accentuated the Mongols' positive contributions; this essay, too, has generally emphasized the favorable aspects of Kublai's reign. However, as early as Ögödei's reign, violence and military conquest were integral to the Mongol empire, and the destruction that the Mongols wrought ought not be ignored.

The invasions against Japan and Java were the most disastrous decisions. The Japanese shogun's unwillingness to submit to the Mongols prompted Kublai to initiate two ill-considered assaults, one in 1274 and another in 1281 (the 1274 expedition may also have been intended to cut off trade between Japan and the Southern Song dynasty, which Kublai was in the process of conquering) (see Chapter 33, fig. 33.1). Navies were not the Mongols' forte, and Kublai's demands for rapid dispatch of the 1281 expedition probably led to the use of some ships that were adequate for river travel but not for rigorous ocean voyages. Tensions erupted between the Chinese and Mongol

commanders. One of the convoys that were to link up in Hakata Bay off the northwestern coast of Kyushu, failed to arrive on time, which created tactical problems and exacerbated the lack of esprit de corps with non-Mongol troops, who were not committed to the expedition. Then, on August 15 and 16 1281, a disastrous typhoon struck, sinking many of the ships[51] (see Chapters 32, 33). Thousands of sailors drowned; according to the Yuan dynastic history, almost half of the 140,000 forces perished, but scholars believe that both figures are probably inflated.[52]

Still failing to appreciate the risks of naval expeditions, Kublai dispatched another convoy to Java in 1292. The Mongol troops, who were not accustomed to the tropical heat and jungle terrain, were unable to pacify Java and withdrew within a year.[53] Although campaigns in Southeast Asia (in modern Cambodia, Myanmar, and Vietnam) had some initial success, the oppressive heat, the guerilla wars launched against his troops, and the tropical infectious and parasitic diseases wore down his forces and caused them to abandon occupation of most of these lands within a few years of the initial conquest. These costly campaigns—scarcely netting any gains but consuming vast resources—as well as the plethora of public works projects initiated by Kublai added to the court's expenditures.

Administrators from Central Asia and Tibet recruited to raise the funds needed to pay for these projects increased the income accruing to the government, but, in the process, alienated much of the population. Ahmad, a Central Asian Muslim, increased taxes on both agriculture and commerce, targeting merchants, in particular. He imposed state monopolies on gold, silver, tea, salt, iron, vinegar, and liquor. Policies that sought to maximize revenue in sales of these commodities were essential, but they antagonized previous supporters of the government, who accused Ahmad of profiteering, nepotism, and corruption. The night of 10 April 1282, a cabal of Chinese officials assassinated him, and with a combination of evidence, both incriminating and reliable, persuaded Kublai of Ahmad's reputed treachery. Sangha, who was most likely of

Tibetan origin, dominated the government from 1282 to 1291. He particularly incensed Chinese officials by his aggressive recruitment of foreigners into the government, his support for the pillaging of the Southern Song imperial tombs, and desecration of the corpse of one of the Song emperors. His Chinese opponents, using both trustworthy and unreliable information, convinced Kublai of Sangha's perfidy, leading to the execution of the financial administrator in 1291.[54] However, the damage to Kublai's reputation among his Chinese subjects had been done and led to greater unrest at the end of his reign and of his successors' rules.

Wars against other regimes in the Mongol empire also generated enormous expenses, exacerbated this unrest, and may have contributed to Kublai's weariness, illness, and death.

A conflict with the Mongol khan of Central Asia over territories along their common borders persisted throughout Kublai's reign. Moreover, Kublai needed to send troops to crush revolts in Tibet and in Manchuria. These setbacks, together with old age and a lifestyle of excessive indulgences of food and drink resulted in serious ailments. On 18 February 1294, in his eightieth year, Kublai Khan died.

Kublai bequeathed an ambiguous legacy to his Mongol successors as emperors of China. On the one hand, his public works projects, fostering of most Chinese religions, and his patronage of drama and the arts, as well as his support of increased contact with other civilizations, offered a model for his descendants as rulers of China. On the other hand, his military expeditions and profligate lifestyle burdened them with debts, which eventually led to increased taxes and inflation. His efforts at sinicization alienated traditional Mongols who supported nomadic pastoral culture and its martial values. Struggles between the advocates of sinicization and the old style of life continued throughout the rest of the Mongol era in China and weakened the Yuan dynasty. Wars with the Mongol khan of Central Asia undermined the unity of the Mongol domains, creating serious problems for his

27.11 Mongol Officials Playing Backgammon
This woodblock print from a 14th-century Chinese encyclopedia, *Shilin guangji*, depicts two Mongol officials enjoying a game of backgammon, or *shuanglu*, in a Chinese palace. First played in India, the game became popular throughout Eurasia and was known in China since the third century.

successors. While Kublai's grandson succeeded him, succession struggles, leading to assassinations, weakened the Yuan dynasty. Kublai's accomplishments and his dream for an eternal empire were tarnished by the last phase of his reign. Although his vision was never fully realized, Kublai Khan, not Genghis Khan, extended the Mongol conquest to its greatest dimensions, while simultaneously initiating its disintegration by overspending and poor military planning.

1. Polo 1938, 185.
2. Boyle 1971, 168.
3. Bar Hebraeus 1932, 398.
4. Franke 1952.
5. Rossabi 1979.
6. Song 1976, 59.
7. Thiel 1961.
8. Yao 1964.
9. Boyle 1971, 262–65.
10. Harada and Komai 1941.
11. Polo 1938, 187.
12. Serruys 1974.
13. Rossabi 1988, 174.
14. Polo 1938, 205.
15. Gernet 1962.
16. Jagchid and Bawden 1965.
17. Song 1976, 4544–45.
18. Song 1976, 176.
19. Franke 1976, 34.
20. Franke 1976, 36.
21. Song 1976, 127–28; Hambis 1957.
22. Petech 1990.
23. Ratchnevsky 1937–72.
24. Arlington and Lewisohn 1935.
25. Song 1976, 1892–1902.
26. Chan 1967, 133.
27. Liu 1992.
28. Lo 1954.
29. Elman 2000.
30. Rossabi 1981.
31. Hucker 1966, 27.
32. Meng 1967.
33. Song 1976, 81.
34. Inosaki 1956.
35. Rossabi 1988, 122–24.
36. Polo 1938, 239.
37. Pelliot 1951; Harris 2007.
38. Sen 2006.
39. Rossabi 1992.
40. Allsen 2001.
41. Nakano 1971; Jing 1994.
42. Allsen 2001.
43. Komaroff and Carboni 2002.
44. Ch'en 1979.
45. Pope 1952.
46. Crump 1980.
47. Li 1965.
48. Pope 1952; Medley 1974.
49. Pelliot 1951; Watt and Wardwell 1997.
50. Smith 2000.
51. Ishii 1990.
52. Conlan 2001.
53. Bade 2002.
54. Rossabi 1988.

28. Emissaries East and West: Rabban Sauma and Marco Polo

MORRIS ROSSABI

MARCO POLO (1254–1324) and Rabban Sauma (d. 1294) were virtual mirror images of one other. The Venetian merchant is probably the most famous voyager in world history, and, for many centuries, his account of his travels provided Europeans with their most comprehensive view of China. The Nestorian monk Rabban Sauma, who traveled at precisely the same time as Marco, is the first man documented to reach Europe from China (fig. 28.1). His account of his travels offered to East Asia a window on the Byzantine empire and Western Europe. To be sure, the motivations for their journeys differed. Marco traveled both out of a spirit of adventure and to foster trade with China. Rabban

Sauma set forth on a religious pilgrimage to the Holy Lands and ended up as an envoy from the Mongol rulers of Iran to Europe. The travels of both men across Eurasia reveal the close contact among the civilizations of China, the Middle East, and Europe brought about by the *Pax Mongolica* (Mongolian Peace).

Marco Polo

Marco's father Niccoló Polo and his uncle Maffeo Polo preceded him in reaching China in the early 1260s. They originally intended a commercial foray into Byzantium, Iran, and Central Asia, but wars among the various khanates, as well as banditry along the route caused them to divert their travels in the direction

of China. There, they met the great Mongol ruler Kublai Khan, who was so impressed with these intrepid voyagers that he commissioned them to bring oil from the Holy Sepulcher and one hundred learned Christians from Europe on a return trip to China. He said that he wanted literate and skilled Christians to teach his subjects about the religion and to convert them, but a likelier explanation is that he wanted to recruit the scholars to help in ruling China because the Mongols preferred foreign advisors to the Chinese. Niccoló and Maffeo brought the oil but were unable to persuade other Christians to join them on their return voyage. Instead they were accompanied by their son and nephew Marco, who left his native city of Venice at the age of seventeen and reached China at twenty-one. This precocious youngster proved to be a much better "gift" to Kublai than the learned Christians.

Marco remained in China with has father and uncle for sixteen years, from 1275 to 1291, during which he made numerous observations about the marvels he witnessed. He writes about the splendid new city of Daidu (the area of modern Beijing, "Great Capital") built on Kublai's orders. He tells of the banquets for 10,000 people at the court, and the postal system, which could deliver urgent messages between stations at the rate of 250 miles a day.[1] His description of Kublai's summer palace at Shangdu not only inspired Samuel Taylor Coleridge to call the city "Xanadu" in his famous poem, but also tallies well with Iranian and Chinese accounts. Marco's purported eyewitness accounts of imperial hunts also jibe with other reports.

The range of Marco's interests

28.1 The Book of Marco Polo
Cosmographia breve introductoria en el libro de Marco Paulo (A Brief Introduction to the World from a book by Marco Polo) reads the title of this Spanish version of Polo's book, printed in 1503. The cover shows the Polos above a harbor scene, framed by a border of interlaced plants, flowers, animals, and cherubs. Marco Polo's adventures in Asia created a sensation in Europe, and while they did not accurately describe Mongol Asia, they stimulated interest in exotic eastern lands at the same time Western Europe was discovering the Americas.

and descriptions is astonishing and cannot be summarized in this brief survey. He was the first Westerner to notice the Chinese use of coal and of paper money. Hangzhou, the capital city of the Southern Song dynasty (1127–1279), which the Mongols had occupied, dazzled him. Marco's hometown of Venice, with a population of less than 100,000, could not compare with this highly sophisticated city, with perhaps 1 to 1.5 million inhabitants. Situated around the West Lake, Hangzhou boasted an advanced sewage and water system, restaurants serving extraordinary Chinese delicacies, and theaters producing some of the finest plays in the Chinese tradition.[2] Marco's description of this capital city meshes with those found in Chinese local histories and gazetteers. Marco even recounts specific events at the court, which are confirmed in Chinese and Iranian histories. He provides an engaging and accurate narrative about the rise and fall of Ahmad, a Central Asian Muslim whom Kublai had selected to head his financial administration and to raise the revenues required for Mongol infrastructure projects in China and additional military campaigns. Sexual practices and the selection of mates in the regions through which he traveled also fascinated him, particularly the Great Khan's requirement that a concubine have sweet breath, smell fresh, and sleep without snoring.

Marco exaggerated his role and influence at Kublai's court, leading to several egregious errors and prompting some later writers to question whether he even reached China. His attempt to take credit for a Mongol victory over the Southern Song dynasty and his claim that Kublai appointed him governor of a Chinese region are untrue. There is also no evidence that Kublai commissioned him to travel throughout China to provide reports on conditions in various domains. These dubious assertions do not detract from the value of his account as much as they reveal the somewhat convoluted process by which Marco's exploits were published. The book popularly attributed to him was actually written by a storyteller named Rusticello who, fortunately for history, shared a prison cell with Marco after they both were captured by the Genoese in a skirmish with the Venetians. Rusticello may have omitted many of Marco's observations, and Marco may have been selective in his account to his cellmate and sought to impress future readers by inflating his significance to the Mongols. The editorial process inherent in this form of transmission may similarly explain his omission of unusual aspects of Chinese civilization, such as bound feet, the Chinese writing system, and the use of chopsticks. Recently discovered evidence from Chinese and Iranian sources has confirmed that Marco did, in fact, reach China. Marco's *Description of the World* became extraordinarily popular and, in part, inspired Christopher Columbus to seek a sea route to the East Indies.

28.2 Sainte-Chapelle
Rabban Sauma's European travels in the late 1280s took him to Constantinople, Naples, Genoa, Rome, Paris, and Bordeaux, and he met with the kings of France and England. As a Nestorian Christian he was especially impressed with the grandeur of Europe's cathedrals. Sainte-Chapelle, built to house relics Louis IX had acquired on his Crusades and consecrated in 1248, had been standing for more than forty years, and even without the famous stained-glass rose window, installed in the 15th century, it would have been a marvel to behold.

Rabban Sauma

The Nestorian Christian monk Rabban Sauma departed China at about the same time that Marco reached Daidu in the late 1270s. In the fourth century, the Catholic Church had declared Nestorian Christianity heretical because it diminished the role of the Virgin Mary and challenged the concept of a coequal Trinity: the Nestorians argued that the Father had to be superior to the Son. Rabban Sauma and a fellow monk left their home in Daidu to make a pilgrimage to the Christian Holy Lands. They traveled, with almost no hindrances, via the Silk Roads through Central Asia and on to Iran, another indication of the relative ease of travel that was facilitated by Mongol domination of much of Asia. When the two monks reached Iran, its Mongol rulers told them that the Muslim Mamluks controlled the Holy Lands and that they could not fulfill their dreams of visiting early Christian sites. Frustrated by this impediment to their pilgrimage, the two monks decided to remain in the Middle Eastern Nestorian community, which was much larger than the one in their Chinese homeland. Bar Markos, Rabban Sauma's traveling companion, eventually became Catholicos, the Nestorian patriarch, in the region.

In 1287 the Mongol ruler of Iran conceived an alliance with the European Christian monarchs to destroy the Mamluk dynasty, their common enemy. He proposed that the Europeans attack Egypt and the Holy Lands from the north and that his troops open a second front from the east. Having been impressed by the Nestorian voyager from China, he selected Rabban Sauma as his emissary to present his plan to the Christian rulers of Europe. The Iranian khan also counted on Rabban Sauma's Christian beliefs to be an asset in his diplomatic mission to Europe. The Nestorian monk reached Constantinople, Naples, Genoa, and Rome; he met with the College of Cardinals in Rome, with the king of France in Paris, and with the king of England in Bordeaux. King Edward I of England was particularly enthusiastic, and Rabban Sauma returned to Iran, believing that he had forged an alliance. Shortly thereafter, Edward I faced rebellions in Scotland and Wales, and the French King Philip IV faced internal disturbances and became embroiled in conflicts with the Italian city-states. Both abandoned their commitments to an alliance with the Mongols.[3]

Rabban Sauma's diplomatic mission was a failure, but he left an indelible historical footprint. His account of his travels was lost and rediscovered in Northwest Iran in the late nineteenth century. In his narrative, he focuses mostly on the theological debates he undertook with Catholics and the religious sites he visited (fig. 28.2), but he also described the curriculum at the University of Paris and commented on what he perceived to be the appalling simplicity of the burial of European monarchs, among many other subjects. His account is a fertile counterpoint to Marco Polo's work and offers a rare European perspective on Asia.

1. Olschki 1960.
2. Gernet 1962.
3. Rossabi 1992.

28.3 *Arghun in his Garden*
Rabban Sauma and Bar Markos were among the first Asian travelers to visit the West. Being Nestorian Christians from Kublai's capital, they wanted to visit the Holy Land but were blocked from traveling there by Mamluk military advances. This scene in Rashid al-Din's 14th-century *Jami' al-Tavarikh* (Compendium of Chronicles), shows Arghun, who became khan in 1284, dispatching Sauma to Europe. His mission, to explore a Mongol-European alliance against the Mamluks, failed, but Rabban Sauma's writings, lost until the late 19th century, gave the Ilkhanate and Mongol Asia its first descriptions of Europe in accounts that were decidedly more factual than Polo's.

29. Ibn Battuta

ROSS E. DUNN

DURING THE AGE OF MONGOL DOMINANCE, European Christians traveled back and forth across Eurasia in small numbers, but the trails and sea lanes of the Eastern hemisphere thronged with Muslims. The majority of Muslim travelers had commercial errands to accomplish, but others ventured abroad as soldiers, diplomats, imperial messengers, artisans, pilgrims, Sufi wanderers, and scholars. The celebrated Moroccan traveler Abu Abdallah Ibn Battuta (1304–13) had at least three goals in mind when, in 1325, he left his hometown of Tangier, a busy port on the Strait of Gibraltar, to make the *hajj*, or holy pilgrimage to Mecca.

Born into a family of legal scholars, Ibn Battuta took to the road at the age of twenty-one, not only to perform the *hajj* but also to study law in some of Islam's prestigious colleges and to find spiritual enlightenment in the company of learned Sufi mystics. When he started out, he probably intended to pursue law and the religious sciences in Cairo or Damascus, then, diplomas in hand, return to Morocco to a well-paying job as a jurist.

Travel plans, however, can change. After he completed his first *hajj* in 1326, Ibn Battuta made a long, looping excursion through the Ilkhanate, the Mongol state that ruled Iran and Iraq. That trip, a sightseeing expedition more than a study tour, launched him on a nearly three-decade career of adventure travel from the Ukraine to Tanzania and from China to West Africa. He visited dozens of colleges and Sufi centers, served in the judiciary of the sultan of India, married (and divorced) several women, fathered children, faced mortal dangers, and witnessed the court ceremonial of three great Mongol khans. When he

finally returned home in 1354, he produced, on orders from his Moroccan sovereign, a narrative of his career on the road. His lengthy *Rihla*, or Book of Travels, stands alone as a detailed and compelling account of Eurasia and Africa in the second quarter of the fourteenth century.

Though he could not have predicted his luck, Ibn Battuta picked a propitious moment to make a world tour. The Mongol wars of conquest were long over, the international trade routes hummed with activity, Muslim communities continued to proliferate in Asia and Africa, and large, reasonably stable states dominated much of the hemisphere.

The three Mongol courts that Ibn Battuta visited had, by the time he arrived on the scene, adopted Islam as the royal religion. This state of affairs served him well. Mongol and Turkic rulers whose recent ancestors had been shamanists and horse herders needed badly to surround themselves with venerable theologians, jurists, artists, and other cognoscenti, who would model civilized Islamic standards. Ibn Battuta never became an accomplished doctor of law. But he was nonetheless an *'alim*, or man of the learned class, and he commanded respect as a speaker and writer of Arabic, the language of the Prophet. Consequently, he nearly always received a warm welcome among rulers eager to ratify themselves as proper Muslim princes and champions of Islamic law and practice.

Although Ibn Battuta had only brief encounters with potentates of the house of Genghis, the *Rihla* gives us vivid and valuable descriptions of the sprawling khanates of Persia-Iraq, the Golden Horde, and Chaghadai. He also reports on

29.1 Qutb Minaret
Ibn Battuta arrived in Old Delhi, in northern India, after crossing western Asia from Sarai in the Golden Horde. He remained in Delhi for about eight years in the 1330s, serving the Turkic sultan in administrative and diplomatic capacities. The Qutb complex, now mostly in ruins but designated a UNESCO World Heritage Site, included a mosque, a huge iron pillar, and the Qutb minaret, built in the late 12th century by Qutb-ud-din Aibak, the first ruler of the Slave dynasty, and his successor, Iltutmish. Standing 72.5 meters high, it is the tallest brick minaret in the world and one of the premier examples of Indo-Islamic architecture.

numerous meetings, and sometimes revealing tête-à-têtes, with Mongol governors and generals. He toured the Ilkhanid realm between 1326 and 1327, when it was under the rule of Abu Said (r. 1316–35), a young man of about his own age. Ibn Battuta had only a glimpse or two of the khan during a stay in Baghdad, but he heaps praise on him for his sober Muslim piety.

Heading across the West Asian steppes toward India in 1332 (or 1334, depending on one's interpretation of the chronology of the *Rihla*), the journeyer met Ozbeg, Khan of the Golden Horde, at a royal encampment just north of the Caucasus Mountains. Devout Muslim that he was, Ozbeg gave an audience to the itinerant legal scholar. So did the four *khatuns*, or royal wives. Ibn Battuta notes in the *Rihla* that these women exercised considerable political power in their own rights,

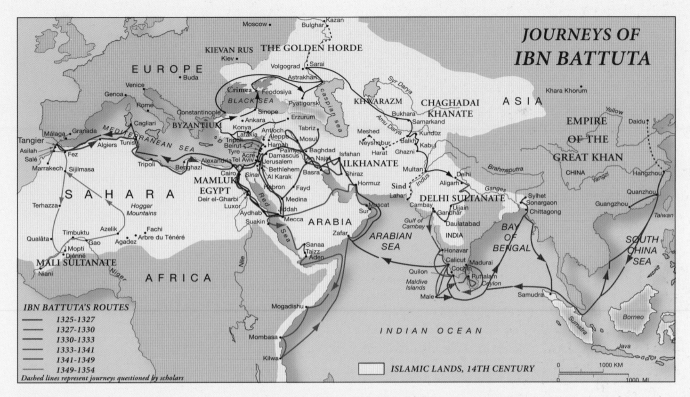

JOURNEYS OF IBN BATTUTA

IBN BATTUTA'S ROUTES
- 1325-1327
- 1327-1330
- 1330-1333
- 1333-1341
- 1341-1349
- 1349-1354

Dashed lines represent journeys questioned by scholars

ISLAMIC LANDS, 14TH CENTURY

1000 KM

1000 MI

and they commanded great wealth:

In front of [the wagon of] the *khatun* are ten or fifteen pages, Greeks and Indians, who are dressed in robes of silk gilt, encrusted with jewels, and each of whom carries in his hand a mace of gold or silver . . . Behind the *khatun's* wagon there are about a hundred wagons, in each of which there are four slave girls full-grown and young . . . Behind these wagons are about three hundred wagons, drawn by camels and oxen, carrying the *khatun's* chests, moneys, robes, furnishings, and food."[1]

Continuing on toward India in 1333 (or 1335), Ibn Battuta had a brief meeting at Samarkand with Tarmashirin, Khan of Chaghadai. This ruler, having made Islam the state religion, receives commendation in the *Rihla* as "a man of great distinction,"[2] though his short reign ended in rebellion and factional war not long after Ibn Battuta's visit.

The Moroccan spent about eight years in India, most in the employ of the regime of Muhammad Ibn Tughluq, the Türkic sultan of Delhi fig. 29.1). Ibn Battuta fell in and out of favor with this sovereign,

but, in 1341, he received an appointment to lead a state embassy from Delhi to the court of the Great Khan Toghon Temür in Mongol China. Unfortunately, this mission ended in a maritime disaster off the southern coast of India. Ibn Battuta, however, eventually continued to East Asia on his own, or so he claims. Historians have been skeptical of the description of China in the *Rihla* on several counts. For example, Ibn Battuta alleges to have witnessed the funeral of the Great Khan in Beijing in 1346, but this is impossible because Toghon Temür reigned without interruption from 1333 to 1368. The *Rihla* account of the southern coast of China has some credibility, but Ibn Battuta certainly did not reach Daidu.

Returning to Morocco in 1347, and after expeditions to both southern Spain and the West African empire of Mali in the ensuing eight years, Ibn Battuta moved to Fez in 1354 to write the *Rihla* in collaboration with a young literary scholar. Meanwhile, all hell broke loose, as it were, across the Eastern hemisphere. The Black Death swept across Inner

29.2 Travels of Ibn Battuta

Ibn Battuta, a native of Tangier, Morocco, on the Strait of Gibraltar, became one of the most widely traveled and influential historians of the medieval era. He was also an accomplished administrator and legal scholar who left highly reputable historical accounts. Part of his success was timing: he traveled during a quiescent period of the early 14th century after the turmoil of the Mongol conquests had subsided and before the onslaught of the Black Death in 1347–48. His *Rihla* (Book of Travels) was written in 1354.

Eurasia, the Mediterranean lands, and Europe in 1347 and 1348; production and trade slumped in many regions. By 1368, the four Mongol khanates—Mongolia and China, the Middle East, Russia, and western Asia, plus the Delhi sultanate and several other large states—had either collapsed or seriously deteriorated. As these crises proliferated, Ibn Battuta busied himself with a quiet judgeship somewhere in Morocco. He died in 1368 or 1369, lucky to have left the road when he did.

1. Ibn Battuta 1958–2000, vol. 2, 485–86.

2. Ibn Battuta 1958–2000, vol. 3, 556.

30. The Yuan Synthesis

CHINESE INFLUENCE ON THE MONGOL CULTURE (1271–1368)

François Louis

IT TOOK THREE GENERATIONS OF MONGOL LEADERS more than sixty years to conquer China. On the eve of the Mongol invasions, China was divided into two states: Jin (1115–1234), occupying the northern half, and Song, the southern half. Genghis Khan first invaded the Jin state in 1210, and his grandson Kublai concluded the protracted conquest in 1276, when he annexed Hangzhou, the capital of the Southern Song dynasty (1127–1279) and the largest, most prosperous metropolis in Asia. For the Mongol elite and its foreign allies, China was a cashbox, there for the taking. Not until the 1250s did the Mongols begin to govern China in a manner that did not simply exploit its resources but also sustained them.[1] The main change came with Kublai Khan. As he curtailed his aspiration to rule all of the Mongol empire and concentrated on "just" the eastern part, he moved his court to China, began building a new capital at Daidu (modern Beijing), and assumed the trappings of the Chinese monarchy. In 1271, he declared himself emperor of the Yuan dynasty.

When Kublai's Mongol elite exchanged military camps for urban courts, and *ger* (yurts) for Chinese palaces, their lifestyles changed significantly. While certain symbols of sedentary imperial power, such as Chinese palace architecture, were simply adopted by the conquerors with little alteration, smaller Chinese luxuries such as silk fabrics, jewelry, costumes, and utensils were now manufactured in a new, hybrid style that reflected Mongol priorities. These transportable types of goods that had traditionally conveyed status and power in nomadic Mongol society now gave the Mongol court in China its distinctive look.

In 1280, just one year after the last Chinese holdouts had surrendered, Kublai commissioned a Chinese court painter to depict him enjoying his new power (fig. 27.1).[2] Significantly, the emperor and one of his four wives are shown not in a formal portrait perched on thrones, but as nomadic nobility on horseback. In a depiction unthinkable among Song royalty, the empress not only mingles with male courtiers, but also engages in falconry. The imperial couple is distinguished from the other courtiers (none of whom is Chinese) by a stunning display of luxury items made in the imperial workshops. They wear layers of silk robes patterned in gold and silver, and gem-encrusted gold jewelry adorns both their belts and their horse gear. This clothing style set a new standard. Even after the native Ming dynasty (1368–1644) overthrew the Yuan, the Chinese court nobility

30.1 Stoneware Jar
This Yuan-dynasty wine jar was manufactured in northern China and is decorated with a phoenix and peony pattern. Following the tradition of the Cizhou kilns in Hebei, the vessel was first covered with a white slip layer; then the design was carved out, revealing the darker clay body underneath; finally the vessel was dipped in a clear glaze and fired. In 1958 this jar was one of the first to be discovered in the ruins of a Yuan city in Tuchengzi near Jining, sixty miles west of Hohhot.

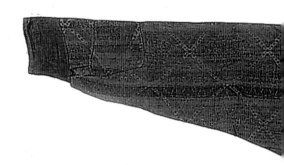

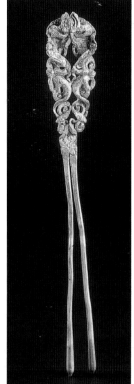 

continued to wear robes decorated with dragons and gem-studded belt plaques.

Portable wealth in the form of glistening gold, gems, pearls, and, above all, patterned silks had been particularly important to the Mongols long before the time of Kublai Khan.[3] However, prior to the Mongol con-quests, most of these precious goods had been hard to come by because of limited access to raw materials and to specialized artisans. When it came to manufacturing, nomadic societies traditionally consisted of generalists: almost everyone knew how to make everything needed to survive, and highly specialized industries did not exist. Before their conquests, the Mongols had to rely on their sedentary neighbors to pro-vide them with commodities produced by trained artisans and complex technologies. This changed once Genghis, and subse-quently Ögödei, began to "collect" highly skilled artisans during their campaigns. They transferred these specialists to new, multicultural court workshops in North

China and Mongolia. In this way, the Mon-gol elite obtained permanent access to rare commodities, which in turn, bolstered their power and status. Moreover, by merging artistic traditions from both Central Asia and China, the Mongol workshops also began to manufacture luxuries that reflected Mongol preferences for the first time. Al-though many of these luxuries ended up in trade as commodities, the Mongol courts ordered them primarily for ceremonial court attire and as political currency. As gifts they could secure loyalties, help establish political alliances, encourage trade relation-ships, or seal family ties at weddings.[4]

The most celebrated products of the ear-ly workshops in Mongolia are the beautiful golden silk brocades, or *nasij*, as they were called throughout the Mongol empire (fig. 30.4). The name is a shortened form of the Arabic phrase for "cloth of gold and silk." *Nasij* are glistening treasures with bold, innovative designs woven on drawlooms from silk and from gold threads made from a fine paper or leather core wrapped with thin gold foil.[5] As Mongol power expand-ed, *nasij* came to be produced in Mongol court workshops from Baghdad to Beijing. When Kublai settled into his new palaces in China in the late 1260s, he brought with him silk weavers and other luxury arti-sans from the workshops in Mongolia.[6]

In administrative structure, the imperial workshops established for the Yuan court in China differed little from those of earlier

30.4 Robe of Gold Brocade
Gold brocade *(nasij)* was the most expensive silk fabric made under Mongol auspices. This *nasij* robe was discovered in a tomb in Mingshui in Inner Mongolia and dates to the 13th–14th centuries. The fabric was woven by Central Asian artisans and is patterned with rosettes within rhomboid lozenges. The yellow silk lining has designs of rearing lions back-to-back, shown in the detail (right).

dynasties. Now, however, they were overseen by foreign specialists, and some were particular to Mongol rule, such as the fur workshops and the great number of silk and goldsmithing workshops (fig. 30.2).[7] A vast amount of the silk, gold, gems, and jades was used for religious articles, most notably to benefit the priests of the Tibetan Sa-skya clan. This Buddhist clergy had successfully taken charge of the Mongols' spiritual salvation. In return, it was given not only powerful oversight of China's religious institutions and political control over Tibet, but an enormous portion of the Yuan dynasty's fortune as well. Records from 1289 and 1310 reveal that more than half of the state revenue went to the Tibetan clergy and to the building of Buddhist institutions. While such figures may seem exaggerated, recent scholarship contends that they are not far from accurate.[8] Indeed, it is in Tibet where the most extraordinary luxury products sponsored by the Yuan court have survived. The imperial tombs of the Yuan dynasty may yield further evidence of Mongol wealth, but to date their whereabouts remain unknown.

While the Mongol conquest of China affected both the conquerors and the trappings of the Chinese court, it also left its mark on Chinese material culture at large. In two areas it brought about changes of historic proportions: in the practice of painting and the production of ceramics. Under the Mongols, painting for the first time came to be widely practiced by China's intellectual elite. Although Chinese scholars had occasionally dabbled as painters before the Yuan era, painting was essentially a professional occupation performed by specially trained artisans. A result of the transformation of

the Chinese elite under the Mongols, "literati painting" would become one of China's most noble traditions. (The term "literati painting" was not coined until the late sixteenth century). Of even greater import was the invention and successful marketing of blue-and-white porcelain. Not only did this type of ware remain the staple of China's ceramics industry, it also influenced ceramics production all over the world, from Southeast Asia, to the Middle East, to Europe. Today, the finest blue-and-white porcelains from Yuan China are the most valuable Chinese antiquities of all time. In 2005 a jar was sold in London for a staggering $27.7 million, setting the auction record for Asian antiquities (fig. 30.9).[9]

Ceramics

The once-burgeoning ceramics industry of northern China was devastated in the wars of the early thirteenth century. Under the Yuan dynasty it produced little more than traditional low-end wares for local markets (fig. 30.1). The ceramic kilns of southern China, in contrast, flourished without interruption, driven by a steadily growing international demand. For centuries, many of their wares were shipped to the big coastal trading ports of Ningbo and Quanzhou, where they were loaded onto large vessels sailing to Japan, Southeast Asia, and the Islamic world.[10] With the Yuan conquest the lucrative business of ceramics trading simply moved from the hands of the Song dynasty to the agents of the Yuan administration, most notably to the Muslim merchants and entrepreneurs appointed to collect local taxes. What had already been a corrupt business, with local officials habitually overtaxing potters and merchants,[11] became under the Mongols a "deregulated" bonanza.[12]

Hundreds of thousands of ceramics were exported overseas during the Yuan dynasty. Several shipwrecks attest to this, the most important of which was discovered in 1976 near the Korean coast of Sinan. That ship, which sank on its way to Japan shortly after 1323,[13] carried more than 20,000 ceramic pieces (almost all of them green- or brown-glazed stoneware), along with thousands of other goods such as exotic woods, bronze, and silver. In addition to supplying the international markets, southern ceramics also served the markets in northern China; the same types of stoneware found on the Sinan shipwreck were also discovered in the Mongol metropolises of Daidu,

Shangdu, and Khara Khorum (fig. 30.7).

Although the Mongol elite showed little inclination to use ceramics for eating and drinking, preferring instead expensive gold and silver vessels, certain ritual aspects of Chinese court life required ceramics. Ceramic offering vessels were used in temples, in private worship, and in funerals. Fine ceramic cups and dishes were used by lower-ranking court officials for banquets,[14] and some ware may also have been intended as diplomatic gifts or imperial trade goods. To secure such court supplies, in 1278, the Yuan government, established a special porcelain manufacturing office in Fuliang near the rich kaolin clay deposits in what is today the Jingdezhen area in remote Jiangxi province in southern China. The area was at the time one of the large, primarily commercial ceramic centers with more than 300 kilns. From Fuliang the Yuan court initially commissioned porcelains with a pale bluish glaze (*qingbai*), the typical products of the kilns. But over the subsequent decades, imperial sponsorship transformed the kilns into China's new center of technological innovation. While kilns in other parts of China continued to produce old-fashioned heavy stoneware,

the Fuliang kilns expanded on the innovation of making thin, high-quality porcelain from a white clay that, when fired, becomes extremely hard and dense. The administration was intent on obtaining very white porcelain, and the kilns responded in two ways: they managed to make the old bluish celadon glazes almost clear, and they developed a distinct, high-fired porcelain with an opaque white glaze, the so-called *shufu* ware.[15] Pieces for imperial use decorated with dragons, which could be modeled in relief or painted, show them with five claws.

Experiments were also conducted with different mineral pigments for the painted decorations (fig. 30.8). Around 1320 a satisfying and efficient combination of materials was found: unfired vessels were painted with cobalt, covered with a transparent glaze, and then fired. At the appropriate high temperature, which only an experienced kiln master could gauge properly, the cobalt decoration turned a dark blue, permanently protected under the glaze. The technology was groundbreaking. For the first time, a superior product with a durable pictorial decoration could be mass-produced easily and cheaply.

Although scholarship on the matter is still imprecise, it appears that the mass production of blue-and-white porcelain did not result primarily from court demand, but rather from the commercial interests of local officials and merchants with overseas connections.[16] There are several reasons to think so. Unlike earlier Fuliang wares, a great number of the blue-and-white pieces were made in Middle Eastern shapes and exported to Muslim communities. Cobalt itself had rarely been used in Chinese kilns before, but it had been a favorite pigment in Middle Eastern ceramic production for centuries; most of the cobalt used by the Fuliang potters was actually imported from the West. The beginning of blue-and-white production, moreover, coincides with a period of decreased court control of the kilns, which had been put under local tax authority in 1324, greatly stimulating the commercialization of what was then the most technologically advanced ceramics industry in China. Blue-and-white wares were, of course, also produced for the Chinese market (such as

30.6 Raft Cup
This unusual silver sculpture by Zhu Bishan, a Chinese Yuan artist (1300–after 1362), is a wine cup depicting an inebriated Chinese scholar floating on a tree trunk. Raft cups became signature works of Zhu Bishan, a famous silversmith active in Suzhou toward the end of the Yuan period. Such art contrasts with the earlier Yuan genre of restrained contemplation.

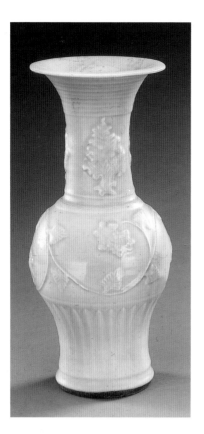

30.7 Longquan Celadon Vase
Longquan ceramics with their characteristic jade-green celadon glazes were produced widely in China during the 12th–13th century Song dynasty and were traded widely throughout East and Southeast Asia and the Philippines. Production continued in southern China into the Yuan dynasty. This vase was made in the 14th century at the kilns in Longquan in southern China and was found in a grave in Inner Mongolia.

30.8 Porcelain Dish
This blue-and-white under-glaze porcelain dish from the mid-14th century was made at the Jingdezhen kilns in northern China where this ware began to be produced using cobalt oxide dyes during the Northern Song dynasty (960–1127). This piece has a central stag motif surrounded by complex bands of floral patterns. Hand-painted designs of such complexity required the service of master artists. Because Chinese preferred small dishes and bowls for eating, large dishes such as this one from the collection of the Topkapi Palace Museum in Istanbul, were primarily made for export to western Asia and the Middle East.

the jar sold in 2005). They were frequently decorated with scenes from famous theater plays. In 1352 the kilns were lost to Chinese insurgents. But the subsequent wars over dynastic succession slowed production for only a brief period, and the victorious Ming dynasty eventually continued to patronize the kilns. International export, however, was severely curtailed until the beginning of the fifteenth century.

Material Culture of the Chinese Elite

The Chinese elite underwent a complex transformation under Mongol rule. Kublai had already begun to assemble Chinese advisors in the 1250s, and these men subsequently became the architects of his new government. They came from all walks of life and were recruited mainly from the impoverished and war-torn northern parts of China. While the government they built obviously served the interests of the foreign elite, it also secured wealth and influence for their own families. By the time Kublai annexed the flourishing Song empire in the south, a Chinese political elite of northerners was already well in place and the old

southern elite, Confucian scholars in particular, were demoted to a subordinate political role, profiting little from the Mongol redistribution of wealth.[17]

Although they retained their high social status—in many cases their family estates––the politically oppressed southern intellectuals came to view a glittering display of wealth as morally unsavory and inappropriate for their new social situation. Unlike the typical members of the multicultural ruling elite, who engaged in conspicuous consumption, the majority of the southern scholar-elite rediscovered frugality as a meaningful Confucian virtue and found renewed appeal in Daoist and Chan-Buddhist ideas of simplicity and reclusion. Accordingly, the articles they valued lacked material glamour but were rich in cultural meaning: antiquities, old paintings, calligraphies, and books.

Ni Zan (1306–1374), one of the seminal scholar-painters of the era, represents these ideals most famously. A wealthy landlord, he chose the lifestyle of a refined ascetic, paring away all that was unessential in both his life and his art to strive for the ideal of "unembellished naturalness"

30.9 Porcelain Vessel
This Yuan vessel may have been used for Yuhuchun, a famous ancient wine, and is decorated with a blue underglaze painting of a four-clawed dragon. The vessel was found in a grave in Wutonghua, Wengniute province, north of Chifeng, Inner Mongolia, and has been reconstructed.

(*pingdan*).[18] A contemporary portrait depicts him in front of a screen painted with a barren ink landscape in his characteristic style (fig. 30.10). Next to him is a pile of old scrolls and on a table a few refined antiquities. To the right of the painting is an inscription by Zhao Yu (1283–1350), a noted Daoist priest and close friend of the family, praising Ni's elegant form of reclusion.

At the other end of the spectrum of southern Chinese elite were men like Lü Shimeng (1234–1304). Lü came from a family whose members all made their career in the military, a fact that made them socially rather different from Confucian intellectuals, who usually served in the civil administration. Lü had been vice minister of war in the Song government and was directly involved in the diplomatic exchange that led to the final handover of the Song capital, Hangzhou, in 1276. Lü was quick to change allegiance to the victorious Yuan dynasty and for that was rewarded with lucrative military posts.[19] Although criticized by some contemporaries as a traitor, he remained a politically influential figure much courted by the local cultural elite. The renowned literary historian Fang Hui (1227–1307), for instance, wrote Lü's epitaph, and his tomb, containing dozens of exquisite gold, jade, and silver items, constitutes one of the richest archaeological discoveries of Yuan China to date.[20]

Although the giving of recommendations and precious gifts in exchange for favors and loyalties had always held a certain place in Chinese culture, under the Mongols this system became the main form of social and political advancement (fig. 30.6). For those within government, obtaining elite patronage was crucial because the Mongols assigned administrative posts on the basis of personal recommendations, family connections, ethnicity, religious affiliation, and coercive persuasion. They saw no need for a public examination system that offered an impartial path to high office, as had been the custom in China for more than five hundred years. Even after the examination system was reintroduced in 1315, it unfairly favored the foreign elite and could not replace the importance of social connections. But even for those who rejected government service, the simple fact that the Mongols had reconfigured the ruling elite required the rebuilding of social connections.[21]

In this environment of social realignment, paintings became prominent interpersonal agents and commodities. Valuable heirlooms now came in handy as bribes,[22] as did certain cultural skills of the old scholar class, including expertise in medicine, cosmology, calligraphy, and painting. Some highly talented Chinese scholars painted for the court or government as regular artisan-subjects fulfilling commissions. But much more frequently, Yuan intellectuals painted for influential officials whose patronage they sought, or for friends whose loyalty they appreciated, or whose favors they needed to repay. The latter three categories of works, oftentimes difficult to distinguish from one other, are now considered the finest forms of Yuan art—private paintings that suitably express individual cultivation and the connection between maker and recipient. The styles developed for this manner of art emphasized the linear features of calligraphy as well as self-referential subject matter, such as landscapes and bamboo. Personal dedications inscribed on paintings become routine at this time in the history of Chinese painting.

The most influential scholar-painter of the Yuan era was Zhao Mengfu (1254–1322) (fig. 30.11). Zhao was not only one of the most brilliant southern scholars and a member of the extended Song imperial family but also the highest-ranking Chinese government official from the southern elite. Thus, he stood squarely at the cen-

ter of Yuan cultural politics. Having spent his youth among the many disenfranchised intellectuals in Hangzhou, he followed Kublai's call to improve government and, in 1287, took up high office at the court. Zhao became an influential advocate for a more humane, Confucian government and was instrumental in fostering cultural exchange between the northern and southern elites. After Kublai's death in 1294, he headed the Confucian Schools in the Hangzhou region, a prestigious position topped only by his subsequent directorship of the National Academy in the capital. As is to be expected, Zhao's rich oeuvre consists of numerous paintings and calligraphies created as gifts to flatter important members of the court elite, along with many works dedicated to friends. In all of his works, Zhao strove to revive ancient models, giving them a highly erudite yet indirectly subversive feel. Even his depictions of horses, which likely appealed to the foreign elite, were closely modeled on masterpieces from the Tang (618–907) and Northern Song (960–1127) periods.[23]

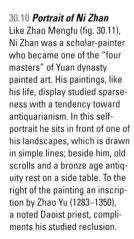

30.10 *Portrait of Ni Zhan*
Like Zhao Mengfu (fig. 30.11), Ni Zhan was a scholar-painter who became one of the "four masters" of Yuan dynasty painted art. His paintings, like his life, display studied sparseness with a tendency toward antiquarianism. In this self-portrait he sits in front of one of his landscapes, which is drawn in simple lines; beside him, old scrolls and a bronze age antiquity rest on a side table. To the right of the painting an inscription by Zhao Yu (1283–1350), a noted Daoist priest, compliments his studied reclusion.

30.11 *Autumn Colors on the Qiao and Hua Mountains*
Zhao Mengfu, while serving in various official capacities in the Yuan administration, developed a distinctive style of scroll painting that combined landscapes with calligraphy and stamp impressions, creating works that have the feel of an informal artist's notebook. This image from a scroll prepared in 1296 shows only the landscape portion of a much longer scroll. His art was frequently dedicated to friends or officials in order to strengthen social connections. This scroll was painted for Zhou Mi, a friend and connoisseur of ancient paintings, and depicts Zhao's ancestral lands, which Zhou had visited.

Just how essential painting skills were in Yuan social life can be gleaned by looking at Zhao Mengfu's family. Never before in Chinese history had cultural prominence and painting gone hand in hand in such obvious ways. Zhao's wife, Guan Daosheng (1262–1319), renowned for her depictions of bamboo and landscapes,[24] was the first woman to achieve lasting fame in the history of Chinese painting.[25] Moreover, both Zhao Mengfu's older and younger brothers were renowned calligraphers and painters, as were his son Zhao Yong, a local prefect, and his grandsons Zhao Lin and Wang Meng, the latter now celebrated as one of the "Four Great Masters" of Yuan China.[26]

In sum, the conventional view of the Mongols as brutal and uncultured barbarians needs to be re-evaluated. The Mongols were important patrons and consumers of the Chinese arts and crafts of painting, porcelain, and textiles. Moreover, aware of the Asian and Middle Eastern demand for Chinese porcelain and textiles, they fostered trade in these commodities, leading to considerable artistic, intellectual, and scientific diffusion across Eurasia.

1. Allsen 1989.
2. Hearn 1996, 269–71.
3. Allsen 1997.
4. Allsen 1997.
5. Watt and Wardwell 1997.
6. Allsen 1997, 35.
7. Jing 1994.
8. Jing 2004.
9. Melikian 2005.
10. Ho 2001.
11. Tichane 1983, 43–48.
12. So 2000.
13. Keith 1979; Seoul 1985.
14. Ho 1994–95.
15. Addis 1980–81; Fung Ping Shan Museum 1992.
16. Oriental Ceramic Society of Hong Kong 1984; Liu 1993.
17. Mote 1994.
18. Hearn 1996, 311–19.
19. Fang 2003.
20. Wenwu 1959.
21. Smith 1992.
22. Weitz 1997.
23. Li 1965; McCausland 1999.
24. Weidner et al. 1988.
25. Weidner et al. 1988.
26. Hearn 1996.

نه

دیگر وزن نمایه که اندر نمایه از نبعد سه روز پدید آید و به از سپیده خیزد و زود خورد و طمعه او باشد

اندر صورت سیمرغ

سیمرغ اندر دار محیط باشد اندر جزیرها بزدیکی خط استوا و مردم بدان جای نزسند و هوای خوش دارد

عنقا

31. Chinese Influence on Iranian Art in the Mongol Empire

Willem J. Vogelsang

IN 1219 Genghis Khan and his Türko-Mongolian army invaded the southern precincts of Central Asia and eastern Iran. Within a few years, the Mongols had defeated all opposition, killed hundreds of thousands of people, and devastated the cities and much of the countryside, including the irrigation systems. In doing so, they also spurred profound changes in the artistic traditions of the Middle East.

During the eleventh and twelfth centuries, under the Türkic-descended Seljuk rulers of Iran, Persian craftsmen and artists refined their arts and crafts to unprecedented heights. Seljuk ceramics include the famous luster and *mina'i* (enameled) wares, very costly to make because they required two firings in the kiln.[1] Artisans, especially those in eastern Iran, produced beautifully inlaid metalwork in large quantities.[2] Luxury textiles of magnificent silks feature elaborate figural designs. The Seljuks also are credited with great advances in architecture, in particular, the classic mosque with four, roofed iwan, a dominant feature of Iranian architecture to this day.

Frequent contacts with East Asia were the norm during this period, when travel and trade were conducted oversea and overland along the so-called Silk Road. Chinese ceramics were quite popular in the Middle East, prompting Middle Eastern potters to imitate them.[3] They covered their pottery with white clay slip to approximate the bright white of Chinese porcelain and developed tin glazes to replicate the colors. Eventually, Seljuk potters invented "fritware," composed of a mixture of ground quartz, white clay, and glass frit that, when fired, produced a hard and translucent white body very similar to Chinese porcelain and could easily be covered with a glossy and transparent alkaline glaze.

Contacts between Iran and East Asia strengthened after the Mongol conquest, with Mongolian traders often acting as intermediary. The Mongols had been in contact with the Chinese for many generations via trade networks, conquest, and other forms of exchange, but Genghis Khan's formal occupation of large parts of China by 1215 intensified China's influence on the Mongol world. Next, he turned his attentions to the west and defeated Ala al-Din Muhammad, the Khwarazm-shah, ruler of South Central Asia and eastern Iran and successor to the Seljuk kings. After Genghis Khan's death in 1227, his son Ögödei Khaghan (r. 1229–41) pursued Mongol advances into Russia and west to the Adriatic. The Anatolian Seljuks were subsequently defeated in 1242–43 at the battle of Köse-Dagh in modern Turkey.

The Middle Eastern conquests were brought to a temporary conclusion by Hülegü (c. 1217–65), son of Tolui, and grandson of Genghis Khan. He was sent by his brother,

31.1 The *Simurgh*
This *simurgh,* a fabulous winged creature of benevolent intent and female gender, is from the *Manafi'-i hayavan* (On the Usefulness of Animals) and dates to c. 1297–1300. The Chinese phoenix image used by early Ilkhanids was transformed into the traditional Iranian *simurgh* in Iran and began to appear on pottery and in other media. The mechanism for this transfer may have been phoenix images on imported Chinese textiles and ceramics.

31.2 The Phoenix
A more direct transfer of the Chinese phoenix is seen in glazed hexagonal tiles from Takht-i Sulaiman, an Ilkhanid summer palace in Iran. The underglaze painting method used here is similar to that developed in China during the Northern Song period and is employed here on Iranian fritware. The transfer of the phoenix motif may have been connected with the trade of Iranian cobalt oxide. Chinese potters used this Iranian mineral to produce the deep blue color in their underglaze porcelains, which in turn were exported to Ilkhanid Iran carrying phoenix and other motifs.

the Great Khan Möngke (r. 1251–59), with a huge army to occupy much of the Middle East. He crossed the Amu Darya River (the classical Oxus River) on 1 January 1256, and quickly moved west. He defeated the Ismailis (*Hashshashins* or Assassins) of the Iranian Elburz mountains at the fortress of Alamut later that year. In February 1258, he took Baghdad and killed the last of the Abbasid rulers. Hülegü subsequently occupied Aleppo and Damascus, but he returned to Iran when he was informed of the death of his brother Möngke Khaghan, and after some of his troops were defeated by the Egyptian Mamluks at the battle of Ayn Jalut in Palestine in 1260. The Mongols never managed to reconquer the entire Middle East; they were stopped by the powerful Mamluks under Sultan Baibars (r. 1260–77) and his successors. Hülegü and his descendants permanently settled in Iran, in the northwestern region of Azerbaijan. The dynasty he established became known as the Ilkhanid, meaning "subordinate khanate," to clarify its status with respect to the Great Khan of the Mongols in Mongolia and China. For the later part of the thirteenth centu-

ry the Mongol emperor was the great Kublai Khan (r. 1260–94), brother of Hülegü, who resided in northern China and who founded the Yuan dynasty (see Chapter 27).

The Mongol conquest of southern Central Asia and Iran brought Iran firmly back into the orbit of Central Asian culture, reversing a trend that started with the Muslim conquest of the country in the mid-seventh century. With the re-orientation of Iranian culture toward the east and northeast, contacts with China intensified. Both Ögödei Khaghan and Möngke Khaghan oversaw the forced migration of craftsmen from one corner of the empire to another. However, after 1270, these forced migrations waned and local schools of craft arts began to develop. Throughout the Mongolian empire, textiles were one of the most important items of trade, and it is very likely that many Chinese motifs that became popular in the art of Ilkhanid Iran were transmitted through this medium.[4] Textiles are relatively easy to transport, and precious textiles, especially the golden cloth of the Mongols (*nasij*), were often used for expensive gifts and even became a form of currency.

Contacts were established in various ways. Marco Polo recounts the mission Kublai Khan gave him to bring a Mongol princess bride to the court of the Ilkhanid ruler Arghun (r. 1284–91).[5] Many of these exchanges were based on the Ilkhanid's nominal recognition of Kublai Khan as overlord. The early Ilkhanids held land in China that provided them a regular income. Only when the Ilkhanid ruler Ghazan (r. 1295–1304) converted to Islam did the symbolic submission to the Yuan rulers end. Even so, business relationships continued as before.

There were many parallels between the hemispheres of the Mongol world. Both the Mongols in China (the Yuan dynasty) and the Mongols in Iran (the Ilkhanids) preferred to hire administrators and other servants from outside. The Yuan rulers preferred non-Chinese administrators, hence many Persian-speaking Muslims were employed in China. One flourishing fourteenth-century Chinese seaport, modern Quanzhou, had a Muslim quarter

31.3 Sultanabad Ware
Chinese influence is also seen in Sultanabad ware, like this vessel depicting phoenixes in flight. Use of a green or grey slip had not been known in pre-Mongol Iranian ceramic tradition. This ware may have originated during the 13th–14th century as an Iranian imitation of Yuan celadon in which a pale green glaze was applied over an Iranian fritware body.

with mosques and a Muslim cemetery. The Ilkhanid rulers employed many Buddhists, Christian Nestorians, and Jews. Hülegü married a Nestorian woman; one of his sons, later Ilkhan Abaqa, married an illegitimate daughter of Michael VIII, the Byzantine emperor. Famous Ilkhanid administrators included the Jewish-born physician, Rashid al-Din (1247–1318), who composed the famous *Compendium of Chronicles* (*Jami' al-Tavarikh*), commissioned by Ilkhan Ghazan and completed in 1310 during the reign of his brother Öljeitü (r. 1304–16). The multicultural citizenry of Mongol Iran formed a cosmopolitan market eager for "foreign" artistic motifs and techniques.

Contrary to traditional Chinese practices, the Yuan dynasty actively promoted commercial contacts with the outside world. An emissary of Ilkhan Ghazan returned from the Yuan court in 1298 with Chinese silks. Crafts and materials, ceramics, perhaps even book scrolls, but especially, silks went west in the hands of Chinese craftsmen, businessmen, or officials.[6] Iranian art of the time includes traditional Chinese symbols for sovereignty, good luck, and

wealth. Both Yuan and Ilkhanid rulers employed special devices and colors to buttress their positions of leadership and authority.

One of the finest adaptations of Chinese motifs is found in the architecture of the Ilkhanid summer palace of Takht-i Sulaiman.[7] This beautiful site to the south of Tabriz in what was the Iranian province of Azerbaijan is built around a crater lake at the top of an extinct volcano, a location once used as the coronation site of pre-Islamic Sassanid kings. The second Ilkhanid ruler, Abaqa (r. 1265–82), a son of Hülegü, rebuilt the site, then called Sughurlukh, in traditional Persian four-iwan style with the lake in the center substituting for the usual courtyard. German excavations revealed the palace floors and walls decorated with tiles and stucco painted or carved with animals and plants. The northern pavilion attached to the west iwan was decorated with star- and cross-shaped tiles of alternating dark and light turquoise glaze. Many of the tiles are painted in the so-called *lajvardina* style (named after the dark blue color of the glaze, *lajvard* being the Persian word for lapis lazuli), in red, white, and black. Other tiles have designs in relief that are completely covered with gold leaf. The star-shaped tiles feature Chinese-style landscapes of trees and clouds as well as dragons, phoenixes, lions, deer, and peonies—symbols of royal power and of prosperity. The dragon chasing a flaming pearl is a well-known Chinese motif, as is the phoenix shown with outstretched wings (fig. 31.2). The dragons at Takht-i Sulaiman are particularly interesting, in that they are shown with four claws, instead of the five claws reserved for Chinese imperial objects, probably out of deference to the higher authority of Kublai Khan as the Yuan emperor.

Dragons and phoenixes are found on Yuan-period Chinese textiles, suggesting they were the primary medium for the transmission of Chinese motifs to Ilkhanid Iran.[8] The tiles at Takht-i Sulaiman decorate inside walls, where textiles often filled the same function. Perhaps most intriguing is that these royal symbols of Chinese derivation were combined at the summer palace with scenes and verses from the *Shahnama* (Book of Kings), the classic devoted to Iranian royal

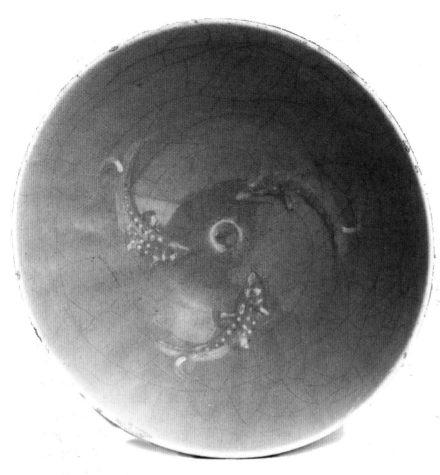

31.4 Green Bowl
The influence of Chinese celadon porcelains is also seen in this underglaze green-slip fritware bowl dating to the first half of the 14th century.

into the Iranian *simurgh*, a flying mythical creature of equally auspicious character. Therefore, while Chinese influence regarding motifs is clear, Chinese potters never decorated their vessels in this manner. Persian potters translated the image from its original Chinese media, most likely textiles, into new uniquely Persian creations.

Chinese influence can be seen on other types of pottery produced in Iran. During the late thirteenth and the fourteenth centuries, Persian potters imitated Chinese celadons by applying a pale green glaze to a fritware body. Greenish Sultanabad ware may have been an attempt to adapt Chinese celadon.[10] Another example of Persian mistranslation of Chinese symbols appears on a large bowl in the collection of the Metropolitan Museum of Art (fig. 31.4). The interior of the bowl is painted with three fish. In China, fish symbolize wealth and are mostly shown in pairs. To the artisan responsible for the painting, three fish was simply a pleasing and exotic embellishment.

Chinese motifs had perhaps their greatest influence on the Persian "art of the book." Illustrations in Ilkhanid manuscripts often show Chinese influence, especially in the rendering of mountain landscapes. Chinese treatment gave Persian artists new ways to indicate space. In one Ilkhanid miniature, *Bahman Meeting Zal*, the background is indicated by tufts of grass that form overlapping planes and provide depth to the picture (fig. 31.5). The trees in Ilkhanid miniatures are often gnarled and leafless, recalling some found in Chinese paintings. The curved "cloud collars" used in decorative borders must also derive from the Chinese. Overall, Ilkhanid art displays a new spirit stimulated by foreign motifs. The earliest Ilkhanid manuscript to clearly exhibit these characteristics is a copy of the *Manafi'-i hayavan* (On the Usefulness of Animals), made in Maragha, south of Tabriz, at the end of the thirteenth century and now housed in the Pierpont Morgan Library (fig. 31.1). The illustrations in the manuscript show a new élan; they are naturalistic, with very clear colors, and full of vigor. The animals are shown as living creatures, rather than caricatures, and they are seen against a realistic back-

glory. When building their palace, Ilkhanid rulers used all the symbols available to assert their sovereignty and their links with their Yuan overlords, without neglecting to imply their place in the royal history of Iran.

Ilkhanid pottery also adopted the Chinese phoenix device for more pedestrian wares. Fourteenth-century Sultanabad pottery, a fritware usually covered with a greenish or grey slip, is known for its clumsy application of Chinese motifs (fig. 31.3). Sultanabad vessels are characterized by naturalistic decoration, painted under a thick overglaze, that is completely different from pre-Mongol wares exhibiting arabesques and other stylized motifs. Sultanabad patterns include the phoenix, often shown in pairs or groups of three, as well as dragons, mandarin ducks (a Chinese symbol of marital bliss), peonies, bands of clouds, and lotuses set against a background of leaves. Similar groups of phoenixes appear on Yuan lacquerware and silk textiles, as mentioned.[9] While the phoenix at the palace of Takht-i Sulaiman was employed as a royal symbol for the early Ilkhanids, its use on clay vessels begins its transformation

31.5 *Bahram Meeting Zal*
The encounter with Chinese painting styles and motifs caused major changes in Iranian art, as seen in this illustration from the 1330 version of the Great Mongol *Shahnama* (Book of Kings). In this scene illustrating ancient Persian oral tradition about King Bahram, perspective is created by the use of overlapping planes of grass tufts. Iranian artists began to imitate such Chinese conventions as leafless trees, gnarled bark, and Chinese-style clouds and grass.

grounds of some of the illustrations show water indicated by imbrications and mountains and trees that recall Chinese examples. One of the paintings from the London manuscript, entitled *The Mountains between Tibet and India*, has conventional Chinese-style peaks (fig. 23.1). An early fourteenth-century version of the *Compendium*, now in the National Library, Berlin, contains a landscape in Chinese style. The river is indicated by curling waves that end in crests, and the trees are leafless and gnarled. Also reminiscent are the stylized rock formations in blue, green, and red. Finally, there is the "Great Mongol *Shahnama*," which probably dates to the 1330s. This book was taken apart by the Belgian dealer, Georges Demotte (1877–1923) in the early twentieth century and its folios are spread all over the world.[11] Some of the illustrations also show Chinese-style landscapes and symbolic imagery such as dragons.

In short, the Mongol conquest and the subsequent rule of the Ilkhanid khans opened the Iranian art world to outside influences, most importantly from Central Asia and Yuan China. Textiles may have been the principal means by which Chinese motifs entered the repertoire of Iranian craftsmen, but other goods, from porcelains to painted scrolls, contributed to the unique synthesis that is Ilkhanate art. The Mongol conquest that inflicted enormous casualties across the Muslim world also invigorated Iranian art, pushing it toward realism, use of vibrant color, and the acceptance of the background as an integral part of illustration.

ground that is decidedly Chinese in manner.

Another manuscript germane to this discussion is a version of the *Compendium of Chronicles*, mentioned above. The manuscript is dated to 1314, and what remains of it is housed in the Edinburgh University Library and in the Khalili Collection, Nour Foundation, London. The book was commissioned by Ilkahns Ghazan and Öljeitü and probably once included more than five hundred illustrations. Featured in the illustrations are textiles with Chinese motifs recalling those painted on Sultanabad pottery and figures wearing Chinese-like garments with Chinese emblems, including the cloud collar. The back-

1. Allan 1971, 30–35.
2. Blair and Bloom 2000, 344–45.
3. Allan 1971, 8–17.
4. Komaroff 2002, 169–95.
5. Rossabi 2002, 33.
6. Komaroff 2002, 181–83.
7. Masuya 2002.
8. Komaroff 2002, 176.
9. Komaroff 2002, 178.
10. Komaroff 2002, 176.
11. Hillenbrand 2002, 155–67.

宣授高麗國儒學提舉都會議中贊修文殿大學士贈謚文成公安　珦真

越延祐五年二月　日降

宥古其目云都會議中贊修文殿大
學士安珦有崇設學校之功亦於

夫子廟庭圖形致祭崇鄉興州守散
郎崔琳依其目摹寫一軀將安之

于鄉校時嗣子于器遼承之鎮邊崔
君送以示之於是焚香拜手乃爲

之贊曰

先君當日振儒風

上命圖形

文廟中一幅丹青照斋梓四時邊豆

荟膚功

　　　　　　是年秋九月　日贊

慶尚全羅州道巡撫鎮邊使匡靖大夫檢校僉議評理無判典儀寺事上護軍安于器拜題

32. A Marriage of Convenience

GORYEO-MONGOL RELATIONS IN THE THIRTEENTH AND FOURTEENTH CENTURIES

GEORGE L. KALLANDER

WHEN THE GORYEO (Koryŏ) dynasty (935–1392) first encountered the Mongols in 1218, Koreans already had a long history of interaction with mainland empires. The previous Korean kingdoms of Paekchae (18 BCE–660 CE), Gogureyŏ (37 BCE–678 CE), and Silla (57 BCE–935 CE) were all influenced by the political, intellectual, and cultural winds of the continent. Since the time of Tang-dynasty China (618–907), Korea had sent diplomatic missions to the Chinese capital, adopted the Chinese dynastic calendar and reign titles, and submitted the names of new kings to the emperor for investiture, among other deferential rituals that defined its tributary status in the East Asia. For continental empires, a cordial relationship with the peninsula ensured a reliable defensive partner against potential invaders from the north. Without the threat of Korea joining an alliance with northern tribes, China had no need to station large numbers of troops along the northeastern frontier and could, therefore, invest resources into defending more volatile border regions and suppressing internal disorder. Being recognized as the rulers of "All Under Heaven" earned Chinese emperors greater domestic and international legitimacy. An emperor needed an empire, and a tributary relationship with Korea bolstered the image of China as the center of civilization. From Korea's perspective, China was an ally. The country benefited from limited trade and the latest Chinese scientific, scholarly, and religious developments, all with little or no interference in internal affairs.

32.1 Portrait of An Hyang
An Hyang (1243–1306) founded Neo-Confucianism in Korea and is responsible for introducing the Song version of this faith to the Goryeo kingdom. While visiting China, he transcribed the *Zhuzi shu*, a famous interpretation of Confucian literature. He used his copy of this work, along with portraits of its author, Zhu Xi, and Confucius, in his movement to revitalize Confucian practices in Korea. In 1304 he founded the Confucian shrine Munmyo.

This relationship changed drastically when the Mongols ascended to power in East Asia. Active Goryeo resistance against the "barbarians" repeatedly brought Mongol armies to the peninsula, until Korea's full acceptance of Mongol demands turned the relationship between the Yuan and Goryeo courts into a family affair.

Intermarriages between the Yuan and Goryeo

The Goryeo kingdom was important to the Mongols in their struggle for domination in East Asia. The Mongol rulers of the Yuan dynasty invested men, horses, and blood in first subduing Goryeo and, later, co-opting the elite into the Mongol Yuan empire. The Goryeo submission would bring legitimacy to Mongol leaders; fill coffers with annual tribute; secure the Mongol eastern flank against Chinese Southern Song loyalists, the Jurchen Jin dynasty, and Khitan tribes; and build an alliance for subjugation of the Japanese islands. From the beginning of the con-

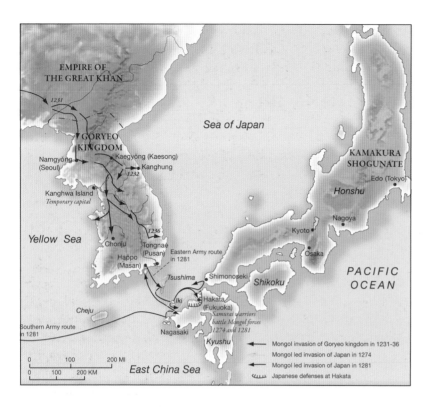

32.2 Mongol Invasion of Korea
Mongols invaded the Goryeo kingdom in 1231–36 but did not absorb these lands into the Mongol empire, preferring to allow the kingdom to exist as a vassal state in return for tribute and official favors. One of the "favors" demanded was participation in the Mongol-led invasions of Japan in 1274 and 1281. For details on the Yuan-led invasions of Japan in 1274 and 1281, see fig. 33.2.

quest in 1218 to the final submission in 1269, the Goryeo court relied upon island defenses, fortified towns, guerilla warfare, and diplomatic stalling tactics in its attempt to resist Mongol demands. The latter tactics included severing relations with the Southern Song dynasty, dispatching a crown prince—the future Goryeo King Chungnyeol (r. 1274–1308)—to the Mongol capital (1259), and promising the return of the king and court to the capital from a temporary residence on Kanghwa Island, fully realized in 1270.

Goryeo leaders had two options: fight the Mongols to preserve the integrity of the king and risk dynastic collapse, or submit, which would preserve the dynasty but dilute the bloodline of the monarchy. Despite the unprecedented destruction and loss of life brought upon the peninsula through repeated invasions, the defection of many to the Mongol side, and the governing of the north by Mongol military commanders (*darugachi*), the Goryeo court managed to resist the Mongols until the reign of King Weonjong (r. 1259–74), when military leaders who opposed full submission were defeated in factional battles. In 1270 the court fully conceded to Mongol demands by returning to the capital at Kaegyeong

(near modern-day Kaeseong) on the mainland. Upon the death of Weonjong four years later, the Korean crown prince married Kublai Khan's daughter in Daidu.[1]

The Mongols first arrived in 1218 on the peninsula ostensibly to aid the Goryeo against invading Khitan armies. Although the Goryeo initially agreed to submit to a tributary relationship, the mysterious, yet timely, death of a Mongol envoy near the Goryeo frontier, in 1224, provided the court and ruling military family with an opportunity to sever relations. To punish the Goryeo and force complete submission, the Mongols dispatched troops to the peninsula. From 1232 until 1270, the Mongol armies campaigned in Korea, unleashing social and political turmoil (fig. 32.2). With the court safely removed to Kanghwa Island—which offered protection because the Mongols had no skills to move their armies across a body of water—and a military clan fearful of loss of its own political power, Goryeo rulers resisted. From Kanghwa, the court called on the population to hide in mountains and islands, enlisted Buddhist monks to carry out acts of piety to support the country, such as recarving the woodblocks used to print the Buddhist canon (*Tripitaka*), which the Mongols had burned, and even called on Buddhist monks to resist the invaders through force. Resistance brought little success: devastation and political instability ensued. When the court retreated from the capital in 1232, uprisings in provinces in the north and south broke out. The destruction of farmlands, homes, and countless lives was unprecedented. Tens of thousands were killed, forced to relocate, or taken as slaves. Because of the turmoil and breakdown of resistance, many Koreans, especially in the north, had no choice but to surrender and go over to the Mongol side. Promises of submission, reluctant agreements with Mongol commanders, and political foot dragging by the court brought Mongol armies back to the peninsula repeatedly until peace was agreed upon in 1259, when the crown prince was sent to the Mongols.

From Chungnyeol's reign (began 1274) and throughout the Yuan period, as Goryeo kings became more and more Mongolized,

32.3 Stoneware Vessel
This wine bottle from the 13th-century Goryeo dynasty is made of stoneware with black and white inlays under a celadon glaze. The use of stamped motifs, such as the wild aster flowers on this vessel, was a common type of decoration during this period.

the ethnic composition of the Korean royal family became blurred. Through intermarriage with Mongol Yuan princesses and adopting Mongol customs, including Mongol fashion and the shaved pate of Mongol males, Goryeo kings almost fully Mongolized. From the time of King Chungseon (r. 1308–13), they also adopted Mongol names to use in official correspondence with the Yuan imperial court. For this reason, Korean kings of the Yuan period are frequently termed "figureheads" and criticized by contemporary historians for spending more time taking part in hunts and other Mongol cultural practices than ruling the dynasty. Although such criticism is understandable, it ignores the importance of cultural identity to the Mongols. Mongol emperors in China and their relatives in Korea celebrated a connection to the Mongol homeland, an important wellspring of cultural identity and a place of refuge should the empire one day fall. Without the clothes, the hair, and lifestyle to preserve a distinctive Mongol identity, over time the ruling families would have assimilated into the larger populations of China and Korea, thus eliminating any privileges as a separate ruling class.

The new relationship between the Yuan and Goryeo dynasties altered the way the Korean court and elite perceived themselves. Parochial attitudes gave way to greater awareness that Korea was part of a much larger empire. King Chungnyeol and his Mongol wife were the first to blur ethnicity and civilization. When she journeyed to Korea in 1274, the new Goryeo queen brought her sheepskins to hang from the doors and ceilings. Even King Chungnyeol's Mongol attire prompted the official Yu Cheonu (1209–1276) to voice his Confucian displeasure: "If the king wears Mongol robes when he leaves the fortress, the commoners will be surprised and think it's very strange."[2] After a long discussion at the court, Mongol dress and hairstyle were adopted.

Members of the elite imitated the royal family by enjoying the benefits of empire. Travel between the Goryeo and Yuan capitals became more frequent. In China, scholar officials from Goryeo came into contact with new people and scholarship, bringing back with them Mongol customs and Chinese learning. But inclusion into the Yuan empire also brought greater responsibility and demands on Goryeo, more exacting than the tributary relationships with previous Chinese empires. The Mongol favor for Goryeo women, as well as the decline in the population from famine and invasions, worried officials, who advocated that restrictions against men taking several wives be lifted to repopulate the country. "The male population," stated the bureaucrat Paek Yu, "has been decimated but there are still many women. This is why the Mongols take so many. There is danger that the pure Goryeo stock will become diluted by the mixture of wild blood."[3]

Invasions of Japan

Korea soon became the perfect staging platform for the Mongols' two attempted invasions of Japan in 1274 and 1281 (fig. 32.2). Not only is the southern portion of the Korean peninsula the closest land mass to the Japanese islands—one may cross the Korean Straits without ever losing sight of land—but the close familial relationship between the Yuan and Goryeo courts facilitated Mongol plans. By orders of Kublai Khan, conveyed through his new son-in-law King Chungnyeol, tens of thousands of Koreans were mobilized for war.[4] Koreans were involved in preparing for both invasions through the construction and manning of ships—Koreans were skilled shipbuilders who had, even earlier, assisted the Mongols in crossing the Yangzi River in

32.4 Gyeongcheonsa Temple Pagoda
This marble pagoda of ten superimposed temples has a peripatetic history. It was erected ca. 1348 at a now-destroyed temple and removed to Japan during that country's occupation of Korea. In 1960 it was returned to Korea and has been designated a national treasure, in part because its carvings preserve information on Goryeo-period wooden temple architecture. Today it stands in the National Museum of Korea.

campaigns against the Southern Song dynasty. In the first invasion, an army of 25,000 Mongol and Chinese troops, along with 8,000 Goryeo soldiers and 6,700 boatmen and navigators, sailed on 900 boats. The second invasion was equally impressive. The Chinese sources exaggerate perhaps in claiming that 40,000 Mongol-Goryeo-Chinese and 100,000 tribal soldiers, along with 900 warships, were mobilized. During the invasions of Japan, Korean soldiers fought bravely against the Japanese.[5] In the early days of the second invasion, one contingent of Korean officers is reported to have severed the heads of 300 Japanese soldiers. But Mongol-Goryeo-Chinese troops also had to combat sickness along with the defending Japanese samurai, as disease killed 3,000 troops. They suffered heavy losses: the ensuing typhoons swept away more than 100,000 allied troops in both campaigns—along with Kublai's dreams of subjugating Japan.

The origins of Kublai's plans for Japan are hard to determine. Certain historians claim that a Korean by the name Jo I (dates unknown) convinced Kublai to invade the islands.[6] But the evidence is ambiguous, at best.[7] What is certain is that as early as 1266, Kublai dispatched an envoy to Japan, whom the Koreans were requested to escort, to deliver a letter addressed to the "King of Japan." That missive announced that Kublai had received the Mandate of Heaven and proposed, under a thinly veiled threat of war, that the Mongol empire and Japan should enter into friendly relations.[8] From the very beginning, the Goryeo court was more interested in acting as a diplomatic peacemaker between the Mongol empire and Japan—any military plans against the islands would surely have

placed a heavy burden on Korea. Although Kublai hoped to resolve the matter through diplomacy, in 1270, when Japan continued to ignore Mongol envoys, he ordered Korea to begin military preparations. The Goryeo court made one last attempt at peace in 1272 by sending an unofficial envoy to Japan, to no avail.[9] The stage was set for war.

Although both invasions failed and Japan was saved from being overrun by foreign troops, the Mongols had demonstrated the strength of their empire, rather than its weakness. In both forays, they were able to work with allies, gather large forces of men and materiel, and move them across the Korean Straits. Despite the outcome, the Mongols do not appear to have been compromised by the loss of resources that went into both attempts. From the Korean perspective, the ultimate significance was the dynasty's full participation in a foreign invasion. For good or ill, Korea was an active participant in empire.

Cultural Diffusion and Empire

The transmission of Neo-Confucian thought based on the teachings of the Song theorist Zhu Xi (1130–1200) was the major political and cultural contribution to Korea in the Mongol Yuan period. The rise of the Jurchen-Jin dynasty in northern China cut Goryeo off from the intellectual developments taking place in the Southern Song. Links between Chinese and Korean schools of Confucianism were reestablished during the late thirteenth century as Goryeo was integrated into the Mongol empire. Under Kublai's patronage, Neo-Confucian studies prospered in the Yuan dynasty and the marital ties between the Goryeo and Mongol courts facilitated the absorption of this new form of study in Korea. Kublai sent as a gift to the Goryeo king a 1,000-volume Neo-Confucian collection. When King Chungseon returned from Daidu to ascend the throne, he brought with him a library of four thousand books.

The close relations between the Yuan and Goryeo courts allowed Koreans more opportunities to travel to China, and they returned with the latest in Neo-Confucian scholarship. On a journey to Daidu in

1289, King Chungnyeol was accompanied by An Hyang (1243–1306), a famous Confucian scholar of the Office for the Promotion of Confucian Studies (*Yuhak jegosa*) (fig. 32.1). In the Yüan capital, An Hyang devoted his full attention to the study of the newly circulating works of Zhu Xi. Once back in his Goryeo domain, Chungseon sent additional students to southern China in 1303, not only to learn more about Zhu Xi's teachings, but also to acquire additional material related to Neo-Confucianism. Under An's guidance, Confucian studies in Goryeo rebounded. The government rebuilt the Royal Confucian Academy (*Seoggyungwon*) as government-officials who would assist in building a new dynasty in Korea after the demise of Mongol power in East Asia at the end of the fourteenth century.

32.5 Bodhisattva Avalokiteshvara
This 14th-century hanging scroll depicts Avalokitesvara, the bodhisattva associated with compassion, seated near the water. The elegant pose of the deity and the delicate use of color are characteristic of Korean Buddhist painting of this period.and follows Chinese prototypes.

Rupture in Relations

Because of familiarity between the courts, fostered by intermarriage, as well as the close proximity between the capitals, Mongol emperors often interfered in Korean affairs. Some involvement was welcome: for example, when the Mongol army returned to Korea in 1290 to help Goryeo defend the frontier against marauding tribes. But many decrees attempted to change Goryeo customs. The Mongols criticized Korean practices and attempted to forbid marriage between men and women of the same surname within the royal and elite classes, as well as marriage between matrilateral cousins. The Mongols even criticized slavery, a mainstay of pre-modern Korean society, and demanded the king free children of mixed slave marriages.

When the Goryeo kingdom overcame Mongol domination following the rise of the Ming (1368–1644), scholars within the government argued for the removal of all Mongol customs and rules that had been adopted. Neo-Confucian thought is, arguably, the greatest and most lasting consequence of this period of Korean history. Although the Mongols did not develop Neo-Confucianism, their practice of religious and scholarly tolerance under the patronage of Kublai Khan and later Yuan emperors provided Neo-Confucianism room to flourish in China and Korea. The Joseon dynasty (1392–1910) began a process that put into practice the Neo-Confucian principles the Mongols had helped transmit to Korea; eventually this lead to the Confucianization of Korean society in the centuries that followed.

1. *Goryeosa* 1998.
2. *Goryeosa* 1998, 27, Wonjong 15.
3. *Goryeosa* 1998, 106.
4. *Goryeosa jeoryo* 1968, 20.
5. *Goryeosa jeoryo* 1968, 20.
6. Yamada 1916; Kim 1998, 199.
7. Hori 1967, 87–88.
8. *Goryeosa jeoryo* 1968, 18.
9. *Goryeosa* 1998, 27, Wonjong 13/1 and 13/4.

DELGADO · SASAKI · HAYASHIDA

33. The Lost Fleet of Kublai Khan

MONGOL INVASIONS OF JAPAN

James P. Delgado

Randall J. Sasaki

Kenzo Hayashida

UNDER THE DESCENDANTS OF GENGHIS KHAN, the Mongols pushed out of their homeland in a series of successful battles and political alliances, expanding Mongol power into the Middle East and Asia. On some occasions, the vaunted Mongolian war machine failed. In the famous battle of Ayn Jalut in September 1260, Mamluk forces from Egypt destroyed the Mongol army. Almost all agree that the greatest military disaster to befall the Mongols, however, was the loss of their navy in Kublai Khan's campaigns against Japan in 1274 and 1281. Some accounts suggest that more than 4,000 ships and 100,000 men were lost in the final 1281 debacle.

The Mongol invasions of Japan soon entrenched themselves into Japanese and Western folklore. In the West, the published accounts of Marco Polo's travels in China reached an audience who thrilled to tales of marvelous "Cipangu" (Japan) and how the Khan's fleet met with a tremendous storm that wrecked Kublai's dreams of conquest. In Japan, the fortuitous arrival of a seasonal typhoon was parlayed into a potent myth of how Japan's ancestral gods, called to protect their shores by the emperor and priests, had answered those prayers with a divine wind, or *kamikaze,* that smashed Kublai's ships into kindling. A rebirth of nationalism in the late nineteenth and early twentieth century focused attention anew on the story of the *kamikaze* and inspired intense Japanese interest in finding relics of the invasions. During the last decades of the twentieth century, that quest was translated into archaeological investigations, with surprising and spectacular results. Historical analysis of contemporary Japanese and Chinese accounts has also helped separate fact from myth: an illustrated handscroll completed for samurai Takezaki Suenaga in or around 1291, known today as the *Mōko shūrai ekotoba* (Mongol Invasion Scroll), and Thomas Conlan's 2001 study of a rare illustrated account of the two invasions are important sources of information (figs. 33.2, 10).

Marco Polo claims that Kublai decided to invade Japan to gain its riches: "Of so great celebrity was the wealth of this island, that a desire was excited in the breast of the grand khan . . . to make the conquest of it, and to annex it to his dominions."[1] The actual reasons were undoubtedly far more complex. Motivated by his own contested succession to the rank of Great Khan, which raised questions about his ability to conquer and rule as a worthy successor, Kublai sought to annex Song China to the Mongol empire. In 1268 Kublai launched an invasion of China. This victory would take eleven years to complete and came only by adopting new tactics of naval warfare

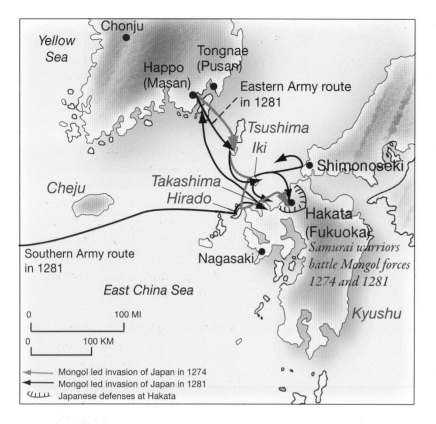

33.1 Yuan Invasions of Japan, 1274 and 1281
Even before his defeat of the Song empire in 1276, Kublai Khan had marshaled Yuan forces for an invasion of Japan. The attack in 1274, launched from Korea with 900 Korean ships and 25,000 men, failed to gain a foothold and forces were withdrawn. After the capitulation of the southern Song, Kublai launched a much larger attack by combining a Yuan and Korean fleet from Korea with a Song fleet from the south. The late arrival of the Song force, along with lack of coordination, Japanese resistance, and a severe storm, resulted in great losses of ships and men.

to supplement the force of arms on land.

The Song dynasty (960–1279) at that time had a large navy and extensive trade networks that ranged from Asian coastal waters to Indonesia and India.[2] As this international trade flourished, such coastal cities as Quanzhou and Ningbo joined the ranks of China's richest cities. Customs duties from the goods that flowed through these ports became a major source of income for the Song.[3] During this period China introduced revolutionary new technologies such as the magnetic compass and gunpowder, which immediately found their way into naval warfare. Maritime prosperity and a powerful navy did not protect the Song from internal dissension and political decay, nor from land-based invaders from the north.

Those invaders, the Mongols, gradually spread their control into northern China and Korea. Spurred by Kublai's dreams of conquest and his own interest in Chinese trade, politics, and culture,[4] the Mongols faced the Song in the southern maritime provinces. Kublai began a strategy of attrition, weakening the Song gradually, attacking them by land and cutting off their maritime trade with Korea and Japan.[5] Korea suffered Mongol

invasion as early as 1231 (fig. 32.2). Initial Korean resistance provoked a prolonged conflict that led to considerable loss of life before the Korean king started to capitulate in 1259, agreeing to an alliance in which he retained his throne but became a vassal and accepted Mongol troops in Korea (see Chapter 32). In 1267 Kublai sent an emissary to Japan with a letter demanding a trade relationship and submission to Mongol authority, implying the use of force. The Japanese court and military government, the *bakufu*, refused to answer, and subsequent Mongol emissaries were rebuffed in what was tantamount to a declaration of war.

The Invasion of 1274

Kublai's war against the Song in China progressed after the Mongols adopted naval warfare. In the five-year siege of the Song River port city of Xiangyang, Kublai's forces, advised by Song defectors, used a naval force to wrest control of the river and cut off supplies to the defenders. In March 1273, Xiangyang fell, and the river became a highway of war as Mongols poured into the Song heartland. Kublai decided the time was ripe to strike at Japan. In January 1274, he ordered the Koreans to build 900 ships.[6] The *Yuanshi*, the official Chinese court history that records Kublai's reign, describes three types of vessels—300 cargo ships, 300 landing craft, and 300 miscellaneous small boats—all to be ready by the beginning of summer. Meanwhile, Kublai assembled his army—20,000 Mongols and Northern Chinese who were already stationed in Korea, and 6,000 Koreans. An additional complement of from 6,700 to 15,000 sailors manned the fleet.

The Khan's combined forces left Korea in late summer, striking across the narrow Straits of Tsushima toward Kyushu, the southernmost of the major Japanese islands. After a quick conquest of the Tsushima and Iki islands (fig. 33.1), the fleet proceeded to Hakata Bay (today's Fukuoka), site of Japan's principal trading port and home to a substantial expatriate Chinese trading community.[7] Hakata fell easily and the Mongols burned it before advancing inland. Engaged in battle by Japanese defense forces, the invaders fought a series of land actions, which are depicted in detail in the scroll *Mōko shūrai eko-toba*.[8] Japanese accounts stress a vigorous defense and claim that wounding the Mongol commander forced the fleet to retreat. It is also assumed that Kublai's non-Mongol troops were not enthusiastic about supporting the invasion, and with the onset of Japanese resistance and storm conditions, made a hasty retreat.

The retreat of 1274 may have had more to do with Mongol strategy than Japanese resistance. Kublai probably did not intend a full-scale invasion to subjugate all of Japan; his main objective was to weaken Song trade by destroying Hakata. By realizing this primary goal, the invasion of 1274 was a marked success. Doubtless Kublai's forces would have continued their quest inland had they not faced determined Japanese resistance, but they withdrew and Kublai turned his attention to the final conquest of the Song. Joined by growing numbers of Song defectors, including most of the navy, Kublai's forces took the capital and pursued Song loyalists along the southern Chinese coast, occupying various ports before a climactic naval battle in 1279 ended all Song resistance. That year Kublai finally became uncontested ruler of all China, and his new dynasty, the Yuan, remained in control for nearly a century.[9]

Fearing that the Mongols would return with a greater force, the Japanese military government ordered reinforcements to Hakata and constructed a series of defensive walls along the beaches (fig. 33.4). Japanese concerns were well warranted. Kublai again sent emissaries seeking Japan's submission. The Japanese authorities, emboldened by the quick retreat of the Mongol forces, their victory in 1274, and their increased defenses, beheaded a Mongol envoy.[10] In response, Kublai ordered another invasion.

The Invasion of 1281

The plan for the second invasion called for 900 ships from Korea and 3,500 ships from the Yangzi Delta port of Ningbo. The sizes of the Korean fleet, known as the Eastern Army, and the fleet from Ningbo, the Southern Army, have been variously estimated, with conflicting figures. The Eastern Army consisted of about 40,000 troops and 17,000 non-combatant sailors, while the Southern Army reputedly sailed with 100,000 troops and 42,000 sailors.[11] The fleets were to rendezvous in the Straits of Tsushima at Iki Island in mid-June and then

33.2 Japanese Samurai Attack Yuan Fleet
The *Mōko shūrai ekotoba* (Mongol Invasion Scroll) painted in 1291 illustrates the Mongol-led attacks on Japan in 1274 and 1281.

33.3 Commander's Seal
One of the most definitive finds recovered from Takashima is this bronze seal found by a fisherman on the beach at Kozaki Harbor. Its inscription, written in 'Phags-pa, the official script of the Yuan empire, reveals it to be the seal of a Mongolian commander whose ship must have been wrecked at this location.

strike the nearby islands and the Japanese mainland.[12]

The Eastern Army sailed first, reaching Tsushima and Iki in early summer. The islands were again conquered, and the fleet gained control of the Straits. Some accounts suggest they then advanced to Hakata Bay, where they were rebuffed by the Japanese defenders and retreated to wait for the Southern Army (fig. 33.1). The force from Ningbo did not reach Japan until late July, arriving at Hirado Island. The combined force left Hirado for Imari Bay, south of Hakata, massacring the inhabitants of Takashima Island to use it to bypass the defenses at Hakata Bay.

Depictions of the second invasion from the *Mōko shūrai ekotoba* mostly show battle scenes fought at sea. While the Japa-

nese did not possess a navy, a small coastal defense force of commandeered fishing vessels and other craft struck at the invaders. Boarding actions, hand-to-hand fighting, and the use of fire ships to set warships ablaze compelled the Mongols to crowd their ships into a tightly packed anchorage. This proved to be their undoing. When a typhoon struck the area after a few days of fighting, the invading fleet was crushed. The official Korean court history, the *Goryeosa*, comments, "About 100,000 troops of the Southern Army came, but they met with large wind, and all the Southern Army died."[13] Most of the Eastern Army seems to have returned safely to Korea, perhaps because they had much smaller vessels than the large ocean-going supply ships sent from China.

The Southern Army lost an unknown number of ships and, according to Chinese sources, as many as 60,000 to 70,000 troops. Many who survived the typhoon fought against each other to get on board vessels that survived and escape Japanese retribution. In the wake of the storm, the defenders avenged themselves on the survivors, executing thousands. The belief that the victory was enabled by a gift of the gods would last for centuries.

Archaeological Discovery of the Invasion

The events of 1281 did not immediately end Kublai's plans to subjugate Japan. He ordered new conscriptions and additional ships for a third invasion, but shortage of timber and internal opposition to further overseas ventures finally dissuaded him. The maritime legacy of his reign, which ended with Kublai's death in 1294, was sullied by continuous, largely unsuccessful invasions of Japan, Vietnam, and Java. The rediscovery of the archaeological legacy—in the waters off Takashima—awaited the invention of modern technology.

Largely forgotten in the centuries following 1281, the story of the Mongol invasions was revived in the late nineteenth century. During the Meiji period, the *Mōko shūrai ekotoba* surfaced from a private family collection and joined the

33.4 Hakata Bay Defense
Stone walls and other defenses were erected at Hakata Bay by samurai forces to defend Japan against the Yuan invasion. This modern construction is part of a Japanese memorial to these events.

33.5 Buddha Preaching
This large sculpture of Buddha came up in a fisherman's net from the waters around Takashima Island more than 200 years ago. The bronze was probably cast in Korea and may have been aboard one of the vessels that sank during the 1281 invasion. The statue resides in a local shrine on Takashima Island.

treasures of the Imperial Household; books written by modern authors reacquainted both Japanese and Westerners with perspectives on the invasion, the "divine wind," and Japanese resistance.[14] Japanese archaeologists excavated and restored portions of the Hakata Bay defense walls, and memorials and religious monuments were erected in Fukuoka, site of ancient Hakata.

Meanwhile, the local people had never forgotten the history of Takashima. More than a century ago a bronze statue of Buddha (fig. 33.5), most likely made in Korea, had come up in a fisherman's net, and Chinese ceramic pots often appear in nets today.[15] Japanese scholars proposed that the

bay be investigated, and marine engineer Torao Mozai used a sonar system he had helped develop to survey the waters around Takashima in the early 1980s.[16] While he did not find any of the wrecks, Mozai discovered many artifacts relating to the Mongol invasion, including storage jars, stone anchor stocks, and bricks. During the survey, a fisherman came forth with a square bronze object he had found several years before (fig. 33.3). Inscribed in 'Phags-pa script, it proved to be the personal seal for a commander in the Mongol army.[17] This artifact even convinced skeptics that the Mongols had come to Takashima and led to worldwide media attention and establishment of a nationally protected site along 7.5 km of the island's southern shoreline and extending 200 meters out to sea. Mozai's work, which ended in the 1980s, pointed the way for a new generation of professional marine archaeologists. Their surveys and excavations demonstrated the full archaeological potential of the site and recovered many artifacts, including stone anchor stocks, bricks, storage jars (known as *shijiko*), and small fragments of ships' hulls that originated in southern China.

Redevelopment in 1994 of the small fishing port at Kozaki harbor, where the bronze seal was found, offered an opportunity for new surveys and excavations. The new work revealed four wooden anchors fitted with stone stocks that were aligned in the same direction, an alignment consistent with positioning taken by vessels being driven ashore in a storm.[18] Discovery of the anchors in 20 meters of water, at approximately 100 meters from the shore, indicated the seabed was undisturbed and that other remains might be found in situ.

Carbon-14 dating of the wood shows that these anchors were made during the time of the invasions; the wood species and the type of stone used for their stocks suggested a southern China origin, perhaps Fujian province.[19] Unlike other stone anchor stocks that had been found previously in Hakata Bay and other regions of Japan, which were formed with a single stone stock,[20] the stone stocks of the Takashima anchors were cut in half and lashed to a wooden frame. This type of anchor was not known previously

33.6 Arrows
Underwater excavations at Kozaki harbor brought up many finds attributable to the naval battles around Takashima island, including this corroded conglomerate of iron crossbow arrowheads.

33.7 Windlass Fragments
The only remains of vessels from the lost fleet found to date are fragments of planking and pieces of the reel-like device that served as a windlass to raise and lower anchors in the bow of the ship. The vessels were probably pulverized by the storm and swept away by ocean currents.

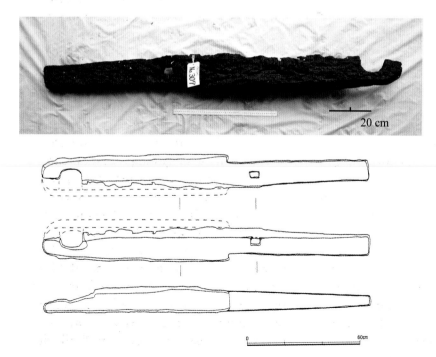

in Japan. The four anchors are of different sizes, which range in weight from smallest to largest by a factor of ten, and would have been used on different types and sizes of vessels. It has been estimated that the smallest anchor could have held a vessel less than 15 meters in length, while the largest would accommodate a vessel up to 40 meters long.[21]

New excavations of Kozaki harbor in 2000 finally revealed substantial remains. Nearly 500 hull fragments, including part of a bulkhead, a step for a ship's mast, and fragments of large and small timbers have been brought to the surface, but there is still no sign of an intact vessel. Only four

of the fragments were still fastened together, and only 6 percent of the timbers were complete. All others were fragments, the majority less than 1.5 meters in length, which makes it difficult to say much about the vessels from which they derive.[22] More diagnostic are fragments of a mast step, windlass, and other shipboard items, which infer some general features of the vessels and ships' equipment (fig. 33.7). Excavation also recovered storage jars, lacquerware, and ceramic bowls, and weapons including swords, crossbow bolts, fragments of leather lamellar armor, and helmets (fig. 33.6).[23]

Perhaps the most significant find was a ceramic ball filled with scrap iron and gunpowder, called a *tetsuhau* (fig. 33.11). This bomb was probably thrown from a trebuchet, and when it exploded, iron shrapnel would tear through the enemy. The *Mōko shūrai ekotoba* handscroll illustrates exploding *tetsuhau* wounding the samurai Suenaga and his horse (fig. 33.10). Prior to the Takashima discovery of an artifact confirming the existence of these weapons in that battle, however, it was thought the depiction might have been added by a later painter.[24] The Takashima *tetsuhau* are now the world's oldest known explosive maritime ordnance and are most likely a Chinese invention, a legacy, like the fleet that carried it, of the Song dynasty.

A Chinese origin is also likely for many of the ceramics that were recovered, including coarse storage jars and pieces of highvalue porcelain, which were probably used by commanders. The few pieces of Korean celadon that were found, as well as the large volume of Chinese ceramics, are consistent with contemporary references that suggest most of the Korean vessels survived the *kamikaze* and returned home with their troops and contents, while the Southern Army was lost with their Chinese ships (fig. 33.8, 9).

A critical question debated by scholars is the number of ships involved in the Mongol invasions. Unfortunately, there is no archaeological means to verify whether the account of 4,400 ships in 1281 is exaggerated, but the archaeological work does provide information about the composition of Kublai Khan's navy. Some vessels were

33.8-9 Porcelain Bowls
Various porcelain bowls were recovered during the underwater excavations at Kozaki harbor, including a light-colored bowl of the Goryeo period (upper) and a light brown glazed bowl similar to wares from southern China. The former probably arrived with the Eastern (Korean) fleet while the latter may have come with the Southern Army from China.

clearly Korean, while others were probably former Song naval forces that had been absorbed into the Yuan-Mongol navy. Analysis of the hull timbers suggests a diverse fleet divided into large support ships, warships, and landing craft, conforming to the historical record. The ships that carried provisions to the front were made in Quanzhou, Yangzhou, and in Hunan province, all along the Yangzi River, towns that built medium and small miscellaneous-purpose vessels with round and flat-bottoms. The Korean vessels were much smaller and had flat bottoms suitable for inland waters.[25] Several large timbers from a V-shaped hull typical of Quanzhou ships were also found.

These vessels may have been 30 or 40 meters in length. The majority of timbers, however, are from small or medium-sized vessels, and included frames, bulkheads, and planks, most likely from vessels built along the Yangzi River. Hull planks, possibly from the bottom of Korean-built vessels, are also present, as well as fragments of fasteners characteristic of Korean shipbuilding.

Kublai Khan, whom Marco Polo observed was an astute planner, must have studied the shipbuilding traditions of his empire and organized his fleet accordingly. He is reported to have said: "Ships from the *Song* are big but not strong; Korean ships are small but strong."[26] These findings conform to that aphorism: flat-bottomed Korean vessels were used as landing craft to gain initial control of the beaches. They were supported by the Southern Army's deep-hulled cargo ships from Fujian province, which carried reinforcements, provisions, and weapons. The vessels from the Yangzi River valley, intermediate in size, functioned to support the troops and to help establish and maintain the invasion.

Because historical documents mention the construction and repair of vessels, as well as pressing merchant and pirate vessels into service, some scholars surmise that the fleet might have been shoddy and ill prepared. The archaeological evidence on this subject is inconclusive. Many of the hull elements display careful craftsmanship: a six meter-long bulkhead was constructed with care, its timbers fastened at regular intervals with closely spaced nails fitted into a carved recess. However, several timber fragments have nails placed in close intervals; another has nails placed in random directions. Other timbers appear to have too many nails, suggesting that these timbers had been recycled or repaired and that some vessels employed reused parts. One provocative artifact is a small wooden tag carrying the inscription: "In the first year of . . . [this object] has been inspected and repaired by . . . [name of the official]." It is difficult to say what was repaired; however, the tag indicates that a piece of large equipment, perhaps even a vessel, may have been inspected for use in the invasion. While the

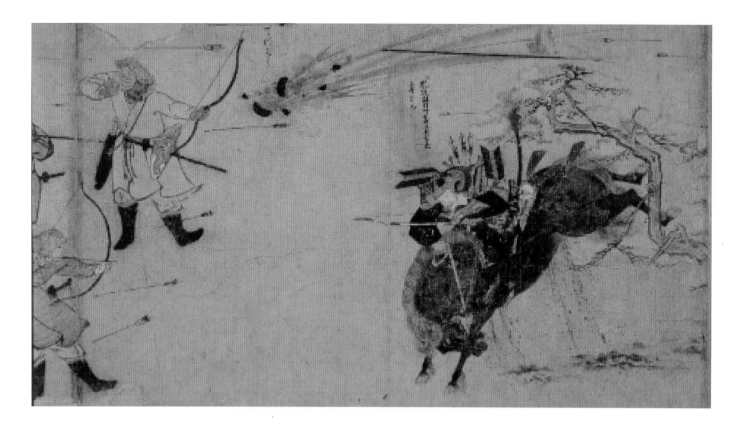

33.10 Exploding *Tetsuhau*
This section of the *Mōko shū rai ekotoba* (Mongol Invasion Scroll) illustrates a battle scene. A samurai and his horse are being wounded by iron flak from a *tetsuhau*, a ceramic bomb filled with iron shrapnel. Such weapons would have been hurled by mechanical slings similar to trebuchets.

33.11 *Tetsuhau:* Cramic Bombs
Divers recovered ceramic bombs from the Takashima underwater site. These finds document the earliest use of maritime explosives anywhere in the world.

tag demonstrates some recycling and several timbers show evidence of reuse and repair, it is impossible to extrapolate how many vessels, or how much of any individual vessel, underwent repair, so the fleet's fitness to sail and fight remains an open question.

The fleet's choice of Imari Bay and Takashima, sparsely populated areas, are appropriate for an anchorage and a beachhead. What Kublai's forces had not anticipated was the possibility of a seasonal typhoon. The anchors aligned with their cables stretching toward shore show conclusively that a storm drove these vessels ashore, where they were ground up in the surf. The mapping of finds on the bottom documents a very disturbed site, with pieces of wood and other artifacts tumbled as if in a blender. The condition of the wood suggests this was the result of a single storm, because seven centuries of storms would have completely pulverized the fragile remains (fig. 33.12).

Conclusions and Expectations

The Hakata and Takashima finds provide an enticing glimpse into historical events of great importance. Japanese resistance at Hakata and the loss of the much larger Chinese–Mongol fleet and army at Takashima in 1281 proved to be a major turning-point, signaling the containment of Mongol expansion, much as the loss of the Spanish Armada in 1588 brought an end to Spain's expansionist hopes in Europe. The Takashima finds confirm the location of the invasion of 1281; the positions of the anchors and cables, lack of intact wrecks, and the dispersed, pulverized nature of vessel fragments strongly point toward the destruction of the fleet in a major storm. Recovery of the bronze seal of the Mongol commander, southern Chinese ceramics, a Buddha statue, and Korean celadon, confirm and amplify the textual histories describing southern Chinese, Korean, and Mongol participation in these events.

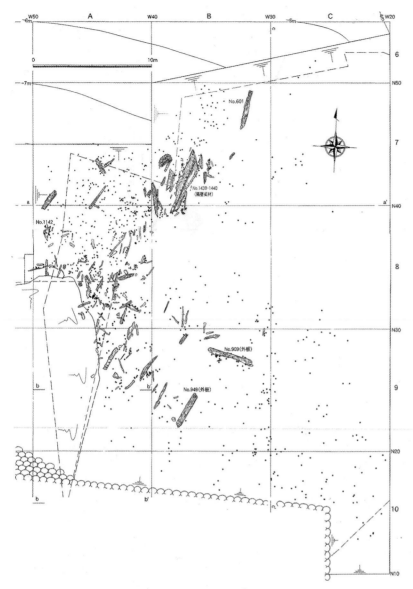

W50 A W40 B W30 C W20

No.601

No.1439·1440
(隔壁梁材)

No.1142

No.909(外板)

No.949(外板)

33.12 Takashima Underwater Site
Underwater research sponsored by the Takashima Board of Education has excavated only a small 30 x 30 meter area of the vast sea floor around the island. The excavations have recovered ship fragments and artifacts dating to the lost fleet. More work will be needed to realize the potential of this important historical site.

equipment. Because it is unlikely that major new historical resources will be forthcoming, archaeological research may be the only way to achieve significant new understanding. At present, only a small portion of the Takashima sea floor has been searched. Even in a near-shore zone where finds have been scrambled by surf and currents, objects of painted wood, leather armor, and other materials have been found, buried in deep mud with high levels of preservation. The promise of an intact hull of an invading ship, providing an even more tangible link to Kublai Khan's ill-fated invasions of Japan, will continue to draw archaeologists to Kyushu until it is found, preserved in the mud.

1. Polo 1958, 244.
2. Lo 1955, 1969.
3. Lo 1969, 64–69; Shiba 1983, 105–6.
4. Rossabi 1988, 28.
5. Hatada 1965; Hori 1974; Rossabi 1988; Saeki 2003.
6. Hatada 1965; Ota 1997.
7. Saeki 2003, 94l; Batten 2006.
8. Conlan 2001.
9. Rossabi 1988, 208.
10. Hatada 1965, 130.
11. Ota 1997, 48.
12. Saeki 2003,140; Hatada 1965, 139.
13. Ota 1997, 42.
14. Yamada 1916.
15. Takashima Board of Education 1984, 1.
16. Mozai 1982; 1983.
17. Takashima Board of Eduction 1996, 116–17.
18. Takashima Board of Education 1996, 32.
19. Suzuki et al. 2001, 131–34.
20. Wang 2000, 145–50.
21. Yamagata 1996, 128–30.
22. Sasaki 2005.
23. Delgado 2003; Takashima Board of Education 2003.
24. Conlan 2001, 73.
25. Sasaki 2006.
26. Ota 1997, 76.

The recovery and preservation of materials relating to the invasions have confirmed historical facts and made important contributions to scholarship and public education about a much-mythologized past. The analysis of the scattered remains has shown potential for answering such long-standing historical questions as Mongol political intentions, preparedness of the fleet, its provisioning and strategy, and, most of all, the nature and origins of its vessels and

34.1 Mapping Mongolia
Modern surveying using Global Positioning System (GPS) equipment can produce geodetic data with a precision better than 5 cm. Here, Tugsuu Amgalantugs operates an Ashtec/Magellan GPS Rover unit.

34. Forensics in the Gobi

THE MUMMIES OF HETS MOUNTAIN CAVE

BRUNO FROHLICH

TSEND AMGALANTUGS

DAVID R. HUNT

JANINE HINTON

ERDENE BATSHATAR

FIVE HUNDRED AND FIFTY YEARS AGO, nine mummified bodies—adult males and females, children, and infants of an extended family—were deposited at the entrance to the empty Hets Mountain Cave in the southern Gobi Desert. The corpses had been executed by strangulation, hanging, or garroting and had marks of other traumatic injury. Before being placed in the cave, the bodies had been left in the open to decompose and had been picked over by birds of prey. The dry wind of the desert had rapidly mummified the soft tissue, so the bodies were intact. Someone had decided that the remains should be brought to the cave for interment.

In 1974 local herdsmen discovered the contents of the cave, located ten kilometers north of the border between Inner Mongolia (China) and present-day Mongolia, and contacted the Mongolian government in Ulaan Baatar.[1] Eight years later, the Mongolian Academy of Science sent archaeologist N. Ser-Odjav and physical anthropologist D. Tumen to investigate. They reported that earlier visitors had disturbed the cave, but that it still contained twelve bodies, including seven children between newborn and seven years, four males and females around 30 years old, and one 60-year-old male. According to their report, ceramics, several wooden plates, and a pair of women's pants were also found, although their present location is unknown.

The investigation lapsed, and the bodies remained in the cave for more than twenty years, attracting tourists and looters. Prompted by reports of vandalism and theft, scientists from the Mongolian Academy of Sciences and the Smithsonian Institution were asked to revisit the cave to assess its contents (fig. 34.1). On May 26, 2004, the five-member team of Naran Bazarsad, Natsag Batbold, Tsend Amgalantugs, and Erdene Batshatar from the Institute of Archaeology of the Mongolian Academy of Sciences, and Bruno Frohlich from the Smithsonian Institution, made its way through the unforgiving desert of weathered rock formations, gravel, sand, and a few obstinate shrubs in the southwestern corner of Domogobi province.

The team entered the cave through a small circular opening and found several tunnels separated by two rock platforms within the first 2.4 meters below the entrance. From the first platform, a 4.2-meter vertical tunnel connects to a second platform, and, from there, a 2.4-meter-long tunnel slopes at a 45-degree angle toward the entrance of the cave chamber. In all, the cave is 17 meters long.

The human remains constituted five groups. Two groups included remains of complete bodies, most of them still in their original position and location. The majority of the bodies were well preserved with

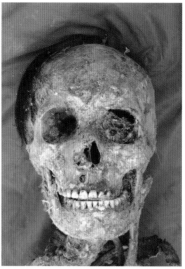

34.2 Hets Mountain Cave
Human bodies were found in two groups in Hets Mountain Cave in the southern Gobi Desert. One group, seen here, included adult males, females, and children; another included only infants.

34.3 Female Skull
Lacerated remnants of flesh indicate the bodies had been cleaned by birds and small animals on the surface before they were placed in the cave.

most of the skeletal tissue present and 10 to 80 percent of the soft tissue intact. The excellent state of preservation of the soft tissue appears to have resulted from a rapid process of natural mummification.[2]

Candle wax and match boxes testified to recent visitors to the cave. Heads of some mummies had been removed. In one of the larger groups, partly articulated bodies were stacked on top of each other (fig. 34.2). One corpse seemed to be in a sitting position, but its head and some extremities were missing. Bodies lay in heaps, suggesting a quick disposal of the remains without any kind of ritual activity. Ligaments on the figures were well preserved, and, on some, there were muscle, skin, intestinal tissue, organs, nails, and hair (fig. 34.3).

Three articulated bodies of infants under two years of age (classified as Group 3) were found about five meters west of the group described above. Preservation of the children was excellent, particularly the soft tissue in the chest and abdomen, but none of these bodies had heads. Body parts and individual bones belonging to Group 3 were later found in several other places in the cave. Once the remains were removed from the cave for closer examination the team could determine the cause of death, where head and/or neck tissue was present.

Most of the people had been murdered by hanging, strangulation, or other trauma. In several cases, ropes were still attached tightly around the collar. The neck of a 40-year-old female apparently had been snapped backward over a rigid object such as a piece of wood (fig. 34.4). She had severed the end of her own tongue, likely in the course of her killing, as the cut marks matched the arch of her row of teeth. Another individual found with a severed tongue seems to have met the same fate. As *The Secret History of the Mongols* describes, Mongolian custom in the time of Genghis Khan proscribed the spilling of blood.[3] Similar ideas may have dictated the methods of bloodless killing observed in the victims of the Hets Mountain Cave. Although it is reasonable that most, if not all, the individuals were killed by hanging, strangulation, or neck-breaking, we cannot verify the cause of death of individuals whose heads are missing. Later, however, we were able to identify the means of murder from CT examination of internal lesions (fig. 34.5).

Based on our evidence, we believe that the deceased victims had been buried outside the cave, and later moved. Bodies and extremities were found "frozen" in postures that could not have been their original positions at the time of death. Some upper and lower extremities were contorting the torso, a result not induced by their being heaped in the cave. If the individuals had been killed and left there to decompose, we would have found the bodies compressed and all torsos, heads, and extremities in positions dictated by gravity. Equally telling was the fact that the brain tissue of all the mummies was in a cranial location that was not close to the ground (fig. 34.6). Since gravity would have pulled the brain tissue downward soon after the killing took place, and because brain tissue shrinks and accumulates in the part of the corpse's brain case closest to the ground, it is obvious that this process took place before the bodies were placed in the cave. On exposed tissue, pecking by birds had roughened the surface, or removed it down to the bone. Given the state of certain outer

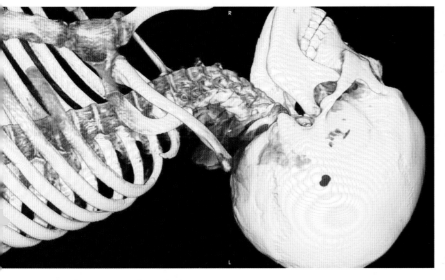

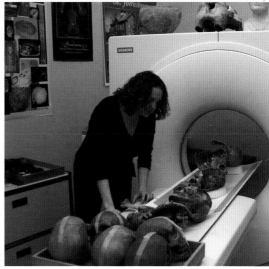

tissue of the mummies, the bodies must have been scavenged before placement in the cave.

After arrival in Ulaan Baatar, the mummies were stored at the Institute of Archaeology for a year. In June 2005, they were air-freighted to the Smithsonian Institution for detailed study. Our research was accomplished in a non-destructive, non-invasive manner, using X-ray and CT technology as often as possible. We collected samples in the field for dating, DNA, and nutrional analyses. We performed radiometric dating, pathological examination, anthropological description, establishment of genetic relationship (DNA analysis), and reconstruction of diet by stable isotope analysis, as well as intensive study of the historical records.[4] By the spring of 2006, we had completed the majority of our data collection; the mummies were flown back to Mongolia to a repository selected by the Mongolian Academy of Sciences.

Without objects accompanying the bodies, we had no clues to the culture or social status of the individuals. Fortunately, the bone was so well preserved that we were able to establish the dates of their deaths by radiometric analyses. The results range from 1301 to 1651 CE, spanning the 350 years from the end of the Mongolian empire (1206–1368) to the end of the Ming dynasty (1368–1644). The average of six C-14 samples placed the mummies within the Ming dynasty between 1435 and 1454, with the most significant dates centered at 1450.

What was the cause of these violent deaths? We turned to historical record to posit the circumstances of the scientific data. From the end of the Mongolian empire through the Yuan and Ming dynasties, political conflict, cultural crisis, and economic turmoil marked the Hets region. With Genghis Khan's death, the Mongolian empire was divided into political and regional factions known as khanates, which became increasingly more independent from each other. In 1271, Kublai Khan initiated the Yuan dynasty, which took political and economic control of the Gobi Desert and Outer Mongolia. The center of power shifted from Khara Khorum, the original seat of Mongol power, to Daidu (early Beijing) in China. Based on textual sources, scholars believe that this political shift along with severe winters may have effected Mongolian pastoralist subsistence strategies and led to famines and malnutrition throughout the Mongolian steppe populations.[5] Records indicate that agricultural products, primarily grains, were imported from China to Mongolia to stem the crisis. In 1368, political control over China passed back to the Chinese, the successor Ming dynasty, who, later, successfully invaded Mongolia, though power across the steppe was left in the hands of competing steppe elite.

The political conditions under which the Hets Mountain people were living may provide context for these murders. During the Yuan dynasty, the Gobi tended to be influenced by north-south forces or events; during the Ming dynasty, east-west dynamics were more dominant. These ruptures may have had a significant impact on food

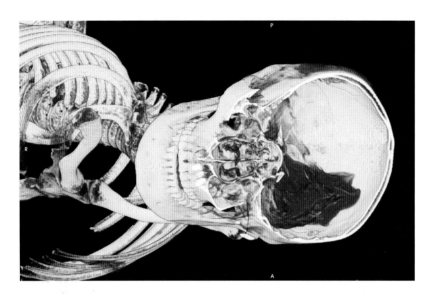

34.6 Reconstructive Imaging
CT images allow researchers to view internal anatomical features like the mummified brain tissue shown here in red. The location of this tissue on the left side of the braincase indicates that the body remained on its left side for a considerable period after death. Because the body was not found in this position, it must have been moved from its original position.

supplies used by the herder populations of the Mongol Gobi. Analysis of the diet of these victims, based on proportions of agricultural versus animal-based foods, may yet reveal a more precise understanding of the lives, the execution, and the deposition of the mummies. Scalp hair was collected from the mummies for dietary evidence. Plants consumed in the diet can be determined from hair, as well as bone, based on how much carbon dioxide within the hairs is converted into sugar through photosynthesis. Groups of plants, when consumed by an herbivorous or omnivorous animal, can be identified. C3 plants are related to cold and dry environments and C4 plants to warmer and more humid environments. Analysis of this sort can assist in establishing whether the victims had been short- or long-term residents of the burial region of the Hets Mountain. When the stable isotope results are compared to those of individuals from two other regions of the Gobi and the Altai, it is clear that the mummified group's dry-weather diet differed significantly from individuals in the other regions, possibly within the last few weeks of their lives.

Did each mummy group within the cave represent a different family group? It appears that genetically related individuals were scattered across the different piles

of corpses. We analyzed DNA samples from four different individuals across the three burial groups; DNA evidence proves that some the mummies are related.[6]

The Hets Mountain Cave victims are beginning to reveal their secrets. Further research and development of new analytical methods will undoubtedly tell us more about who these people were and how they lived. Sadly, lack of cultural and detailed historical context makes it difficult, if not impossible, to understand why they were killed. Location itself is a clue: The central Gobi, lying between more productive economic zones with larger populations and political centers in northern Mongolia and northern China, has always been a demanding and dangerous place to live. Despite the harsh environment, this corner of the Gobi has been traversed for millennia by parties intent on raiding or war. Violence in the region persisted into the twentieth century. In the 1920s, American explorer Roy Chapman Andrews and his American Museum of Natural History expedition discovered ancient humans and far older mammals and dinosaurs, but they also battled marauding bandits and thieves in a land that was largely ungoverned and unruly. Border wars between Chinese and Russian soldiers in the mid-twentieth century are said to have taken many thousands of lives. Frontier warfare, subsistence stress in an arid and unpredictable environment, or feuding between rival clans—all common occurrences throughout Mongolian history—are among the many plausible contexts for the slaughtered of individualsHets Mountain Cave.

1. Bazarsad et al. 2005; Frohlich et al. 2005
2. Frohlich et al. 2008.
3. Onon 2005.
4. Turner et al. 2007; Zuckerman et al. 2007.
5. Bazarsad et al. 2005; Endicott 2005; Groussett 2002; Ross 2006; Zuckerman et al. 2007.
6. Frohlich et al. 2008.

35. Cave Burials of Mongolia

Ulambayar Erdenebat

ONE OF THE UNIQUE TRADITIONS of the Mongolian nomads a thousand years ago was the burying of their dead in caves and rock shelters. Burial sites from ancient times are spread widely across the territory of modern Mongolia, most in areas with mountains, rock-strewn outcrops, and ridges.[1] Burial caves are found in locations that range from the steppe lands to the northern forests bordering on Siberia to the southern Gobi Desert.[2] They often provide valuable information about the individuals who are interred there and about the culture in which they lived.

Cave burials were not the only mortuary activity of the Mongols. Numerous earthen pit burials—typically marked on the surface by a stone mound, ring, or oval—are also known and are probably the more common form of interment.[3] Why were some deceased placed in rock shelters and others buried in the earth? Archaeologists still do not have the answer.

In a cave burial, the dead man or woman is placed directly on the stone surface in a natural grave chamber, where the body either is left exposed to the air or sparingly covered by rocks and sand. In some cases, a stone embankment was built up around the body, possibly to mimic an earthen burial pit, or simply to protect the body and grave

35.1 Tsagaan Khanan Finds
The dry air of the Gobi Desert helped preserve these 14th-century artifacts recovered from a burial in Tsagaan Khanan cave. They include a necklace strung with plant seeds, seed cases, coral, and multicolored glass beads; an hourglass-shaped silk pouch; and a comb and ring.

furnishings. Often, it is difficult to reconstruct exactly the original arrangement of a cave burial because of human or animal intrusions.[4]

Cave burials are not easy to locate, even when using trusted archaeological techniques such as systematic survey of the landscape. Burial caves are often known to local herders who have lived in these areas all of their lives and may have discovered them while herding. Because natural crevices, hollows, and holes were used for burying the dead, there are usually no exterior signs that a place is in fact a burial chamber.[5] The burials are frequently in higher elevations on peaks or ridges that have expansive views of the surrounding landscape. The chosen rock overhangs, shelters, and caves often are small and inconspicuous with openings oriented toward the south or east, and, oc-

casionally, to the west. Normally, the deceased is found in the cave or crevice with arms at the sides and legs fully extended. Although the orientation of the body in the rock alcove or cave depends somewhat on the configuration and size of the geological feature chosen for the burial, the predominant orientations of the body are to the east, north, northeast, and northwest, which are also the most common orientations for earthen pit burials.

So far, no evidence of cremation has been found in any of the rock burials, though this has been documented elsewhere as one of many treatments used during the Mongol empire.[6] Burial caves usually contain the body of one person, and with a few sensational exceptions (see Chapter 34), mass burials are not part of the Mongol tradition.[7] Sometimes, there is a single stone chamber used for multiple burials over long periods of time, perhaps because the place became known as a sacred and important burial site. One cave did have eight bod-

35.2 Coffin from Artsat Del
Reports of a burial near the top of Artsat Del Mountain in Bayankhongor province, southwestern Mongolia, led archaeologists to a crevice containing this wooden casket. It was so tightly closed that little dust had found its way inside.

35.3 Horse Gear
For more than 4,000 years, Mongolians and other steppe peoples have depended on horses as their primary means of transport. Owning a horse and equipping it according to cultural standards, status, or position defined one's social identity both in life and in death. The sacrifice of horses and/ or burial of horse remains, saddles, bridles, and other gear was considered necessary for maintaining one's social position in the afterlife. Analysis of horse gear recovered from Dugui Tsakhir and Artsat Del provides clues about the social standing of the deceased. This drawing illustrates the types of horse gear similar to that found in the Artsat Del burial.

ies deposited over an estimated five hundred years, each individual dressed in clothing and wrapped in silk, felt, leather, or birch bark.[8]

Ancient Mongol corpses have also been found in coffins or other wooden constructions, within rock shelters or caves. The dead were sometimes placed into caskets made of wooden planks or fashioned from two halves of a large hollowed-out log (fig. 35.2). Caskets have been discovered that were made from the hide of a large bull stretched onto a lashed wooden frame. Others exhibit an underlying support or "death bed" assembled from the wooden parts of a cart or from the wooden lattice of a nomadic tent, or *ger*. In other instances, the deceased was laid on a wooden framework and covered with reeds, straw, and woven branches to protect the body. Cave burials with wooden frameworks made from carts suggest that the body was taken to the ridge top or mountain crevice in a

cart, which was then disassembled and included as part of the funeral process.

The scientific study of cave burials in Mongolia began in the mid-1920s. Since then, more than thirty burial caves have been recorded. In each case, the greatest care has been taken to ensure that the contents are protected and that the excavations are conducted to the highest standards. Eight of these sites have been dated by radiocarbon analysis to between CE 370 and 1630, though based on artifact styles, some cave burials probably date to time periods prior to and after this radiocarbon range.

Grave furnishings found in cave burials provide a wealth of information about nomadic technology and everyday life. A deceased male is often accompanied by saddles, bridles, whips, quivers, bows, arrows, swords, and flint stones for starting fires (fig. 35.3). A deceased

female may be surrounded by jewelry, scissors, a mirror, a knife, spindles for wool, and containers made of tree roots, birch bark, or pottery (fig. 35.1). Cave burials may also contain animal bones—most commonly, the tibia and anklebone of a sheep—left as offerings as part of the mortuary ritual.

The contents of the burial caves are of great historical value because many of them are extremely well preserved on account of the arid and cool climate of Mongolia. For example, birch-bark quivers and felt boots have been recovered from cave burials in excellent condition, while similar artifacts in earthen pit burials decayed long ago and remain as only fragments or outlines in the surrounding soil. The assemblages of objects, personal clothing (fig. 35.4), and wooden structures from cave burials provide us with an image of how rich and varied mortuary practices were during the medieval period. They also offer us a wealth of biological data on ancient populations, including health, diet, DNA, and, in

35.4 Silk *Deel*
This red silk *deel* was found at the Ikh Nartyn Chuluu burial site in the eastern Gobi Dornogobi province. Once a personal treasure of the owner, such fragmentary materials often become treasures to archaeologists because of the information they can provide on fabric type, source, and period of manufacture. The silk fabric and design allowed this *deel* to be dated to the 13th-14th century.

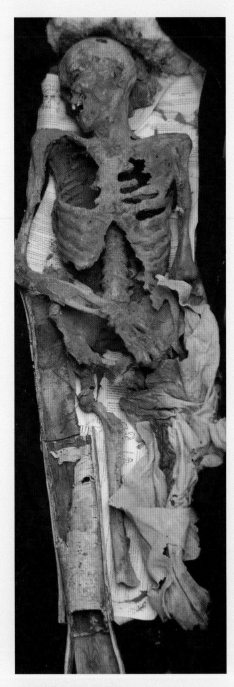

35.5 Dugui Tsakhir Mummy
These remains were found at the Dugui Tsakhir cave in Bayankhongor province. Such bodies can be studied with a variety of methods to investigate ancient disease, genetic relationships, age, physical trauma, cause of death, and other questions. Mongolians do not object to the use of human remains for historical and scientific research, or their display for educational purposes, provided the remains receive respectful treatment.

some cases, even the facial features of the deceased when human tissue has preserved by aridity. With the right environmental conditions, the natural drying or freeze drying of corpses in a burial cave can mummify human remains (fig. 35.5).

A startling example of how well preserved a burial context can be after many centuries is the Artsat Del cave burial in Bayankhongor province, southwestern Mongolia. In the summer of 1999, local nomads chasing a wounded wolf came upon an ancient burial ground in the sacred mountains of Artsat Del and reported their important discovery to officials. Two years later, in the fall of 2001, a Mongolian–German archaeological team arrived at the area to document this fascinating site. After extensive mountainside reconnaissance with the assistance of local herders, the site was relocated at an elevation of 2,686 meters above sea level. The burial was near the top of one of the mountain's many limestone peaks in a small crevice that could only be entered by bending low and shuffling inside.[9]

By flashlight, the archaeological team saw a wooden coffin oriented to the northwest with wooden fragments of a yak cart leaning against its sides. The casket was thickly covered with fine Gobi dust and the excrement of birds and mice. The casket was made of thin planks of wood that were bound by leather straps and so well fitted that no gaps showed between them. The archaeologists documented the scene with drawings, photographs, and samplings of the soils and wood. The coffin lid was carefully removed.

For the first time in more than one thousand years, the face of a nomad appeared in the faint beams.

He lay supine with his face up, his head resting on the low curve of a wooden horse saddle covered in leather. To the left of the man's head was a fine birch-bark box, empty of its original organic contents. There were also saddle attachments, bronze decorations, stirrups, and pieces of a bridle. The rider was also equipped with weapons, a long steel sword, and a compound bow. Across his body lay a beautifully preserved birch-bark quiver with an impressive variety of arrowheads and nineteen complete arrows with all feathers still in place.

The rituals of Mongolian cave burial are still obscure because mortuary practices are complex and always entwined with the ideology, cosmology, politics, as well as the public and private rites of the living. From the earliest days, however, it is clear that nomadic peoples chose to bury their dead in places of importance and honor. Many ancient beliefs that impart spiritual significance to mountains and that link caves with the sacred depths of the earth, persist in current nomadic culture. As the grave of the rider at Arts Del Mountain reveals so poignantly, the Mongolian cave burial shows the highest respect for the honored dead.

1. Erdenebat and Bayar 2004.
2. Kyzlasov 1986.
3. Honeychurch and Amartuvshin 2006, 272–73.
4. Perlee 1959, 3.
5. Menes and Bilegt 1992.
6. Crubezy et al. 2006.
7. Erdenebat and Khurelsukh 2007.
8. Erdenebat 2001.
9. Erdenebat and Pohl 2005b, 81–89.

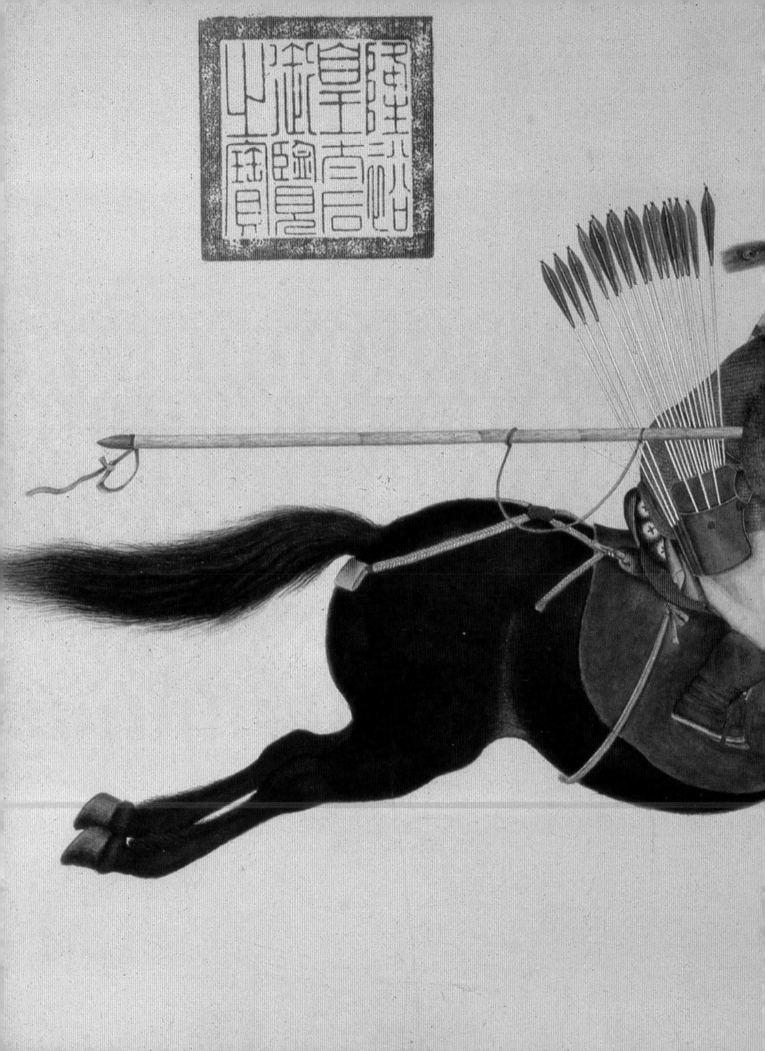

PART V

GENGHIS KHAN'S LEGACY

< **Previous Pages** *Ayush's Charge*
This charging Mongolian cavalry officer named Ayush is part of a larger work by Giuseppe Castiglione, an Italian Jesuit who went to China as a missionary in 1715 and became court painter at the Imperial Palace in Beijing. He became famous for his paintings of horses and other animals and initiated the Chinese to Western painting techniques. This painting illustrates a battle between Mongol forces fighting for the Qing against rebellious Zunghar Mongolians in western Xinjiang in 1755.

36.1 Chengde
During the Qing dynasty, Manchu domination of Mongolia played out through a complex web of relations involving Khalkha and western Mongol groups, Tibet, and Russia. This illustration painted in 1754 by Giuseppe Castiglione, Ignatis Sichelbart, and Jean Denis Attiret at Chengde, in northwestern China, shows the location where Mongol and Qing leaders received visiting allies and envoys. One of the visitors at this event was Amursana, a Zunghar Mongolian leader who briefly allied with the Qing Manchu dynasty but was soon betrayed by them, leading to the Zunghar rebellions and Qing counterattacks of 1754–57.

36. Mongolia from Empire to Republic, 1400 to 1921

Pamela K. Crossley

When the Yuan dynasty collapsed in 1368, the Mongols in China had no obvious place to which they could retreat. Long-standing enmity with the Chaghadai Mongols in Central Asia cut off that direction of escape. Many Mongols chose to stay in China, where a small number served as scholars and officials in the early Ming bureaucracy. A larger number served in the Ming military, which was patterned on the lines established by Kublai in the 1200s. A significant Mongol population remained garrisoned in the far southwestern province of Yunnan. Today, there are more than six thousand descendants of these Mongols who speak a dialect derived from Mongolian.

Mongols who returned to Mongolia in the fourteenth century faced competition from other Mongols such as the Oyirads and the Buryats, who had remained comparatively autonomous during the Genghis and Yuan periods, largely because of their peripheral locations. The largest of the federations withdrawing across the northern border from China were the Six Tümen, as they were called in Chinese records. These federations considered themselves the continuation of the Yuan empire, and in some records referred to themselves as the Northern Yuan. Although they revered the line of Genghis's descendants and regarded them as uniquely eligible to be Great Khan, over the course of almost a century this group had little centralization or unity and no recognized capital.

In western Mongolia, a distinct cultural zone emerged. The "Four Oyirads" (*dörböd Oyirad*) saw themselves as having distinct origins, distinct religious beliefs, and a distinct language from other Mongol groups.

Their ancestors had supported Arigh Böke, the loser in the great civil war that had preceded Kublai's ascent to power. In the ensuing two centuries, geography brought the Oyirads into a close relationship with Tibetan religious elites and gave them a growing familiarity with Islam.[1] In the middle 1400s the Oyirads had concentrated enough power to put pressure on eastern Mongols, on Ming China, and on Central Asia. In 1449 the Oyirad ruler, Esen Khan, felt sufficiently emboldened to attack the Ming capital at Beijing. The Ming emperor was captured and held for almost a year. Esen proceeded to gain momentary dominance over the eastern Mongols by murdering the current khan, who descended from Genghis. In the aftermath Esen himself was murdered and the power center he had created in western Mongolia and eastern Turkestan began to fail.

Partly in response to the threats from the west and pressure from Ming China, the eastern Mongols began to rebuild their pow-

36.2 Ikh Zuu Monastery
In the late 1570s, the Mongol leader Altan Khan and the leading Tibetan lama agreed to share political and religious authority in Mongolia. They cemented their relationship by becoming joint patrons of a new monastery in Hohhot, Inner Mongolia, which Altan had made his capital city. The Ikh zuu monastery, seen here, grew into a sprawling complex surrounding a three meter–tall silver Buddha that the Dalai Lama had donated. Hohhot, already a cultural and political center on the Mongolia and China border, also became a thriving religious center.

er and re-create some centralization in the later 1400s. Mandukhai Khatun, the widow of the deposed Great Khan Mandaghol, oversaw a Genghis revival by declaring her great-great nephew Dayan as Great Khan; Mandukhai Khatun herself led the eastern Mongol troops against the Oyirads to enforce the boy ruler's status.[2] By the time of Dayan's death in 1532, the overt conflict between the descendants of Genghis and the Oyirads had divided Mongolia's geography, religion, and culture. The Great Khanship remained within a single lineage among the descendants of Genghis and was based upon rule over a southeastern group of Mongols known as the Chahar federation. The eastern Mongols recovered the region of Khara Khorum from the Oyirads and continued to push their former overlords back ever westward. At the same time, their pressure upon northern China was continuous and in 1550 resulted in another assault upon Beijing that wrested well-defined border and commercial agreements from the Ming court.

This eastern Mongolia ascendancy was the foundation for the brilliant rule of the Great Khan Altan, who established many of the cultural features of modern Mongolia such as the adoption of Buddhism, the founding of the capital Hohhot, and keeping the Mongolian groups united. Altan was a descendant of Genghis and born in 1507. As he gained power, he became an acting regent of the young Great Khan and established Hohhot within his ancestral territo-

ries. The site was located in what is now Inner Mongolia, which was the historical nexus of cultural and economic contact between China and Mongolia (fig. 36.2).

Before Altan's time, eastern Mongols had been united mostly by their observance of the cult of Genghis and of older shamanic rituals, as well as recognition of living descendants of Genghis as the only eligible class from which the Great Khan could be selected. Altan noted that among the Oyirads, Buddhism had become a significant unifying force. He invited Songnam Gyamtso, an elder of the Dge-lugs (hereafter Reformed) sect to eastern Mongolia in 1576, and the great lama arrived in 1578. Altan Khan rewarded the Reformed leader with the title Dalai (in Mongolian, "oceanic," "universal") lama ("teacher," in Tibetan) and recognized him as the third in a series of reincarnated religious teachers. The Dalai Lama, in return, acknowledged Altan Khan as Great Khan, proclaiming him to be reincarnations of both Kublai Khan and Manjusri, the bodhisattva of wisdom. Both men became patrons of a sprawling new monastery at Khökö khota (Hohhot) and Yeke zuu (modern Ikh zuu), which features a silver Buddha, nearly ten feet high (approximately 3 meters), donated by the Dalai Lama. Within sixty years of its founding, Hohhot's religious and economic activity had drawn a population of more than 150,000.

By the time of Altan's death in 1582, Tibetan Buddhism and rule by Genghis's descendants of the eastern Mongols had been cemented in partnership.[3] As a popularly familiar and practiced religion, Reformed Buddhism spread from Altan's home territories to the rest of eastern Mongolia. Commentary by Chinese observers reveals that the spread was slow and that shamanic traditions were not displaced easily.[4] By the late sixteenth century there was evidence that Buddhism had reached the eastern Buryats, the most remote of the significant Mongol federations, though their conversion was not complete until the middle seventeenth century. Western Buryats remained shamanists (fig. 36.5). As Buddhism spread, the government of Altan and his

36.3 Ulaan Butong _Ovoo_
This large _ovoo_ monument marks the battlefield where Mongolians under Galdan fought a large Chinese army to a standstill in 1690. The standing stone in the foreground is not a typical component of _ovoo_ monuments, so it is likely that the _ovoo_ was placed at a spot that had special significance long before this battle.

successors ferociously suppressed shamanism. It was legally forbidden; shamans who did not desist were executed, and Mongols who practiced shamanic rituals were fined. Popular shamanic deities were absorbed as Reformed bodhisattvas, and Buddhist lamas insisted that the spirits were more effectively addressed through Buddhist prayer than by shamanic superstition (see Chapter 6).[5]

The Great Khanship remained with Genghis's descendants among the eastern Mongols. By the very early seventeenth century, the great eastern federations of Chahar and Khalkha were each centers of power unto themselves. The Great Khanship was most strongly associated with the Chahar, who maintained Altan's capital at Hohhot. When Lighdan, of the Chahar federation, became Great Khan in 1604, he resolved that eastern Mongolia would be reunited. The immediate result, however, was competition for leadership and further fragmenting of the eastern federation, which created new opportunities for interference in eastern Mongol affairs by the Oyirads. Mongols and their herds moved toward Manchuria, northern China, Turkestan, and Tibet to avoid Lighdan's impositions. Defections and

resistance weakened the Chahar forces. The Jurchen khanate based in Manchuria declared war on Lighdan in 1632. His death in 1634 gave victory to the Jurchens and was a watershed event in the history of Mongolia[6] because between 1634 and 1636 the Jurchens absorbed not only a large part of the Chahar population but, equally important, the symbols, rituals, and historical narrative of the Great Khan. The result was creation of the Qing empire of the Jurchens—now known as the Manchus—in 1636.

Qing assimilation of Mongols and of the heritage of the Great Khan was not simple or orderly. The new empire intended to bring Chahar nobles into its own aristocratic ranks and to create "banners" within its armed forces for all Mongol recruits. These banner units, which were the foundation of Qing military and administrative function, were by 1636 in the process of being designated by cultural group, with compatible educational programs and commanders chosen from within the group. But, as in the days of Dayan Khan and of Lighdan himself, many Mongols were quick to notice that the real effect was to establish leaders over them who were considered reliable by the throne—in

36.4 Red Cash: Coins of the Zunghar Mongols
The Zunghar khanate, which coalesced in the early 17th century as a union of Oyirad tribes in the Altai mountain region of Xinjiang province in China and eastern Kazakhstan, was crushed in the mid-18th century by the Qing dynasty. Copper coins, widely called "red cash," were made in this region from the 17th to the 20th century. These teardrop coins date to the 17th century.

this case, the throne of the alien Qing empire. In the years after the collapse of the Chahar Great Khanship and its absorption by the Qing, Chahar nobles led sporadic rebellions, always ferociously suppressed by the Qing. When the empire conquered north China in 1644, the Chahars and Khorchins were firmly allied to the invading forces. They aided not only in the ongoing conquest of China, but later in the direct conquest of Mongolia itself, and still later of Turkestan. Their ancestral territories, including Altan's capital at Hohhot, became the framework for what is now "Inner Mongolia."[7]

During this period of dominion over eastern Mongolia the distinct culture of the Khalkhas, the most populous federation among the Mongols, became recognized as the standard culture of modern Mongolia. Much of this cultural evanescence revolved around Zanabazar. He was born in 1635 to one of the descendants of Genghis among the Khalkha and began to study Reformed Buddhism when very young. In 1640, at the age of five, Zanabazar was recognized by the Dalai Lama as a *khutughtu*, or reincarnation of a venerated teacher. The Qing government, to which Zanabazar's family was loyal, also recognized him as the Bogdo Gegen and administrator of the Khalkhas. Zanabazar was multiply gifted. He is perhaps best known as a sculptor, with many magnificent cast works still surviving—including the huge Buddha figure he created for his own temple at his capital of

Urga (modern Ulaan Baatar). He also created new prayers and songs for his monks and invented a new script *(soyombo)* that could be used for writing Mongolian, Tibetan, and Sanskrit. He died in 1723, leaving the Khalkha with a tradition of religious distinction and political eminence.

In western Mongolia, Eastern Turkestan, and western Tibet, the Qing conquest of the Khalkas was viewed with alarm. After the defeat of their eastern enemy, Lighdan Khan, the Oyirads had attempted to recentralize under the regime known as Zunghar (fig. 36.4). In origin the Zunghar were largely Oyirad, but had absorbed a significant number of other Mongol groups, Kazakhs, and Tibetans. In 1671 a period of political unrest among the Zunghars ended with the acceptance of Galdan, who had returned from studies in Tibet, as supreme Zunghar khan. Galdan's struggle to consolidate his power led indirectly to the alienation of some western groups, such as the Torghud branch known later as the Kalmyks, who migrated as far as the Volga valley to escape the troubles. Until his death in 1697, Galdan would fight not only the Khalkhas and the Qing but enemies in his own khanate, indeed in his own family, which constantly distracted him from his military goals with assassination attempts and sabotage.[8] Galdan intended to subjugate the Khalkha Mongols to the east, as his ancestor Esen Khan had once done. The Kangxi emperor of the Qing attempted both

36.5 Buryat Shaman
The Buryats, a large Mongol ethnic group that lives in northern Mongolia and southern Siberia has a strong shamanist tradition. This Buryat woman, described in Russian records as a shaman, was photographed in 1905 wearing medals and huge strings of beaded earrings. Her ritual staffs are ornamented with bells and animal skins.

small band of followers, he fled as far as the Altai Mountains before dying in May 1697.[9]

The defeat of Galdan secured Qing control over Khalkha, but did not lead to the submission of Zungharia. Galdan's successors (and enemies) turned their ambitions westward, conquering parts of Eastern Turkestan and Tibet. In the 1740s they entered a brief truce with the Qing that took the Altai Mountains as the border between the empire and Zungharia. But within a decade, troubles in Zungharia gave the Qing an opening for a massive assault that finally extended the Qing military domain to all Mongolia, Eastern Turkestan, and Tibet. For the remainder of the eighteenth century, notable uprisings against the empire gave voice to Mongol outrage over the foreign conquest. The Qing tendency to appoint Mongol khans of their own liking to rule over Mongols particularly stung. The Zunghar prince Amursana, who for a time joined the Qing in their campaigns of conquest, turned his back on them in 1755 (fig. 36.1). His cousin Galden Ceren, rushing to join Amursana's rebellion, cursed the Khalkha who remained loyal to the Qing despite the empire's deep assault on Mongolian traditions of rule. Those curses did not all fall on deaf ears, and within months, the Khalkha were also in revolt, led by Chingunjav. But Qing forces crushed the rebellions within a year, and the name "Zunghar" —a memory of the political unity of western Mongolia—was thereafter banned from Qing official documents.

After the rebellion, the Qing decreed that in the future the Bogdo Gegen would be born within Tibet, not in Mongolia. Nevertheless, the establishment of the Bogdo Gegen's court, bureaucracy, and monks in the general vicinity of Urga (the Russian corruption of Orgoo, now Ulaan Baatar) gave Khalkha a new economic significance. Tensions between the expanding Russian and Qing empires had been resolved by treaties in 1689 and 1727. These treaties established trading ports on the borders and greatly increased the security and ease of transporting goods.

The Mongols called Urga Ikh Khüree meaning "great camp," a reference to the tent settlement of the Bogdo Gegen. Chi-

to negotiate with Galdan and to lure him into open conflict. In 1690 Galdan and the imperial forces fought to a standstill at Ulaan Butong, and to the Qing emperor's outrage, Galdan escaped (fig. 36.3). Then in 1696 the Qing forces, many armed with muskets, caught Galdan in a two-pronged attack at Juun Mod (Jao Modo). His forces scattered, his wife was killed, and his political enemies at home refused to shelter him. With a very

36.6 The Potala at Chengde
The Potala temple, built by the Qing leaders in 1767–71 as a summer residence, resembles the Dalai Lama's residence in Lhasa. The complex was a gesture of goodwill to the Qing's Tibetan subjects and used for special Lamaist rites that could be attended only by the Qing imperial family, by Mongol visitors and retainers, and by the Tibetan clergy.

nese traders from Beijing and from Shanxi province set up shops outside the religious compound. Most of the goods were those bound for the border—silk bolts and finished silk clothes, porcelain bowls and figurines, as well as buttons, wooden bowls, and cups that were popular with Mongol shoppers. The better Chinese shops also carried European imports, including cotton goods, watches, thermometers and barometers, and mechanical toys. Mongols camping at Urga sold horses, milk and *airag*, hides, luxury furs, felt, wool, rhubarb, ginseng, firewood, and hay; a few were set up as blacksmiths. In the nineteenth century Russian traders and a few residents arrived, and a new Russian consulate was established in 1863. The monks, the greater part of the population, lived in a central complex organized around the impressive Gandan monastery, with a great market square before it and a separate compound for the secular population adjacent to it. The Russian explorer Nikolai Prezhevalsky stopped in Urga in 1879 and in 1882, noting that between those years the

number of people had increased very sharply while the number of camels and horses had fallen disastrously low.[10] In 1892 the Russian scholar Alexei Pozdneyev estimated the total population at Urga was between 16,000 and 20,000.[11] Urga was by far the largest urban complex in the Khalkha lands, and in all of Mongolia, second only to the city of Guihua—the successor to Altan's old capital, Hohhot, which was now a major nexus of the Chinese trade with Mongolia, as well as an administrative center for the Chinese population of the area, and a major Qing military installation.[12]

At the beginning of the twentieth century, alienation among Mongolia's population was transformed through a combination of local and long-distance processes. Economic exploitation by both Chinese and by Russians; a continuing assault upon Mongol social traditions, political values, and culture; and the stimulation of new ideas of nationalism—all contributed to resistance movements that surpassed the political scope of the earlier insurgencies of the Qing period.[13]

Within a century of their formal submission to the Qing, grazing lands in Khalkha had been transferred from khan to khan by state fiat, and the overall amount of land available for pasturing had declined because of the Qing policy of encouraging the immigration of Chinese farmers who turned irrigable land to agriculture. Firms based in China were given licenses to virtually monopolize the trade in horses, furs, textiles, and grains between Khalkha and China, allowing them insuperable leverage in controlling the development of both Guihua and Urga.

Although the Khalkha khans were given partial jurisdiction over the trade by the Qing court, they rarely exercised oversight or administration, so that dubious land deals, high rents and interest rates, and monopolization of capital by China-based financial interests impoverished a large portion of the population. By the turn of the twentieth century Khalkha was in social and economic crisis, and poor Mongols made public prayers to Genghis for help. Zungharia, including Eastern Turkestan, was a site of nearly constant unrest. In 1826, 1846, 1857, and 1864–78, the territory was racked by large-scale uprisings—mostly led by Muslims, many of combined Türkic and Mongol descent—and equally devastating suppression that took a major toll on both the Qing treasury and its international reputation. In 1884 the empire attempted to tighten its grip on the region by formally incorporating it as the province of Xinjiang.

The Buryats, among the most remote of the Mongols, turned out to be critical to the Mongol future. By the beginning of the twentieth century the Buryats were undergoing a political crisis of their own, caused by the weakening of Russian rule in eastern Asia and the imminent demise of Qing rule in the Khalkha territories. Buryat students attending Russian universities brought back the radical ideas of autonomy and nationalism already spreading across much of Russian Eurasia and Central Asia. Though new demands for local autonomy arose among the Buryats in the later nineteenth century, there was no serious movement for secession from Russia until 1901, when legislation protecting native lands was rescinded. Secession, nationalism, and pan-Mongolism became the touchstones for the creation of new cultural sensibilities and political forms.[14]

Though Mongols east and west remained a formidable military challenge to the Ming and Qing empires, no leader achieved a reunification of all of Mongolia during this period. Instead, the pattern of Qing conquest followed by the imposition of Qing policy defined two zones in Mongolia: an inner zone, strongly bound to China's economy, centered at the large urban concentration at Hohhot; and an outer zone, sometimes riven by political rivalries, and urban only at the modest city of Urga. These centuries of political and cultural transitions introduced the fundamental features of modern Mongolia—the standard language based upon Khalkha dialect, the predominance of Tibetan Buddhism coexisting with a persisting minor interest in shamanism, and the combined political and spiritual preeminence of the Bogdo Gegen. As the Qing empire faltered and dreams of Mongol political independence stirred, these features became the foundation upon which nationalists both in Mongolia and in Inner Mongolia built their ideals of Mongol identity.

1. Halkovic 1997.
2. Goodrich and Fang 1976.
3. Moses 1997.
4. Xiao 1972.
5. Moses 1997.
6. Moses 1997.
7. Bawden 1968.
8. Hummel 1943.
9. Perdue 2005.
10. Pozdneyev 1997.
11. Pozdneyev 1997.
12. Jankowiak 1992.
13. Crossley 2006.
14. Bawden 1976.

37. Buddhism in Mongolia

Shagdaryn Bira

Land-locked Mongolia is often considered one of the most isolated nations on earth. For thousands of years Mongolian peoples had practiced shamanism, revering the spirits of nature and ancestors that influenced their lives of hunting, fishing, and herding (see Chapter 6). Today, vestiges of this naturalistic religion are still present, often coexisting with Buddhism. During its premodern history, however, nomadic Mongolia entered the flow of cultures, ideas, and information issuing from sedentary Indo-Iranian, Sino-Tibetan, and Eurasian civilizations. One of the most powerful philosophies to reach Mongolia was Buddhism, which first appeared during the early period of Genghis Khan's reign.

The Uyghurs, one of the most advanced early nomadic peoples, created their own powerful kingdom in Mongolia in the eighth and ninth centuries. After the collapse of the Uyghur kingdom, Uyghurs moved to Eastern Turkestan but maintained close relations with the Mongols. Several centuries later Genghis Khan borrowed their script, based on an ancient Phoenician Aramaic system of writing to create the first Mongolian written language. As a result, Buddhism spread to Mongolia through the written as well as the spoken word, and in time all the Buddhist sutras were translated into Mongolian.

The Tibetan Buddhism practiced by the Xi Xia (Tanghuts) in northwestern China caught the attention of the Mongol elite after Genghis Khan conquered the Xi Xia state in 1227 (see Chapter 21). Under Kublai Khan, the newly established Yuan dynasty in China entered a relationship with the chief lama of Tibet in which the emperor would stand as the temporal guarantor of the spiritual authority of the Grand Lama, an alliance that persisted, in a see-saw balance of power, throughout the successive Ming and Manchu Qing dynasties. In 1269, Kublai commissioned the Tibetan 'Phags-pa lama to produce an official script conceived for all the Mongol domains (see Chapter 11).

According to the stone inscription of 1346 commemorating the restoration of a Buddhist temple begun in 1235 under Genghis's son and successor Ögödei Khaghan, a stupa covered with a five-story pavilion was built at the Mongol capital of Khara Khorum together with several other Buddhist temples (see Chapters 18, 19). In Khara Khorum Buddhists lived alongside Nestorian Christians and Muslims. Mongolian khans were strong adherents to the policy of religious tolerance. According to William of Rubruck, a Franciscan friar who visited the Mongol court, Möngke Khaghan, Genghis's grandson, told him: "We Mongols believe that there is but one God, by Whom we live, and by Whom we die, and towards Him we have an upright heart. . . . But just as God gives different fingers to the hand, so has He given different ways to men."[1] Chinese sources note the arrival during the reign of Ögödei of the Kashmiri monk Namu and his brother. Namu remained in Mongolia throughout the reigns of Ögödei's successor khaghans, Güyüg and Möngke. Möngke appointed Namu State Preceptor (Guoshi) as minister of Buddhist affairs and gave him a jade seal. Namu was much honored at the Mongolian court and was awarded the lordship of ten thousand Kashmiri households. He maintained good terms with

37.1 Egiin Gol Stele
This late 19th to early 20th century stele stands along a road near the Egiin Gol River in Bulgan province. The upper three lines are inscribed with a Buddhist prayer written in modern Tibetan, but the bottom lines are rendered in an old Mongol script. This stele rests atop a 3,000-year-old *khirigsuur*. The inscription was likely placed here as a way to integrate this Bronze Age monument into the Buddhist religious sphere.

Khublai Khan, Möngke's younger brother. During the debates between Buddhists and Daoists in China, Namu, together with the 'Phags-pa lama, convinced Kublai to favor Tibetan (Tantric) Buddhism over Daoism, and allowed shamanistic Mongolian traditions to persist. The 'Phags-pa lama was anointed Imperial Preceptor (Dishi). The khans attached special significance to Tibetan Buddhism because it served to counterbalance Confucianism in securing their domination over China. Kublai appointed Buddhists, Nestorian Christians, and Muslims to his bureaucracy. Tibet enjoyed special status both as a vassal of China and vessel of Buddhist ideology and Indian cultural traditions.

The 'Phags-pa lama was schooled both in Buddhist doctrine and in the Buddhist literary tradition, especially in epistolary writings composed in poems and hymns by ancient Indian sages, Nagarjuna, Matrceta, Cabdragoming, and others. In his own numerous writings, 'Phags-pa glorifies Kublai Khan by prescribing to him the attributes of great patrons, as Indian sages had earlier lauded the rulers Ashoka, Kanishka, and others.

Buddhism and Later Mongol History

After the disintegration of the Yuan empire at the end of the fourteenth century, when the Mongols had withdrawn to their native territory, shamanism regained the dominant position in Mongolia's religious belief. Even so, the Mongol link to Tibetan Buddhism was not severed. During the second half of the sixteenth century, a major revival occurred, leading to massive conversion among the population and intense rivalry among Mongol leaders promoting different sects of Tibetan Buddhism. Monasteries were built in different parts of Mongolia; Buddhist learning spread; and the cultural links between Mongolia and Tibet grew stronger. These contacts were aided by a kind of religious and political alliance. At an historic meeting in 1586, Altan Khan, the ruler of the northern Mongols, and the third Dalai Lama of Tibet agreed to establish a so-called "Patron and Preceptor" arrangement, along the lines of the model initiated by Kublai Khan.

Meanwhile, a new power was emerging in another remote region northeast of China—the Manchus, who would rule the Chinese empire as the Qing dynasty (1644–1911). The Manchus manipulated Tibetan Buddhism in their empire-building policy toward neighboring countries, first in Mongolia. Over time, the Manchu rulers exploited divisions and lack of central leadership within Mongolia. Playing on their ethnic and cultural affinity to the Mongols, the Manchus declared themselves the rightful inheritors of the family line of Genghis Khan and launched a propaganda campaign promoting their desire to restore the great empire of the Genghissids, even claiming to have recovered the legendary state seal of the great Mongolian khans (see Chapter 36).

When the Mongols were in danger of being annihilated during a great struggle between the eastern and western Mongols, the Bogdo Gegen (Living Buddha) Zanabazar (1635–1723), head Buddhist and a member of the Golden Family of Genghis Khan, decided to submit to Manchu control. The Manchu victors declared themselves the true patrons of Buddhism and established close contact with the Dalai Lama of Tibet. By the beginning of the twentieth century, 750 monasteries were flourishing in the Khalkha region of Mongolia, and lamas constituted a fifth of its population (see Chapter 5).

Although their Manchu rulers claimed to be the lawful khans of the Mongols, Mongolian chroniclers forged a fabulous genealogy of Indian, Tibetan, and Mongolian rulers by which the Golden Family of Genghis Khan could be traced back to the king Mahasammata (Great Chosen One), the first in a lineage that spawned the Shakya clan from which the historic Gautama Buddha (Shakyamuni) was descended. They even constructed a special genre of historical writing about the so-called Three Buddhist Monarchies—India, Tibet, and Mongolia—that was in practice until recent times. Great Mongolian khans were declared to be reincarnations of various Buddhist deities, Genghis Khan being the reincarnation of Vajrapani and Kublai Khan a second coming of Manjushri.

Translations of Buddhist sutras and treatises by Mongolian lamas belong to the Manchu period. The two great collections of Mahayana Buddhist writings, known in Mongolian as the *Ganjur* (the *Vinaya*,

37.2 Ruins of Orgoonii Khural
During the late 16th to 19th centuries, Buddhism became a powerful political and religious force in Mongolia. Hundreds of monasteries were established and large numbers of Mongolians became lamas. All but a few monasteries are now in ruins, some destroyed by factional strife in the 18th–19th centuries, but most during early 20th-century revolutionary battles and Communist purges of the 1930s.

37.3 Gimpil Darjaalan Monastery
Décor once typical of many Mongolian monasteries has been preserved in the elaborate architecture, wall paintings, and hangings in Gimpil Darjaalan Monastery in Erdenedalai. Today, this monastery in the stark Gobi Desert is a thriving tourist attraction and a Buddhist religious center.

Sutra, and *Tantra* in 108 volumes) and the *Tanjur* (philosophy, commentary, and secular scholarship in 225 volumes), were fully translated into Mongolian and published by means of woodblock printing in Beijing by 1749 in multilingual editions in Tibetan, Manchu, Chinese, and Mongolian. Both works have been highly esteemed, even worshipped, by Mongols as treasures of ancient Indian wisdom. The *Tanjur* is of special importance, containing works on philosophy, logic, grammar, poetics, prose, medicine, astrology, art, and other fields. From the Indian Sanskrit, the language of the Indian Buddhist texts, come many words in Mongolian, including botanical and medicinal terms, even the names of the planets.

Manchu domination of Mongolia lasted more than two hundred years in northern Mongolia and nearly three hundred years in southern Mongolia. Paradoxically, the more Manchus tried to consolidate their power in Mongolia, the more the Mongols became spiritually and culturally alienated from their Manchu rulers, who were, at the time, adopting a Confucian Chinese ethos. With strong encouragement from the Manchus, the Buddhist leaders of Mongolia—Khutugus and Khubilgads, the great sacred lamas and their reincarnations—overshadowed even the secular authorities, who were the real inheritors of the Golden Family of the Ghengissids. They mastered not only the minds of the Mongols, but owned enormous shares of the country's resources, including massive herds of cattle and horses as well as rich agricultural lands. At the turn of the twentieth century, when rival khans were again sparring for control, the eighth Bogdo Gegen, Jebtsundamba Khutugtu, was the only respected central authority in Mongolia. Supported by a wider circle of ecclesiastics, the Bodgo Gegen took power just as the Manchu empire was collapsing in 1911, declared Mongolian independence, and made overtures to the United States, Japan, and other countries. Bogdo Gegen was proclaimed Bogdo Khan with the title "Elevated by the Many" and given the Sanskrit name, Mahasammata, after the Indian king. Two hundred years after the first Bogdo Gergen Zanabazar was forced to submit Mongolia to Manchu domination, the last Bogdo Gegen, was able to restore its independence. Bogdo Gegen ruled Mongolia as a theocratic state until 1921; he died in 1924. The title was eliminated by the socialists, who systematically wrested power from the influential Buddhist establishment. What began as a socialist-supported propaganda and harassment campaign against the monasteries and Buddhist elite in the 1920s and early 1930s ended as a brutal military purge in which thousands of monks were executed and hastily buried in mass graves (fig. 37.2). By 1938 Buddhist resistance to the socialist government was entirely eradicated, and countless monasteries lay in ruins, reduced to dust by Soviet dynamite.

Mongolians believed that the Bogdo Gegens, through a series of reincarnations, had the right to claim not only the sacred genealogy of reincarnations of the Buddha's learned disciples, who originated in

37.4 Sum Khokh Burd Temple
Isolation was a value easily maintained in this 18th-century Buddhist temple, which is located on a small island in a desert marsh in Dundgov province.

THEODORE G. SCHURR

India, but also of the Golden Family of Genghis Khan in Mongolia. In this way, Indo-Tibetan Buddhism eventually was transformed into an important component of Mongolian nationalism. The leaders of the so-called People's Revolution in 1921, supported by Communist Russia, championed the slogan "Restore State and Religion in Mongolia." Even the totalitarian secular regime that ruled Mongolia for the succeeding seventy years, though it decimated Mongolia's Buddhist ranks and destroyed most of its monasteries, occasionally tried to exploit Indian connections and Buddhist sentiments. India was the first non-communist country with which Mongolia established diplomatic relations after 1955.

With the democratic reforms that started in 1990, Mongolia has begun a new period of Buddhist revival alongside modernization (fig. 37.3). However, the Buddhism of twenty-first-century Mongolia will certainly not follow the course of Tibetan Buddhism as it existed under the Manchus. Present-day Mongolia needs more radical reforms in all spheres of social, political, and religious life. While some continue to promote the historical Tibetan Buddhist model of a theocracy, Tibetan Buddhism is unlikely to arbitrate Mongolian national and cultural identity in today's international world.

This essay is adapted from the author's paper "The Indo-Mongolian Relationship: A Retrospective Outlook on Buddhism" delivered to the Indo-Mongolian Society, New York, in May 1998.

1. Dawson 1955, 195.

IN RECENT YEARS it has become possible to track the geographic movements of human populations over long periods of time using shared genetic markers and the emergence of new mutations. These advances in genetic tracking suggest that sixteen million people, nearly one-tenth of all Central and East Asian men, have a common forefather. That ancestor may have been Genghis Khan. Was Genghis Khan, whose name means "universal ruler," also the "universal father" of large swaths of Central and East Asia?

Although all humans have the same basic DNA, small variations make up about 0.1 percent of a person's genetic heritage. These variations are the result of small mutations that take place over time. Some mutations lead to inherited diseases and birth defects; others seem to have little physical expression. The rate of these mutations can be tracked and estimations can be made on how long ago the original mutation took place.[1]

A team of geneticists from China, Mongolia, Pakistan, Uzbekistan, and Great Britain collected blood samples from more than two thousand men in sixteen communities spread throughout what was formerly the Mongol empire.[2] They looked at the patterns of genetic variation in these samples and found that a cluster of Y chromosomes carried a common genetic signature, which indicates they were closely related to one another through a single "founder" chromosome. This cluster of chromosomes was far more common than would be expected by chance.

By estimating the rate of mutation in this chromosome cluster, geneticists determined that it originated in a common male ancestor—the "founder"—about one thousand years ago. A likely candidate for this male ancestor was a descendent of Genghis Khan and his close male relatives. The prevalence of this cluster could be a consequence not only of the many women that he and his male relatives impregnated through marriage, concubinage, or rape, but also because the Mongols decimated the original male population in their march across Central Asia.[3]

Through this approach researchers have investigated the influence of Türkic and Mongolic peoples on the cultural and biological landscape of the steppe and taiga regions of Eurasia over the past two millennia. While the Türkic and Mongolian groups show some similarities in language and culture, they are distinct and separate ethnic groups.[4] Mongolians probably originated in the region encompassing modern Mongolia, whereas Türkic-speaking groups apparently emerged in the Altai-Sayan region of south-central Siberia.[5] The impact of the expansions of these groups from their original homelands can still be observed in their cultural and demographic legacy—in the languages and modern populations of West Asia and northern Eurasia, and in the political organization, subsistence traditions, and artistic expression of the peoples living there.

The genetic legacy of the Türkic and Mongolian groups that moved west from present-day Mongolia and south-central Siberia is also visible in the DNA of the populations now living in the area formerly under the Mongolian empire. The two marker systems most widely used in such studies are the mitochondrial DNA (mtDNA), which

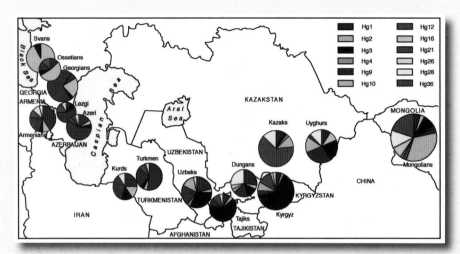

38.1 Y-Chromosome Frequencies
This map shows haplogroup frequencies in populations from the Middle East and Western and Central Asia. The circle area is proportional to sample size; haplogroup color codes are indicated in the key.

is maternally inherited, and the non-recombining region of the Y-chromosome (NRY), which is paternally inherited. Because mtDNA and NRY do not recombine, they accumulate mutations sequentially along female and male lines, respectively. By reconstructing the historical pattern of mutations (markers) in these parts of the human genome, scientists can determine the paths by which groups moved from place to place and date these movements by estimating the time that these markers arose, using known mutation rates for mtDNA and NRY.

Paternal lineages, also known as haplogroups, have been defined in different human populations. The Y-chromosome evolves more slowly than the mtDNA, but has accumulated sufficient variation to differentiate specific branches of the paternal genealogy.[6] Based on their mutational characteristics, NRY haplogroups can be arranged in a network reflecting their pattern of

evolution and phylogeographic (ancestor-descendant) relationships to each other. The current distribution of these haplogroups and their constituent haplotypes allows researchers to reconstruct the migration history of human populations over the past 100,000 years.[7] In other words, the distribution of the NRY haplogroups and their subbranches in different geographic areas, and the genealogical connections between them, as shown by the patterns of genetic markers they possess, allow scientists to determine the region in which different paternal lineages arose, as well as when they were introduced into other locations outside the source area.

One of the first studies of Y-chromosome variation involving Mongolians was a broad genetic survey of West and Central Asian populations, conducted by Tatiana Zerjal and colleagues in 2002.[8] This analysis identified a variety of different paternal haplogroups that arose in either East or West Eurasia. Mongolians had haplotypes from primarily haplogroups C and K (~70%), which are two of the oldest lineages in Central and East

Asia, as well as low frequencies of others (D, N3) that are common in North-East Asia. They also had low frequencies of other haplogroups, including some (e.g., J, P, R1a1) that are more commonly seen in Near East and West Asian populations. This latter set of haplogroups was likely contributed by steppe nomad populations moving into East Asia from the west (Fig. 38.1).

In addition to establishing this general pattern of population affinities, in 2003 Zerjal and a larger team identified a specific branch of NRY haplogroup C (now called C3c) with several unusual features.[9] This branch (Fig. 38.2) had a unique mutational pattern relative to others present in haplogroup C, and appeared as a large central node with a number of short branches extending from it. The starlike pattern of the branch indicated that it had recently arisen through a founder event, and then was spread fairly rapidly across the area in which it is now found. This founder haplotype was observed in sixteen populations throughout a large region of Central and East Asia and occurred at high frequency there (Fig. 38.3).

The pattern of sequence variation observed in the C3c sublineage suggested that it originated in Mongolia more than 1,000 years ago. Because this sublineage was also concentrated within the boundaries of the original Mongol empire, researchers hypothesized that Genghis Khan (c. 1162-1227) and his male relatives were responsible for disseminating it throughout this region. During the twelfth and thirteenth centuries, Genghis's sons, grandsons, and other members of his clan expanded the Mongolian heartland into an empire stretching from southern China and the Pacific coast of Asia through the western steppe and taiga and into Hungary and western parts of Russia. The initial phase of Mongol conquest involved the defeat of local tribes that were competing for power and one hundred years of Mongol population expansion, political domination, and economic integration of broad stretches of Central and East Asia. These practices, together with the Mongol custom of cementing political alliances though spousal exchanges of women, left a lasting Mongol imprint on the genetics of peoples in these subjugated lands. As a consequence, some sixteen million men living in Central and East Asia now carry the haplotypes belonging to this paternal lineage.

While this genetic imprint is perhaps the largest one that can be attributed to a single male individual or his kin group, it did not affect the majority of people living at the time of the Mongol empire. As shown by numerous genetic studies many different NRY haplogroups are found in males from East Asia as well as other regions of the world.[10] In fact, those men

who now bear the C3c sublineage represent only 0.4% of the world's population of four billion, not one-fifth (which would be 80,000,000 persons), as has been asserted in the popular media. Thus, claims of genetic ancestry tracing back to Genghis Khan by persons of non-Asian descent should be viewed with skepticism.

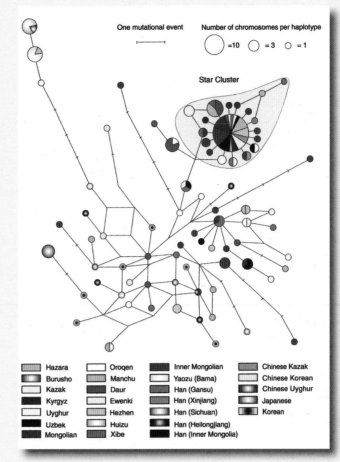

38.2 **Star-cluster Haplotype**
This diagram illustrates the variation in Y-chromosomal haplogroup C*(xC3c). Circles represent lineages; their size is proportional to their frequency in the population sampled; and color indicates population of origin. Lines represent microsatellite mutation differences.

1. NIH website, http://www.nigms.nih.gov/Publications/Factsheet_GeneticVariation.htm; National Coalition for Health Professional Education in Genetics; http://www.nchpeg.org/raceandgenetics/index.asp

2. Wade, 2003.

3. Travis 2003, p. 91.

4. Golden 1992; Janhunen 2003; Morgan 2007; Spuler 1989.

5. Golden 1992.

6. Jobling and Tyler-Smith 2003.

7. Underhill et al. 2000; Y-Chromosome Consortium 2002.

8. Zerjal et al. 2002.

9. Zerjal et al. 2003.

10. Underhill et al. 2000.

38.3 **Star-cluster Distribution**
This map shows the distribution of star-cluster (C3c) Y-chromosomes in relation to the extent of Genghis Khan's empire at the time of his death in 1227. Populations are shown as circles with an area proportional to sample size; star-cluster chromosomes are indicated by green sectors.

PETER K. MARSH

MYAGMAR SARUUL-ERDENE

WRITING IN 1907, Theodore Roosevelt showed that he was no great fan of the medieval Mongols, who "have ever been so hideous and on the whole so noxious to mankind. The Mongols were savages as cruel as they were brave and hardy." The Mongol soldiers who charged into Europe, he continues, must have appeared to those "who cowered in horror before them," as "squat, slit-eyed, brawny horsemen, 'with the faces like the snouts of dogs,' [who] seemed as hideous and fearsome as demons, and as irresistible by ordinary mortals."[1] At the same time, he cautioned that "full understanding of the history of the Mongol people is necessary to all who would understand the development of Asia and of eastern Europe."[2] Roosevelt's preface was written for Jeremiah Curtin's *The Mongols: A History*,

one of several books from the first half of the twentieth century that spread knowledge about Genghis Khan and the Mongol empire to a broad audience. These history books drew upon the increasing number of newly discovered documents to update the interpretation of the Mongol empire.

Images of the Mongols through History

In emphasizing the "ruthless cruelty" and "savage nature" of Genghis Khan and the Mongols, Roosevelt was continuing a tradition that has deep historical roots. As early as the thirteenth century European Christians were describing the invading Mongols as "hostile and blood-thirsty barbarians." They burst into European consciousness out of nowhere, prompting many to connect their appearance to ancient fables and stories of monsters and half-human beasts that were believed to exist outside the boundaries of Western civilization. Rumors spread throughout Europe and the Middle East that the Mongols ate human flesh, dogs,

and snakes (fig. 39.1).[3] Some Christians saw signs that Genghis Khan could have been the Antichrist and that his arrival heralded the coming of the Apocalypse.[4] Many of these descriptions may have been driven by ulterior motives, but they do convey the depth of fear and confusion that many felt in Russia, Europe, and the Middle East.

That European attitudes toward the Mongols were not monolithic, however, is evident in the writings of succeeding generations. Geoffrey Chaucer, more than a century after Genghis Khan's death, wrote fawningly about him, describing the "King of Tartary" as noble, wise, merciful, and "blest by Fortune's smile."[5] Christopher Columbus was fascinated by Marco Polo's journey to Kublai Khan's Cathay in 1271. He mentions in his journals that he carried a copy of Polo's *Travels* on his voyage in 1492, when he fully expected to land in China and meet the Mongol khans.

By the time of the Enlightenment, European attitudes towards Asians, in general, and the Mon-

39.1 *The Chronica Majora*

This illustration from *Chronica Majora*, an illustrated medieval manuscript attributed to Matthew Paris, deals with English history from 1240 to 1253, when rumors of Mongol attacks on Russia and eastern Europe were rampant. The illustration shows Mongols killing captives and roasting and eating their flesh.

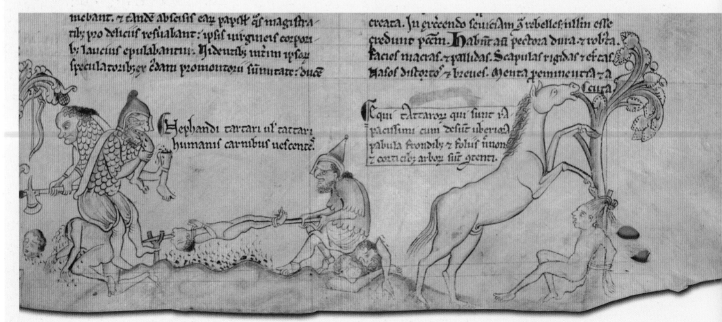

gols, in particular, had darkened considerably. Voltaire chose Genghis Khan as the subject of his tragedy *L'Orphelin de la Chine* (1755; the London premiere of *The Orphan of China* was held in 1759), in which he becomes a "bloody conqueror" and "destructive tyrant" who is "yet no more /Than a wild Scythian soldier; bred to arms /And practiced in the trade of blood." He and his soldiers are "wild sons of rapine, / Who live in tents, in chariots, and in fields." They "detest our arts, / Our customs, and our laws; and therefore mean /To change them all." Wherever they go, Voltaire continues, "they spread destruction round them."[6] While Voltaire likely used Genghis Khan as a literary foil to attack the French king, his construction of him as a symbol for the world's evils caught on with other writers.[7] Such portrayals continued up to the twentieth century. Russian historians have long characterized the period of Mongol occupation known as the "Tatar Yoke," as one of destruction, death, and stagnation. In eastern Europe, particularly in Poland, the Ukraine, and Hungary, Genghis Khan is broadly remembered for the destruction his armies brought upon their lands.

Russian, European, and American Cinema

It is perhaps not surprising that film-makers would turn to the history of the Mongols for inspiration. One of the earliest films to tell the story of the medieval Mongols was the Russian film *Storm Over Asia* (1928) directed by V. I. Pudovkin. Although evoking the terror of Genghis Khan's invasions, the film is not about Genghis Khan but about one of his heirs, a simple Mongol hunter

named Bayar (the Buryat-Mongol actor Enkhijinov) who becomes caught up in a revolutionary struggle to rid his homeland of foreign occupiers. The film ends with Bayar's words: "Oh, my people, rise, in your ancient strength, and free yourselves." With the rise of Stalin in the mid 1920s, such exhortations were no longer allowed in any Soviet or Mongolian films, making *Storm Over Asia* the first—and last—Soviet film that mentions Genghis Khan in a positive light.

By the 1930s Soviet propaganda began to portray the Mongols in very different ways. Genghis Khan and his heirs became petty aristocratic thugs who seized power in the thirteenth century and suppressed the freedoms of the common Mongols. This attitude toward the Mongol "aristocracy" is evident in a scene from Sergei Einsenstein's *Alexander Nevsky* (1938), a film about a battle between Russian foot soldiers and mounted Livonian knights on a frozen Russian lake in 1242. In one scene before the battle, a Mongolian prince humiliates the Russians, but their leader, Nevsky, cautions them not to retaliate, explaining later, "It is not time to fight them. We have more dangerous enemies right now." In his film *Andrey Rublev* (1969), the famous Soviet-era director Andrei Tarkovsky

At her feet, The Conqueror laid all the riches of Cathay... and for a hundred years, their children ruled half the world!

39.2 Howard Hughes Presents *The Conqueror*
This 1956 Technicolor, cinemascope production took liberties with historical fact: "At her feet, the Conqueror laid all the riches of Cathay...For a hundred years, their children ruled half the world." In 1956, movie-goers were presented with a Western fantasy world, one in which John Wayne's claim to "conquer like a barbarian" was not met with guffaws. Today's Genghis Khan movies use Asian actors, but only one, so far, has been Mongolian.

uses the character of Andrey Rublev to explore the influence of Mongol invasions on Russian society. The Mongols are portrayed as brutal, bloody, and cruel, sacking the village of Vladimir and killing everyone who took refuge in a Christian church. The Mongol sacking of that city under the leadership of Batu Khan in 1238 was indeed brutal, but these portrayals echo formulaic medieval fables meant to emphasize the brutality of the Mongols.[8]

European films about Genghis Khan and the medieval Mongols are often much more historically imaginative. The Italian film *I Mongoli* (1961) takes as its subject the Mongol siege of the Polish city of Krakov in 1241, which it depicts as being led by Genghis Khan (Roldano Lupi) and his son Ögödei (Jack Palance). That neither Khan actually participated in this campaign is only one of its many inaccuracies. Egyptian-born Omar Sharif plays the title role in the joint West German–Yugoslavian production, *Genghis Khan* (1965). Despite the big name actors, the film is rife with historical fabrications, such as a scene where Temüjin's best friend, Jamukha (Steven Boyd) kidnaps Temüjin's love, Börte (Françoise Dorléac). Although drawing upon ideas from *The Secret History of the Mongols*, the confusion of names, relationships, and events bends historical fact to fit a scriptwriter's dramatic narrative.

Hollywood proved to be no better in its depiction of the medieval Mongols in productions throughout the twentieth century, including *The Adventures of Marco Polo* (1938), *The Black Rose* (1950), *The Golden Horde* (1951), and *The Conqueror* (1956). Billed as "fiction based on fact," *The Conqueror*, featuring John Wayne as Genghis Khan, never aimed to tell a historically accurate story (fig. 39.2).[9] The inventions begin with Genghis Khan's capture of the fiancée of the chieftain of the Merkid tribe, Börte (Susan Hayward), which sets off a series of romantic encounters and battle scenes. The stilted dialogue and poor acting is exemplified by an encounter between John Wayne and Susan Hayward in which he booms, "There are moments for action, then I listen to my blood. I feel this Tartar woman is for me. My blood says take her!" In another scene Genghis

39.3 A Genghis Khan Video Game
Nintendo produced this video game in 1993. The beards and mustaches look Asian, but the facial features still have a European cast.

Khan and his officers enjoy an evening of relaxation in the palace of a Chinese prince, which includes an "Oriental dance" featuring "a clutch of scantily clad charmers."[10] Such an image alludes to the stereotype of unbridled sexuality of Oriental despots that was central to Coleridge's depiction of Kubilai Khan's "stately pleasure-dome" in his poem called "Kubla Khan" (1797).

Films released in the early 2000s have gone to the other extreme of glorifying Genghis. Sergei Bodrov's *Mongol* (2007) depicts the Mongol ruler as a heroic figure and downplays the killings and massacres for which he was responsible. It even erroneously claims that he released a specific captive, one of his blood brothers, with whom he had broken and then fought. He actually had his former ally killed in a gruesome fashion. In another ridiculous episode, his wife purloins a key that permits Genghis to escape from a cage and captivity. The film ludicrously portrays him as generous and benevolent and as being forced to make war to survive.

Video Games

As technology improved throughout the 1990s, game creators dreamed up ever more sophisticated—and erroneous—depictions of other worlds. In one of the earliest of these strategy games, *Genghis Khan II* (Nintendo 1993), each player controls an army, one of which is Mongol, and must assess the strengths and weaknesses of each in determining the proper tactics and strategies needed to achieve world conquest (fig. 39.3). Later versions of strategy games gave players not only better graphics, but more responsibilities. In *Medieval I and II: Total War* (Sega 2002, 2006) and *Shogun-Total War: Mongol Invasion* (Sega 2000), a player must not only lead an army but ensure there is enough food for the people in the communities they control, that the taxes are collected, religious temples maintained, and so on. In *Age of Empires: Age of Kings* (Microsoft 2006) and *Civilization IV* (2K Games 2005) players have the opportunity to re-enact scenes from the lives of famous historical figures. Players who select Genghis Khan re-enact his unification of the Mongol tribes and invasion of China, and try their hands at maintaining a global empire. While immersing players in Mongol history and important personalities and events, these games also perpetuate long-held Western stereotypes of the Asian as "other."

Mongolian Barbecue

Mongol stereotypes have also helped to fuel the spread of Mongolian barbecue restaurants in which customers select raw meats, vegetables, seafood, salads, and sauces for cooking in a single bowl by a "master griller." The origin of Mongolian barbecue is disputed, but it was likely developed in Taiwan or China and from there spread throughout Asia and to the United States, reaching California in the 1960s.[11] The owner of a Ventura County, California, restaurant argues that Genghis Khan and his soldiers used their iron helmets and shields to prepare their food. "For meals," he writes, "nuts, berries, roots and wild game were thinly-sliced for quick cooking and placed inside helmets over open flames—[and thus] the roots of Mongolian barbecue were born—a truly native meal, typical of the diet of the rugged Mongolian nomad."[12]

What is more important to these restaurant owners than historical accuracy was to provide their patrons with an exciting and unique dining experience. One restaurant describes itself as bringing diners "one of the world's least known but most original eating experiences."[13] Another restaurant claims that the aromas of Mongolian barbecue will help diners "understand how this tasty dish helped Genghis Kahn [sic] conquer China."[14] And still another boasts that it is architecturally designed to evoke "feelings of being in an open Mongolian tent and the pleasure of a sumptuous meal."[15] Like the creators of video games, Mongolian restaurants make a business of reinforcing the perception of the Mongols as uncivilized outsiders.

Genghis Khan in Historical Fiction

Giving readers a sense of what life was like for Genghis Khan and his soldiers has become popular theme in historical fiction. Referring to his *Genghis: Birth of an Empire* (2007a), Conn Iggulden describes good historical fiction as "deliberately filling in the gaps" to help the reader imagine the story being told and making it "very, very vivid."[16] Though centuries old, Iggulden sees the life of Genghis Khan as a very human survival story. Other historical fiction like *The Earth Is the Lord's: A Tale of the Rise of Genghis Khan* (1975) by Taylor Caldwell and *The Blue Wolf: The Epic Tale of the Life of Genghis Khan and the Empire of the Steppes* (2003) by Frederic Dion, also try to personalize his rise to power and to give greater depth to the caricatures that predominate in Western popular culture. Florence Prusmack's *Khan: A Romantic Historical Novel Based on the Early Life of Ghenghis Khan* (1992) even seeks to explore Genghis Khan as a caring father and husband, as well as a charismatic military commander.

Recent Western scholars and journalists have begun to question these popular perceptions. Jack Weatherford's *Genghis Khan and the Making of the Modern World* (2004) has done much to encourage many people to reconsider their own assumptions about the man and to reflect upon the positive roles he played in modern world history. His work, in turn, follows by nearly a decade the controversial decision by *The Washington Post* to name Genghis Khan the "Man of the Millennium"[17] citing his role in shaking up the known world of the thirteenth century in ways that would lead to the development of the modern world. In Mongolia itself, Genghis Khan has become a powerful nationalist icon since the nation sloughed off Soviet domination in 1990. To many Mongolians, he and his achievements represent the power of the Mongols as a people, a power that exists independently of the West and that asserts Mongol uniqueness on the global stage. However, even this "heroic" Genghis Khan of the early twenty-first century may be just another historical construction that is, ultimately, no closer to the man himself than was the "evil" construction that Theodore Roosevelt referred to in the beginning of the twentieth century. What runs through all of these depictions is the persistent power of Genghis Khan to spur our imaginations.

1. Curtin 1908, xii.
2. Curtin 1908, xv.
3. Jackson 2005, 140, 149.
4. Jackson 142, 144.
5. Chaucer 1993, 284–85.
6. Voltaire 1901.
7. Weatherford 2004, 256.
8. Jackson 2005, 145.
9. Weiler 1956.
10. Weiler 1956.
11. Lipson 1969.
12. Anonymous 2003. 47.
13. Mongolian Barbecue Restaurant n.d.
14. Mongolian Barbecue Blogspot 2006.
15. Kublai Khan Monglian Restaurant 2004.
16. Iggulden 2007b.
17. Achenbach 1995.

40.1 Genghis in Steel

This massive 40-meter steel statue of Genghis, erected as part of the 800th anniversary project, stands on the Tuul River outside Ulaan Baatar. Genghis sits confidently on his horse, looking northeast towards Khentii province, his homeland. Tourists can climb to the top inside the figure and look out through the eyes of one of the world's greatest conquerors, imagining what they would have done had they been Genghis Khan.

40. Today's Genghis Khan

FROM HERO TO OUTCAST TO HERO AGAIN

Nomin Lkhagvasuren

"So, where are you from?" an American asked me.
"Mongolia"
"That's in Latin America, right?"
"Well, actually it's in Asia. Have you ever heard of Genghis Khan?"
"Oh, that Mongolia—sure, the Mongolia of Genghis!"

Arriving in Ulaan Baatar, the capital of Mongolia, without knowledge of the native language is not to be feared: one only need know "Genghis Khan." The brightly lit Genghis Khan International Airport is ready to receive the Mongolian Airlines jet, which may also be named the "Genghis Khan." Inside, the airport lobby is decorated with large portraits of the Great Khan and his descendants. Outside, buses from the luxurious Genghis Khan Hotel might be parked, awaiting guests. On the way to Ulaan Baatar, the road passes Genghis's Urguu tourist camp, and further down, a huge portrait of Genghis Khan etched into the side of Bogdo Mountain, facing the city. Visible in the large central square of Ulaan Baatar is a huge bronze statue of Genghis Khan. Bars around the square sell pints of local Genghis beer or shots of Genghis vodka and, of course, these beverages can be enjoyed nearby in the popular Grand Khan pub. The Mongolian money that pays for your drinks has yet another famous image of Genghis, drawn at the order of Kublai Khan in 1270—shaded pink, blue, green, or purple for various denominations (fig. 40.5).

Such demonstrations of veneration of the Great Khan, the father of the Mongolian nation, became possible only after 1990, with liberation from Soviet control over Mongolia and the withdrawal of thousands of Russian troops and tanks. For 300 or so years, Mongolia had been under foreign domination and the Great Khan's historical presence as a national symbol of unity was not always welcome. The Manchu Qing dynasty that ruled Mongolia from 1644 to 1911 ensured that Mongolian princedoms remained divided and isolated. Aristocrats of the Genghis lineage were left to rule local territories, while Mongolian intellectuals were free to compose textual studies of a proud Mongolian history. Unfortunately, these works were inaccessible to the majority of Mongolian nomads, most of whom were illiterate.

In the seventeenth century the spread of the Tibetan Mahayana School of Buddhism resulted in Undur Gegen Zanabazar (1635–1723) being proclaimed the first Bogdo Gegen (Living Buddha) of Mongolia in 1640. The Manchus honored Zanabazar as a descendant of Genghis Khan. Although they were respectful of the traditional worship of Tenggeri, Genghis Khan, and natural spirits, they used the spread of Buddhism to strengthen their control over the Mongolian population,[1] forbidding a centralized religious and state administration and requiring monasteries and temples to remain small and isolated. During this period Buddhist

40.2 Genghis Khan Enthroned
Temüjin's receipt of the title Genghis Khan at the *khuriltai* of 1206 is seen as the beginning of Mongolian statehood, and the 800th anniversary of this event became the focus of a huge national celebration in 2006. Genghis was at the center of every undertaking, beginning with the new façade on the parliament building. A huge bronze statue of Genghis Khan, flanked by seated figures of Ögödei and Kublai and mounted figures of famous generals, replaced the Soviet-style mausoleum of Mongolia's revolutionary heroes, D. Sukhbaatar and Kh. Choibalsan, at the center of a massive columned façade.

Mongolians viewed Genghis Khan as the human reincarnation of the Buddhist diety Vajrapani (see Chapter 37).[2]

Mongolia and the Soviets: Genghis Banished

The fall of the Qing dynasty in 1911, and the brief rise of a Buddhist theocracy, was but a taste of genuine political independence before the year 1921 brought a socialist revolution to Mongolia. In 1924 Mongolia became a Soviet satellite state with the proclamation of the Mongolian People's Republic and establishment of a one-party authoritarian political system. The government began a campaign to eradicate popular worship of the Great Khan, replacing him with such revolutionary heroes as D. Sukhbaatar.

World War II came like a sudden storm to the eastern steppes of Mongolia, beginning with the Khalkhyn Gol battle in 1939. A combined Mongolian–Soviet effort defeated and repelled the invading Japanese forces and awoke the nation's patriotic spirit. Mongolia was a steadfast supporter of the Soviets in the war against fascism. In order to bolster national effort, the Mongolian propaganda machine, much like its parent in the Soviet Union, began producing martial propaganda in the form of public art, movies, and theater about the patriots of Mongolia and its legendary warrior kings and queens.

Following the war, the Mongolian Peo-

ples Revolutionary Party, fearful of growing nationalist sentiment fired by the wartime patriotism and propaganda, reinforced the Soviet ideology of internationalism, particularly in schools. Genghis Khan was portrayed as a ruthless warrior and a representative of feudal aristocracy. On the other hand, the post-war period also saw academician Ts. Damdinsuren convert *The Secret History of Mongols* (see Chapter 14) into a Cyrillic script version that could be read by every Mongol. This important publication had an initial release of 10,000 copies in 1947 and became a required part of the school curriculum. Over the next few years, 230,000 copies of *The Secret History* were issued, a number that almost equaled every household in the country. Although Genghis Khan was always acknowledged as founder of the Mongolian state, official interpretations emphasized Genghis's destruction of the peoples of Asia and Europe and the negative influence of his military conquests on the development of Mongolia itself. "There were times when [any] favorable word . . . mentioned about the Mongol Empire of the XIIIth century . . . was considered praise [for the] cruel feudal conquests, the expression of nationalism, and a threat to the unbreakable friendship between the peoples of Mongolia and the Soviet Union."[3]

A good example of the political ideology of these times was the celebration of the 800th anniversary of Genghis Khan's birth in 1962. Inspired by exhortations coming from prominent Mongolian historians, the Party's Central Committee issued a resolution in 1961. The highlight of the anniversary was to be an international conference of scholars, artists, and local and foreign media. The conference was wildly popular. Not only was the conference room full, but people had to stand along the stairs, down to the foyer and out on the patio of the Central Library, where, next to a statue of Stalin, they listened to the proceedings on a loudspeaker. In the debate following the official speech, a wide variety of views were expressed, and afterwards several participants, including the famed historians, Ts. Damdinsuren, Sh. Natsagdorj, and the leading politician and conference or-

ganizer, D. Tomor-Ochir, were put on the Party's blacklist, branded as "nationalists," and demoted or even banished from the capital city. Contrary to plans, the proceedings were never published.[4] A simple stone monument to Genghis Khan was erected in Khentii province, with his words, "Let my body not rest, but let my state be strong." The Central Committee ordered the monument to be destroyed, but silent resistance on part of those who were to perform this task resulted in the demolition being postponed time and again,[5] and so it stands today.

The Genghis Revival
The political upheaval of 1990 opened the floodgates holding back Mongolia's long-denied desire for independence and a distinct national identity. At last, Mongols could mention the name of the Great Khan in public without fear of censure or prosecution. Public interest in Mongolian history surged; old ideological texts and curricula were revised; and writers and artists, free to express their views for the first time in modern history, exercised newfound creativity and explored new media and venues. The first Mongolian film about Genghis Khan, *Under the Power of the Eternal Heaven,* was produced; a pop band called Genghis Khan took off with its hit song of the same name; painters, actors, composers, and designers created works inspired by Genghis Khan. All were full of pride in belonging to the nation that once ruled much of the known world.

Inevitably, this initial euphoria became inflated and somewhat overdone. Institutions like the World Academy of Genghis Khan, led by a man claiming to be a direct descendant of Genghis Khan, and the World Academy of the Eternal Tenggeri appeared, promoted in the new sensation-driven media. Although dismissed by scholars, they claimed research expertise, popularized Genghis's philosophy and life, and nominated as academy members a local fashion model, a politician, and Bill and Hillary Clinton among many others. A great number of Mongols claimed to be descendants of Genghis Khan's Borjigin clan, and a craze for naming newborns Genghis, Temüjin, and Börte swept across the nation. Shamanism and worship of Tenggeri and Genghis Khan, long suppressed by the Soviet-backed Mongolian government, sprang into the open and with it the tradition of venerating the spirits of local mountains and hills by constructing *ovoos* (ceremonial rock piles) decorated with colorful blue silken cloths called *khadag,* as well as such personal items as discarded crutches, money, and even empty vodka bottles. Tasteless events and awards invoked Genghis Khan's name or image, and prizes fashioned after medieval styles were awarded. Shamanic worship of Genghis Khan's spirit had become very popular.

The process of Genghis's revival also unleashed new possibilities for political ad-

40.4 *Naadam* Wrestling
Mongolian wrestling is a featured event in the *naadam* celebrations. Men compete in a three-piece costume including briefs, shirtless sleeves, and ornamented leather boots. Winners receive formal titles, perform an eagle dance, and throw milk curds to the cheering audience.

40.5 Mongolian Currency
An artist's rendition of a youthful Genghis Khan appears on several denominations of Mongolian currency.

vantage and commercial gain. The Democratic Party based its 2008 parliamentary election campaign on a slogan calling for the awakening of the 2.6 million "Genghis Khans" living in Mongolia. The party's leader, Ts. Elbegdorj, said, "Genghises, look around: how do you live? The Democratic party entered Mongolian democratic history along with Temüjin, with Genghis."[6] The National New Party came out with slogans of worship for Genghis Khan and emphasis on respect for the state. Political commercials declared their parties were responsible for renewing national pride in the name of Genghis Khan. Businesses used Genghis in their advertising to attract customers. An Ulaan Baatar newspaper wrote, "We have been over-using Genghis Khan's name . . . Our state and government leaders and politicians use his name when traveling here and there . . . and businesses enrich themselves using Genghis's name on various labels they produce and consequently filling up their pockets."[7]

The 800th Anniversary of the Great Mongolian State, 1206–2006

Genghis-themed events reached their zenith in 2006 during the celebration of the 800th anniversary of Temüjin's investiture as Genghis, khan of all the Mongols, which is now recognized as the creation of the Great Mongolian State. Official celebrations lasted the entire year and were supported by the state and by a newly established nongovernmental "Genghis Khan Fund." A 40-foot high monument to the Great Khan in Ulaan Baatar, an idea first advanced by accused nationalist D. Tomor-Ochir in 1962, was completed in 2006. This monument in front of the parliament building depicts the Great Khan on a throne as the central figure in a complex frieze that includes the seated figures of Ögödei and Kublai and mounted figures of famous generals from that era (fig. 40.2). Its construction, which required removing the Soviet-styled mausoleum containing the preserved bodies of D. Sukhbaatar, the Mongolian revolutionary hero, and his comrade, H. Choibalsan, was perhaps the most controversial and debated of all symbols of the reawakened Mongol state. The project started with a 10 billion togrog (around $7 million) budget, but is believed to have cost twice that amount by the time it was finished.

The 800th anniversary was commemorated by the creation of a special edition of *The Secret History of the Mongols* decorated with precious stones for display in the House of Parliament. Dozens of books on Mongolian history, nomadic life, and traditions were published and dozens of Genghis-themed exhibitions, symposia, and conferences were organized. A Japanese-Mongolian film about Genghis Khan was produced, and the operas *Queen Börte*, and *Queens of Great Khans*, and the first Mongolian rock-opera, *Genghis Khan*, were staged. A drama entitled *Fistful of Blood* by the Mongolian writer and

40.6 *Naadam* **Horse Race**
The 800th anniversary National Celebration in 2006 carried on the ancient traditions of "manly sports"—Mongolian wrestling, archery, and horseracing. Here two young riders are encouraged toward the finish line by older relatives. *Naadam* races are held throughout the country, but the Ulaan Baatar event is the largest, with hundreds of riders joining the competition.

poet B. Lkhagvasuren was performed and the history of Genghis Khan and medieval Mongolia was popularized via mass media throughout the countryside provinces.

A pragmatic side to these widespread celebrations involved attracting and entertaining foreign tourists. Events staged for foreigners included a mock battle deploying 500 soldiers and horses dressed in Mongol-era costumes, which was organized by a Japanese company, and a flamboyant opening to the summer games that featured thirteenth-century wooden carts and period clothing. A giant statue of Genghis Khan on horseback, equipped with an internal escalator affording access to a panoramic view, was erected next to a model thirteenth-century settlement (figs. 40.1, 40.3). All of these events stirred the imaginations of contemporary Mongols and foreigners alike. Then Prime Minister M. Enkhbold reported that these events led to a 12 percent increase in tourism in 2006 compared with the previous year, attracting some 380,000 tourists from 176 countries.[8]

The anniversary celebrations produced the greatest outpouring of national reverence for the Great Khan's memory in the modern history of Mongolia. Genghis Khan permeated every aspect of Mongolian life that year. Some said it was too much, while some celebrated the revival of national pride. Some disliked the appearance of Genghis kitsch and the use of his name and image for every kind of merchandising. In the view of historian B. Punsaldulam of the Mongolian Academy of Sciences, the euphoria surrounding the Great Khan has been like a dough that has risen above the bowl, but with time settles down. Genghis Khan is everywhere in Mongolia once again, 800 years after he created the nation. He will always be in the hearts of Mongols, but we now look forward to a time when he is not on every single billboard, label, and television commercial.

1. Dashbadrakh 2004.
2. Bira 2006, 95–96.
3. Ishjamts 1998, 51.
4. Ishjamts 1998.
5. Baljinnyam and Nagaanbuu 2007, 29–33
6. Elbegdorj 2008.
7. Chuluuntsetseg 2005.
8. Baljinnyam and Nagaanbuu 2007, 6.

Acknowledgments

THE EFFORT TO BRING *Genghis Khan and the Mongol Empire* to press took initial form in the spring of 2007, when William Fitzhugh approached Don Lessem about organizing a book to support Lessem's exhibition on the same subject. At that time, the exhibition was focused primarily on Genghis Khan, with a secondary interest in Kublai Khan, Genghis's grandson and founder of the Yuan dynasty in China. Lessem was receptive and facilitated the organization of an editorial team that included Morris Rossabi of the City University of New York and Columbia University, and William Honeychurch of Yale University. Our early discussions of content and organization benefited from the editorial and production expertise of Letitia Burns O'Connor and the design perspective offered by Dana Levy, both of Perpetua Press, Santa Barbara.

It became clear from our initial meetings that the book we wanted to produce should include topics of historical interest broader than Genghis Khan's Mongolia and Yuan China. During the past decade several popular biographies on Genghis Khan have appeared; museum exhibitions have featured topics relating to the Mongols; and films, websites, and children's books have been sparking curiosity about Genghis Khan and his successors. While all of these were geared toward specific audiences, we envisioned a more comprehensive book on Genghis Khan and the Mongol empire that would consider the genesis of the empire together with its geographic, cultural, and historical aftermath—in short, an exploration of the Mongols' cultural and historical legacy.

Following these themes we solicited manuscripts from a range of experts. We were not able to include all whom we approached, and we thank those for their forbearance. As the project developed it grew larger than the financial resources available, and when the exhibit was required to open at the Houston Museum of Natural Science eight months earlier than expected, it seemed the project might falter until Don Lessem agreed to take on the roles of publisher and sponsor. Later, the University of Washington Press agreed to act as distributor. Our work has also benefited from support provided by the exhibition team at the Houston Museum of Natural Science, which arranged the artifact loan from the State Hermitage Museum, St. Petersburg, and photographed a number of objects from the exhibition for the volume at the request of the editors.

Under Don Lessem, Dino Don, Inc., developed the exhibition, working on the selection of loans; negotiating with private collectors, institutions, and governments; and arranging photography for loans from institutions in Mongolia. We thank Dino Don, Inc. Director of Operations Juliana Flower for her considerable effort in all of these areas. We gratefully acknowledge the lenders to the exhibition in the front pages of the volume. We especially thank photographer Oktyabri Dash of Ok Photo Company for his many fine images of museum objects and Mongolian landscapes. Photographers Gordon Wiltsie, Jamsranjav Bayarsaikhan, Gankhuyag Natseg, and David Ertl also contributed wonderful photographs of modern Mongolia, and they are acknowledged along with the many other individuals and institutions listed in our illustration index who are responsible for the incredible variety of images included in this publication. A special note of thanks is owed to Larry and Pat Gotuaco, Arthur Leeper, Vahid and Cathy Kooros, and the the Qinxuan Collection, who contributed important objects from their private collections to the exhibition and allowed us to publish them.

The task of selecting illustrations began with suggestions from the publication's contributing authors, many of whom also provided their own photographs. Abigail McDermott conducted the lion's share of the illustration research, and negotiated with copyright holders, with assistance from Cara Seitchek. Kohei Tsumori of Dai Nippon Printing Co., Ltd. helped secure the images of the *Mōko shūrai ekotoba* from the Sannomaru Shozokan (Museum of Imperial Collections) in Japan. Yue Shu at the Freer Gallery of Art and Arthur M. Sackler Gallery Library assisted Abigail McDermott with her illustration research and communicated with copyright holders in China. Paul Taylor and the Asian Cultural History Program in the Department of Anthropology of the Smithsonian Institution's National Museum of Natural History advised the editors on appropriate illustrations from Korea's Goryeo period and facilitated communication with the National Museum of Korea.

Abigail McDermott also researched and oversaw the preparation of the publication's many maps, which were expertly drawn by Marcia Bakry, renowned artist and illustrator in the Department of Anthropology, Smithsonian Institution. In addition, librarians Maggie Dittemore and James Haug of the Department of Anthropology, Smithsonian Institution, assisted William Fitzhugh in his research. Donald Hurlbert and his colleagues in the National Museum of Natural History Photograph Services Office provided photographic and imaging assistance. Finally, Department of Anthropology, Smithsonian Institution, budget managers Nancy Shorey, Zaborian Payne, and Michelle Reed, and department Chairman J. Daniel Rogers, himself a contributor to the volume, and Associate Chair Laurie Burgess, supplied encouragement and administrative support.

As with every publication, much of the coordination and production effort fell to the editorial team. We owe a great debt of thanks to Morris Rossabi for serving as Co-Editor, for contributing his own scholarship, and for drawing on his network of scholar colleagues. Co-Editor William Honeychurch brought extensive knowledge of Mongolian archaeology along with crucial editorial scrutiny. Dana Levy worked miracles with the images and handsome design of the book. Jane Oliver provided additional editorial oversight to the text and bibliography. Kathy Talley-Jones contributed editorial expertise to the essays and compiled the index. In addition to her role as editor and content advisor, Letitia Burns O'Connor expertly interfaced with authors and other members of the team. Her friendship, dedication, and editorial pen produced whatever literary merit is evident here. I owe her a deep debt of gratitude for serving as multipurpose editor and overall project advisor. I owe a similar debt to Abigail McDermott, who in addition to her many other duties, kept our complicated project on track. It is impossible to overstate our gratitude to the volume's authors for both their erudition and literary gifts and for their indulgence during the long effort of bringing this book to fruition.

From start to finish, our project was enabled by the continued interest and support of Don Lessem, who, in the midst of financing and producing a major international exhibition, encouraged our work with his distinctive brand of tough love when it would have been easier to walk away. We hope the end product exceeds his expectations and fulfills his desire to bring the story of Genghis Khan and Mongolia to wider public attention.

WILLIAM W. FITZHUGH
Editor

Object Checklist and Illustration Credits

An asterisk following the image title indicates an object that appears in the exhibition.

The abbreviation SI/NMNH stands for Smithsonian Institution National Museum of Natural History.

COVER
Naadam race
Darkhad Valley, Mongolia
Photograph © Gordon Wiltsie
MG 0856H

PAGE 1
Whistling arrow*
Gold inlay on silver; 28.7 cm; 14th c.
Courtesy of Vahid and Cathy Kooros, with the cooperation of the Museum of Fine Arts, Houston
TR: 983-2003

PAGE 2
Erdene Zuu monastery with clouds
Khara Khorum, Ovorkhangai province, Mongolia
Photograph © David Ertl, Cologne

PAGE 4
Kül Tegin stele
Marble; 42 cm; 8th c.
Arkhangai province, Mongolia
Courtesy of the Institute of Archaeology of the Mongolian Academy of Sciences
T-005

Portrait of Genghis Khan
Ink on silk; 116.1 cm; Yuan dynasty, 14th c.
Courtesy of the National Palace Museum, Taiwan
zhonghua 000324-1 bis 8

PAGE 5
Silver-gilt plate with Genovese coat of arms
Silver, gilding; 30 cm. diam; 14th–15th c.
Found in 1895 in the North Caucasus region
Photograph © The State Hermitage Museum, St. Petersburg
Kub-991

Portrait of Kublai Khan
Ink on silk; 116.1 cm; Yuan dynasty, 14th c.
Courtesy of the National Palace Museum, Taiwan
zhonghua 000324-1 bis 8

Genghis Khan on horseback
Tov province, Mongolia
Photograph by J. Bayarsaikhan

PAGE 8
Nambaryn Enkhbayar
President of Mongolia
Photograph courtesy of the Embassy of Mongolia, Washington, DC

PAGE 9
Khasbazaryn Bekhbat
Extraordinary and Plenipotentiary Ambassador of Mongolia to the USA
Photograph courtesy of the Embassy of Mongolia, Washington, DC

PAGE 11
Genghis Khan attacks the Khwarazmian empire in 1219
Mural painted for the exhibit
Image © Yu Shan

PAGE 12
Rabbit-motif trunk*
Lacquer over leather core; 63.5 cm; 15th–16th c.
Courtesy of Arthur Leeper, Belvedere, California

PAGE 13
Seal with wooden handle*
Wood and silver on iron; 11.4 cm; 14th c.
Courtesy of Vahid and Cathy Kooros, with the cooperation of the Museum of Fine Arts, Houston
TR: 984-2003

PAGE 14
Silver *dirnam* coin*
Silver; 2.4 cm diam.; ca. 1281–5
Minted for Hülegü Khan
Courtesy of Vahid and Cathy Kooros, with the cooperation of the Museum of Fine Arts, Houston
TR: 932-2005

Silver *dirnam* coin*
Silver; 1.9 cm diam.; ca. 1262
Minted for Alghu Khan; from Transoxiana
Courtesy of Vahid and Cathy Kooros,

with the cooperation of the Museum of Fine Arts, Houston
TR: 923-2005

Silver *dirnam* coin*
Silver; 1.6 cm diam.; ca. 1225-7
Minted for Genghis Khan; Shazna mint
Courtesy of Vahid and Cathy Kooros, with the cooperation of the Museum of Fine Arts, Houston
TR: 915-2005

Gold double *dinar* coin*
Gold; 2.2 cm; ca. 1331-2
Minted for Abu Said; from Tabriz
Courtesy of Vahid and Cathy Kooros, with the cooperation of the Museum of Fine Arts, Houston
TR: 944-2005

Gold double *dinar* coin*
Gold; 2.4 cm diam.; ca. 1300-1
Minted for Mahmud Ghazan; from Shiraz
Courtesy of Vahid and Cathy Kooros, with the cooperation of the Museum of Fine Arts, Houston
TR: 935-2005

Gold *dinar* coin*
Gold; 2.4 cm diam.; ca. 1221
Minted for Genghis Khan; Shaza mint
Courtesy of Vahid and Cathy Kooros, with the cooperation of the Museum of Fine Arts, Houston
TR: 914-2005

PAGE 15
Saddle cloth fragment*
Silk embroidery; 93 cm; 13th–14th c.
Courtesy of Arthur Leeper, Belvedere, California

PAGE 16
Fresco fragment*
Pigment on plaster; 52.1 cm; 13th c.
Courtesy of Vahid and Cathy Kooros, with the cooperation of the Museum of Fine Arts, Houston
TR: 282-2009

PAGE 17
Lacquered-leather travel trunk*

Lacquered leather with iron fittings; 71.1 cm; 13th–14th c.
Courtesy of Arthur Leeper, Belvedere, California

PAGE 18
Lacquer saddle*
Black, red, and yellow lacquer over wood core; 45.7 cm; 13th–14th c.
Courtesy of Arthur Leeper, Belvedere, California

PAGE 22
Fig. 1.1 The Horidal Saridag Mountains
Lake Khovsgol, Mongolia
Photograph © Gordon Wiltsie
MG 7890H

PAGE 24
Fig. 1.2 Map of the Mongol Empire at its greatest extent, ca. 1276
Prepared by Marcia Bakry, SI/NMNH
After Rossabi 1988: 111.
Map courtesy of SI/NMNH

PAGE 25
Fig. 1.3 The Fra Mauro Map
Parchment; 2 m diam.; ca. 1450
Circular planisphere drawn by Fra Mauro
Courtesy of the Biblioteca Nazionale Marciana, Venice

PAGE 26
Fig. 1.4 Khara Khorum tortoise
Khara Khorum, Ovorkhangai province, Mongolia
Photograph by William W. Fitzhugh, SI/NMNH

PAGE 27
Fig. 1.5 Ulan Tolgoi
Khovsgol province, Mongolia
Photograph by William W. Fitzhugh, SI/NMNH

PAGE 29
Fig. 1.6 Man's boots*
Leather; 35 cm; 19th–20th c.
Photograph © Oktyabri Dash, Ok Photo Company, Mongolia

Courtesy of the National Museum of
Mongolia
D92-4-4

PAGE 30
Fig. 1.7 Engraved s;.ilver medalion*
Silver; 12.8 cm; 13th–14th c.
Sukhbaatar province, Mongolia
Photograph © Oktyabri Dash, Ok
Photo Company, Mongolia
Courtesy of the National Museum of
Mongolia
Y2006-6-34

PAGE 31
Fig. 1.8 Casting spoon*
Cast copper; 5.4 cm; 14th c.
Khara Khorum, Ovorkhangai
province, Mongolia
Courtesy of the Institute of Archaeology
of the Mongolian Academy of Sciences
Kar 2-361

PAGE 32
Fig. 1.9 Arrowheads*
Iron; 13th–14th c.
Photograph © Oktyabri Dash, Ok
Photo Company, Mongolia
Courtesy of the National Museum of
Mongolia
Y97-2-29

PAGE 33
Fig. 1.10 S.V. Kiselev illustrations of
Khara Khorum artifacts
After Kiselev 1965: 169.

PAGE 35
Fig. 1.11 Blue and white plate*
Porcelain (Qinghua kiln); diam. 28
cm; 13th c.
Khara Khorum, Ovorkhangai prov-
ince, Mongolia
Courtesy of the Institute of Archae-
ology of the Mongolian Academy of
Sciences
Kar 2-9761

PAGE 37
Camel harnessed to Genghis tent
Photograph by Owen Lattimore
Courtesy of the Peabody Museum of
Archaeology and Ethnology, Harvard
University
2004.24.36199

PAGE 39
Fig. 1.12 Mongolian musicians in re-
constructed 13th-c. Mongolian village
Tov province, Mongolia
Photograph by Gankhuyag Natsag

PAGE 40
Lake Dood Nuur
Darkhad Valley, Northern Mongolia
Photograph © Gordon Wiltsie
MG 3270H

PAGE 42
Fig. 2.1 Horse herder with lasso
Photograph © Oktyabri Dash, Ok
Photo Company, Mongolia

PAGE 44
Fig. 2.2 Gobi Desert sand dunes
Photograph by James Bosson

PAGE 45
Fig. 2.3 Mongolian steppe grasslands
Photograph by James Bosson

PAGE 46
Fig. 2.4 Map of the ecological zones
of Asia
Prepared by Marcia Bakry, SI/NMNH
Map courtesy of SI/NMNH

PAGE 47
Fig. 2.5 Historical photograph of a
postal service cart
Between Kiakhta and Ourga, Mongolia
Photograph by Stéphane Passet, 13
July 1913
Image © Musée départemental
Albert-Kahn, Paris
A3946

PAGE 48
Fig. 2.6 Woman's snuff bottle and
pouch*
Corral, iron, silk; 19th–20th c.
Photograph © Oktyabri Dash, Ok
Photo Company, Mongolia
Courtesy of the National Museum of
Mongolia
Y64-1-72/ Y64-1-78

Fig. 2.7 Meat drying on ger lattice
Photograph by James Bosson

PAGE 49
Fig. 2.8 Erecting a ger
Darkhad Valley, Mongolia
Photograph © Gordon Wiltsie
MG 2242dH

PAGE 50
Fig. 3.1 Climactic profiles graph
Data from http://www.weatherbase.com/
Prepared by Paula Hoffman

PAGE 51
Fig. 3.2 Tsaatan reindeer
Northern Mongolia
Photograph © Gordon Wiltsie
MG 1974H

PAGE 52
Fig. 3.3 Winter camp
Photograph © Oktyabri Dash, Ok
Photo Company, Mongolia

PAGE 53
Fig. 4.1 Ancient larch tree
Photograph by Biligbaatar Nazad

PAGE 54
Fig. 4.2 Tree-ring temperature record
graph
Prepared by Gordon C. Jacoby

PAGE 56
Fig. 5.1 Mountain camp milking
Photograph © Oktyabri Dash, Ok
Photo Company, Mongolia

PAGE 58
Fig. 5.2 Map of modern Mongolia's
officially recognized ethnic groups
Prepared by Marcia Bakry, SI/NMNH
After Rinchen 1979: Map 23.
Map courtesy of SI/NMNH

PAGE 59
Fig. 5.3 Saddle*
Wood, silver, leather, iron; 40 cm;
19th–20th c.
Photograph © Oktyabri Dash, Ok
Photo Company, Mongolia
Courtesy of the National Museum of
Mongolia
Y2001x-5-2

PAGE 60
Fig. 5.4 Making milk tea
Photograph © Gordon Wiltsie
MG 6425H

Fig. 5.5 Making aaruul (cheese)
Photograph © Oktyabri Dash, Ok
Photo Company, Mongolia

PAGE 61
Fig. 5.6 Iron pot
Iron; 40 cm diam; Yuan dynasty
Photograph © The Inner Mongolia
Museum and Inner Mongolia Univer-
sity, China

PAGE 62
Fig. 5.7 Woman's headdress*
Silk, cotton; 138 cm; 19th–20th c.
Photograph © Oktyabri Dash, Ok
Photo Company, Mongolia
Courtesy of the National Museum of
Mongolia
Y64-3-54

PAGE 63
Fig. 5.8 Woman's hat*
Silk, jewel, corral; 23 cm; 19th–20th c.
Photograph © Oktyabri Dash, Ok
Photo Company, Mongolia
Courtesy of the National Museum of
Mongolia
Y98-1-2

PAGE 64
Fig. 6.1 Shaman's robe
Skin, copper, iron, silk and cloth; 177 cm
Chenbaerhu Banner, Hulunbeier City,
Inner Mongolia, China
Photograph © The Inner Mongolia
Museum and Inner Mongolia Univer-
sity, China

PAGE 66
Fig. 6.2 Biluut rock art image of shaman
Khoton Lake, Bayan Olgii province,
Mongolia
Photo by William W. Fitzhugh,
SI/NMNH

PAGE 67
Fig. 6.3 Buryat shaman
Photograph by Manduhai Buyandelger

PAGE 68
Fig. 6.4 Drum-beater*
Skin, wood, iron; 12 cm; 19th–20th c.
Photograph © Oktyabri Dash, Ok
Photo Company, Mongolia
Courtesy of the National Museum of
Mongolia
D1397

Fig. 6.5 Shaman's hat*
Cotton, feather; 70 cm; 19th–20th c.
Photograph © Oktyabri Dash, Ok

Photo Company, Mongolia
Courtesy of the National Museum of
Mongolia
D1397

PAGE 69
Fig. 6.5 Shaman's costume*
Cotton, iron; 186 cm; 19th–20th c.
Photograph © Oktyabri Dash, Ok
Photo Company, Mongolia
Courtesy of the National Museum of
Mongolia
D1397

PAGE 70
Fig. 6.6 Modern Mongolian masked
shaman
Darkhad Valley, Mongolia
Photograph © Gordon Wiltsie
MG 2409H

PAGE 71
Fig. 6.7 Modern shamans
Photograph © B. Chadraabal, 2009

PAGE 72
Fig. 7.1 Marco Polo before Kublai
Khan
Manuscript detail from Le Livre
des Merveilles du Monde (Travels of
Marco Polo), ca. 1412
Courtesy Bibliothèque nationale de
France, Paris
Ms. fr. 2810, folio 3

Fig. 7.2 Mongolian fiddler from
"Chinggis 800" festival
Photograph by Donald E. Hurlbert,
SI/NMNH

PAGE 73
Fig. 7.3 Morin khuur or horsehead
fiddle*
Wood, skin, horse hair; 115.5 cm;
ca. 1989
Photograph © Oktyabri Dash, Ok
Photo Company, Mongolia
Courtesy of the National Museum of
Mongolia
Y89x-9-3

PAGE 74
Fig. 8.1 Satellite photo of Xiongnu-
period frontier settlement
Southern Gobi Desert, Mongolia
Courtesy of the Institute of Archaeology
of the Mongolian Academy of Sciences

PAGE 76
Fig. 8.2 Salkhit cranium
Salkhit site, Northeast Mongolia
Photograph by Bruno Frohlich,
SI/NMNH

Fig. 8.3 Bayanlig hunting art
Bayankhongor province, Southwest
Mongolia
Photograph by William Honeychurch

PAGE 77
Fig. 8.4 On Khot khirigsuur with
horse burial mounds
Lake Khoton, Bayan Olgii province,
Mongolia
Photo by William W. Fitzhugh,
SI/NMNH

PAGE 78
Fig. 8.5 Open work belt plaque
Bronze; 11.5 cm; ca. Late First Millennium BCE
Photograph by William Honeychurch
Courtesy of the Dundgobi Provincial Museum, Mandalgovi, Mongolia
Dundgobi X35

Arrowheads
Bronze; ca. First Millennium BCE
Baga Gazaryn Chuluu, Dundgobi province, Mongolia
Photograph by William Honeychurch
Courtesy of the Institute of Archaeology of the Mongolian Academy of Sciences
Field Catalog - BGC-SMF 2006

Knife with animal-style decorations
Bronze; 22 cm; ca. Early to Middle First Millennium BCE
Photograph by William Honeychurch
Courtesy of the Dundgobi Provincial Museum, Mandalgovi, Mongolia

PAGE 79
Fig. 8.6 Biluut ceremonial figures
Khoton Lake, Bayan Olgii province, Mongolia
Photograph by Richard Kortum, East Tennessee State University

PAGE 80
Fig. 8.7 Ulan Tolgoi deer stone
Lake Erkhel, Khovsgol province, Mongolia
Photograph by William W. Fitzhugh, SI/NMNH

PAGE 81
Fig. 8.8 Square burial
Selenge River, Mongolia
Photograph by William W. Fitzhugh, SI/NMNH

PAGE 82
Fig. 8.9 Ulaan Tolgoi Deer Stone 5
Lake Erkhel, Khovsgol province, Mongolia
Photograph by William W. Fitzhugh, SI/NMNH

Fig. 8.10
Egyptian Bes figurine
Faience; 2.5 cm; 2nd–1st c. BCE
Photograph by Chunag Amartuvshin
Courtesy of the Institute of Archaeology of the Mongolian Academy of Sciences
Field Catalog - BGC-EX05.02, SMF

Egyptian amulet (*Manus Ficus* symbol)
Faience; 2.1 cm; 2nd–1st c. BCE
Photograph by Chunag Amartuvshin
Courtesy of the Institute of Archaeology of the Mongolian Academy of Sciences
Field Catalog - BGC-EX05.02, SMF

PAGE 83
Fig. 8.11 Tsagaan Asga deer stones
Western Mongolia
Photograph by William W. Fitzhugh, SI/NMNH

PAGE 84
Fig. 9.1 Türkic figure
Selenge River, Mongolia
Photograph by William W. Fitzhugh, SI/NMNH

PAGE 86
Fig. 9.2 Map of the Türkic empire
Prepared by Marcia Bakry, SI/NMNH
After Vainshtein 1989: 58.
Map courtesy of SI/NMNH

Fig. 9.3 Türk empire–period horse bits and stirrups
Iron; 7th–8th c.
From the Bilgä Khaghan treasure
Courtesy of the National Museum of Mongolia

PAGE 87
Fig. 9.4 Kül Tegin head sculpture
Marble; 42 cm; 8th c.
Khashaat, Arkhangai province, Mongolia
Courtesy of the Institute of Archaeology of the Mongolian Academy of Sciences
T-005

PAGE 88
Fig. 9.5 Bilgä Khaghan Stele
Stone; 132 cm; 8th c.
Khashaat sum, Arkhangai province, Mongolia
Courtesy of the National Museum of Mongolia

PAGE 90
Fig. 10.1 *Budonjar's wives and his sons Buka and Buktal*
Manuscript illustration from *The History of the Mongols*, ca. 1590
Photograph © Werner Forman / Art Resource, NY

PAGE 92
Fig. 10.2 Pingo mound with rider
Near Tsagaan Asga, Bayan Olgii province, Mongolia
Photograph by William W. Fitzhugh, SI/NMNH

PAGE 93
Fig. 10.3 Map of Central Asian Tribal Distribution, ca. 12th c.
Prepared by Marcia Bakry, SI/NMNH
After Dawson 1980: 237.
Map courtesy of SI/NMNH

PAGE 94
Fig. 10.4 *Camp scene*
Ink on paper; 36.4 cm; 14th c.
Attributed to Muhammad Siyah Qalam
Courtesy of the Topkapi Palace Museum, Istanbul
TSMK H. 2153, folio 8b

PAGE 95
Fig. 10.5 Altai camels
Altai Mountains, Bayan Olgii province, Mongolia
Photograph by William W. Fitzhugh, SI/NMNH

PAGE 96
Naadam race
Darkhad Valley, Mongolia
Photograph © Gordon Wiltsie
MG 0856H

PAGE 98
Fig. 11.1 *Genghis Khan with his four sons*
Persian miniature; 16th c.
Photograph by Lutz Braun.
Image © British Library Board. All Rights Reserved
Or. 3222, f.43v

PAGE 100
Fig. 11.2 Map of Genghis Khan's Campaigns, 1209-27
Prepared by Marcia Bakry, SI/NMNH
After Edwards 1996: map supplement.
Map courtesy of SI/NMNH

PAGE 101
Fig. 11.3 Genghis Stone
Granite; 210 cm; 1224-5
Photograph © The State Hermitage Museum, St. Petersburg
Inv. No. BM-728

PAGE 102
Fig. 11.4 *Portrait of Genghis Khan*
Ink on silk; 116.1 cm; Yuan dynasty, 14th c.
Courtesy of the National Palace Museum, Taiwan
zhonghua 000324-1 bis 8

PAGE 105
Fig. 11.5 *Genghis Khan at the mosque in Bukhara*
Persian miniature; 14th c.
Image © British Library Board. All Rights Reserved
Or. 2780, f.61

PAGE 107
Fig. 11.6 *The Mongol ruler and his wife sitting on a throne*
Manuscript illustration from *Jami' al-Tavarikh* (Compendium of Chronicles) by Rashid al-Din, ca. 1330
Photograph by Dietmar Katz
Courtesy of Staatsbibliothek zu Berlin - Preussischer Kulturbesitz, Orientabteilung / Art Resource, NY
Diez A Fol 70, No. 10

PAGE 111
Fig. 12.1 *Portrait of Chabi*
Ink on silk; 114.7 cm; Yuan dynasty, 14th c.
Courtesy of the National Palace Museum, Taiwan
zhonghua 000325-1 bis 8

PAGE 112
Fig. 13.1 *Faramurz Pursing the Kabulis*
From the Great Mongol *Shahnama* (Book of Kings), ca. 1330s
Photograph by Herve Lewandowski; collection of the Musée du Louvre
Réunion des Musées Nationaux / Art Resource, NY
7095

PAGE 113
Fig. 13.2 Desert horsemen
Photograph © Oktyabri Dash, Ok Photo Company, Mongolia

PAGE 114
Fig. 13.3 Bridle bit*
Iron; 17 cm; 13th–14th c.
Bayankhongor province, Artsat del, Mongolia
Photograph © Oktyabri Dash, Ok Photo Company, Mongolia
Courtesy of the National Museum of Mongolia
Y2001-8-5

Fig. 13.4 Stirrups*
Iron; 18 cm; 13th–14th c.
Bayankhongor province, Artsat del, Mongolia
Photograph © Oktyabri Dash, Ok Photo Company, Mongolia
Courtesy of the National Museum of Mongolia
Y2001-8-1

PAGE 115
Fig. 13.5 Saddle
Wood, leather, bone; 57.5 cm; 14th c.
Khuiten Khoshuu, Khentii province, Mongolia
Courtesy of the Institute of Archaeology of the Mongolian Academy of Sciences
M-112

PAGE 116
Fig. 14.1 Site of Genghis Khan's defeat of the Naiman
Zag-Baidragiin bulcheer, Bayankhongor province, Mongolia
Photograph © Michael Gervers 2006
2006.01 428

PAGE 120
Fig. 14.2 Opening Pages of the *Yuan Chao Bi Shi*
Changsha: Ye shi guan gu tang
长沙：葉氏觀古堂 [1908]
Courtesy of the Harvard-Yenching Library, Harvard University, Cambridge

PAGE 121
Fig. 14.3 Horseman in winter
Darkhad Valley, Mongolia
Photograph © Gordon Wiltsie
MG 4532H

PAGE 123
Fig. 14.4 Mirror with landscape design*
Cast copper; 10.9 cm diam.; 12th–13th c.
Khara Khorum, Ovorkhangai province, Mongolia
Courtesy of the Institute of Archaeology of the Mongolian Academy of Sciences
Kar 2-533

Page 124
Fig. 15.1 Landscape in the Orkhon River Valley, Mongolia
Photograph © David Ertl, Cologne

Page 126
Fig. 16.1 Shargiin Gobi panorama
Photograph © Oktyabri Dash, Ok
Photo Company, Mongolia

Page 128
Fig. 16.2 Gol Mod II
Khanuy River Valley, Mongolia
Photograph by William W. Fitzhugh,
SI/NMNH

Page 129
Fig. 16.3 Stupa at Kherlem Bars City,
ca. 10th c.
Dornod province, Mongolia
Photograph by Amelia Yonan
Courtesy of J. Daniel Rogers,
SI/NMNH

Fig. 16.4 Khar Balgas reconstruction
Prepared by Marcia Bakry, SI/NMNH
After Tkachev 1987: 116.

Page 130
Fig. 16.5 Excavation at Uglugchiin
Kherem, ca. 12th–14th c.
Khentii province, Mongolia
Photograph by J. Daniel Rogers,
SI/NMNH

Fig. 16.6 Pharaonic maskette
Possibly obsidian; 20 cm; 13th–14th c.
Khara Khorum, Ovorkhangai prov-
ince, Mongolia
Courtesy of the Institute of Archae-
ology of the Mongolian Academy of
Sciences
M-144

Page 131
Fig. 16.7 Feng Yuan Cheng Tu
Illustration from Yuan dynasty
Chang'an zhi tu
After Steinhardt 1988: 88.

Page 132
Fig. 17.1 Map of the Khentii Homeland
Prepared by Marcia Barkry, SI/
NMNH
Based on a map prepared by
Noriyuki Shiraishi
Map courtesy of SI/NMNH

Fig. 17.2 Serven Khaalga rock
inscription
Serven Khaalga Mountain, Khentii
province, Mongolia
Photograph by Noriyuki Shiraishi

Fig. 17.3 Serven Khaalga inscription
rubbings
Serven Khaalga Mountain, Khentii
province, Mongolia
Prepared by Noriyuki Shiraishi and
Toshihiko Miyake

Page 133
Fig. 17.4 Distant view of Avraga site
Kherlen River Valley, Khentii prov-
ince, Mongolia
Photograph by Noriyuki Shiraishi

Page 135
Fig. 17.5 Aerial photograph of Platform 1

Avraga site, Khentii province, Mongolia
Photograph by Noriyuki Shiraishi

Fig. 17.6 Avraga site plan
Prepared by Noriyuki Shiraishi

Page 134
Fig. 17.7 Fragment of a measuring
device
13th–14th c.
Avraga site, Kherlen River Valley,
Mongolia
Photograph by Noriyuki Shiraishi

Fig. 17.8 Charred grain
Millet, barley and wheat grains
Avraga site, Khentii province, Mongolia
Photograph by Noriyuki Shiraishi

Page 136
Fig. 18.1 Excavation at the Khara
Khorum crossroads
Khara Khorum, Ovorkhangai prov-
ince, Mongolia
Photograph © David Ertl, Cologne

Page 138
Fig. 18.2 Aerial photograph of Khara
Khorum and Erdene Zuu monastery
Khara Khorum, Ovorkhangai prov-
ince, Mongolia
Photograph © Deutsches Archäolo-
gisches Institut/MDKE

Page 139
Fig. 18.3 Decorative clay roof tiles
Khara Khorum, Ovorkhangai prov-
ince, Mongolia
Photograph by Ernst Pohl

Page 140
Fig. 18.4 Deer-shaped Belt Decora-
tion*
Jade; 6.7 cm; 14th c.
Khara Khorum, Ovorkhangai prov-
ince, Mongolia
Courtesy of the Institute of Archae-
ology of the Mongolian Academy of
Sciences
Kar 2-259

Fig. 18.5 Dragon-head ornament*
Carved antler; 8.5 cm; 13th c.
Khara Khorum, Ovorkhangai prov-
ince, Mongolia
Courtesy of the Institute of Archae-
ology of the Mongolian Academy of
Sciences
Kar 2-2552

Page 141
Fig. 18.6 Hand mirror*
Cast copper alloy; 19.4 cm; 13th c.
Khanan, Khentii province, Mongolia
Courtesy of the Institute of Archae-
ology of the Mongolian Academy of
Sciences
M-120

Fig. 18.7 Qingbai kiln lion*
Porcelain; 13.5 cm; 14th c.
Khara Khorum, Ovorkhangai prov-
ince, Mongolia
Courtesy of the Institute of Archaeology
of the Mongolian Academy of Sciences
Kar 2-448

Page 142
Fig. 18.8 Storage vessel in situ
Khara Khorum, Ovorkhangai prov-
ince, Mongolia
Photograph by Ernst Pohl

Fig. 18.9 Seated Buddha Sakyamuni
Kar*
Bronze, wood base; 3.5 cm; 13th c.
Khara Khorum, Ovorkhangai prov-
ince, Mongolia
Courtesy of the Institute of Archae-
ology of the Mongolian Academy of
Sciences
Kar 1-02/2102

Page 143
Fig. 18.10 Bodhisattva head*
Green-glazed terracotta; 11.6 cm;
13th c.
Khara Khorum, Ovorkhangai prov-
ince, Mongolia
Courtesy of the Institute of Archae-
ology of the Mongolian Academy of
Sciences
Kar 1-00/173

Fig. 18.11 Jun kiln bowl*
Glazed ceramic; 18 cm. diam.; Song
or Yuan dynasty
Khara Khorum, Ovorkhangai prov-
ince, Mongolia
Courtesy of the Institute of Archae-
ology of the Mongolian Academy of
Sciences
Kar 2-9763

Page 144
Fig. 18.12 Bracelet*
Gold alloy; 7 cm. diam; 14th c.
Khara Khorum, Ovorkhangai prov-
ince, Mongolia
Courtesy of the Institute of Archae-
ology of the Mongolian Academy of
Sciences
Kar 2-1697

Bracelet mold*
Cast copper; 11.1 cm; 14th c.
Khara Khorum, Ovorkhangai prov-
ince, Mongolia
Courtesy of the Institute of Archae-
ology of the Mongolian Academy of
Sciences
Kar 2-1445

Page 145
Fig. 18.13 Seal of office*
Copper alloy; 7.3 cm; 14th c.
Khara Khorum, Ovorkhangai prov-
ince, Mongolia
Courtesy of the Institute of Archae-
ology of the Mongolian Academy of
Sciences
Kar-2-1581

Fig. 18.14 Silver coin
Silver; ca. 1237–8
Photograph by Stefan Heidemann.
Courtesy of the Oriental Coin Cabi-
net of Jena University

Page 146
Fig. 19.1 Aerial view of Khara Khorum and Erdene Zuu monastery
Khara Khorum, Ovorkhangai province, Mongolia

Photograph © Deutsches Archäo-
gisches Institut/MDKE

Page 147
Fig. 19.2 Khara Khorum digital ter-
rain model
Khara Khorum, Ovorkhangai prov-
ince, Mongolia
Prepared by Karlsruhe University of
Applied Sciences, Germany
Image © Deutsches Archäologisches
Institut/MDKE

Fig. 19.3 Aerial view of Khar Balgas
Orkhon River Valley, Arkhangai
province, Mongolia
Photograph © Deutsches Archäologisches Institut/MDKE

Page 148
Fig. 19.4 Palace area excavation
trench
Northern profile; August 2004
Khara Khorum, Ovorkhangai prov-
ince, Mongolia
Photograph © Deutsches Archäolo-
gisches Institut/MDKE

Fig. 19.5 Buddhist clay reliefs in situ
Khara Khorum, Ovorkhangai province, Mongolia
Photograph © Deutsches Archäologisches Institut/MDKE

Fig. 19.6 Fragment of a temple fresco
Khara Khorum, Ovorkhangai province, Mongolia
Photograph © Deutsches Archäologisches Institut/MDKE

Page 149
Fig. 19.7 Trench stratigraphy
Under the Erdene Zuu monastery
wall; 2005
Khara Khorum, Ovorkhangai prov-
ince, Mongolia
Photograph © Deutsches Archäolo-
gisches Institut/MDKE

Fig. 19.8 Aerial image of Erdene Zuu
with 2005 excavation areas
Khara Khorum, Ovorkhangai province, Mongolia
Photograph © Deutsches Archäologisches Institut/MDKE

Fig. 19.9 Blue-and-white tea bowl
Qingbai kiln ceramic; Yuan dynasty,
14th c.
Khara Khorum, Ovorkhangai province, Mongolia
Photograph © Deutsches Archäologisches Institut/MDKE
Courtesy of the Institute of Archaeology, Mongolian Academy of Sciences
KAR1-04/8-10-23

Page 150
Fig. 20.1 Illumination from William
of Rubruck's Itinerarium, ca. 1300
The Parker Library
Image courtesy of the Master and
Fellows of Corpus Christi College,
Cambridge
MS 66A, f. 67r.

Winter Palace, St. Petersburg, Russia
Photograph © The State Hermitage Museum, St. Petersburg
Rep6 Kazany

PAGE 190
Fig. 26.1 *The Mongols under Hül- egü cross the Tigris river and conquer Baghdad in 1258*
Illustration from a manuscript of Rashid al-Din's *Jami' al-Tavarikh* (Compendium of Chronicles), ca. 14th c.
Image courtesy Staatsbibliothek zu Berlin - Preussischer Kulturbesitz, Orientabteilung / Art Resource, NY
Diez A fol.70, no. 7

PAGE 192
Fig. 26.2 Caracole tactic
Illustration © Dick Gage for *Military History* magazine

Fig. 26.3 Feign retreat
Illustration © Dick Gage for *Military History* magazine

PAGE 193
Fig. 26.4 Mongolian cavalry
Re-enactors formed in a *jaghun* or one hundred-man unit
Photograph by Timothy May

Fig. 26.5 Mongol horses
Photograph by Timothy May

PAGE 194
Fig. 26.6 The Citadel of Aleppo
Aleppo, Syria
Photograph by Timothy May

Fig. 26.7 Helmet*
Iron; 24 cm diam.; 15th–16th c.
Photograph by Timothy May
Courtesy of the National Museum of Mongolia

PAGE 195
Fig. 26.8 Firearm*
Iron; 44.4 cm; 13th–14th c.
Photograph © Oktyabri Dash, Ok Photo Company, Mongolia
Courtesy of the Military Museum of Mongolia
Y-96-12-5

PAGE 196
Fig. 26.9 Bow, arrows, and quiver*
Wood, birch bark, iron; 115 cm; 13th–14th c.
Shiluustei sum, Zavkhan province, Mongolia
Photograph © Oktyabri Dash, Ok Photo Company, Mongolia
Courtesy of the National Museum of Mongolia
Y2004-2-1

PAGE 197
Fig. 26.10 Sword*
Iron; 80.7 cm; 13th–14th c.
Photograph © Oktyabri Dash, Ok Photo Company, Mongolia
Courtesy of the Military Museum of Mongolia
Y-91-6-1

Fig. 26.11 Spearhead*
Iron; 27.6 cm; 13th–14th c.
Photograph © Oktyabri Dash, Ok Photo Company, Mongolia
Courtesy of the Military Museum of Mongolia
Y-00-3-12

Fig. 26.12 Porcelain bombs or mines
Clay filled with metal shards; 18.5 cm diam.; Yuan dynasty
Photograph © The Inner Mongolia Museum and Inner Mongolia University, China

Fig. 26.13 Liquor bottles
10.5 cm diam.; Yuan dynasty
Photograph © The Inner Mongolia Museum and Inner Mongolia University, China

PAGE 198
Fig. 26.14 Plate armor*
Iron, cotton; 72 cm; 13th–14th c.
Photograph © Oktyabri Dash, Ok Photo Company, Mongolia
Courtesy of the Military Museum of Mongolia
Y-99-1-666

PAGE 199
Fig. 26.15 Chain-mail armor*
Iron; 92 cm; 13th–14th c.
Photograph © Oktyabri Dash, Ok Photo Company, Mongolia
Courtesy of the National Museum of Mongolia
Y63-1-4

PAGE 200
Portrait of Kublai Khan
Ink on silk; 116.1 cm; Yuan dynasty, ca. 14th c.
Courtesy of the National Palace Museum, Taiwan
zhonghua 000324-1 bis 8

PAGE 202
Fig. 27.1 *Kublai Khan Hunting*
Painted hanging scroll by Liu Guandao, ca. 1280
Ink and colors on silk; 182.9 cm; Yuan dynasty
Courtesy of the National Palace Museum, Taiwan

PAGE 204
Fig. 27.2 Map of the Mongol conquest of China
Prepared by Marcia Bakry, SI/NMNH
After Edwards 1996: map supplement.
Map courtesy of SI/NMNH

Page 206
Fig. 27.3 *Sheep and Goat*
Painted handscroll by Zhao Mengfu, ca. 1300
Ink on paper; 48.7 cm; Yuan dynasty
Courtesy of the Freer Gallery of Art, Smithsonian Institution, Washington, DC
F1931.4

PAGE 207
Fig. 27.4 *Kublai Khan on a hunt*

Manuscript detail from Marco Polo's *Le Livre des Merveilles du Monde* (Travels of Marco Polo), ca. 1412
Courtesy Bibliothèque nationale de France, Paris
Ms. fr. 2810, fol.42 v.

PAGE 209
Fig. 27.5 Bronze messenger pass or *paiza*
Bronze; 11 cm diam.; 13th–14th c.
Photograph © Oktyabri Dash, Ok Photo Company, Mongolia
Courtesy of the National Museum of Mongolia
D2634

PAGE 210
Fig. 27.6 Bronze weight
Bronze; 14.2 cm; Yuan dynasty
Photograph © The Inner Mongolia Museum and Inner Mongolia University, China

PAGE 211
Fig. 27.7 Bronze coin*
States *da yuan tong bao* (currency of the Great Yuan); Phags-pa script
Bronze; 4.13 cm diam.; ca. 1310
Courtesy of the Qinxuan Collection, San Francisco, California

PAGE 212
Fig. 27.8 Stem cup
Gold; 9.8 cm. diam; Yuan dynasty
Photograph © The Inner Mongolia Museum and Inner Mongolia University, China

PAGE 214
Fig. 27.9 Detail from *Kublai Khan Hunting*
Painted hanging scroll by Liu Guandao, ca. 1280
Ink and colors on silk; 182.9 cm; Yuan dynasty
Courtesy of the National Palace Museum, Taiwan

PAGE 215
Fig. 27.10 *Kublai Khan dining*
Manuscript detail from Marco Polo's *Le Livre des Merveilles du Monde* (Travels of Marco Polo), ca. 1412
Courtesy Bibliothèque nationale de France, Paris
Ms. fr. 2810, fol. 39 r.

PAGE 216
Fig. 27.11 Two men playing *shuanglu* (backgammon)
Wood block illustration in the *Shilin guangji*; Yuan dynasty
After Li 2002: 74.

PAGE 217
Fig. 28.1 Title Page of a Spanish version of the *Book of Marco Polo*, ca. 1503
Image © The Granger Collection, New York
ID: 0037175

PAGE 218
Fig. 28.2 Interior of Sainte-Chapelle, Paris

Photograph © Scala / Art Resource, New York

PAGE 219
Fig. 28.3 *Arghun in his Garden*
Manuscript illustration from *Jami' al-Tavarikh* (Compendium of Chronicles) by Rashid al-Din, ca. 1430-34
Courtesy Bibliothèque nationale de France, Paris
Persian supplement 1113, folio 204v

Page 220
Fig. 29.1 Qutb Minaret
Delhi, India
Photograph © Gordon Wiltsie
DL 1505H

PAGE 221
Fig. 29.2 Map of the travels of Ibn Battuta
Prepared by Marcia Bakry, SI/NMNH
After Abercrombie 1991: 12–13.
Map courtesy of SI/NMNH

PAGE 222
Fig. 30.1 Jar with phoenix and peony pattern
Stoneware; 22 cm; Yuan dynasty
Northern China
Photograph © The Inner Mongolia Museum and Inner Mongolia University, China

PAGE 224
Fig. 30.2 Gold hairpins
Gold; 15.5 cm; Yuan dynasty
Photograph © The Inner Mongolia Museum and Inner Mongolia University, China

Fig. 30.3 Camel-bone belt
Bone; 120 cm; Yuan dynasty
Photograph © The Inner Mongolia Museum and Inner Mongolia University, China

PAGE 225
Fig. 30.4 Robe made of gold brocade
Gold and silk brocade; 246 cm; 13th c.
Mingshui, Inner Mongolia, China
Photograph © The Inner Mongolia Museum and Inner Mongolia University, China

PAGE 226
Fig. 30.5 Chemise with an embroidered robe
Silk; 107 cm; Yuan dynasty
Inner Mongolia, China
Photograph © The Inner Mongolia Museum and Inner Mongolia University, China

PAGE 227
Fig. 30.6 Raft cup
Work of Zhu Bishan, ca. 1345
Hammer silver; 20.5 cm
Chabei, Guangdong, China

PAGE 228
Fig. 30.7 Longquan celadon vase
Celadon glaze; Yuan dynasty
Longquan kilns, Southern China
Photograph © The Inner Mongolia

Museum and Inner Mongolia University, China

Fig. 30.8 Blue-and-white dish
Underglaze painted porcelain; 46.5 cm diam.; 14th c.
Jingdeshen kilns, Northern China
Courtesy of the Topkapi Palace Museum, Istanbul
TSM 15/1420

PAGE 229
Fig. 30.9 Blue-and-white *yuhuchun* vase
Porcelain; 18 cm; Yuan dynasty
Photograph © The Inner Mongolia Museum and Inner Mongolia University, China

PAGE 230
Fig. 30.10 *Portrait of Ni Zan*
Ink and color on paper; ca. 1340
Courtesy of the National Palace Museum, Taiwan

PAGE 231
Fig. 30.11 *Autumn Colors on the Ch'iao and Hua Mountains*
Painted handscroll by Zhao Mengfu, ca. 1296
Ink and color on paper; 90.2 cm; Yuan dynasty
Courtesy of the National Palace Museum, Taiwan

PAGE 232
Fig. 31.1 *The Simurgh*
Manuscript illustration from *Manafi'-i hayavan* (On the Usefulness of Animals), ca. 1297-1300
Copied at Maragheh, Iran
Courtesy of The Pierpont Morgan Library, New York
MS M. 500, fol. 55 recto.

PAGE 234
Fig. 31.2 Hexagonal tile with phoenix
Underglaze painted fritware; ca. 1270
Takht-i Sulaiman, Iran
Courtesy of Bildarchiv Preussischer Kulturbesitz / Art Resource, New York
I.1988.10

PAGE 235
Fig. 31.3 Bowl with phoenixes in flight
Sultanabad ware; 14th c.; Iran
Photograph by Herve Lewandowski; collection of the Musée du Louvre
Courtesy of the Réunion des Musées Nationaux / Art Resource, New York
8177

PAGE 236
Fig. 31.4 Bowl with three fishes
Fritware painted under a transparent glaze; 26.6 cm diam.; 14th c.
Ilkhanate period; Iran
Courtesy of The Metropolitan Museum of Art, H.O. Havenmeyer Collection
Gift of Mrs. Horace Havenmeyer, in memory of her husband, Horace Havemeyer, 1959
Image © The Metropolitan Museum of Art, New York
59.60

PAGE 237
Fig. 31.5 *Bahram Meeting Zal*
Manuscript illustration from the Great Mongol *Shahnama* (Book of Kings), ca. 1335-40
Ilkhanate period; Iran
Photograph by Yves Siza
Image © Musée d'art et d'histoire (Cabinet des dessins), Collection Pozzi, Geneva
Inv. no. 1971-107/2

PAGE 238
Fig. 32.1 *Portrait of An Hyang*
Silk scroll; 84 cm; copy of a 13th–14th c. original
Courtesy of the National Museum of Korea
tŏksu 3968

PAGE 240
Fig. 32.2 Map of the Mongol Invasion of Korea, 1231-6
Prepared by Marcia Bakry, SI/NMNH
Map courtesy of SI/NMNH

PAGE 241
Fig. 32.3 Celadon bottle
Stoneware, black and white inlays; 35.6 cm; 13th c.
Goryeo period; Korea
Gift of Charles Lang Freer
Courtesy of the Freer Gallery of Art, Smithsonian Institution, Washington, DC
F1907.76

PAGE 242
Fig. 32.4 *Gyeongcheonsa Pagoda*
Marble; 1350 cm; ca. 1348
Goryeo period, Korea
National Treasure of Korea no. 86
Courtesy of the National Museum of Korea
pongwan 6753

PAGE 243
Fig. 32.5 Hanging scroll depicting *Avalokiteshvara*
Ink, color and gold on silk; 98.4 cm; 14th c.
Goryeo period; Korea
Gift of Charles Lang Freer
Courtesy of the Freer Gallery of Art, Smithsonian Institution, Washington, DC
F1904.13

PAGE 244
Detail from *Mōko Shūrai ekotoba* (Mongol Invasion Scroll)
Handscroll; 23 m; ca. 1291
Kyushu Island, Japan
Courtesy of the *Sannomaru Shozokan* (Museum of Imperial Collections), Tokyo

PAGE 246
Fig. 33.1 Map of Yuan-led Invasions of Japan in 1274 and 1281
Prepared by Marcia Bakry, SI/NMNH
Map courtesy of SI/NMNH

PAGE 247
Fig. 33.2 Detail from *Mōko Shūrai ekotoba* (Mongol Invasion Scroll)

Handscroll; 23 m; ca. 1291
Kyushu Island, Japan
Courtesy of the *Sannomaru Shozokan* (Museum of Imperial Collections), Tokyo

PAGE 248
Fig. 33.3 Bronze seal
Bronze; 4.4 cm; ca. 1277
Kozaki Harbor, Takashima Island, Japan
Courtesy of the Matsuura Board of Education, Nagasaki prefecture, Japan

Fig. 33.4 Reconstructed defensive wall
Hakata Bay, Fukuoka prefecture, Japan
Photograph by Randall Sasaki
Courtesy of Fukuoka City Board of Education, Fukuoka prefecture, Japan

PAGE 249
Fig. 33.5 Statue of *Amitabha Tathagata*
Bronze, Goryeo period style; 77 cm; 10th–13th c.
Takashima Island, Nagasaki prefecture, Japan
Photograph by Randall Sasaki
Courtesy of the Matsuura Board of Education, Nagasaki prefecture, Japan

PAGE 250
Fig. 33.6 Bundle of arrows
Wood, iron; 30 cm
Kozaki Harbor, Takashima Island, Japan
Photograph by Randall Sasaki
Courtesy of the Matsuura Board of Education, Nagasaki prefecture, Japan

Fig. 33.7 Windlass reel and drawing
Wood; 176 cm
Takashima Island, Nagasaki prefecture, Japan
Courtesy of the Matsuura Board of Education, Nagasaki prefecture, Japan

PAGE 251
Fig. 33.8 Bowl from South China
Porcelain; 14.8 cm diam.
Takashima Island, Nagasaki prefecture, Japan
Photograph by Randall Sasaki
Courtesy of the Matsuura Board of Education, Nagasaki prefecture, Japan

Fig. 33.9 Goryeo bowl
Longquan kiln celadon porcelain; 17.4 cm diam.
Takashima Island, Nagasaki prefecture, Japan
Photograph by Randall Sasaki
Courtesy of the Matsuura Board of Education, Nagasaki prefecture, Japan

PAGE 252
Fig. 33.10 Detail from *Mōko Shūrai ekotoba* (Mongol Invasion Scroll)
Painted handscroll; 23 m; ca. 1291
Kyushu Island, Japan
Courtesy of the *Sannomaru Shozokan* (Museum of Imperial Collections), Tokyo

Fig. 33.11 *Tetsuhau* bombs
Ceramic; avg. 15 cm diam.

Kozaki Harbor, Takashima Island, Japan
Photograph by Randall Sasaki
Courtesy of the Matsuura Board of Education, Nagasaki prefecture, Japan

PAGE 253
Fig. 33.12 Drawing of anchors as found on the seabed in Kozaki Harbor
Courtesy of the Matsuura Board of Education, Nagasaki prefecture, Japan

PAGE 254
Fig. 34.1 GPS surveying in Mongolia
Khovsgol province, Mongolia
Photograph by Bruno Frohlich, SI/NMNH

PAGE 256
Fig. 34.2 Hets Mountain cave mummies
Southern Gobi Desert, Mongolia
Photograph by Bruno Frohlich, SI/NMNH

Fig. 34.3 Mongolian female
Southern Gobi Desert, Mongolia
Photograph by Bruno Frohlich, SI/NMNH

PAGE 257
Fig. 34.4 CT scan of female vertebrae
Image by Bruno Frohlich, SI/NMNH

Fig. 34.5 Siemens Somatom CT (CAT) scanner
Photograph by Bruno Frohlich, SI/NMNH

PAGE 258
Fig. 34.6 Reconstructive imaging of brain case
Image by Bruno Frohlich, SI/NMNH

PAGE 259
Fig. 35.1 Beaded necklace and pouch
Glass, corral, seeds, silk; 57 cm; 14th c.
Tsagaan Khanan cave, Umnugobi province, Mongolia
Courtesy of the Institute of Archaeology of the Mongolian Academy of Sciences
M-025 and M-031

Fig. 35.2 Wooden casket*
1.7 m; 13th–14th c.
Artsat Del mountain, Bayankhongor province, Mongolia
Courtesy of the Dornogobi Province Museum, Mongolia

PAGE 260
Fig. 35.3 Illustration of medieval horse trappings
Drawing by O. Angaragsuren
Courtesy of the Institute of Archaeology of the Mongolian Academy of Sciences

Fig. 35.4 Red silk *deel* (robe)*
Silk; 158 cm; 13th–14th c.
Nartiin Khad, Dornogobi province, Mongolia
Photograph by Ulambayar Erdenebat
Courtesy of the Dornogobi Province Museum, Mongolia

Works Cited

Abercrombie, Thomas J.
1991
"Ibn Battuta: Prince of Travelers." Photographs by James L. Stanfield. *National Geographic* 180, no. 6: 3–49.

Abramowski, Waltraut.
1976
"Die chinesischen Annalen von Ögedei und Güyük: Übersetzung des 2. Kapitels des *Yüan-shih*." (Chinese records on Ögödei and Güyüg: Translation of chapter 2 of the *Yuanshi*). *Zentralasiatische Studien* 10: 117–67.

1979
"Die chinesischen Annalen des Möngke: Übersetzung des 3. Kapitels des *Yüan-shih*" (Chinese records on Möngke: Translation of chapter 3 of the *Yuanshi*). *Zentralasiatische Studien* 13: 7–71.

Achenbach, Joel.
1995
"The Era of His Ways: In Which We Choose the Most Important Man of the Last Thousand Years." *The Washington Post*, 31 Dec., F01.

Addis, Sir John.
1980–81
"Porcelain-stone and Kaolin: Late Yuan Developments at Hutian." *Bulletin of the Oriental Ceramic Society* 45: 54–66.

Aisin-Gioro, Ulhicun.
2006
"The Stone-Carved Jurchen Inscriptions on the Nine Peaks Cliff of Mongolia." In *Research on Inscriptions of Jin Dynasty in Mongolia. Report of the Scientific Research Project Grant-in-Aid JSPS*, ed. Noriyuki Shiraishi. Niigata: Niigata University.

Alexander, David.
1992
The Arts of War: Arms and Armour of the 7th to 19th Centuries. Vol. 21 of *The Nasser D. Khalili Collection of Islamic Art.* London: Nour Foundation in association with Azimuth Editions and Oxford University Press.

Allan, J. W.
1971
Medieval Middle Eastern Pottery. Oxford: Ashmolean Museum.

Allard, Francis, and Diimaajav Erdenebaatar.
2005
"Khirigsuurs, Ritual and Mobility in the Bronze Age of Mongolia." *Antiquity* 79, no. 305: 547–63.

Allsen, Thomas T.
1987
Mongol Imperialism: The Policies of the Grand Qan Möngke in China, Russia, and the Islamic Lands, 1251–1259. Berkeley: University of California Press.

1989
"Mongolian Princes and Their Merchant Partners, 1200–1260." *Asia Major* 2: 83–126.

1994
"The Rise of the Mongolian Empire and Mongolian Rule in North China." In *Alien Regimes and Border States, 907–1368*, vol. 6 of *The Cambridge History of China*, ed. Herbert Franke and Denis Twitchett. Cambridge; New York: Cambridge University Press.

1997
Commodity and Exchange in the Mongol Empire: A Cultural History of Islamic Textiles. Cambridge; New York: Cambridge University Press.

2001
Culture and Conquest in Mongol Eurasia. Cambridge; New York: Cambridge University Press.

2002
"The Circulation of Military Technology in the Mongolian Empire." In *Warfare in Inner Asian History, 500–1800*, ed. Nicola Di Cosmo, vol. 6 of *Handbook of Oriental Studies*, section 8: *Central Asia*. Leiden: Brill.

2006
The Royal Hunt in Eurasian History. Philadelphia: University of Pennsylvania Press.

Amitai, Reuven.
2005
"The Resolution of the Mongol-Mamluk War." In *Mongols, Turks and Others: Eurasian Nomads and the Sedentary World*, ed. R. Amitai and Michal Biran. Vol. 11 of *Brill's Inner Asia Library.* Leiden; Boston: Brill.

Anonymous
2003
"Walk this way to Wok 'N' South." *Ventura County Star* (March 6), 47.

Arlington, L. C., and William Lewisohn.
1935
In Search of Old Peking. Peking: Henri Vetch.

Atwood, Christopher Pratt.
2004
Encyclopedia of Mongolia and the Mongol Empire. New York: Facts on File Library of World History.

Ayalon, David.
1971–73
"The Great Yasa of Chingiz Khan: A Reexamination." *Studia Islamica* 33: 97–140; 34: 151–80; 36: 113–58; 38: 107–56.

Bade, David W.
2002
Khubilai Khan and the Beautiful Princess of Tumapel: The Mongols between History and Literature in Java. Ulaan Baatar: A. Chuluunbat.

Baljinnyam, B., and Nagaanbuu, N.
2007
Ih Mongol Uls 800 (The great Mongolian state [at] 800). Ulaan Baatar: ADMON.

Banzarov, Dorji [Dorzhi].
1891
Chernaya Vera ili Shamanstvo u Mongolov I Drugiye Stat'I Dorji Banzarova (Black beliefs or shamanism of the Mongols and other articles by Dorji Banzarov). Ed. G. N. Potanin. St. Petersburg: Press of the Imperial Academy of Sciences.

1991–92
Black Belief, or Shamanism among the Mongols and Other Articles.

Trans. Jan Nattier, and John R. Kreuger. *Mongolian Studies*, Journal of the Mongolia Society 7: 53–91.

Bar Hebraeus (1236–1286).
1932
The Chronography of Gregory Abu'l Faraj, the Son of Aaron, the Hebrew Physician, commonly known as Bar Hebraeus: Being the First Part of His Political History of the World, Translated from the Syriac by Ernest A. Wallis Budge, ed. and trans. Ernest A. Wallis Budge. 2 vols. London: Oxford University Press; H. Milford.

Barfield, Thomas.
1981
"The Hsiung-nu Imperial Confederacy: Organization and Foreign Policy." *Journal of Asian Studies* 41: 45–61.

2001
"Steppe Empires, China, and the Silk Route: Nomads as a Force in International Trade and Politics." In *Nomads in the Sedentary World*, ed. Anatoly Khazanov and André Wink. London: Curzon Press.

Barkmann, Udo B.
2002
"Qara Qorum [Karakorum]: Fragmente zur Geschichte einer vergessenen Reichshauptstadt" (Karakorum: fragments of history from a forgotten imperial capital). In *Qara Qorum-City (Mongolia) I. Preliminary report of the excavations 2000–2001*, eds. Helmut R. Roth and Ulambaja [Ulambayar] Erdenebat; co-ed. Ernst Pohl and Eva Nagel. Vol. 1 of *Bonn Contributions to Asian Archaeology.* 2nd rev. and enl. ed. Bonn: Institute of Pre- and Early Historical Archaeology.

Batten, Bruce L.
2006
Gateway to Japan: Hakata in War and Peace, 500–1300. Honolulu: University of Hawai'i Press.

Bawden, Charles R.
1968
The Modern History of Mongolia. New York: Praeger.

1989
The Modern History of Mongolia. London: Kegan Paul International.

Bazarsad, N., B. Frohlich, N. Batbold, and D. Hunt.
2005
"Fourteenth Century Mummified Human Remains from the Gobi Desert, Mongolia." In *The Deer Stone Project: Anthropological Studies in Mongolia 2002–2004*, eds. William W. Fitzhugh, Jamsranjav Bayarsaikhan, and Peter K. Marsh. Washington, DC: Arctic Studies Center, National Museum of Natural History, Smithsonian Institution; Ulaan Bataar: National Museum of Mongolian History.

Beckingham, Charles F.
1977
"In Search of Ibn Battuta." *Asian Affairs* 8: 263–77.
1993
"The *Rihla*: Fact or Fiction?." In *Golden Roads: Migration, Pilgrimage and Travel in Mediaeval and Modern Islam*, ed. I. R. Netton. Richmond, UK: Curzon Press.

Bemmann, Jan, and Ernst Pohl, eds.
2009
"KAR 2 – Excavations in the Chinese Craftsmen-Quarter at the Main Road." In *Mongolisch-Deutsche Karakorum-Expedition (MDKE)* 1. *Forschungen zur Archäologie Aussereuropäischer Kulturen* (Research on the archaeology of non-European cultures) 8. Wiesbaden: Reichert.

Bemmann, Jan, Hermann Parzinger, Ernst Pohl, and Damdinsuren Tseveendorj, eds.
2009
Current Archaeological Research in Mongolia. Papers from the First International Conference on "Archaeological Research in Mongolia" held in Ulaanbaatar, August 2007. Bonn Contributions to Asian Archaeology 4.

Berger, Patricia Ann, and Terese Tse Bartholomew.
1995
Mongolia: The Legacy of Chinggis Khan. London: Thames and Hudson in association with the Asian Art Museum of San Francisco.

Bergholz, Fred.
1993
The Partition of the Steppe: The Struggle of the Russians, Manchus and the Zunghar Mongols for Empire in Central Asia, 1619–1758. New York: Peter Lang.

Bira, Sh[agdaryn].
1999
"Qubilai Qa'an and 'Phags-Pa bLama." In *The Mongol Empire and Its Legacy*, ed. Reuven Amitai-Preiss and David Morgan. Leiden: Brill.
2004
"Mongolian Tenggerism and Modern Globalism: A Retrospective Outlook on Globalisation." Lecture delivered to the Royal Asiatic Society, London, 10 October 2002 on the occasion of his receiving the Denis Sinor Medal, and published in *Journal of the Royal Asiatic Society* series 3, 14, no. 1: 3–12.
2006
Some Problems of the History of Mongolian Statehood. Ulaan Baatar: Interpress.

Biran, Michal.
1997
Qaidu and the Rise of the Independent Mongol State in Central Asia. Richmond, UK: Curzon.
2005
The Empire of the Qara Khitai in Eurasian History: Between China and the Islamic World. Cambridge: Cambridge University Press.

Blair, Sheila, and Jonathan Bloom.
2000
"Decorative Arts." In *Islam: Art and Architecture*, ed. Markus Hattstein and Peter Delius. Cologne: Könemann.

Blockley, R. C., trans.
1985
see Menander.

Blokhin, V. G., and L. V. Yavorskaya.
2006
Arkheologiya zolotoordynskikh gorodov Nizhnego Povolzh'ya (Archaeology of the Golden Horde cities of Nizhnee Povolzh'e: The Lower Volga region). Volgograd: Volgograd State University Press.

Boldbaatar, Jigjidiin, and David Sneath.
2006
"Ordering Subjects: Mongolian Civil and Military Administration," In *Imperial Statecraft: Political Forms and Techniques of Governance in Inner Asia 6th – 20th Centuries*, ed. David Sneath. Bellingham, WA: Western Washington University.

Bosworth, C. E.
1968
"The Political and Dynastic History of the Iranian World (A.D. 1000–1217)." In *The Saljuq and Mongol Periods*, vol. 5 of *The Cambridge History of Iran*, ed. J[ohn] A. Boyle. Cambridge: Cambridge University Press.

Boyle, John A.
1971
Successors of Genghis Khan. New York: Columbia University Press.

Boyle, John A., trans.
1958
see Juvaini.

Brantingham, Jeffrey, Andrei Krivoshapkin, Li Jinzeng, and Ya. Tserendagva.
2001
"The Initial Upper Paleolithic in Northeast Asia." *Current Anthropology* 42 (5): 735–46.

Brend, Barbara.
1991
Islamic Art. London: British Museum Press.

Brigham-Grette, J., and S. A. Elias.
2001
"David M. Hopkins: An Inspiration to Multidisciplinary Science" [Beringian Paleoenvironments: Festschrift in Honour of D. M. Hopkins]. *Quaternary Science Reviews* 20 (1–3): 1–3.

Brose, Michael C.
2005
"Uyghur Technologists of Writing and Literacy in Mongol China." *T'oung Pao* 91: 4–5; 396–435.
2007
Subjects and Masters: Uyghurs in the Mongol Empire. Bellingham, WA: Center for East Asian Studies, Western Washington University.

Bruun, Ole, and Ole Odgaard.
1996
"A Society and Economy in Transition." In *Mongolia in Transition: New Patterns, New Challenges*, ed. Ole Bruun and Ole Odgaard. Nordic Institute of Asian Studies, *Studies in Asian Topics*, no. 22. Richmond, UK: Curzon Press.

Budge, Ernest. A. Wallis, trans.
1932
see Bar Hebraeus.

Buell, Paul D.
1979a
"Sino-Khitan Administration in Mongol Bukhara." *Journal of Asian History* 13: 121–51.
1979b
"The Role of the Sino-Mongolian Frontier Zone in the Rise of Cinggis Qan." In *Studies on Mongolia: Proceedings of the First North American Conference on Mongolian studies*, ed. Henry G. Schwarz. Bellingham, WA: Western Washington University.
1980
"Kalmyk Tanggaci People: Thoughts on the Mechanics and Impact of Mongol Expansion." *Mongolian Studies* 6: 41–59.
1993
"Sübötei Ba'atur." In *In the Service of the Khan: Eminent Personalities of the Early Mongol–Yüan Period (1200–1300)*, ed. Igor de Rachewiltz, Hok-lam Chan, Hsiao Ch'i-ch'ing, and Peter W. Geier. Wiesbaden: Otto Harrassowitz Verlag.
2003
Historical Dictionary of the Mongol World Empire. No. 8 of *Historical Dictionaries of Ancient Civilizations and Historical Eras.* Lanham, MD: The Scarecrow Press.

Bulag, Uradyn.
2002
The Mongols at China's Edge: History and the Politics of National Unity. World Social Change series. Lanham, MD: Rowman and Littlefield Publishers.

Bullis, Douglas.
2000
"The Longest Hajj: The Journeys of Ibn Battuta." *Saudi Aramco World* 51, no. 4: 3–39.

Buyandelger, Manduhai.
1999
"Who Makes the Shaman?: The Politics of Shamanic Practices among the Buriats of Mongolia." *Inner Asia* 1: 121–44.
2004
"Between Hearth and Celestial Court: Gender, Marginality, and the Politics of Shamanic Practices among the Buryats of Mongolia." Ph.D. diss. Harvard University.
2007
"Dealing with Uncertainty: Shamans, Marginal Capitalism, and the Remaking of History in Post-socialist Mongolia." *American Ethnologist* 34, no. 1: 127–47.

Caldwell, Taylor.
1975
The Earth Is the Lord's: A Tale of the Rise of Genghis Khan. New York: Amereon Ltd.

Campi, Alicia.
2006
"The Rise of Cities in Nomadic Mongolia." In *Mongolians from Country to City: Floating Boundaries, Pastoralism and City Life in the Mongol Lands*, ed. Ole Bruun and Li Narangoa. Honolulu: University of Hawai'i Press.

Chambers, James.
1979
The Devil's Horsemen: The Mongol Invasion of Europe. London: Atheneum.

Chaucer, Geoffrey.
1993
"The Squire's Tale." In *The Canterbury Tales*, trans. Ronald L. Ecker and Eugene J. Cook. Palatka, FL: Hodge & Braddock.

Chan Hok-lam.
1967
"Liu Ping-chung (1216–1274): A Buddhist-Taoist Statesman at the Court of Khubilai Khan." *T'oung Pao* 53: 98–146.

Chen Bingying.
1985
Xixia wenwu yanjiu (Studies of Xixia archaeology). Yinchuan: Ningxia renmin chubanshe.

Ch'en, Paul Heng-chao.
1979
Chinese Legal Tradition under the Mongols. Princeton: Princeton University Press.

Christian, David.
2000
"Silk Roads or Steppe Roads?: The Silk Roads in World History." *Journal of World History* 11 (1): 1–26.

Chuluuntsetseg, Ch.
2005
"L. Erdenebulgan: It is Clear that a Great State Has Created the Memorial Complex for a Particular Reason." *Udriin Sonin*, no. 098, 22 Apr.

Cleaves, Francis Woodman.
1952
"The Sino–Mongolian Inscription of 1346." *Harvard Journal of Asiatic Studies* 15: 1–123.
1955
"The Historicity of the Baljuna Covenant." *Harvard Journal of Asiatic Studies* 18, no. 2: 357–421.

1982
The Secret History of the Mongols: For the First Time Done into English out of the Original Tongue and Provided with an Exegetical Commentary. Cambridge, MA; London: Harvard University Press for the Harvard-Yenching Institute.

Conlan, Thomas.
2001
In Little Need of Divine Intervention: Takezaki Suenaga's Scrolls of the Mongol Invasions of Japan. Trans., and with an interpretive essay. Ithaca: NY: Cornell University Press.

Cook, Edward R., and Leonidas Kairiukstis, eds.
1990
Methods of Dendrochronology: Application in the Environmental Sciences. Dordrecht: Kluwer Academic Publishers.

Coppens, Y., D. Tseveendorj, F. Demeter, Ts. Turbat, and P. Giscard.
2008
"Discovery of an Archaic Homo Sapiens Skullcap in Northeast Mongolia." *Comptes Rendus Palevol* 7: 51–60.

Cordier, Henri.
1893
"Situation de Ho-lin en Tartarie. Manuscrit inédit du Père A.Gaubil, S.J., publié avec une introduction et des notes. (The location of Ho-lin in Tartary. From an unpublished manuscript of Jesuit priest A. Gaubil, published with an introduction and notes)." *T'oung Pao* 4 : 33–80.

Crossley, Pamela Kyle.
2006
"Making Mongols." In *Empire at the Margins: Culture, Ethnicity, and Frontier in Early Modern China,* ed. Pamela Kyle Crossley, Helen F. Siu, and Donald S. Sutton. Berkeley: University of California Press.

Crubezy, E., F. Ricaut, H. Martin, D. Erdenebaatar, H. Coqueugnot, B. Maureille, and P. Giscard.
2006
"Inhumation and Cremation in Medieval Mongolia: Analysis and Analogy." *Antiquity* 80: 894–905.

Crump, James I.
1980
Chinese Theater in the Days of Kublai Khan. Tucson: University of Arizona Press.

Curtin, Jeremiah.
1908
The Mongols: A History. Boston: Little, Brown and Company.

Dars, Sarah.
1972
"L'Architecture Mongole Ancienne" (Early Mongolian architecture). *Etudes Mongoles* 3: 162–223.

Dashbadrakh, Dorjgotov.
2004
Manjiin turuus Mongolyn shashny talaar yavuulsan bodlogo, ur dagavar (Manchu State Policies Regarding Religion in Mongolia and their Conse-

quences). Ulaan Baatar: Institute of History, Mongolian Academy of Sciences.

Dashdorj, D., and S. Tsoodol.
1971
Ardyn duu khögjmiin suu bilegtnüüd (The geniuses of folk song and music). Ulaan Baatar: State Publishing House.

Davi, Nicole K., Gordon C. Jacoby, Ashley E. Curtis, and Nachin Baatarbileg.
2006
"Extension of Drought Records for Central Asia Using Tree Rings: West Central Mongolia." *Journal of Climate* 19: 288–99.

Davidson, Ronald M.
2005
Tibetan Renaissance: Tantric Buddhism in the Rebirth of Tibetan Culture. New York: Columbia University Press.

Davydova, A. V.
1995
Ivolginskii Arkheologicheskii Kompleks: Ivolginskoe Gorodishche. (The Ivolga archaeological complex: Ivolga fortress). St. Petersburg: AziatIKA.

Dawson, Christopher, ed.
1955/1980
The Mongol Mission: Narratives and Letters of the Franciscan Missionaries in Mongolia and China in the Thirteenth and Fourteenth Centuries. Translated by a nun of Stanbrook Abbey. London; New York 1955: Sheed and Ward; reprinted 1980 as: *Mission to Asia: Narratives.* In the series Medieval Academy Reprints for Teaching. Toronto; Buffalo: University of Toronto Press in association with the Medieval Academy of America.

1980
The Mongol Mission. Reprint, New York: AMS Press.

De Rachewiltz, Igor.
1971
Papal Envoys to the Great Khans. London: Faber and Faber Ltd. Stanford, CA: Stanford University Press.

1983
"Turks in China under the Mongols: A Preliminary Investigation of Turco-Mongol Relations in the 13th and 14th Centuries." In *China among Equals,* ed. Morris Rossabi. Berkeley: University of California Press.

1993
"Some Reflections on Činggis Qan's Jasagh." *East Asian History* 6: 91–104.

De Rachewiltz, Igor, trans.
2004
Yuan chao bi shih, The Secret History of the Mongols: A Mongolian Epic Chronicle of the Thirteenth Century. Historical and philological commentary by Igor de Rachewiltz. 2 vols. *Brill's Inner Asian Library,* vol. 7. Leiden: Brill.

Delgado, James P.
2003
"Relics of the Kamikaze." *Archaeology Magazine* 56, no. 1: 36–42.

Derevianko, Anatoly.
1994

"Central and Northern Asia During the Neolithic." In *History of Humanity: Prehistory and the Beginnings of Civilization,* ed. S. J. De Laet, vol 1. Paris: UNESCO Publishing.

Derevianko, A[natoly], and D. Dorj.
1992
"Neolithic Tribes in Northern Parts of Central Asia." In *History of Civilization of Central Asia: The Dawn of Civilization, Earliest times to 700 BC,* ed. A. H. Dani and V. M. Masson. Paris: UNESCO Publishing.

Di Cosmo, Nicola.
1994
"Ancient Inner Asian Nomads: Their Economic Basis and its Significance in Chinese History." *Journal of Asian Studies* 53: 1092–1126.

2002
Ancient China and Its Enemies: The Rise of Nomadic Power in East Asia History. Cambridge: Cambridge University Press.

2006
"The Origins of the Great Wall." *The Silk Road* 4: 14–19.

———, ed.
2009
Military Culture in Imperial China. Cambridge, MA: Harvard University Press.

Dien, Albert.
1991
"A New Look at the Xianbei and Their Impact on Chinese Culture." In *Ancient Mortuary Traditions of China: Papers on Chinese Ceramic Funerary Sculptures,* ed. George Kuwayama. Los Angeles: Los Angeles County Museum of Art.

Dion, Frederic.
2003
The Blue Wolf: The Epic Tale of the Life of Genghis Khan and the Empire of the Steppes. New York: Thomas Dunne Books.

Dobrovits, Mihály.
2005
"The Great Western Campaign of the Eastern Turks (711–14)." *Acta Orientalia Academiae Scientiarum Hungaricae* 58, no. 1: 179–85.

Drompp, Michael R.
2005
"Imperial State Formation in Inner Asia: The Early Turkic Empires (6th to 9th Centuries)." *Acta Orientalia Academiae Scientiarum Hungaricae* 58, no. 1: 101–11.

Dunn, Ross E.
1993
"Migrations of Literate Muslims in the Middle Periods: The Case of Ibn Battuta." In *Golden Roads: Migration, Pilgrimage and Travel in Mediaeval and Modern Islam,* ed. I. R. Netton. Richmond, UK: Curzon Press.

2001
"Ibn Battuta and Muslim Cosmopolitanism in the Fourteenth Century." *Hadeeth ad-Dar* (Dar al-Athar al-Islamiyyah, Ministry of Information, Kuwait) 12: 10–13.

2005
The Adventures of Ibn Battuta, a Muslim Traveler of the Fourteenth Century. Rev. ed. Berkeley: University of California Press.

Dunnell, Ruth.
1991
"The Fall of Xia: Sino-Steppe Relations in the Late 12th–Early 13th Centuries." In *Rulers from the Steppe: State Formation on the Eurasian Periphery,* vol. 2, ed. Gary Seaman and Daniel Marks. Los Angeles: University of Southern California Ethnographics Press.

1992
"The Hsia Origins of the Yüan Institution of Imperial Preceptor." *Asia Major,* 3rd ser., 5 (1): 85–111.

1994
"Hsi-Hsia." In *The Cambridge History of China,* vol. 6, ed. Denis C. Twitchett and Herbert Franke. Cambridge: Cambridge University Press.

1996
The Great State of White and High: Buddhism and State Formation in Eleventh-Century Xia. Honolulu: University of Hawai'i Press.

Dupuy, Trevor N.
1980
The Evolution of Weapons and Warfare. Indianapolis: Bobbs-Merrill.

Eckert, Carter, et al.
1990
Korea Old and New: A History. Seoul: Ilchokak, for the Korea Institute, Harvard University, and Harvard University Press.

Edwards, Mike.
1996
"Genghis: Lord of the Mongols." *National Geographic* 190, no. 6: 2–37.

Egorov, V. L.
1985
Istoricheskaya geografiya Zolotoi Ordy v XIII–XIV vv. (Historical geography of the Golden Horde in the thirteenth and fourteenth centuries). Moscow: Nauka (Akademiia nauk SSSR) Publishers.

Elbegdorj, Tsakhiag.
2008
"Excerpts from the Public Greeting by the Democratic Party Leader, Tsahiagiyn Elbegdorj, made on 1 January 2008." *Shine Erkh Chuluu,* January, No. 1/06.

Elman, Benjamin.
2000
A Cultural History of Civil Examinations in Imperial China. Berkeley: University of California Press.

Elverskog, Johan.
2006
Our Great Qing: The Mongols, Buddhism and the State in Late Imperial China. Honolulu: University of Hawai'i Press.

2006
"The Legend of Mount Muna." *Inner Asia* 8, no. 1: 99–122.

Emsheimer, Ernst.
1991
"Earliest Reports about the Music of

the Mongols." In *Studia Ethnomusicologica Eurasiatica (Festschrift to Ernst Emsheimer on the occasion of his 80th birthday)*, vol. II. Stockholm: Musikhistoriska Museet.

Endicott, E.
2005
"The Mongols and China: Cultural Contacts and the Changing Nature of Pastoral Nomadism (Twelfth to early twentieth centuries)." In *Mongols, Turks and Others: Eurasian Nomads and the Sedentary World*, ed. Reuven Amitai and M. Biran. Leiden; Boston: Brill.

Enkhtuvshin, B. , and B. Ochir.
2006
Genghis Khan Encyclopedia. Sciences of Mongolia series. Ulaan Baatar: Sogoo.

Erdenebat, Ulambayar.
2001
"Mongol orny agujn archeologijn sudalgaany uchir kholbogdol (A rationale for cave archaeological research in Mongolia)." *Studia Museologica* 4, no. 3: 8–24.

Erdenebat, Ulambayar, and D. Bayar.
2004
"Eine mittelalterliche Felshoehlenbestattung aus der suedlichen Mongolei (A medieval cave burial from southern Mongolia)." *Beitraege zur Allgemeinen und Vergleichenden Archaeologie* (Contributions to general and comparative archaeology) 24: 45–66.

Erdenebat, Ulambayar, and Ernst Pohl.
2005a
"Aus der Mitte der Hauptstadt: Die Ausgrabungen der Universität Bonn im Zentrum von Karakorum (From the middle of the capital: excavations of Bonn University in the center of Karakorum)." In *Dschingis Khan und seine Erben: Das Weltreich der Mongolen* (Genghis Khan and his heirs: The empire of the Mongols), ed. Claudius C. Müller and Henriette Pleiger. Bonn; Munich: Kunst und Ausstellungshalle der Bundesrepublik Deutschland & Staatliches Museum für Völkerkunde München.
2005b
"Felsspalten- und Hoehlenbestattungen in der Mongolei (Rock crevice and cave burials in Mongolia)." In *Dschingis Khan und seine Erben: Das Weltreich der Mongolen* (Genghis Khan and his heirs: The empire of the Mongols), ed. Claudius C. Müller and Henriette Pleiger. Bonn; Munich: Kunst und Ausstellungshalle der Bundesrepublik Deutschland & Staatliches Museum für Völkerkunde München.

Erdenebat, Ulambayar, and S. Khurelsukh.
2007
"Nartyn khadny orshuulga (A rock shelter burial at the Nartyn site)." *Studia Archaeologica* 24, no. 23: 332–59.

Erdenebaatar, Diimaajav.
2004
"Burial Materials Related to the History of the Bronze Age on the Ter-

ritory of Mongolia." In *Metallurgy in Ancient Eastern Eurasia from the Urals to the Yellow River*, ed. K. M. Linduff. Lewiston, NY: Edwin Mellen Press.

Erdenetuya, Urtnasun.
2002
"Ovoo üüdekhiin zan üil selt orshiv sudryn tukhai (Regarding a sutra for the establishment of a new *ovoo*)." *Ugsaatny Sudlal (Ethnology)* 14 (2): 1–5.

Etler, Dennis.
1996
"The Fossil Evidence for Human Evolution in Asia." *Annual Review of Anthropology* 25: 275–301.

Evstratov, I. V.
1997
"O zolotoordynskikh gorodakh, nakhodivshikhsya na mestakh Selitrennogo i Tsarevskikh gorodishch (opyt ispol'zovaniya monetnogo materiala dlya lokalizatsii srednevekovykh gorodov Povolzh'ya) (On the Golden Horde cities that were located at the ancient cities of Selitrennoe and Tsarevskoe [An experience in using currency material for locating medieval cities of the Volga area])." In *Epokha bronzy i rannii zheleznyi vek v istorii drevnikh plemen yuzhnorusskikh stepei* (The Bronze and Iron Ages in the history of the early tribes of the southern Russia steppes), vol. 2. Saratov: Saratov University Press.

Fairservis, Walter.
1993
Archaeology of the Southern Gobi of Mongolia. Durham, NC: Carolina Academic Press.

Fang, Cheng-hua.
2003
"Military Families and the Southern Song Court: The Lü Case." *Journal of Sung–Yüan Studies* 33: 49–70.

Farquhar, David M.
1990
The Government of China under Mongolian Rule. Münchner ostasiatische Studien 53. Stuttgart: Franz Steiner.

Fedorov-Davydov, G. A.
1976
Iskusstvo kochevnikov i Zolotoi Ordy: Ocherki kul'tury i iskusstva narodov Evraziiskikh stepei i zolotoordynskikh gorodov (The Art of the nomads and the Golden Horde: Essays on the culture and art of the peoples of the Eurasian steppe and cities of the Golden Horde). Moscow: Izdatel'stvo "Iskusstvo."
1984
The Culture of the Golden Horde Cities. Trans. H. Bartlett Wells. BAR International Series 198. Oxford: BAR (British Archaeological Reports).
1994
Zolotoordynskie goroda Povolzh'ia (The Golden Horde cities of the Volga region). Moscow: Izdatel'stvo Moskovskogo Universiteta.
2003
Denezhnoe delo Zolotoi Ordy (Mon-

etary affairs of the Golden Horde). Moscow: Paleograf Publishers.

Fedorov-Davydov, G. A., and N. M. Bulatov.
1989
Keramicheskaia masterskaia Selitrennogo gorodishcha (A ceramic workshop at the ancient city of Selitrennoe). In *Sokrovishcha sarmatskikh vozhdei i drevnie goroda Povolzhia* (The hoard of a Sarmatian leader and the early cities of Povolzh'e [the Volga region]), supervising ed. K. A. Smirnov. Moscow: Nauka (Akademiia nauk SSSR) Publishers.

Fitzhugh, William W.
2009
"The Mongolian Deer Stone-Khirigsuur Complex: Dating and Organization of a Late Bronze Age Menagerie." In *Current Archaeological Research in Mongolia: Papers from the 1st international conference on Archaeological Research in Mongolia held in Ulaanbaatar, August 2007*, ed. Jan Bemmann, Hermann Parzinger, Ernst Pohl, and Damdinsuren Tseveendorj. Bonn: Bonn University.

Fitzhugh, William W., Jamsranjav Bayarsaikhan, and Peter K. Marsh, eds.
2005
The Deer Stone Project: Anthropological Studies in Mongolia 2002–2004. Washington, DC: Arctic Studies Center, National Museum of Natural History, Smithsonian Institution; Ulaan Bataar: National Museum of Mongolian History.

Fletcher, Joseph F., Jr.
1986
"The Mongols: Ecological and Social Perspectives." *Harvard Journal of Asiatic Studies* 46, no. 1: 11–50.

Fragner, Bert.
1997
"Iran under Ilkhanid Rule in a World History Perspective." In *L'Iran face à la domination mongole*, ed. D. Aigle. Tehran: Institut Français de Recherche en Iran.

Franke, Herbert.
1952
"Could the Mongol Emperors Read and Write Chinese?." *Asia Major* n.s. 3, no. 1: 28–41.
1976
Sung Biographies. 4 vols. Wiesbaden: Franz Steiner Verlag.

Fritts, Harold C.
1976
Tree Rings and Climate. London; New York; San Francisco: Academic Press.

Frohlich, Bruno, N. Bazarsad, D. Hunt, and N. Batbold.
2005
"Human Mummified Remains from the Southern Gobi Desert: Preliminary Report on the Finds of Ten Executed Individuals Dating to the End of the Great Mongolian Empire." In *Journal of Biological Research, Proceedings V World Congress on Mummy Studies*, 80, no. 1: 167–70.

Frohlich, Bruno, M. Zuckerman, T. Amgalantugs, D. Hunt, Andrew S. Wilson, T. P. Gilbert, R. Chambers, H. M. Coyle, B. Falkowski, E. Garofalo, and E. Batshatar.
2008
"Human Mummified Remains from the Gobi Desert: Current Progress in Reconstruction and Evaluation." In *Proceedings VI World Congress of Mummy Studies* (Canary Islands, Feb. 20–24, 2007), ed. Pablo Atoche Peña, ConradoRodríguez Martín, and M.Ángeles Ramírez Rodríguez. Canary Islands: Academia Canaria de la Historia.

Frohlich, Bruno, Ts. Amgalantugs, J. Littleton, D. Hunt, J. Hinton, E. Batshatar, M. Dickson, T. Frohlich, and K. Goler.
2009
"Bronze Age Burial Mounds *(Khirigsuurs)* in Hovsgol aimag, Mongolia: A Reconstruction of Biological and Social Histories." In *Current Archaeological Research in Mongolia: Papers from the 1st international conference on Archaeological Research in Mongolia held in Ulaanbaatar, August 2007*, ed. Jan Bemmann, Hermann Parzinger, Ernst Pohl, and Damdinsuren Tseveendorj. Bonn: Bonn University.

Fung Ping Shan Museum, ed.
1992
Jingdezhen chu tu Wu dai zhi Qing chu ci zhan, Xianggang Feng Pingshan bo wu guan ji Jingdezhen shi tao ci kao gu yan jiu suo lian he zhu ban / Ceramic finds from Jingdezhen kilns (10th–17th century), Jointly presented by the Jingdezhen Institute of Ceramic Archaeology and the Fung Ping Shan Museum, the University of Hong Kong. Hong Kong: Jingdezhen Institute of Ceramic Archaeology; Fung Ping Shan Museum, University of Hong Kong.

Genden, Togoochiin.
1999
Gurvan Tumen Hunii Am' (The life and death of thirty thousand people). Ulaan Baatar: Shuvuun Saaral Publishing.

Gernet, Jacques.
1962
Daily Life in China on the Eve of the Mongol Invasion, 1250–1276. Trans. H. M. Wright. New York: Macmillan.

Gibb, H. A. R., ed.
1958–94
The Travels of Ibn Battuta A.D. 1325–1354, Translated with Notes from the Arabic Text. Ed. C. Defrémery and B. R. Sanguinetti. Vols. 1–3, Cambridge: Cambridge University Press for the Hakluyt Society, 1958, 1961, and 1971. Vol. 4: Translation completed with annotations by C. F. Beckingham. London: Hakluyt Society, 1994.

Gibb, H. A. R., ed. and trans.
1958–2000
see Ibn Battuta.

Gilberg, Rolf, and Jan-Olof Svantesson.
1996
"The Mongols, Their Land and His-

tory." In *Mongolia in Transition: New Patterns, New Challenges*, ed. Ole Bruun and Ole Odgaard. Nordic Institute of Asian Studies, *Studies in Asian Topics*, no. 22. Richmond, UK: Curzon Press.

Golden, Peter B.
1982
"Imperial Ideology and the Sources of Political Unity amongst the Pre-Chinggisid Nomads of Western Eurasia." *Archivum Eurasiae Medii Aevi* 2: 37–76.
1992
An Introduction to the History of the Turkic Peoples: Ethnogenesis and State Formation in Medieval and Early Modern Eurasia and the Middle East. Wiesbaden: Otto Harrassowitz.

Goncharov, E. Yu.
2000
"Staryi i Novyi Sarai: stolitsa Zolotoi Ordy (novyi vzglyad na izvestnye istochniki) (Old and new Sarai: The capital of the Golden Horde [A new look at known sources])." In *Sbornik statei* (Collected Essays), vol. 1 of *Trudy po arkheologii: Stepi Evropy v epokhu srednevekov'ya* (Works in archaeology: The steppes of Europe during the Middle Ages). Donetsk: Donetsk State University Press.

Goodrich, L. Carrington, and Chao-ying Fang.
1976
Dictionary of Ming Biography, 1368–1644. New York: Columbia University Press.

Goryeosa.
1998
see *Koryŏsa.*

Goryeosa jeoryo.
1968
see *Koryŏsa chŏryo.*

Graff, David.
2002
"Strategy and Contingency in the Tang Defeat of the Eastern Turks, 629–30." In *Warfare in Inner Asian History (500–1800)*, ed. Nicola Di Cosmo. Leiden: Brill.

Grekov, Boris Dmitrievich, and Aleksandr Iurevich Iakubovksii.
1950
Zolotaia Orda i ee padenie (The Golden Horde and its fall). Leningrad: Izdatel'stvo Akademii nauk SSSR.

Groussett, Réné.
2002
Empire of the Steppes: A History of Central Asia. Reprint of 1970 edit. translated by Naomi Walford. New Brunswick, NJ; London: Rutgers University Press.

Grove, Jean M.
1988
The Little Ice Age. London: Routledge, Kegan, Paul.

Guthrie, R. D.
1990
Frozen Flora of the Mammoth Steppe: The Story of Blue Babe. Chicago: University of Chicago Press.

Haining, Thomas H.
1999
"The Vicissitudes of Mongolian Historiography in the 20th Century." In *The Mongol Empire and Its Legacy*, ed. Reuven Amitai-Preiss and David Morgan. Leiden: Brill.

Hall, John W., and Jeffrey P. Mass, eds.
1974
Medieval Japan, Essays in Institutional History. New Haven; London: Yale University Press.

Halkovic, Stephen A., Jr.
1997
The Mongols of the West. Indiana University Publications, Uralic and Altaic series. London: Routledge, Curzon.

Halperin, Charles J.
1985
Russia and the Golden Horde: The Mongol Impact on Medieval Russian History. Bloomington: Indiana University Press.
2003
"Ivan IV and Chinggis Khan." *Jahrbücher für Geschichte Osteuropas* 51: 481–97.

Hambis, Louis.
1957
"Notes sur l'histoire de Corée à l'époque mongole" (Notes on the history of Korea during the Mongol period). *T'oung Pao* 45: 151–218.

Harada Yoshito, and Komai Kazuchika.
1941
Jōto: Mōko doronnōru ni okeru gendai toshi no chōsa/Shang-tu: The Summer Capital of the Yüan Dynasty in Dolon-Nor, Mongolia. Harada Yoshito vol., vol. 2 of *Tōho kōkōgaku sōkan* (Publications on East Asian Archaeology). Tokyo: Toa-Koko Gaku-kai; Hatsubai zauhō kankōkai.

Harris, Peter, trans.
2007
Zhou Daguan: A Record of Cambodia: The Land and Its People. Seattle: University of Washington Press.

Hatada Takashi.
1965
Genkō: Mōko teikoku no naibu jijo (The Mongol Invasion: Circumstances inside the Mongol Empire). *Chūkō shinsho*, no. 80. Tokyo: Chuo koronsha.

Hattstein, Markus, and Peter Delius, eds.
2000
Islam: Art and Architecture. Cologne: Könemann.

Hearn, Maxwell K.
1996
"Reunification and Revival" and "The Artist as Hero." In *Possessing the Past: Treasures from the National Palace Museum, Taipei*, ed. Wen Fong and James C. Y. Watt. New York: The Metropolitan Museum of Art.

Heidemann, Stefan, et al.
2006
"The First Documentary Evidence for

Qara Qorum from the Year 635/1237–38." *Zeitschrift für Archäologie Aussereuropäischer Kulturen* (Journal on the archaeology of non-European cultures) 1: 93–102.

Heissig, Walther.
1980
The Religions of the Mongols. Trans. Geoffrey Samuel. Berkeley: University of California Press; London: Routledge and Kegan Paul.

Henthorn, William E.
1963
Korea: The Mongol Invasions. Leiden: E. J. Brill.
1971
A History of Korea. New York: The Free Press.

Heywood, Colin J.
2000
"Filling the Black Hole: The Emergence of the Bithynian Atamanates." In *The Great Ottoman–Turkish Civilization*, vol. 1, ed. K. Çiçek, et al. Ankara: Yeni Türkiye.

Hiebert, Fredrik T[almage].
1994
Origins of the Bronze Age Oasis Civilization in Central Asia. Foreword by C. C. Lamberg-Karlovsky; preface by V. I. Sarianidi. In *Bulletin* (American School of Prehistory Research). Cambridge, MA: Peabody Museum of Archaeology and Ethnology.

Hillenbrand, Robert.
1999
Islamic Art and Architecture. London: Thames and Hudson.
2002
"The Arts of the Book in Ilkhanid Iran." In *The Legacy of Genghis Khan: Courtly Art and Culture in Western Asia, 1256–1353*, ed. Linda Komaroff and Stefano Carboni. New York: The Metropolitan Museum of Art; New Haven; London: Yale University Press.

Ho, Chuimei.
1994–95
"Social Life Under the Mongols as Seen in Ceramics." *Bulletin of the Oriental Ceramic Society* 59: 33–47.
2001
"The Ceramic Boom in Minnan During Song and Yuan Times." In *The Emporium of the World: Maritime Quanzhou, 1000–1400*, ed. Angela Schottenhammer. Leiden: Brill.

Holmgren, Jennifer.
1986
"Observations on Marriage and Inheritance Practices in Early Mongol and Yuan Society, with Particular Reference to the Levirate." *Journal of Asian History* 20, no. 2: 127–92.

Honeychurch, W., and Chunag Amartuvshin.
2006
"States on Horseback: The Rise of Inner Asian Confederations and Empires." In *Archaeology of Asia*, ed. Miriam Stark. Malden, MA: Blackwell.
2007
"Hinterlands, Urban Centers, and

Mobile Settings: The 'New' Old World Archaeology from the Eurasian Steppe." *Asian Perspectives* 46 (1): 36–64.

Honeychurch, William, and Joshua Wright.
2008
"Asia North and Central: Prehistoric Cultures of the Steppes, Deserts, and Forests." In *Encyclopedia of Archaeology*, ed. Deborah Pearsall. London: Elsevier Publishing.

Honeychurch, William, Joshua Wright, and Chunag Amartuvshin.
2009
"Re-Writing Monumental Landscapes as Inner Asian Political Process." In *Monuments, Metals, and Mobility: Trajectories of Complexity in the Late Prehistory of the Eurasian Steppe*, ed. Bryan Hanks and Kathryn Linduff. Cambridge: Cambridge University Press.

Hopkins, D. M., J. V. Matthews, Jr., C. S. Schweger, and S. B. Young, eds.
1982
Paleoecology of Beringia. New York: Academic Press.

Hori, Kyotsu.
1967
"The Mongol Invasions and the Kamakura Bakufu." Ph.D. diss. Columbia University.
1974
"The Economic and Political Effects of the Mongol Wars." In *Medieval Japan: Essays in Institutional History*, ed. John W. Hall and Jeffrey P. Mass. New Haven: Yale University Press.

Hrbek, Ivan.
1962
"The Chronology of Ibn Battuta's Travels." *Archiv Orientalni* 30: 409–86.

Hucker, Charles O.
1966
The Censorial System of Ming China. Stanford: Stanford University Press.

Hultèn, Eric.
1937
Outline of the History of Arctic and Boreal Biota During the Quaternary Period: Their Evolution During and After the Glacial Period as Indicated by the Equiformal Progressive Areas of Present Plant Species. Stockholm: Bokförlags Aktiebolaget Thule.

Hummel, Arthur W., ed.
1943
Eminent Chinese of the Ch'ing Period. Washington, DC: U.S. Government Printing Office.

Humphrey, Caroline.
1979
"The Uses of Genealogy: A Historical Study of the Nomadic and Sedentarized Buriats." In *L'Equipe Ecologie et Anthropologie des Sociétés Pastorales* (Pastoral production and society). Cambridge: Cambridge University Press; Paris: Maison des Sciences de l'Homme.
1983
Karl Marx Collective: Economy, So-

ciety and Religion in a Siberian Collective Farm. Cambridge: Cambridge University Press.

1994
"Shamanic Practices and the State in Northern Asia: Views from the Center and Periphery." In Shamanism, History and the State, ed. N. Thomas and C. Humphrey. Ann Arbor: University of Michigan Press.

1996
Shamans and Elders: Experience, Knowledge and Power among the Daur Mongols. Oxford: Oxford University Press.

Humphrey, Caroline, and Altanhuu Hürelbaatar.
2005
"Regret as a Political Intervention: An Essay in the Historical Anthropology of the Early Mongols." Past and Present 186: 3–45.

Hung, William.
1951
"The Transmission of the Book Known as The Secret History of the Mongols." Harvard Journal of Asiatic Studies, 14: 433–92.

Hüttel, Hans-Georg.
2004
"Im Palast des ewigen Friedens: Die mongolisch-deutschen Ausgrabungen im Palastbezirk von Karakorum (In the Palace of Eternal Peace: the Mongolian-German excavations in the palace district of Karakorum)." In Expeditionen in vergessene Welten (Expeditions to forgotten worlds), vol. 10 of 25 Jahre archäologische Forschungen in Afrika, Amerika und Asien (Twenty-five years of archaeological research in Africa, America, and Asia), ed. AVA-Forschungen. Aachen: Linden Soft.

2008
"Ausgrabungen des DAI und der MAW in Karakorum 2005–2006. (Excavations of the German Archaeological Institute and the Mongolian Academy of Sceinces at Khara Khorum, 2005–2006)." Zeitschrift für Archäologie Aussereuropäischer Kulturen (Journal on the archaeology of non-European cultures) 2: 402–12.

2009
"Royal Palace or Buddhist Temple? On Search for the Karakorum Palace." In Current Archaeological Research in Mongolia: Papers from the 1st international conference on Archaeological Research in Mongolia held in Ulaanbaatar, August 2007, ed. Jan Bemmann, Hermann Parzinger, Ernst Pohl, and Damdinsuren Tseveendorj. Bonn: Bonn University.

Hymes, Robert P.
1987
"Not Quite Gentlemen? Doctors in Sung and Yüan." Chinese Science 8: 9–76.

Ibn Battuta.
1958–2000
The Travels of Ibn Battuta, A.D. 1325–1354. Trans. and ed. H. A. R. Gibb. 5 vols. Cambridge: Hakluyt Society at the University Press.

2003
"Iz opisaniya puteshestvii Ibn Batutty (From a description of the travels of Ibn Batutta): Zolotaya Orda v istochnikakh (The Golden Horde in the source materials)." In Arabskie i persidskie sochineniya: Sbornik materialov, otnosyashchikhsya k istorii Zologoi Ordy, v perevodakh V. G. Tizengauzena (Arabian and Persian compositions: A collection of materials related to the history of the Golden Horde, in the translations of V. G. Tizengauzen Sostavlenie, vvodnaya stat'ya i kommentarii R. P. Khrapchevskogo [Compilation, introduction of the article, and commentaries by R. P. Khrapchevskii]), vol. 1. Moscow: Nauka (Akademiia nauk SSSR) Publishers.

Iggulden, Conn.
2007a
Genghis: Birth of an Empire. New York: Delacorte Press.

2007b
"Conn Iggulden, Interview," YouTube (Posted 24 May 2008), <http://www.youtube.com/watch?v=zE2zJdVCbsw>, accessed 20 June 2009.

Inosaki Takaoki.
1956
"Gendai shasei no seijiteki kōsatsu." (Examination of the government of Yüan society). Tōyōshi kenkyū 15, no. 1: 1–25.

IISNC (International Institute for the Study of Nomadic Civilizations).
2006
History and Culture of the Mongols. First Edition. Ulaan Baatar: IISNC–UNESCO, Admon.

IPCC
2007
Climate Change 2007: The physical science basis, Summary for Policy Makers. <http://ipcc-wg1.ucar.edu/>, accessed 20 June 2009.

Ishii Susumu.
1990
"The Decline of the Kamakura Bakufu." In The Cambridge History of Japan, vol. 3, ed. Kozo Yamamura. Cambridge: Cambridge University Press.

Ishjamts, N.
1998
Tuuhyin Zarim Uguullyin Emhetgel (A compilation of historical essays). Ulaan Baatar: GCom.

Jackson, Peter.
1978
"The Dissolution of the Mongol Empire." Central Asiatic Journal 22: 186–244.

2005
The Mongols and the West, 1221–1410. The Medieval World series. Harlow, UK; New York: Pearson-Longman.

Jackson, Peter, and David Morgan, eds.
1990
see Rubruck.

Jacobson, Esther, Vladimir Kubarev, and Damdensurenjin Tseevendorj.

2001
Mongolie du Nord-ouest Tsagaan Salla/Baga Oigor (Mongolia from the northwest: Tsagaan Salaa/Baga Oigor). Paris: De Boccard.

Jacoby, Gordon, Nachin Baatarbileg, Nicole Davi, Ashley Curtis, and Rosanne D'Arrigo.
2009
"A Central Asian Millennial Temperature Record based on Tree Rings from Mongolia." Quaternary Research. In revision.

Jagchid, Sechin, and Charles R. Bawden.
1965
"Some Notes on the Horse Policy of the Yüan Dynasty." Central Asiatic Journal. 10: 3–4; 246–68.

Jagchid, Sechin, and Van Jay Symons.
1989
Peace, War, and Trade Along the Great Wall: Nomadic-Chinese Interaction through Two Millennia. Bloomington: Indiana University Press.

Jahn, Karl.
1969
"Paper Currency in Iran." Journal of Asian History 4, no. 2: 101–35.

Janhunen, Juha, ed.
2003
The Mongolic Languages. Routledge Language Family series. London: Routledge Curzon.

Jankowiak, William R.
1992
Sex, Death, and Hierarchy in a Chinese City: An Anthropological Account. New York: Columbia University Press.

Jenkins, Gareth.
1974
"A Note on Climate Cycles and the Rise of Chinggis Khan." Central Asiatic Journal 18: 217–26.

Jettmar, Karl.
1994
"Body-Painting and the Roots of the Scytho-Siberian Animal Style." In The Archaeology of the Steppes: Methods and Strategies, ed. B. Genito. Naples: Instituto Universitario Orientale.

Jiangsu sheng wenwu guanli yuanhui.
1959
see Wenwu.

Jing Anning.
1994
"The Portraits of Khubilai Khan and Chabi by Anige (1254–1306), A Nepali Artist at the Yuan Court." Artibus Asiae 54, nos. 1, 2: 40–86.

2004
"Financial and Material Aspects of Tibetan Art under the Yuan Dynasty." Artibus Asiae 64, no. 2: 213–41.

Jobling, Mark. A., and Chris Tyler-Smith.
2003
"The Human Y Chromosome: An Evolutionary Marker Comes of Age." Nature Reviews Genetics 4: 598–612.

Juvaini [Juvaynî], 'Ata-Malik.
1912–37
[13th century] "Ta'rikh-I Jahan-Gusha (The history of the world conqueror)." E. J. W. Gibb Memorial Series 16, ed. Mirza Muhammad Qazvini. London: Luzac.

1958
History of the World Conqueror. Translated by John A. Boyle. 2 vols. Manchester: Manchester University Press.

Kahn, Paul.
1984
The Secret History of the Mongols: The Origin of Chingis Khan. Adapted. San Francisco: North Point Press.

1998
The Secret History of the Mongols: The Origin of Chingis Khan. Expanded ed. Boston: Cheng & Tsui.

Kano, Tetsuya.
2005
"Animal bone finds from Platform No.1 at the Avraga Site." In Avraga 1: Occasional Paper on the Excavations of the Palace of Genghis Khan, ed. Shimpei Kato and Noriyuki Shiraishi. Tokyo: Doseisha.

Kaplonski, Christopher.
2004
Truth, History, and Politics in Mongolia: The Memory of Heroes. London: Routledge Curzon.

Kato, Shimpei.
2005
"On the Shaofan Ritual at the Avraga Site." In Avraga 1: Occasional Paper on the Excavations of the Palace of Genghis Khan, ed. Shimpei Kato and Noriyuki Shiraishi. Tokyo: Doseisha.

Kazakevich, V. A.
1934
Souremennaia mongol'skaia toponimika (Modern Mongolian toponymy). Trudy mongol'skoi komissii (Works of the Mongolian Committee) 13. Leningrad: Izd-vo Akademii nauk SSSR.

Keith, Donald H.
1979
"Yellow Sea Yields Shipwreck Trove: A 14th-Century Cargo Makes Port at Last." National Geographic 156, no. 2: 230–43.

Kessler, Adam.
1993
Empires Beyond the Great Wall: The Heritage of Genghis Khan. Los Angeles: Natural History Museum of Los Angeles County.

Khatanbaatar, P., B. Jargal, W. Honeychurch, and Ch. Amartuvshin.
2007
"Khunnugiin bulshnaass ilersen khar' garaltai oldvoruud (Artifacts of foreign origin discovered in a Khunnu burial)." Arkheologiin Sudlal 4 (24): 305–22.

Kim Tang-t'aek.
1998
Wŏn kansŏp ha ŭi Koryŏ chŏngch'isa (The political history of Koryŏ under Yuan intervention). Seoul: Ilchogak.

Kiselev, Sergej [Sergei] Vladmirovich, and Institut arkheologii (Akademia nauk SSSR), eds.
1965
Drevnemongol'skie Goroda (Ancient Mongolian cities) Moscow: Nauka (Institut Arkheologii, Akademiia nauk SSSR). [For a summary of Kiselev's work in English, see Phillips 1969].

Komaroff, Linda.
2002
"The Transmission and Dissemination of a New Visual Language." In *The Legacy of Genghis Khan: Courtly Art and Culture in Western Asia, 1256–1353*, ed. Linda Komaroff, and Stefano Carboni. New York: The Metropolitan Museum of Art; New York; London: Yale University Press.

Komaroff, Linda, and Stefano Carboni, eds.
2002
The Legacy of Genghis Khan: Courtly Art and Culture in Western Asia, 1256–1353. New York: The Metropolitan Museum of Art; New York; London: Yale University Press.

Konovalov, P.B.
1976
Khunnu v Zabaikal'e (The Khunnu of Zabaikal'e). Ulan-Ude: Nauka (Institut Arkheologii, Akademiia nauk SSSR).

Koryŏsa.
1998
(History of the Koryŏ dynasty; [completed 1451]). Seoul: Yŏllin taeit'ŏbaeise yŏnguwŏn. Access to the *Koryŏsa* database is available through LibraryWeb, Columbia University Libraries, at <http://www.columbia.edu/cu/lweb/eresources/databases/2552377.html> accessed 20 June 2009.

Koryŏsa. chŏryo.
1968
(Essential history of the Koryŏ dynasty). Seoul: Minjok munhwa ch'ujinhoe.

Kramarovsky, M[ark]. G.
2001
Zoloto Chingisidov: kul'turnoe nasledie Zolotoi Ordy (Gold of the Chingisids: The cultural heritage of the Golden Horde). St. Petersburg: Slaviya Publishers.

2005
"Zolotaya Orda kak tsivilizatsiya (The Golden Horde as civilization)." In *Zolotaya Orda: Istoriya i kul'tura* (The Golden Horde: History and culture). St. Petersburg: Slaviya Publishers.

2006
"Khyng-oglan: kon'udachi, Verkhovaya loshad' Chingisidov (XIII–XV vv.) (Khyng-oglan: 'The Good Luck Horse,' The saddle horse of the Chingisids [13th–15th centuries])." In *"Poltsarstva za konya . . ." Loshad' v mirovoi kul'ture: Proizvedeniya iz sobraniya Gosudarstvennogo Ermitazha, Katalog vystavki* ("A Kingdom for My Horse . . .": The horse in world culture, Art work from the collection of the State Hermitage Museum, Catalog of exhibits). St. Petersburg: Slaviya Publishers.

2007
"Kubok iz Azaka: O polikhromii v keramike Zolotoi Ordy" (Goblet from Azak: Polychrome ceramics of the Golden Horde). In *Srednevekovaya arkheologiya evraziiskikh stepei* (Medieval Archaeology of the Eurasian Steppes), vol. 1. Kazan: Institute of History.

2008a
"Dzhuchids 1207–1502: tri etapa samoidentifikatsii (The Juchids of 1207–1502: Three stages of self identification)." In *Vo dvortsakh i v shatrakh: Islamskii mir ot Kitaya do Evropy, Katalog vystavki. Izdatel'stvo Gosudarstvennogo Ermitazha* (In palaces and in tents: The Islamic world from China to Europe, Catalog of exhibits, State Hermitage Museum). St. Petersburg: State Hermitage Museum.

2008b
"Sel'dzhukskie poyasa v Krymu i na Severnom Kavkaze v XIV v. (Seljuk girdles in the Crimea and in the northern Caucasus in the fourteenth century)." In *Sbornik nauchnykh trudov* (Collection of Scientific Works), no. 39 of *Antichnaya drevnost' i srednie veka* (Antiquity and the Middle Ages). Ekaterinburg: Urals State University Press.

Kramarovsky, M. G., and V. D. Gukin.
2007
Otchet ob arkheologicheskikh issledovaniyakh srednevekovogo poseleniya Bokatash II v 2005 godu (An account of archaeological investigations of the medieval site of Bokatash II in 2005), no. 4. St. Petersburg: State Hermitage Museum.

Kublai Khan Mongolian Barbecue.
2004
Kublai Khan Mongolian Barbecue Restaurant, <http://pachome2.pacific.net.sg/~mongolianbbq>, accessed 20 June 2009.

Kunishita Hirosato.
1921–22
"Gensho ni okeru teishitsu to zensō to no kankei ni tsuite" (On the relationship of the early Yuan emperors and the Buddhist monks). *Tōyō gakuhō* 11: 547–77; 12: 89–124, 245–49.

Kychanov, E. I.
1997
More znachenii, ustanovlennykh sviatymi (The sea of meanings established by the saints). Facsimile edition, translated from Tanghut, with foreword, commentary and appendices. St. Petersburg: Petersburg Orientalia.

1998
"Tangut Buddhist Books: Customers, Copyists, and Editors." *Manuscripta Orientalia* 4: 3, 5–9.

1999
Katalog tangutskikh buddiiskikh pamiatnikov (Catalogue of Tanghut Buddhist monuments). Kyoto: Kyoto University Press.

Kyzlasov, I. L.
1986
"Novyj vid pogrebal'nykh pamyatnikov Yujnoj Sibiri (A new type of burial monument of South Siberia)." In *Materialy po archeologii Gornogo Altaya* (Materials on the archaeology of the Gorno-Altai region). Gorno-Altaisk: Nauka (Akademiia nauk SSSR) Publishers.

Lamb, Harold.
1927
Genghis Khan: The Emperor of All Men. Garden City, NY: International Collectors Library.

Lamb, Hubert H.
1995
Climate, History and the Modern World. 2nd edition. London: Routledge.

Lane, George.
2003
Early Mongol Rule in Thirteenth-Century Iran: A Persian Renaissance. London: Routledge Curzon.

Latham, J. D.
1969
"Notes on Mamlûk Horse-Archers." *Bulletin of the School of Oriental and African Studies (BSOAS)* 32: 257–69.

Latham, Ronald, trans.
1958
see Polo.

Lattimore, Owen.
1936
"The Shrine of a Conqueror," *The Times* (London), 13 Apr.

1938
"The Geographical Factor in Mongol History." *The Geographical Journal* 91, no. 1: 1–16.

Ledyard, Gari.
1963
"Early Koryŏ–Mongol Relations." M.A. thesis. University of California.

Lee, Ki-Baek
1984
New History of Korea. Cambridge, MA: Harvard University Press.

Lei Runze, Yu Cunhai, and He Jiying.
1995
Xixia fota (Buddhist temples with pagodas of the Xixia dynasty [1038–1227]). Vol. 1 of *Zhongguo gu dai jian zhu* (Architecture of ancient China). Beijing: Wenwu chubanshe.

Levin, Theodore, and Valentina Suzukei.
2006
Where Rivers and Mountains Sing: Sound, Music, and Nomadism in Tuva and Beyond. Bloomington: Indiana University Press.

Levine, Marsha.
1999
"The Origins of Horse Husbandry on the Eurasian Steppe." In *Late Prehistoric Exploitation of the Eurasian Steppe*, ed. Marsha Levine, Yuri Rassamakin, Aleksandr Kislenko, and Nataliya Tatarintseva. Cambridge: McDonald Institute for Archaeological Research.

Li, Chu-tsing.
1965
The Autumn Colors on the Ch'iao and Hua Mountains: A Landscape bu Chao Meng-fu. Ascona, Switzerland: *Artibus Asiae*, supplement 21.

Li, Dong.
2002
"Suspicions Regarding What Are Alleged to be Glass and Agate Weiqi Chess Pieces." *China Archaeology and Art Digest* 4, no. 4: 63–78.

Li Zhichang (1193–1256).
1931
The Travels of an Alchemist: The Journey of the Taoist Ch'ang-ch'un from China to the Hindukush at the Summons of Chingiz Khan, Recorded by his Disciple Li Chih-ch'ang. Trans. and annot. Arthur Waley. London: Routledge & Kegan Paul, Ltd.

Linghu Defen.
1971 [635] *Zhou shu* (History of the Northern Zhou). 3 vols. Beijing: Zhonghua shuju.

Lipson, Larry.
1969
"Café Ramblings." *Valley News and Green Sheet*, 31 Jan., 28.

Liu, Cary.
1992
"The Yüan Dynasty Capital, Ta-tu: Imperial Building Program and Bureaucracy." *T'oung Pao* 78: 264–301.

Liu Xinyuan.
1993
"Yuan Dynasty Official Wares from Jingdezhen." In *The Porcelains of Jingdezhen: Colloquies on Art and Archaeology in Asia* 16, ed. Rosemary E. Scott. London: Percival David Foundation of Chinese Art.

Liu Xu, et al.
1975 [945]
Jiu Tang shu (Classic Tang history). 16 vols. Beijing: Zhonghua shuju.

Liu Yuquan.
2002
"Xixia dui Dunhuang yishu de teshu gongxian" (The special contributions of Xixia to Dunhuang art). *Guojia tushuguan xuekan* (National Library Bulletin), *Xixia wenzhuanhao* (Special issue devoted to Xixia): 176–79.

Lo Jung-pang.
1954
"The Controversy over Grain Conveyance during the Reign of Qubilai Qaqan (1260–94)." *Far Eastern Quarterly* 13, no. 3: 263–85.

1955
"The Emergence of China as a Sea Power During the Late Sung and Early Yüan Periods," *Far Eastern Quarterly* 14: 489–503.

1969
"Maritime Commerce and Its Relation to the Sung Navy," *Journal of the Economic and Social History of the Orient* 12, no. 1: 57–101.

Love, Ronald S.
1991
"'All the King's Horsemen': The

Equestrian Army of Henri IV, 1585–1598." *Sixteenth Century Journal* 22, no. 3: 510–33.

Lynn, John A.
1985
"Tactical Evolution in the French Army, 1560–1660." *French Historical Studies* 14, no. 2: 176–91.

Mackerras, Colin.
1990
"The Uighurs." In *The Cambridge History of Early Inner Asia*, ed. Denis Sinor. Cambridge: Cambridge University Press.

Mackintosh-Smith, Tim.
2001
Travels with a Tangerine: A Journey in the Footnotes of Ibn Battutah. London: John Murray.

2003
The Travels of Ibn Battutah. London: Picador.

2005
The Hall of a Thousand Columns: Hindustan to Malabar with Ibn Battutah. London: John Murray.

Man, John.
2005
Genghis Khan: Life, Death and Resurrection. London: Bantam Press.

Marsh, Peter K.
2009
The Horsehead Fiddle and the Cosmopolitan Reimagination of Tradition in Mongolia. New York: Routledge.

Marshak, B[oris] I.
1994
"K voprosu o sel'dzhukskoi torevtike (On the question of Seljuk torevtika)." *Vostochnoe istoricheskoe istochnikovedenie i spetsial'nye istoricheskie distsypliny* (Eastern historical source studies and special historical disciplines) 2. Moscow: Vostochnaja Literatura.

Marshall, Robert.
1993
Storm from the East: From Ghenghis Khan to Khubilai Khan. Berkeley: University of California Press.

Martin, Henry Desmond.
1970
The Rise of Chingis Khan and His Conquest of North China. Baltimore: Johns Hopkins University Press.

Martynyuk, Aleksey V.
2002
Die Mongolen im Bild: Orientalische, westeuropäische und russische Bildquellen zur Geschichte des Mongolischen Weltreiches und seiner Nachfolgestaaten im 13.–16. Jahrhundert (The Mongols in portrait: Eastern, West European, and Russian picture sources in the history of the Mongolian empire and its descendant states in the thirteenth to sixteenth centuries). Hamburg: Verlag Dr. Kovač.

2004
"Rus' i Zolotaya Orda v miniatyurakh Litsevogo letopisnogo svoda" (The Rus and the Golden Horde in the miniatures of the Litsevoy Chronicle). *Rossiiskie i slavyanskie issledovaniya:*

Sbornik nauchnykh statei (Russian and Slavic investigations: Collection of scientific articles) 1. Minsk: Belorussian University.

Masuya, Tomoko.
2002
"Ilkhanid Courtly Life." In *The Legacy of Genghis Khan: Courtly Art and Culture in Western Asia, 1256–1353*, ed. Linda Komaroff and Stefano Carboni. New York: The Metropolitan Museum of Art; New Haven; London: Yale University Press.

Matsuda Koichi.
2006
"Serven-Khaalga kanji meibun to Uljagawa no tatakai (The Chinese inscription on the rock of Serven Khaalga and the battle along the Ulja River)." In *Research on Inscriptions of Jin Dynasty in Mongolia: Report of the Scientific Research Project Grant-in-Aid JSPS*, ed. Noriyuki Shiraishi. Niigata: Niigata University.

May, Timothy.
2004
"The Mechanics of Conquest and Governance: The Rise and Expansion of the Mongol Empire, 1185–1265." Ph.D. diss. University of Wisconsin-Madison.

2006a
"The Training of an Inner Asian Nomad Army in the Pre-Modern Period." *The Journal of Military History* 70, no. 3: 617–35.

2006b
"Jamuqa and the Education of Chinggis Khan." *Acta Mongolica* 6: 273–86.

2007
The Mongol Art of War. London: Pen and Sword Publications.

McCausland, Shane.
1999
"Zhao Mengfu (1254–1322) and the Revolution of Elite Culture in Mongol China." Ph.D. diss. Princeton University.

Medley, Margaret.
1974
Yüan Porcelain and Stoneware. New York: Pitman Publishing Co.

Melikian, Souren.
2005
"Chinese jar sets record for Asian art." *International Herald Tribune*, 12 July.

Melville, Charles P.
1990
"'Padshah-i Islam': The Conversion of Sultan Mahmūd Ghazan Khan." In *Pembroke Papers I: Persian and Islamic Studies in Honour of P.W. Avery*, ed. C. P. Melville. Cambridge: University of Cambridge Centre of Middle Eastern Studies.

1999
The Fall of Amir Chupan and the Decline of the Ilkhanate, 1327–37: A Decade of Discord in Mongol Iran. Bloomington: Indiana University Press.

Menes, G., and L. Bilegt.
1992
"Ob odnom skal'nom pogrebenij

XII-XVI vv. iz bassejna reki Kerulen (About one rock crevice burial of the 12th-16th centuries from the Kerulen River basin.)." In *Pyatyj mejdunarodnyj kongress mongolovedov* (Fifth international congress of Mongolists) 3:155–59.

Meng Ssu-ming.
1967
Yüan-tai she-hui chieh-chi chih-tu (The social class system in Yüan times). Reprint. Hong Kong: Lungmen shu-tien.

Miller, David B.
1989
"Monumental Building as an Indicator of Economic Trends in Northern Rus' in the Late Kievan and Mongol Periods, 1138–1462." *The American Historical Review* 94: 360–90.

Miniaev, S., and L. Sakharovskaia.
2007
"Elitnyi Kompleks zakhoronenii Siunnu v padi Tsaram (An elite burial complex of the Xiongnu in the Tsaram Basin)." *Rossiiskaia Arkheologiia* 1: 194–210.

Miyake, Toshihiko.
2005
"Coins Collected from the Avraga Site." In *Avraga 1: Occasional Paper on the Excavations of the Palace of Genghis Khan*, ed. Shimpei Kato and Noriyuki Shiraishi. Tokyo: Doseisha.

Mongolian Barbecue Restaurant.
n.d.
"About Us." *Mongolian Barbecue Restaurant*, <http://www.themongolianbbq.com>, accessed 20 June 2009.

Mongolian Barbecue Blogspot.
2006
"Mongolian BBQ Recipe," *Mongolian Barbecue Blogspot* (posted 16 Oct.), <http://mongolian-bbq.blogspot.com>, accessed 20 June 2009.

Morgan, David O.
1985
"The Mongols in Syria, 1260–1300." In *Crusade and Settlement*, ed. P.W. Edbury. Cardiff: University College, Cardiff Press.

1986a
"The 'Great Yasa of Chingiz Khan' and Mongol Law in the Ilkhanate." *Bulletin of the School of Oriental and African Studies* 49, no. 1: 163–76.

1986b
The Mongols. The People of Europe series. Oxford; New York: B[asil] Blackwell.

1996
"Mongol or Persian: The Government of Ilkhanid Iran." *Harvard Middle Eastern and Islamic Review* 3, nos. 1, 2: 62–76.

1997
"Rasid al-Din and Gazan Khan." In *L'Iran face à la domination mongole*, ed. D. Aigle. Tehran: Institut Français de Recherche en Iran.

2001
"Ibn Battuta and the Mongols." *Journal of the Royal Asiatic Society* ser. 3, no. 11, 1: 1–11.

2007
The Mongols. Oxford: Basil Blackwell Publishers.

Moriyasu, T., and A. Ochir.
1999
Provisional Report of Researches on Historical Sites and Inscriptions in Mongolia from 1996 to 1998. Tokyo: Society of Central Eurasia Studies.

Moses, Larry.
1997
The Political Role of Mongol Buddhism. Uralic and Altaic series, Indiana University. London: Routledge Curzon.

Mote, Frederick W.
1994
"Chinese Society Under Mongol Rule, 1215–1368." In *Alien Regimes and Border States, 907–1368*, vol. 6 of *The Cambridge History of China*, ed. Herbert Franke and Denis Twitchett. Cambridge: Cambridge University Press.

Moule, A. C., and Paul Pelliot, trans.
1938
see Polo.

Mozai, Torao.
1982
"The Lost Fleet of Khubilai Khan," *National Geographic* 162, no. 5: 634–48.

1983
"The Mongol Invasion Fleet of 1281: Recent Underwater Archaeological Finds." *Journal of the Pacific Society* 18: 24–53.

Müller, Claudius C., and Henriette Pleiger, eds.
2005
Dschingis Khan und seine Erben: Das Weltreich der Mongolen (Genghis Khan and his heirs: The empire of the Mongols). Bonn; Munich: Kunst und Ausstellungshalle der Bundesrepublik Deutschland & Staatliches Museum für Völkerkunde München.

Murzaev, E. M.
1954
Die mongolishe Volksrepublik: Physischegeographische Beschreibung (The Mongolian Peoples Republic: a description of physical geography). Gotha: VEB Geographisch-Kartographische Anstalt.

Nagel, Eva.
2002
"A secretary's seal of the ministry of revenue issued in April 1372." In *Qara Qorum-City (Mongolia) I. Preliminary report of the excavations 2000–2001*, ed. Helmut R. Roth and Ulambaja [Ulambayar] Erdenebat; co-ed. Ernst Pohl and Eva Nagel. Vol. 1 of Bonn Contributions to Asian Archaeology. 2nd rev. and enl. ed. Bonn: Institute of Pre- and Early Historical Archaeology.

Nakano, Miyoko.
1971
A Phonological Study on the 'Phagspa Script and the Meng-ku Tzu-yün. Canberra: Australian National University Press.

Nam, Seng Geung.
1994
"A Study of Military Technics [*sic*] of the Thirteenth Century Mongols." *Mongolica* 5: 196–205.

Namnandorj, O.
1956
Research on Mönkh Khan's Inscription Monument and Palace. Ulaan Baatar: Publication of the State.

Nasonov, Arsenii Nikolaevich.
1940
Mongoly i Rus': Istoriia tatarskoi politiki na Rusi (The Mongols and Rus': The history of Tartar policies in Rus'). Moscow: Izdatel'stvo Akademii nauk SSSR.

National Institutes of Health
NIH website, <http://www.nigms.nih.gov/Publications/Factsheet_GeneticVariation.htm; National Coalition for Health Professional Education in Genetics; <http://www.nchpeg.org/raceandgenetics/index.asp>, accessed 20 June 2009.

National Palace Museum, ed.
1971
Gu gong tu xiang xuan cui/Kokyū zuzō sensui/Masterpieces of Chinese Portrait Painting in the National Palace Museum. Vol. 11 of *Guo li gu gong bo wu yuan/Collection of the National Palace Museum*. Taipei: National Palace Museum.

2001
Da Han de shi ji: Meng Yuan shi dai de duo yuan wen hua yu yi shi/Age of the Great Khan: Pluralism in Chinese Art and Culture Under the Mongols. Ed. Shi Shouqian, and Ge Wanzhang. Taipei: National Palace Museum.

Natsagdorj, Sh.
1978
Mongolyn Feodalizmyn Undsen Zamal (The fundamental lines of Mongolian feudalism). Ulaan Baatar: State Publishing House.

Navaan, D.
2005
"The Tavan Tolgoi Site, Ongon sum, Sukhbaatar Aimag." No. 44 of *Relics, Excavation, State and Meaning in the Jinghiz Khan Age. Korea and Eastern Asia (III)*. The 6th International Conference. Seoul: Korea University.

Nelson, Albert R.
2000
Bioarchaeology of the Joint Mongolian-American Egiin Gol Expedition Burial Sample: 2000 Field Season. Physical anthropology analysis report. Ulaan Baatar: Mongolian Institute of History.

Ningxia wenwu kaogu yanjiusuo (Institute of Archaeology and Cultural Relics of Ningxia Hui Autonomous Region), ed.
2005
Baisigou Xixia fangta (The Xixia quadrilateral pagoda in the Baisigou Valley). Beijing: Wenwu chubanshe.

Noll, Richard.
1983

"Shamanism and Schizophrenia: A State Specific Approach to the 'Schizophrenia Metaphor' of Shamanic States." *American Ethnologist* 10, no. 3: 443–59.

Novgorodova, E.
1982
Ulangom: Ein skythenzeitliches Graberfeld in der Mongolei (Ulangom: A Scythian-period cemetery in Mongolia). Wiesbaden: Harrassowitz.

Oba Osamu.
2001
Hyouchakusen monogatari (Tale of being adrift at sea). Tokyo: Iwanami shoten.

Obata, Hiroki.
2007
"Avraga iseki shutsudo no shokubutsu izontai ni tsuite/On the Botanical Remains from the Avraga Site." In *Preliminary Report on Japan–Mongolia Joint Archaeological Expedition "New Century Project" 2006*, ed. Noriyuki Shiraishi. Niigata: Niigata University.

Odkhuu, S.
2006
Mongol dakh' Chingis Sudlalyn Tovchoon (A summary of Mongolian research on Chingis [Genghis Khan]). Ulaan Baatar: Huh Sudar Printing.

Olbricht, Peter, and Elisabeth Pinks, trans.
1980
see Zhao Gong.

Olschki, Leonardo.
1960
Marco Polo's Asia. Berkeley: University of California Press.

Onon, Urgunge, trans. and annot.
2005
The Secret History of the Mongols: The Life and Times of Chinggis Khan. Ulaan Baatar: Bolor sudar.

Oriental Ceramic Society of Hong Kong, ed.
1984
Jingdezhen Wares: The Yuan Evolution. Hong Kong: Oriental Ceramic Society.

Osawa, Masami.
2005
"One of the Forms of Iron Producing in the Mongol Empire Obtained from Forge-related Objects Found at Avraga Site." In *Avraga 1: Occasional Paper on the Excavations of the Palace of Genghis Khan*, ed. Shimpei Kato and Noriyuki Shiraishi. Tokyo: Doseisha.

Ostrowski, Donald.
1998
"The Tamma at the Dual-Administrative Structure of the Mongol Empire." *Bulletin of the School of Oriental and African Studies* 61: 262–77.

1990
"The Mongol Origins of Muscovite Political Institutions." *Slavic Review* 49: 525–42.

Ota Kouki.
1997
Mōko shuūrai: Sono gunjiteki kenkyō (Study of military aspects of the Mongol invasion). Tokyo: Kinseisha.

Ouyang Xiu, and Song Qi.
1975.[1060].
Xin Tang shu (New Tang History). 20 vols. Beijing: Zhonghua shuju.

Pachkalov, A. V.
2001
"K voprosu ob interpretatsii epiteta al-Dzhedid (po materialam gorodov Ulusa Dzhuchi) (On the question of interpretation of an epithet of al-Jedid [Based on materials from the cities of the Ulus Jochi])." *Povolzh'e v srednie veka: Tezisy dokladov Vserossiiskoi nauchnoi konferentsii, posvyashchennoi 70-letiyu so dnya rozhdeniya Germana Alekseevicha Fedorova-Davydova (1931–2000)* (Povolzh'e [The Volga region] in the Middle Ages: Theses of reports of the all-Russian scientific conference, commemorating the 70th birthday of the German Alekseevich Fedorov-Davydov [1931–2000]). Nizhnii Novgorod: State Pedagogical University.

Paderin, Innokentii V.
1874
"O Karakorume i drugikh razvalinakh bliz Orkhona (On Khara Khorum and other ruins near the Orkhon)." *Izvestiia Russkogo Geograficheskogo Obshchestva* (Newsletter of the Russian Geographical Society) 9, no.10: 355–60.

Pan, Yihong.
1997
Son of Heaven and Heavenly Qaghan: Sui–Tang China and its Neighbors. Bellingham, WA: Western Washington University Press.

Payne, Ann.
1990
Medieval Beasts. New York: New Amsterdam.

Payne-Gallway, Ralph.
1973
The Projectile-Throwing Engines of the Ancients and Turkish and Other Oriental Bows. Totowa: Rowman and Littlefield.

Pederson, Niel, Gordon C. Jacoby, Rosanne D'Arrigo, Edward R. Cook, Brendan M. Buckley, Chemultin Dugarjav, and Renchin Mijjidorj.
2001
"Hydrometeorological Reconstructions for Northeastern Mongolia Derived from Tree Rings, 1651–1995." *Journal of Climate* 14 (5): 872–81.

Pegg, Carole.
2001
Mongolian Music, Dance, and Oral Narrative. Seattle: University of Washington Press.

Pelliot, Paul.
1951
Mémoires sur les coutumes du Cambodge de Tcheou Ta-kouan (version nouvelle). Paris: Adrien–Maisonneuve.

1959–73
Notes on Marco Polo. 3 vols. Paris: Imprimerie Nationale.

Pelliot, Paul, and Louis Hambis, trans.
1951
see Shengwu.

Perdue, Peter C.
2005
China Marches West: The Qing Conquest of Central Eurasia. Cambridge, MA: Harvard University Press.

Perlee, Khodoo.
1959
"Negen sharilyn tukhaj (About one burial)." *Studia Mongolica* 1, no. 15.

1961
Mongol Ard Ulsyn ert, Dundad Ueiin Knot Suuriny Tovchoon (An overview of ancient and medieval period settlements in the Mongolian People's Republic). Ulaan Baatar: Mongolian Academy of Sciences.

Petech, Luciano.
1990
Central Tibet and the Mongols. Rome: Instituto Italiano per il Medio ed Estremo Oriente.

Petrov, Andrej E.
2005
"La mémoire de la bataille de Kulikovo dans l'idéologie de l'État russe des XVᵉ-XVIᵉ siècles." *Cahiers du Monde Russe* 46, nos. 1, 2: 305–26.

Phillips, Eustace D.
1969
The Mongols. London: Thames & Hudson.

Pigg, Stacey Leig.
1996
"The Credible and the Credulous: The Question of 'Villagers' Beliefs' in Nepal." *Cultural Anthropology* 11, no. 2: 160–201.

Piotrovskii [Piotrovsky], Mikhail Borisovich, ed.
1993
Lost Empire of the Silk Road, Buddhist Art from Khara Khoto (X-XIIIth century). Milan: Thyssen-Bornemisza Foundation and Electra Editrice.

Piotrovskii [Piotrovsky], Mikhail Borisovich, et al., eds.
2000
Altyn urda khaézinaélaére/Sokrovishcha Zolotoi ordy: Katalog vystavki (The treasures of the Golden Horde). Contrib. by Mark G. Kramarovsky, Mikhail Borisovich Piotrovskii, and V. I. U. Matveev. Exh. cat. St. Petersburg: Slaviya.

Pohl, Ernst.
2009
"Interpretation without excavation: Topographical mapping on the ground of the Mongolian capital Karakorum." In *Current Archaeological Research in Mongolia. Papers from the First International Conference on "Archaeological Research in Mongolia" held in Ulaanbaatar, August*

2007, ed. Jan Bemmann Hermann Parzinger, Ernst Pohl, Damdinsuren Tseveendorj. Bonn: Bonn University.

Pohl, Ernst, and Ulambayar Erdenebat.
2002
"Karakorum 2: Archäologie im Stadtzentrum" (Karakorum 2: Archaeology in the city center). In *Qara Qorum-City (Mongolia) I. Preliminary report of the excavations 2000–2001*, ed. Helmut R. Roth and Ulambaja [Ulambayar] Erdenebat. Ernst Pohl and Eva Nagel. Vol. 1 of *Bonn Contributions to Asian Archaeology*. 2nd rev. and enl. ed. Bonn: Institute of Pre- and Early Historical Archaeology.

Polo, Marco.
1903
The Book of Ser Marco Polo, the Venetian, Concerning the Kingdoms and Marvels of the East. 2 vols. 3rd ed. rev. in light of recent discoveries by Henri Cordier. London: John Murray.
1938
The Description of the World. Trans. and ann. A[rthur] C[hristopher] Moule, and Paul Pelliot. 2 vols. London: George Routledge & Sons, Ltd.
1958
The Travels of Marco Polo. Trans. and with intro. by Ronald Latham. Harmondsworth, UK: Penguin Books, 1958.

Pope, John Alexander.
1952
Fourteenth-Century Blue-and-White: A Group of Chinese Porcelains in the Topkapu Sarayi Müzesi, Istanbul. Washington, DC: Freer Gallery of Art.

Pozdneyev [Pozdneev], Alexei [Aleksei] M.
1883
Mongol'skaia letopis' "Erdeniin erikhe." Podlinnyi tekst s perevodom i poiasneniiami, zakliuchaiushchimi v sebe materialy dlia istorii Khalkhi s 1636 po 1736 g. (The Mongolian chronicle "Erdeniin erikhe." Genuine text with translation and notes containing the materials for the history of Khalkha from 1636 to 1736). St. Petersburg: Academy of Sciences.
1997
Mongolia and the Mongols: Presenting the Results of a Trip Taken in 1892 and 1893. Indiana University Publications. Uralic and Altaic series. London: Routledge Curzon.

Pratt, Keith.
2007
Everlasting Flower: A History of Korea. London: Reaktion Books.

Prusmack, Florence.
1992
Khan: A Romantic Historical Novel Based on the Early Life of Ghenghis Khan. Fort Pierce, FL: Ashby-Ferguson.

Radloff, Wilhelm.
1892
Atlas der Alterthümer der Mongolei (Atlas of the antiquities of Mongolia). St. Petersburg: Academy of Sciences.

Rakhimzianov, Bulat R.
2005
"Nasledie Zolotoi Ordy v formiro-

vanii Rossiiskogo gosudarstva (The legacy of the Golden Horde in the formation of the Russian State)." *Cahiers du Monde Russe* 46, nos. 1, 2: 29–38.

Rashid al-Din [Tabib].
1946–60 [ca. 1309]
Sbornik letopiseĭ (Compendium of Chronicles). Translated from the Persian to Russian by L. A. Khetagurova. Moscow: The Academy of Sciences of the USSR.
1998 [ca. 1309]
[*Jami'al-tavarikh*] *Rashiduddin Fazlullah's Jami'u't-tawarikh, Compendium of Chronicles.* Spine title *Rashiduddin Fazlulla, Jami'u t-tawarikh*; added title p. *Câmi u't-Tevârîh.* Trans. and annot. by Wheeler M. Thackston. Vol. 45 of *Sources of Oriental Languages and Literatures, Central Asian Sources* 4. Cambridge, MA: Harvard University, Department of Near Eastern Languages and Civilizations.
2003 [ca. 1309]
"Izvlecheniya iz 'sbornika letopisei' Rashid al-Dina (Extracts from *Compendium of Chronicles* by Rashid al-Din)." In *Zolotaya Orda v istochnikakh: T. I. Arabskie i Persidskie sochineniya: Sbornik materialov, otnosyashchikhsya k istorii Zolotoi Ordy v perevodakh V. G. Tizengauzena.* (Arabian and Persian compositions: Collection of materials belonging to the history of the Golden Horde in the translations of V. G. Tizengauzen, vol. 1 of The Golden Horde in the sources,) Compilation, introduction to the essay, and commentary by R. P. Krapchevskii. Moscow: Nauka (Akademiia nauk SSSR) Publishers.

Ratchnevsky, Paul.
1968
"The Levirate in the Legislation of the Yüan dynasty." In *Tamura Hakushi shōju tōyōshi ronsō: Tamura Hakushi taikan kinen jigyōkaihen* (Asiatic studies in honor of [Dr.] Tamura Jitsuzō on the occasion of his sixty-fourth birthday), ed. Tamura Hakushi taikan kinen jigyōkai. Kyoto: n.p.
1991
Genghis Khan: His Life and Legacy. Trans. Thomas Haining. Oxford: Blackwell Publishing.

———, ed.
1937–72
Un Code des Yuan (A Yuan code). [The *Yuanshi* of Song Lian (1310–1381)].
Annot. and comm.. by Paul Ratchnevsky. 2 vols. *Bibliothèque de l'Institut des hautes études chinoises*, vol. 4. Paris: Presses Universitaires de France.

Riasanovsky, Valentin.
1965
Fundamental Principles of Mongol Law. Reprint. Bloomington: Indiana University.

Rinchen, B.
1979
Mongol Ard Ulsyn Ugsaatny Sudlal, Khelnii Shinjleliin Atlas (Ethnographic and linguistic atlas of the Mongolian People's Republic). Ulaan Baatar: Academy of Sciences.

Robinson, Kevin D., Mark B. Abbott, Michael F. Rosenmeier, S. Nergui, and William W. Fitzhugh.
2009
"A 2400 Year Record of Lacustrine Productivity from a Small Lake in the Baroon Taiga Mountains, Northern Mongolia." *Journal of Paleolimnology*: In revision.

Rogers, J. Daniel, Erdenebat Ulambayar, and Mathew Gallon.
2005
"Urban Centres and the Emergence of Empires in Eastern Inner Asia." *Antiquity* 79: 801–18.

Ross, J.
2006
"Evidence of Violent Death Adds Mystery to Mummies Found in Remote Mongolian Cave." *Inside Smithsonian Research* 11: 6–7.

Rossabi, Morris.
1979
"Khubilai Khan and the Women in His Family." In *Studia Sino-Mongolica: Festschrift für Herbert Franke*, ed. Wolfgang Bauer. Wiesbaden: Franz Steiner Verlag.
1981
"The Muslims in the Early Yüan Dynasty." In *China under Mongol Rule*, ed. John D. Langlois. Princeton: Princeton University Press.
1988
Khubilai Khan: His Life and Times. Berkeley: University of California Press.
1992
Voyager from Xanadu. New York: Kodansha.
2002
"The Mongols and Their Legacy." In *The Legacy of Genghis Khan: Courtly Art and Culture in Western Asia, 1256-1353*, ed. Linda Komaroff and Stefano Carboni. New York: The Metropolitan Museum of Art; New Haven; London: Yale University Press.
2005
Modern Mongolia: From Khans to Commissars to Capitalists. Berkeley: University of California Press.

Roth, Helmut R., and Ulambaja [Ulambayar] Erdenebat, eds.
2002
Qara Qorum-City (Mongolia) I. Preliminary report of the excavations 2000–2001. Co-ed. Ernst Pohl, and Eva Nagel. Vol. 1 of *Bonn Contributions to Asian Archaeology.* 2nd rev. and enl. ed. Bonn: Institute of Pre- and Early Historical Archaeology.

Roux, Jean-Paul.
1993
Histoire de l'Empire Mongol. Paris: Fayard.

Rubruck, Friar William of [Willem van Ruysbroeck].
1990 [13th century, *Itinerarium*]
The Mission of Friar William of Rubruck: His Journey to the Court of the Great Khan Möngke, 1253-1255. Trans. Peter Jackson. Intro., notes, and appendices by Peter Jackson with David Morgan. In *Works issued by the Hakluyt Society* 0072-9396, 2nd

ser., no. 173. London: Hakluyt Society.

Rudenko, K.
2005
"Kazanskii drakon: obraz i simvol (Kazan dragon: Form and symbol)." *Tatarskaya arkheologiya: Kazan' i Kazanskoe khanstvo* (Tartar archaeology: Kazan and the Kazan khanate) nos. 1, 2: 14–15.

Rudenko, S. I.
1962
Kul'tura khunnov i Noinulinskie kurgany (Khunnu culture and the Kurgans of Noin Ula). Moscow: Nauka (Institut Arkheologii, Akademiia nauk SSSR).
1970
Frozen Tombs of Siberia; The Pazyryk Burials of Iron Age Horsemen. Berkeley: University of California Press.

Saeki Koji.
2003
Mongoku shōrai no shōgeki (The impact of the Mongol Invasion). Tokyo: Chuo koronsha.

Sagaster, Klaus.
2005
"Karakorum Nr.108: die chinesisch-mongolische Inschrift von 1346 aus Erdeni joo. (Karakorum no. 108: the Chinese-Mongolian inscription of 1346 from Erdene Zuu)." In *Dschingis Khan und seine Erben.* (Genghis Khan and his heirs: The empire of the Mongols) ed. Claudius C. Müller and Henriette Pleiger. Bonn; Munich: Kunst und Ausstellungshalle der Bundesrepublik Deutschland & Staatliches Museum für Völkerkunde München.

Samosiuk, Kira Federovna.
2006
Buddiiskaia Zhivopis' iz Khara-Khoto, XII-XIV Vekov, Mezhdu Kitaem I Tibetom: Kollektsiia P.K. Kozlova (Buddhist paintings from Khara-Khoto, XII-XIV centuries, between China and Tibet: The collection of P. K. Kozlov). St. Petersburg: The State Hermitage Museum.

Sarantsatsral, Ts.
2006
"*The Secret History of the Mongols*" and Its Translations into Foreign Languages. Ulaan Baatar: Bembi San Publishing House.

Sasaki, Randall.
2005
"The Legend of Kamikaze: Nautical Archaeology in Japan." *The INA Quarterly* 32, no. 1: 3–8.
2006
"Where the Vessels Were Built: Reconstructing the Mongol Invasions of Japan." *The INA Quarterly* 33, no. 3: 16–22.

Savel'eva, E[lena]. A[lekseevna].
1987
Vymskie mogil'niki XI–XIV vv. (Mounds of the Vym River valley of the eleventh to fourteenth centuries). Supervisory ed. Igor Vasilevich Dubov. Leningrad: Leningrad University.

Scott, Keith.
1975
"Khitan Settlements in Northern Mongolia: New Light on the Social and Cultural History of the pre-Chingisid Era." *The Canada–Mongolia Review* 1, no. 1: 5–28.

Sen, Tansen.
2006
"The Yuan Khanate and India: Cross-Cultural Diplomacy in the Thirteenth and Fourteenth Centuries." *Asia Major* 3rd ser., 19, nos. 1, 2: 299–326.

Seoul.
1985
Relics Salvaged from the Seabed Off Sinan. Ed. Bureau of Cultural Properties, Ministry of Culture and Information of the Republic of Korea. Seoul: Dong Hwa.

Serruys, Henry.
1974
Kumiss Ceremonies and Horse Racing: Three Mongolian Texts. Wiesbaden: Otto Harrassowitz.
1987
The Mongols and Ming China: Customs and History. Ed. Françoise Aubin. London: Variorum.

Shen Congwen.
1997
Zhongguo gudai fushi yanjiu (Studies on ancient Chinese costume). Shanghai: Shanghai shudian chubanshe.

Shengwu.
1951 [13th century]
[*Shengwu qinzhenglu.*] *Histoire des campagnes de Gengis Khan: Chengwou ts'in-tscheng lou.* Trans. and ed. Paul Pelliot and Louis Hambis. Leiden: E. J. Brill.

Shi Jinbo.
1993
Xixia fojiao shilue (History of Xixia Buddhism). Reprint of 1988 edition. Taipei: Commercial Press.

Shi Jinbo, and Yasen Wushouer.
2000
Xixia he Huihu huozi yishua yanjiu (Studies on Xixia and Uyghur moveable-type printing). Beijing: Shehuikexueyuan chubanshe.

Shiba, Yoshinobu.
1983
"Sung Foreign Trade: Its Scope and Organization." In *China Among Equals: The Middle Kingdom and Its Neighbors, 10th–14th Centuries,* ed. Morris Rossabi. Berkeley: University of California Press.

Shiraishi Noriyuki.
2001
Chingisu kan no kōkogaku (Archaeological studies on Genghis Khan). Tokyo: Doseisha.
2002
Mongoru teikoku shi no kōkogaku teki kenkyō (Archaeological studies on the history of the Mongol Empire). Tokyo: Doseisha.
2004
"Seasonal Migrations of the Mongol Emperors and the Peri-urban Area of

Kharakhorum." *The International Journal of Asian Studies* 1, no. 1 (Jan.): 105–19.
2006
"Avraga Site: The 'Great Ordu' of Genghis Khan." In *Beyond the Legacy of Genghis Khan,* ed. Linda Komaroff. Leiden; Boston: Brill.

Silk Road.
2006
"Tombs of Chingisids Are Still Being Found . . . An Interview with Senior Archaeologist Professor Dorjpagma Navaan." *The Silk Road* 4, no. 1, summer.

Sima Qian [ca. 145–ca. 86 BCE].
1993
Records of the Grand Historian, Han Dynasty, by Sima Qian. Trans. from the *Shi ji* by Burton Watson. 2 vols., rev. ed. Records of Civilization, Sources and Studies series, no. 65. Hong Kong; New York: Renditions–Columbia University Press.

Simukov, Andrei D.
1936
"Materialy po kochevomu bytu naseleniya MNR" (Materials concerning the nomadic life of the population of Mongolia). *Sovremennaya Mongoliya* (Contemporary Mongolia) 2 (15): 49–57.

Sinor, Denis.
1971
"On Mongol Strategy." In *Proceedings of the Fourth East Asian Altaistic Conference,* ed. Ch'en Chieh-hsien. Tainan, Taiwan: Dept. of History, National Ch'engkung University.
1981
"The Inner Asian Warriors." *Journal of the American Oriental Society* (*JAOS*) 101, no. 2: 133–44.
1990
"The Establishment and Dissolution of the Türk Empire." In *The Cambridge History of Early Inner Asia,* ed. Denis Sinor. Cambridge: Cambridge University Press.

Skaff, Jonathan Karam.
2002
"Western Turk Rule of Turkestan's Oases in the Sixth through Eighth Centuries." In *The Turks,* ed. H. Inalcik. Ankara: Yeni Türkiye.
2004
"Survival in the Frontier Zone: Comparative Perspectives on Identity and Political Allegiance in China's Inner Asian Borderlands during the Sui–Tang Dynastic Transition (617–630)." *Journal of World History* 15, no. 2: 117–53.
2009
"Tang Military culture and Its Inner Asian Influences." In *Military Culture in Imperial China,* ed. Nicola Di Cosmo. Cambridge, MA: Harvard University Press.

Skelton, R. A., Thomas E. Marston, and George D Painter.
1965
The Vinland Map and the Tartar Relation. New Haven: Yale University Press.

Smith, John Masson, Jr.
1970

"Mongol and Nomadic Taxation." *Harvard Journal of Asiatic Studies* 30: 46–85.
1984
"'Ayn Jalut: Mamluk Success or Mongol Failure?." *Harvard Journal of Asiatic Studies* 44, no. 2: 307–45.
1993–94
"Demographic Considerations in Mongol Siege Warfare." *Archivum Ottomanicum* 13: 329–35.
1996
"Mongol Society and Military in the Middle East: Antecedents and Adaptations." In *War and Society in the Eastern Mediterranean, 7th and 15th Centuries,* vol. 9. of *The Medieval Mediterranean Peoples, Economies, and Cultures, 400–1453,* ed. Yaacov Lev. Leiden: Brill.
2000
"Dietary Decadence and Dynastic Decline in the Mongol Empire." *Journal of Asian History* 34, no. 1: 35–52.

Smith, Paul J.
1992
"Family, Landsmann, and Status-Group Affinity in Refugee Mobility Strategies: The Mongol Invasions and the Diaspora of Sichuanese Elites, 1230–1330." *Harvard Journal of Asiatic Studies* 52, no. 2: 665–708.

Sneath, David.
1999
"Spatial Mobility and Inner Asian Pastoralism." In Caroline Humphrey and David Sneath, *The End of Nomadism?: Society, State and the Environment in Inner Asia.* Durham, NC: Duke University Press.
2002
"Custody and Property: Land, Indigenous Understanding, and the Conceptual Basis of Development Policy in Pastoral Mongolia." In *Markets and Moralities: Ethnographies of Postsocialism,* ed. Caroline Huphrey and R. Mandel. London: Routledge.
2007
"Ritual Idioms and Spatial Orders: Comparing the Rites for Mongolian and Tibetan 'Local Deities'." In *The Mongol-Tibet Interface: Opening New Research Terrains in Inner Asia,* ed. U. Bulag and H. Deimberger. Leiden: Brill.

So, Billy K. L.
2000
Prosperity, Region, and Institutions in Maritime China: The South Fukien Pattern, 946–1368. Cambridge, MA; London: Harvard University Asia Center and Harvard University Press.

Sokrovishcha Zolotoĭ ordy.
2000
see Piotrovskii.

Song Lian, et al.
1976 [14th c.]
Yuanshi (History of the Yuan). 15 vols. Beijing: Zhonghua shuju.

Spuler, Bertold.
1985
Die Mongolen in Iran (The Mongols in Iran). Leiden: E. J. Brill.

1989
History of the Mongols. Reprint of 1972 *History of the Mongols, Based on Eastern and Western Accounts of the Thirteenth and Fourteenth Centuries.* Trans. from the German by Helga and Stuart Drummond. Berkeley: University of California Press; New York: Dorset Press.

Steinhardt, Nancy S.
1988
"Imperial Architecture Along the Mongolian Road to Dadu." *Ars Orientalis* 18: 59–93.

Strahlenberg, Philipp Johan von.
1730
Das nord-und ostliche Theil von Europa und Asia, in so weit solches das gantze Russische Reich mit Siberien und der grossen Tatarey in sich begreiffet, in einer historisch-geographischen Beschreibung der alten und neuren Zeiten nebst einer noch niemahls ans Licht gegebenen Tabula polyglotta von zwey und dreyssigerley Arten tartarischer Völcker Sprachen und einem kalmuckischen Vocabulario, sonderlich aber einer grossen richtigen Land-Charte von den benannten Ländern (An historico-geographical description of the north and eastern parts of Europe and Asia, but more particularly of Russia, Siberia, and Great Tartary; both in their ancient and modern state; together with an entire new polyglot-table of the dialects of 32 Tartarian nations). Stockholm: Selbstrverl.

Suzuki, Kazahiro, Hirotaka Oda, Mitsuhiko Ogawa, Etsuko Niu, Akiko Ikeda, Toshio Nakamura, and Akiko Matsuo.
2001
"C14 Dating of Wooden Anchors and Planks Excavated from Submerged Wrecks Located at Takashima in Imari Bay, Nagasaki Prefecture." *Proceedings of the Japan Academy, Series B, Physical and Biological Sciences* 77, no. 7: 131–34.

Takashima Board of Education.
1984
Tokonami kaitei iseki (Excavation report on Tokonami Underwater Site).
1996
Takashima kaitei iseki (Excavation report on Takashima) 3.
2003
Takashima kaitei iseki (Excavation report on Takashima) 8.

T'ang, C.
1981
"Agrarianism and Urbanism, and Their Relationship to the Hsiung-nu Empire." *Central Asiatic Journal* 1, 2: 110–20.

Tao Jing-shen.
1976
The Jurchen in Twelfth-Century China: A Study of Sinicization. Seattle: University of Washington Press.

Tasmagambetov, Imangali, and Zaĭnolla Samashev.
2001
Saraichik. Almaty: Berel.

Tataro-mongoly.
1970
see Tikhvinskii.

Taussig, Michael.
1997
The Magic of the State. New York; London: Routledge.

Tekin, Talat.
1968
A Grammar of Orkhon Turkic. Bloomington: Research Center for the Language Sciences, Indiana University.

Thackston, Wheeler, trans.
1998–99
see Rashid al-Din.

Thiel, Joseph.
1961
"Der Streit der Buddhisten und Tao-isten zur Mongolenzeit (The struggle between Buddhists and Daoists in Mongol times)." *Monumenta Serica* 20: 1–81.

Thomsen, Vilhelm L.
1893
"Déchiffrement des inscriptions de l'Orkhon et de l'Iénisséi." *Bulletin de l'Académie royale des sciences et des lettres de Danemark*, 285–299.

1919–31
Samlede Afhandlingar (Collected essays [on philology]). 4 vols. Copenhagen: Kristiana, Gyldendal.

Tichane, Robert.
1983
Ching-te-chen: Views of a Porcelain City. Painted Post, NY: New York State Institute for Glaze Research.

Tikhvinskii, Sergei Leonidovich, ed.
1970
Tataro-mongoly v Azii i Evrope: Sbornik statei (The Tatar-Mongols in Asia and Europe: A Collection of Articles). Moscow: Nauka (Akademiia nauk SSSR) Publishers.

Tkachev, V.
1987
"Nomadic Capitals in Central Asia." *Information Bulletin* (Moscow: Nauka): 114–18.

Togan, Isenbike.
1998
Flexibility and Limitation in Steppe Formations: The Keräit Khanate and Chinggis Khan. Leiden: Brill.

Tombs of Chingisids.
2006
see Silk Road.

Toynbee, Arnold Joseph.
1934–61
A Study of History. 12 vols. London; New York: Oxford University Press.

Travis, John.
2003
"Genghis Khan's Legacy?." *Science News* 163 (8 Feb.): 91.

Trepavlov, V. V.
1993
"Status 'belogo tsarya': Moskva i tatarskie khanstva v XV–XVI vv. (Sta-tus of the 'White Sovereign': Moscow and the Tatar Khanates in the fifteenth and sixteenth centuries)." In *Rossiya i Vostok: problemy vzaimodeistviya* (Russia and the East: Problems of Interaction), part 1. Moscow: Turan Publishers.

2002
Istoriya Nogaiskoi Ordy (History of the Nogai Orda). Moscow: Vostoch-naia Literatura.

Tseveendorj, D.
1980
Chandmany Soel (Chandman culture). Ulaan Baatar: Academy of Sciences.

Tseveendorj, D., L. Dashnyam, A. Ochir, and N. Urtnasan, eds.
1999
Historical and Cultural Monuments on the Territory of Mongolia. Ulaan Baatar: Mongolian Academy of Hu-manities.

Tseveendorj, D., B. Guchinsuren, B. Tsogtbaatar, and Ya. Tserendagva.
2001
Omnogov' aimgiin Khanbogd sumyn nutag dakh' Ivanhoe Mines Mongo-lia kompanii Oyu Tolgoi ashiglaltyn talbaid khiisen arkheologiin maltlaga sudalgaany ajilyn tailan (Report of the 2001 archaeological excavations at the Ivanhoe Mines Company com-mercial development area, Khanbogd sum, Omnogov' aimag). Ulaan Baatar: Mongolian Academy of Sciences, In-stitute of Archaeology.

Tseveendorj, D., D. Bayar, Ya. Tserendagva, and Ts. Ochirkhuyag.
2003
Mongolyn Arkheologii (Archaeology of Mongolia). Ulaan Baatar: Institute of Archaeology.

Tseveendorj, D., N. Batbold, and T. Amgalantugs.
2006
"Mongolanthropus buyuu nen ertnii Mongol khun (Mongolanthropus, a particularly early Mongolian homi-nin)." *Arkheologiin Sudlal* (Archaeo-logical Research) 3 (23): 5–10.

Tseveendorj, D., V. Molodin, G. Parzinger, M. Bayarsaikhan, and G. Lkhundev.
2007
"Mongol Altain monkh tsevdgiin bulshny sudalgaa" (Research on per-mafrost burials in the Mongolian Altai). *Arkheologiin Sudlal* (Archaeo-logical Research) 4 (24): 167–87.

Tuotuo, et al.
1975 [1344]
Jinshi (Jin dynastic history). Shangwu yinshu guan Bona edn. Ed. and re-printed. Beijing: Zhonghua shuju.

Turner, B. L., M. K. Zuckerman, B. A. Carlson, J. D. Kingston, G. J. Armelagos, D. R. Hunt, T. Amgalan-tugs, and B. Frohlich.
2007
"Prisoners of War or Victims of Raids?: Population Dynamics and Their Relationship to Dynastic Upheaval in Southern Mongolia c. 1300–1350 AD." Paper presented at 77th Annual Meeting of the As-sociation of Physical Anthropologists. Cleveland: American Association of Physical Anthropologists.

Underhill, Peter A., Peidong Shen, Alice A. Lin, Li Jin, Giuseppe Passarino, Wei H. Yang, Erin Kauff-man, Batsheva Bonné-Tamir, Jaume Bertranpetit, Paolo Francalacci, Muntaser Ibrahim, Trefor Jenkins, Judith R. Kidd, S. Qasim Mehdi, Mark T. Seielstad, R. Spencer Wells, Alberto Piazza, Ronald W. Davis, Marcus W. Feldman, L. Luca Cavalli-Sforza, and Peter J. Oefner.
2000
"Y Chromosome Sequence Variation and the History of Human Popula-tions." *Nature Genetics* 26: 358–61.

Vainshtein, Sevyan I.
1980
Nomads of South Siberia: The Pasto-ral Economies of Tuva. Cambridge: Cambridge University Press.

1989
"The Turkic Peoples, Sixth to Twelfth Centuries." In *Nomads of Eurasia*, ed. Vladimir N. Basilov. Seattle; Lon-don: National History Museum of Los Angeles County and University of Washington Press.

Varvarovskii, Iu. E.
2000
"K voprosu o 'teorii dvukh Saraev' i lokalizatsii goroda Giulistana (On the question of the 'Theory of Two Sarais' and the location of the city of Gulistan)." *Arkheologicheskie vesti* 7: 251–65.

Vernadsky, George.
1953
The Mongols and Russia. New Ha-ven: Yale University Press.

Vladimirtsov, Boris Iakovlevich.
1969
The Life of Chingis Khan. Trans. by D. S. Mirsky. Reprint of 1930 ed. New York: Benjamin Blom.

Voltaire.
1901
"The Orphan of China." In *The Dramatic Works of Voltaire*. Vol. 15. Trans. William F. Fleming. New York: E. R. Du Mont.

Wade, Nicholas.
2003
"A Prolific Genghis Khan, It Seems, Helped People the World," *New York Times*, 11 Feb.

Waley, Arthur, trans.
1931;1938
see Li Zhichang.

Wang, Guanzhuo.
2000
Zhongguo Gu Chuan Tu (Catalogue of ancient Chinese ships). Beijing: san San lian shu dian.

Ward, Rachel M.
1993
Islamic Metalwork. London: British Museum Press for The Trustees of the British Museum.

Watson, Burton, trans.
1993
see Sima Qian.

Watt, James C. Y.
2003
"A Note on Artistic Exchanges in the Mongol Empire." In *The Legacy of Genghis Khan: Courtly Art and Cul-ture in Western Asia, 1256–1353*, ed. Linda Komaroff and Stefano Carboni. New York: The Metropolitan Muse-um of Art, 2003; New York; London: Yale University Press.

Watt, James C. Y., and Anne E. Wardwell.
1997
When Silk Was Gold: Central Asian and Chinese Textiles. New York: The Metropolitan Museum of Art, 1997.

Weatherford, Jack [McIver].
2004
Genghis Khan and the Making of the Modern World. New York: Crown Publishers.

Wei Zheng.
1973 [656].
Sui shu (History of the Sui). 6 vols. Beijing: Zhonghua shuju.

Weidner, Marsha, et al.
1988
Views from Jade Terrace: Chinese Women Artists, 1300–1912. Indianap-olis: Indianapolis Museum of Art.

Weiler, A. H.
1956
"Screen: 'The Conqueror,' John Wayne Stars in Oriental 'Western.'" *The New York Times*, 31 Mar., 13.

1974
Medieval Russia's Epics, Chronicles, and Tales. 2nd ed. New York: Dutton.

Weitz, Ankeney.
1997
"Notes on the Early Yuan Antique Art Market in Hangzhou." *Ars Orientalis* 27: 27–38.

Wenwu.
1959
"Jiangsu wuxian yuan mu qingli jian-bao" (Preliminary report on the dis-covery of a Yuan tomb in Wu county, Jiangsu province). *Wenwu* (Cultural relics)/*Wen wu bian ji wei yuan hui bian*: 19–24.

Winkelman, Michael.
1986
"Trance States: A Theoretical Model and Cross-Cultural Analyses." *Ethos* 14, no. 2: 174–203.

Xiao Daheng.
1972
Beilu fengsu (Customs of the northern slaves). Taipei: Guangwen shuju.

Xu Cheng, and Du Yubin.
1995
Xixia ling (The Xixia tombs). Beijing: Dongfang chubanshe.

Yakovlev, Ya. A.
2006
"Novaya nakhodka (pamyatnika)

zolotoordynskoi torevtiki iz Surgutskogo Priob'ya (A New Find [of sites] of the Golden Horde Torevtika from the Surgut Ob area). *Rossiiskaya arkheologiya* (Russian Archaeology), 2. Moscow: Nauka (Akademiia nauk SSSR).

Yamada, Nakaba.
1916
Ghenkō: The Mongol Invasion of Japan. New York: E.P. Dutton; London: Smith, Elder and Co.

Yamagata Kinya.
1996
"Bunken kara mita gendai senpaku to sobi ni tsuite (A documentary study of the Yuan-era ships and its equipment)." In *Takashima kaitei iseki* (Excavation report on Takashima) 8: 128–30.

Yang, Bao, Achim Braeuning, Kathleen R. Johnson, and Shi Yafeng.
2002
"General Characteristics of Temperature Variation in China During the Last Two Millennia." *Geophysical Research Letters* 29, no. 9:1324. DOI: 10.1029/2001GL014485.

Yao Congwu.
1964
"Yuan Xianzong (Mengge Han) di daju zheng Shu yu ta zai Hezhou Diaoyu Cheng di zhansi (The great expedition against Shu led by Emperor Xianzong [Möngke Khan] of the Yuan and his death at the battle of Diaoyu Cheng near Hezhou)." *Wenshi zhe xuebao* 14: 61–85.

YCC (The Y Chromosome Consortium)
2002
"A Nomenclature System for the Tree of Human Y-Chromosome Binary Haplogroups." *Genome Research* 12: 339–48.

Young, S[teven]. B.
1982
"The Vegetation of Land Bridge Beringia." In *Paleoecology of Beringia*, ed. D. M. Hopkins, J. V. Matthews, Jr., C. S. Schweger, and S. B. Young. New York: Academic Press.

1994
To the Arctic: An Introduction to the Far Northern World. New York: John Wiley.

2005
"Modern Vegetation of the Hovsgol Region of Mongolia: A Possible Key to the Demise of the Ice Age Mammoth Steppe of the Arctic." In *The Deer Stone Project: Anthropological Studies in Mongolia 2002–2004*, eds. W. Fitzhugh, J. Bayarsaikhan, and P. Marsh. Washington, DC: Arctic Studies Center, Smithsonian Institution.

Yule, Henry, trans.
1903
see Polo.

Yuwen Maochao.
1986 [12th century]
Da Jin guozhi (Great Jin state chronicle). Guoxue wenku edn. Edited and reprinted. Beijing: Zhonghua shuju.

Zenkovsky, Serge A., trans. and ed.
1974
Medieval Russia's Epics, Chronicles, and Tales. 2nd ed. New York: Dutton.

Zerjal, Tatiana, R. Spencer Wells, Nadira Yuldasheva, Rusian Ruzibakiev, and Chris Tyler-Smith.
2002
"A Genetic Landscape Reshaped by Recent Events: Y-Chromosomal Insights into Central Asia." *American Journal of Human Genetics* 71: 466–82.

Zerjal, Tatiana, Yali Xue, Giorgio Bertorelle, R. Spencer Wells, Weidong Bao, Suling Zhu, Raheel Qamar, Qasim Ayub, Aisha Mohyuddin, Songbin Fu, Pu Li, Nadira Yuldasheva, Ruslan Ruzibakiev, Jiujin Xu, Qunfang Shu, Ruofu Du, Huanming Yang, Matthew E. Hurles, Elizabeth Robinson, Tudevdagva Gerelsaikhan, Bumbein Dashnyam, S. Qasim Mehdi, and Chris Tyler-Smith.
2003
"The Genetic Legacy of the Mongols." *American Journal of Human Genetics* 72: 717–21.

Zhang, P.Z., Cheng, H., Edwards, R.L., Chen, F.H., Wang, Y.J., Yang, X.L., Liu, J., Tan, M.,Wang, X.F., Liu, J.H., An, C.L., Dai, Z.B., Zhou, J., Zhang, D.Z., Jia, J.H., Jin, L.Y., Johnson, K.R.
2008
"A Test of Climate, Sun, and Culture Relationships from an 1810-year Chinese Cave Record." *Science* 322: 940–942.

Zhao Gong, Xu Ting, and Peng Daya.
1980[from the 13th-century origs.

Meng Da bei lu; Hei Da shi lue.]
Meng-Ta pei-lu und Hei-Ta shih-lüe: chinesische Gesandtenberichte über die frühen Mongolen 1221 und 1237. Forewords by Erich Haenisch and Yao Congwu. Comp. and commentary by Peter Olbricht and Elisabeth Pinks. Introduction by Werner Banck. Vol. 56 of *Asiatische Forschungen* (Research on Asia). Wiesbaden: Harrassowitz.

Zhilina, Natal'ia Viktorovna.
2001
Shapka Monomakha: Istoriko-kul'turnoe i tekhnologicheskoe issledovanie (The Cap of Monomakh: A Historical-Cultural and Technical Study). Moscow: Nauka (Akademiia nauk SSSR) Publishers.

Zhi-Yong Yin, Xuemei Shao, Ningsheng Qin, and Eryuan Liang.
2007
"Reconstruction of a 1436-year Soil Moisture and Vegetation Water Use History Based on Tree-ring Widths from Qilian Junipers in Northeastern Qaidam Basin, Northwestern China." *International Journal of Climatology* 28: 37-53.

Zilivinskaya, E. D.
2003
The Golden Horde Mosques: Toward an Archaeology of Buildings. Contexts and Concepts. Ed. Gunilla Malm. BAR (British Archaeological Reports) International Series 1186.

2006
"K voprosu o mnogogrannykh v plane pogrebal'nykh pamyatnikakh v Zolotoi Orde (On the question of burial sites of the Golden Horde multifaceted in plan)." In *Krupnovskie chteniya" po arkheologii Severnogo Kavkaza: Tezisy dokladov.* XXIV ("Krupnovskie Readings" in the archaeology of the northern Caucasus: Theses of reports), 24. Moscow: Nauka (Akademiia nauk SSSR) Publishers.

Zuckerman, M. K., B. L. Turner, B. A. Carlson, J. D. Kingston, G. J. Armelagos, D. R. Hunt, T. Amgalantugs, and B. Frohlich.
2007
"Diet and Disease in Times of War: Analysis of Mummified Human Remains from Southern Mongolia c. 1300–1350 AD." Paper presented at 77th Annual Meeting of the Association of Physical Anthropologists. Cleveland: American Association of Physical Anthropologists.

Index

Praise for other Odyssey Books & Maps...

"Thorough and beautifully illustrated, this book is a comprehensive—and fun—window into Afghan history, culture, and traditions. A must-have for travel readers and a gripping read for anyone with even a passing interest in Afghanistan."
—Khaled Hosseini, author of *The Kite Runner*

"It is one of those rare travel guides that is a joy to read whether or not you are planning a trip."—*New York Times*

"Don't leave home without *Angkor* by Dawn Rooney."—*San Francisco Chronicle*

"The bible of Bhutan guidebooks..."—*Travel & Leisure*

"Luce Boulnois's volume is another welcome resource about the Silk Road, valuable to serious scholars, tourists and armchair travelers alike...combining traditional history leavened with first-hand travel accounts, other primary sources and word portraits of historical personalities. The tra ction by Bradley Mayhew reflects the wisdom of an experienced modern Silk Road traveler. It is very succinct and broadly impressionistic, packed with practical advice and information."—*Orientations*

"Odyssey fans tend to be adventurous travelers with a literary bent. If you're lucky enough to find an Odyssey Guide to where you're going, grab it."—*National Geographic Traveler*

"Quite excellent... No one should visit Samarkand, Bukhara or Khiva without this meticulously researched guide."
—Peter Hopkirk, author of *The Great Game*

"A beautiful book..."—Peter Hessler, author of *River Town*

"...poetic prose that captures the very essence of the brave, proud people of Afghanistan..."—*New York Times*

"The Odyssey guide is a good read, full of historical background; the one to read before you go..."—*Times* (London)

"I especially recommend *The Silk Road*"—*Forbes Magazine*

"For coverage of Chongqing and the Gorges, and of the more placid and historically notable sites below Yichang and downriver to Shanghai, [this book] is unrivalled."—Simon Winchester

"Nothing is as insightful as a comprehensive guidebook. Correspondents I know rely on them, but few of us like to admit it. The best one I've encountered on *Georgia* is Roger Rosen's Georgia published by Odyssey."—Robert D. Kaplan, in *Eastward to Tartary*

"...Essential traveling equipment for anyone planning a journey of this kind..."—*Asian Wall Street Journal*

"Like the colorfully layered matryoshka doll, this indispensable travel guide is packed with style and character. It not only provides a cornucopia of practical information and cultural insight, but takes the traveler on a splendid journey through the extensive map of the Russian soul."—Isabel Allende

"His panoramic shots of mountain valleys are dizzying and lovely; so too are his photographs of religious ceremonies, with the villagers dressed in their finery."—*New York Times*

"If travel books came with warnings, the one for AFGHANISTAN: A COMPANION AND GUIDE would read, 'Caution: may inspire actual voyage.' But then, this lavishly produced guide couldn't help do otherwise—especially if you're partial to adventure."—*TIME*, August 22nd 2005

"Above all, it is authoritative and as well-informed as only extensive travels inside the country can make it. It is strong on the history. In particular the synopsis at the beginning is a masterly piece of compression."—*The Spectator*

"A gem of a book"—*The Literary Review*

"The *Yangzi* guide is terrific"—*Longitude Books*

"...It's a superb book, superbly produced, that makes me long to go back to China..."—John Julius Norwich

"Odyssey have invented a wonderful format for guidebooks that deserves to change the genre forever."—William Dalrymple

"It is an understatement to say that this book comes at a period of great popular and academic interest in Afghanistan. The publishing frenzy since 2001 has focused almost entirely on terrorism, drugs, warlordism and human rights abuses. This book...goes a long way towards humanising both the country and its people—and giving greater confidence that the country might be firmly put on the road to recovery."—*Asian Affairs Journal*

"...It might seem madness to publish a guide of nearly 800 pages to a country that is still on the Foreign Office 'blacklist' but this one, strong on history and sumptuously produced, can be enjoyed even by adventurers who never leave their armchair..."—*Daily Telegraph*

"...Colorful, practical guide, well illustrated with many astonishing photographs. Provides an in-depth general introduction to this kingdom's history, culture and ecology, with a comprehensive itinerary ranging from the major cities to the remotest monasteries..."
—*Traveller*

"...A stunning guide, packed with history, that no visitor to Iran should be without"
—Christina lamb, foreign affairs correspondent, *Sunday Times* (London)

Readers should note that printing plates used for the
first printing of this book were mislaid and as a result
we have had to makes use of files not always up to
our usual standards. Nevertheless the co-publishers
feel that the importance of keeping the work in print
out-weighs all other considerations

Genghis Khan and the Mongol Empire

was originally produced by
Perpetua Press, Santa Barbara, California

Designed by
Dana Levy

Edited by
Letitia O'Connor,
Jane Oliver and Kathy Talley-Jones

Typeset in Sabon, Univers, and Skia fonts

This printing by
Twin Age Ltd, Hong Kong
twinage@netvigator.com